The Ancient World

P9-AFF-555

Caspian Sea

Black Sea

CAUCASUS MTS.

Danube

...I MTS.

Byzantium

ANATOLIA

Tigris

Nineveh

ASSYRIA

GREECE Athens

Euphrates

Tigris

CYPRUS

SYRIA

Babylon

PHOENICIA

Sidon

Tyre

...terranean Sea

PALESTINE

Jerusalem

LIBYA

ARABIAN DESERT

Memphis

Nile

EGYPT

Red Sea

0	210	420 Miles
0	210	420 KM

C.E. Byzantine Empire

Survey of
HISTORIC
COSTUME

Survey of
HISTORIC
COSTUME

PHYLLIS G. TORTORA   SARA B. MARCKETTI

Fairchild Books An Imprint of Bloomsbury Publishing Inc.

BLOOMSBURY
LONDON · NEW DELHI · NEW YORK · SYDNEY

Fairchild Books
An imprint of Bloomsbury Publishing Inc

1385 Broadway   50 Bedford Square
New York   London
NY 10018   WC1B 3DP
USA   UK

www.bloomsbury.com
FAIRCHILD BOOKS, BLOOMSBURY and the Diana logo
are trademarks of Bloomsbury Publishing Plc

First edition published 1989

Second edition published 1994

Third edition published 1998

Fourth edition published 2005

Fifth edition published 2010

This edition first published 2015

© Bloomsbury Publishing Inc, 2015

Library of Congress Cataloging-in-Publication Data
Tortora, Phyllis G.
Survey of historic costume / Phyllis G. Tortora, Sara B. Marcketti. — Sixth edition.
pages cm
ISBN 978-1-62892-167-0 (hardback)
1. Clothing and dress—History. I. Marcketti, Sara B. II. Title.
GT580.T67 2015
391.009—dc23
2014032833

ISBN: HB: 978-1-62892-167-0

Typeset by Lachina
Cover Design by Eleanor Rose and Sam Clark
Printed and bound in Singapore

CONTENTS

EXTENDED CONTENTS

PREFACE

We are delighted to present the sixth edition of *Survey of Historic Costume*, now celebrating its 25th anniversary as a best-selling textbook for the study of fashion history. We are pleased to introduce new co-author Sara B. Marcketti, Associate Professor at Iowa State University, who has taught History of European and American Dress and Twentieth Century Dress History courses since 2005 and is an associate director of the university's Center for Excellence in Learning and Teaching. She brings a wealth of scholarship, knowledge, and teaching experience to this edition. Marcketti is delighted to join esteemed Professor Emerita Phyllis Tortora in this revision. This edition is supported by a new multimedia resource—*STUDIO: Survey of Historic Costume*—which provides a digital study tool directly related to the content of the book, including online self-quizzes with results and personalized study tips, flashcards with definitions and image identification, chapter videos and images, maps, a timeline, and activities to help students master concepts and improve grades.

NEW TO THIS EDITION

One goal of this edition is to refine the historic content and help students draw connections between themes and dress history. We have decreased the length of part openers and made chapters a more manageable length. A new Chapter 20, The New Millennium, places greater emphasis on major fashion events of this century, making this book as current as possible and more relevant to the study of fashion today.

In addition to streamlining and updating the text for 2014, this edition includes two new features. Decorative and Fine Arts tables of previous editions have been incorporated into new, illustrated chapter-opening timelines. Each timeline spread quickly orients the student in the era's history, including political, economic, social, technological, decorative and fine arts, and cultural events.

Survey of Historic Costume is a basic text for readers who need an overview of the history of costume in the Euro-American world. We make no attempt to survey the vast topic of historic costume in all parts of the world. Our purpose is to present a *survey* of Euro-American dress rather than an infinitely detailed picture. At the same time, it is our intention to make that picture as complete as possible within the limitations of space. Thus, another key change to this edition is introduction of global dress through a new Global Connections boxed feature, which demonstrates cross-cultural interactions of dress and clothing.

FEATURES

The consistent organization and parallel contents across chapters provide a systematic way for students to read and learn the information. Each chapter contains the following features.

Timeline

The one-page chapter chronologies of previous editions have been expanded in this edition to full-spread, illustrated timelines, which coordinate with six themes that appear in the chapters: fashion and textiles; politics and conflicts; decorative and fine arts; economics and trade; technology and ideas; and religion and society. Illustrations from the chapter-opening timeline appear again at relevant points in the chapter, drawing clear connections to chapter topics and adding depth to the chapter.

Chapter Organization

We must view the dress of each era within the context of the period. To assist readers who may have a limited background in history, a brief summary of the major historical developments related to the chapter is provided both in the chapter opener pages and in the text.

Clothing is a part of the basic equipment for everyday life, and so each chapter makes note of some of the important aspects of the lives of the people of the time. Where the arts, specific individuals, events, or societal values can be seen to have influenced styles, they are discussed. The technology and economy of the production and distribution of fabrics often influence dress; therefore, changes in technology for the making of cloth and items of dress, and in the economic systems of production and distribution, are noted. As the fashion industry becomes more complex, changes in its organization and function are stressed.

After the setting has been delineated, specific styles of each period worn by men, women, and children are described. Organization and contents are parallel in all chapters, and all elements of dress, ranging from undergarments to accessories, are included for every period. In this way, a rather detailed picture of costume can be provided even within the space limitations imposed on a single volume. Each chapter concludes with a summary of the themes evident in the dress of the period.

Illustrations

The history of dress is in major part a visual history. In this sixth edition, 90 percent of the photographs are full color, with black and white reserved for important illustrations not available in color.

Readers need depictions of costume from original source materials not only to understand unfamiliar terms, but also to supplement the general, survey approach of the text. The captions of the illustrations not only identify various parts of the costume and provide the contemporary names for elements of the styles, but also identify the aspects of the pictures that provide supporting evidence to the costume historian of the nature of costume in this period. The material in the captions of illustrations is as important as the contents of the book and should be read as carefully as the text.

Tables

Survey includes both illustrated and descriptive tables. Illustrated tables summarize material briefly and effectively. These are usually line drawings based on primary source materials. We have chosen to use clean line drawings without color, because these can often provide a clearer idea of the structure of the item than a photograph. **Illustrated Tables** depict important accessories, footwear, and headwear that were predominant during the period, and **Visual Summary Tables** show clear line drawings of the fashionable silhouettes and details of the period. Types of descriptive tables include those listing names of style, influential designers, and fashion influences from the period.

Global Connections

Global Connections is a new boxed feature that illustrates how items from one culture have influenced another. Usually, items will relate to influences on Euro-American dress, but in a few examples readers will see the influence traveling in another direction. The photographs are of items that originated or were in use during the time periods discussed in each chapter. Our objective in these features is to make readers aware that no culture, present or past, is without some connections to other cultures around the globe. By showing images and physical objects that demonstrate cross-cultural influence, students are able to holistically understand the ways in which the world has influenced Western dress.

Contemporary Comments

Each chapter includes at least one box in which comments from contemporary sources on some aspect of clothing are reproduced. These quotations are intended to provide readers with a flavor of the attitudes toward clothing that individuals of the period held as well as contemporary descriptions.

Modern Influences

This feature appears throughout the book and depicts a recent fashion that has been influenced by some aspect of dress from the period surveyed in that chapter.

Notes and References

A list of references used by the authors is placed at the end of each chapter.

Terminology

Historic costume reference books and materials (particularly for some of the early periods where actual records are confusing, contradictory, and scarce) show marked differences in terminology and content. We have attempted to present as accurate a summary as possible and one that we hope is free from the tendency to present largely apocryphal stories of the origins of styles as fact. When such material is introduced, it is clearly labeled as questionable or as legend.

In this text, the terms **clothes** and **clothing** are synonymous and mean wearing apparel. **Dress** is a general term that includes not only garments and accessories, but also aspects of personal appearance that can be changed, such as grooming, and management of parts of the body such as hair, manipulation through piercing, decoration by tattooing, or addition of cosmetics and fragrances. **Style** is the predominant form of dress of any given period or culture. Styles may persist for very long or shorter periods of time. The term **fashion** is used synonymously with *style* after the latter part of the medieval period. It implies styles of relatively short duration. **Costume** is used as a synonym for dress by those who work in the museum field and by many scholars who study historic dress. Some scholars prefer the use of the word *dress*, because to many people, *costume* means dress used in the theater, in dance, or for masquerade.

Several tools have been provided for readers. Many of the words for items of historic costume are not English terms. Where the pronunciation of these terms is not obvious, a **phonetic pronunciation** of the word is provided in parentheses just after the word. The **index** is organized so that it can be used as a glossary of terms. Terms printed in boldface type are defined within the text; the page numbers printed in bold type immediately after these words in the index are the pages on which these words are defined or explained.

Bibliography

A bibliography at the end of the book lists some of the many books written about historic costume. This bibliography does not include books dealing with techniques of theatrical costuming or sociocultural aspects of dress.

NEW ONLINE STUDENT RESOURCES

Survey of Historic Costume STUDiO

This new multimedia resource provides a digital study tool directly related to the content of *Survey of Historic Costume*. Consisting of online self-quizzes with results and personalized study tips, flashcards with definitions and image identification, chapter videos, world maps, a timeline, and much more, *Survey of Historic Costume STUDIO* will enhance learning, aid in instruction, and may result in better long-term retention for students.

STUDIO access cards are offered free with new book purchases and also sold separately through Bloomsbury Fashion Central (www.BloomsburyFashionCentral.com).

Student Resources

- Watch chapter videos that bring historic costume topics and concepts to life.
- Study smarter with online self-quizzes featuring scored results and personalized study tips.
- Review concepts with flashcards of terms/definitions and image identification.
- Learn context with a comprehensive timeline spanning the ancient world to present day, including key moments in fashion and textiles, politics and conflicts, decorative and fine arts, economics and trade, technology, and religion, plus the evolution of silhouettes over time.
- Enhance geographic knowledge with world maps showing the ancient world and modern world.
- Browse the Fashion Designer Index for an alphabetized list of key designers with brief bios.
- Branch out with links to fashion museums, costume collections, and online resources.

Survey of Historic Costume Student Study Guide

ISBN 9781628922349 | Sold separately on www.BloomsburyFashionCentral.com

This student study guide is designed to help students effectively navigate *Survey of Historic Costume* and provide a tool that enables students to identify, synthesize, and retain the text's core information. Following the chapters of the textbook, the Student Study Guide includes chapter objectives, key terms, historic snapshots, chapter summaries, chapter quizzes, image-analysis exercises, garment analysis worksheets, glossary of key terms, and a fashion garment guide—a "mini" dictionary identifying basic garment terminology with illustrations. By providing a consistent approach to all of the chapters in this text, the guide provides a vehicle that enhances the journey students will take through time and place, making the study of historic costume accessible, memorable, and exciting.

Instructor Resources

Now easily accessible through www.BloomsburyFashion Central.com.

- Access to all STUDIO content, eBook versions of *Survey of Historic Costume*, 6th Edition, and *Student Study Guide*
- Image library with every illustration and photo from the book
- PowerPoint slides for each chapter
- Test Bank including multiple choice, true/false, and essay questions for each chapter with answer key
- Instructor's Guide including sample syllabi and units based on the timeline in the book, chapter objectives, discussion questions, additional research projects, assignments, and information about sources of video materials that complement and amplify this book and web sites that provide information about costume, as well as suggested teaching strategies and evaluative techniques

ACKNOWLEDGMENTS

No person, even after a lifetime of study, can be expected to be knowledgeable in all aspects of historic costume solely on the basis of his or her own research. Fortunately, there are many individuals whose specialized work has been invaluable in the preparation of a broad survey of this type. It is important that these sources be given special acknowledgment. Readers who are interested in any of these periods may wish to consult these sources.

Elizabeth Barber's books on prehistoric textiles, the books of Mary Houston and Lillian Wilson on costume of the ancient world and the more recent work on Egyptian dress of Gillian Vogelsang-Eastwood and Judith Sebesta and Larissa Bonfante on Roman dress added new information. Larissa Bonfante's illuminates Etruscan costume and related Greek styles.

For the medieval period, Joan Evans's work on costume of the Middle Ages and the fine handbook by Phillis and Cecil Willet Cunnington were invaluable. Eunice Rathbone Goddard's work on French costume of the 11th and 12th centuries also provided useful information, as did works by Francoise Piponnier and Perrine Mane, and Desoree G. Koslin and Janet E. Snyder. A recent addition to scholarship about the Middle Ages that is helpful in understanding the beginnings of fashion change is Sarah-Grace Heller's *Fashion in Medieval France*.

Elizabeth Birbiri's fine study of Italian Renaissance costume provided not only detailed information but also a wealth of excellent illustrative materials, as did the work of Jacqueline Herald. For the 16th through the 19th centuries, the several volumes of handbooks on costume by the Cunningtons, and that by Phillis Cunnington and Alan Mansfield for the 20th century, were among the most useful of the materials cited. Not only were they a superlative source for detailed information, but they were also a helpful tool for cross-checking conflicting information.

For menswear of the 20th century, the *Esquire Encyclopedia of 20th Century Men's Fashion* was by far the most useful secondary source an author or researcher could find, with its wealth of detailed information quoted directly from the fashion press and its many illustrations from the periods covered in this book. For women's fashions in the 20th century, probably the most extensive reference prepared to date is *Vogue History of 20th Century Fashion*. For information about fashion designers, *Who's Who in Fashion*, fifth edition, by Holly Price Alford and Anne Stegemeyer, was invaluable.

Underclothing has been thoroughly illustrated and explored in the books by C. W. Cunnington, Nora Waugh, and Elizabeth Ewing. Waugh's work is especially helpful in its inclusion of quotations from the literature of various periods concerning different types of undergarments. For some specialized material in the area of bathing costume, Claudia Kidwell's monograph was useful, as was the work she and Margaret Christman did on American ready-to-wear.

The works of François Boucher and Millia Davenport should be noted for their wealth of illustrative material drawn from sources from the various periods, although we recommend that readers approach these books armed with a magnifying glass.

A number of scholars have explored the many complex changes that fashion has undergone in the 20th and 21st centuries. We note particularly the work of Ted Polhemus, Amy de la Haye, and Cathie Dingwall on "style tribes"; Diana Crane's insightful work on the contemporary fashion system; and Valerie Steele's corpus of work.

Books on subjects related to fashion and fashion design in the recent past have proliferated. There are too many of excellent quality to list them.

Having begun by citing some of the books to which we are indebted, we also acknowledge libraries that were especially helpful from the first edition to this edition: the Costume Institute Library of the Metropolitan Museum of Art; the Pierpont Morgan Library in New York City; the research library of the New York Public Library; the Queens College Library; the Port Washington Public Library; the library of the Fashion Institute of Technology; Alderman Library and Darden Graduate School of Business Administration Library, University of Virginia; the Charlottesville branches of the Jefferson-Madison Regional Library; the Westchester Public Library system; and the libraries of Westchester Community College and Iowa State University.

Some individuals also deserve special recognition. Two whose work is still an integral part of this book are no longer living. Keith Eubank, co-author from the first to the fifth edition, died before the current edition revision was begun. His work on the historical contexts of the periods remains and is still appreciated. The late Vincent Tortora took many of the photographs used in this and previous editions and also reviewed and corrected phonetic pronunciations. His encouragement and contributions made this book possible.

Special thanks also to the Marcketti and Brubacher families who provided matchless support throughout the revision process and more. We appreciate the willingness of designer Rob Hillestad, who provided photographs of his fine work. We are also grateful that the Huntington Historical Society, Huntington, New York, has continued to permit reproduction of images from its collection. Other important assistance in finding illustrative material came from the Cleveland Museum of Art. Commercial image banks were very helpful, especially Art Resource. Dover Publications has been very generous in permitting reproduction of images from its books. Thanks to Daniel Castro of Daniel Castro Photography for the beautiful cover image.

We cannot thank individually all of our colleagues and friends who contributed in many ways, but we would like to note that the International Textile and Apparel Association (ITAA), the Costume Society of America (CSA), and the Textile Society of America (TSA) have consistently provided settings for the reporting of new research and the interchange of ideas with colleagues from around the world, and these opportunities to hear about the latest scholarship have been much appreciated.

A number of anonymous reviewers had offered suggestions over the many years during which the first edition was developed, and their input continues to influence subsequent editions. Prior to publication of the first edition, Elizabeth Ann Coleman, curator, author, and scholar, did a careful reading and made excellent suggestions for the chapters on the 19th and 20th centuries.

We express grateful thanks, also, to the many users and readers of previous editions who have made helpful suggestions for revisions. Among those who have consistently offered sound advice are Patricia Warner, retired from the University of Massachusetts at Amherst, Patricia Cunningham of the Ohio State University, and Linda Welters of the University of Rhode Island, who offered valuable critiques and suggestions and willingly shared resources. Other experienced scholars and teachers were very helpful in considering additions to the ancillary materials, including Jose Blanco, University of Georgia; Sheryl Farnan-Leipzig, Metropolitan Community College; Anne Bissonette, University of Alberta, Canada; Janet Blood, Indiana University of Pennsylvania; Susan J. Torntore, Colorado State University; Amanda Lensch, Iowa State University; and Carmen Keist, Western Illinois University. Reviewers selected by the publisher were also very helpful and we gratefully thank them: Jennifer Banning, Illinois State University; Ali Basye, Art Institute of Seattle; Vicki Bolan, University of the Fraser Valley; Jill Carey, Lasell College; M. Kathleen Colussy, The Art Institute of Florida; Kathleen Evans, The New England Institute of Art; Rhonda R. Gorman, Texas Women's University; Janice S. Jenny, Herkimer County Community College; Catherine Amoroso Leslie, Kent State University; Donna Meester, University of Alabama; Diana Saiki, Ball State University; Elizabeth Cole Sheehan, Fisher College, Lasell College, Mount Ida College, Newbury College, and New England Institute of Art; Emily Stoehrer, Fisher College; Alexandra Jordan Thelin, Montclair State University; and Andrea Varga, SUNY New Paltz. Thanks are also due to the many instructors who participated in online surveys and offered their thoughtful feedback on past editions of the book; we rely on you immensely as we strive to meet your students' needs.

Olga T. Kontzias, former Executive Editor of Fairchild Books, was associated with this book from its first edition until her retirement in 2013. Her role in the evolution of this book is gratefully acknowledged and appreciated. Always ready to support new ideas and to offer ideas of her own, she made the work a pleasure.

Fairchild Books is now a part of Bloomsbury Publishing's Visual Arts Division. Kathryn Earle, Head of Visual Arts, Priscilla McGeehon, Publisher, and Amanda Breccia, Acquisitions Editor, launched the work on the new edition and spearheaded the online resources and videos. An excellent and supportive staff, including Joseph Miranda, Editorial Development Director; Edie Weinberg, Art Development Editor; Karen Fein, Development Editor; Sue Howard, Photo Researcher; Kiley Kudrna, Editorial Assistant; and Bina Abling and Yelena Safronova, Illustrators, carried the work along. Special thanks to Josh Barinstein of Zenergy Films for his fabulous work creating the new videos. A debt of gratitude to Amanda Lensch for her help preparing the historic garments for the videos, all of which would not be possible without the support and resources of Iowa State University, the Apparel, Events, and Hospitality Management Department, and the Textiles and Clothing Museum.

2014

Phyllis Tortora
Sara Marcketti

CHAPTER ONE
Introduction

THE ORIGINS OF DRESS

Beads are possibly the most plentiful examples of dress from early periods. According to Dubin (2009), the oldest beads found so far are those in Sikul Cave in Israel on Mount Carmel. These beads, made of shells, have been dated to 108,000 BCE (Dubin, 2009). Other examples from c. 36,000 to 28,000 BCE show beads strung in quantity on something like a cord or animal sinew, quite possibly onto garments and head coverings now long disappeared.

From the post–ice-age or the Upper Paleolithic period, approximately 35,000 to 12,000 years ago, stylized depictions of humans have been found in sculpture; statuettes; incised figures on bone, horn, and antler; and incised and painted art in caves or on rocks. Although many of the sculpted statuettes (c. 25,000 BCE) are unclothed, some of them appear to be wearing elements of dress that were most likely made from fibers (Barber, 1991). Hairnets, caplike headgear, string skirts, and bands above and below the breast and around the back are visible (see Figure 1.1).

Archeologists have concluded that the headgear in particular appeared spirally hand woven, made much in the way a basket might be. The string skirt was made by tying cords made from twisted plant fibers with loose or frayed ends to another cord that formed a belt. The bandeaux appeared to be made by twining, and its parts were probably sewn together at the

points where they intersected (Adovasio, Soffer, and Page, 2009).

Additional excavations have presented evidence of textile weaving in the form of textile imprints on unfired and fired clay fragments. Archeologists have reported that the textile imprints, dated at between

FIGURE 1.1 This Venus of Willendorf statuette appears to be wearing headgear or hairnetting. Dated to c. 24,000–22,000 BCE, it was discovered at a Paleolithic site in Austria in 1908. (HIP/Art Resource, NY.)

29,000 to 24,000 years ago, exhibit variations in the size of interlacings and in the weaves used. This led them to speculate about possible end uses, including woven garments. These imprints were found near eyed needles, some of which archeologists believe are too small to have been used on hides, arguing that "this likely reflects working on woven textiles and/or embroidering rather than conjoining animal hides" (Soffer, Adovasio, and Hyland, 2000, 514).

The oldest actual textile fiber archeologists have discovered dates to about 30,000 years ago. The flax fibers discovered in a cave in Georgia, a country at the crossroads between Europe and Asia, appear to have been twisted in complex ways, indicating to archeologists that the fibers had been spun (Kvavadze et al., 2009). Perhaps used for cording, clothing, and basketry, the fibers were dyed in a color range including yellow, red, blue, violet, black, brown, green, and khaki.

Sandals and slip-on shoes have been found from c. 8,300 BCE at the Arnold Research Cave in Central Missouri (see Figure 1.2). The specimens include varying materials, styles, and construction techniques (Kuttruff, DeHart, and O'Brien, 1998). The wearing of shoes, though, is almost certainly older than the oldest

extant shoes. For example, a weakening of small toe bones found in 40,000-year-old human fossils has been cited as evidence of early shoe use (Trinkaus and Shang, 2008). Based on visual and artifact evidence, humans most probably wore dress made from fur, skins, and fibrous materials held together in some type of textile construction (Tortora, 2015).

There are places in the world where clothing is not essential for survival, and yet most cultures use some form of dress. Psychologists and sociologists have suggested four basic motivations for wearing clothes: decoration, protection, modesty, and status. Of these four reasons, decoration is generally acknowledged to be primary.

Most cultures use dress to denote status, but this function probably became attached to dress after clothing first came into use. Just what constitutes modesty differs markedly from society to society, and what is modest in one part of the world may be immodest in another. Modesty, too, may have become associated with dress after its use became widespread.

Protection from the elements is needed, it would seem, for survival, but humans seem to have had their origins in warm, not cold, climates. Furthermore, shelter and fire also provide warmth, and people from

FIGURE 1.2 Leather footwear constructed in moccasin style discovered at the Arnold Research Cave in central Missouri. The shoe, dated to 8,300 BCE, includes grass lining. (University of Missouri Museum of Anthropology.)

various geographic areas have differing responses to the temperature of their surroundings.

Another type of protection may be related to the origins and functions of dress: supernatural protection, or protection against spiritual dangers that are thought to surround each individual. Good-luck amulets and charms are worn in most cultures. Aprons used to protect the genitals from physical harm and from witchcraft may have evolved into skirts or loincloths in some areas.

The reasons for believing decoration to be a primary, if not the most primary, motive in human dress are compelling. Although using dress as protection against the elements and evil spirits is not universal, decoration of the human body is. There are cultures in which clothing as such does not exist, but there are no cultures in which some form of decoration does not exist. The logical conclusion is that decoration of the self is a basic human practice. Dressing the body may have grown out of this decoration of the self; protection, modesty, and status may have been important motivations for the elaboration and development of complex forms of dress.

LIMITATIONS TO THE DESIGN OF GARMENTS

As with any medium, the design of clothing is subject to limitations. Garments have some functional aspects. Except for costumes that have only a ceremonial purpose, the wearer must be able to move, to carry the weight of the garment, and, often, to perform certain duties while wearing the clothing. The duties assigned to an individual have a direct influence on the kind of dress he or she can wear. Affluent men and women with servants to do the work of the household are able to dress in one way, while the servants dress in costumes more appropriate to the labors they perform.

There are other limitations as well. Although paint and ornaments alone can serve as the prescribed dress in some cultures, more complex dress evolved in most societies. Early human may have used skins. The draping qualities of skins are different from that of cloth and would therefore impose certain restrictions on the shapes of garments that could be constructed.

Once people learned to spin yarns and weave fabrics, these techniques were employed to make clothing. Before the advent of manufactured fibers in the 20th century, only natural materials were available for use. Each of these had inherent qualities that affected the characteristics of fabrics that could be made from it. Some materials such as barkcloth, which is made of the inner layer of the bark of trees, are relatively stiff; other fibers such as cotton, wool, or linen are more flexible.

People in isolated regions were limited to the use of local materials. Trade between regions brought materials from one part of the world to another. Silk was little known in Europe until the Romans imported it from India and China around the beginning of Christianity. Cotton does not grow in the cool northern climate of Europe, so it was not until after the Crusaders imported limited quantities of cotton fabrics from the Near East that cotton cloth was known in medieval Europe.

The word *costume* tends to be used in museums and by historians who study what people wear. The word *dress* has been defined quite precisely as anything that individuals do to modify the body, anything they attach to the body, and anything they place around the body (Eicher and Roach-Higgins, 1992). As used in this text, the words *costume* and *dress* are generally synonymous.

Dress is generally constructed by either draping or tailoring. **Draped dress** is created by the arrangement around the body of pieces of fabric that are folded, pleated, pinned, or belted in different ways. Draped clothing usually fits the body loosely. Draped garments were probably developed after people learned to weave cloth.

By contrast, the use of skins or leather likely led to the development of **tailored dress**. In tailored garments, pieces are cut and sewn together. They fit the body more closely and provide greater warmth than do draped garments; hence, they are more likely to be worn in cool climates. Draped garments are more characteristic of warm climates. Some costume combines elements of both draping and tailoring.

Technology has had an important impact on dress. Some regions developed spinning and weaving skills to a far greater extent than did others. Many of the changes in dress that came about in Europe and North America after the 18th century can be directly or indirectly attributed to such developments as mechanized spinning and weaving, the sewing machine, and the emergence of the American ready-to-wear industry. The resulting mass production probably helped simplify styles and speed up fashion changes.

Costume is also limited by the mores and customs of the period. The word *costume* derives from the same root as the word *custom*. Persons who violate the dress customs of their culture or even those of their socioeconomic class are often considered to be deviant or asocial—perhaps even mad. George Sand, a French female writer of the 19th century who dressed in men's clothing, was considered to be decidedly eccentric; later women such as writer Radclyffe Hall in the early 20th century used masculine dress to express sexual identity (Marcketti and Angstman, 2013). Even in the postmodern world of "anything goes," there still exist norms of dressing, particularly within subgroups.

COMMON THEMES IN COSTUME HISTORY ACROSS TIME

A **theme**, in the sense that the word is used here, is "a recurring or unifying subject or idea" (*Webster's New World Dictionary*, 1988). One can identify many themes related to dress. Although the ways in which various themes emerge, develop, and have an impact on dress differ from period to period, a thematic approach to the study of dress may facilitate the comparison of historical periods and aid in understanding how and why styles developed and changed.

In the pages that follow, specific themes are identified and discussed. These themes are printed in small capital letters so that they will be readily identifiable. The themes that emerge from what is known of costume in any period are often most clear when that period is viewed retrospectively. For this reason, although each chapter will touch on many themes, a final section of each chapter will summarize, highlight, and discuss some of the themes that stand out for that period.

Individual humans rarely live in isolation but gather together in social groups. The interactions of individuals living together and communicating on many levels have strong influences on how people dress. SOCIAL LIFE, SOCIAL CLASS STRUCTURE, SOCIAL ROLES (including those related to GENDER), and CHANGES OR PATTERNS IN SOCIAL BEHAVIOR (what modern terminology might call LIFESTYLES) comprise one set of important themes in the study of dress. As these themes play out, many of the functions of dress are evident.

Functions of Dress in the Social Context

Throughout history, clothing has served many social purposes. It has been used to differentiate between the sexes and to designate age as well as occupational, marital, and socioeconomic status, group membership, and other social roles that individuals played.

Designation of Gender Differences

One of the most fundamental aspects of dress in most societies is that custom decrees that the dress of men and women be different. These differences reflect culturally determined views of the social roles appropriate to each sex. No universal customs exist that dictate the specific forms of dress for each gender. What is considered appropriate may differ markedly from one civilization or one century to another. From the Late Middle Ages until the 20th century in western Europe, for example, skirted garments (with a few exceptions such as kilts) were designated as feminine dress, and breeches or trousers, as male dress.

Understanding the part clothing plays in reflecting gender-related issues requires some knowledge about relationships between the sexes in a particular cultural context. Costume historians have explored the topic of gender and dress, paying attention to the complex and intricate interplay of attitudes toward gender roles and the dress of men and women (Kidwell and Steele, 1989; see this publication for a lengthy exploration of the topic of gender and dress).

Designation of Age

Sometimes clothing serves to mark age-associated changes. In western Europe and in European settlements in North America, for example, boys and girls often were dressed alike in their earliest years, but once they reached a designated age, a distinction was made between the dress of boys and girls. In England during the Renaissance, this stage was celebrated in a ritual called **breeching**, when a 5- or 6-year-old boy was given his first pair of breeches.

Age differentiation may, as in the preceding example, be an established procedure, but it is often less a ritual than an accepted part of the mores of a society. Throughout the 19th century, for example, younger girls wore shorter costumes than their adolescent sisters. During the 1920s and 1930s, wearing knickers marked a stage of development between childhood and adult life for many young men.

Designation of Status

A uniform or a particular style of dress frequently designates occupational status. In England, even today, lawyers wear an established costume when they appear in court. Police officers, firefighters, postal workers, and some of the clergy are but a few of those whose dress may identify them as members of a particular profession. Sometimes the uniform also serves a practical function, as, for example, the firefighter's waterproof coat and protective helmet or the construction worker's hard hat.

Dress designating occupational status is not limited to a uniform. For many years, particularly during the 1950s and 1960s, men employed by certain companies in the United States were required to wear white shirts with ties to work. Colored shirts were not permitted. Young lawyers who, on first entering the practice of law, went to a menswear store and requested "a lawyer's suit" found that the salespersons knew exactly what they wanted.

Marital status may be indicated by customs of dress. In western society, a wedding ring worn on a specific finger signifies marital status. Among the Amish, an American religious group, married men wear beards while unmarried men do not. For many centuries, it was customary for married women to cover their hair, while young unmarried women were permitted to go without head coverings.

In some cultures or during some historical periods, certain types of clothing have been restricted to individuals of a particular rank and social and economic status. These restrictions were sometimes codified into **sumptuary laws**, which restricted the use of, or expenditures on, luxury goods such as clothing and household furnishings. During the 14th century in England, those who worked as servants to "great men" were required to limit the cost of their clothing, and they were not permitted to wear any article of gold or silver, embroidery, or silk (Scott, 1975). In ancient Rome only the male Roman citizen was permitted to wear the costume called the *toga*, which identified his sociopolitical status.

Identification of Group Membership

Dress is also used to identify an individual as belonging to a particular social group. A uniform or insignia may be adopted formally by that group and kept for its members alone, as in the uniforms of fraternal groups such as the Masons or Shriners or religious groups such as the Amish of today or the Puritans of the 17th century. At other times, group identification is demonstrated by an informal kind of uniform, such as those adopted by adolescents who belong to the same clique or the zoot suits worn by certain groups of young people during the early 1940s.

Ceremonial Use of Clothing

Ceremonies are an important part of the structure of most societies and social groups. Designated forms of dress are frequently an important part of any ceremony. Sociologists speak of rites of passage, ceremonies marking the passage of the individual from one status to another. Often these require wearing designated garments. Specific costumes exist in modern American society that are considered appropriate for weddings, baptisms, burials, mourning, and graduation. Other ceremonies that serve to strengthen the community, called *rites of intensification*, may involve special clothing. For example, when the bicentennial of the founding of a town is celebrated, townspeople often dress in the costumes of the period of the founding of the town. Many significant moments of life are accompanied by wearing culturally specified ritual dress.

Enhancement of Sexual Attractiveness

Clothing is also a means of enhancing sexual attractiveness. In some cultures this is quite explicit, with clothing focusing attention on women's breasts or men's genitals. In many periods women have padded dresses to make the bosom appear larger or have worn dresses with very low necklines designed to call attention to the breasts. At other times the waist, the hips, or the legs have been emphasized. James Laver (1950), a well-known costume historian, believed that fashion changes in women's dress were a result of shifting erogenous zones. His theory was that women uncovered different parts of the body selectively in order to attract men; for example, as men became used to seeing more of the breasts, this area lost its interest and power to excite and therefore was covered while another area, such as the hips, was emphasized.

Laver also suggested that sexual attractiveness might lie in other aspects of dress. Men in modern western society, he said, are considered attractive when they appear affluent and successful.

Clothing as a Means of Social Communication

The foregoing discussion of the functions of dress leads to the conclusion that dress serves as a means of communication. To the person who is knowledgeable about a particular culture, dress is a silent language. It tells the observer something about the organization of the society in which it is worn. It discloses the social stratification, revealing whether the society is one with rigid delineations of social and economic class or is

a classless society. For example, the political leaders in the African Ashanti tribe once wore distinctive dress marking their special status. Any subject who wore the same fabric pattern as the king was put to death. In contrast, the costume of American political leaders does not differ from that of most of the rest of the population. The political distinctions between the two cultures—one an absolute monarchy, the other a democracy—are mirrored in their clothing practices.

Other aspects of social organization may manifest themselves in dress. The garments worn by religious leaders may distinguish them from worshippers or may show no differentiation. The roles of men and women may be distinctly identified by dress (as in some Islamic countries that require women to be veiled). Alternatively, when the social roles of men and women are not clearly defined, there may not be sharp distinctions in the customary dress of the sexes. For example, since the 1920s in Europe and North America, women have been free to wear trousers, a garment previously nearly exclusively reserved for men (Waugh, 1964).

The Historical Context

Most writings about historic dress provides modern readers with some context for the period in which costumes were worn. In this text, the introductory section of each chapter, "Historical Background," establishes that context. Within the historical background of each period, one of the recurring themes is POLITICS, a term that refers to government. Governments and political leaders often have a strong impact on the lives of individuals under their influence and can affect clothing styles either directly or indirectly. Such political influences may range from laws restricting the wearing of actual items of dress or regulation of clothing-related industries to the desire of individuals or groups to imitate clothing worn by a charismatic political leader. Examples of the impact of politics on dress include the banning of imported Kashmir shawls by Napoleon in the early 19th century, the revival of interest in homburg hats that followed President Eisenhower's wearing of this hat to his inauguration, or the popularity of fashion designer Charles Worth in the mid-1800s after Empress Eugénie began wearing clothes he had designed.

Unfortunately, another common theme in history is CONFLICT, often the cause of wars. Warfare may restrict access to the raw materials needed for apparel, or it may produce the opposite effect: Through exposure to other societies, new materials and ideas can be introduced, resulting in the expansion of apparel alternatives. For example, nylon disappeared from the consumer market during World War II, when it was diverted for use in wartime equipment; the trench coat, an item of military dress, was adopted after World War I; and following conflicts in the Middle East from the 1990s onward, camouflage was worn.

Another important theme in history is ECONOMIC EVENTS, which include TRADE. Economic events may be the result of political policy or may be shaped by unexpected occurrences, such as disease or the discovery of valuable natural resources. Such themes were evident when the Depression of the 1930s was accompanied by a shift from ornate, decorative clothing to more subdued styles, or when the opening of the silk trade with China by the Romans by the end of the first century BCE made this fabric available to the upper class Romans.

Another theme closely related to economics is the PRODUCTION AND ACQUISITION OF TEXTILES AND APPAREL. Textiles are the raw materials from which many elements of dress are created. This theme is quite literally woven throughout the history of costume. One dramatic example from the 19th and early 20th centuries is the development of mass production of clothing in the United States, which made possible the modern fashion industry.

The theme of TECHNOLOGY is often related to the production of textiles and apparel. Technology may also have an impact on such areas as transportation, communications, or the production of consumer goods, each of which, in turn, may influence dress. Examples range from the invention of the sewing machine, without which mass production would have been impossible, to the development of the automobile, which probably encouraged the wearing of shorter skirts by women.

As has been noted, dress can be a form of communication, but it is also the subject of communication. Information about dress can be transmitted through a variety of MEDIA OF COMMUNICATION. Over the centuries, the media by which information has been transmitted have changed. The impact of those changes on dress is another theme to be explored. Photography, motion pictures, and television can be cited as examples of 19th- and 20th-century media that both communicated information about dress and also influenced it.

Cross-Cultural Influences

In an article suggesting new approaches to the teaching of history of costume, Jasper and Roach-Higgins (1987) reminded us that unless we include the historical traditions of Asia, the Near East, Africa, and North and South America before Columbus, we are studying the history of western costume. Throughout the history of western dress, influences from other parts of the world have appeared. When explorers, traders, soldiers, tourists, and immigrants visited regions new to them, the local practices contrasted with those of their own culture. As one of the most visible manifestations of culture, dress immediately draws the attention of strangers, just as the dress of the visitor commands the attention of those being visited. Judgments are made on both sides of this cultural divide, and when an element or type of dress is viewed as attractive or interesting or useful, it may be subsequently incorporated into the dress of local residents or visitors. For example, a new style might appear after the invasion of one country by another, or a new fiber or fabric might come into use after trade opens between countries. When historical documents and illustrations are available, they may provide quite specific evidence about how, why, and where an influence or a new style originated. Some influences are subtle; others are obvious.

Roach and Musa (1980) called styles that incorporate components from several cultures **mixtures**. Erekosima and Eicher (1981) suggested the term **cultural**

authentication to identify the process "whereby elements of dress of one culture are incorporated into the dress of another" (48). Usually the culturally authenticated style is changed in some way. Only rarely are entire garments adopted. The steps in cultural authentication, according to Erekosima and Eicher, are *selection* of an item of dress from another culture, *characterization* of the item by giving it a name, *incorporation* of the item into its possessions by a particular group, and *transformation* of the item by making some changes from the original.

The fashion designer who incorporates ethnic styles into fashionable garments is participating in cultural authentication of the styles that inspired the design, just as the fashionable ladies of the Empire period did when they "borrowed" Middle Eastern turbans for their headdress in the early 19th century.

Many cultures and ethnic groups have contributed to and influenced all aspects of life in the western world. The study of historic costume can sometimes provide a visual representation of some of these multicultural contributions. Hence, the theme of CROSS-CULTURAL INFLUENCES IN DRESS grows out of recognition that western society, or any one country or other political entity within that society, cannot exist in isolation. As cultures come into contact with one another, there is a reciprocal infusion of new ideas, and much of this cross-cultural material is culturally authenticated, resulting in styles that are mixtures. Examples of cross-cultural influences are present in almost every period: the introduction of tunics to ancient Egypt from abroad, Middle Eastern influences on Renaissance dress, and Chinese influences on American fashions after President Nixon visited China in the early 1970s. For this reason, each chapter that follows includes a discussion of specific dress items from around the world that were influenced by or contributed to western clothing practices of the period.

Geography, the Natural Environment, and Ecology

Factors such as GEOGRAPHIC LOCATION, the NATURAL ENVIRONMENT, and ECOLOGY (the relationship of humans to their physical environment) may emerge as themes that are evident in dress. Examples can be seen in preferences for tailored clothing in cold climates and draped clothing in warm environments, or in contemporary avoidance of fur by some consumers as a means of protecting endangered species.

Clothing as an Art Form

Expression through the arts is rooted in a particular culture and historical period. Conventions or customs determine the form and content of art in any given period. Although the human impulse toward expressing feelings through art is universal, the specific expression of an era is determined by a complex mixture of social, psychological, and aesthetic factors often called the **zeitgeist**, or spirit of the times.

The artists or designers of a given period all experience many of the same influences; therefore, it is not surprising that different art forms from the same era may display similar qualities. These similarities may occur in the decorative motifs that are used; in scale, form, color, and proportion; and in the feelings evoked by works of art. This phenomenon is certainly true of clothing, and likenesses between dress and architectural forms, furnishings, and the other visual arts are often pointed out. Writers speak of the visual resemblance of the tall, pointed headdresses of northern European women of the Late Middle Ages to the tall spires of Gothic cathedrals. The elaborate trimmings applied to Victorian women's dresses have been likened to some of the decoration applied to Victorian furniture. The spare, straight lines of early modern architecture and the work of cubist painters are seen as related to the straight, somewhat square lines of women's clothing in the 1920s, clothing that is frequently ornamented with art deco designs similar to those used in architecture and interior design of the period. The result may be expressed as yet another theme for examination: THE RELATIONSHIPS BETWEEN COSTUME OF A PARTICULAR ERA AND DEVELOPMENTS IN THE FINE AND APPLIED ARTS.

The modern apparel industry assigns the role of creating new design ideas to fashion designers. Some designers are exceptionally innovative, generating exciting new ideas that the public finds to be in keeping with the current zeitgeist. When this happens, a designer may help move current fashion in a new direction, a theme that might be called THE RELATIONSHIP BETWEEN COSTUME AND THE WORK OF INDIVIDUAL ARTISTS AND DESIGNERS. Examples of such influential designers include Paul Poiret before World War I, Gabrielle Chanel in the 1920s, Madeleine Vionnet in the 1920s and 1930s, and Christian Dior in the post–World War II period.

At the same time, clothing offers the designer or the wearer a medium of expression with its own forms and techniques. The lines, textures, colors, proportions, and scale of fabric designs and the shapes of garments can and have varied enormously at different times and in different places throughout history. Ideals of human beauty change with changes in the zeitgeist. Often individuals use clothing to attempt to conform to the physical ideal of human beauty at a particular time.

Another theme in historic costume grows out of the tendency for dress to play a role in REVIVALS of interest in earlier styles. This phenomenon of deriving contemporary styles from those of an earlier time period may result from factors such as a culturewide interest in ideas or art of an earlier period, from the popularity of films or books, or from political events. Whatever the cause, revivals in clothing styles have been especially notable over the past two centuries and deserve attention. For this reason, each chapter closes with a discussion of how and where the styles of the period under study survived and were later revived.

The Phenomenon of Fashion in Western Dress

The word *fashion* is often used interchangeably with the words *costume, dress,* and *clothing.* **Fashion** is more precisely defined as a taste shared by many for a short period of time. Although fashion as a social phenomenon is not limited to clothing (it can be observed in such diverse aspects of modern life as the design of automobiles, houses, or furniture; in literary styles; and in vacation destinations), it is very much

a feature of 20th- and 21st-century clothing styles. It is also a characteristic of **western dress**, the dress prevalent in western Europe and Euro-America since the Middle Ages.

Although acceptance of a style by a large and influential part of the population is characteristic of all periods, frequent change of these styles is not. Although occasional exceptions can sometimes be observed in earlier periods, it is generally agreed that fashion as a pervasive social phenomenon first appeared in western Europe in the Middle Ages. The precise date when fashions began changing more rapidly is debated, but it is clear that by the 15th century, style changes were occurring at least every several decades instead of taking a hundred or more years.

Scholars who have investigated fashion as a social phenomenon agree that for fashion change to occur, a society must have sufficient affluence for a reasonably large number of people to participate in the fashion process, a class structure that is open enough to allow movement from one social class to another, and a means of communication of fashion information. The history of western dress in the Middle Ages and later is a history of fashionable dress worn by affluent people.

As a social phenomenon, FASHION is a theme integral to all periods after the Middle Ages. This focus on fashionable rather than utilitarian dress is particularly true of the centuries preceding the French Revolution, which began in 1789. Little documentation of the clothing worn by the poor existed in earlier times. Their clothing was worn until it was no longer serviceable. Their portraits were not painted, and they rarely appeared in other art works of these periods. For the 19th through 21st centuries, far more evidence of costume for all levels of society has been preserved, particularly from the documentation of daguerreotypes, photographs, the moving image, and the Internet (Severa, 1987; Tortora, 2015). Then, too, a far wider proportion of the population was wearing fashionable dress. Recent scholarship has shed some light on the dress of slaves, of the rural and urban poor, and of others who by necessity or by choice did not follow fashion.

By the early 20th century, clothing was mass produced and, especially in the United States, a complex industry developed that linked together textile production, clothing design and manufacture, and retail distribution of clothing. This **fashion system** has made fashionable clothing available in a wide variety of price ranges. As a result, for most of the 20th and 21st centuries, men and women of all income levels have tended to follow current fashions. Consequently, the history of dress is that of fashionable clothing.

The tendency of most consumers to follow one predominant style line began to change in the decades after the 1960s, leading some to predict "the end of fashion." Fashion did not disappear, but rather became more segmented. As a result, the fashion production and distribution system underwent changes. In such periods, and in periods when fashion changes are abrupt or radical, certain aspects of the theme of FASHION may demand special attention.

Fashionable Dress and Folk Dress

Folk costume is, for purposes of this discussion, defined as the dress of the European peasant class. European **folk costume** had its major flowering and development in the 18th and 19th centuries. The European peasant was the farmer or agricultural worker who lived in rural areas or villages. Like urban dwellers, peasants could be quite affluent, moderately well off, or very poor. The terms *ethnic costume* or *traditional costume* are sometimes used to refer to folk dress.

During the 18th and 19th centuries and in some areas into the 21st century, local communities used traditional textiles and dress forms as a means of setting themselves apart from others. Through the vocabulary of folk dress, individuals proclaimed themselves as part of a region or town. Conservative and traditional in its outlook, peasant society stressed conformity and stability rather than change. The Romantic movement in the arts in the 19th century and the adoption of folk costume by royalty in some countries helped reinforce interest in local dress (Snowden, 1979). Although folk dress has sometimes influenced fashionable dress and fashionable elements may appear in folk

styles, folk dress in western Europe diverges from the mainstream of fashionable dress and is not covered in this book; it is too complex and varied a subject to be included in a general survey of western dress.

SOURCES OF EVIDENCE FOR THE STUDY OF HISTORIC COSTUME

The study of costume, then, must take into account the socioeconomic structure of a society, the customs relating to dress, the art of the period, and the technology available for the production of both fabrics and clothing itself. To obtain this information, the costume historian must utilize the evidence he or she can garner from a variety of sources. Because these SOURCES OF INFORMATION ABOUT COSTUME, another ongoing theme in the study of costume, so often determine what is known about costume, this topic is given special attention in each chapter.

The sources of evidence used by the costume historian are plentiful for some periods and relatively scarce for others. The further back one goes in history, the less clear and abundant is the historic record. For periods before the 16th century, the major sources of information are sculpture and painting and, sometimes, written records. Rarely does fabric remain, although there are a few examples of fabrics or clothes discovered at burial sites. Archeological evidence is usually limited to durable items: jewelry, buttons, pins, or decorations.

Written records may amplify the visual records, especially in periods when visual evidence is scarce. For example, historians studying the origins of fashion have generally placed the beginnings of fashion change in the 14th century. However, one author (Heller, 2007) who studied literature of the 11th and 12th centuries noted that French works of fiction called *romances* describe characters who are keen to keep up with fashion and wear fashionable clothes. Artistic representations of dress in this period are somewhat limited, and she argued that this leads to a mistaken belief that following fashion does not appear until later. Those who study the dress of antiquity, especially in Greece and Rome, often benefit from also studying the writings of those periods.

After the invention of the printing press in the 1500s, written and pictorial records of European costume became more abundant, with even more material added after the widespread adoption of daguerreotypes in the 19th century. Fabrics and individual items of costume have been preserved since the early Renaissance, although the supply becomes plentiful only around the 18th century. Many items of dress from the early 19th century to the present day have been preserved in museums and costume collections.

To obtain a complete picture of dress in a given era, historians must assemble evidence from all of the sources available. These sources must be checked against others, including written as well as pictorial records. Even so, the student of historic costume should be aware of some of the problems involved in obtaining accurate dates for particular styles.

Because many of the representations of costumes from the 18th century and earlier periods come from art works, the artistic conventions of a given period may interfere with accurate representations of dress. For example, it is believed that Egyptian artists depicted women in tight-fitting garments that in actuality were probably worn in a less form-fitting version. Artists such as Gainsborough and Rembrandt enjoyed dressing the individuals who were sitting for portraits in fanciful, imaginary costumes. Some paintings of earlier historical scenes depict figures dressed in costumes the artist imagined were worn at the time. French painters of about 1800 dressed figures in scenes from Greek and Roman history according to their perceptions of Greek or Roman styles, with varying historical accuracy.

Sometimes the attribution of a painting to a particular country or date may be in error. Also, standards of modesty may preclude the depiction of certain items of costume, such as underclothing, leaving the costume historian without a record of the appearance of such garments.

Even when fashion magazines of the 19th, 20th, and 21st centuries are consulted, one must remember "proposed" styles were often shown that may not necessarily have been actually worn at the time. It is a fairly safe assumption that many women copied the fashion plates shown therein, and yet Elizabeth Ann Coleman, curator emeritus at Boston Museum of Fine Arts, pointed out that even though skirts with lavish panels of decoration appeared in fashion magazines of the crinoline period, few, if any, costumes in collections show this characteristic. Fashion magazines stress the ideal and not necessarily the real (1972).

Written material can also be difficult to interpret. Fashion terms with one meaning may take on a different meaning at a later time. When used before 1800, the term *pelisse* usually implied an outdoor garment with some fur trim or lining. In the 19th century, a pelisse was still an outdoor garment but did not necessarily have fur associated with it. The precise meaning of some terms is lost. The words *kalasiris* in Egypt and *cote-hardie* in the Middle Ages are examples of words that have been given a number of different definitions by various costume historians. Writers of earlier periods often used color and fabric names that are no longer understood.

The interpretation of written material cannot always be taken literally, which is particularly true of sumptuary laws that restricted the use of spending on luxury items. These laws were not always enforced. Although such laws may express a certain attitude toward social stratification, society was not always prepared to obey or impose them.

Even photographs must be viewed with a skeptical eye. Many photographs are not reliably dated. People generally dressed in their best clothing to be photographed, so these pictures may not be representative of all types of clothing. Fashion photographs share some of the problems of fashion drawings in showing proposed styles. In addition, camera angles may purposely distort the proportions of garments.

Finally, one must treat actual garments that remain with some degree of skepticism. Dating of some items may be inaccurate. Individuals who donate items to costume collections may give the date of an item on the basis of the ages of the owners during the last years of their lives rather than at the time the garments were actually worn. Then, too, a garment may have been remodeled several times, thereby making it difficult to assign an accurate date.

The dating of historic costume, therefore, requires corroborative evidence from a variety of sources. For this reason, one may encounter discrepancy between different writings about historic costume concerning the precise practices in periods where evidence is scarce or fragmentary.

Summary

Readers can follow the themes identified in the foregoing discussion through the chapters of this text. Headings within each chapter help identify material related to some of these themes; however, not all themes will be evident or important in all periods, especially in periods when data about costume are lacking or unclear or the historical record is incomplete.

Finally, recurring topics do not exist in isolation. Factors that influence dress are often the result of many interconnecting themes. A brief look at one rather simple example serves to illustrate this point. In 1947, following the end of World War II, designer Christian Dior showed a collection that came to be known as the New Look, because it represented a pronounced change from the styles of the wartime years. In considering the speed with which these stylistic changes were adopted, one can identify a number of themes that, working together, helped to promote the new style. Among the themes that can be identified are these: THE RELATIONSHIP BETWEEN COSTUME AND THE WORK OF AN INDIVIDUAL DESIGNER, evident in the presence of a talented and perceptive designer, Christian Dior; ECONOMIC EVENTS, which made possible the renewal of production of luxury textile fabrics and their availability to Dior; and the active participation of various MEDIA OF COMMUNICATION, as the fashion press not only named the style but promoted its adoption worldwide.

Far more complex relationships can be identified in each of the periods examined in this text. These complex interactions help make the study of historic costume so fascinating.

REFERENCES

Adovasio, J. M., Soffer, O., & Page, J. (2009). *The invisible sex: Uncovering the true roles of women in prehistory.* Walnut Creek, CA: Left Coast Press.

Barber, E. J. W. (1991). *Prehistoric textiles.* Princeton, NJ: Princeton University Press.

Coleman, E. A. (1972). *Changing fashions, 1800–1970.* Brooklyn, NY: Brooklyn Museum Bookshop.

Dubin, L. S. (2009). *The history of beads from 100,000 BCE to the present.* New York: Abrams.

Eicher, J. B., & Roach-Higgins, M. E. (1992). Describing dress: A system of classifying and defining. In R. Barnes & J. B. Eicher (Eds.), *Dress and gender: Making and meaning in cultural context* (pp. 8–28). Washington, DC: Berg.

Erekosima, T., & Eicher, J. (1981). Kalabari "cut-thread" and "pulled-thread" clothing: An example of cultural authentication. *African Arts, 14*(2), 48–51, 57.

Heller, S. G. (2007). *Fashion in medieval France.* Rochester, NY: Brewer.

Jasper, C. R., & Roach-Higgins, M. E. (1987). History of costume: Theory and instruction. *Clothing and Textiles Research Journal, 5*(4), 1–6.

Kidwell, C. B., & Steele, V. (Eds.). (1989). *Dressing the part.* Washington, DC: Smithsonian Institution Press.

Kuttruff, J. T., DeHart, G., & O'Brien, M. J. (1998). 7,500 years of prehistoric footwear: Tianyuan and Sunghir. *Journal of Archeological Science, 35*, 1928–1933.

Kvavadze, E., Bar-Yosef, O., Belfer-Cohen, A., Boaretto, E., Jakeli, N., Matshevich, N., & Meshveliani, T. (2009). 30,000 year old wild flax fibers. *Science, 325*(5946), 1359.

Laver, J. (1950). *Dress*. London, UK: Albemarle.

Marcketti, S. B., & Angstman, E. T. (2013). The trend for mannish suits in the 1930s. *Dress 39*(2), 135–152.

Roach, M. E., & Musa, K. E. (1980). *New perspectives on the history of western dress: A handbook*. New York, NY: NutriGuides.

Scott, A. F. (1975). *Everyone a witness: The plantagenet age*. New York, NY: Crowell.

Severa, J. (1987). *Dressed for the photographer: Ordinary Americans and fashion, 1840–1900*. Kent, Ohio: Kent State University Press.

Soffer, O., Adovasio, J. M., & Hyland, D. C. (2000). The "Venus" figurines: Textiles, basketry, gender, and status in the upper Paleolithic. *Current Anthropology, 41*(4), 511–537.

Snowden, J. (1979). *The folk dress of Europe*. New York, NY: Mayflower.

Theme. (1988). In *Webster's New World Dictionary*. Cleveland, OH: Simon & Schuster.

Tortora, P. G. (2015). *Dress, fashion and technology: From prehistory to present*. New York, NY: Bloomsbury.

Trinkaus, E., & Shang, H. (2008). Anatomical evidence for the antiquity of human footwear from Arnold Research Cave, Missouri. *Science, 281*, 72–75.

Waugh, N. (1964). *The cut of men's clothes, 1600–1900*. New York, NY: Theatre Arts Books.

PART ONE

The Ancient World

The roots of Western Civilization are to be found in the area around the Mediterranean Sea, a region that gave rise to a series of civilizations that formed the artistic, religious, philosophical, and political basis of Western culture. The valley of the Nile River and the land between the Tigris and the Euphrates rivers were the locations of some of the earliest agriculturally based urban societies.

About 3,500 years before Christ, a civilization flourished in the region that the Greeks would later call Mesopotamia, "the land between the waters" (the Tigris and Euphrates), which approximates modern-day Iraq. This region became the home of a people called the Sumerians. Over the next 2,500 years, the center of civilization and the site of political power spread gradually northward into Babylonia and Assyria.

The first civilization that was established at Sumer developed the city-state, the first example of urban planning, including cobbled streets and multistory buildings (the Tower of Babel); a system of canals for irrigation; and, most importantly, a form of writing. During the Babylonian domination of Mesopotamia, the first written collection of laws was drafted, the Code of Hammurabi, and a level of mathematics was achieved that was unsurpassed until the Renaissance.

Concurrently, about 3000 BCE in the Nile River Valley, the Egyptians were developing another center of culture, a civilization that endured for almost 3,000 years. Also between 2000 and 1400 BCE, the island of Crete (the home of a people known as the Minoans) became the center of an important Mediterranean civilization. Minoan civilization was marked by a high standard of housing and material possessions; organized production of food, textiles, and other products; and a vigorous trade with remote regions. The Minoans eventually extended their cultural influence to mainland Greece. This mainland area included the town of Mycenae, home of a people called the Mycenaeans. After about 1400 BCE, the Mycenaeans, in a reversal of power, came to dominate not only the mainland but also Crete.

Soon after 1200 BCE, the Dorians, a wave of invaders that historians believe came from regions to the north, overwhelmed the Mycenaean civilization, and Greece entered a Dark Age about which little is known. During the Archaic Age of the seventh through fifth centuries BCE Greek colonists left their homes to found colonies in the Mediterranean area. The Classical Age of Greece in the fifth and fourth centuries BCE, the period of the great philosophers and playwrights and Greek democracy, ended in the early 300s after the Greeks, led by Alexander the Great, conquered much of the eastern Mediterranean regions.

The westward colonization that extended Greek art and culture influenced the Etruscans, who were a people living in the Italian peninsula. The Etruscans dominated central Italy from 800 BCE until they were absorbed by the Romans in the third century BCE. The Romans went on to triumph over the other civilizations surrounding the Mediterranean. Eventually the Roman legions conquered not only North Africa and the Middle East but also the lands extending as far northeast to the Danube River and northwest into much of Britain.

Table I.1 compares the periods and duration of each of these civilizations. As the table shows, some of these peoples reached their peak of power and development at the same time. Others flowered and then declined while new centers of influence were rising. Some cultures borrowed liberally from one another, such as the Greeks, the Etruscans, and the Romans, while others, such as Egypt and Mesopotamia, although in contact, evolved in different directions.

Figure I.1 shows the locations of the most important of the civilizations of antiquity.

Although each of the Mediterranean cultures had its own distinctive forms of various items of dress, a number of basic garment types can be identified that were common to most of these cultures. The Mediterranean basin possesses a warm climate in which draped clothing is more comfortable than fitted clothing. With a few notable exceptions, garments of the region consisted of a draped length of square,

TABLE I.1 Civilizations of the Ancient World

TIME PERIOD	MESOPOTAMIA	EGYPT	CRETE	GREECE	ETRURIA	ROME
4000–3000 BCE	Sumerian civilization	Unification of Egypt				
3000–2000		Old Kingdom				
2000–1000	Rise of Babylonia	Middle Kingdom	Minoan civilization	Mycenaean civilization		
		New Kingdom	Mycenaean			
1000–800	Rise of Assyria			Dark Age		
800–600		Decline of Native Egyptian civilization	Greek civilization	Homeric (Archaic) period	Rise of Etruscan civilization	
600–500	Neo-Babylonian period					Etruscan kings of Rome
500–400	Persian conquests of Asia and Middle East			Golden Age		Roman Republic
400–300	Greek conquests	Greek conquests		Alexander the Great		
300–200					End of Etruscan Confederation	
200–CE 0					Roman Empire	Roman Empire
0–300	Roman domination	Roman domination	Roman domination	Roman domination		

FIGURE I.1 Locations of the civilizations of the ancient world in the Mediterranean region.

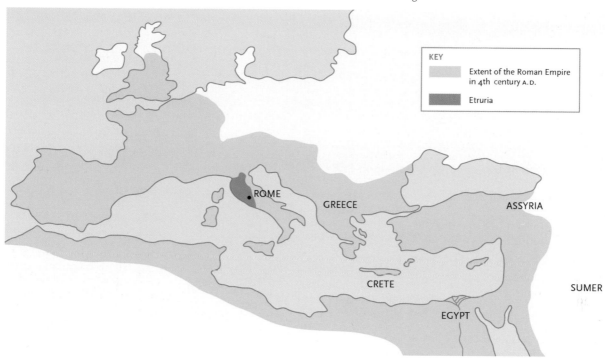

rectangular, or semicircular fabric. When fastening was required, these draped garments were closed with pins or by sewing. The general term used by archeologists for a pin that was used in holding a garment together is a Roman word, **fibula**.

These draped garments can be further subdivided into loincloths, skirts, tunics, shawls, cloaks, and veils. The **loincloth** was a length of cloth wrapped to cover the genitals. The **skirt**, in the ancient world, began at the waist or slightly below and hung loosely around the body. Skirts were worn by both men and women and varied in length. **Tunics** were simple, one-piece, and often T-shaped garments with openings for the head and the arms. Tunics were usually long enough to cover the torso and, like skirts, were made in many different lengths.

Rectangles, squares, or ovals of fabric were commonly combined with skirts or tunics. These **shawl**-like garments ranged from pieces that covered only the upper body to larger squares that were wrapped to cover the entire body. Large squares of fabric tied or pinned at the neck, rather like a modern cape, served as a **cloak** or outdoor covering. **Veils**, smaller rectangles than either shawls or cloaks, were

worn to cover the head and, sometimes, part of the body. Veils were worn almost exclusively by women.

Terminology from these periods can be confusing, as different authorities use different phonetic terms for words that modern people have never heard pronounced and with which readers are unfamiliar. For this reason descriptions of dress must rely upon using the closest modern equivalent for the garment in order that the reader can relate the unfamiliar term to one that is more familiar. Sometimes modern terms have taken on connotations that are misleading or confusing when that term is applied to historic dress. For example, the term *skirt* is associated with an item of women's clothing. In the ancient world, however, both men and women wore what could be described as skirts. As a result, many sources will refer to the skirt as worn by men as a *kilt*, even though *kilt* is actually a Scottish word for a specific style worn by men. For this reason the authors have chosen to use the nearest equivalent modern word descriptive of the form of the item of dress. This is with the exception of those instances where an ancient word has come into modern usage, such as *toga* (from Latin) or *chiton* (from the Greek).

	3500 BCE	3300–1900 BCE	2500–1500 BCE	c. 1938–1600 BCE
FASHION AND TEXTILES		Sumerian towns and cities give rise to refined skills and technologies in the textile arts		
POLITICS AND CONFLICTS		Lower and Upper Egypt unite (2925–2575 BCE) Old Kingdom in Egypt (2575–2130 BCE)	Sargon and Akkadians conquer Sumerian civilization (2334–2279 BCE) First intermediate period in Egypt (2130–2080 BCE)	Middle Kingdom in Egypt; Egyptians extend political and cultural influence into Palestine and south along the Nile
DECORATIVE AND FINE ARTS				
ECONOMICS AND TRADE			Mesopotamians trade with Indus Valley civilization	Servants carry gifts and offerings
TECHNOLOGY AND IDEAS	Mesopotamians found first cities; cuneiform writing develops	Hieroglyphic writing develops		King Hammurabi develops code of law (1792–1750 BCE)
RELIGION AND SOCIETY		Building of the first step pyramid	Building of the first "pure" pyramids	

CHAPTER TWO

The Ancient Middle East

c. 3500–600 BCE

1630–1540 BCE	1479–1477 BCE	1470–11TH CENTURY BCE	12TH CENTURY BCE–332 BCE
Second Intermediate period Conquest of Egypt by Hyksos (1630 BCE)	Egypt expands under Thutmose III	New Kingdom	Egyptian power declines Assyrians conquer Egypt (670 BCE) Chaldean Babylon (625–539 BCE) Persians conquer Mesopotamia (525 BCE) Greeks conquer Egypt (332 BCE)
	Skilled artisans work with ivory veneers and ebony wood		

The first civilizations in the Middle East were located in Mesopotamia, in the region between the Tigris and Euphrates rivers (the name *Mesopotamia* means "between rivers"). At the same period that the early Mesopotamian civilization was developing between these rivers, the Nile River became the site of the Egyptian civilization.

HISTORICAL BACKGROUND

Mesopotamia

The greater part of ancient Mesopotamia occupied the area extending from the Persian Gulf to near the borders between modern Iraq and Turkey. Towns and cities first developed in the southern parts of the region. Thanks to the rich, fertile plains created by the deposits from the two rivers, agriculture and herding produced sufficient food to enable the establishment of towns and cities where residents developed complex social organizations.

The people called the Sumerians entered the area from the northeast about 3500 BCE. They founded the first cities in southern Mesopotamia. The Sumerian civilization (3500–2500 BCE) invented a form of writing that enabled them to keep records of their activities, codify laws, and transmit knowledge (Figure 2.1). The Sumerians never developed a strong political organization and remained only a loose confederation of city-states that came under the domination of a northern neighbor, Akkad, led by Sargon (c. 2334–2279 BCE), who extended Akkadian influence into Asia Minor. The Amorites, new invaders from the west, conquered Sumer and Akkad and established a new empire with the capital at Babylon. These Babylonians created an autocratic state. During the reign of King Hammurabi (c. 1792–1750 BCE), they extended their control northward. His famous law code, dealing with almost every facet of life, influenced later Middle Eastern law codes, including Mosaic law.

Babylonian power declined after about 1700 BCE as a series of invaders attacked the empire. Control of the region seesawed back and forth among the invaders until after 1000 BCE, when a powerful Assyrian army from the upper Tigris River conquered Babylonia. The Assyrians developed the first great military machine consisting of a large standing army equipped with superior weapons, including iron swords. Their empire, which stretched into Syria, Palestine, and even Egypt, was the largest the Near East had seen. The cruelties of the hated and feared Assyrians led their enemies to conspire against them. This brought about their downfall. In 612 BCE, the armies of the Chaldeans, who now ruled Babylonia, destroyed Nineveh, the capital of Assyria, thereby ending the Assyrian empire. In time, Chaldean Babylon fell to a new and greater power, the Persians under Cyrus in 539 BCE.

Chaldean Babylon was notorious for its luxury and wealth. The Chaldeans constructed the Hanging Gardens, a terraced roof garden considered one of the seven wonders of the ancient world. Motivated by their religion, the Chaldeans became the most competent astronomers in Mesopotamian history. Their records of the movements of the heavenly bodies were maintained for more than 350 years.

FIGURE 2.1 As the civilization of the Sumerians grew more complex, they invented a form of writing known as cuneiform to keep records and transmit knowledge. This tool was very useful to manufacturers and merchants of textiles. (Dorling Kindersley/Getty Images)

Egypt

Deserts and seas protected the land of Egypt from foreign invaders. Agriculture flourished thanks to the annual flooding of the Nile, which left behind a rich deposit of soil that made fertilizers unnecessary. These factors enabled the development of an advanced civilization.

The ancient Egyptian kingdoms flourished from about 3200 BCE until about 300 BCE, when Greeks led by Alexander the Great conquered Egypt. Historians have divided Egyptian history into six periods: the early dynastic period, the Old Kingdom, the first intermediate period, the Middle Kingdom, the second intermediate period, and the New Kingdom. Within each period are a number of dynasties or sequences of rule by members of the same family.

During the early dynastic period (c. 2925–2575 BCE), two separate kingdoms that bordered the Nile were united under the first pharaoh, or king. The first pyramid, a step pyramid, was constructed (Figure 2.2). Pyramids were intended not only to be the tombs of the pharaohs but also a sign that the Egyptian state was indestructible. The newly unified state required that records be kept. To meet this need the earliest form of Egyptian writing was invented.

FIGURE 2.2 Building of pyramids in Egypt began in the Old Kingdom with a pyramid that rose in a series of steps. These pyramids served as burial places for the pharoah and as an illustration of the indestructibility of the Egyptian state.

By the time of the Old Kingdom (2575–2130 BCE), the powers of the pharaohs had become unlimited, and pyramid building had become the chief activity of the monarchy. The pyramids were astounding feats of engineering, dwarfing monuments from other eras. The great pyramid of Cheops, which reached the height of 481 feet, contained more than two million limestone blocks fitted together with great precision. Some weighed more than 15 tons. But pyramid building exhausted the government's revenues. Weak pharaohs lost control of the government, and local nobles, usurping power, began to act like petty kings.

The succeeding first intermediate period (c. 2130–2080 BCE) was a time of turmoil, civil war, and disorder. Tombs of the pharaohs were looted, and bandits robbed travelers; desert tribes invaded Egypt.

Pharaohs of the 11th and 12th dynasties established the Middle Kingdom (c. 1938–1600 BCE) and united the country after ending the period of anarchy. A stronger central government was restored; public works that benefited the population replaced pyramid building. Egyptian influence was extended into Palestine and south along the Nile. As prosperity returned, wealth became more widespread among the Egyptian people. This period ended with the first serious threat from abroad.

The second intermediate period (c. 1630–1540 BCE) brought revolts by the nobility and a weakening of the pharaohs' power. About 1630 BCE, a nomadic people from western Asia, the Hyksos, seized control of Egypt. The Hyksos, who brought horse-drawn chariots and new weapons, soon adopted Egyptian customs and ways, including the power and title of pharaoh. The Egyptians launched a revolt against the hated Hyksos under the leadership of the founder of the 18th dynasty, finally driving them from Egypt. In the period of the New Kingdom (1470–11th century BCE, also called the period of Empire), Egypt became a strong, military power under the pharaoh Thutmose III (1504–1450 BCE). His leadership of 17 military campaigns expanded Egyptian rule eastward to the Euphrates. Thutmose III made Egypt a powerful force in the eastern Mediterranean region. The new monarchy restored temples and built luxurious palaces. Earlier art forms that had been stylized and monumental became more natural and realistic.

By the 12th century, Egyptian power had declined and society had decayed; the empire was disappearing as foreign powers conquered Egypt. The Persians invaded in 525 BCE. Egypt stagnated, its glory far in the past. In 332 BCE, Alexander the Great, a Greek from Macedonia, conquered Egypt, ending Persian rule. Successive periods of Egyptian history were marked by domination first by Greece and then by Rome. A truly native Egyptian civilization had ended (Figure 2.3).

Details of the life and history of Egypt are more complete than those for Mesopotamia over the same period. Like the Mesopotamians, the Egyptians had a form of writing, known as hieroglyphic, which historians have deciphered. Written records provide an abundant source of information about Egyptian life and religion. The Egyptians not only believed in life after death but also buried personal possessions (e.g., tools, furniture, food, and drink) with the dead so that they might use them in the afterlife. The hot, dry climate of the desert where prominent Egyptians were buried preserved these objects, often in excellent condition. In addition, many of the temples and tombs contained paintings and sculpture, but unlike the Mesopotamians whose art generally emphasized the ceremonial aspects of life, the Egyptians painted and sculpted individuals engaged in a variety of daily tasks (see Figure 2.12).

DIFFERENCES IN THE EGYPTIAN AND MESOPOTAMIAN CIVILIZATIONS

One of the most outstanding aspects of Egyptian civilization is the relative slowness with which changes occurred. It is not that there were no significant changes in the 3,000 years during which this civilization existed, but they took place so gradually that they seemed almost

FIGURE 2.3 As Egyptian civilization declined, other states ruled Egypt. During the period that Greece under Alexander the Great was the ruling power, Egyptians adopted Greek styles of dress. (Alinari/Art Resource, NY)

imperceptible, even over several hundred years. For almost 3,000 years, Egyptian civilization was scarcely affected by foreign cultural and political influences. According to historian Fairservis (1962), "Between the Egypt of the Pyramid Age and that of Cleopatra were many differences, but many of these seem superficial, for much of the hard core of Egyptian thought and institutions was comparatively unchanged after some 25 centuries" (84–85).

The civilizations of Mesopotamia display greater diversity when viewed over a period of 3,000 years. One reason for these differences may be the geographical unity of the landscape in Egypt, in contrast to a variety of landscapes and types of terrain in Mesopotamia. Egypt was a narrow strip of land set in the valley of the Nile where annual floods maintained the fertility of the land. Deserts on either side provided security from invasion, while throughout Egypt farmers carried on the ceaseless routine of agriculture. In Mesopotamia, regions differed more. Each area supported specific crops, and each crop required special skills and care. The necessary labor force, the investment of capital, and the organization of agriculture were different in each region. For example, flocks had to be moved seasonally, but grain crops required long-term storage and distribution throughout the year. Some crops required long-range planting and planning, while others could be sown and harvested in a short time.

These differences also accounted for some variations between the dress of the two cultures. While the climate in Egypt was relatively warm and uniform throughout the year, that of Mesopotamia was more variable, including both high-altitude areas where warm clothing was required at some times of the year and hot, desert areas.

Another difference was the degree to which each culture was subjected to outside influences. Both traded abroad to obtain raw materials unavailable within the boundaries of the region. With trade came outside influences. Egypt, however, was less open to outside influences because of the sea and the desert, natural barriers that provided security from foreigners. Mesopotamia lacked natural barriers to invasion, and

foreign invaders entered periodically. Some came to dominate the region and adopted many traditions of the native people. In this way traditions were perpetuated, but at the same time new ideas were also incorporated into the culture. Egypt maintained a continuity in political and religious tradition that was seriously threatened from outside only once, by the Hyksos.

MESOPOTAMIAN CIVILIZATION

This review of the history of the Mesopotamians is divided into three periods: Early Sumerian (c. 3500–2500 BCE), Later Sumerian and Babylonian (c. 2500–1000 BCE), and Assyrian (c. 1000–600 BCE). Relatively little is known of the earliest period of Sumerian history. The record is clearer during the latter part of the period and it is possible to obtain a better picture of some aspects of life, in general, and of dress in particular.

Social Structure

The Babylonian culture was based on the earlier Sumerian civilization, and the social structure of the Babylonians was similar to that of the Sumerians. Social classes were clearly defined. The nobility stood far above all the rest of society. Babylonian society was divided into those who were free; an intermediate class of people who might be called "the poor," who were "worth little"; and the slaves, who were "worth nothing." The free made up a sort of middle class of artisans, tradesmen, lesser public officials, and laborers. Farmers were generally part of the intermediate or poor class. Slaves were relatively few in Sumer, but by the time of the Babylonians they had grown in number as they became an increasingly necessary part of the workforce. Slaves could be foreign captives, the children of slaves, or wives or children of free men sold into slavery to meet the debts of the father of the family. Adopted children who disgraced their adoptive parents could also be sold into slavery (Contenau, 1954).

The Family

The family was patriarchal in structure. Marriage was a contractual arrangement generally made to cement an economic alliance between two families. By this contract, a man had a principal wife but could, and usually did, keep one or more concubines as well. Divorce was easily obtained if the principal wife was unable to have children.

The art that remains from Sumer and Babylonia indicates that the position of women was a subordinate one. Representations of men predominate, and illustrations of women—usually goddesses, priestesses, or queens—are relatively rare. Women were not completely without rights, however, as Babylonian legal codes extended to them the right to testify in court cases and provided some degree of economic protection in the case of the death of a husband.

Although children had no legal rights, letters written on clay tablets and sent from children of the upper classes to their parents reveal that they felt free to demand the clothing or jewelry that they considered appropriate to their rank. One boy wrote to his mother:

> From year to year the clothes of the young gentlemen here become better, but you let my clothes get worse from year to year. Indeed you persisted in making my clothes poorer and more scanty. At a time when in our house wool is used up like bread, you have made me poor clothes. The son of Adididdinam whose father is only an assistant of my father has two new sets of clothes while you fuss even about a single set of clothes for me. In spite of the fact that you bore me and his mother only adopted him, his mother loves him, while you do not love me. (Oppenheim, 1967, 67)

Another boy wrote to his father:

> I have never before written to you for something precious I wanted. But if you want to be like a father to me, get me a fine string full of beads, to be worn around the head it should be full [of beads] and it should be beautiful. If I see it and dislike it, I shall send it back! Also send the cloak, of which I spoke to you. (Oppenheim, 1967, 85)

Fabrics and Cloth Production

The cloak and the new sets of clothes these boys asked for were most likely made of wool. The chief products of Mesopotamia are described as barley, wool, and oil. These fabrics were produced not just for domestic consumption, but were traded to other regions as well. Flax is occasionally mentioned in the ancient records, but although fragments of linen have been found in excavations and there were skilled linen weavers, linen was clearly less important than wool, which is mentioned often along with quotes for current prices. Clothes, tapestries, and curtains were made of wool. One contract has been found that describes the period of apprenticeship for a weaver as 5 years, an exceptionally long time when compared with the training of other artisans. However, the variety of fabrics and the decorations applied to them seem to have been quite complex, so the weaver may have had to master quite a complicated system of manufacture (Leix, 1938).

In writing about women's work in the ancient world, Barber (1994) noted that in the 19th century BCE women often played an important role in producing Mesopotamian textiles. Women seem to have been responsible for spinning and weaving, while men may have completed the dyeing and finishing (Figure 2.4). Although men traveled long distances to trade in textiles, women often supervised local textile production and took care of aspects of business close to home.

FIGURE 2.4 Back strap looms were an early technology for weaving textiles. With the yarns wrapped around the waist, the weaver could increase or decrease the tension needed on the lengthwise by changing position. (© Gianni Dagli Orti/Corbis)

SOURCES OF EVIDENCE ABOUT SUMERIAN COSTUME

The evidence for details of the costume of Mesopotamia is largely derived from visual materials. Depictions of individuals are found on seals (small engraved markers used to press an identification into clay and wax). These seals had scenes of Sumerian mythology incised or cut into them. A few wall paintings survive, as do small votive statuettes of worshippers left at shrines as substitutes for the worshippers themselves, to provide a sort of perpetual presence of the individual at the temple. Some impressions of Sumerian dress can be gained from these rather limited remains and from the excavation of Sumerian tombs.

MESOPOTAMIAN/SUMERIAN COSTUME: c. 3500–2500 BCE

Costume Components for Men and Women

Garments

Skirts, worn by both men and women, were the major item of dress seen in the art of this era. In the earliest period, these were probably made of sheepskin with the fleece still attached. A Greek word, **kaunakes**, has been applied to this fleece or fleecelike fabric. Lengths varied: Servants and soldiers wore shorter lengths; royalty and deities were depicted in longer lengths. Skirts apparently wrapped around the body. When fabric ends were long enough, an end of the fabric length was passed up, under a belt, and over one shoulder (Figure 2.5). Even after sheepskin had been supplemented by woven cloth, the cloth was fringed at the hem or constructed to simulate tufts of wool on the fleece (Figure 2.6).

Fragments of cloth from an excavation of the tomb of a queen showed that she and her attendants wore a bright red, heavy woolen fabric at the time of their deaths.

Belts were located at the waist to hold skirts in place. They appear to have been wide and padded.

Cloaks were probably made from animal skins, leather, or heavy, felted cloth and covered the upper part of the body.

Hair and Headdress

Shaving the head was a practice of several Mediterranean cultures, including the early Mesopotamian and the Egyptian. Very likely this was a means of discouraging vermin and for comfort in the hot climate. Mesopotamian men are depicted both clean shaven and bearded. Sometimes their heads are bald (see Figure 2.6). Both men and women might have pulled their long hair into a **chignon** (*sheen'yon*), a bun of hair at the back of the neck, which was held in place by a **fillet** (*fil'it*), another name for a headband. Alternatively, they also wore their hair falling straight to the shoulders and held in place by a fillet. Over their heads, soldiers wore closely fitted helmets with pointed tops that may have been made of leather.

Jewelry

From archeological evidence it appears that some royal women apparently wore elaborate gold jewelry. An excavation at the city of Ur from c. 2800 BCE unearthed a beautiful gold and jeweled crown (Figure 2.7), made

FIGURE 2.5 Praying figure. Mesopotamian, Sumerian, c. 2200 BCE. Sumerian man wearing a kaunakes garment in the form of a wrapped skirt. The end of the skirt is thrown over his left shoulder. Both men and women wore the same type of garment. (Erich Lessing/Art Resource, NY)

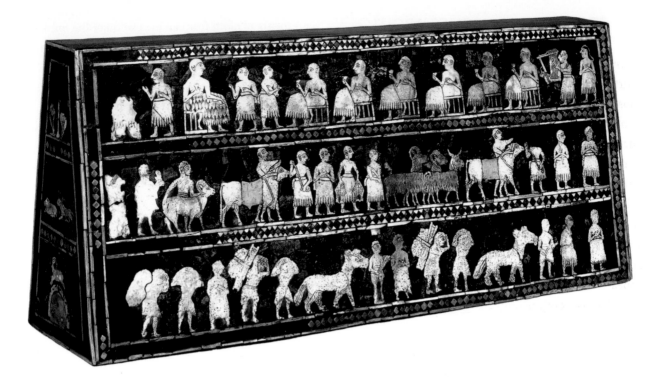

FIGURE 2.6 The seated man in the top row, left side, is wearing a kaunakes skirt, while most other figures are dressed in fringed skirts. A few of the laborers in the lowest panel appear to be wearing loincloths or very short skirts. (© The Trustees of The British Museum/Art Resource, NY)

with delicate leaves and flowers, and massive gold necklaces and earrings. Comparable items have not been found for later periods, nor are they depicted in the art of the period.

COSTUME OF MESOPOTAMIANS/LATER SUMERIANS AND BABYLONIANS: c. 2500–1000 BCE

Styles evolved slowly, and sharp distinctions cannot be made between garments of the later Sumerian and early Babylonian periods. Costume generally increased in complexity. Although men's and women's dress continued to utilize similar elements, evidence indicates a trend toward greater distinctions in the clothing for each gender. Skirts continued in use. Shawls, woven rectangles or squares of fabric, were draped in various ways. Tunics were worn.

FIGURE 2.7 Woman's headdress and jewelry, including a comb, hair rings, hair ribbons, and earrings found during the excavation of the tomb of what was probably a royal woman in Ur, Mesopotamia, about 2800 BCE. The ornaments were made of gold and the gemstones lapis lazuli and carnelian. (Courtesy of Penn Museum, Image #152100)

Costume Components for Men

Garments

Skirts, loincloths, and tunics probably made up the most common items of dress for the poor. The nobility or mythological figures were depicted wearing a draped garment described by Houston (1964) as made from a square of fabric about 118 inches wide and 56 inches long. Figure 2.8 depicts Ur-Ningirsu, son of Gudea, a ruler of c. 2120 BCE wearing a draped cloth. Sumerian and Babylonian art depicts these garments as smooth surfaced, without draped folds, but this is probably an artistic convention. Not only do the woven fabrics appear to fall without folds, but even faces, skin, and arms have smooth planes and lack detail. Fabrics are fringed or have woven or embroidered edging.

Hair and Headdress

Before 2300 BCE, men are shown both clean shaven and with beards. Later, men are depicted only with beards. Hats are turbanlike and closely fitted at the crown, with a small brim or padded roll at the edge (see Figure 2.8).

Footwear

Feet usually are shown as bare or with sandals, which would have provided covering in rough terrain. Archeologists have found a clay model of a leather shoe that dates from c. 2600 BCE with a tongue, upward curve to the toe, and a pompom on the toe. Born (1940) suggested that such shoes may have originated in mountainous areas where there was snow and that they may have been brought from there to Mesopotamia. This style of shoe seems to have taken on a ceremonial function, being reserved in sculpture for a heroic figure representing the king. "The peaked shoe with a pompom,"

said Born (1940), "is probably to be regarded as a regal attribute" (1210).

Costume for Specialized Occupations

Military Dress

From depictions of armies and military leaders, we can identify the elements of the dress of soldiers. Skirts were probably made of woven fabric. Fringed decoration around the lower edge persisted in military dress. Shawls were worn with skirts. The center of the shawl was placed across the left shoulder, with the ends crossing the chest and carried back to be knotted over the right hip.

Soldiers wore helmets made of leather or metal, sometimes with horn-shaped decorations. Footwear consisted of sandals, which were worn when rough terrain made foot coverings necessary.

Costume Components for Women

Garments

The kaunakes garment persisted for a time for women, but gradually became associated with religious figures (goddesses, priestesses, or minor deities). In this period, garments were cut to cover the entire body, not just one shoulder as in earlier periods. Evidence is inadequate to be certain of the specific design, but possible constructions were a skirt in combination with a short cape cut with an opening for the head or a tunic with openings for the head and arms.

FIGURE **2.8** Statuette of Ur-Ningirsu, Son of Gudea. Mesopotamia, Neo-Sumerian. c. 2100 BCE. The garment shown here was probably made from a rectangular length of fabric wrapped around the body. On his head is a closely fitted hat with a small brim or padded roll. (Erich Lessing/Art Resource, NY)

Houston (1964) reconstructed two additional garment forms (Figure 2.9). Her suggestions are based on evidence from statues such as those in Figure 2.10 in which the lines shown on the statue are also visible in the proposed reconstruction. This statue wears a head covering characteristic of one of the areas in this region. This headdress covers all of the hair except for a narrow section across the forehead. The woman wears a closely fitted necklace; the statue originally had earrings of precious metal or shell, which have not survived.

Hair and Headdress

The chignon held in place with a fillet continued in use; in some representations, hair appears to be confined in a net.

Footwear

Bare feet were common. The well-to-do wore sandals.

Jewelry

A tightly fitted, dog-collar type of necklace made from several rings of metal was shown most often. Archeologists have found beads that originated from as far away as the Indus Valley of India (see Global Connections).

COSTUME OF MESOPOTAMIANS/LATER BABYLONIANS AND THE ASSYRIANS: c. 1000–600 BCE

The Assyrians adopted Babylonian costume; thus, a clear break between the late Babylonian and early

(a)   (b)

FIGURE 2.9 Houston suggests these reconstructions for Babylonian women's costume. (a) Costume is draped from a rectangle of fabric. Point 2 is placed at center front, points 1 and 3 are drawn under the arms, segment 2–3 crossing over 1–2 in back. Points 1 and 3 are pulled over the shoulder to hang down at each side in front. (b) Costume is draped from a rectangle with one end curved. A small fold of fabric (shaded area) is made at the top. Square corner at point 1 is draped across the right shoulder to the back, across the back and under the left arm, across the front again, passing under the drape of point 1. Point 3 is pulled across the back again and pinned over the shoulder to point 2 in the front. Section 3–4 falls in a drape behind the shoulder to the ground. (Courtesy of Fairchild Publications, Inc.)

Global Connections

The Mesopotamians traded with people living on the coast of what is now India during the Indus Valley civilization (2500–1500 BCE). The beads of this necklace would have been part of that trade, which included not only jewelry made of gold, copper, lapis lazuli, ivory, and various types of shells, but also cotton textiles. A prized commodity made in the Indus Valley, cotton samples found by archeologists indicate that the weavers were highly skilled and understood how to dye the cloth using mordants, substances that improved the intensity and performance of the dyestuff. In return, the Mesopotamians shipped wool to cities on the Indus Valley coast. (© RMN-Grand Palais/Art Resource, NY)

Assyrian styles cannot be seen. Patterns of change in costume history are generally evolutionary. In these early periods, lack of detailed knowledge gives the impression that changes occured slowly over time.

Although the Assyrian leaders adopted the styles of the Babylonians, they added to their decoration. Woven or embroidered patterns are seen in great profusion on the costumes of the king and his chief officials. Cross-cultural contacts through trade or warfare may have had the effect of introducing new style ideas or new materials, thereby having an impact on dress.

FIGURE 2.10 Head and upper body of woman wearing the kind of garment shown in Figure 2.9a. The edges of the neck and drape covering the shoulders are ornamented with what appears to be a type of braid or embroidery. She wears a closely fitted necklace of several strands, and her wavy hair is visible around the edges of the head covering. (© RMN-Grand Palais/Art Resource, NY)

Although the Assyrians continued the tradition of wearing wool garments, King Sennacherib (c. 700 BCE) is said to have introduced cotton to Assyria. He spoke of having "trees bearing wool" in his botanical garden, but there is no solid evidence for the use of cotton by the Assyrians (Barber, 1991).

Costume Components for Men

Garments

The word *tunic* has come into English from Latin and is used here, and subsequently, as a generic term for a T-shaped garment with openings at the top for the head and arms. Textile historian and linguist Elizabeth Barber (1994) suggested that the Latin word *tunica* derived from a Middle Eastern word for linen. She noted that the earliest tunics seem to have been made of linen and that in some areas tunics first appeared just after wool came into use. She concluded that linen tunics were probably adopted as an underlayer to prevent irritation of the skin by wool garments.

Tunic-type garments were an essential part of dress in all of the civilizations of antiquity. Tunics from different civilizations showed variations in cut, construction, and fit; in length; in whether or not they had sleeves; and in the length of those sleeves. Tunics could be made from any type of fabric, although

FIGURE 2.11 Assyrian King Ashurnasirpal II, c. 883–859 BCE, wears his hair long in the style of his period. He is bearded. Over his long tunic he wears a fringed shawl that wraps around his body. He holds a mace, a symbol of his authority, in his left hand and a sickle, a weapon related to Assyrian mythology, in his right hand. (© The Trustees of The British Museum/Art Resource, NY)

when worn next to the body, they were more likely to be linen.

At some point, the Assyrians replaced the skirts and draped garments characteristic of the earlier Babylonian period with tunics. Perhaps the tunic, a closely fitting garment more suitable for cooler climates, was borrowed from nearby mountain people (Figure 2.11).

Royalty wore floor-length tunics beneath several long, fringed shawls. Draping of shawls around the body juxtaposed horizontal, vertical, and diagonal arrangement of fringes and was sufficiently complex to inhibit movement. It is likely that these costumes were for state occasions and that everyday clothing, even for royalty, may have been simpler. In scenes depicting hunting or warfare, the king's costume has less encumbering drapery.

In any civilization, the dress of royal figures is set apart by differences in style, costlier materials, greater elaboration in its decoration, or by the emblems of power in the form of a special headdress, a staff, or a scepter. Often the costume of royalty is specified by tradition and does not necessarily reflect current styles. Mesopotamian artists depicted the garments of the king as covered with what appears to be embroidery, although some authors have suggested that these designs may have been woven. Priests determined the specific garment worn by the king on any given day. The Assyrians believed that some days were favorable and some unfavorable; therefore, a priest would prescribe the most auspicious garment, including its color and fabric. On some unfavorable days, the king was not permitted to change his clothing at all.

Tunics for the laboring classes were worn with a belt and little decoration and ended above the knee. Soldiers wore them knee length with armor.

Hair and Headdress

Men were bearded, with the hair and beard arranged in small curls thought to have been achieved with the help of curling irons. The king's beard was longer than that of other men, and supplemented with a false section (see Figure 2.11). Lower class men had shorter beards and hair.

Among the hat styles was a high brimless hat similar to the **fez** or **tarbush**, a modern-day, traditional Arab style worn in southwest Asia or northern Africa that is shaped like a truncated cone. In Assyrian art this hat is sometimes depicted with broad bands of fabric hanging down the back. The king wore a higher, straighter version similar to hats worn in later centuries by Persian royalty and by Eastern Orthodox Christian priests in the 20th century.

Footwear

Sandals, depending on whether they were to be given heavier or lighter use, had thicker or thinner soles, respectively. Closed shoes are depicted, though less commonly than sandals. High boots are shown on horsemen, probably as protective footwear for the aggressive Assyrian military forces.

Jewelry

Earrings, bracelets, and armlets were worn. Decorative motifs used for jewelry often resembled those seen on patterned fabrics.

Costume for Specialized Occupations

Military Dress

Soldiers wore a short tunic, a corselet of mail, and a wide belt. The mail of this period was probably made by sewing small metal plates onto leather or heavy cloth. Representations of soldiers indicate that sometimes mail covered only the upper torso, while at other times entire tunics were covered in mail. Helmets fit the head closely, coming to a peaked point

at the back of the head. Both sandals and high boots were worn.

Costume Components for Women

Few representations of women are found in Assyrian art. Although the status of women in Sumer and Babylon had been relatively low, Babylonian wives did participate actively when families were engaged in commercial production of textiles. Under Assyrian law, women's right to testify in court was taken away, and some of the Babylonian protection extended to women in regard to property rights was removed. Historians see this as evidence of a possible influx of new people whose customs differed from those of the native population.

Garments

Women wore tunics that were cut with somewhat longer sleeves than those for men. Fabrics used for women's tunics were elaborately patterned. Women also wore fringed shawls draped around the body.

Hair and Headdress

Population and attitude changes may have affected customs surrounding the wearing of veils by women. Assyrian legal codes contained references to wearing veils. In Assyrian and late Babylonian times, the veil was considered to be the distinguishing mark of a free, married woman. Slaves and prostitutes were not permitted to wear veils, and a concubine could wear a veil only when she accompanied the principal wife. Some representations show the veil hanging over the hair on either side of the face, but apparently veils covered the face in public. This custom persists today in some areas of the Middle East, and although the reasons for veiling women are no longer specifically related to marital status, one can see that wearing the veil is a tradition of long duration in the area.

Hairstyles show considerable variety. Earlier styles for Assyrian women are elaborately arranged. Later styles were simplified to curly, shoulder-length hair.

Footwear

Both sandals and closed shoes are depicted.

Jewelry

Jewelry consisted of necklaces, earrings, bracelets, and armlets.

Costume for Children: c. 3500–600 BCE

Sources do not provide any solid information about children's clothing. Children occupied a subservient position in the family. In Babylonia, the father of the family had the right to sell his children into slavery or leave them on deposit with a creditor as security for repayment of a loan. Their costume was probably minimal. When clothing was worn, it may have consisted of the simplest of the adult garments: a loincloth, a skirt, or a tunic. Children of the upper classes probably wore clothing like that of their parents.

EGYPTIAN CIVILIZATION

Egyptian culture and dress developed in quite different ways from that of the Mesopotamian civilizations. Researchers can use extensive evidence about Egyptian life and dress from works of art, real objects, and written records.

Social Structure

The hierarchy of Egyptian society has been compared to the shape of the pyramids. The pharaoh (a hereditary king) was at the top of this pyramid. His chief deputies and the high priests were at the next level. Below them were a host of officials of lesser status who were associated either with the court or the administration of towns and cities.

Other important positions were occupied by the scribes, comparable to the white-collar workers of today, such as department managers, bookkeepers, accountants, clerks, and bureaucrats. They were attached to the courts, city administrations, religious organizations, and the military. These occupations provided an avenue of upward mobility within Egyptian society.

The artisans, a vast throng of skilled workers, such as painters, sculptors, architects, furniture makers, weavers, and jewelers, were a step below the scribes.

Servants, laborers, and the large number of peasants who tilled the land provided the agricultural base on which the upper levels of the social pyramid rested. Slaves were foreign captives, not native Egyptians. Some, like the Hebrew slave Moses, were able to attain freedom and rise to relatively high station, but this was rare (Figure 2.12).

The Upper Classes

Costume served to delineate social class, even though much of Egyptian costume was relatively simple. The draping, the quality of the fabrics, and the addition of costly jewelry and belts distinguished the garments of the upper from those of the lower classes.

Upper class families lived in luxuriously furnished houses. By today's standards, the quantity of furniture was small, but pieces were decorated with beautiful inlays and worked metal (Figure 2.13). Homes were spacious with carefully tended gardens.

Artists often depicted social gatherings at home during the New Kingdom. Men and women dressed lavishly for these occasions, wearing long, full, pleated gowns, vivid cosmetics, and brightly colored jewelry and headdresses. Musicians, acrobats, and dancing girls entertained. Cones of scented wax were set on the heads of guests. As the evening progressed these wax cones would melt, run down over the wigs, and perfume the air (see Figure 2.14, page 39).

The hot climate made cleanliness essential for comfort. Upper class Egyptians had high standards of personal cleanliness, bathing two or more times each day. In some periods, heads were shaved and wigs worn, possibly as a means of keeping the head clean and free from vermin. Class distinctions in grooming practices are evident in Egyptian art. Higher standards of grooming were expected of the upper classes. Workmen are shown in paintings with a stubbly growth of beard, while upper class men are invariably clean shaven.

The Family

Marriage was a civil contract; divorce was easy to obtain. Multiple marriages were not common, although many well-to-do men had a harem or at least several

FIGURE 2.12 Egyptian wall painting, c. 1415 BCE. A variety of costume types. Within the picture can be seen a woman in a sheath dress, various examples of schentis worn without upper body coverings, two workers dressed only in loincloths, sheer tunics of varying lengths worn over or under a schenti. (Image copyright © The Metropolitan Museum of Art. Image source: Art Resource, NY)

concubines. Some wall paintings show scenes of warm, close family life. Fathers and mothers caress the young, and small children play happily with toys or pets.

SOURCES OF EVIDENCE FOR EGYPTIAN COSTUME

Egyptian Art

Many of the buildings of ancient Egypt are gone, the stones used by subsequent generations for building later structures. The massive pyramids remain, as do a number of temples. Statues and carved wall reliefs are still found in these buildings. Although art historians identify various styles that changed over

FIGURE 2.13 With its ivory veneer and ebony wood, this chair from c. 1450 BCE demonstrates the ability of furniture makers to craft fine furniture. (Image copyright © The Metropolitan Museum of Art. Image source: Art Resource, NY)

time in Egyptian art, these changes are hard for the nonspecialist to detect. Fortunately for the costume historian, Egyptian artists depicted people going about their daily activities; much of the information about Egyptian costume has been gained through such art.

Artists probably did not always depict costume with absolute fidelity. Artists followed strict guidelines that governed the proportions of sculpture and relief depictions of important figures. These conventions derived from the Egyptian system of measurement. In relief carvings and wall paintings the conventional pose shows shoulders to the front, head and legs facing to the right or left. Clothing is often shown frontally, while legs face to one side (Iversen, 1975). It is likely that the representation of some costume forms in art may have lagged behind their actual adoption; others may not have been depicted at all.

Then, too, artists depicted lower status individuals as smaller in size than those who were more important. As a result, these figures sometimes have been mistakenly identified as children.

The Contents of Tombs

Much of Egyptian art has been preserved in tombs where painters decorated the walls with scenes from daily life and the afterlife. Personal possessions and models of useful objects were placed in tombs. The dead, awakening to the afterlife, would be well supplied with everything necessary for a comfortable existence.

Private housing has not survived, because houses were made from mud brick that erodes. Homes and workplaces and the activities that took place there can be seen, because some paintings in the tombs do show private houses.

Archeologists made a particularly valuable discovery when the tomb of King Tutankhamen was excavated in the 1920s. The tombs of many pharaohs had been robbed of much of their treasure, but this tomb of a young king dating from c. 1350 BCE had remained undisturbed for thousands of years.

Egyptian tombs have sometimes yielded items of dress that seem to have no counterpart in paintings or statuary, such as the multicolored garments and elaborately decorated sandals found in the excavation of the tomb of Tutankhamen. These might have been ceremonial garments, special funeral garments, or actual items from the king's wardrobe.

During the periods of Greek and Roman dominance, pharaohs were represented in art dressed in the styles of the Old Kingdom, and yet records indicate that the rulers of the period actually dressed in Greek and Roman styles (Mertz, 2008). One of the basic costumes for women is a straight, fitted garment of tubular form. Paintings and statues show this garment fitting so tightly around the body that the wearer would be virtually unable to walk. Woven fabrics do not cling so closely to the body, and as far as research can ascertain, the Egyptians had not developed techniques such as knitting that would permit such a close fit; consequently, we can hypothesize that artistic convention required the garment be shown as exceptionally tight fitting.

Research by Gillian Vogelsang-Eastwood (1993), a textile archeologist, has added significantly to what is known of Egyptian costume. Combining evidence from actual garments excavated by archeologists with a careful study of Egyptian artists' depictions of clothing, she has published the most complete summary of what is known about Egyptian clothing to date. Vogelsang-Eastwood also reproduced garments and had students put on copies in order to see how they might actually have been worn. The result has been some new ideas that challenge certain prevailing views of Egyptian dress. Many of her proposals are discussed in subsequent sections of this chapter. In spite of the wealth of evidence available and continuing research, our knowledge about the clothing of Egypt is still incomplete.

Egyptian Decorative Motifs

In any historic period, certain similarities can be observed in the various art forms (see Chapter 1, pages 8–9, for a discussion of clothing as an art form). In Egypt these similarities are most obvious in decorative motifs, most of which are derived either from the natural world or from religious symbolism. These motifs appear in the decoration of temples and tomb chambers, on furniture and utilitarian objects, and in clothing, most often in jewelry or decorative accessories of clothing.

The Egyptians had an abiding faith in magic and believed that by representing symbols of religious figures in jewelry, the positive qualities of the deity would be transferred to the wearer. The **scarab**, a symbol of a beetle that represented the sun god and also rebirth, was a popular motif. The hawk appears often as another symbol of the sun god. The sacred cobra, called the **uraeus**, was the symbol of Lower Egypt, and the vulture was the symbol of Upper Egypt. Used together on royal headdress and in jewelry, the two symbolized the unification of Lower and Upper Egypt under the pharaohs. The **eye of Horus**, a stylized representation of the human eye, symbolized the moon. The lotus blossom, papyrus blossom, and animal forms that were native to the area were also translated into decorative motifs.

CONTRIBUTIONS OF ARTISANS TO COSTUME

The workmanship of artisans was of exceptional quality. Of special interest to the study of historic costume are the weaving and jewelry-making crafts.

Textile Production and Technology

Thanks to the hot, dry climate of Egypt, actual pieces of fabric have been preserved in Egyptian tombs. **Linen**, the fiber most used by Egyptians, is cloth made from a fiber that is removed from the stems of the **flax** plant. The fiber may be called flax until it has been removed and cleaned for use in spinning, after which it is usually called linen. Wool was considered ritually unclean and was not worn by priests or by visitors to sanctuaries, or for burial. Herodotus, a Greek historian of the fifth century BCE who traveled in Egypt, reported that wool was used for some outer garments. Although a recent archeological find indicated that silk may have been present in Egypt as early as 1000 BCE, silk was not widely used in Egypt until the fourth century CE, well after the periods discussed here (Wilford, 1993). Cotton cloth, too, reached Egypt only after Egyptian power had declined.

Linen is difficult to dye to colors that will not fade unless substances called **mordants** are used to fix the colors. Egyptian dyers were apparently unfamiliar with mordants until the New Kingdom period; therefore, most Egyptian clothing was made in the natural, creamy-white color of linen or bleached to a pure white.

Spinning and weaving techniques were well developed as early as the Old Kingdom. During the Old and Middle Kingdoms, Egyptians used a horizontal ground loom to weave fabrics of varying widths. Weaving consists of interlacing lengthwise (called **warp** yarns) and crosswise (called **weft** or **filling**) yarns. The place at the sides of a fabric where a weft yarn turns to make its return trip across the fabric is called the **selvage**. By looping or adding extra yarns, decorative elements can be introduced at the selvage. At each end of the cloth, where the weaving has stopped, the ends of the warp yarns remain. These can be cut off, can remain as fringe, or can be tied into tassels. Egyptian weavers used these decorative selvages, fringes, and tassels to ornament their clothing.

Flax was raised on the large estates owned by wealthy Egyptians where cloth needed by the estate was also woven. Lacking a cash economy, the Egyptians used textiles as a type of currency when trading for other goods (Barber, 1994, 200). Men processed the flax stems to remove the fibers; then women spun the fibers into yarns and wove the yarns into cloth. Men did a final cleaning of the finished cloth by either boiling it or washing it in the river, where they had to be on the lookout against attack by dangerous crocodiles.

Some fine, closely woven fabrics have been found with thread counts as high as 160 threads in the lengthwise direction and 120 threads in the crosswise direction (Casson, 1975). The finest sheer organdy fabrics of the 19th and 20th centuries rarely have thread counts as high as 150 in the lengthwise and 100 in the crosswise directions (*American Fabrics Encyclopedia*, 1972).

Pleated linen fabrics appear in art and in actual garments. Pleats were probably made on a grooved board or other surface. Cloth would have been pressed into the grooves, and the pleats fixed by the application of starch or sizing (Stead, 1986). Pleats were made horizontally, vertically, or in a sort of herringbone effect that was produced by pleating a fabric in one direction, then turning the fabric and pleating it again in the other direction.

The earliest fabrics decorated with ornamental tapestry-woven designs date from after 1500 BCE, as do wall paintings of a new type of loom, a vertical loom. Barber (1994) suggested that this new technology may have been taught to the Egyptians by foreign captives. Although the vertical looms did not replace the older horizontal looms, they did make weaving of more elaborately patterned fabrics possible.

The items excavated from the tomb of King Tutankhamen included robes made of beaded fabric, others with woven and embroidered patterns, and still others with appliqué. These artifacts reveal that the arts of fabric construction included skill in beading, pattern weaving, embroidery, and appliqué.

Jewelry

Gold jewelry was prized by the Egyptians. Silver was not found in Egypt and had to be imported; therefore, its use was limited. The Egyptians did not make glass until after the 18th Dynasty, but glazes made from ground quartz, natural volcanic glass, and imported glass were used in jewelry (Stead, 1986). Semiprecious and precious stones such as carnelian, lapis lazuli, feldspar, and turquoise were worked into large, multicolored round collars, **pectorals** (*decorative pendants*), earrings, bracelets, armlets, and hair or head ornaments. Religious symbols appear often in jewelry, as well as in art. Archeological finds attest to the high level of skill of jewelers and to the widespread use of jeweled personal ornaments.

EGYPTIAN COSTUME: c. 3000–300 BCE

Costume may express the relationships between the individual and his or her natural and social environments.

As the social structures of society evolved, dress was one means of manifesting visually one's personal power, dignity, or wealth. The climate of Egypt did not require clothing for warmth. Most garments consisted of pieces of fabric, usually square or rectangular, that were draped and tied around the body. Raw, unfinished edges of cut cloth were turned under and hemmed. Clothing forms for all ages and classes were relatively simple, with minimal sewing and construction required. Only a few garments actually had **seams** (places where one piece of cloth was joined to another by sewing).

Clothing identified distinctions in social status. These were evident not so much in the types of clothing worn but rather in the quality of the materials used and in the amount of clothing owned by the individual. Slaves, peasants, and lower class people lacked personal wealth, power, and status (hence they would not have needed a great variety of clothing items). But what clothing they did have was not different in shape or construction from that of the upper classes. Table 2.1 summarizes the types of garments worn during the various Egyptian periods.

Costume Terminology

Although the Egyptians had a written language, hieroglyphics, it is not possible to ascertain what names Egyptians gave to individual garments. Costume historians have assigned names to some of these garments. In some cases those names derive from words that have been associated with Egyptian civilization in some way; in other cases names have been made up based on the style or the function of garments. In this text the authors use descriptive modern English terms for costume items but also mention those names that appear frequently in costume histories so that readers will know what is meant if they encounter these words in other publications.

The term **kalasiris** (or **calasiris**) serves to illustrate some of the problems of terminology. As readers can see in Contemporary Comment 2.1, the Greek historian Herodotus mentioned a garment which he said the Egyptians called a *calasiri*. He described it as a fringed tunic. Many costume historians apply this term to a closely fitted garment, also called a **sheath dress**, which

TABLE 2.1 Egyptian Garments

PERIOD	MEN	WOMEN
Old Kingdom (2575–2130 BCE)	cloth loincloths; short, wraparound skirts; long, narrow aprons; long cloaks; sashes and straps; sandals	cloth loincloths; wraparound skirts of various types; wraparound sheath dresses; beadnet dresses; V-necked dresses; shawls and long cloaks; sashes and straps; sandals
Middle Kingdom (c. 1938–1600 BCE)	cloth and leather loincloths; wraparound skirts of various lengths; long, narrow, and triangular aprons; short shawls and long cloaks; sashes and straps; sandals	cloth loincloths; wraparound skirts of various types; wraparound sheath dresses; bead-net dresses; V-necked dresses; shawls and long cloaks; sashes and straps; sandals
New Kingdom (1470–11th century BCE)	cloth and leather loincloths; wraparound skirts of various lengths; sometimes layered, sashed, wraparound skirts; triangular aprons; bag tunics; knotted and wraparound cloaks of various kinds; sashes and straps; sandals	cloth loincloths; wraparound skirts of various types; wraparound sheath dresses; wraparound dresses of more complex construction; bag tunics; shawls and long cloaks; sashes and straps; sandals

Note: Based on data from Vogelsang-Eastwood, G. (1993). *Pharaonic Egyptian clothing*. Leiden, The Netherlands: E. J. Brill, p. 180.

was worn by women; others apply it to tunics; and still others apply it to both tunics and closely fitted dresses.

Costume Components for Men

Loincloth

Linen loincloths were under or outer garments shaped and worn like triangular diapers. Strings were attached for tying the garment around the waist, although sometimes a separate sash was also wrapped around the waist. Often loincloths were the sole garment worn by laborers (Figure 2.12). Actual examples of leather loincloths have also been found. A few are solid leather, but most of them consist of a network of leather with solid sections of leather as reinforcement at the waist and over the buttocks. These network loincloths were generally depicted worn over cloth loincloths.

Apron

Vogelsang-Eastwood (1993) defined aprons as separate items that covered the genital area and were worn alone over a skirt or some other garment or over a loincloth and under a skirt. She described them as being made of one or more pieces of cloth attached to a belt, sash, or band that fastened around the waist. No actual examples of this garment have been found in Egypt, although examples exist in the nearby region of Nubia, which was subject to Egyptian influences. Illustrations show men dressed only in aprons, but

when these garments are combined with skirts (see Figure 2.13), it is difficult to ascertain whether they are separate garments or a part of the skirt construction. Art from the Middle and New Kingdoms, especially, frequently showed men wearing skirts with large, projecting triangular aprons. Because no actual examples of such garments have been found, the question of whether these were separate aprons or simply the way that the ends of the wrapped skirt were arranged remains unanswered.

Wrapped Skirt

A wrapped skirt, the length, width, and fit of which varied with different time periods and social classes, served as a major garment for men throughout all of Egyptian history. Costume historians have called this costume a **schenti**, **shent**, **skent**, or **schent**. Others use the term **kilt**. (A kilt is a short skirt worn by Scotsmen, and some authors use this term as a means of distinguishing between male and female dress, calling the same garment a *skirt* when worn by women). A number of different skirts for men can be seen in Figures 2.12 and 2.14. The following variations can be identified:

- In the earliest periods, the skirt was generally knee length or shorter and fitted closely around the hips. Some were pleated and some had a diagonal line across the front, which sources have suggested was achieved by rounding one end of the fabric. No curved fabrics have been found, however,

Contemporary Comments 2.1

EGYPTIAN COSTUME AS DESCRIBED BY HERODOTUS

The Greek historian Herodotus (484–425 BCE). traveled extensively. One of the places he visited was Egypt. The following are his observations on the clothing practices of the Egyptians.

In other countries the priests have long hair, in Egypt their heads are shaven; elsewhere it is customary, in mourning for near relatives to cut their hair close; the Egyptians, who wear no hair at all at any other time, when they lose a relative, let their beards and the hair of their heads grow long. . . .

. . . Their men wear two garments apiece, their women but one. [Book II, Chapter 36]

. . . They wear linen garments, which they are specially careful to have always fresh washed. . . .

. . . [Of priests] Their dress is entirely of linen, and their shoes of the papyrus plant: it is not lawful for them to wear either dress or shoes of any other material. . . . [Book II, Chapter 37]

. . . They wear a linen tunic fringed about the legs, and called calasiris; over this they have a white woollen garment thrown on afterwards. Nothing of woollen, however, is taken into their temples or buried with them, as their religion forbids it. [Book II, Chapter 81]

and Vogelsang-Eastwood (1993) pointed out that by taking the end of a square piece of fabric and pulling it up to tuck into the waist, a curved shape is produced. Thus, it seems likely that the ornamental effect was achieved through draping.

- Middle Kingdom styles show the skirt elongated, sometimes reaching to the ankle, with shorter versions for work, for soldiers, or for hunters. A double skirt, the underlayer opaque and outer layer sheer, appeared and continued in use into the New Kingdom. Some depictions show what appear to be pleats.

- New Kingdom styles had pleated skirts, both shorter examples that tended to fit more closely and long skirts that were quite full. Large, triangular decorative panels were located at the front of some skirts.

By following the lines of pleats in garments shown on statues, it is possible to gain some understanding of how the fabrics were draped. In one version, a length of fabric appeared to have been pleated along its long direction. The pleats were arranged horizontally across the back, then pulled up, diagonally, to the waistline in front where the ends were tied or passed over each other. They hung downward at center front to form a pleated panel (Houston, 1964).

Upper Body Coverings

In very early representations, we may see the skin of a leopard or lion fastened across the shoulders of men. In later periods, fabric replaced skins for the construction of upper garments. Wearing animal skins was reserved for the most powerful element in society: kings and priests (Figure 2.14). Finally, even the skins were no longer worn, but were replaced by ritual garments made from cloth simulating animal skins. Leopard spots were painted onto the cloth. The Egyptian belief in magic seems to underlie this practice. The Egyptians believed that wearing the skin

FIGURE 2.14 Apuy, a sculptor of the New Kingdom period, and his wife receiving an offering. Men and women wear sheer, pleated linen gowns with wide bead collars. Man making the offering wears a leopard skin with a pleated linen schenti. All wear wigs; those of the men are shorter than those of the women. A scented cone of wax is placed on their heads. The fingernails and toenails of both men and women are polished, their eyes outlined in kohl. The men wear sandals. (Image copyright © The Metropolitan Museum of Art. Image source: Art Resource, NY)

of a fierce beast magically transferred the powers of the animal to the wearer.

In the Middle and New Kingdoms men wore a short fabric cape that fastened at center front. Not unlike a cape, a wide necklace made from concentric circles of precious or semiprecious stones might have been worn alone, over a linen gown, over a short cape, or with a corselet (see Figure 2.14). The **corselet** was sleeveless, probably a decorative form of armor, and might be either strapless or suspended by small straps from the shoulders (see Visual Summary Table, page 48).

Men were sometimes depicted wearing narrow straps wrapped around the upper part of the body. The method of wrapping varied. Sometimes straps ran diagonally over one shoulder, sometimes across both shoulders, and sometimes they were also wrapped around the waist or at various points on the chest. They were most likely a practical garment used to prevent perspiration from running down the body. Women were only rarely shown wearing straps, and

then usually when engaged in physical activity, such as dancing or acrobatics.

Tunic

During the New Kingdom a number of new elements entered dress, probably as a result of cross-cultural contacts with the Near East, the invasion of the Hyksos, or the expansion of the Egyptian empire into the area west of Egypt.

Longer tunics, similar to those of Mesopotamia, appeared in Egypt about the time of the New Kingdom. As depicted on wall paintings, they are made with or without sleeves and often of sheer, almost transparent, linen. Artists showed loincloths or a short skirt underneath or skirts wrapped over tunics (see Figure 2.13).

Long, Wrapped Garments

The earliest wrapped garments appeared on depictions of both men and women of all classes from the earliest period up until the Middle Kingdom. Later, wrapped garments seem to be associated only with women, gods, and kings. Possible ways of wrapping the fabric are depicted in Figure 2.17.

During the New Kingdom, men appeared in long, loose, flowing garments of sheer pleated linen (see Figure 2.14). The precise construction of these garments is not clear from most of their representations. The following alternatives have been suggested:

- full tunic worn loose or belted,
- skirt with cape or shawl, or
- wrapped shawl.

Shawls and Cloaks

Shawls, consisting of squares or rectangles of fabric that wrapped around the upper part of the body and did not extend below the waist, were shown on both men and women. Longer cloaks, which probably were worn for warmth, also appeared. Some of these were wrapped around the body in various ways, while others had ends tied together over one shoulder.

Costume Components for Women

Skirts

Paintings often show skirts on lower class women at work. Slaves and dancing girls are also depicted occasionally without clothes or with a small cloth strip covering the genitals and held up with a narrow waistband (see Figure 2.18).

Wrapped Dress or Sheath and Bead-Net Dresses

Costume historians have described the most common garment for women of all classes as a sheath dress. This garment appears as a closely fitted tube of fabric beginning above or below the breasts and ending around the lower calf or ankle (Figure 2.15). It appears to have had one or two straps holding it over the shoulders. Many authors have commented about the tightness of this garment and have noted that it fits so tightly that it would have been difficult not only to get into but also to wear. For this reason it has been suggested that artists depicted the garment in a conventional rather than a realistic manner.

Vogelsang-Eastwood (1993) argued persuasively that this garment was probably a wraparound dress (see Figures 2.15 and 2.17a) and that the shoulder straps were separate garments. As evidence, she noted that no sheath dresses have been found in any excavations but that lengths of cloth with patterns of wear consistent with wraparound dresses have been found in fairly substantial numbers. This assertion also solves the problem of the varying placements of the top of the garment, because the cloth could have been wrapped around the body at any point above or beneath the breasts or at the waist. Separate straps could have been placed in any of a variety of ways.

Scholars are uncertain about the techniques used to decorate the fabrics of sheath dresses, which were often elaborately patterned. Speculations include painted designs, appliqués, leather, feathers, beadwork, or woven designs. From the evidence in the Tutankhamen tomb, we know that skill in beadwork was well developed. A pair of gloves of woven fabric with a design similar to those seen on many of the sheaths was discovered in the same tomb. Actual bead-net dresses have been found in tombs (Figure 2.16). Some of the patterned effects seen on closely fitting dresses (see Figure 2.15) could have been achieved by placing a bead-net dress over a wrapped dress.

Pleated and Draped Wrapped Long Dress

Though at first glance, the sheer, pleated robes of men and women look alike, careful examination reveals that their draping and arrangement were different. Some women's styles covered the breasts, and others left them exposed (see Figure 2.4). These garments were the most complex worn by Egyptian women. A number of scholars have suggested ways in which these sheer, pleated garments may have been wrapped. See Figure 2.17b and c for some of these suggestions.

Tunics and V-Necked Dresses

Women, like men, wore loosely fitted tunics. Women of a lower economic class, such as musicians, often wore these garments (Figure 2.18).

FIGURE 2.15 Model of a girl of the Middle Kingdom (XI Dynasty) wearing a closely fitted sheath dress and a wide, faience collar. She bears a basket of offerings for a funeral. Trade goods were also often borne by servants. (Image copyright © The Metropolitan Museum of Art. Image source: Art Resource, NY)

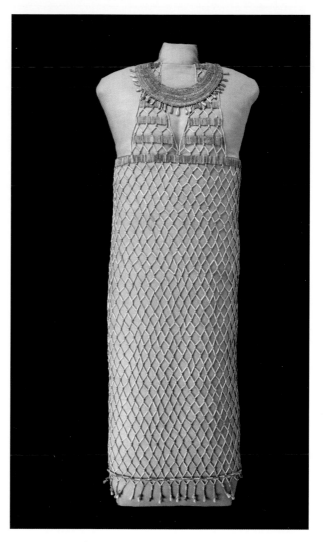

FIGURE 2.16 Beadnet dress from Giza. It has been suggested that these dresses were placed over a wraparound garment such as that shown in Figure 2.17a. (Beadnet dress. Egyptian, Old Kingdom, Dynasty 4, reign of Khufu, 2551–2528 B.C. Findspot: Egypt, Giza, Tomb G 7440 Z Faience Overall: 44 x 113cm (17 5/16 x 44 1/2in.) Mount: 139.7 x 31.8 x 17.8 cm (55 x 12 1/2 x 7 in.) Museum of Fine Arts, Boston Harvard University—Boston Museum of Fine Arts Expedition 27.1548.1 Photograph © 2014 Museum of Fine Arts, Boston. All rights reserved.)

Among the most numerous garments found in women's tombs are V-necked dresses, with or without sleeves. The simple sleeveless version of this dress, which may be either pleated or plain, began to appear during the Old Kingdom. The sleeved version is more complex, with a tubular skirt joined to a yoke. Figure 2.19 shows two examples of this dress.

Shawls and cloaks of similar types were worn by women and men.

With so much of Egyptian clothing being made from lengths of cloth wrapped around the body, sashes helped to hold clothing in place. Both men and women are depicted wearing sashes, although men seem to wear sashes more often. Surviving examples are made of rope; plain-weave linen, sometimes with fringes or tassels; and elaborately designed tapestry or double-weave fabrics. For upper class individuals dressed in white linen, sashes and men's decorated aprons are sometimes the only ornamentation and color, other than that provided by jewelry.

Costume Components for Men and Women

As a result of the relatively simple styles of clothing and the limited range of colors of fabrics, elements of dress and ornamentation—such as jewelry, footwear,

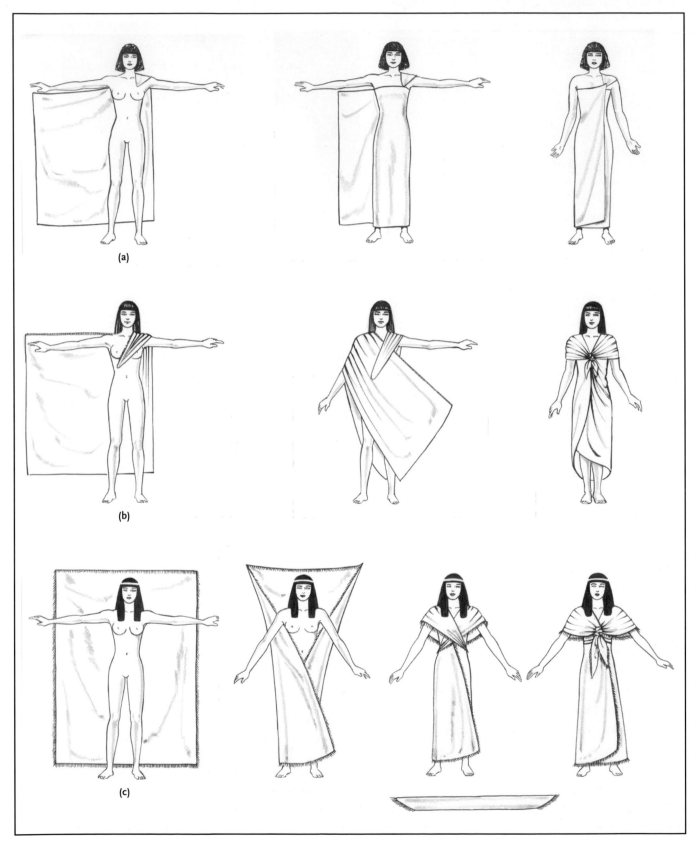

FIGURE 2.17 Suggested ways of draping some items of Egyptian wrapped costume: (a) The wraparound garment for men or women; (b) and (c) two alternatives for creating a woman's draped gown. (Courtesy of Fairchild Publications, Inc.)

FIGURE 2.18 Wall painting of musicians from the New Kingdom (Dynasty VIII). Figures on the extreme left and right wear sheath dresses and have cones of wax on their heads. The flute player wears a kalasiris. (Image copyright © The Metropolitan Museum of Art. Image source: Art Resource, NY)

hairstyles, cosmetics, and tattoos—are particularly noticeable. Some evidence that tattooing was not uncommon, especially for women, has been found on clay statuettes and on mummies. The earliest tattoos were abstract, geometric forms. Later tattoos were generally motifs or figures related to religion, particularly the god Bes, know as a protector of the home and of women's and children's concerns (Pointer, 2005). Evidence of tattooing for men is absent.

Hair and Headdress

Men were usually clean shaven. However, the beard was a symbol of maturity and authority and was, as a consequence, worn (or at least depicted on paintings and sculpture) not only by adult male rulers but also by young kings and even by Queen Hatshepsut, who ruled around 1500 BCE. During some periods, men shaved their heads as well. It was less common, though not unknown, for women to shave their heads.

Wigs were worn over the shaved head or over the hair. The shape, length, and arrangement of wigs varied from period to period. More expensive wigs were of human hair; cheaper ones were made of wool, flax, palm fiber, or felt. Most wigs were black in color, although blue, brown, white, or some gilded examples exist. Even when wigs were relatively short, women's tended to be longer than men's. Their styling ranged from simple, long flowing locks to complex braiding, curls, or twists. It is likely that wigs were worn because they were decorative and could more easily be made into complicated styles than could real hair. Furthermore, in the hot Egyptian climate some individuals probably found it comfortable and convenient to wear wigs over shaved heads or short hair. This also made it easier to avoid getting head lice (see the wigs in Figures 2.14 and 2.15).

Much of Egyptian headdress was ceremonial or symbolic. See Illustrated Table 2.1 (page 46) for depiction and summary of the major head-covering styles and their functions.

Footwear

Only high-status persons wore sandals, while low-status individuals went barefoot. Sandals were made of rushes woven or twisted together. Some examples from royal burials are elaborately decorated. The high status of the wearer was demonstrated by superior workmanship, increased decoration, and finer materials (Figure 2.20; see also Figure 2.14).

FIGURE 2.19 V-necked linen dresses from Deshasha, Egypt. (Copyright Petrie Museum of Egyptian Archaeology, University College London, UC31182, UC31183)

Jewelry

With New Kingdom gowns, jewelry or jeweled belts were the main sources of color. Belts and decorated aprons often provided the only touches of color on clothes made of plain white linen. Beads, leatherwork, appliqué, and woven designs could all be used to construct the highly ornate decorative belts and aprons that were an integral part of Egyptian costume.

Wide, jeweled collars covered most of the chest and had a counterweight at the back to balance the heavy section in front. These collars appear in art from the Old Kingdom up to and beyond the New Kingdom. Other ornaments worn at the neck were **pectorals** (ornaments that hung down on the chest), single **amulets** (charms worn around the neck to ward off evil), or plaques with mounted amulets.

Some **diadems** (*crowns*) or fillets placed on the head held flowers. Others copied flowers in metal and polished stones. Armlets, bracelets, and anklets were all worn, though only in the New Kingdom were they all worn simultaneously.

Possibly another of the contributions of the Hyksos to Egyptian styles, earrings are a late addition to Egyptian jewelry. First worn by women, they seem eventually to have also been used by men. In the 1977–1978 exhibit of artifacts from the tomb of Tutankhamen, it was suggested that earrings may have been worn by young boys but abandoned in manhood ("Treasures of Tutankhamen," 1972, 39).

Cosmetics

Both men and women decorated their eyes, skin, and lips. Red ochre pigment in a base of fat or gum resin was used to color lips. Fingernails and toenails were polished and buffed. **Henna**, a reddish hair dye, may have been used to color nails. Scented ointments were applied to the body.

Eye paint had cosmetic, symbolic, and medicinal functions. Eye painting represented the eye of the god Horus, considered a powerful charm, and the line formed around the eye helped to protect against the glare of the sun. Some written records include medical prescriptions for eye paints. In the Old Kingdom green eye paint predominated; in the Middle Kingdom both green and black paints were used; by the New Kingdom black **kohl** (made of galena, a sulfide of lead) had replaced green. Red ochre was used as rouge and probably a lip color (Pointer, 2005).

Costume Components for Children

The children who are depicted in Egyptian paintings were generally the offspring of wealthy or royal families. These representations and the numerous toys found in Egyptian tombs indicate that children were regarded with interest and warm affection. Education was provided for boys—the very rich had private tutors, the less affluent went to temple schools. Children of the lower classes were taught a trade or craft, while sons of peasants labored in the fields with their fathers.

Dress for the very young was minimal. Little boys are depicted as naked except for an occasional bracelet or amulet; little girls wear necklaces, armlets, bracelets, anklets, and sometimes earrings. Some pictures show girls wearing a belt at the waist (see Figure 2.18). After beginning school, boys apparently were dressed in skirts or tunics or, among the lower classes, probably in a loincloth. Girls apparently continued to go naked until close to the time they reached puberty, after which they dressed like their mothers.

Special hairstyles for children appear. In some representations, the head is completely shaved; in others part is left unshaven. The long locks of hair that grew in the unshaven part of the head were arranged in curls or braids. The children of the pharaoh wore a distinctive hairstyle called the **lock of Horus** or the **lock of youth** in which one lock of hair remained on the left side of the head. This lock was arranged carefully in braids over the ear (Illustrated Table 2.1, page 46).

Costume for Specialized Occupations

Costume for specialized occupations showed some minor variations from the basic Egyptian styles.

Military Dress

The ordinary foot soldier of ancient Egypt wore a short skirt. In the New Kingdom representations, an additional stiffened triangular panel is shown at the front, possibly to protect the vulnerable genitals. A helmet, made of padded leather, covered the head. The soldier carried weapons and a shield. In some instances a sleeveless armored corselet supported by straps was shown. This garment covered the chest and is thought to have been made of small plates of bone, metal, or leather sewn to a linen body. Most soldiers are depicted as barefooted.

When the pharaoh dressed for war, he wore the costume typical of his era plus the special insignia of his rank: a special crown, called the *blue war crown* (see Illustrated Table 2.1) and a false beard. When at war, the king carried weapons. After the adoption of chariots for warfare, the pharaoh was often represented riding in a chariot while a servant preceded him, carrying his sandals.

FIGURE 2.20 From left to right: Shawl, of linen, from the Late Period (Dynasty XXI); kerchief from the New Kingdom (Dynasty XVII); child's linen garment, made like the description by Herodotus of the kalasiris, from the Late Period; sandals for a child and for an adult from the New Kingdom (Dynasty XVIII). (Image copyright © The Metropolitan Museum of Art. Image source: Art Resource, NY)

Religious Dress

The costume of priests did not differ much from that of ordinary Egyptians. Priests were usually depicted with shaven heads. One of the insignias of the priesthood was either a real or simulated leopard skin draped over the shoulders.

Gods and goddesses are shown in Egyptian art dressed as ordinary mortals but wearing special headdresses or carrying symbols of their divinity. In the New Kingdom, goddesses were dressed in the older, fitted sheath style, and they often appeared alongside mortals dressed in the pleated robe. It may have been a convention to show these divinities in costumes that emphasized their timelessness. The pharaoh, who was considered to be divine, frequently appears wearing the special headdress or insignia of the gods.

Illustrated Table 2.1

Some of the Headdresses Worn in Ancient Egypt

Red crown of Lower Egypt: worn by pharaohs to symbolize rule over Lower Egypt

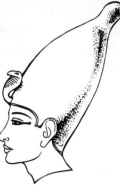

White crown of Upper Egypt: worn by pharaohs to symbolize rule over Upper Egypt

Pschent crown of Lower and Upper Egypt: worn by pharaohs to symbolize rule over Lower and Upper Egypt; consisted of a combination of the crowns of Lower and Upper Egypt

Hemhemet crown: worn by pharaohs who used it only rarely, on ceremonial occasions, possibly because it was so awkward and unwieldy

Blue or war crown: worn by pharaohs to symbolize military power or when going to war; in the New Kingdom, this headdress was worn more often than the double crown; made of molded leather and decorated with gold sequins, it had a uraeus at the center front

Nemes headdress: worn by rulers from the Old to the New Kingdom; a scarflike construction that completely covered the head, was fitted across the temple, hanging down to the shoulder behind the ears, and with a long tail at center back that symbolized a lion's tail; the shape of the Nemes head covering is similar to a simple, scarflike head covering owned by the Metropolitan Museum (see Figure 2.15)

Falcon or vulture headdress: worn by queens or goddesses; shaped like a bird of prey with the wings falling down at the side of the head and framing the face

Flat crown: appears on depictions of Queen Nefertiti, a New Kingdom queen, who apparently wore this head covering over a shaved head

Lock of youth: worn by children of the royal family

Uraeus: worn by kings and queens; a representation of a cobra, which was a symbol of royal power; could be worn on a headband, or as part of another headdress

Dress for Musicians, Dancers, and Acrobats

Entertainers, such as dancers and acrobats, are often shown naked or wearing only a band around the waist. Musicians, both male and female, wore the simpler costume forms of the period. During the New Kingdom this would have been a full, very sheer tunic, or calasiri (see Figure 2.18).

Summary

Themes

Although we are separated from the Mesopotamian and Egyptian cultures by thousands of years and we do not have a complete view of the lives of these ancient peoples, some of the themes discussed in Chapter 1 emerge in this broad overview of 3,000 years of Mesopotamian and Egyptian costume.

The stability of costume in Egypt compared with more frequent changes in Mesopotamia can be related to themes such as POLITICAL CONFLICT with its accompanying wars and invasions, ECONOMIC EVENTS such as patterns of trade, and the CROSS-CULTURAL CONTACTS that resulted from warfare and trade. Mesopotamia, more open geographically to both invaders and traders, showed more frequent costume changes, whereas Egypt, more geographically isolated, experienced important changes only in relatively rare instances, such as the adoption of the tunic after the invasion of Egypt and subsequent political control by the Hyksos, a foreign people.

SOCIAL LIFE, SOCIAL ROLES, SOCIAL CLASS STRUCTURE, and CHANGES OR PATTERNS IN SOCIAL BEHAVIOR undoubtedly shaped clothing practices in both of these civilizations. The most obvious examples are in the differences in the quality and variety of apparel worn by upper classes and lower classes and in those items such as headdresses that designated status (Illustrated Table 2.1, page 46). However, because our knowledge of social life of these periods is limited in many ways, we undoubtedly overlook nuances in dress that must have been obvious to people living at the time.

In Egypt and Mesopotamia, the themes of PRODUCTION OF TEXTILES, ECOLOGY, and THE ARTS AND DRESS come together. Linen, a fabric that was comfortable in the heat of a tropical climate and that could be made into soft, sheer, drapable fabrics, was the primary material from which garments were made throughout the history of this civilization. Mesopotamian costume, too, continued to utilize one fiber to a considerable extent: wool, which made a fabric of greater bulk and warmth than did linen. (In the later periods, both cotton and linen seem also to have been added to the materials from which Mesopotamians made their clothes.)

Egyptian costume began with the simple loincloth or skirt for men and a straight, closely fitted, wrapped dress (sheath) or a skirt for women. Throughout the history of this civilization, although the forms of these costumes grew more elaborate and more decorative and although additional types of garments were added, the basic aesthetic preference for clothing that complemented the natural lines of the body was retained. By contrast, Mesopotamian clothing was designed not to complement the body but to cover it. The early kaunakes skins and full-length garments, the draped styles of the later Babylonians, and the shawls that wrapped the Assyrian kings covered the body with layers of fabric that obscured its natural lines. These differences have been attributed not only to geographical or ecological differences but also to differences in standards of taste. Leix (1938) pointed out that Egyptians loved clarity of form in life and art, while the Babylonians loved pomp and luxury. This latter preference is reflected in the heavy fabrics, rich patterns, and elaborate fringes of Mesopotamian styles. Furthermore, moral reasons, possibly expressed as different views of modesty in dress, may also have influenced styles. Mesopotamian religions show a greater preoccupation with ethical problems than do those of Egypt.

Visual Summary Table

Major Mesopotamian and Egyptian Garments

Sumerian man and woman in
kaunakes-type garments
(3300–2500 BCE)

Babylonian man
(2500–1000 BCE)

Assyrian ruler
(1000–600 BCE)

Royal Egyptian boy in draped skirt,
corselet, and wearing his hair in
the lock of youth (New Kingdom)

Egyptian women in (a) draped gown
(New Kingdom) and (b) sheath dress
(Old Kingdom through New Kingdom)

Egyptian wearing a tunic
(New Kingdom)

LEGACIES OF MESOPOTAMIAN AND EGYPTIAN DRESS

The decline of the Assyrian civilization did not totally obliterate all traces of Mesopotamian costume. At least one element of dress persisted in the region and, eventually, found its way into other parts of the world. The high-crowned headdress worn by Assyrian kings was adopted by the Persians. From its use in Persia, it eventually found its way into the costume of the Eastern Orthodox Christian priests.

Certain other aspects of Mesopotamian costume utilized not only by the Sumerian, Babylonian, or Assyrian people but also more generally throughout the Near East have survived into more recent times. The custom of requiring women to wear a veil outside of the home is one example. It has also been suggested (although it cannot be documented) that the kaunakes fabric in the form of a garment worn by shepherds and other rustic folk may have come into European art to symbolize people from little known or distant lands of the Middle East.

Egyptian dress did not long survive the Greek and Roman domination of Egypt, although it was used for the formal portraits of the last pharaohs and Queen Cleopatra. Instead, the Egyptians adopted first Greek, then Roman, styles. In several instances, however, ancient Egyptian fashions have influenced 20th-century styles. The first was in 1920 when the discovery of the tomb of King Tutankhamen gave rise to a short-lived vogue for Egyptian-inspired fabrics, jewelry, and to a lesser extent, women's fashions. The exhibit of artifacts from this same tomb in 1977–1978 also motivated fashion and jewelry designers to orchestrate a revival of Egyptian-inspired products. This, too, proved to be a short-term fashion. Individual fashion designers may find inspiration in elements of Egyptian dress, as in the couture design in Modern Influences (page 49).

REFERENCES

American Fabrics Encyclopedia of Textiles. (1972). Englewood Cliffs, NJ: Prentice-Hall.

Barber, E. J. W. (1991). *Prehistoric textiles.* Princeton, NJ: Princeton University Press.

Barber, E. J. W. (1994). *Women's work: The first 20,000 years.* New York, NY: Norton.

Born, W. (1940). Footwear of the ancient orient. *CIBA Review,* 1210.

Casson, L. (1975). *Daily life in ancient Egypt.* New York, NY: American Heritage.

Contenau, G. (1954). *Everyday life in Babylon and Assyria.* London, UK: Edward Arnold.

Fairservis, W. A., Jr. (1962). *The ancient kingdoms of the Nile.* New York, NY: New American Library.

Houston, M. G. (1964). *Ancient Egyptian, Mesopotamian, and Persian costume.* New York, NY: Barnes and Noble.

Iversen, E. (1975). *In canon and proportions in Egyptian art.* United Kingdom, Warminster: Aris and Phillips.

Leix, A. (1938). Babylon-Assur: Land of wool. *CIBA Review,* 12, 406.

Mertz, B. (2008). *Red land, black land.* New York, NY: William Morrow.

Oppenheim, A. L. (1967). *Letters from Mesopotamia.* Chicago, IL. University of Chicago Press.

Pointer, S. (2005). *The artifice of beauty.* CITY, UK: Sutton.

Stead, M. (1986). *Egyptian life.* Cambridge, MA: Harvard University Press.

Treasures of King Tutankhamen. (1972). [Catalog of the exhibition of the British Museum]. London, UK: British Museum.

Vogelsang-Eastwood, G. (1993). *Pharaonic Egyptian clothing.* Leiden, The Netherlands: Brill.

Wilford, J. N. (1993, March 16). New finds suggest even earlier trade on fabled silk road. *New York Times,* p. C1.

MODERN INFLUENCES

Egyptian dress and decorative motifs have inspired contemporary fashion designers. This spring 2004 design by John Galliano for Christian Dior shows clear Egyptian influences, especially in the colorful neckpiece.

(Charles Platiau/Reuters/Corbis)

	2900–1200 BCE		1200–800 BCE	
FASHION AND TEXTILES				
POLITICS AND CONFLICTS	Early Minoan period; City of Knossos develops (2900–2100 BCE)	Myceneans dominate (1400–1200 BCE)	Dark Age of Greece (1200–750 BCE)	
DECORATIVE AND FINE ARTS			Homer writes *Iliad* and *Odyssey* (before 700 BCE)	
ECONOMICS AND TRADE	Traders of Middle Minoan period carry goods to other Mediterranean regions (2100–1600 BCE)			
TECHNOLOGY AND IDEAS				
RELIGION AND SOCIETY		Minos, legendary ruler of Crete, is associated with bulls near the start of the Late Minoan period (1600–1100 BCE)	First Olympic games in Greece (776 BCE)	

CHAPTER THREE

Crete and Greece

c. 2900–100 BCE

800 BCE–399 BCE	399 BCE–100 BCE

Herodotus reports on causes of the change from Doric to Ionic chiton styles (484–425 BCE)

Chitons of the era are distinct from earlier periods (after 323 BCE)

Archaic period (650–480 BCE)

Alexander the Great (356–323 BCE)

Hellenistic period followed by decline of Greek power (after 323 BCE)

Classical Age sees flowering of Greek fine and applied arts (500–323 BCE)

Life of Socrates (470–399 BCE)

The remains of the Minoan civilization can be found on the Mediterranean island of Crete, whereas traces of the Mycenaean civilization that succeeded them are found on the mainland, which is now part of modern Greece. The unique dress of these early people did not survive the dark ages that preceded the archaic Greek period. The culture of the classical period that followed influenced the arts, philosophy, and political thought of many later periods in western world history. Likewise, the styles of Greek classical-period dress have continued to inspire design up to the present time.

HISTORICAL BACKGROUND: MINOAN AND MYCENAEAN CIVILIZATIONS

On the narrow island of Crete in the eastern Mediterranean, another civilization flourished over much the same period of time as that of the Egyptians and Mesopotamians. Named for their legendary king, Minos, the Minoan people enjoyed peace and prosperity from c. 2900 to 1450 BCE and developed an elegant culture (Figure 3.1).

The Minoans were a prosperous seafaring people who carried on an active trade with Egypt, Syria, Sicily,

FIGURE 3.1 As the center of Minoan government, the city of Knossos was the site of many handsome palaces and dwellings in which the citizens enjoyed a high standard of living and comfort. (Photograph by Vincent R. Tortora)

and Spain. The Minoan people are depicted in the wall paintings of Egypt; their pottery and other traces of their contact with foreign lands have been discovered in Asia Minor, mainland Greece, and islands in the Aegean Sea. Their cities had no fortifications; they depended on their naval fleet for protection. The pleasure-loving, secure life of the Minoan people was caught by their artists in delicate, brightly colored frescoes that have been found on the walls of excavated palaces in Crete and on the island of Thera. The crowning achievement of Crete was the palace of Knossos. Its many rooms gave rise to the legend that a labyrinth under the palace housed a fearsome creature, half man and half bull, that devoured prisoners.

English archeologist Sir Arthur Evans (1963, ch. 4) first revealed the rich civilization of Crete. He divided Minoan history into three main periods: Early Minoan (c. 2900–2100 BCE), Middle Minoan (c. 2100–1600 BCE), and Late Minoan (c. 1600–1100 BCE). The Minoans maintained political control not only over Crete but also over what is today mainland Greece. During most of the Middle Minoan period, the mainland people, named for their most powerful city-state, Mycenae, gradually grew stronger. In a reversal of political control, the Mycenaeans (*My-seh-ne'ans*) had come to dominate Crete and the Minoan people by c. 1400 BCE.

The Mycenaean civilization extended throughout Greece, centered in more than 300 towns. These towns spread out around the palaces, which each king tried to make a monument to his power and glory. The palaces were decorated with magnificent frescoes of great artistic and technical quality. The remains of these towns reveal works of architecture and large-scale engineering projects, which so astounded later generations of Greeks that they thought the walls of the Mycenaean cities and palaces had been built by giants. Other sources of information about the Mycenaeans include grave sites in which artifacts of gold and silver reveal a wealthy and sophisticated civilization.

At the end of the 13th century, a mysterious "sea people" (whose origins are not known by historians) devastated the eastern Mediterranean area and ruined trade in a series of piratical raids. Many Mycenaean cities and towns suffered. Mycenae survived another century before it was destroyed, probably by Dorian invaders from the north. The population declined throughout Greece. Among the Mycenaean cities, Athens survived, although it was somewhat impoverished. Greece entered a dark age at the beginning of the 13th century BCE about which little is known. The Minoan civilization disappeared at about the same time.

SOCIAL ORGANIZATION AND MATERIAL CULTURE

Evidence about the organization and structure of Minoan and Mycenaean society is fragmentary. Apparently, the Minoans had what amounted to a two-class society, with the ruling classes separated from the common people by a great gulf. No genuine middle class developed in ancient Greece.

Women occupied a higher place in society than in most early cultures. They enjoyed equality with men, and they were not secluded in the household but participated with men in public festivals. They engaged in athletics, often joining men in a favorite Minoan sport, vaulting over bulls. The position of women in Minoan civilization was an exception in the ancient world, possibly reflecting the importance of female deities. The major figure in Minoan religion was the mother goddess. At the same time, unlike Egypt, where queens ruled as pharaohs in some periods, the rulers of Crete were invariably men (Figure 3.2).

Standards of material comfort were high for the wealthy. The remains of several excavated palaces reveal that the private apartments were well lighted, decorated with wall paintings (*frescos*), and even had running water piped into bathrooms.

The Mycenaeans imitated many aspects of Minoan decoration and styles, but their social organization seems to have differed somewhat. Little is known of the manner of life of the ordinary citizen. Wealth apparently

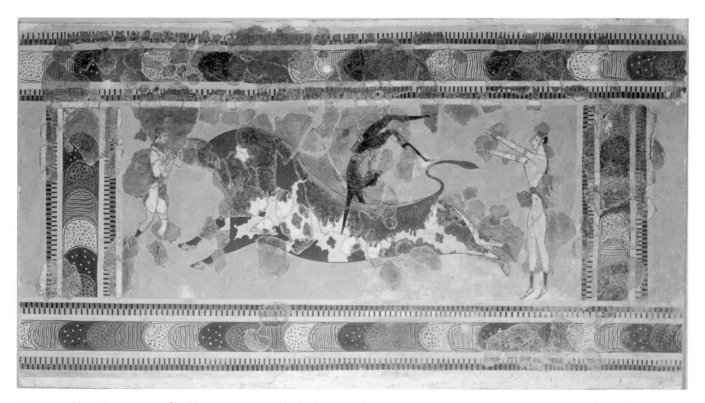

FIGURE 3.2 The Minoan sport of bull leaping, practiced by both men and women, required protective garments to keep them from being injured by the horns of the bull. (Scala/Art Resource)

was concentrated among the nobles in the king's court. There was a slightly lower class of nobility and a large group of craftsmen, peasants, and shepherds.

Sources of Information about Costume

As a result of the close contact between Mycenaeans and Minoans, both groups wore essentially the same styles of clothing from the Middle Minoan period until the Later Minoan period. Most of the evidence for costume during the Minoan civilization comes from the statuary and wall paintings discovered in Crete. Some frescoes and statuary of the period have also been found in mainland Greece.

The costume of the small statuettes of Minoan goddesses and priestesses is depicted in good detail. The dress of these statues has been taken to be characteristic of the dress of upper class women. Wall paintings of general scenes of Minoan life confirm these details. Men's costume is more often shown on wall paintings than in statuary. Many of the wall paintings have been restored, with details reconstructed from fragments of the original paintings, so that inaccuracies may have been incorporated into the restorations.

Textile Production and Technology

Barber (1994) described a Minoan village in which evidence has been uncovered for spinning, weaving, and dyeing linen and wool textiles. Minoan wall paintings and clay figurines depict brightly colored, elaborately patterned garments. Barber's (1991) careful analysis of evidence about Minoan textiles showed that many of the design motifs seen in Minoan art could have been woven easily. Others, more difficult and time consuming, are also technically possible with the types of looms in use. A few could have been achieved only by tapestry weaving, by embroidery, or by painting on textiles. Color was used lavishly, and skill in textile dyeing must have been well developed. Archeological evidence shows that chemical mordants used to fix dyes on linen were imported to Crete.

Egyptian wall paintings of traders dressed in Minoan garments provide evidence of trade between Egypt and Crete. A seafaring people, the Minoans undoubtedly traveled widely around the Mediterranean trading their textiles for other goods.

MINOAN COSTUME: 2900–1100 BCE

In commenting on many of the objects from the early Greek civilizations that archeologists have found, a Greek archeologist George Mylonas (1966) said, "these may be likened to the illustrations of a picture book for which the scholar must provide the text" (136). This text, however, can be widely divergent and highly subjective in its interpretations. Precisely the same comment can be made about the representations of costume from the Minoan period. The lack of any body of literature, legal texts, or religious writings and even the fragmentary nature of many of the paintings from this period leave the costume historian at a loss as to the precise function of many items of dress. The conclusions that are drawn are, therefore, somewhat tentative.

Scholars differ as to whether the dress of Minoans was more tailored and fitted or more draped. Clearly, some depictions show closely fitted, shaped garments that would appear to be more tailored, while others show simpler, more draped styles (Figure 3.3). Houston (1966) suggested that the tailored costume of the Minoans (Figure 3.4) may have evolved from the early use of leather for clothing.

Attempts have been made to reconstruct Minoan dress based on wall paintings and sculpture. Barber (2000), an expert on early textiles, noted that the appearance of a garment depends very much on the fibers and fabrics used. She criticized efforts at reconstruction that have not used textile fibers and fabrics of the same types that would have been used by the Minoans.

Costume Components for Men and Women

Garments

The garment worn closest to the skin was the loincloth, a fitted garment that covered much the same area as a pair of modern athletic briefs. A similar costume (called the **perizoma** in Greek) was worn by Greeks and

Etruscans (see Figure 4.1, page 77). Loincloths were depicted as worn by men and by women athletes. Men and women performed athletic leaps over the horns of bulls. For this activity they both wore loincloths, which, when used for this purpose, were reinforced at the crotch to protect against the horns of the bulls.

Men wore skirts. Some were short, ending at the thigh. These apparently wrapped around the body and generally ended in a point with a suspended, weighted tassel at center front or center back. They are shown as being made of elaborately patterned fabric (see Figure 3.3). Marcar (2005), in a detailed analysis of all the known representations of Minoan dress, identified a men's garment that has the appearance of modern-day shorts. But in examining these depictions, she could find no indication of seams at the side or at the crotch and concluded that these were wrapped and draped skirts, which she called "kilts," because they resemble somewhat the Scottish men's skirt, or kilt. Other skirts are depicted in longer lengths, ending either below the knee or at the ankle. Some men's skirts also appear to be made of sheep fleece, not unlike the Mesopotamian kaunakes skirt.

Women's skirts were bell shaped and had at least three different forms. One version was fitted at the waist, and flared gently to the ground (see Figure 3.4). Another style (Figure 3.5) seemed to have been made of a series of horizontal or V-shaped ruffles or flounces, with each successive ruffle wider in circumference than the one above it. In drawings and sculpture, a third form (Figure 3.6) shows a line down the center of women's skirts. Some scholars have interpreted this as a bifurcated garment similar to modern culottes. This may, however, have been an artistic convention used to depict V-shaped ruffles or could be the overlapping edge of a wrapped skirt. Women are also shown wearing sheep-fleece skirts.

Women's costume had a unique aspect. Smoothly fitted bodices, laced or otherwise, fastened beneath the breasts, leaving the breasts exposed (see Figure 3.4). Because most depictions of this breast-exposing style are of priestesses, some authorities believe ordinary women covered the breasts with sheer fabric (Boucher, 1987). Most bodices had sleeves that fit the arms closely. A few examples have small puffs at the shoulders.

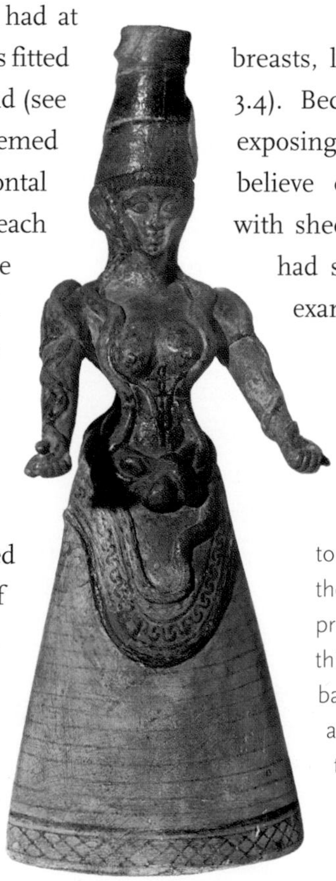

FIGURE 3.3 Restored frescoes from the palace at Knossos depict men from Crete who wear wrapped skirts with a tassel at the front. (Photograph by Vincent R. Tortora)

FIGURE 3.4 Female Minoan snake deity, dressed in a garment typical of those depicted for women. The bodice has short, slightly puffed sleeves and is open to below the breasts. Whether all women bared their breasts is not clear, but figurines of either priestesses or goddesses are represented with this bodice style. The flared skirt with horizontal bands is one of three common skirt types. An apronlike covering extends from below the waist to the hip area. See also Figures 3.5 and 3.6. (Scala/Art Resource, NY)

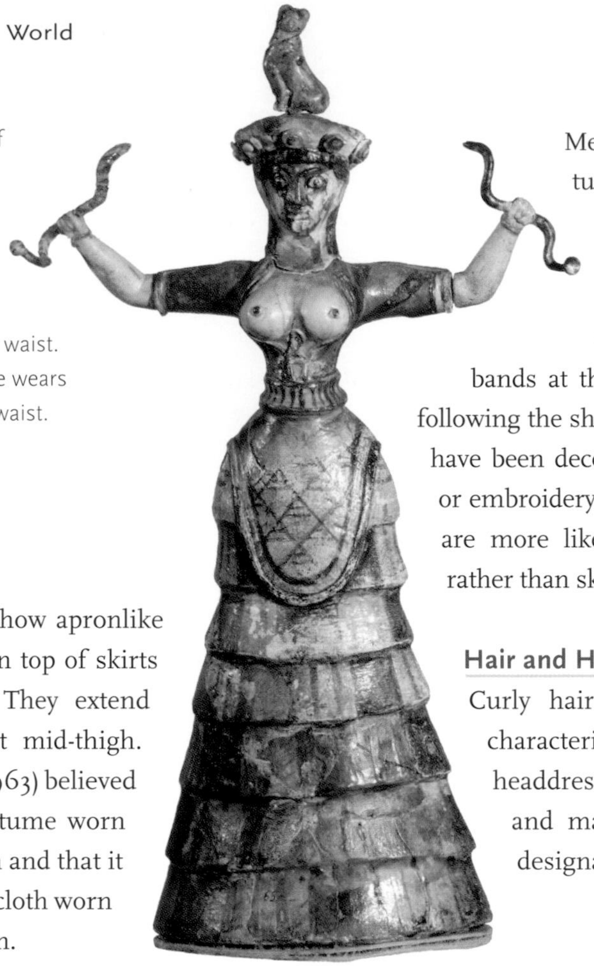

FIGURE 3.5 In another depiction of a snake goddess, here is a skirt apparently made from rows of ruffles. Her bodice is made of patterned fabric or fabric with ornamented applied bands, and she has a round, rolled belt at the waist. Like the goddess in Figure 3.2, she wears the apronlike covering below her waist. (Erich Lessing/Art Resource, NY)

Paintings and sculpture show apronlike garments worn by women on top of skirts (see Figures 3.4 and 3.5). They extend in front and back to about mid-thigh. Archeologist Arthur Evans (1963) believed that this garment was a costume worn in religious rituals by women and that it derived from a primitive loincloth worn originally by men and women.

Poncholike capes were usually worn by men in combination with skirts. These capes covered the upper part of the body and appeared to consist of a rectangle of fabric, folded in half, with an opening cut for the head. Both men and women wrapped shawl-like garments made from animal skins or heavy wool around the body in cold weather.

Tight, rolled belts were apparently made from fabric or leather and decorated with metal. Belts were worn by men and boys from the earliest periods and adopted by women during later Minoan periods. Because Minoan men are shown with abnormally small waists (which may have been an artistic convention), some authorities speculate that these belts may have been placed on young boys from age 12 or 14 in order to constrict the development of the waist.

Men and women wore T-shaped tunics with long or short sleeves. Women's tunics were long; men's were long or short. Tunics were generally decorated with patterned bands at the hem, along the sides, and following the shoulderlines. These bands may have been decorative selvages, woven tapes, or embroidery (Figure 3.7). Mycenaean men are more likely to be depicted in tunics rather than skirts or loincloths.

Hair and Headdress

Curly hair was apparently an ethnic characteristic. Probably much of the headdress had religious significance and may have served as a symbol designating priest or priestess status.

FIGURE 3.6 A third type of skirt is seen in wall paintings. The exact construction is unclear. Some scholars suggest that the garment may have been wide-legged trousers, but it seems more likely that it is a wrapped skirt. (Detail: Scala/Art Resource, NY)

FIGURE 3.7 Figures depicted on a sarcophagus from the 14th century BCE at Hagia Triada, Crete, show a procession of two women and a man. The woman at the left wears a sheepskin skirt and a fitted bodice. The man and woman at the right are wearing long tunics decorated with trimming that may be woven braid. (Courtesy of Fairchild Publications, Inc.)

Men wore their hair long and curly or short and cut close to the head. Sometimes men tied their hair into a braid or lock at the back of the head; sometimes they held it in place with a fillet. Hat styles included elaborate, possibly ritual types: high, round, and crownlike with a tall plume; turbans; small caps; and wide-brimmed hats.

Women's long, curled hair was often held in place with a fillet or elaborate arrangement of plain or jeweled bands (see Illustrated Table 3.1, page 58). Hats ranged from high, tiered, brimless styles to beretlike flat hats.

Footwear

Men and women wore sandals or shoes with pointed toes that fitted the foot closely and ended at the ankle. Athletes (bull leapers) wore a soft shoe with what appears to be a short sock or ankle support. Archeologists have found that the floors of Minoan palaces show little wear from shoes, while entrance stairs are worn away from the passing of shod feet, leading to the conclusion that people went barefoot indoors but wore shoes outside.

Jewelry

Men and women wore rings, bracelets, and armlets. Women wore necklaces. Although earrings were found in Minoan graves, they are not generally depicted in the art.

Cosmetics and Grooming

Women apparently used eye makeup and, probably, lip coloring. Men were clean shaven.

Costume Components for Children

Little evidence exists for the costume of children. Boys depicted in the paintings found on Thera wear little clothing: A fishing boy wears nothing; those boxing have strings around their waists. Their heads are shaven except for some locks of hair. One statuary group from Mycenae shows a small boy of perhaps about 3 or 4 years of age dressed in a floor-length skirt and wearing a necklace and a padded, rolled belt. Probably children wore simple costumes such as skirts or tunics. After puberty they undoubtedly assumed adult clothing.

TRANSITIONS IN THE DOMINANT STYLES

Some costume historians have pointed out parallels between the tiered skirts of Minoan women and the fringed kaunakes garments of Mesopotamia. Similarities also exist in elements of language between Crete and the Middle East. Cretan traders traveled extensively throughout the Mediterranean area both to the east and to Egypt in the south (see Global Connections). Certainly the Cretan traders reached the areas of Asia Minor where the kaunakes garments were worn, but even if the origin of the tiered skirt for Minoan women was to be found in the Middle East, the forms that evolved during the height of Minoan civilization differ markedly from the dress of Mesopotamia and Egypt during concurrent periods.

Sometime during the dark ages after the close of the Minoan–Mycenaean period, the fitted, full-skirted costume for women disappeared. Just how long it

Illustrated Table 3.1

Examples of Hairstyles and Headdress Worn by Men and Women in Greece

Youthful male figure with
short, curly hair from
Classical period

Bearded philosopher from
Classical period

Youth wearing a petasos

Youth wearing a
Phrygian bonnet

Women's hairstyles depicted on Archaic Greek sculpture

Woman's hairstyle
depicted in Minoan
wall painting

Women's hairstyles and headdress from Classical period depicted on vase paintings

Thomas Hope. Reprinted from *Costumes of the Greeks and Romans* by Thomas Hope with permission by Dover Publications, Inc.

Global Connections

Most likely created in Crete or Greece, this statue dating from c. 640–630 BCE wears a closely fitted dress of uncertain type, perhaps most like an Egyptian sheath dress or a Greek Doric peplos of the archaic period (see Figures 3.9 and 3.10). She wears a Minoan-type wide belt. Her hair has the appearance of an Egyptian wig. Not typical dress of either the Egyptians, Minoans, or Greeks, the garment provides evidence of active contact between Greece and Egypt during the Minoan and archaic Greek periods. Such contact led to the combination of Egyptian, Cretan, and archaic Greek dress elements into an artist's sculpture of a mythical woman, probably the acolyte of a goddess. (Gianni Dagli Orti/The Art Archive at Art Resource, NY)

persisted after the beginning of the dark ages and how it came to be supplanted by the later Greek styles is unknown. By the time political control of Crete had passed to the Mycenaeans, the elaborately patterned fabrics declined in use, giving way to plain cloth with simpler edgings. Barber (1991) speculated about this development, saying, "One wonders if the Mycenaeans cheerfully bought up and wore the sumptuous Minoan fabrics as they began to take over affairs on Crete, but then allowed the local native industry to fade" (330).

After a period of more than 400 years, mainland Greece emerged from the dark ages into the archaic period. By this time costume in general and the costume of women in particular had altered dramatically.

HISTORICAL BACKGROUND: GREEK CIVILIZATION

Written records vanished during the dark ages. The political history of the period does not exist.

Intellectual achievements were limited to epic ballads, sung perhaps by wandering bards, which were eventually woven into a cycle familiar to modern readers from the poems attributed to Homer, *The Iliad* and *The Odyssey*. Although he related stories about the heroes of the Trojan War, which occurred during the Mycenaean period, Homer's epic poems describe the life and customs of his own times, probably before 700 BCE.

As the dark ages ended and Greece entered the archaic period, c. 650–480 BCE, the Greek people began to prosper as their culture revived. Village communities evolved into independent city-states that would provide the first type of democratic government with elections, juries, and government by citizens of the city-state.

In the classical age, c. 500–323 BCE, Greece enjoyed a golden age, one of the most creative eras in the history of western civilization. Greek philosophers such as Socrates, Plato, and Aristotle pondered the nature of the universe, the meaning of life, and ethical values. Tragic dramatists such as Aeschylus, Sophocles, and Euripides wrote dramas for the public dealing with the nature and fate of man. The Greeks developed "history," a new literary form, which related and analyzed past experiences. Greek sculpture glorified the human body; using new techniques to build in marble, the Greeks created architectural masterpieces.

Even before the classical age, Greeks had for centuries been establishing colonies throughout the Mediterranean. The first were on the western coasts of present-day Turkey, which the Greeks called Ionia. Greek settlements had also been established in Sicily, throughout southern Italy, and as far west as southern France. These centers of Greek culture and trade helped to spread Greek culture. Etruscan costume (the Etruscans were a people living on the Italian peninsula whose civilization predated that of the Romans) shows many resemblances to that of the Greeks, as do the later Roman styles. At the same time, Greek dress borrowed from the regions with which the Greeks came into contact, particularly from the Middle East.

Greek influence was spread also by the conquests of Alexander the Great of Macedonia (356–323 BCE), whose father had brought Greece under his control. Alexander carved out an empire that stretched from Greece and Egypt in the west to the shores of the Indian Ocean in the east. After Alexander's death his empire fell apart; Greek influence waned while that of the Romans began to expand. The period following Alexander's death is known as the Hellenistic period and is generally dated from c. 300 to 100 BCE. Gradually, the Romans supplanted the Greeks as the dominant force in the Mediterranean region, although the art and the wisdom of Greece continued to influence the world long after its political power was eclipsed.

Social Organization

Society in the time of Homer was made up of nobility and commoners. Households were largely self-sufficient, each one producing its own food and clothing textiles. A man's home was, quite literally, his fortress, protected by walls against the raiders who frequently attacked the Greek settlements near the sea.

By the classical age, a period for which written and art records abound, Greek communities had grown into city-states and had developed a far more sophisticated and urban organization. The population of Athens, the most famous city-state in Greece, consisted of men (the active citizens), their dependent women and children, resident foreigners, and slaves.

An ordinary Athenian lived in a small, unpretentious house made of sun-dried brick that lacked central heating and running water (Figure 3.8). A man might attend the assembly of the law courts when not engaged in work. According to Roebuck (1966),

FIGURE 3.8 The high-level skills in the fine and applied arts of Greece appeared as well in home furnishings, such as this klysmos chair that has been the basis of furniture design in such Euro-American periods as the Renaissance and the Empire periods. (Munson-Williams-Proctor Art Institute/Art Resource, NY)

his recreation was found in the festivals and public facilities like gymnasiums, which were provided by the city. Luxuries of diet, clothing, and furniture were for the very rich, although they, too, lived relatively simply. In democratic Athens extravagance and ostentation were quick to attract attention and draw censure. (366)

In the classical age, women occupied a subordinate position, but judging from the writings of Homer they had a rather open, companionable relationship with men. The general view of the place of women in classical times has been that women lacked political power and had little control over their own destinies. It has been said that from birth to death they were under the control of some man. Even widows or divorced women, although they retained title to their inherited property, had to be supervised by their nearest male relative.

Marriages were arranged, and monogamy was the rule. Girls married at about age 14 to men who were usually about age 30. Scholars believe the average life span for women was about 40 years. Husbands did not consider their wives as equals, socially or intellectually, and did not appear with them in public. Secluded in the household, the wife oversaw the running of the home, where she was responsible for the children, food, and clothing. By spinning and weaving fabrics and making clothing, she made a very real contribution to the economy of the household.

Scholars differ as to how freely women could move around the city outside the home. The current belief is that women were able to carry out at least some activities outside the home. They obtained water from the town fountains, attended public speeches, visited religious sanctuaries, and participated in religious festivals. Some of these activities included both genders, but others were strictly for women. They could visit close friends and were permitted to attend tragic plays but not comedies, perhaps because those tended to be bawdy. As Reeder (1995) noted,

In all movements outside the home, a woman was supposed to be inconspicuous to the point of invisibility, and although the use of the veil is not yet well understood,

she was probably expected upon leaving her house to wrap her mantle or a veil around her head so that it obscured part of her face and neck. (20)

This practice may have come to Greece from Ionia and the Near East c. 530 BCE, along with such styles as the Ionic form of dress. This veiling symbolized the subjugation of women to their husbands. Scholars see evidence for this custom in a large number of statues of women that have been found in which veils are pulled down at least partially over the face (Galt, 1931) and in references in the writing of poets such as Homer.

In Sparta, the largest and the most militaristic Greek city-state, women were less restricted, a state of affairs other Greeks found disquieting. The historian Plutarch described Spartan women as bold, masculine, and overbearing and seemed shocked at the notion that they spoke openly "even on the most important subjects" (Durant, 1966, 84).

Connelly (2007), in *Portrait of a Priestess*, has shown that the office of priestess was one area in which women could attain status equal to that of men. Although there were exceptions, female priestesses presided over the cults of goddesses and male priests over those of gods. To be qualified to become a priestess, women had to come from affluent families of high social rank. Some appointments were hereditary. The duties included the care of the sanctuary, especially tending to the holy things kept there. Priestesses had to pay for some of the supplies used in ceremonies. They took part in processions. Often depicted carrying trays of holy objects, priestesses made liquid offerings called libations to the goddess (Figure 3.9). They offered prayers, and participated in sacrifices and ritual feasting.

Laws relating to appropriate dress for participation in religious rites were inscribed within sanctuaries. These were not universal, but were developed locally and were different for different cults. In many sanctuaries white garments, which were associated with purity, were required. In some places of worship limits were placed on the cost of clothing. Purple (only

FIGURE 3.9 Depiction of a family performing sacrifices, c. 530 BCE. Women are dressed in blue Doric peplos with red cloaks. Young boys wear himationlike draped cloaks. (Scala/Art Resource, NY)

available in very costly fabrics), flower-decorated, or black garments; sandals; and rings were prohibited in another place. Some temples confiscated dress that violated prohibitions on decorated robes. In art, it is not possible to identify priestesses by their clothing, but some of the objects they carry signify their status. One in particular, the key to the sanctuary, seems to have been almost universal. Unlike a modern key, it was a large, long, narrow piece of metal with a sharp right-angled turn and often a circular garland hung from it.

Another group of women not subject to the constraints of married women were the prostitutes. The lowest class of prostitutes lived in brothels, often in seaports. They dressed in such lightweight clothing that literary references described them as "naked." Nudity for women was not socially acceptable. A slightly higher class of courtesans were the "flute girls" who entertained with music and dancing at the otherwise all-male parties that were customary. These women are often depicted on vase paintings where some are shown clad in ordinary dress, some in special short dancing costumes, and others in the nude. The highest class of courtesans was the *hetairi*; the literal translation of the word is

"companions." These women moved freely among men. They were often better educated than ordinary women, and some were known for their skill in philosophical disputation or for their literary efforts. A few became quite famous. Many dyed their hair blonde (the predominant hair color among Greek women was dark). The law appears to have required them to wear specially decorated robes to distinguish them from respectable women.

In the Hellenistic period (c. 300–100 BCE) after the death of Alexander the Great in 323 BCE, the status of women seems to have risen somewhat. Female nudity in art increased. It is not likely that women ever appeared nude in public. Women were treated more openly and sympathetically in drama, and, interestingly, the influence of the hetairi on Athenian life diminished.

Fabrics and Cloth Production

Spinning and weaving were considered fit occupations for queens and goddesses. In Homer's *Odyssey*, Ulysses' faithful queen, Penelope, promises to choose a new king for Ithaca after she has finished weaving a shroud or burial sheet. After each day of weaving, at night she secretly unravels the work that she has done in order to avoid taking a new husband. Athena, goddess of wisdom, patroness of the city of Athens, and patroness of artisans, is credited in Greek mythology as being the first woman to work with wool. As part of the religious ceremonies held in Athens every 4 years in honor of the goddess, a magnificently patterned garment, the **sacred peplos**, was carried in procession to the temple to be placed upon her statue. It was woven by two women selected from those who participated in fertility rites associated with the cult of Athena.

Sheepherding was practiced in the mountainous Greek peninsula. Those sheep provided wool for weaving. The Greeks also used linen, particularly after the sixth century BCE. Linen use seems to have come to Greece from Egypt by way of Asia Minor, particularly from the Ionian region where many Greeks had settled. Greece imported most of the linen used from the Middle East and Egypt. The island of Cos was known for the production of silk in the late Greek period. Some scholars believe that the silk produced there was made by weaving with yarns unraveled from fabrics imported from China by way of Persia, but it is more likely that this was silk made from the cocoons of wild native silkworms and not cultivated silk. Cotton fiber was apparently brought to Greece by the soldiers of Alexander the Great. Alexander's troops also encountered silk banners in warfare, used to confuse the enemy by waving them during battle. Import of Chinese silk obtained from Persian traders began about the time of Alexander. For the most part, however, Greek clothing was made from wool or from linen (Faber, 1938).

The visual evidence for Greek styles often comes from marble statues that have been bleached white over the centuries or from vase paintings that do not show color. As a result it is often mistakenly assumed that Greek clothing had little color. Fabrics were colored with dyes obtained from plants, minerals, and shellfish. Decoration of fabrics during weaving or by embroidery was common. Greek women were gifted weavers, and they were talented in embroidery.

Skill was developed in pleating fabrics, and some sort of clothes press existed for smoothing and flattening fabrics and pressing in pleats. Fabrics were bleached with the fumes of a sulfur compound. Because Greek costume was draped, not cut and sewn, the fabric was probably woven to the correct size and did not require cutting (Figure 3.10).

Women manufactured all of the family clothing and covers for beds, cushions, and chests. Women making cloth at home generally carried out all of the steps in the process with the possible exceptions of dyeing and fulling (see Figure 3.10). **Fulling** is a process whereby wool fabrics are washed and shrunk to produce a dense, close weave. Both dyeing and fulling were processes that produced strong, unpleasant odors and required space and a good supply of water; therefore, they were not especially suited to urban households. When textiles were produced commercially for sale in the marketplace, the labor was divided into specialties that included wool combers, flax preparers, yarn spinners, dyers, fullers, and, when necessary, tailors to do the cutting and sewing.

FIGURE 3.10 Athenian women, c. 560 BCE (left to right), preparing wool, folding cloth, spinning yarn, weaving on an upright warp-weighted loom, and weighing wool fiber. These women are dressed in the form-fitting Dorian peplos of the Archaic period. (Image copyright © The Metropolitan Museum of Art. Image source: Art Resource, NY)

SOURCES OF EVIDENCE FOR THE STUDY OF GREEK COSTUME

The sculpture and vase paintings of Greece provide evidence concerning the costume of ancient Greece. However, records from the early archaic period are unclear. The art of that time was highly stylized (called *geometric art*) and provides little information about dress. The statuary of the later archaic period becomes more representational, allowing scholars to draw some conclusions regarding dress. The later periods, particularly the classical period, abound in representations of costume in sculpture and painting.

The Greeks developed the concept of ideal human form and proportions. Polyclitis, a sculptor (c. 450 BCE), wrote an influential treatise about his view of the appropriate standard of proportions for sculptors. Through Greek art and writings, this Greek ideal, a figure about $7^1/_2$ heads high with the hipline at wrist level halfway down the body, continued to influence ideas about perfect male and female proportions in subsequent periods and became a part of the heritage of classical influences in the western world.

Although Greek vase painting and sculpture provide plenty of evidence about the construction of clothing, the conventions of Greek art limit information about color in dress. Greek marble statues had been colorfully painted, but over the centuries that color has been bleached away. Major Greek vase painting styles include black figure painting, with black figures on an orange-red background; red figure painting, with red figures on black background; and white ground vases. Only on these latter vases can one see color.

Nudity was not acceptable to the Minoans, the Mycenaeans, or the Homeric Greeks. Tradition records the date of c. 720 BCE as the time when Greek men began to participate in athletic events in the nude (Bonfante, 1977). Athletic games in Greece were part of religious ritual; therefore, athletes performing in the nude competed in a religious context. Furthermore, the Greek ideal stressed perfection of the body and the soul. At about the same time that nudity came into athletics, artists began to make representations of the male nude.

Depiction of female nudity did not follow. Although in earlier periods the ideal of the well-formed female body was clearly visible beneath the sculpted, softly flowing draperies of the costume, women participated in athletics or attended the games only in the city of Sparta. Women dancers and acrobats wore, at the minimum, a perizoma (*loincloth*) and usually also a band covering the breasts. After 400 BCE, attitudes toward women seem to have become somewhat less restrictive, and artists sculpted some of the now famous nude or partially nude statues of women such as the Venus de Milo.

GREEK COSTUME: 650–100 BCE

The garment called the *tunic* heretofore was called a **chiton** (*ky'tn*) by the Greeks. Although many of the earliest depictions of Greek chitons give the impression of a garment sewn together at the shoulders and under the arms, later versions were not necessarily sewn, but often were created by taking a single rectangle of fabric and wrapping it around the body, securing it at the shoulders with one or more pins (see Figures 3.9 and 3.10). Variations in the appearance of chitons were often achieved by belting the chiton at any of several locations, by creating and manipulating a fold over the top of the fabric, and by varying the placement of the pins at the shoulder.

Full-length chitons were woven to the same size no matter how tall or short the person who was to wear the garment. Lengths could be easily adjusted by increasing or decreasing the size of the overfold.

Over the chiton, Greek men and women placed shawls or cloaks. Some of the overgarments were decorative; others were utilitarian. The summary and illustrations that follow describe the major costume forms in use during the archaic, classical, and Hellenistic periods of ancient Greek history. Various authors use conflicting terminology to identify different types of chitons. The terms used here are those that seemed to the authors to be most consistently used by reliable sources.

TABLE 3.1 Types of Chitons Worn by Greek Men and Women

NAME OF STYLE	WORN BY	LENGTH	FIT	FABRIC	DURATION
chitoniskos	men	usually short, between hip and thigh	close to body, similar in shaping to the Doric peplos	usually patterned wool	Archaic period to c. 550 BCE
Doric peplos [Fig. 3.9 and 3.10]	women	to ankles	close to body, fastened with large straight pin at shoulder	usually patterned wool	Archaic period to c. 550 BCE
Ionic chiton [Fig. 3.11 and 3.12]	men women	short or long long, to ground	full, longer sleeves, fastened with many small brooches at shoulder	lightweight wool or pleated linen	550–480 BCE, less often from 480–300 BCE
Doric chiton [Fig. 3.13]	men women	short, with few exceptions long	narrower than Ionic, without sleeves, fastened with one brooch (fibula) at shoulders	wool, linen, or silk	400 to 100 BCE 450 to 300 BCE
Hellenistic chiton [Fig. 3.14]	women	long	similar to Doric chilton, but narrower, often belted just below bosom	lightweight wool, linen, or silk	300 to 100 BCE
exomis [Visual Summary Table]	working-class men and slaves	short	fastened over one shoulder	sturdy, durable fabric, probably wool	throughout all Greek periods

Costume Components for Men and Women

The Chiton

Greek art and literature indicate that the chiton underwent a number of changes over time. Table 3.1 summarizes the variations in the type of chitons worn by men and women at various times. Chitons are shown in Figures 3.11, 3.12, 3.13, and 3.14.

The Greek author Herodotus claimed the Doric style (see Figure 3.11) of the archaic period was abandoned because of an incident toward the beginning of the sixth century BCE. Athenian women supposedly used their dress pins to stab to death a messenger who brought the bad news of the almost total destruction of an Athenian military force in battle. According to Herodotus, the Ionic chiton, which did not utilize these large, sharp pins, was mandated as a result. Contemporary Comments 3.1 contains Herodotus's description of the scene.

Geddes (1987) related men's change from the Ionic chiton to the Doric chiton in the classical period to changes in social and political attitudes. He believed that the luxurious fabrics and elaborate draperies of the full Ionic chiton had offered many opportunities for the display of a man's wealth.

Beginning in the late fifth century BCE, Greek political thought and practices encouraged values such as fitness, equality, and a sense of "thinking alike" that required, at the least, less flaunting of wealth. The Doric chiton, which had simple, relatively straight lines, was seen to best advantage on a fit body. It did not lend itself to ostentatious display, making it a style more in keeping with these new values.

FIGURE 3.11 Figure from a Greek vase by Thomas Hope (18th century). Woman fastens the shoulder of her Doric chiton. Notice the small weights at the end of the drapery that falls from her right shoulder. (Reprinted from *Costumes of the Greeks and Romans* by Thomas Hope with permission by Dover Publications, Inc.)

FIGURE 3.12 Only rarely does Greek art show colors of costumes. Here, a woman wearing a gold-colored Ionic chiton has a lavender chlamydon over her shoulder. (Image copyright © The Metropolitan Museum of Art. Image source: Art Resource, NY)

FIGURE 3.13 Woman in Ionic chiton over which she wears a chlamydon. (The Atalanta Lekythos (Funerary Oil Jug), 500-490 BCE. Attributed to Douris (Greek). Painted white-ground terracotta; 31.8 cm. The Cleveland Museum of Art, Leonard C. Hanna, Jr. Fund 1966.114)

FIGURE 3.14 *Dancing Lady*, Greek, c. 50 BCE. Greek woman wears the Hellenistic chiton, which is belted, typically, high under the breasts and made of lightweight fabric that molds the body lines. (Dancing Lady, c. 50 BC. Greece, Alexandria (?), 1st century BC. Marble; 85.4 cm. The Cleveland Museum of Art, John L. Severance Fund 1965.24)

The Himation

Just when the word **himation** (*hi-mat'e-ahn*) came to be applied to a large rectangle of fabric that wrapped around the body is not entirely clear (see Figures 3.15 and 3.16). This garment has been compared to the wrapped shawls of Mesopotamia. An earlier version worn in the archaic period seems to have been called a **chlaina** (Evans, 1964). Under the name *himation*, this garment was in wide use by the late fifth century BCE. Various methods of draping the himation are depicted by artists. The most common way of wearing it seems to have been with the upper corner covering the left shoulder, the bulk of the fabric wrapped across the back, passed under the right arm, and draped over the left shoulder or carried across the left arm. Both women and men wore this garment over a chiton. Philosophers and older gods are depicted in the himation alone, without a chiton beneath, but whether this was an artistic convention or actual practice is unclear. Geddes (1987) suggested that the popularity of the himation may have been related to an emphasis on athletic fitness, because it was easily taken off for sports and just as easily put back on.

Other Garments

The perizoma (*per-i-zo'ma*), Greek for a loincloth, was a garment worn by men either as an undergarment or for athletic contests (see Figure 4.1, page 77). Greek vases depict women with bands of cloth wrapped around the upper torso. Depending on how the bands were placed, they either bound or supported the breasts. Stafford (2005) reported seeing these bands and also a garment that looks much like a 21st-century sports bra depicted on vases showing women athletes. These garments seem to be similar to a Roman garment called the *strophium* (see Figure 4.14, page 89).

The **diplax** (*dy'plax*), a small rectangle of fabric worn by women, especially over the Ionic chiton, was draped in much the same way as the himation. The chlamydon (*kla'mi-don*) was a more complicated form of the woman's diplax in which fabric was pleated into a fabric band (see Figure 3.12).

Various styles of cloaks and capes were worn for cool weather. The most notable example was the **chlamys** (*kla'mis*), a rectangular cloak of leather or wool pinned over the right or left shoulder. Worn by men over a chiton, especially for traveling, it could be used as a blanket for sleeping at night (see Figure 3.16).

Hair and Headdress for Men

In the archaic period, long or medium-length hair and beards predominated, whereas in the classical period, young men wore short hair and no beards and older men longer hair and beards. See Illustrated Table 3.1, page 58, for a cross-section of hairstyles for the period.

Types of hats often shown in art included fitted caps and the **petasos** (*pet'a-sos*), usually worn with the

FIGURE 3.15 Greek youth wearing himation. (© Vanni Archive/ Art Resource, NY)

chlamys. Its wide brim provided shade in summer or kept rain off the head. Though not Greek styles, **Phrygian** (*frig'ee-an*) **bonnets**, brimless caps with a high padded peak that fell forward, were often depicted. Phrygian bonnets in Greek art identify wearers as foreigners from the Middle East. This type of hat reappears in European styles in the Middle Ages.

Both men and women wore the **pilos** (*pi'los*), a narrow-brimmed or brimless hat with a pointed crown.

Hair and Headdress for Women

In the archaic period, women wore their hair long in curling tresses with small curls arranged around the face. In the classical period, it was pulled into a knot or chignon at the back of the head. See Illustrated Table 3.1, page 58, for a cross-section of hairstyles for the period.

Fillets, scarves, ribbons, and caps were used to confine the hair. Paintings and sculpture of women depict veils that were worn over the head and are sometimes shown pulled across to cover the face.

Footwear

Both men and women wore sandals. Men also wore fitted shoes, ankle high or mid-calf length, or, for travel or warfare, leather boots that laced up the front (Figures 3.15 and 3.16).

FIGURE 3.16 Fifth-century BCE Greek vase shows (from left to right) a woman in an Ionic chiton with a shawl drawn over her head; a naked cupid; a goddess in a Doric chiton; a woman in an Ionic chiton, a veil over her head and a cloak over her shoulders; two men in chlamys and petasos; and a man in a himation. Older men are bearded; the youth is clean shaven. (Image copyright © The Metropolitan Museum of Art. Image source: Art Resource, NY)

Jewelry

More often worn by women than men, jewelry consisted of necklaces, earrings, rings, decorative pins for fastening the chiton, and brooches.

Cosmetics

Statues and vase paintings do not reveal the extent to which makeup was worn. Writings of the period do, however, record the use of perfumes. Contemporary Comments 3.2 reprints passages from *The Iliad* and *The Odyssey* that describe not only some of the clothing worn by women, but also cosmetics and jewels.

Costume Components for Children

Infants were wrapped in **swaddling clothes** (bands of fabric wrapped around the body) and wore closely fitted, peaked caps. Swaddling babies, a common practice throughout Europe until the 19th century, was thought to prevent deformity of children's limbs. Because the Greeks emphasized bodily perfection, they probably held similar beliefs. A few representations of infants, perhaps older ones, show them wrapped in loose cloth draperies rather than in swaddling bands.

Sometimes small boys are depicted in the nude. School-age boys wore short chitons, either belted or

Contemporary Comments 3.2

HOMER DESCRIBES WOMEN'S GROOMING AND DRESS

In The Iliad, *Homer describes how Hera, a goddess, beautifies herself so that she may persuade the god Zeus to do something she wishes.*

She went to her chamber. . . . There entering she drew shut the leaves of the shining door, then first from her adorable body washed away all stains with ambrosia [a sweet-smelling substance], and next anointed herself with ambrosial sweet olive oil, which stood there in its fragrance beside. . . . When with this she had anointed her delicate body and combed her hair, next with her hands she arranged the shining and lovely and ambrosial curls along her immortal head, and dressed in an ambrosial robe that Athene [another goddess] had made her carefully, smooth, and with many figures upon it, and pinned it across her breast with a golden brooch, and circled her waist about with a zone [belt] that floated a hundred tassels, and in the lobes of her carefully pierced ears she put rings with triple drops in mulberry clusters, radiant with beauty, and, lovely among goddesses, she veiled her head downward with a sweet fresh veil that glimmered pale like the sunlight. Underneath her shining feet she bound on the fair sandals. [Book 14, lines 169–186]

In The Odyssey, *an epic describing the adventures of Odysseus, a Greek warrior, suitors who believe Odysseus is dead give presents to his wife Penelope. These gifts include clothing and jewels.*

. . . every man sent a squire to fetch a gift—Aninoos a wide resplendent robe, embroidered fine, and fastened with twelve brooches, pins pressed into sheathing tubes of gold; Eurymakhos, a necklace wrought in gold, with sunray pieces of clear glinting amber. Eurydamas's men came back with pendants, ear-drops in triple clusters of warm lights; and from the hoard of Lord Polyktor's son, Peisandros, came a band for her white throat, jewelled adornment.

Homer. (2011, trans.). *The iliad of Homer* [R. Lattimore, trans.]. Chicago, IL: University of Chicago Press.
Homer. (1961, trans.). *The odyssey* [R. Fitzgerald, trans.]. Garden City, NY: Doubleday.

unbelted. Girls' chitons were arranged much as those of older women and belted in a variety of ways. Both boys and girls wore himations; those for girls were worn over a chiton, and those for boys, either alone or over a chiton.

For protection outdoors, art of the period depicts small, rectangular cloaks with clasps on the right shoulder. Another warm garment was a long cape with a pointed hood that either closed in front or had an opening through which it could be slipped over the head.

Hair and Headdress

Small children and boys had short hair. Older girls dressed their hair in the same way as women. Boys and girls wore a flat-crowned hat with a heavy roll as a brim. Girls wore a high, peaked hat with a flat, stiff brim.

Footwear

Children were often shown barefoot. Foot coverings included sandals and closed shoes.

Jewelry

Children wore earrings, necklaces, and bracelets, especially those in the form of a serpent.

Costume for Specialized Occupations or Occasions

Wedding Dress

The Greek bride's costume for weddings was laden with symbolism (Figure 3.17). The wedding garment had some areas that were dyed purple with a costly dye obtained from a rare type of mollusk called the *murex*. The bride wore a belt tied with a double knot known as a bridal or **Hercules knot**. The loosening of this knot, which took place on the wedding night, was both a symbol of and a necessary preface to the sexual union of the bride and groom. Her veil, which was either a mantle pulled up over the back of the head or a separate veil, was colored yellow-

FIGURE 3.17 Woman preparing for her wedding. The attendant at the left is handing her the stephane, or bridal crown. The bride, on the right, has a belt—tied with a bridal knot—around her waist and is in the process of donning her bridal veil. (Manner of: the Meidias Painter. Oil flask (lekythos) in the form of an acorn with scene of bridal preparations. Greek, Classical Period, 410–400 B.C. Place of Manufacture: Greece, Attica, Athens Ceramic, Red Figure. Height x diameter: 16.2 x 6 cm (6 3/8 x 2 3/8 in.) Museum of Fine Arts, Boston Anonymous gift 95.1402 Photograph © 2014 Museum of Fine Arts, Boston. All rights reserved)

orange with the dye from the saffron plant. Saffron was associated with women because of its use as a medicine for menstrual problems. The **stephane**, or bridal crown, was placed over the veil. The veil covered the bride's face before and during the ceremony and was lifted when the ritual unveiling of the bride, the **anakalypteria**, took place. The bride and the groom had not seen each other before this unveiling, and this part of the ceremony is thought to have symbolized the bride's willing acceptance of the groom.

Both bride and groom were also crowned with laurel wreaths, a religious symbol with divine associations that was intended to glorify the weddings of mortals. The bride also wore special sandals called **nymphides** and decked herself with elaborate jewelry (see Figure 3.17). Finally, the bride presented the groom with a tunic, a **chlanis**, she had woven herself. This gift probably symbolized her mastery of an essential housewifely skill.

Military Dress

Military costume during both the archaic and classical periods varied from one city-state to another but usually included some form of protective clothing worn over a tunic. In the archaic period, soldiers wore cloaks of rough wool. They protected themselves with such devices as breastplates made from metal plates or disks mounted on fabric corselets and held up by shoulder straps. Helmets made of either leather or bronze that had chin straps and high crests were intended to make warriors look more fearsome. **Greaves**, shaped leather or metal protectors for the lower legs, and wide metal belts and shields provided additional protection.

In the classical period, chlamys-style cloaks were worn. Protective devices for common soldiers included a leather **cuirass** (*kwi-ras'*)—a modern term for a closely fitted, shaped armor that covered the body—a metal belt, and greaves. Heavily armed infantry wore a metal or leather cuirass with a row of leather tabs hanging down from the cuirass at the waist to protect the lower part of body (Figure 3.18). Helmets, worn either with or without crests, became more protective with extended pieces to cover the cheekbones, nose, jaws, and neck. In both periods men either went barefoot or wore high boots.

FIGURE 3.18 Greek soldier wearing leather cuirass with suspended leather panels. Note that the cheek guards of the helmet are raised. When in use, these panels would fold down to protect the side of the face. The soldier wears greaves on his legs. (Reprinted with permission by Dover Publications, Inc..)

Theatrical Dress

The theater was important in Greece and eventually acquired a traditional style of costume through which the theatergoer could immediately identify the characters. Male actors played all of the parts in both comedies and tragedies. Tragic actors wore a tragic mask, with either tall wigs or tufts of hair fastened to it, and thick-soled platform shoes. Kings, queens, gods, goddesses, happy characters, tragic figures, and slaves were each identified by a specific style of dress, special insignia, or color.

Summary

Themes

Although lack of precise information about Minoan life and culture limits our ability to explore themes related to social life, we can readily see the impact on dress of themes such as the PRODUCTION OF TEXTILES and related TECHNOLOGY. Skills related to weaving and dyeing, especially of wool fibers, made possible the wide variety of highly ornamented fabrics used in Minoan dress. TRADE, exporting textiles and importing dyestuffs to and from other Mediterranean countries, was another factor that contributed to the development of Minoan styles. The resulting CROSS-CULTURAL INTERCHANGES may also have influenced some specific garments, such as shoes and sheep-fleece skirts.

Minoan POLITICAL CONTROL of Mycenae helped to spread Minoan-influenced styles to the mainland of Greece. Eventually, POLITICAL CONFLICT in the form of the conquest of the Minoans and the Mycenaeans

by outside forces closed off information about these people for a number of centuries.

The archaic and classical Greek periods provide more fertile territory for identification of important themes.

Some of the variations in the forms of the chiton illustrate themes such as POLITICS, CROSS-CULTURAL INFLUENCES, and CHANGES IN SOCIAL VALUES. The Ionic chiton was a style with non-Greek origins, most probably a Middle Eastern style adopted by Greeks in Ionia, a settlement at the far eastern end of the Mediterranean. From Ionia the style spread to the mainland, where it supplanted the Doric style. Following war with Persia, a period of intense interest in the Greek past, and a denigration of Middle Eastern styles apparently led to a rejection of the Ionic chiton in favor of the Doric chiton, which represented a revival of the older, native Doric styles. For men, the simpler Doric chiton was more compatible with the social value of equality than the more elaborate Ionic.

The shape and construction of costume for men and for women in Greece was not markedly different. Nevertheless, the theme of GENDER ROLES does appear in the dress of brides and in the veil for married women.

Many writers have commented on similarities between certain aspects of Greek ARTS AND DRESS. These similarities are especially notable in architecture. Decorative motifs often appear both on buildings and as ornamentation on garments. Tall, slender Doric and Ionic building columns with their fluted surfaces have been compared to the long, pleated tubular chitons worn by the Greeks.

LEGACIES OF GREEK DRESS

The travels of the chiton do not end with the decline of Greek power. The spread of Greek settlements and Greek culture throughout the Mediterranean world resulted in the adoption of many elements of Greek costume by contemporary Egyptians, by the Etruscans, and, later, by the Romans in Italy.

By way of Roman costume, Greek costume can be said to have served as a basis for the costume of Romanized Europe for the six centuries following the death of Alexander the Great. It can even be argued that its influence in certain aspects of dress can be felt until the latter part of the Middle Ages. Moreover, Greek influence on dress was not limited to the civilizations that coexisted with classical Greece. Elements of classical art have been revived during the Renaissance (15th and 16th centuries), the Neoclassical period (18th century), and the Empire period (early 1800s). In this latter period a method of belting the dress high, under the bustline, was copied from Hellenistic chiton styles (see Figures 11.3 and 11.5, pages 309 and 311). Called the **Empire waist**, this Greek-inspired style was revived periodically by fashion designers of the 20th and 21st centuries, many of whom looked to historic periods for design inspiration. The soft, flowing lines of the Greek styles seem to appeal particularly to lingerie designers and designers of evening dress.

REFERENCES

Barber, E. J. W. (1991). *Prehistoric textiles*. Princeton, NJ: Princeton University Press.

Barber, E. J. W. (1994). *Women's work: The first 20,000 years*. New York, NY: Norton.

Barber, E. J. W. (2000). [Letter to the editor]. *Archaeology* (Nov.–Dec.), 6.

Bonfante, L. (1977). *Etruscan dress*. Baltimore, MD: Johns Hopkins University Press.

Boucher, F. (1987). *20,000 years of fashion*. London, UK: Thames and Hudson.

Connelly, J. B. (2007). *Portrait of a priestess: Women and ritual in ancient Greece*. Princeton, NJ: Princeton University Press.

Durant, W. (1966). *The life of Greece. The story of civilization* (Vol. 2). New York, NY: Simon & Schuster.

Evans, A. (1963). Scenes from Minoan life. In J. Hawkes (Ed.), *The world of the past*. New York, NY: Knopf.

Evans, M. M. (1964). Greek dress. In M. Johnson (Ed.), *Ancient Greek dress*. Chicago, IL: Argonaut.

Faber, A. (1938). Dress and dress materials in Greece and Rome. *CIBA Review*, p. 297.

MODERN INFLUENCES

This dress from Jenny Packham's spring 2015 bridal show has an obvious ancestor in the Greek Doric chiton. Designers often draw inspiration for white wedding dresses from the dress of ancient Greece seen on ancient white marble statues.

(Mitra/WWW/© Conde Nast)

Visual Summary Table

Major Greek Garments

Doric peplos
(c. 550 BCE)

Ionic chiton
(c. 550–480 BCE)

Doric chiton
(c. 400–100 BCE)

Himation

Chlamys (*cloak*) and petasos (*hat*)

Exomis

Galt, C. (1931). Veiled ladies. *American Journal of Archeology,* 35(4), 373.

Geddes, A. G. (1987). Rags and riches: The costume of Athenian men in the fifth century. *Classical Quarterly,* 37(ii), 307–331.

Houston, M. G. (1966). *Ancient Greek, Roman, and Byzantine costume.* London, UK: Adam & Charles Black.

Marcar, A. (2005). Reconstructing Aegean Bronze Age fashion. In L. Cleland, M. Harlow, & L. Llewellyn-Jones (Eds.), *The clothed body in the ancient world* (p. 34). Oxford, UK: Oxbow.

Mylonas, G. (1966). *Mycenae and the Mycenaean world.* Princeton, NJ: Princeton University Press.

Reeder, E. D. (1995). Women and men in classical Greece. In E. Reeder (Ed.), *Pandora: Women in classical Greece.* Princeton, NJ: Princeton University Press.

Roebuck, C. (1966). *The world of ancient times.* New York, NY: Scribner's.

Stafford, E. J. (2005). Viewing and obscuring the female breast: Glimpse of the ancient bra. In L. Cleland, M. Harlow, & L. Llewellyn-Jones (Eds.), *The clothed body in the ancient world* (pp. 96–110). Oxford, UK: Oxbow.

	800–480 BCE			79 BCE
FASHION AND TEXTILES				
POLITICS AND CONFLICTS	Etruscan civilization superior to nearby tribes has developed (800 BCE)	The city of Rome evolves into a metropolis (753 BCE)	Kings rule Rome, including Etruscan kings (753–509 BCE)	Roman Republic ends when Julius Caesar becomes dictator
DECORATIVE AND FINE ARTS				
ECONOMICS AND TRADE			Etruscan dress shows Greek influences arriving with trade during the archaic Greek period (c. 550 BCE)	
TECHNOLOGY AND IDEAS				
RELIGION AND SOCIETY	Etruscan wall paintings in tombs (800 BCE)			

CHAPTER FOUR

Etruria and Rome

c. 800 BCE–400 CE

44 BCE–395 CE | 476 CE

Roman Empire assigns special dress according to status (31 BCE–395 CE)

Assassination of Julius Caesar (44 BCE)
Augustus becomes Emperor in 27 BCE; forms the Roman Empire

Rome divides into eastern and western empires (395 CE)

Last western emperor of Rome deposed

Roman villas furnished with handsome furniture and floor mosaics (31 BCE–395 CE)

Roman engineers build aqueducts to carry water from the countryside into cities throughout the empire (first century CE)

Romans worship a number of gods (79 CE)

Greek influence was strong in the Etruscan towns that developed on the Italian peninsula. Etruria received Greek goods through trade, and the style of Etruscan (*ih-trus'can*) dress grew similar to that of the Greeks. The Etruscans were among the first people to be overcome by their ever more powerful Roman neighbors. The Roman Empire eventually dominated the Mediterranean region and most of the European continent. In its form and configuration, Roman dress was similar to both Greek and Etruscan forms; however, within these forms, Roman clothing incorporated elements that proclaimed the status of the wearer.

HISTORICAL BACKGROUND: THE ETRUSCANS

Prehistoric human occupants of the Italian peninsula migrated to Italy from many different places: Africa, Sicily, Spain, France, the Danube Valley, and Switzerland. They left no written records and are known only through archeological remains. These remains tell us they were pastoral people who tilled the soil, wove clothing, and made pottery and bronze implements. Among the pre-Roman peoples who migrated into Italy, none left a deeper impression than the Etruscans.

In certain areas of the Italian peninsula, a culture had developed by about 800 BCE that was more complex in organization than that of its neighbors. The Romans called these people **Etruscans**. The Etruscans had developed superior skills and artistic production. Eventually their territory stretched as far north as the region near the present-day city of Venice. The most important settlements in Etruria were concentrated in the western area that today is bounded on the north by Florence and on the south by Rome, roughly corresponding to the current Italian region of Tuscany.

Other immigrants also entered Italy. By the latter part of the eighth century BCE, Greek colonies had been established in Sicily and in southern Italy. By the sixth century BCE the Greeks reached the northern limits of their colonization, the southern boundary of Etruria. (It was the Greeks who gave the name *Italy* to

the region, naming it after an early king of one of the native tribes.)

In addition to the Etruscans and the Greeks, other native tribes populated the Italian peninsula. One of these tribes, the Latins, lived in an area near the mouth of the Tiber. At some point, possibly in the eighth century BCE, on one of the hills near the river, a colony of these people established a settlement that became the city of Rome. But the Romans, as these people were to be known to history, did not become an important political force in the Mediterranean until about the third century BCE when they subjugated the Etruscans.

The origins of the Etruscans are shrouded in mystery. They may have emigrated from Asia Minor, or they may have been an indigenous people, native to the Italian peninsula. Because of their superiority in arms and fighting ability, they were able to seize strategic points along the coast. From there they pushed inland, conquering vital sites from which they could control the local population. Eighteen fortified cities have been found. The 12 most important cities, ruled by kings and nobles, formed a loose confederation. The characteristics of the Etruscans, who were dominant, military, and aristocratic, but numerically a minority, enabled them to overcome their rivals.

The Etruscans left abundant records of their lives in wall paintings, in statues, and in the objects that they placed in their elaborate necropoli, or grave cities. Although they had a written language using a Greek alphabet, the limited numbers and types of inscriptions have not allowed full understanding of grammar and vocabulary. Consequently, terms related to Etruscan costume will be given in Greek- or Latin-based words. Based on the archaeological evidence, scholars have divided Etruscan civilization into archaic and classical periods.

The chief Etruscan towns had been founded by the middle of the seventh century BCE. Not only did the Etruscans improve the arable land and plant vineyards and olive groves, but they also mined and smelted iron ore, exploited deposits of copper, traded throughout the Mediterranean area, and amassed great wealth. In building their cities, they utilized a form of city planning. When a new site for a city was selected, they laid out the towns in a checkerboard pattern with two main streets intersecting at right angles.

Social Life

We know relatively little of Etruscan family life. Women seem to have occupied a position of greater importance in Etruscan society than did either Greek or Roman women. Roman writers frequently sneered about the foolishness of the Etruscans in granting their women such privileged status. Many of the funerary statues and paintings show men and women reclining together on couches at banquets with expressions and attitudes of warm affection. Family groups are depicted in relaxed, informal poses. Some recently excavated terra-cotta statues of children are among the most delightfully realistic statues from antiquity of infants and small children.

Art and Trade

The art of the Etruscans showed strong Greek influences, particularly during the sixth and fifth centuries BCE when Greek colonies were well established in southern Italy. Clearly Greece and Etruria had an active and close trading relationship. The scenes of daily life depicted by the Etruscans, however, portrayed Etruscans, not Greeks—indicated by the inclusion of some dress styles and conventions that are peculiar to the Etruscans and by the way in which respectable women are depicted as dining and appearing with men in public. The Etruscan tomb paintings were done in color so the observer can see the characteristic use of vivid color and pattern in clothing. Although much of the art of Etruria was of local production, rich Etruscans also purchased imported art objects from abroad, especially from Greece, and many of these were placed in the tombs with their owners.

ETRUSCAN COSTUME: C. 800–200 BCE

Costume Components for Men and Women

Garments

The Etruscan perizoma (*par-e-zo-ma'*) was a loincloth (like that worn by Minoans and Greeks) that was worn alone as an outer garment by laborers or other

physically active men. It was worn as an undergarment under a short, shirtlike chiton or a slightly longer chiton also called a tunic (Figure 4.1). The Etruscans apparently did not share Greek acceptance of male nudity.

The Etruscan versions of the chiton worn by men and women were essentially the same as those worn by Greeks. The most common length for men was to the thighs, but longer versions were also depicted. The Doric peplos was made in woven plaid or decorated with what may have been embroidery (Figure 3.9 on page 62 shows the general shape and form of the Doric peplos). Subsequently, a chiton cut fuller than

FIGURE 4.1 Figure from the land of Cyprus, c. seventh–sixth centuries BCE, wears a perizoma (*loincloth*) of the type worn by both the Greeks and the Etruscans.

FIGURE 4.2 Woman depicted on an Etruscan sarcophagus is dressed in a Doric chiton with a purple-bordered shawl draped around her body, over her shoulders, and drawn over her hair. Her jewelry includes a tiara, earrings, a necklace, bracelets, and finger rings.
(© The Trustees of the British Museum/Art Resource, NY)

the Doric peplos and with pleats appears in Etruscan art. According to Bonfante (2003) this chiton may be a forerunner of the later Ionic chiton. She pointed out that the Ionic chiton appeared in Etruria slightly earlier than in mainland Greece and suggested that both Greece and Etruria may have adopted the style independently from a third source, the Ionian region of the Near East.

Both Ionic and Doric chitons were worn between 580 BCE and the beginning of the Roman period, c. 300 BCE. However, Greek and Etruscan chitons are often difficult to tell apart (Figure 4.2). Etruscan chitons consistently tend to be shorter and less voluminous than Greek. Some appear to have sleeves cut and sewn into the garment, giving garments a closer fit and a less draped appearance (Figures 4.3 and 4.4). During the classical period of the Etruscans, upper class Etruscan ladies wore a badge of status consisting of a fringe or tassel that hung down at the front and back of each shoulder.

Wraps for the body were among the most distinctive styles developed by the Etruscans. Varieties included a heavy woolen cloak for men, which was similar to the Greek chlamys. It fastened at one shoulder. Etruscans wore the himation, adopted after it first appeared among the Greeks. The most original of the Etruscan mantles was the **tebenna** (*ta'ben-a*), a

FIGURE 4.3 *Dancer of Maenad* [a mythological figure in the form of a young girl], Italy, Etruscan, late sixth century BCE. Etruscan garments such as this one often show more shaping in the cut of the sleeves and a more fitted line through the body than the Greek costume of a comparable period. This figure also wears characteristic Etruscan pointed-toed shoes and the tutulus, a high-crowned, small-brimmed hat. (Candelabrum Stand of a Dancing Maenad, 525-500 BCE. Italy, Etruscan, late sixth Century BC. Bronze; 18.8 cm. The Cleveland Museum of Art, Purchase from the J. H. Wade Fund 1953.124)

FIGURE 4.4 A mythological Etruscan figure from a tomb in the Etruscan town of Tarquinia wears a short tunic that, like some Etruscan garments, fits the body closely. (Scala/Art Resource, NY)

rounded mantle worn by men and women. *Tebenna* is a Greek rendering of what was probably an Etruscan word. This garment seems to have been woven with curved edges in a roughly semicircular or elliptical form. It was draped in various ways: (1) like a chlamys, (2) worn back-to-front with the curved edge hanging down in front and the two ends thrown back over the shoulder, or (3) like a himation (Figure 4.5a–c). This

garment is thought to have been a forerunner of the Roman toga (*to'ga*), a semicircular draped garment symbolizing Roman citizenship.

Hair and Headdress

Men in the archaic period wore medium-length hair and pointed beards; in the postarchaic period, hair was short and faces were clean shaven. During the archaic

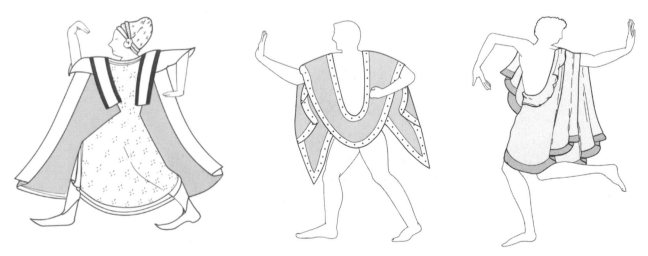

FIGURE 4.5 Three of the varied styles of mantles worn by the Etruscans: (a) a capelike garment worn by women that had long tabs hanging down in the front; (b) a tebenna, worn with the curved edge hanging down in the front and the two ends thrown over the shoulders; (c) a tebenna, draped over one shoulder, in a manner much like the himation. Compare the draping of (c) to that of the toga in (a). The tebenna is thought to have been the precursor of the toga. (Courtesy of Fairchild Publications, Inc.)

period women arranged their hair in a single braid at the back or in long, flowing tresses. In postarchaic periods women's hairstyles were like those of Greek women.

Distinctive styles of headwear included wide-brimmed hats similar to the petasos for men and fillets to confine the hair for both men and women. On festive occasions men and women wore a crownlike headpiece. Both genders wore high-crowned brimless hats; men's styles often were peaked (see Figure 4.4), while women wore the tutulus, with a rounded crown (see Figure 4.3).

Footwear

Both men and women wore sandals. Another style, often red in color, covered the foot up to the ankle and had an elongated toe that curled upward (see Figure 4.3). Bonfante (2003) suggested this style may have survived from Mycenae and come by some unknown route to Etruria from Greece in the sixth century BCE, when they first appeared.

Jewelry

Necklaces, earrings, decorative brooches, and fibulae appear in painting and sculpture. They were more often worn by women than men. Jewelry was either of local origin or imported from abroad.

COSTUME COMPONENTS FOR CHILDREN

So far as anyone can tell, there were no specialized costumes for children. Small children went naked in warm weather. Young boys dressed in short tunics (see Figure 4.10, page 86). Specific evidence of the dress of young girls is lacking, but probably they wore chitons similar to those of Greek girl children.

HISTORICAL BACKGROUND: THE ROMANS

Early Roman history was closely intertwined with that of Etruria. Kings ruled Rome during the early years of Roman history. Several of these kings were Etruscan, but in 509 BCE revolution ended the reign of Etruscan kings in Rome. Etruscans and Romans battled each other, one by one, until the cities of Etruria lost their independence and became another of the many ethnic strands woven into Roman Italy (Figure 4.6).

The Roman Republic (509–27 BCE) had a conservative government with two consuls elected annually. The consuls exercised the executive powers and commanded the armies in times of war. Rome also had a senate and a popular assembly.

FIGURE 4.6 The city of Rome began as a small settlement on the banks of the Tiber River and grew into an enormous metropolis, as seen in this model. (© Vanni Archive/ Art Resource, NY)

Under this form of government, Rome fought a series of wars that expanded Roman control over all of Italy. Rome and Carthage, whose empire stretched across North Africa, quarreled over Sicily. This led to the first wars of conquest beyond the Italian peninsula that, in time, produced the Roman Empire (see Figure I.1, page 17). Ultimately under the Republic, Roman-dominated lands included much of North Africa, large areas of the Middle East, eastern Europe up to the Danube River, and most of continental Europe (Figure 4.7).

Rome became a wealthy, complex society. However, the strain of warfare on society and the economy led to social strife. The rivalry of ambitious generals led to civil war, and ultimately one of the generals, Julius Caesar, was appointed dictator for life.

After Caesar's assassination in 44 BCE, Augustus, his grandnephew and adopted son, won out over all rivals in a struggle for power, and he became the first Roman emperor in 27 BCE. Augustus laid the foundations for an empire that would give the Mediterranean world 200 years of prosperity and peace, the *Pax Romana* (Roman Peace). Augustus and his successors added territory to the Empire in Arabia, Africa, Germany east of the Danube, and in Britain. Not until the third century CE would decline set in, culminating in the fall of the Roman Empire. Factors contributing to the decay of the empire included the flawed quality and competence of the emperors, military anarchy and civil wars, the failure of the economy, and the collapse of Roman society. The migration of the German tribes into the empire in search of land and provisions added to these problems.

Emperor Constantine built a new capital, Constantinople (now called Istanbul), in the eastern portion of the empire c. 325 CE, signaling the decline of the western Roman Empire. In 395 the naming of two Roman emperors, one for the east and one for the west, split the empire. Each portion became involved in separate struggles for survival. In the west, where German chieftains had begun to establish Germanic kingdoms, a barbarian chieftain deposed the last emperor in 476. The eastern Roman Empire, wealthy

FIGURE 4.7 As Roman cities grew in size, Roman engineers applied their skills to the building of aqueducts to move water from the countryside into the city. (Photograph by Vincent R. Tortora)

and secure, grew into the powerful and influential Byzantine Empire.

Social Life

During the early imperial period, the population of the city of Rome is estimated to have been more than a million people, consisting of Roman citizens, their families, their slaves, and foreigners (Friedlander, 1936). Only men were citizens, but citizens could be rich, middle class, or poor. By the second century, perhaps 90 percent of the residents of Rome were of foreign extraction, though many foreigners were residents of Roman provinces to whom citizenship had been extended (Casson, 1975).

The well-to-do population lived in town houses built around a sunny courtyard and decorated with colorful frescoes, or in large, comfortable apartments located on the ground floor of buildings that rose from four to nine stories high The less affluent and the poor lived in the tall apartment buildings on the higher floors, sometimes under crowded conditions, with poor lighting, bad ventilation, and the constant threat of disastrous fires.

FIGURE 4.8 Elaborate beds served not only for sleeping but also could be used as a place to recline when dining. (Image copyright © The Metropolitan Museum of Art. Image source: Art Resource, NY)

Members of the aristocracy lived in large, well-furnished households composed of relatives, servants who were often freed slaves, and household slaves (Figure 4.8). Heading every Roman family was the oldest male member, the *pater familias*. The pater familias was the sole owner of family possessions, including those of his children and also of his grandchildren. He decided whom his children would marry. If a marriage was not a success, it could be dissolved very easily. Married women of middle class or higher status supervised the children and the household, the size and complexity of which depended on the family's socioeconomic status. Wealthy families often had villas in the countryside where they might practice their religious rites (Figure 4.9).

Social Distinctions and Dress

According to Bonfante (1994), "Dress for a Roman often, if not primarily, signified rank, status, office, or authority" (5). Roman literary sources indicate that a married Roman woman wore a distinctive item of costume: the *stola* (see Figure 4.17, page 92). When her husband became a pater familias, she became the *mater familias*. On achieving this status, she then began to dress her hair in a distinctive hairstyle called the *tutulus*. If she were widowed, she wore a dark, square cloak for at least a year after her husband's death.

In spite of socioeconomic differences among Romans, the primary distinction made in Roman society for men was between the citizen and the noncitizen. This status was clearly marked by dress. The male citizen was entitled to wear the **toga**, a draped, elliptically shaped mantle that probably evolved from the Etruscan tabenna. Slaves, foreigners, and chaste adult women were prohibited from wearing this costume.

The emperor and the imperial court were at the very top of Roman society, and the upper classes more or less faithfully mirrored the manners and customs of the court of the day. Upper class men generally belonged to one of the civil and military orders. The most important of these were the senators. Second in importance were the knights (referred to by historians as the equestrian orders). Beginning in Republican times, senators were distinguished by their dress.

FIGURE 4.9 Romans worshiped a number of different gods, holding ceremonies of worship in their homes. Sometimes their homes were decorated with depictions of those ceremonies, such as this one preserved by the eruption of Mt. Vesuvius. (© Scala/Art Resource, NY)

Their tunics (and those of the emperor) had broad purple bands that extended vertically from hem to hem across the shoulders. These bands were called **clavi** (*clah'vee*), the plural form of **clavus** (*clah'vus*). Furthermore, senators wore shoes with laces that wrapped around the leg halfway to the knee. The tunics of knights had slightly narrower purple bands, and they wore a gold ring that signified their rank.

After the end of the first century BCE, it became customary for all male members of the nobility to wear clavi on the tunic.

The remainder of the citizenry had no special insignia aside from the toga, although a number of special types of togas were worn for certain occasions or to designate particular roles (Table 4.1). Foreigners wore the costume of their native land, and slaves wore tunics.

TABLE 4.1 The Appearance and Significance of Various Types of Togas

TYPE OF TOGA	APPEARANCE	SIGNIFICANCE
toga pura or toga virilis	plain white, undecorated wool	worn after the age of 16 by the ordinary male Roman citizen
toga candida	this was the toga pura lightened to an exceptional white	worn by candidates for office; the word candidate derives from this term
toga praetexta	with a purple border about 2–3 inches wide	worn by the young sons (until age 16) and daughters (until age 12) of the nobility and by certain adult magistrates and high priests
toga pulla	black or dark-colored toga	supposedly worn for mourning
toga picta	purple with gold embroidery	assigned on special occasions to victorious generals or others who distinguished themselves in some way
toga trabea	apparently multicolored, striped toga	assigned to augurs (religious officials who prophesied the future) or important officials

Note: Based on material in Wilson, L. M. (1924). *The Roman toga.* Baltimore, MD: Johns Hopkins University Press.

Fabrics and Clothing Production

Throughout Roman history wool was the major fiber used for clothing, and flax, the second most important. It is clear from literary sources that by the time of the Roman Republic, quite varied types of fabrics and ready-made garments were available in the marketplace. Used clothing was cut into patches and made into cloaks or quilts for slaves.

Linen or wool fabrics could be gauzelike or tightly woven. Some may have had a soft pile or a tapestrylike weave. Well-to-do individuals could purchase luxurious linen goods from Egypt. Cotton was first mentioned in Roman writings around 190 BCE, although it was probably imported earlier. It was often mixed with linen to make a fabric that draped better than linen but had a handsome, fairly lustrous surface when pressed. Wool and cotton were also blended.

By the end of the first century BCE, silk was available to the wealthy. Imported from China through northern India, silk was so expensive that is was generally mixed with other fibers, especially linen. On those very rare occasions when a garment was made entirely of silk, it was valued at its own weight in gold (Sebesta, 1994b).

Fabrics were dyed to a wide range of colors. Among the most important dyestuffs were those used to produce the shade of purple required for the clavi of men's tunics and the borders of certain togas.

Although women were closely associated with fabric production and many Roman women did weave cloth for their families, the textile industry was not a home craft, as it had been in Greece. Large estates often produced their own cloth. Here the work was done mostly by women in a workshop called a **gynaeceum**, many of whom were slaves (Herlihy, 1990). Much of the weaving, dyeing, and finishing was carried out in business establishments that might employ as many as 50 or 100 people, both men and women. These "factories" were located in many towns throughout the empire. Both fabrics and garments were imported to Rome from all parts of the empire and beyond. Some cities were especially well known for making certain types of cloth or items of clothing.

A cloak from Modena was considered superior to one from Laodicia, or a tunic from Scythia, better than one from Alexandria (Jones, 1960).

Wealthy families probably had their clothing needs provided by the slaves of the household, but evidence concerning trades in Roman times indicates that there was also a thriving "ready-to-wear" business. A dialogue in a Greek–Latin book reflects the nature of bargaining that went on in these shops (Friedlander, 1936, 148):

"I am going to the tailor."
"How much does this pair cost?"
"One hundred denarii."
"How much is the waterproof?"
"Two hundred denarii."
"That is too dear; take a hundred."

Tailors were accused of adjusting their prices for winter garments according to the severity of the season.

Specialization among shoemakers was apparently sufficiently great that differentiation was made between shoemakers, bootmakers, sandal makers, slipper makers, and ladies' shoemakers. Jewelry-craft members included workers in pearls and diamonds, gold and silversmiths, and ringmakers. In Rome, each craft was concentrated in a different district of the city.

SOURCES OF EVIDENCE FOR THE STUDY OF ROMAN COSTUME

Information about Roman dress comes from Roman art, Roman literature, and archeological excavations. Remarkable artifacts were preserved when the cities of Pompeii and Herculaneum were buried by the eruption of Mt. Vesuvius, a nearby volcano, in 79 CE.

Greek artists were brought to Rome to work, often as slaves. Many Roman statues were copies of sculptures created by earlier Greek artists. As a result, Roman art showed strong Greek influences, and it is not always clear whether the individuals depicted are actually Roman. On the other hand, Roman portrait sculpture (often executed by Greek sculptors working in Rome) emphasized a realism not to be found in

Global Connections

Zubarah, now abandoned, lies on the coast of modern Qatar. From this inhospitable Persian Gulf site, fine pearls—like these worn by a woman in Romanized Egypt around the second century CE—were exported throughout the Roman empire, proving to be a lucrative source of trade for the pearl divers of Zubarah. Pearls have been a treasured decorative element for millennia and were especially prized by the Romans. But the quality of these treasures varies significantly. Archeologists consider Zubarah to be the source of the highest quality of pearls before, during, and after the Roman period. (Gianni Dagli Orti/The Art Archive at Art Resource, NY)

the more idealized copies of Greek works. Many of these statues are portraits of individuals and depict the appearance, hairstyles, and garb of upper class Romans (see Global Connections).

Very sophisticated painting techniques had also developed. **Frescoes**, paintings on plaster, were extensively utilized in decorating the interiors of buildings, but relatively few of these art works have survived. Those that have been found provide some indication of the colors used in Roman costume, although artists may have been limited in the pigments available for painting or colors may have faded. One of the favorite ways of decorating buildings was with mosaics, pictures created from small pieces of colored stone. Here, too, people might be depicted.

Literary works, especially plays and satires, provide the names of garments; insight into current attitudes toward particular styles; and how they were bought, worn, or used to create an impact on friends (see Contemporary Comments 4.1).

Written material also reveals some of the uncertainties about Roman costume, especially concerning the costume of Roman women. Although a number of authors make reference to specific elements of women's dress, visual sources are confusing and individual scholars have interpreted this material differently.

ROMAN COSTUME FOR MEN AND WOMEN

The basic form of the chiton, called a *tunic* by the Romans, was adopted from the Greeks, possibly by way of Etruscan dress (Figure 4.10). The most distinctive Roman costume form, the toga, was apparently Etruscan in origin. These adopted costumes, however, took on Latin names and elements that reflected the Roman character.

In describing clothing, the Romans made a distinction between garments that were "put on"

FIGURE 4.10 Roman men and boys of all classes wore the tunic. For working classes and the poor the tunic would have been of sturdy durable fabric. For the more affluent, the form would have been similar to the garment worn by this butcher but made from higher quality fabric. (Gianni Dagli Orti/The Art Archive at Art Resource, NY)

(*indutus*) and garments that were "wrapped around" (*amictus*). Indutus was worn underneath or closest to the skin (e.g., the tunic), and amictus might be considered outerwear (e.g., the toga or the himation). Over time the toga took on symbolic meaning and its use became increasingly restricted. Roman sources indicate that initially both women and men wore togas, men wearing theirs over a loincloth. By the second century BCE, the toga was a garment worn over a tunic by adult males. Laws passed in the middle of the first century restricted its use to male Roman citizens. The earlier use for both men and women was preserved in the practice of having freeborn boys and girls wear togas with purple borders (**toga praetexta**); girls until they reached puberty (around 12 years) and boys until age 14 to 16, after which they donned the white **toga virilis** of the citizen (Stone, 1994). At the time of the Emperor Augustus, any adult female

wearing a toga was considered a prostitute, and women who had been divorced for infidelity were required to wear togas (Sebesta, 1994b). Togas for special uses had distinctive names, shapes, modes of decoration, colors, and forms of drapery (see Table 4.1).

The earliest toga, the basis of later styles, was draped from a length of white wool fabric, roughly semicircular in shape, with a band of color around the curved edge. Wilson (1924), in a lengthy study of the Roman toga, determined that the early toga was shaped as depicted in Figure 4.11a.

By the imperial period the shape of the toga had evolved to that shown in Figures 4.11b and 4.12, and its draping had become more complicated. Two new features were added (see Figure 4.11). The **sinus** was formed from the overfold of the imperial toga. The overfold was rolled into loose folds as it crossed the back of the body; as it emerged from under the right arm, the folds were loosened, causing the overfold to fall almost to the knee, rather like a draped apron. The other new feature was the **umbo** (literally translated as *knob*). Created by pulling a clump of fabric up from the first, concealed, part of the toga that had been placed vertically from floor to shoulder, the umbo may have helped to hold the toga drapery in place, but seems ultimately to have become a decorative element. In its first development, before it became too large and open, the sinus was used as a sort of pocket in which to carry things. After the sinus enlarged, the umbo served this purpose. Before entering a sacred area, men sometimes pulled the overfold up and over the head at the back to form a sort of hood (Stone, 1994; see Figure 4.13).

It required care to apportion the folds of a toga properly and to balance the bulk of the fabric. Carcopino (1940) commented:

The toga was a garment worthy of the masters of the world, flowing, solemn, eloquent, but with over-much complication in its arrangement and a little too much emphatic affectation in the self-conscious tumult of its folds. It required real skill to drape it artfully. It required unremitting attention if the balance of the toga were to be preserved in walking, in the heat of a discourse, or amid the jostling of a crowd. (155)

Contemporary Comments 4.1

ROMAN POET OVID OFFERS ADVICE ON GROOMING AND DRESS

In The Art of Love, *the Roman poet Ovid offers advice on grooming and dress in order to attract the opposite sex.*

To men he says:

Don't be crimping your locks with the use of the curling iron,

Don't scrape the hair off your legs, using the coarse pumice stone, . . .

Men should not care too much for good looks; neglect is becoming . . .

Let your person be clean, your body tanned by the sunshine,

Let your toga fit well, never a spot on its white,

Don't let your sandals be scuffed, nor your feet flap around in them loosely,

See that your teeth are clean, brush them at least twice a day,

Don't let your hair grow long, and when you visit a barber, patronize only the best, don't let him mangle your beard,

Keep your nails short, and don't ever let them be dirty,

Keep the little hairs out of your nose and ears,

Let your breath be sweet, and your body free from rank odors . . . [Book One, pp. 120–121]

To women:

. . . I do not recommend flounces,

Do not endorse the wools reddened with Tyrian dye.

When you have such a choice of cheaper and pleasanter colors, you would be crazy to use only one costly display.

There is the color of sky, light-blue, with no cloud in the heavens,

There is the hue of the ram, rearing the golden fleece,

There is the color of wave, the hue of the Nereids' raiment,

There is the saffron glow worn by Aurora at dawn,

All kinds of colors: swans-down, amethyst, emerald, myrtle,

Almond, chestnut, and rose, yellow of wax, honey-pale—

Colors as many as flowers born from new earth in the springtime,

When the buds of the vine swell, and old winter has fled,

So many colors, or more, the wool absorbs; choose the right ones—

Not every color will suit everyone's differing need.

If your complexion is fair, dark-gray is a suitable color; . . .

If you are dark, dress in white . . .

Also, I need not remind you to brush your teeth night and morning.

Need not remind you your face ought to be washed when you rise.

You know what to apply to acquire a brighter complexion—

Nature's pallidest rose blushes with suitable art.

Art supplies the means for patching an incomplete eye-brow,

Art or a beauty-spot, aids the cheeks that have never a flaw.

There's nothing amiss in darkening eyes with mascara,

Ash, or the saffron that comes out of Cilician soil. . . .

Don't let your lover find the boxes displayed on your dresser,

Art that dissembles art gives the most happy effect.

Who wants to look at a face so smeared with paint that it's dripping,

Oozing sluggishly down into the neck of the gown? [Book Three, pp. 158–159]

Ovid. (1957, trans). *The art of love* [R. Humphries, Trans.]. Bloomington, IN: Indiana University Press.

The toga was required dress during most of the imperial period for audiences with the emperor, at the spectacles that were staged in the Roman arena, and for any event where a citizen appeared in an official capacity. The heavy garment was probably uncomfortably hot in summer. To keep it white required frequent cleaning, which must have caused the toga to wear out quickly. Martial, a satirical poet, was constantly complaining about having a threadbare toga that he must replace.

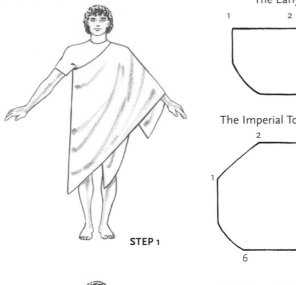

STEP 1

STEP 2

STEP 3

a

The Early Toga

The Imperial Toga (full size)

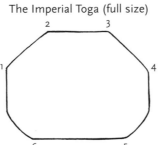

The Imperial Toga (folded)

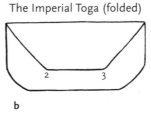

b

FIGURE 4.11 (a) Steps for draping the early form of the toga. Step 1: The toga is placed over the shoulder with point 1 below the knee. Step 2: Point 3 is drawn across the back, under the right arm and up to the left shoulder. Step 3: Point 3 is thrown across the left shoulder and arm to hang down in back of the left shoulder. Point 1 is obscured by draping the bulk of the toga across the front of the body. (Courtesy of Fairchild Publications, Inc.) The imperial toga (4.11b) was draped in essentially the same way, except that the fold created an extra drapery at the front of the body. (Courtesy of Fairchild Publications, Inc..) The fold, the sinus, and the umbo (pockets formed by pulling part of the side fold to the front) can be seen in Figure 4.12.

FIGURE 4.12 Roman wearing the imperial toga over a tunic. The draped pouch at the front is the sinus. A darker area near his neck may have been purple and that would indicate he is a magistrate. (Alinari/Art Resource, NY)

FIGURE 4.13 Roman citizen in the center is participating in a religious rite and wears his toga pulled over his head, according to religious custom. His tunic bears two broad purple clavi. The two figures on either side represent household spirits. (Photograph by Vincent R. Tortora)

It is not surprising, then, to learn that less cumbersome versions of this garment gradually developed. One variant, called the **balteus** (*belt*), developed after the second century CE. Bringing the section under the right arm higher and twisting the top into a sort of beltlike band eliminated the umbo. The ***toga with the folded bands*** evolved from this style. The overfold was folded back and forth upon itself until a folded band of fabric was formed at the top of the semicircle. These folds were probably held in place by stitching or pinning. When draped around the body, the folds created a smooth, diagonal band across the breast to the shoulder (Figure 4.14).

When etiquette grew more lax during the late empire, men felt free to wear garments other than the toga for important occasions. Many Roman men preferred an evolved form of the Greek himation (in Latin, **pallium**), which was a broad rectangle draped around the shoulders, crossed in front, and held in place with a belt.

ROMAN COSTUME: 500 BCE–400 CE

Costume Components for Men

Garments

In Latin, the loincloth was referred to as **subligar** (*subli'gar*), and was probably comparable to the Greek perizoma, serving as an undergarment for middle and upper class men and a working garment for slaves.

Roman versions of the tunic ended around the knee, were short sleeved, and T-shaped. Tunics served as underclothing or a nightshirt for upper class men; belted tunics served as the usual street costume for poor men. By the first century CE of the empire, these variations were noted: (1) tunics cut shorter in front than back and (2) shorter versions for manual laborers and the military.

Several layers were worn in cold weather, one as an undergarment (interior tunic) and one as an outer

FIGURE 4.14 Toga with the folded bands. (Redrawn from The Arch of Constantine by Thomas Hope with permission by Dover Publications, Inc.)

garment (superior tunic). Those sensitive to cold wore two under tunics. Emperor Augustus is said to have worn four layers. Personal style also affected how the tunic was worn. Horace, a Roman writer, described two extremes: "Maltinus minces about with his tunic trailing low, another has it hoisted obscenely up his crotch" (Rudd, 1973, 33).

During the third century CE tunics had lengthened and covered the lower leg, reaching to the shin. This longer length continued in use to the end of the empire, although the military and working men wore the practical, shorter length. The toga, that essential garment for male citizens, was worn over a tunic.

Cloaks and capes served as outdoor garments for cold weather and were made with or without hoods. The most important cloaks cited by various sources were:

- **paenula** (*pie-new'la*): a heavy wool cloak, semicircular in shape, closed at the front, with a hood;
- **lacerna** (*la-cer'na*): rectangular, with rounded corners and a hood;

FIGURE 4.15 Women participating in an athletic competition are wearing what is probably the kind of undergarments worn by women of Rome. (Photograph by Vincent R. Tortora)

- **laena** (*lie'na*): a circle of cloth folded to a semicircle that was thrown over the shoulders and pinned at the front;
- **birrus** (*beer'rus*) or **burrus** (*bur'rus*): resembling a modern, hooded poncho, cut full and with an opening through which the head was slipped; and
- **paludamentum** (*pa-lu-da-men'tum*): a large white or purple cloak similar to the Greek chlamys, worn by emperors or generals.

Costume Components for Women

The individual elements of costume for adult women were similar to those of Greek women and consisted of undergarments, several layers of tunics, and outer mantles. Roman literary sources provide the Latin names of these garments, but it is not always possible to tell precisely how the garments appeared, and individual scholars have come to different conclusions concerning some aspects of women's clothing.

Garments

Undergarments for women consisted of a loincloth (called **subligaria**—the feminine form of *subligar*) and a band of fabric, the **strophium** that supported the breasts. A mosaic in Sicily shows female athletes in what looks like a two-piece, modern bathing suit (Figure 4.15). It is thought these women are each wearing the subligaria and the strophium. There are also works of art in which cupids help the goddess Venus to tie her strophium. In attempting to reproduce Roman costume, Goldman (1994) experimented with a long, narrow piece of fabric. She found that

> the band would be most efficiently used as a brassiere by bringing the ends around the body from the back so that each long end crossed in front, supporting the breasts. These ends then continue around to the sides to the back, where they are tucked inside the wrapping to be held securely in place. (235)

The tunic (Latin, *tunica*) was the basic garment for women in Rome and had much the same appearance as the Greek chiton. Women's tunics reached to the ankle or to the floor. Like men, women wore an under tunic and an outer tunic. The under tunic was not seen in public. It served as a night dress and was worn alone in the privacy of the home.

A draped shawl (counterpart of the Greek himation), the **palla** (*pal'la*) was placed over the outer tunic (Figure 4.16). The palla is depicted as draped either similarly to the toga, casually pulled across the shoulder, or pulled over the head like a veil.

For outdoor wear, women wrapped themselves in cloaks, including the paenula, which was worn when traveling in bad weather.

Garments Designating Social Status for Women

Literary sources make it clear that specific garments were associated with women at various stages of their adult lives. Often the terms for these garments are known, but their precise form may not be. The following are the major garments designating social status for women as described by Sebesta (1994a).

- **Stola** Roman literary sources speak of the stola as a garment reserved for free, married women. Like the toga, it was a garment that denoted status. Scholars have disagreed about its construction. Roman writers use the term **instita** in describing the distinctive dress of a Roman matron. Some scholars have interpreted this as a ruffle at the bottom of the stola that covered the feet; others, as a dress suspended from sewed-on straps. Sebesta argued that this latter description is accurate and described the stola as resembling "a modern slip, though made of fuller material which hung in distinctive folds. . . ." (Sebesta, 1994a, 49).

Roman art shows some examples of a sleeveless outer tunic with straps worn over an under tunic (Figure 4.17), but there are also many other representations of women dressed in garments without these straplike shoulders. Assuming that Sebesta is correct, a number of

FIGURE 4.16 Wall painting that depicts Roman women at home. They are wearing tunics in a variety of different colors with pallas draped over them. (Detail: Erich Lessing/Art Resource, NY)

reasons could account for the relatively small number of images of the traditional stola, and the lack of clarity about its construction. Mythological characters appear frequently in Roman art and such women would not be dressed as Roman matrons. Depictions of women at home usually show them in informal situations where the formal "status" garment would most likely not have been worn. When women are depicted outside the home, they frequently are shown with cloaks that obscure the precise construction of their garments.

- **Veil** Although the palla was not worn exclusively by Roman matrons, they were expected to cover their heads with their pallas when they left their homes.
- **Vitta** A woolen band used to bind her hair was another element of the prescribed dress for Roman matrons.
- **Tutulus** A Roman matron became the mater familias only when her husband became the pater familias. This special status was designated by a special hairstyle, the tutulus. Probably created by drawing the hair to the top of the head and wrapping it in cloth bindings called vittae, the effect was a conical shape similar to the Etruscan women's headdress of the same name (see Figure 4.3, page 78).
- **Rincinium** According to literary sources, widows wore this garment instead of a palla for a year of mourning. It was probably dark colored, but its precise form is unclear.
- **Toga** A women who was divorced on the grounds of adultery was no longer permitted to wear the stola and vittae. Instead she was required to wear a plain toga. There is no indication of how a woman who was divorced for other reasons dressed, nor do we know how unmarried adult women dressed.

Costume Components for Men and Women

Hair and Headdress

In the Republican period women had softly waved hair. By the end of the first century, complex—almost architectural—forms were built up of curls, braids, and

FIGURE 4.17 A pleatlike structure appears at the shoulder of the Roman matron's palla. The woman depicted on this cameo, Livia Drusilla, was the wife of the Emperor Augustus. The empress's dress could have been more elaborate than the simpler pleats of lower status women. (Erich Lessing/Art Resource, NY)

artificial hair. Blonde hair was fashionable. Because dark hair is a common ethnic characteristic among many Mediterranean people, blonde hair had to be achieved through bleaching or wearing wigs made from the hair of blonde northern European captives (see Illustrated Table 4.1 for typical Roman hairstyles).

Roman writers ridiculed the custom of elaborately dressing the hair. Juvenal (as cited in Carcopino, 1940) said, "So numerous are the tiers and stories piled one upon another on her head: in front you would take her for an Andromache; she is not so tall behind; you would not think it was the same person" (57).

During the later empire, women's hairstyles became simplified, with braids or locks doubled up in back and pinned to the top of the head.

Men's hair was cut short and arranged by a barber. Sometimes straight hair was favored; at other times, curls. Men who wished to appear more youthful dyed

Illustrated Table 4.1

Examples of Hairstyles and Headdress Worn by Men and Women during the Roman Empire

Bearded Roman of the
Republican Period

Clean-shaven Roman man with
carefully arranged hair, depicted on
Trajan's column, first century CE

Depiction of the Emperor
Constantine, fourth century CE

Roman women's hairstyles before first century CE

Elaborate hair arrangements of Roman
women from after first century CE

Simpler hairstyle from after
second century CE

their hair. Beards predominated in the Republican years; clean-shaven faces, during the empire—until the reign of Hadrian (c. 120 CE), an emperor who was bearded.

Without sharp-edged steel razors, shaving was a painful and sometimes dangerous experience. Penalties were established for barbers who scarred their clients. A really good barber could become very prosperous. A Roman poet commemorated one barber for his skill. A man's first shave was a rite of passage, celebrated with a religious ceremony. The shaven hairs were deposited in a special container and sacrificed to the gods at a festival to which family and friends were invited (Carcopino, 1940).

Instead of wearing hats, women tended to pull the palla or a scarf over the head. They wore fillets and coronets. Men's hat styles included those similar to the Greek petasos, hoods, and rounded or pointed caps.

Footwear

Men and women wore sandals (in Latin, **solae** [*so'lay*] or **sandalis**), boots, and a slipperlike shoe reaching to the ankle (**soccus**).

Accessories

Women carried fans and handbags. Sun shades were needed for the games held in the arenas, and for this purpose women used either wide hats or parasols that did not fold.

White linen handkerchiefs had different names and functions. The **sudarium** was for wiping off perspiration, veiling the face, or holding in front of the mouth to protect against disease. An **orarium** was a slightly larger version of the sudarium. It became a symbol of rank, and in the late empire was worn by upper class women neatly pleated across the left shoulder or forearm. A **mappa** was a table napkin (guests brought their own napkins when invited for dinner).

Jewelry

Women wore expensive and beautifully crafted rings, bracelets, necklaces, armlets, earrings, and diadems, as well as less costly versions. Of the types of jewelry, men wore only rings.

Cosmetics and Grooming

According to the satirists, cosmetics were used lavishly by both men and women. Practices reported for women included whitening the skin with lead, tinting the lips red, and darkening the eyebrows. One disgruntled lover makes this charge about his mistress: "You lie stored away in a hundred caskets; and your face does not sleep with you" (Carcopino, 1940, 69).

Appearance-conscious men were said to use makeup cream on the cheeks and to paste small circles of cloth over skin flaws. Members of both sexes used perfume.

Large public baths were frequented not only for cleanliness and exercise, but also as a place to socialize and do business. In some periods, baths were segregated by sex; in others, men and women bathed together.

Contemporary Comments 4.1 (page 87) presents excerpts from the Roman writer Ovid's *The Art of Love*, a book in which he offers advice to both men and women as to how to improve one's appearance in order to please the opposite sex.

COSTUME COMPONENTS FOR CHILDREN

Children dressed much like adults of the same sex: boys wearing short tunics, and girls, a garment similar to the stola. At first only the children of noble families wore the toga praetexta, but by 200 BCE legislation had extended the right to wear this garment to all freeborn children. When boys reached the age of 14 to 16, they gave up the praetexta in favor of the toga pura. Girls apparently ceased wearing the toga praetexta after puberty. Some sources have indicated the cutoff was after age 12, and others have said it was age 16 or when they married, whichever came first.

Croom (2002) noted that young girls may have worn a garment called a **supparum**. She pointed to depictions of girls wearing a belted linen garment that looked very much like a chiton with an overfold and suggested that the garment could easily have been lengthened by shortening the overfold.

FIGURE 4.18 Young Roman boy wears the toga praetexta, customary dress for prepubescent Roman boys and girls, and around his neck a bulla, a round charm presented to freeborn boys as infants to protect them against evil. (Gianni Dagli Orti/ The Art Archive at Art Resource, NY)

Infants were swaddled. At the time a freeborn boy was named, a locket, called a **bulla**, made of gold, silver, bronze, or leather and containing charms against the evil eye, was placed around the infant's neck. This was worn throughout childhood (Figure 4.18). From infancy until they reached adult status, girls wore their hair braided and tied with a single woolen band.

COSTUME FOR SPECIALIZED OCCUPATIONS AND OCCASIONS

Military Dress

One of the distinctive elements of the dress of Roman soldiers was body armor worn over a tunic. Such armor might be made from leather bands, from corselets of metal plates, or from disks mounted on fabric or leather. Some armor consisted of large metal plates hinged at the shoulders and molded to fit the body. A wide band of leather rectangles might be suspended from the waist to cover the lower torso. Greaves protected the legs, and helmets protected the head.

During the imperial period, Roman soldiers adopted knee-length trousers that were placed under the tunic in cold weather. These garments were similar to those worn by the Gauls, a northern European tribe. Cloaks provided protection from the weather. Distinctions existed between the dress of officers and ordinary soldiers. Officers wore the **abolla** (*ah-bol'la*), a folded rectangle fastening on the right shoulder. The **sagum** (*sa'gum*), like the abolla, was a single layer of thick wool, generally red. Ordinary soldiers wore it, and in time of war so did Roman citizens. The phrase "to put on the sagum" was synonymous with saying "to go to war." Generals leaving the city of Rome for a military campaign donned the aforementioned paludamentum, larger and thicker than the cloaks of either officers or common soldiers.

Footwear for the military included boots that laced up the front, covering the leg to above the ankle; sandals; and open- and closed-toed shoes.

Dinner Parties

The **synthesis** (*sin-the'-sis*) was a garment worn by men at dinner parties, the precise form of which is a matter of debate. After a careful analysis of the Latin texts, McDaniel (1925) concluded that the synthesis was a lightweight garment worn instead of the toga for dining, because the toga was too heavy and cumbersome to wear when the Romans reclined to eat. The texts that refer to the synthesis imply that the garment had two parts, and McDaniel suggested that these two parts probably consisted of a tunic plus a shoulder garment, such as the pallium. Latin authors speak of the synthesis as bright and colorful.

The synthesis was never seen outside of the home except during the Saturnalia, a public festival in December. One of the characteristics of the Saturnalia was that everything was turned "upside down." For example, masters waited upon their slaves, and gambling games that were normally forbidden were allowed. Wearing the synthesis outdoors may be another example of upsetting tradition that was part of the Saturnalia.

Wedding Dress

Roman bridal costume for women introduced certain elements that have continued to have traditional associations with weddings even until the present day: the veil and orange blossoms. The bridal costume consisted of a tunic woven in a traditional way and tied around the waist with a knotted belt of wool, a saffron-colored palla and matching shoes, and a metal collar. The bride's hair was arranged with six pads of artificial hair, each separated by narrow bands, and over this a veil of bright orange—the **flammeum** (*fla-may'um*)—was worn. The veil covered the upper part of the bride's face. On top of the veil a wreath made of myrtle and orange blossoms was placed.

Religious Dress

Religious garb differed little from the costume of ordinary persons. Vestal virgins, a group of unmarried women assigned to guard the sacred flame kept burning in the temple of Vesta, wore veils that fastened under the chin and six pads of artificial hair separated by bands like those worn by brides. Augurs wore the multicolored, striped toga trabea.

CHANGES IN COSTUME

During the closing century of the Roman Empire, some changes in costume highlighted the erosion of Roman control over the outer limits of its empire. Throughout the imperial period, articles of local, non-Roman dress had tended to survive or be incorporated into Roman clothing in outlying regions. The Gallic cloak, a loose, unbelted tunic worn in Roman Gaul (now France), and trousers, worn by northern barbarian tribes, provide examples of this tendency. As Roman control over the provinces declined, local styles and Roman costume tended to merge even more.

In Rome itself a new variant of the tunic, called the **dalmatic** (*dal-mat'ik*), was adopted (see Figure 5.5, page 111). It was fuller than earlier tunics and had long, wide sleeves. Citizens wore the toga less and less. After the fall of the Roman Empire, the practice of wearing a draped shawl over a tunic survived during the Byzantine Empire and the Early Middle Ages in Europe in a modified form. This garment was, however, more like a Greek himation than a toga.

When the western Roman Empire fell, at the close of the fifth century, the focus of Roman styles shifted eastward to the court in Constantinople where elements of Roman style blended with influences from the east to produce Byzantine styles (discussed in Chapter 5).

Summary

Differences between Greek, Etruscan, and Roman Costume

Much of what were originally Greek clothing styles came to the Romans by way of the Etruscans. Comparisons of Greek, Etruscan, and Roman styles may serve not only to summarize the material in Chapters 3 and 4 but also to point out differences in these three cultures that are reflected in their costume.

Most Greek garments were based on rectangular forms. Roman and Etruscan styles used a greater variety of shapes, with particular emphasis on rounded or elliptical forms. (In this context it is interesting to note that the Etruscans are thought to have originated the round arch, now called the *Roman arch*, whereas the Greeks tended to use the rectangular post-and-lintel construction in their buildings.) Both Roman

Visual Summary Table

Major Roman Garments

Tunic

Toga

Woman in under tunic,
outer tunic, and palla

Woman in under tunic,
stola, and palla

and Etruscan styles relied less than Greek styles on the draping of a single piece of fabric and made greater use of cutting and sewing, although draped elements were also present in the styles of the Italian region. This change and the tendency of the Romans, in particular, to use wool fabrics in preference to linen help to account for the difference in appearance between the free flow of Greek clothing and the heavier draperies of Etruscan and Roman clothes.

Both the Etruscans and Romans used more ornamentation and accessories, and in general they also wore more clothing. The climate may have been a factor (the climate of northern Italy is cooler than that of Greece), but it also reflects a cultural attitude. The Etruscans and Romans did not share the Greek appreciation of nudity or the lightly clad human body.

Themes

From the visual images, which are the major source of information about Etruscan dress, it is obvious

that the theme of CROSS-CULTURAL INFLUENCES played a major role in Etruscan styles. Indeed, during the period when classical Greek culture dominated the Mediterranean region, Etruscan styles hardly differed from the Greek.

Roman dress continues the CROSS-CULTURAL theme. Although the terminology for the basic garment changed from the Greek term *chiton* to the Roman *tunica*, the form of this garment did not change much. To this garment the Romans added the toga, probably derived from their Etruscan neighbors.

The availability of silk in both Greece and Rome was due to the trade with China, where the fibers originated. Silk and other products traveled across a land route now called the Silk Road. However, the Romans and the Chinese traded through middlemen and did not have direct contact; therefore, there is no evidence of stylistic influences from one culture to another.

POLITICAL CONFLICT played a role in Roman dress as well. The conquest of enormous territories brought both the raw materials for textiles and the finished products to Rome and the Romans.

The major theme that plays out in Roman dress, however, is that of the delineation of SOCIAL ROLES. Throughout Roman costume we find evidence of the use of costume to set the individual or the occasion apart. In this context, several come to mind: the special garment for dining, the synthesis; the special costume of senators and of knights; the stola of the Roman matron; and the variety of togas, each with special significance. From childhood to widowhood, Roman dress was full of well-defined symbols.

LEGACIES OF ETRUSCAN AND ROMAN DRESS

Greek, Etruscan, and Roman styles are often called *classical*. Except where a garment, such as the toga, is unique to one civilization, or where terminology assigned to styles makes that connection explicit, the similarities in garment styles of these periods make it difficult to identify the revivals of classical styles as specifically Greek or Roman. For example, a hairstyle of the Directoire period (see Chapter 11) was called the Titus. Titus is the name of a Roman emperor, and the hairstyle was similar to Roman men's haircuts. Artists of the 18th century sometimes dressed the subjects of portraits in some version of a Roman toga, but few revivals of this garment can be found in fashionable dress. However, the word *toga* is often used as a fashion term that describes garments that cover one shoulder and leave the other bare.

The far-reaching influence of classical styles on subsequent periods is discussed on page 72.

REFERENCES

Bonfante, L. (1994). Introduction. In J. L. Sebesta & L. Bonfante (Eds.), *The world of Roman costume* (pp. 3–10). Madison, WI: University of Wisconsin Press.

Bonfante, L. (2003). *Etruscan dress*. Baltimore, MD: Johns Hopkins University Press.

Carcopino, J. (1940). *Daily life in ancient Rome*. New Haven, CT: Yale University Press.

Casson, L. (1975). *Everyday life in ancient Rome*. New York, NY: Heritage.

Croom, A. T. (2002). *Roman clothing and fashion*. Charleston, SC: Tempus.

MODERN INFLUENCES

Designer Alberta Ferretti, based in Milan, Italy, has been known to base her designs on Roman dress. This dress has been inspired by Roman tunics, especially when paired with Roman-like sandals. Ferretti adds a modern touch with the colorful braid belt and embroidery. (Victor VIRGILE/ Gamma-Rapho via Getty Images)

Friedlander, L. (1936). *Roman life and manners under the early empire* (Vol. 1). New York, NY: Dutton.

Goldman, N. (1994). Reconstructing Roman clothing. In J. L. Sebesta & L. Bonfante (Eds.), *The world of Roman costume* (pp. 213–237). Madison, WI: University of Wisconsin Press.

Herlihy, D. (1990). *Opera muliebria: Women and work in medieval Europe*. Philadelphia, PA: Temple University Press.

Jones, A. H. M. (1960). The cloth industry under the Roman Empire. *Economic History Review, 13*(2), 183.

Lawler, A. (2010). The pearl trade. *Archeology, 65*(2), 46–51.

McDaniel, W. B. (1925). Roman dinner garments. *Classical Philology, 20,* 268.

Rudd, N. (Trans.). (1973). *The satires of Horace and Persius.* Baltimore, MD: Penguin Books.

Sebesta, J. L. (1994a). Symbolism in the costume of the Roman woman. In J. L. Sebesta & L. Bonfante (Eds.), *The world of Roman costume* (pp. 46–53). Madison, Wi: University of Wisconsin Press.

Sebesta, J. L. (1994b). Tunica ralla, tunica spissa. In J. L. Sebesta & L. Bonfante (Eds.), *The world of Roman costume* (pp. 65–76). Madison, WI: University of Wisconsin Press.

Stone, S. (1994). The toga: From national to ceremonial costume. In J. L. Sebesta & L. Bonfante (Eds.), *The world of Roman costume* (pp. 13–45). Madison, WI: University of Wisconsin Press.

Wilson, L. M. (1924). *The Roman toga.* Baltimore, MD: Johns Hopkins Press.

PART TWO

The Middle Ages

In 330, Emperor Constantine moved the capital of the Roman Empire to Byzantium, renamed Constantinople, signaling the decline of Rome and the western portion of the empire. It also meant two cultures would develop in the empire, in addition to two lines of emperors. The wealthier, more populous eastern empire was well situated to defend that portion of the empire and dominate trade routes. The western empire, ruled from Rome, was overwhelmed by the mass migration of German tribes, which began at the close of the fourth century and continued throughout the fifth century.

Due to its geographical location, Rome was vulnerable to attacks and was sacked in 410 and several times later in the century. The western emperors moved the capital of the western empire from Rome to Ravenna in 403, hoping that this city on the Adriatic coast, south of Venice, would be more defensible than Rome. Despite attacks, certain elements of Roman civilization and culture survived. The Christian church, which had endured Roman persecution, became the official state church of the Roman Empire in the fourth century, exercising a unifying force in western Europe. After Christianity became the official state religion, some Christians sought a more ascetic form of religion, called *monasticism*. Because the monks had to be occupied with some form of work, copying books by hand became an appropriate form of labor. Monastery libraries preserved Christian and earlier Greek and Roman classical literature, which otherwise would have been lost forever.

The Early Middle Ages, from the fall of the Roman Empire until the ninth century, saw a decline in cultural standards as people lost command of the Latin language. Education for laymen disappeared, producing generations who could neither read nor write. In much of the period, depopulation, poverty, plagues, and isolation affected many areas of Europe; the quality of life declined. Written records from the period are often sparse, and information about dress is especially scarce. With the decline in living standards and the decrease in wealth, works of art were rarely commissioned, except for those intended for the church. Nevertheless, enough evidence remains to construct a general, if not too detailed, picture of life in the early medieval period.

Throughout the Middle Ages the eastern Roman Empire, more often called the Byzantine Empire, thrived, in part because it was based on an efficient bureaucracy and sound economy. Although trade and urban life almost ceased in the west, cities and commerce flourished in the Byzantine Empire. With money obtained from trade, Byzantine officials recruited, trained, and equipped armies that held off attackers. A period of expansion ended in the seventh century when Arab armies invaded Byzantine territories.

Islam, a new religion founded by Mohammed in Mecca in the early seventh century, inspired successors to unite the Bedouin tribes in Arabia into a military force that soon swept across the Middle East. Arab armies, inspired by their new faith and seeking booty and land, conquered present-day Iraq, Syria, and Palestine and pressed on to seize territories as far east as India. On more than one occasion the Arab armies besieged Constantinople. After conquering North Africa, they moved northward through Spain and into southern France, where their expansion was halted in the battle of Tours in 732.

In spite of constant pressure from hostile forces, the Byzantine Empire survived until 1453, when the city of Constantinople and the remains of a once powerful empire fell to a conquering force of Ottoman Turks. In its history of more than a thousand years, the Byzantine Empire developed an artistic and intellectual atmosphere in which styles and ideas of both east and west were merged. Even though the Crusaders and Turks destroyed many of the manuscripts and works of art, Byzantine libraries and art collections ensured preservation of many records and traditions from Greek and Roman antiquity.

In the western Roman Empire, Germanic kingdoms replaced Roman government. These kingdoms, including the Franks, helped fuse Roman and Germanic cultures into a new civilization. In 800, the pope crowned the king of the Franks, Charlemagne, emperor of the Romans. The ceremony symbolized a declaration of independence from the Byzantine Empire and a revival of the Roman Empire, but it was in fact more German than Roman. After his death in 814, Charlemagne's empire, which extended over much of western Europe, disintegrated under the impact of new and more destructive invasions. From the wreckage of the Carolingian empire emerged a feudal society in which local lords controlled small areas. These leaders pledged their personal loyalty to more powerful lords in return for their protection, and above them all was the supreme overlord, the king.

Under feudal monarchies, Europe revived so much that by the 11th century a great military expedition, the First Crusade, sought to regain the Holy Land from the Muslims. Originally proclaimed by Pope Urban II, it was a call for the unruly feudal knights to do battle for a righteous cause. Thousands, both knights and poor people, responded to the call. For centuries Christians had done penance for their sins by going on pilgrimages to holy places. Now the Crusades became a super pilgrimage. From the Middle East, the Crusaders returned to Europe bringing back new products: spices, fabrics, perfumes, jewelry, and ideas.

By the 12th century, trade among the nations of Europe again flourished, and their once-stagnant economies experienced a remarkable revitalization. While the Crusades brought Middle Eastern styles and ideas to Europe, other developments extended European contacts beyond the Middle East to Asia.

The Muslim conquests in the seventh century closed the land routes to Asia until the Mongols swept out of northern China, across western Asia and into Russia in the 13th century. The Mongols, eager for trade and cultural relations with Europe, welcomed enterprising Europeans who dared to travel across Asia to the Mongol capital at Peking. Two Venetian merchants, Nicolo and Matteo Polo, traveled eastward across Asia in 1260 hoping to profit from the reopening of the land route to Asia. No western Christians before the Polo brothers had ever visited China.

The Polo brothers set out for China again in 1271 accompanied by Nicolo's 17-year-old son Marco. The three men journeyed across the deserts and mountains of central Asia for $3^1/_2$ years. Marco Polo even entered the Mongolian civil service, governing a Chinese city for 3 years and traveling to southeast Asia. Marco Polo, his father, and his uncle remained in China and did not return to Europe until 1295 (Figure II.1).

Marco Polo's memoirs, *The Travels of Marco Polo*, appeared in 1307 and became one of the most widely read books in Europe in the 14th and 15th centuries. Marco Polo was the first European to cross the continent of Asia and leave a record of what he had seen and heard. The book aroused great interest in Asia and stimulated the European search for the spices and luxuries of east Asia. This search would lead to the 1492 accidental discovery of the lands of the western hemisphere.

FIGURE II.1 Marco Polo sets out from Venice for east Asia with his uncles. (© RMN-Grand Palais/Art Resource, NY)

By the 1400s the arts, the intellectual life, and the social structure of Europe had been virtually transformed. Some historians and social scientists believe that the phenomenon of fashion in dress in western society began in, or at least accelerated during, the Middle Ages.

Fashion has been defined as "a pattern of change in which certain social forms enjoy temporary acceptance and respectability only to be replaced by others" (Blumer, 1968, 142). *The Dictionary of Social Sciences* (Gold, 1964, 262) described fashion as "a recurring cultural pattern, found in societies having open-ended class systems" and noted that "fashion becomes a matter of imitation of higher by lower classes in the common scramble for unstable and

superficial status symbols." Fashion change no longer originates solely with the upper classes. But at the time of its beginnings, those who sought to be in fashion were typically copying the dress of royalty and the wealthy.

Experts disagree about exactly when individuals developed interest in and began wearing fashionable dress. Bell (1948) pointed out that the increasingly rapid change of dress styles characteristic of Europe after the Middle Ages contrasts with the more static nature of clothing in earlier civilizations. In a study of French fashion, Sarah-Grace Heller (2007) argued that the art and literature of the 11th century make it clear that men and women of this period were very much interested in fashion.

An open-ended class system and the imitation of higher classes by lower classes are both aspects of medieval life in the 13th through the 15th centuries that allowed for the growth of fashion. Peasants who moved from rural areas to cities often became part of the growing middle class. The passage of **sumptuary laws** regulating dress and other luxuries in the 13th to the 15th centuries is evidence of the vain attempts by the nobility to prevent the increasing affluent commoners from usurping those status symbols the nobility considered to be their own (Nicholas, 1974).

Two other conditions contributed to the spread of fashion. In order to imitate those of higher status, the imitator must have sufficient means to afford the latest fashions. A newly affluent middle class, largely merchants and artisans, was emerging. This development provided social mobility and increased affluence for a substantially larger proportion of the population. Finally, increased trade and travel carried fashion from place to place. As the Middle Ages drew to a close, the phenomenon called *fashion* was firmly established, and the duration of the periods that fashionable styles endured grew shorter and shorter. No longer can one speak of styles, such as those of the Egyptians, that lasted for thousands of years. Instead, by the close of the medieval period one speaks of fashions that lasted less than a century (Figure II.2).

FIGURE II.2 By the latter part of the Middle Ages, European courts provided a stage for the display of lavish dress. This 15th-century illuminated manuscript page shows the court of the French Duke of Berry. The duke, at center right in blue, wears a gown woven or embroidered with designs of peacock feathers, a fabric that could have been made along the Silk Road. Some courtiers, or attendants, wear turbanlike headdresses that show Middle Eastern influences. (© RMN-Grand Palais/Art Resource, NY)

REFERENCES

Bell, Q. (1948). *On human finery*. London, UK: Hogarth Press.

Blumer, H. (1968). Fashion. *International encyclopedia of the social sciences*. New York, NY: Macmillan.

Gold, R. L. (1964.) Fashion. *The dictionary of the social sciences*. New York, NY: Free Press.

Heller, S. G. (2007). *Fashion in medieval France*. Rochester, NY: D. S. Brewer.

Nicholas, D. (1974). Patterns of social mobility. In R. L. DeMolen & D. Herlihy (Eds.), *One thousand years: Western Europe in the Middle Ages* (pp. 45–108). New York, NY: Houghton-Mifflin.

	4TH CENTURY	481–511	6TH CENTURY	527–65	EARLY 7TH CENTURY	751	800
FASHION AND TEXTILES	Byzantine styles of dress develop						
POLITICS AND CONFLICTS	Constantinople becomes capital of eastern Roman Empire		Clovis founds Merovingian dynasty			Pepin the Short founds the Carolingian dynasty	Pope crowns Charlemagne emperor of the Romans
DECORATIVE AND FINE ARTS				During the reign of Emperor Justinian, Hagia Sophia is built in Istanbul			
ECONOMICS AND TRADE	Silk Road allows for trade and transmission of ideas			Plagues impact life and commerce. The Plague of Justinian c. 540 swept through Europe, Africa, and parts of Asia.			
TECHNOLOGY AND IDEAS			Secrets of the process of silk production smuggled to Byzantium from China				
RELIGION AND SOCIETY	Roman emperor Constantine converts to Christianity				Mohammed founds Islam		

CHAPTER FIVE

The Early Middle Ages

c. 330–1500

900	11TH CENTURY	12TH CENTURY	1271–1272	1296

Garments begin to fit more closely to the body

Bayeux Tapestry depicts William of Normandy's invasion of England and coronation in 1066

Romanesque architecture reaches its height (c. 1025)

Gothic styles develop in architecture

Feudalism develops

Marco Polo dictates the story of his travels to east Asia

Pope Urban II declares the First Crusade (1095)

The ninth and last crusade

Two distinct cultures developed after the fall of the Western Roman Empire at the close of the fifth century. Byzantium, the eastern seat of the Roman Empire, situated at the crossroads of east and west, influenced both. Roman styles in dress gradually evolved to include more ornate eastern elements. Between the 5th and 13th centuries, European culture melded Roman institutions, the Christian church, and the Germanic tribes that infiltrated the Roman territories. The primary components of both Byzantine and medieval dress were layered tunics combined with a mantle. Their increasingly complex cut and ornamentation signaled a more rapid speed of fashion change.

HISTORICAL BACKGROUND: THE BYZANTINE PERIOD C. 330–1453

In 330, Roman Emperor Constantine moved his capital from Rome to Byzantium, a Greek port city.

The city, renamed Constantinople, became the capital of the Byzantine Empire. Located at the entrance of the Black Sea, the city and its surrounding territories commanded both land and sea trade routes between the west and central Asia, Russia, and east Asia. At the same time, the city was protected by the rugged Balkan Mountains from the invading barbarians who overran Rome and the Italian peninsula.

The location of the capital ensured its survival and determined its character. Situated at the literal crossroads between east and west, the city and the empire of which it was the capital became a rich amalgam of eastern and western art, dress, and culture.

During the reign of the Emperor Justinian from 527 to 565, Byzantium gained control over Italy and southern Spain, all part of Justinian's dream of restoring the Roman Empire to its former greatness (Figure 5.1). By the end of his rule, the Byzantine Empire stretched north through the Balkans to the Danube; east into

FIGURE 5.1 This map shows the extent of the Byzantine Empire under Justinian in the sixth century.

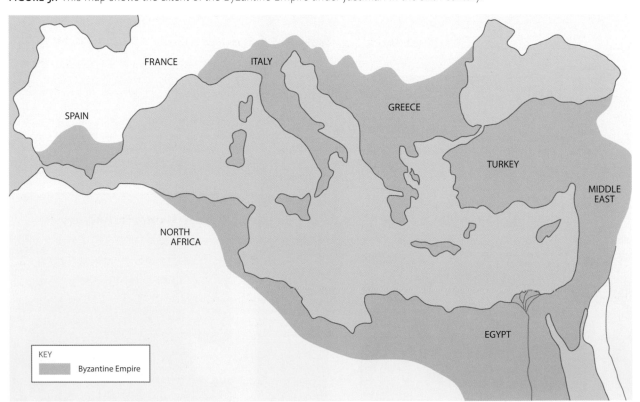

KEY
Byzantine Empire

FIGURE 5.2 Gold coin with portrait of Byzantine Emperor Justinian who ruled from 527 to 565. (bpk, Berlin/Staatliche Museen/Art Resource, NY)

Asia Minor, Syria, and Palestine; and west into Egypt and North Africa, Italy, and southern Spain (Figure 5.2). During the seventh and eighth centuries, its size was reduced, and by the mid-ninth century it comprised only the Greek peninsula and much of modern-day Turkey. Attacks from outsiders and a plague that devastated Byzantium weakened the empire and prohibited its growth. The diminished empire was separated from the rest of Europe to such an extent that Greek replaced the Latin language, and Middle Eastern influences on life and styles became more pronounced.

Throughout its history, Byzantium was constantly at war with a series of enemies: Persians, Arabs, Bulgars, Avars, Seljuq Turks, and, at the end, the Ottoman Turks. In 1204, even crusaders seized Constantinople. They sacked the city, destroyed manuscripts and priceless works of art, and declared a crusader emperor. In 1261 a Byzantine emperor retook Constantinople, but the once-great empire had vanished. Byzantium was reduced to little more than a Balkan state. The artistic and intellectual life of the city revived, but the menace of invasion by the Turks continued. Finally, in 1453, the Ottoman Turks captured Constantinople, destroying the empire.

Social Organization

The Byzantine emperor was both an absolute political ruler and the head of the eastern Church, which had separated from the western Christian church in 1054. A landed nobility made up an important element in the economic life and government of the empire. A well-developed civil service helped the imperial administration function by collecting taxes, administering justice, raising armies, and putting them into the field. Determined by wealth, rather than blood line, ambitious young men could rise from one social group to the next. As such, education was important to wealthy families, most of whom had tutors for their sons. Students could attend schools in some provincial areas, and Constantinople maintained a well-known university.

In the earlier period the status of women was more advanced than in the later phase when ideas from the Near East predominated. Empresses reigned alone or as regents for minor sons, and a number of them exercised great power. At the other end of the social scale were the slaves, both foreign captives and poor people who sold themselves into slavery in order to survive.

Margaret Scott (2007) pointed out that the Byzantine Empire developed very detailed regulations about who wore what and when. Based on these regulations, or **sumptuary laws**, individuals were assigned colors and garments to wear based on their status. In Byzantine artwork, individuals wearing the same color stand next to one another in assigned positions relative to the emperor.

Culture, Art, and Technology

Throughout its history, the city of Constantinople was a center for the preservation of the "antique" (i.e., Greek and Roman) culture. Writings and works of art were actively preserved. Many of these treasures, however, were destroyed when the crusaders and the Turks sacked the city. Other artifacts were saved or carried away by raiders to other places where they escaped destruction. Hagia Sophia (Holy Wisdom), constructed by the Emperor Justinian represented the

FIGURE 5.3 Hagia Sophia, the church of "Holy Wisdom," was built with a technically complex system of vaults and semi-domes. The interior included costly colored marbles and stone inlays. (© Vanni Archive/ Art Resource, NY)

finest example of Byzantine architecture. The interior was decorated with gold leaf, colored marble, bits of glass, and colored mosaics. Mosaics were pictures or designs made from small, colored stones and glass. Similar motifs and decorative elements appeared in Byzantine dress (Figure 5.3).

SOURCES OF EVIDENCE ABOUT COSTUME

The art of the Byzantine Empire provides the major record from which dress information comes. Artists decorated churches with mosaics, many of which still exist. Other special skills included carving of ivory and manuscript illumination or hand painting and lettering. Byzantine art, and its dress, displays a blending of classical and Middle Eastern motifs and forms of decoration.

Much Byzantine art has a religious motif. Religious art favored traditional rather than realistic representations of people. For example, early Byzantine artists depicted the evangelists in the classical costume of fourth-century Romans. This convention persisted to such an extent that many eighth- and ninth-century portrayals resemble those in earlier artwork (Calkins, 1993). Other conventions of Byzantine art include

representing Christ as a king and Mary as a queen, both dressed in royal robes to symbolize their status. Like portrayals of the evangelists, these stereotypes continued in use during the remainder of the Middle Ages; a careful eye is needed to determine whether the figures are wearing contemporaneous dress.

Textile Production and Technology

The Byzantines wove fine textiles. From the fourth to the sixth centuries, linen and wool predominated. Production of silk fabrics was a secret process held first by the Chinese and later by the Koreans and Japanese. Gradually, knowledge of how silk was produced spread westward. Silk fabrics and possibly some raw silk fiber were carried through trade routes to Greece and Rome before the first century BCE, but silk production had been possible only on a very limited scale. Byzantine historians reported that in the sixth century a pair of monks brought the secret of **sericulture** (*silk production*) to the Byzantine emperor. These monks supposedly smuggled a number of silkworm eggs out of China in a hollow bamboo pole and learned how to breed, feed, and raise silkworms (Heichelheim, 1949; Figure 5.4).

From this point until the ninth century (when Greeks in Sicily also began to produce silk), the Byzantines

FIGURE 5.4 Silk woven textile from Byzantium incorporates Persian theme of roosters. (Erich Lessing/Art Resource, NY)

moved his capital to Byzantium, the Roman administrators carried with them Roman dress and customs. With time, Roman influences eroded, and eastern influences prevailed. The evolution of the toga is an example of this process. The toga diminished in use from the third century on. By the fourth century, it was used only for ceremonial occasions by important state officials, such as the emperor and the consuls. Finally, only a vestige of the toga remained—a narrow band of folded fabric that wrapped around the body in the same way as the toga. Eventually, even this was transformed into the emperor's narrow, jeweled scarf.

Costume Components for Men

Garments

The basic garment for men was a tunic (Figure 5.5). Tunics were either short, ending below the knee, or long, reaching to the ground. Long sleeves predominated. Byzantine art shows the Emperor Justinian and other officials in tunics that ended below

produced silk for the western world. The emperor charged enormous prices for the silk; therefore, only the wealthiest Europeans could afford the fabric. Brocades woven in Byzantium often included designs originating in Persia, with Christian subjects depicted in complex woven patterns. When made into garments or wall hangings, these luxurious fabrics might be adorned with precious and semiprecious stones, small medallions of enamel, embroidery, and appliqués (see Global Connections).

Sources reveal clothing was quite expensive in the Byzantine Empire. Through an examination of wills, Ball (2005) found that clothing was often passed down to family members, slaves, and domestic servants. While lack of money restricted the number of garments owned and the fineness of the material, clothing choices for the non-elite went beyond strictly utilitarian decisions.

BYZANTINE COSTUME: 330–1453

Early Byzantine and late Roman costumes are virtually indistinguishable. When the Emperor Constantine

FIGURE 5.5 Tunic from the Byzantine period in Egypt, c. sixth to seventh centuries. This tunic has tapestry-woven decorations in colors on a red ground in the form of clavi over the shoulders, roundels on either side of the tunic and over the shoulders, and segmentae on the sleeves. Woven decorative bands are attached at the cuffs and hem. (Image copyright © The Metropolitan Museum of Art. Image source: Art Resource, NY)

Global Connections

The Silk Road, established by 200 BCE, was a series of land and sea trade routes that traversed over 5,000 miles from China to the Mediterranean and southern Europe (Gordon, 2011). Despite its name, coined in the 1800s, other commodities, such as gold, spices, and plants—as well as technologies, ideas, and religions—were transported. Textile makers and merchants established communities along the Silk Road, and the textiles created indicate diverse origins of motifs

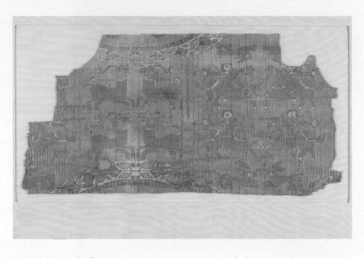

and decorative details (Watt and Wardwell, 1997). This silk fragment, dating to the eighth to ninth centuries, retains the interstices between two rows of roundels. The hunters appear in the Byzantine style, while the floral decoration is reminiscent of silks attributed to Alexandria, Egypt. The abstracted style of the roundels indicates Sogdian (or Iranian) provenance. It is within this textile that we clearly see the international diversity of goods produced, traveled, and consumed along the Silk Road. (Hunters, 8th–9th century. Central Asia, Sogdiana, 8th–9th century Compound twill, silk; overall—height 22.00 cm, width 41.80 cm [height 8 5/8 inches, width 16 7/16 inches]; The Cleveland Museum of Art, Purchase from the J. H. Wade Fund 1974.98)

the knee (Figure 5.6). In later centuries emperors and important court officials appear to have worn full-length tunics (see Figure 5.5), while less important people wore shorter tunics.

Some tunics were decorated with clavi (by now these stripes that originated in Roman dress on either side of the tunic had become ornamental rather than indicative of the wearer's status), circular motifs called **roundels**, and **segmentae** (*seg-men'-tie*), rectangular or star-shaped decorative medallions that were placed in different areas of the tunic.

Tunics of the wealthy were decorated with vertical and horizontal bands that were elaborately patterned with woven designs, embroidery, appliqués, or precious stones. In the early part of the empire, fabrics were usually plain in color, and artisans decorated them with clavi, roundels, segmentae, and banding. As eastern influences gained favor, fabrics

developed overall patterning (Figure 5.7). Working men wore shorter tunics in plainer, less ornamented fabric, often tucked up in a belt to allow for greater mobility.

After 1000 the silhouette changed and tunics were more closely fitted to the body. Generally men wore two tunics: the under tunic with closely fitted sleeves and the outer tunic with shorter, wider sleeves. When the tunic was belted, some of the fabric bloused out and over the belt. Fabrics had overall patterns with bands of jeweled decoration placed at hems and on sleeves, with wide, decorative yokes at the neck (see Figure 5.7). Worn as a leg covering, hose were often light in color, some decorated with horizontal bands of geometric patterns.

The **pallium** (*pal-ee'-um*), also called a **lorum** (*lo'rum*), was a long, narrow, heavily jeweled scarf—possibly evolved from the toga with the folded bands—

FIGURE 5.6 On the left are two men whose short tunics can be seen through the opening in their cloaks. On the right, the Byzantine Empress Theodora wears a paludamentum of purple, a color associated with royalty, while her female retainers are dressed in colorful brocades probably woven from silk produced by the Byzantine silk industry. (Detail: Cameraphoto Arte, Venice/Art Resource, NY)

that became part of the official insignia of the emperor. The empress was also permitted to wear this garment. Initially draped around the shoulders, across the front of the body, and carried over one arm, it eventually became a simpler panel of fabric with an opening for the head, sometimes with a round collarlike construction at the head opening (Figure 5.8).

Hair and Headdress

From the 4th to 10th centuries, men tended to be clean shaven (see Figure 5.6). Later, men were more likely to have beards (see Figure 5.7). Men wore Phrygian bonnetlike styles, or conical caps, and several versions

FIGURE 5.7 Emperor Constantine IX Momomachus ruler from 1042 to 1055 is dressed in an elaborately jeweled garment made of fabric with an overall pattern. His crown has a suspended string of pearls. He is bearded, unlike earlier men who tended to be clean shaven. (Erich Lessing/Art Resource, NY)

FIGURE 5.8. Enameled picture of Archangel Michael, in the Byzantine style, c. 10th to 12th centuries or later. The archangel wears a jeweled lorum or pallium over an ankle-length tunic. (Detail: Scala/Art Resource, NY)

of a high hat with an upstanding brim surrounding a high-crowned turban, a smooth, close-fitting crown, or a soft crown with a tassel at the back. Emperors wore jeweled crowns, often with suspended strings of pearls.

Costume Components for Women

Garments

During the early Byzantine Empire, women continued to wear the Roman tunic and palla. Gradually, the wide, long-sleeved tunic called the **dalmatic**, decorated with

clavi and segmentae, replaced the outer tunic. Women wore the dalmatic over an under tunic with closely fitted sleeves. A simple veil worn over the head replaced the palla for a time. Eventually the palla returned to use in a modified form that wrapped around the body and covered the upper part of the skirt, the bodice, and either one or both shoulders (Figure 5.9).

Although occasional outer garments with long, fitted sleeves are depicted in art in the seventh century and after, for the most part women wore double-layered tunics. The under tunic had long, fitted sleeves and the outer tunic had full, open sleeves cut short enough to display the sleeve of the under tunic. Made from elaborately patterned fabrics, noble and wealthy women's garments were often decorated with jewels. Women of this class also wore jeweled belts and collars (see Figure 5.6).

After 1000, the ornamentation of tunics increased. Variations in sleeve styles included wide, hanging sleeves or sleeves with long bands of fabric forming a sort of pendant cuff. Occasionally, what appears to be a skirt and long, knee-length overblouse is depicted, though this may be just an especially short outer tunic.

Hair and Headdress

Some early representations show women with hair parted in the center, soft waves framing the face, and the bulk of the hair pulled to the back or knotted on top of the head. Otherwise, women's hair is usually covered.

Characteristic hair coverings included veils and turbanlike hats that appeared from the 4th century to the 12th century. The latter style has been described as looking like a cap surrounded by a small tire. Empresses set their royal crowns on top of the hat or on top of their own hair. Royal crowns were heavily jeweled diadems with pendant strings of pearls (see Figure 5.6).

Costume Components for Men and Women

Cloaks

Upperclass men and the empress wore the **paludamentum** (*pa-lud-a-men'tum*), which fastened over the right

FIGURE 5.9 Mosaic from the church of St. Apollinarus in Ravenna depicting women who each wear a white under tunic of the sixth century. A white palla is draped across the shoulders. (Scala/Art Resource, NY)

shoulder with a jeweled brooch. This cloak was distinguished by a large square decoration, the **tablion** (*tablee'on*), in contrasting colors and fabric located at the open edge over the breast (see Figure 5.6). After the 11th century, upperclass men and the imperial family no longer wore the paludamentum outdoors, wearing instead semicircular cloaks fastened at center front.

For common people and women other than the empress, a simple, square cloak replaced the hooded paenula of Roman times for general wear. After the seventh and eighth centuries, a semicircular cloak pinned at the shoulder or at center front came into general use.

Footwear

Shoemakers often made shoes with an open construction and ornamented them with decorations cut out of either cloth (including silk) or leather.

Additional decorations included stones, pearls, enameled metal, embroidery, appliqué, and cutwork. Red apparently was a favored color for empresses and their retinue. Some tied, while others buckled at the ankle. Hose worn under the shoes are visible in some paintings, particularly when the tunics are shorter in length.

Men, not women, seem to have worn boots. Most boots ended just below the calf, although a few boots are depicted as high at the front and lower behind the knee. Some decorated styles were worn by the wealthy. Military figures from the early Byzantine Empire wore Roman-like, open-toed boots; later they adopted a closed boot.

Jewelry

Not just accessories, jewels were an integral part of the dress. Empresses wore wide, jeweled collars over the

FIGURE 5.10 Byzantine mosaic from first half of the sixth century. The woman's elaborate diadem (*crown*) and dress are bordered with alternating black and white tile meant to suggest pearls. Blue glass represents sapphires among the red and green glass gemstones of the necklace and earrings. (Detail: Image copyright © The Metropolitan Museum of Art. Image source: Art Resource, NY)

paludamentum or at the neck of the dress (see Figure 5.6). Other important items of jewelry included pins, earrings, bracelets, rings, and other types of necklaces (Figure 5.10). Jewelers were skilled in techniques of working gold, setting precious stones, enameling, and making mosaics.

HISTORICAL BACKGROUND: WESTERN EUROPE FROM THE FALL OF THE ROMAN EMPIRE TO 900

The Fall of the Roman Empire

Even though Constantinople was nominally the capital of the eastern and western sections of the Roman Empire, events soon resulted in the empire's division between east and west. For centuries, the Germans had been filtering into the Roman Empire in search of land. Many enlisted in the Roman armies, rising to high rank and often becoming commanders. Eventually, entire German tribes migrated into western Europe and North Africa. Other tribes were also on the move. The Roman standard of living attracted northern tribes, and tribes from east of the Danube sought new homelands.

As German tribes entered the empire, many settled down to live alongside the Romans. They intermarried, adopted many Roman customs, converted to Christianity, and established German kingdoms. The fusion of Roman and Germanic cultures made up **medieval** civilization. After the establishment of Germanic kingdoms in the west and the end of any semblance of a Roman empire, the eastern and western sections drifted farther apart, divided by religion, culture, and political systems.

The Merovingian and Carolingian Dynasties

In the west, the Franks were a collection of early Germanic tribes ultimately unified by the brutal Clovis (481–511), who conquered most of modern France and Belgium. Clovis founded the Merovingian dynasty, the successor to the defunct Roman Empire. Eventually, the Merovingian line degenerated into do-nothing kings who allowed the chief minister, titled "mayor of the palace," to actually rule. In 751 a mayor of the palace, Pepin the Short, with the pope's blessing, deposed the Merovingian king and became king.

King Pepin was succeeded by his son, Charles the Great, known to history as Charlemagne (768–814). Charlemagne expanded the kingdom into central Europe and southward into central Italy. He became the dominant figure in western Europe. Contemporaries compared him to the ancient Roman emperors. His greatest achievement was encouraging the establishment of schools to teach reading and writing. He founded a palace school to which he invited European scholars. The high point of his reign came with his coronation on Christmas Day 800, when the pope crowned him emperor of the

Romans. For a time, Charlemagne hoped a marriage with a Byzantine empress would unite the eastern and western empires, but a marriage never occurred. Throughout the period, contacts between the eastern and western empire continued, with Byzantine styles exercising strong influences on European dress (Figure 5.11).

A new culture entered western Europe when the Moors, Muslim Berbers from Morocco, invaded Spain in 711. Within several years they overran Spain (except for northern mountainous areas). Near Tours in southern France, the defeat of a small Muslim force in 732 marked the most northerly advance of Islam in western Europe. Islamic Spain now became part of a free-trade area stretching across the Islamic world from the Middle East through North Africa. Consequently, many new ideas and products (including citrus fruits, almonds, figs, and cotton) entered Europe through Spain.

Charlemagne's success in uniting a western European empire did not last for long after his death in 814. His successors were not strong enough to hold the empire together, and it was once again divided. No single power emerged to replace the ineffective Carolingian kings, the last of whom was deposed in 888. The remnants of Carolingian rule gradually collapsed under the impact of new and more destructive invasions. From the east, hordes of Magyar horsemen devastated the eastern lands of the Carolingian Empire. From the south came the Saracens, Arab raiders, who plundered southern France and coastal Italy. The most destructive of the invaders, the Northmen or Vikings, came from Scandinavia, attracted by the wealth of the Christian churches and the monasteries. They looted and burned, ruthlessly killing their victims. Britain and France suffered the worst spoliation, until about the middle of the ninth century when the plunder gradually ended.

Many areas in the west were depopulated and ruined, impacted by raiders and occurrences of plague, which spread along trade routes. However, a new Europe began to appear. Commerce and town life began to revive; improvements in agriculture helped

FIGURE 5.11 Byzantine inspired styles are evident in this mosaic. (Alfredo Dagli Orti/The Art Archive at Art Resource, NY)

produce an increase in population. The Carolingian Empire was followed by feudal monarchies, the nations of the future.

SOURCES OF EVIDENCE ABOUT COSTUME

Relatively few images from western Europe that depict costume remain from the centuries after the fall of Rome. From the fifth to the eighth centuries, these sources are mostly two-dimensional images depicted in illuminated manuscripts, mosaics, and some rare frescoes in churches. Early Christian art in the west, like that of the Byzantine east, derived from Roman art. As late as the seventh and eighth centuries, religious figures, saints, and angels were often depicted in draped garments borrowed from Roman art. Of the relatively few surviving illuminated manuscripts, the most useful tend to be depictions of German rulers of the 10th and 11th centuries. Others, like the famous *Book of Kells*, that were painted by Celtic monks in the eighth and ninth centuries often contain little figurative art and no clear information about costume. Wills indicate some clothing bequests but provide little detail. The pronouncements of church officials against the wearing of particular forms of dress provide more helpful information (Scott, 2007).

WESTERN EUROPEAN COSTUME: FALL OF THE ROMAN EMPIRE TO 900

During the Roman era, people residing in the provinces had become Romanized in their dress. Men wore tunics and women wore layered tunics covered by pallas. After the fall of Rome, dress retained these Roman elements, but other components were added, elements that derived from the dress of the tribes from northern Europe that had moved west. Barbarian men wore a tunic cut to the knee, combining it with a type of trousers. Coming as they did from colder climates, they used more fur, often as sleeveless vests worn over tunics. Gartered hose, which became part of western, medieval dress, were also derived from tribal dress. The most pronounced change came as garments made from pieces that were cut and sewn replaced draped garments characteristic of the classical era.

The Production of Cloth

The Roman tradition, in which women were the major producers of textiles, continued. Although free women and serfs must have made fabrics at home to meet family needs, large quantities of cloth were produced in a **gynaceaum** or women's workshop. References to women's textile workshops indicate that very young slave and lower-class girls worked at this trade until they reached adulthood, when they left to marry or enter a convent. Most of these workshops were on large estates in rural areas (Herlihy, 1990).

Textiles were produced from linen fibers removed from flax and wool sheered from sheep. Women spun the yarns by hand, wove the fabric on upright looms, and cut and sewed the clothing. Although the Moors had introduced cotton manufacture to Spain in the ninth century, it had not yet spread to the non-Muslim west. Like silk imported from Byzantium, it was largely an upper-class, luxury, imported fabric.

It is possible to determine the colors of fabrics by considering the kind of dyestuffs that were in use. Plant and animal natural dyes would have produced blue, yellow, green, and purple. The Bayeux Tapestry, an embroidered depiction of the Battle of Hastings (in 1066), confirms this. All of the aforementioned colors, except purple, appear in the tapestry. By the 10th century, kermes, made from an egg-bearing insect, produced a red color.

THE MEROVINGIAN AND CAROLINGIAN DYNASTIES

Evidence for the costume of the Merovingian and Carolingian periods is sparse. What is known about costume is of a general nature. Royal figures described by contemporary writers provide a bit of costume information, but little is known of the clothing of commoners.

Costume Components for Men: The Merovingian Period

Clovis, the first of the Merovingian kings of northern France, was crowned in 493. He married a Christian, converted to Christianity, and adopted Byzantine-style dress for his court as a symbol of his change from the status of tribal chief to Christian king. He wore a short tunic, decorated with bands of embroidery or woven design, but without the lavish jeweled decoration of the Byzantine emperors. His hose were tied close to the leg with garters. The paludamentum and a crown completed his regalia. He retained one earlier Frankish practice. The king wore his hair long as a symbol of his rank, while the rest of the men in his court and other subjects cut their hair short.

Tunics worn by Merovingians ended below the knee. Like the tunic worn by King Clovis, they sometimes had bands or ornamentation, worn with or without belts (Figure 5.12). Merovingian cloaks were shaped like the Greek chlamys, fastening over one shoulder. Men also wore hooded capes, which may

FIGURE 5.12 Late fourth- or early fifth-century statuette of a man from the region of Gaul. He wears a knee-length tunic that has an overall pattern and a braid decoration at the neck, the hem, and down the center front. (© Dumbarton Oaks, Byzantine Collection, Washington DC)

have been a later version of the Roman paenula. Gartered hose that spiraled the leg were worn with boots or shoes.

Costume Components for Men: The Carolingian Period

Changes in dress from the Merovingian to the Carolingian period were minor, and elements of Byzantine influence continued to be apparent in the dress of the wealthy and powerful. Men wore tunics and mantles as their primary garments. Tunics changed slightly, narrowing through the upper body and widening in the skirt. Belts were worn over tunics, which remained short except for ceremonial occasions. When tunics were ornamented, clavi and decorative bands were used around the neckline and sleeve edges. The shapes and styles of cloaks did not undergo important changes.

Carolingian kings no longer wore long hair. Men cut their hair below the ears, and adult men wore beards. Footwear included boots, which ended below the calf, and shoes. See Contemporary Comments 5.1, page 120, for a contemporaneous description of Charlemagne and his way of dressing.

Costume Components for Women: The Merovingian Period

Byzantine influences remained strong in the Merovingian dynasty. Generally, women placed loose-fitting shawls or pallalike draperies over tunics.

Archeological excavations of an early sixth century Merovingian tomb in Paris revealed Queen Arnegund's clothes. Enough clothing remained to

permit determination of the various layers of her dress and their general form. A linen shift or chemise was closest to the body. Over this was placed a knee-length under tunic of violet silk, with a jewel-decorated belt. Outermost was a long, outer tunic of dark red silk, opening at the front and closed with richly jeweled pins. A red silk veil was on her head. The thin leather slippers on her feet were worn with cross-gartered linen stockings. Her jewelry included earrings, brooches, silver belt ends and buckles, a long gold pin, and the signet ring that proved her identity (Rice, 1965). Jewelry-making techniques and styles were greatly influenced by Byzantine jewelry. Archeologists have found a number of fine enameled pieces and mountings of large stones.

It is clear royal families imported silk from Byzantium. Common people would have worn linen, which grew well in damp northern climates, or wool from local sheep herders. Cotton had not yet been imported into Europe.

Costume Components for Women: The Carolingian Period

Carolingian costume continued to show strong Byzantine influences. The under tunics included fitted sleeves. Outer tunics often had wider sleeves and bands of ornamentation (Figure 5.13). Covering their hair, adult women placed veils or pallalike shawls over their outer tunics. Jewelry included bracelets and earrings.

CLERICAL COSTUME: THE EARLY MIDDLE AGES

Much of the clerical costume that was to become traditional for Roman Catholic priests, monks, and nuns until the mid-20th century originated during the Early Middle Ages.

Contemporary Comments 5.1

THE DRESS OF CHARLEMAGNE

In his Life of Charlemagne, *Einhard, a Frankish historian who lived at the court of Charlemagne, describes the appearance of the emperor.*

He wore the national dress of the Franks. The trunk of his body was covered with a linen shirt, his thighs with linen pants. Over these he put on a tunic trimmed at the border with silk. The legs from the knee downward were wound with leggings, fastened around the calves with laces, and on his feet he wore boots. In winter he protected his shoulders and chest with a vest made of otter skins and marten fur, and over that he wrapped a blue cloak. He always carried a sword strapped to his side, and the hilt and belt thereof were made either of gold or silver. Only on special holidays or when ambassadors from foreign nations were to be received did he sometimes carry a jewel-studded saber. He disliked foreign clothes, no matter how beautiful they were, and would never allow himself to be dressed in them. Only in Rome was he seen on two occasions in a long tunic, chlamys, and Roman shoes[1]: the first time at the entreaty of Pope Hadrian and the second by request of his successor [Pope] Leo. On high festival days he wore a suite of golden cloth ornamented with jewels. His cloak was fastened by a golden brooch, and on his head he carried a diadem of gold, embellished with gems. On other days, however, his dress was not much different from the common people.

1. The translators noted that this is the costume traditionally worn by Byzantine emperors.

Scherabon Firchow, E. S., & Zeydel, E. H. (Trans.). (1972). *Einhard: The life of Charlemagne* (p. 89). Coral Gables, FL: University of Miami Press.

Dress of Priests

Ecclesiastical costume worn by priests and higher church officials developed gradually from the fourth century to the ninth century. Before the fourth century, priests wore no special costume. Throughout the medieval period, the parish priest who lived in the community was more clearly distinguished by his **tonsure** (*haircut*) than by his everyday dress. Two distinctive haircuts included one in which the top of the head was shaved and a fringe of hair grew around the shaved area. In the other, the forehead was shaved from ear to ear.

Higher ranking clerics wore a more distinctive costume on ceremonial occasions or during church services. By the ninth century the Roman Catholic Church had established a number of items as part of the liturgical costume (Figure 5.14), including the following:

Amice (*am'is*) A strip of linen placed around the shoulders and tied in position to form a collar, which was worn by priests saying mass.

Alb A long white tunic with narrow sleeves and a slit for the head, tied with a belt. The name derived from the Roman *tunica alba* (*white tunic*).

Chasuble (*chahz'you-bul*) An evolved form of the paenula. This round Roman cape, worn by the clergy, included sides cut shorter to allow movement of the arms. A Y-shaped band of embroidery called the **orphrey** extended from each shoulder to meet and form a vertical line in the back and front of the chasuble.

Stole A long, narrow strip of material worn over the shoulder during mass.

Pallium A narrow band of white wool worn by popes and archbishops. Prelates wore the band with one end falling to the front and the other falling to the back. This band evolved from the Greek himation, which lost its shawl-like form and became a narrow band that was a symbol of learning in Roman and then Byzantine styles.

Cope A voluminous cape worn for processions.

Other refinements of costume specific to particular clerical rank or ceremonies, such as colors, cut, fabric, and ornamentation, were made at different periods of the history of the Catholic Church. Church

FIGURE 5.13 In this illuminated manuscript from the late ninth century, Carolingian ruler Charles the Bald's wife and attendant wear long tunics, veils over the head, and bracelets and earrings. (Scala/Art Resource, NY)

FIGURE 5.14 Stone relief of Saint Peter showing clerical dress including orphrey, chasuble, stole, and alb. (V&A Images, London/Art Resource, NY)

law encouraged clerics to "show signs of religious observance [through their dress] and not of luxury" (Izbicki, 2005, 105).

Monastic Dress

The practice of leaving the world to devote oneself to prayer and self-denial began early in the history of the Christian church. After the fourth century, entire communities were formed, often around the person of a particularly holy man or woman. These monasteries or convents did not require specialized costume; their members dressed in the ordinary costume of the poor. Although the costume of most people changed over time, the monks and nuns retained their original dress, thereby distinguishing themselves from the "worldly." Both men and women wore a loose-fitting tunic with long, fairly wide sleeves. This tunic reached to the ground and was belted. Specific colors and cuts varied somewhat from order to order, but the usual colors employed were brown, white, black, or gray.

The monk's costume included a **cowl**, a hood that either was attached to the tunic or was a separate garment. Nuns covered their heads with veils. On first entering convents, women cropped their hair closely. Members of some orders went barefoot; most wore sandals. Eventually, the distinctions among the various orders became quite pronounced, and even the most casual observer could identify the order with which the individual was associated. Some Catholic religious orders still wear garments of the type first adopted in the Middle Ages.

HISTORICAL BACKGROUND: THE 10TH–13TH CENTURIES

Feudal Monarchies

The feudal system developed out of the need for protection as the Carolingian Empire collapsed under the attacks of the Vikings, Magyars, and Saracens. Central government vanished; law and order disappeared. Security was found only in military might. A new invention, the stirrup, revolutionized warfare by combining human and animal power to produce mounted warriors with sword and lance capable of shock combat. These warriors became armored knights on horseback. Knights, who were professional warriors, needed years of training to learn how to handle the horse and the weapons. Such training began in youth, and it was expensive. The knight needed a number of horses bred for warfare, and they required care and training.

Knights were vassals of a lord. The word *vassal* came from a Celtic word meaning "one who serves." To maintain his vassals, a lord granted each of them land, called a *fief* or *fiefdom*, in exchange for military services. The knight lived on his fief when he was not fighting on behalf of his lord. Along with the fief came serfs, who worked the land for the lords and knights. A serf was someone who had lost freedom years before when an ancestor surrendered his freedom and that of his family to a lord in return for protection.

On the local level, the lord and his vassals enforced whatever law and order existed. In theory, the feudal king was the supreme lord and theoretical owner of all the land within his kingdom. The knights owed him allegiance; however, if a vassal challenged him, the monarch had no national army that could be mobilized, so the feudal king had to rely on his other vassals for support.

The feudal lords fought invaders and went to war with other feudal nobles. The armored knight was more likely to be captured and held for ransom than killed. The serfs and peasants suffered more because their lives, homes, and crops could be destroyed in a battle.

Feudal lords and knights built castles on their lands to serve as places of protection, as well as for homes for the lord and his family. At first these castles were structures of wood intended only for defense, but by the 12th century they had become very elaborate. They were uncomfortable, cold, damp, dark, and very windy because the windows in the outer walls were nothing more than slits without glass. As such, layers of clothing and decorative as well as functional wall hangings were utilized for warmth. Onto these castles, as well as shields and clothing, **heraldic devices** were painted and sewn. Possibly originating among families descended from Charlemagne, heraldry spread quickly and became quite common in the 12th century.

Feudalism took various forms in different parts of Europe because it developed from local practices and customs. Originating in northern France, it spread into southern France, Germany, and northern Italy. England did not develop a feudal organization until after Duke William of Normandy invaded England in 1066 and became king of England (Figure 5.15).

Political Developments in Europe

Political developments from 900 to 1300 were exceedingly complex. The reader may be best served by a brief note of some of the more important developments in the different areas of Europe. See Figure 5.16 for a map showing the major political divisions of Europe by the mid-14th century.

The German Dynasties

In Germany, after the German line of the Carolingian emperors died out, a new dynasty emerged from the Duchy of Saxony. Otto I (936–973) invaded Italy, proclaimed himself king and had the pope crown him Holy Roman Emperor in 962. Although the empire was thoroughly German, it was considered to be a continuation of the ancient Roman Empire. After Otto's line ended in 1138 the Hohenstaufen emperors ruled until the last one was executed in 1268. The task of trying to rule Germany, Italy, and Sicily while fighting off rebellious dukes and hostile popes proved too much for the Hohenstaufen dynasty. When the nobles elected the first Hapsburg emperor in 1273, Germany had become a collection of semi-independent principalities instead of a united empire.

Anglo-Saxon and Norman Britain

After the Roman legions had been withdrawn from northwestern Germany, Angles, Saxons, and Jutes

FIGURE 5.15 Scene from the Bayeux Tapestry. (Erich Lessing/Art Resource, NY)

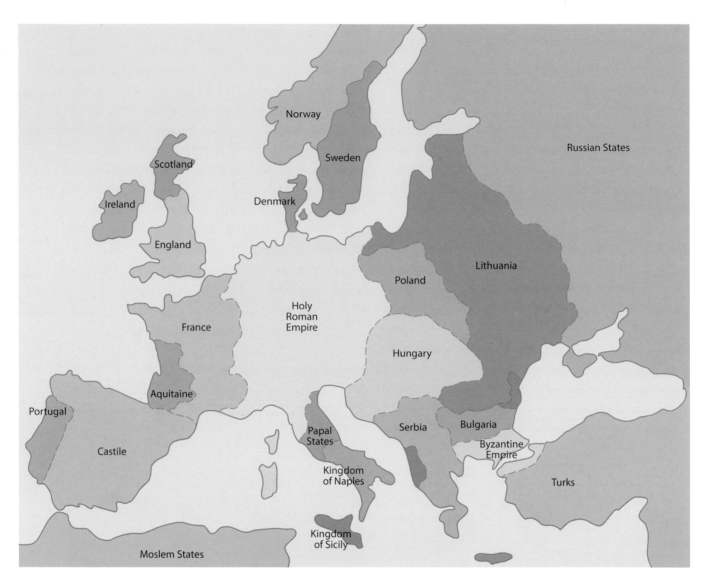

FIGURE 5.16 This map shows the major political divisions of Europe during the mid-14th century. (Courtesy of Fairchild Publications, Inc.)

invaded Britain in the fifth century. They drove the original Britons, the Celts, westward into Wales, Devon, Cornwall, and north into Scotland. The Anglo-Saxons settled down, intermarried, converted to Christianity, and established seven Anglo-Saxon kingdoms. In the ninth century, the Anglo-Saxons suffered an invasion by the Danes (Vikings) who came to plunder and settle. The Anglo-Saxon king, Alfred the Great (871–899), halted the Danes, and his dynasty united Britain under one king. When Alfred's line died out in 1066, William the Conqueror, Duke of Normandy, claimed the throne. He invaded England

and defeated the Anglo-Saxon claimant to the throne in the Battle of Hastings. William I established a feudal system in England that was better organized and more centralized than on the continent of Europe. Under Henry II (1154–1189), one of the greatest of English kings, whose mother was a granddaughter of William I and whose father was of the Plantagenet family, England laid claim to large areas of France. These claims were based on the fact that William the Conqueror had ruled Normandy and Henry II had married Eleanor of Aquitaine, an heiress who controlled a large area of southwestern France. For many years thereafter France and England battled over these claims. The struggle climaxed in the Hundred Years' War (1337–1453), which ended with the English driven from France except for a foothold in Calais. The Plantagenet family ruled over England until 1399.

The French Kings

In France, after the death of Charlemagne, the title of king carried with it little actual wealth or power. The kings were often less powerful than their feudal vassals. The election of Hugh Capet (987–996) as king marked the beginning of the Capetian dynasty, which ruled France for more than 300 years. But not until the 1100s would the French kings begin to increase the power and wealth of the monarchy and to weaken their mighty vassals. By the time that the Capetian line died out in 1328, the French king had become a genuine force in European power politics by consolidating his holdings, subjugating the powerful dukes, and replacing provincialism with unifying national patriotism.

FACTORS RELATED TO DEVELOPMENTS IN COSTUME

Political, social, and economic events can have both direct and indirect influence on clothing styles. The availability of the raw materials from which garments are made, the social stage on which they are worn, and even the practical needs they must satisfy each play a part in their development.

The Crusades

In the 11th century, under the urging of Pope Urban II, the European powers launched the first of nine Crusades against the Muslims. Ostensibly intended to free the holy places of Christendom from the Muslims who now controlled them, the actual motivations for each of the Crusades varied from genuine religious fervor to outright mercenary designs for accumulating wealth and power (Figure 5.17).

By the end of the Crusades in the 13th century, many new products and processes were being imported

FIGURE 5.17 Depiction of crusaders on their travels. (© British Library/HIP/Art Resource, NY)

to Europe. The crusaders learned the technique of printing patterns on textiles from the Muslims, who had learned it from the Coptic people of Egypt. Crusaders brought back foods, spices, drugs, works of art, and fabrics. New fabrics such as muslin, dimity, and silk damask came into use, as did a new fiber, cotton. Many crusaders stopped in Constantinople on their way to and from the wars, thereby continuing the strong Byzantine influences on the dress of the nobility of western Europe. These cross-cultural contacts did not end with the close of the Crusades. Trade expanded, especially between the Italian seaports and the Middle East.

Medieval Castles and Courts

The feudal lord and his family had private quarters in the large, fortified castles. Rooms were poorly ventilated. In winter only a large fireplace provided heat. Woolen garments were desirable not only in winter to combat the cold, but also in summer when castles continued to be damp and chilly. By modern standards, furnishings were simple and not very comfortable; however, crusaders brought back from the east more luxurious items such as carpets, wall hangings, and cushions. In spite of these improvements, multiple layers of clothing provided the most practical way of dressing for comfort.

The institution of knighthood and chivalry, the system for training knights, required that boys learn not only the arts of war but also the manners and customs of the upper classes. Generally, to learn these practices, the young knight had to leave his home and reside in the castle of a powerful lord. These courts, especially those of the dukes and kings, attracted artists, poets, troubadours or wandering singers, musicians, and other entertainers. The courts of southern France were especially noted as centers of artistic, musical, and literary expression. Moreover, they provided a stage for the display of fashion.

Town Life

After the fall of Rome, many formerly thriving urban centers were severely depopulated. During the 10th and 11th centuries, urban life revived. Europe experienced an economic upturn in agriculture, manufacturing of goods, and trade, so that by the 12th and 13th centuries major cities became lively centers that attracted an increased population. Among those residing in towns were wealthy merchants who dressed themselves in styles worn by the nobility. The clergy disapproved of this blurring of class distinctions, saying that "Jesus Christ and his blessed mother, of royal blood though they were, never thought of wearing the belts of silk, gold, and silver that are fashionable among wealthy women" (Gies and Gies, 1974, 47).

Early Indications of Fashion Changes

In the 11th and 12th centuries, a large number of people accepted styles for a relatively short period before a new style predominated—that is, they took part in the social phenomenon called *fashion*. Heller

(2007) saw evidence in the literary works called romances that were written in the 11th century. The characters in these books made it clear that they were striving to achieve a fashionable appearance. Scott (2007) based her belief that fashion was operating by the 12th century on visual evidence and on literary sources in which the clergy railed about men who were clean shaven and who grew their hair long. They complained about the inordinate attention to personal appearance and immodest styles. See Contemporary Comments 5.2, page 134, for a monk's description of clothing. Women, too, were admonished for trying to attract men through the fashionable styles that they wore. From the documentary evidence, it is clear that tailors required special training in order to construct more complex styles, and references were made to clothing cut in the French manner, possibly the earliest acknowledgment of France as a style leader. New fabrics appeared—the word *velvet* appeared for the first time in the late 1200s.

Fabric Production

A major evolution in the organization of textile manufacture took place. In the early Middle Ages women working in Roman-style factories or at home had produced most textiles. By 1300 men did the weaving, and women, the fiber preparation and spinning. Dyeing and fulling (compacting of wool cloth by pounding) were specialized crafts, practiced outside the home. In a study of women's work in the Middle Ages, Herlihy (1990) saw the decline in slavery and the movement of population from rural to urban centers as one of the reasons for these changes. Women's workshops disappeared and textile production moved into the household. Men formerly employed in agriculture needed to find work in the urban centers and took over women's work.

Technological changes accompanied these developments. Since the 10th century, water-powered mills provided the power for fulling wool. By the 12th century, a horizontal loom that allowed the weaver to sit rather than stand replaced the vertical loom. The horizontal loom had foot treadles for moving the lengthwise yarns and a carrier, called a shuttle, for the crosswise yarn. The old hand-spinning method was supplanted by the spinning wheel in the 13th century. This machine apparently came to Europe from India by way of Muslim Spain (Gies and Gies, 1994).

By the 12th century, European craftsmen had established a number of centers for the manufacture of cloth for export. Trade guilds were first established in the 11th century by merchants who wanted to prevent the importation of competing goods. By the 12th century the craftsmen had begun to form their own **guilds**. Only by apprenticing himself to a guild could a young boy become a practitioner of a craft. Guilds were able to regulate the number of artisans and to set quality standards, rates of pay, and regulate working conditions.

Textile trade guild members were permitted to hire their wives and daughters to spin and weave. The widow of a guild member could herself become owner of her late husband's business and a member of the guild. However, pay scales for women were consistently lower than those for men.

Wool was an especially important fiber in the European textile trade. Wool grown in England was considered the finest available. Much English wool was exported to Flanders, where skilled weavers made it into high-quality cloth. Cloth merchants were by no means limited to wool cloth, however. Flax, from which linen fiber was obtained, was grown throughout Europe and used for household textiles and for clothing. Silk production was, by the mid-1200s, a major industry in Italy, Sicily, and Spain. Cotton, originally a product from India, was introduced into Spain by the Moors, so it, too, was available for spinning.

The merchant purchased the raw fiber. After cleaning, carding, and combing, he sold it to the weaver. The weaver's wife spun the yarn with spindle and distaff or, after the 13th century, with a spinning wheel. The weaver created the cloth on a hand loom. Some finishing steps were given to the fabric, and if color had not been added to either the fiber or the yarn, the fabric might be dyed. In some cases, the fabric was sold undyed to skilled dyers from Italy who added the color.

SOURCES OF EVIDENCE ABOUT COSTUME

Europe underwent marked changes in the arts at the same time it experienced this economic awakening. Most of the public art produced was not solely intended as decoration but was designed to tell the generally unlettered population the stories of the Christian faith. Although some of the traditions continued, such as dressing Christ, Mary, angels, and saints in the stereotypical garments that had been depicted in the art of earlier centuries, other factors led artists to include figures dressed in the dress of the artist's own time. Manuscripts incorporated calendars that showed ordinary people doing the work of the various seasons. After the 13th century more manuscripts were produced in urban workshops, not in monasteries, and created by lay artists rather than monks. Then, too, some of these manuscripts dealt with secular themes. Sometimes costumes were based on imagination or on the reports of dress brought back by the returning crusaders. In spite of these limitations, scholars rely on these works of art as the major source of visual evidence of 12th- and 13th-century costume.

Important art forms included illuminated manuscripts and miniatures carved in ivory and wood. Romanesque architecture of the 10th and 11th centuries utilized the work of sculptors as an important element of decoration. After the 1150s Romanesque architecture was superseded by the Gothic style, which predominated until the end of the 1400s. Gothic churches with pointed arches and soaring, graceful structures told stories to the faithful through sculpture and stained-glass windows.

EUROPEAN COSTUME: THE 10TH AND 11TH CENTURIES

Costume Components for Men

Garments

Underclothing consisted of undershirts and under-drawers. Undershirts, sometimes referred to as chemises, were short-sleeved linen garments.

Underdrawers, called **braies** (*brays*), were loose-fitting linen breeches fastened at the waist with a belt (see Figure 5.24 on page 133). Lengths varied, ranging from knee-length to longer ankle-length variations, which were wrapped close to the leg with gartering.

Men often wore two tunics, one over the other: an outer tunic and an under tunic. Usually both were the same length, although sometimes the under tunic was slightly longer and therefore visible at the lower edge of the garment (Figure 5.18).

When short in length, outer tunics were almost always made with close-fitting sleeves. Sometimes sleeves extended over the hand with the excess fabric pushed up into folds above the wrist (Figure 5.19). Long outer tunics were made either with fitted sleeves, or (more often) cut wide and full, allowing the sleeve of the under tunic to show.

Tunic necklines were round or square. These garments usually belted at the waist. The fabrics most frequently used were linen and wool. The poor wore wool almost exclusively. Silk was imported by the very well-to-do.

The length of the tunic and its decoration indicated social class distinctions. Outer tunics of the wealthy were decorated with bands of silk embroidery at neck, sleeves, and hem (Figure 5.20). The nobility and the clergy wore long flowing robes for ceremonial occasions. For hunting and warfare, men of all classes wore more practical short tunics.

Mantles for men were either open or closed. **Open mantles** were made from one piece of fabric that fastened on one shoulder (see Figure 5.18), while **closed mantles** were a length of fabric with a slit to slip the head through (see Figure 5.19).

FIGURE 5.18 Page from a manuscript c. 1050. Men at right wear short tunics with gaitered hose, over which they wear cloaks. The long sleeves of their tunics are pushed up into folds above the wrist. Their hats are in the Phrygian bonnet style. Women on the page wear long tunics and cover their hair with veils. (The Pierpont Morgan Library/Art Resource, NY)

Tenth-century mantles were usually square; in the 11th century semicircular mantles began to appear. For ceremonial events, men in important political or religious positions wore mantles draped like Greek himations.

Hair and Headdress

Young men were clean shaven; older men were bearded (see Figure 5.20). Hair was parted in the middle, falling naturally either straight or in waves at the side of the face to the nape of the neck or below.

Except for helmets worn in war, hoods and Phrygian bonnet styles were the predominant styles

FIGURE 5.20 Byzantine influences appeared in European dress of the upper classes during the Middle Ages. Bands of embroidery on the tunic of the second figure on the left show Byzantine influence, while other figures wear under tunics, and mantles of various solid colors (11th century).
(Detail: The Pierpont Morgan Library/Art Resource, NY)

FIGURE 5.19 Twelfth-century manuscript showing male angel on left and woman on right. Both wear outer tunics and contrasting, lighter colored under tunics. The angel wears an open mantle, the woman is in a closed mantle with light colored veil over her head. (Detail: The Pierpont Morgan Library/Art Resource, NY)

of head coverings. Hats with small, round brims and peaked crowns were depicted on Jewish men as early as the 11th century in works of art. These hats, and also beards, seem to have been part of traditional dress worn voluntarily by Jews. Rubens (1967) suggested that they probably derived from a conical hat worn by non-Muslims in Muslim countries and were introduced into Europe by way of Spain or Byzantium.

Footwear and Leg Coverings

Hose were made of woven fabric, cut and sewn to fit the leg, ending either at the knee or thigh. **Leg bandages** (also called **gaiters**) were strips of linen or wool wrapped closely around the leg to the knee and worn either over the hose or alone (see Figure 5.18). Socks, shorter than hose, were usually brightly colored. Some socks with decorative figures around the upper edges might be placed over the end of the braies, over hose, or worn with leg bandages.

Frequently decorated, boots might be either short to the ankle or longer, reaching to mid-calf. The style for flat, pointed-toed shoes appeared as early as the 10th century. Closely fitted shoes generally ended at the ankle, fastening when necessary with thongs of leather or fabric (Figure 5.21). Some clergymen wore Byzantine-style slippers that were cut low over the instep.

FIGURE 5.21 First half of the 12th century. Fashionable tunics, both short and long, are more closely fitted through the torso in the 12th century, whereas the monk's costume retains the fit and characteristics of an earlier period. With their short tunics, the servants wear hose, over which they place short, striped stockings, and shoes that end at the ankle. (Detail: The Pierpont Morgan Library/Art Resource, NY)

Costume Components for Women

Costume of men and women showed relatively few differences during the 10th and 11th centuries.

Garments

Women wore a loose-fitting linen garment very close to the skin. Called a **chemise** (*chem-eze'*) in French, it was cut longer but otherwise was much like a man's undershirt.

Over this, women wore floor-length under tunics with close-fitting sleeves and an embroidered border at neck, hem, and sleeves. Outermost they placed floor-length outer tunics made with wide sleeves that allowed the under tunic sleeves to show. Usually the outer tunic was pulled up and bloused over a belt (see Figure 5.19).

For outdoors, women wore either open or closed mantles (see Figure 5.19). Some were made as **double mantles** lined in contrasting colors. **Winter mantles** could be fur lined.

Hair and Headdress

Young girls wore their hair loose, flowing, and uncovered. Married (and older) women covered their hair with a veil, which was pulled around the face under the chin, or was open, hanging close to the sides of the face and ending about mid-chest (see Figure 5.19). The rich had silk or fine linen veils; people in the lower classes used coarser linen or wool.

Footwear and Leg Coverings

Hose (*stockings*) tied into place around the knee. Women's shoes were similar to those of men. Women also wore open slippers with bands across the ankle, similar to those worn by some clergymen. **Clogs** were wooden platforms that raised shoes out of the water, mud, or snow. These were placed over leather shoes.

Jewelry

Written records and a few visual depictions indicate wealthy women wore headbands (**circlets**) of gold and neckbands of beads, bracelets, rings, and earrings. Jeweled belts (often called **girdles**) are sometimes depicted in art.

EUROPEAN COSTUME: THE 12TH CENTURY

Historians have identified several changes in styles. Snyder (2002) identified three types of garments shown in art. The first is a tunic worn by lower class men and women that fit a little more closely than in the previous century (see Figure 5.21). The second is a tightly fitted one-piece garment, which Snyder called a **bliaut** (*blee-o'*; man standing at center Figure 5.22) worn by both men and women. The third is a close-fitting garment with an upper section joined to a skirt, the **bliaut gironé** (*blee-o' gee-rohn*) which was limited in its use to upper-class men and women. The latter two garments clung to the body, with many vertical and horizontal folds. The laces of these garments sometimes fell open, revealing the bare flesh beneath. Clerics in the 13th century issued decrees against women revealing too much of their bodies.

In analyzing the evidence from art and from an extant garment that belonged to a Spanish prince (c. 1146), Waugh (1999) concluded that the closer fit of the bliaut was achieved by curving the seams of the section close to the upper body section. **Gores,** or *triangular wedges of fabric,* provided fullness and shaping to the skirt.

Snyder (2002) described the bliaut gironé as more complex in cut than earlier garments, having a fuller skirt that was joined to a separate bodice section. Like the bliaut, it laced shut at the sides. The skirt and bodice joined below the anatomical waistline. The bodice and skirt were sewn together, and an inset bias (diagonal) fabric piece may have been used to ensure a better fit at the hips. Seams were concealed by applied pieces of decorative tape. There is no evidence, however, that sleeves were set in. The bliaut gironé was made of costly silk fabrics such as satin or velvet, embroidered with gold thread, and decorated with precious stones (Figure 5.23).

FIGURE 5.22 Manuscript illustration for a Bible from before 1185 depicts a variety of costumes, including women (left side) with wide, pendant cuffs on their outer tunics. The sleeves of the under tunics are visible at the wrist. Woman at far left wears a closed mantle; the one at the right an open mantle. The man in the center panel wears a bliaut under a mantle lined in fur. (Detail: The Pierpont Morgan Library/Art Resource, NY)

FIGURE 5.23 Romanesque architectural detail, 12th century, France. This bliaut gironé, worn by a figure representing a king, is fitted through the waist to the hip where a finely pleated skirt joins the top. The sleeves are slightly pendant. Both sleeves and neckline are edged in decorative fabric. (Detail: Image copyright © The Metropolitan Museum of Art. Image source: Art Resource, NY)

Costume Components for Men

Garments

Both the under tunic and outer tunic continued to be the basic elements of dress for most men. However, in some representations no evidence can be seen of an under tunic; perhaps in some instances only a single tunic was worn. Sleeves became more varied. The major types were

- close-fitting sleeves with decorative, turned-back cuffs,
- elbow-length sleeves,
- full sleeves on the outer tunic that revealed fitted sleeves on the tunic underneath, and
- sleeves cut fairly close at the shoulders and widening to a full bell shape at the end.

Men continued to wear mantles, as well as loose outer garments, including those with attached hoods. They fastened the mantles with circular brooches.

Hair and Headdress

Most men were bearded and had moustaches. Hair varied in length but usually did not fall below the shoulder. Clergymen railed against the hairstyles adopted by some men who grew their hair long and had small, clipped, and pointed beards. Such critics often viewed these men as effeminate.

For outdoors, men wore hoods or small round hats that had a small stem or tab at the top. The **coif**, a cap that tied under the chin and was similar to a modern baby's bonnet in shape, began to be used in the latter part of the century (Figure 5.24).

Footwear

Leg wrappings, strips of cloth perhaps taken from worn-out garments, were calf and ankle height. Shoes and boots, much like those of the previous century, continued in use. Pointed shoes had been worn in the 10th century, and some upper-class men now adopted shoes with very long points. See Contemporary Comments 5.2, page 134, for a description by a clergyman who disapproved of the new styles of clothing and shoes with extremely long toes.

Costume Components for Women

While costume for lower-class women changed very little, upper-class women's costume evolved such that the chemise, the under tunic, and the outer tunic all fitted the body more closely. Some sculpted representations of the bliaut gironé of this period show fabric that looks as if it may have been pleated, smocked, or crinkled.

Garments

Sleeves of women's bliauts or tunics were even longer and more exaggerated in their cut than those of men. Some illustrations show closely fitting sleeves ending in long, pendant cuffs or bands that hang all the way to the floor. If both under and outer tunics were worn, the sleeves of the garment underneath were usually long and fitted while outer garments had either pendant cuffs, wide cuffs with decorative banding, or sleeves narrow at the top and flaring gradually to end in a bell shape (see Figure 5.22).

The **chainse** (*shens*) was another distinctive type of outer garment for upper-class women. Made of washable material, probably linen, it was long and probably pleated (Figure 5.25). The chainse seems to have been worn alone, without an outer tunic, as a house dress, especially in the late 12th century. It

FIGURE 5.24 Manuscript of about 1240–1260. Lower left panel shows three men harvesting wheat. The man on the right wears only his braies and a small, white coif on his head. His fellow workers wear short tunics or cotes; the man on the left has tucked his into his belt, thereby revealing his braies and the top of his hose, which fasten to the top of his braies. Women in the upper panel wear (from left to right) a cote; a cote with a sideless surcote (which is lifted up to reveal her patterned stockings); and cotes and mantles. The two women in the center of the panels wear wimples. The woman at the far right is wearing a fur-lined mantle. (Detail: The Pierpont Morgan Library/Art Resource, NY)

may have been a summer garment, because it was washable and made of lightweight fabric.

Mantles for the upper classes were long, capelike garments that opened down the front and fastened with a long ribbon that was attached to clasps placed on either side of the front. Some mantles were exceedingly luxurious. A poet described one as made of rose and white cloth from India, woven or embroidered with figures of animals and flowers, cut in one piece, and lined with scented fur. It had a collar

FIGURE 5.25 Garment (possibly a chainse) of crinkled fabric shows a row of lacing up the side, under the arm. (Detail: The Pierpont Morgan Library/Art Resource, NY)

Contemporary Comments 5.2

FASHIONABLE DRESS OF MEN IN THE 12TH CENTURY

Orderic Vitalis, a monk writing in the early 12th century, writes disparagingly of the fashionable styles of the period. In his diatribe against the new styles, he gives one version of the origins of the long, pointed toes for shoes that appear periodically throughout the Middle Ages.

Count Fulk[1] was a man with many reprehensible, even scandalous, habits, and gave way to many pestilential vices. Being a man with deformed feet he had shoes made with very long and pointed toes, to hide the shape of his feet and conceal the growths that are commonly called bunions. This encouraged a new fashion in the western regions, which delighted frivolous men in search of novelties. To meet it cobblers fashioned shoes like scorpions' tails, which are commonly called 'pulley-shoes' [poulaines], and almost all, rich and poor alike, now demand shoes of this kind. Before then shoes always used to be made round, fitting the foot, and these were adequate to the needs of high and low, both clergy and laity. But now laymen in their pride seize upon a fashion typical of their corrupt morals. . . .

Robert, a certain worthless fellow at King Rufus's court, first began to stuff the long 'pulley-toes' and in this way bend them into the shape of a ram's horn. . . . The frivolous fashion he had set was soon imitated by a great part of the nobility as if it had been an achievement of great worth and importance. At that time effeminates set the fashion in many parts of the world. . . . They rejected the traditions of honest men, ridiculed the counsel of priests, and persisted in their barbarous way of life and style of dress. They parted their hair from the crown of the head to the forehead, grew long and luxurious locks like women, and loved to deck themselves in long, overtight shirts and tunics. . . . They add escrescences like serpents' tails to the tips of their toes where the body ends, and gaze with admiration on these scorpion-like shapes. They sweep the dusty ground with the unnecessary trains of their robes and mantles; their long, wide sleeves cover their hands whatever they do; impeded by these frivolities they are almost incapable of walking quickly or doing any kind of useful work. They shave the front part of their head, like thieves, and let their hair grow very long at the back, like harlots. Up to now penitents and prisoners and pilgrims have normally been unshaven, with long beards, and in this way have publicly proclaimed their condition of penance or captivity or pilgrimage. But now almost all our fellow countrymen are crazy and wear little beards. . . . They curl their hair with hot irons and cover their heads with a fillet or cap. Scarcely any knight appears in public with his head uncovered and decently shorn according to the apostle's precept.

1. Count Fulk le Rechin was from France.

Chibnall, M. (Ed. & Trans.). (1973). *The ecclesiastical history of Orderic Vitalis* (Vol. 4) (pp. 187, 189). Oxford, UK: Clarendon Press.

and a border spotted with dark blue and yellow and fastened with jeweled clasps on the shoulder that were made from two rubies (from the poem *Le Roman de Troie,* as cited in Goddard, 1927).

Some cloaks were fur lined or decorated with fur. **Peliçon** (*pel'ee-son*) or **pelice** (*pel'eese*) are terms applied to any of a number of fur-trimmed garments including outer wraps, under tunics, and outer tunics.

Hair and Headdress

Women of the highest classes arranged their hair in two long plaits or braids covered in tubular cases that hung down on either side of the face. These braids sometimes reached almost to the floor, and contemporary records indicate that hairpieces were added in order to reach the fashionable length. Decorative bands of ribbon might be intertwined in the braids or the end of the braid held in a jeweled clasp. Over this a loose veil was placed.

Most women covered their hair entirely and wrapped veils so closely that only the face showed. A linen band called a **barbette** passed down from one temple under the chin and up to the other temple and attached with a standing linen band called a fillet, rather like a crown (see Figure 5.29 on page 137) over which a veil might be draped. Another new development, the wimple, was a fine white linen or silk scarf that covered the neck. The center was placed under the chin and each end was pulled up and fastened above the ear or at the temple. A wimple was generally worn in combination with a veil (Figure 5.26). Not worn by laywomen after the Middle Ages, wimples became part of the dress of many orders of Roman Catholic nuns and continued to be worn until the 1960s.

EUROPEAN COSTUME IN THE 13TH CENTURY

Problems of Costume Terminology

Variety in types of dress increases in the history of costume of the later Middle Ages. This tendency, which began to accelerate in the 13th century, presents the historian with difficulties in terminology. The written records of the period abound in descriptions of items of luxurious dress, but these descriptions are not accompanied by illustrations of the garments or accessories that they describe. The application of these terms to costume leaves the reader with a maze of terms in several languages that cannot be attached to particular garments with complete accuracy. For these reasons the names applied to particular items, or the definition of terms, may conflict in textbooks, costume histories, and journal articles dealing with dress of the Late Middle Ages. Furthermore, modern English words frequently derive from the early names for items, but the modern usage of the term is often markedly different from its original use.

Costume Components for Men

Throughout the 13th century men dressed in garments of functions similar to the preceding century; however, the terminology used to describe this clothing underwent some changes. To summarize, a man wore knee-length or shorter braies (breeches) and a linen chemise (undershirt). Over this he placed a **cote** (*under tunic*) and over the cote, a **surcote** (*outer tunic*). In cold weather or for protection outdoors he added yet another garment, some form of cloak with a more or less fitted cut.

An emphasis on greater modesty in court dress came at the time that Louis IX was king of France. Louis, a very pious man, was the only French king ever to be declared a saint by the Catholic Church. During his reign, court dress became more austere and luxurious display was discouraged.

Garments

Upper-class men wore long cotes; working men wore them short. Two types of sleeves are depicted most frequently. One is long and tightly fitted (Figure 5.27). The other is cut very full under the arm, tapering to a close fit at the wrist. Some costume references call this a **magyar sleeve** (Figure 5.26).

Depictions of surcotes (the outermost tunics) show variations in cut. Some were sleeveless with a round or wide horizontal neckline and wide armholes (the garment was sewn closed under the wide armhole; see Figure 5.26). Others had sleeves to the elbow or three quarters of the way down the arm (see Figure 5.26) or long sleeves cut full and wide under the arm, tapering to the wrist (as described for the cote).

Long surcotes were often slit to the waist to make riding and other movement easier. Even short surcotes and cotes worn without a surcote sometimes had these slits at the front (Figure 5.27).

FIGURE 5.26 Manuscript page, c. 1230, shows a king and queen on the upper panel. The queen, Blanche of France, wears a cote, cut full under the arm, and over it a fur-lined mantle. The king who is her son, St. Louis IX, wears a cote with long, fitted sleeves and a surcote that ends below the elbow with wider sleeves. His mantle closes at the front with a decorative brooch. The author of the book and scribe on the lower panel each wear sideless surcotes. (The Pierpont Morgan Library/Art Resource, NY)

Distinctions between the surcote and some of the cloaks and mantles worn outdoors blur. Major items of outdoor wear included open or closed cloaks or mantles. Mantles placed over the shoulders and fastening across the front with a chain or ribbon remained a symbol of high rank or status.

The **garnache** (*gar'nosh*) was a long cloak with capelike sleeves. Often lined or collared with fur, this garment was open at the sides under the arms (see Figure 5.27).

The **herigaut** (*er-ee-go'*) was a full garment with long, wide sleeves and a slit below the shoulder in front through which the arm could be slipped, leaving the long, full sleeve hanging behind. In some instances the top of the sleeve was pleated or tucked to add fullness to the sleeve (Figure 5.28; from descriptions, the **gardcors**, or **gardecorps** [*gard'-corz*], seems to have been the same kind of garment).

The **tabard** (*tab'erd*) was originally a short, loose garment with short or no sleeves that was worn by monks and lower-class men. In some instances it fastened under the arms either by seaming or with fabric tabs. In later centuries this garment became part of military dress or the dress of servants in lordly households (Figure 5.29). Decorations were applied to the tabard that identified the lord to whom the wearer owed allegiance.

Fitchets, or *slits*, which to the modern eye look like pockets, were made in some of the more voluminous

FIGURE 5.27 Manuscript of about 1240–1260 shows a variety of costumes including a garnache, a cloak with wide, capelike sleeves depicted both in lower left panel and upper right-hand panel. (Detail: The Pierpont Morgan Library/Art Resource, NY)

FIGURE 5.28 Manuscript illuminated after 1262 depicts donors of the manuscript each shown wearing an herigaut. The woman on the right has her hair enclosed in a net, a barbette around her chin, and fillet around her head. (Detail: The Pierpont Morgan Library/Art Resource, NY)

outdoor garments so that one could put his hands inside for warmth or to reach a purse hung from the belt around the waist of the garment beneath.

Hair and Headdress

Hair length was moderate and hair was parted in the center. Younger men wore shorter hair than did their elders. If beards were worn, they were short. Many men were beardless because of the development of a new closed military helmet that completely covered the face. It was uncomfortable if worn over a beard.

FIGURE 5.29 Kneeling Carthusian Monk wearing a tabard, which closes with cloth tabs under the arm. (Kneeling Carthusian Monk, c. 1380-1400. France, Burgundy, Dijon, 14th century. Marble; 24.2 x14.7 x 7.6 cm. The Cleveland Museum of Art, John L. Severance Fund 1966.113)

The most important head coverings were the **coif** and hoods (see Figure 5.27). Some hoods no longer had attached capes. By the end of the 13th century, hoods fitted the head more closely and some were made with a long, hanging tube of fabric at the back. The French called this a **cornette** (*kor'net*); the English, a **liripipe** (*leer'-eh-pip*; see Figure 6.11, page 156).

By the 13th century many Jewish men ceased to wear the traditional Jewish pointed hat and could no longer be clearly distinguished from other Europeans by their dress. Prejudice against Jews led leaders of the Catholic Church to pass edicts requiring that Jews dress in ways that made them clearly identifiable, and wearing this hat became a requirement rather than a voluntary act. Many artists creating works of art for an illiterate audience used symbols such as the pointed hat and beard to identify Jewish characters in biblical stories (the man in the upper right corner of Figure 5.31). During the Late Middle Ages these hats gradually went out of use; anti-Semitic attitudes continued, however. In many communities Jewish men and women were required to wear either distinctive items of clothing or some sort of badge.

Footwear

Both long hose and short stockings were worn, and footed hose increased in use. Closed shoes that buckled or laced, open slippers, shoes open over the top of the foot and having a high tab behind the ankle, and loose-fitting boots rarely above calf height were all worn (see Figure 5.27).

Costume Components for Women

While women did not wear braies, the other garments in their wardrobes corresponded to those of men: a chemise, cote, surcote, and, outdoors, a mantle or cloak.

Garments

Cotes had either fitted sleeves or sleeves cut full under the arm. Surcotes were either sleeved or sleeveless. Sleeved surcotes ended somewhere between the elbow and the wrist and were generally quite wide and full. Sleeveless surcotes were cut with wide armholes through which the cote beneath was visible (see Figure 5.28).

Toward the end of the 13th century more fitted styles replaced the loose, enveloping garments considered proper during the time of Saint Louis. Some women laced the cote (under tunic) tightly to emphasize their figures, which were visible through the wide armholes of the surcote.

Ceremonial open mantles, worn indoors and out were worn by women of high rank (see Figure 5.25). Cloaks such as those of the 11th and 12th centuries continued in use; some of them were hooded for cold weather. Women occasionally wore the herigaut and less often the garnache, which was for the most part a man's garment.

Hair and Headdress

As before, young girls wore their hair uncovered while adult women covered their heads. Long braids (such as those of the 12th century) were no longer seen. Veils and hair nets covered the hair. Barbettes, fillets, and wimples remained, although sometimes they were placed over a hair net instead of a veil (see Figure 5.28).

Footwear

No major changes were to be seen in footwear from that worn in the preceding century.

ACCESSORIES OF DRESS FOR MEN AND WOMEN: 10TH–13TH CENTURIES

Accessories were largely limited to jewelry, wallets, purses or other devices for carrying valuables, and gloves.

According to the Cunnington and Cunnington (1952), until the 13th century, only the nobility and the clergy wore gloves. Kings are sometimes represented wearing jeweled gloves. By the close of the 13th century, gloves seem to have been used more commonly by both men and women. Some were elbow length, others

wrist length. Some women were said to have worn linen gloves to protect their hands from sunburn.

Purses and pouches or wallets were suspended from belts (and, rarely, from the shoulder) or were sometimes worn underneath outer garments (reachable through an opening or slit).

Jewelry

Rarely visible in pictures or statuary, jewelry is described in literary sources. Most important items were rings, belts, clasps used to hold the ribbon that fastened the mantle, and a round brooch—**fermail** (*fair'my*) or **afiche** (*a'feesh*)—used to close the top of the outer tunic, bliaut, or surcote.

Cosmetics

After the Crusades, perfumes and ointments imported from the Middle East came into general use. Cunnington and Cunnington (1952) reported that English women of higher ranks used rouge in the 12th century. If it was imported for use in England where the nobility retained close ties to France and to English territories on the continent, one can be sure it was used on the continent as well. The same source mentioned hair dyes and face creams.

MILITARY COSTUME

Entire books have been devoted to the subject of military costume and armor. The discussion that follows provides only highlights of this topic.

Blair (1972), an authority on armor, suggested that armor be divided according to types of construction: (1) soft armor, made of quilted fabric or leather that has not been subjected to any special hardening process; (2) **mail**, made of interlocked metal rings; and (3) plates of metal, hardened leather, whalebone, or horn. The third category can also be divided into large plates that completely cover areas of the body and are flexible only where necessary for movement of the body, or small plates fastened together to provide more flexible covering.

All three of these forms were utilized in the Greek and Roman armies. During the Early Middle Ages in Europe the plate type of armor seems not to have been used. Blair (1972), in a lengthy study of European armor, wrote that although some forms of small plate armor were used by the Franks and the Vikings,

> *It is probably safe to say that during the period c. 600–1250 when anything other than soft armor was worn, it was in ninety-nine cases out of a hundred made of mail (p. 19).*

Mail in medieval Europe was made of circular rings, each ring having four other rings hooked through it (Figure 5.30).

The **Bayeux Tapestry** is one of the earliest and most important sources of information about the appearance of medieval armor. Dated from the second half of the 11th century, or slightly later, the tapestry depicts not only the events leading to the Battle of Hastings but also the actual battle itself, which took place in 1066. In the tapestry many figures wear knee-

FIGURE 5.31 Soldiers in chain mail with colorful surcotes placed over the mail. The mail covers all parts of the body except the face. (Image copyright © The Metropolitan Museum of Art. Image source: Art Resource, NY)

FIGURE 5.30 Mail shirt, 15th century. This shirt typifies the construction of chain-mail garments, which were the major form of armor in the Early Middle Ages and continued to be used in conjunction with plate armor in the Late Middle Ages as well. (Image copyright © The Metropolitan Museum of Art. Image source: Art Resource, NY)

length shirts of mail, which are split in front for riding. This mail shirt was called a **hauberk** (*ho'berk*) or **byrnie** (*burr'neh*). A hood of mail was worn to protect the neck and head. This may have been a separate piece, but in later armor the hood is made in one with the body of the hauberk for maximum protection of the neck. Some figures also wore leg protectors of mail, or **chausses** (*shos*). Some chausses merely covered the front of the leg while others were more like hose and fitted all around. On the head and over the mail hood, the warrior placed a cone-shaped helmet with a barlike extension that covered the nose.

In the mid-12th century men began wearing a surcote over the armor (Figure 5.31). Possibly the practice originated during the Crusades in an attempt to protect the metal armor from the heat of the Mediterranean sun, a custom possibly copied from Muslim soldiers. In later periods soldiers wore surcotes decorated with a coat of arms that identified the force to which they belonged, a necessary step when faces were covered by helmets.

In the 12th and 13th centuries, armor consisted of a coat of mail—sometimes quite long, other times shorter—hose, and shoes of mail. The sleeves reached over the hands to form a sort of mail mitten. The whole outfit weighed from 25 to 30 pounds and was worn over a padded garment. In the early 13th century, a closed form of helmet developed. Blair (1972) compared it to a modern welder's helmet, except that it was closed in the back, with eye slits and breathing holes, sort of like wearing a large, inverted can over the head. Placed over the chain-mail coif and a small padded skull cap that protected the head from the ridges of the mail, the helmet was worn only for combat as it was too uncomfortable for general wear. In the last half of the 13th century, large

crests in animal or birdlike shapes were placed on top of the helmet to identify the knight.

The use of closed helmets brought about changes in hairstyles. Men wore their hair shorter and were clean shaven in order to avoid the heat and discomfort that came from wearing a closed helmet over a full beard or long hair.

Common foot soldiers were not equipped with chain mail. Their protection was most likely limited to reinforced, quilted coats such as those worn under the armor to which they might add quilted leg guards.

By the end of the 13th century, a change from mail to plate armor had begun.

Summary

Visual Summary

The accompanying Visual Summary Table shows the major garment styles of the Byzantine and early medieval periods.

Themes

Byzantine dress, with its blending of eastern and Roman styles, clearly plays out the theme of CROSS-CULTURAL INFLUENCES. One can also see here the connections between ART AND DRESS. In the decoration of Byzantine styles, with brightly colored embroideries and jeweled ornamentation, one can find an echo of the jewel-like, brightly colored mosaics that decorate Byzantine churches.

CROSS-CULTURAL themes play a dominant role in the history of dress in western Europe from the early medieval period onward. Byzantine decorative elements in dress traveled across Europe to influence the dress of the rich and powerful Merovingian and Carolingian kings and their courts. Even the dress of the common people resulted from a merging of Roman with barbarian dress.

It is often through POLITICAL CONFLICT that CROSS-CULTURAL contacts occur. Crusaders traveling to the Middle East brought back new textiles and garments. The Moorish conquest and occupation of Sicily and

Spain helped to spread new TECHNOLOGIES important for dress, such as the cultivation and processing of cotton and silk fibers or the introduction of the spinning wheel. New garments associated with armor were adopted by civilians as a result of POLITICAL CONFLICT and warfare.

One can also see hints of the theme of SOCIAL CLASS. Thorstein Veblen (1953), a 19th-century economist, argued in his book *The Theory of the Leisure Class* that clothing can be an important means of displaying social class. He spoke of affluence demonstrated through **conspicuous consumption**, the acquisition of items that display the wealth of the wearer, and **conspicuous leisure**. In the 10th to the 13th centuries upper-class men wore long tunics, and lower-class men wore short tunics. These more encumbering garments, in which it would be difficult to do any menial work, could be said to demonstrate conspicuous leisure. With their voluminous sleeves, women's garments of the 12th century were even more restrictive.

LEGACIES OF BYZANTINE AND EARLY MEDIEVAL STYLES

Styles during the Early Middle Ages might be characterized as Roman forms in combination with local forms. In Byzantium, the non-Roman elements

Visual Summary Table

Major Garments of the Byzantine and Early Medieval Periods

Byzantine man,
c. 6th century

Byzantine woman,
c. 6th century

Byzantine man,
c. 11th century

Byzantine woman,
c. 11th century

Medieval European man,
12th century

Medieval European woman,
12th century

Medieval European man and
woman, 13th century

Outer garment called the *garnache*,
between late 13th and early 14th century

Medieval outer garment, called *herigaut*
or *gardecorps*, mid-13th century

came from the Middle East, whereas in Europe the non-Roman elements came from barbarian dress. In both cases, however, the chief components of dress were layered tunics combined with a mantle of some sort.

Byzantine styles influenced European styles among the upper classes. Byzantine silks were purchased, and rulers in Europe adopted Byzantine styles. By copying the Byzantine styles, these rulers brought to their courts a reflection of the wealth and status associated with the court at Constantinople, which had become the most cultured center of the period (see Figures 5.6 and 5.20).

Except for the introduction of sericulture into the west by way of the Byzantine Empire, neither technology for the production of cloth nor basic styles took any great leap forward in Europe during the period before 900. The major changes of the Middle Ages in western Europe were yet to come.

In an extensive study of influences from the dress of the Ottoman Turks, Jirousek (2005) pointed out that many elements of western dress show Ottoman influences, some appearing in the Early Middle Ages. One such feature that she identified as probably Turkish in origin is the hanging sleeve. Another is the coat that opens at the front; this is an innovation, as European outer garments tended to be capes, cloaks, or tunics without front openings that were put on over the head.

In the years between 900 and 1300, costume had evolved gradually from loosely fitted, T-shaped tunics and loose mantles to more closely fitted styles of a more complex cut. As medieval courts became centers of fashionable life, special court dress developed. Made of more costly materials, clothing was often so extreme in cut that it clearly demonstrated that the wearer belonged to a more leisured class. As the economy improved, the manufacture and distribution of fabrics multiplied, and new types of cloth became available. As the merchant class in the towns increased in wealth and numbers, fashionable dress was adopted not only by the nobility but also by the bourgeoisie.

Some elements of styles from the Early Middle Ages served as an inspiration to fashion designers of the 19th through 21st centuries. Notable revivals of medieval styles include cowl necklines and hanging sleeves. The magyar sleeve, cut full under the arm, was revived in the 1930s and the World War II period as the "bat-wing" or "dolman" sleeve. During the late Romantic through the Crinoline periods, hanging sleeves appeared again.

Changes in styles in the High Middle Ages were gradual. A young woman of modest means might be married and, many years later, buried in the same dress, or she might pass it on to her daughter in her will. After the end of the 13th century, this practice was less likely to occur. Fashion, with its rapid changes, was becoming an important aspect of dress, and styles began to change at what must have seemed like a dizzying pace. No wonder that a writer of 1350 was to

MODERN INFLUENCES

Contemporary designers cut in styles and lengths that are very different from the medieval period; nevertheless, the use of fur, tightly fitting leg hose (known as trousers for men today), and even a hood of mail were inspirations to designers Dolce & Gabbana in their fall 2014 menswear collection. Dolce & Gabbana's 2013 and 2014 women's wear collections were also heavily inspired by Byzantium and medieval periods. (© epa european pressphoto agency b.v./ Alamy)

look back on the styles at the end of the 1200s and lament that

> *Once upon a time women wore white wimples, surcotes with hanging sleeves, long full skirts, and decent hoods of cloth or silk. A woman had only three dresses. One for weddings and great feasts, one for Sundays and holidays, and one for every day. Narrow laced shoes and buttoned sleeves were for courtesans; decent women tied their bodices with ribbons and sewed their sleeves, wore their belts high and plaited their hair round their heads* (Evans, 1952, 24–25).

REFERENCES

Ball, J. (2005). *Byzantine dress.* New York, NY: Palgrave Macmillan.

Blair, C. (1972). *European armour.* London, UK: Batsford.

Calkins, R. (1993). *The illuminated books of the Middle Ages.* Ithaca, NY: Cornell University Press.

Cunnington, C., & Cunnington, P. (1952). *Handbook of medieval costume.* London, UK: Faber and Faber.

Evans, J. (1952). *Dress in medieval France.* Oxford, UK: Clarendon Press.

Gies, C., & Gies, F. (1974). *Life in a medieval castle.* New York, NY: Crowell.

Gies, F., & Gies, J. (1994). *Cathedral, forge, and waterwheel.* New York, NY: HarperCollins.

Goddard, E. R. (1927). *Women's costume in French texts of the 11th and 12th centuries.* Baltimore, MD: Johns Hopkins University Press.

Gordon, B. (2011). *Textiles: The whole story.* New York, NY: Thames & Hudson.

Heichelheim, F. M. (1949). Byzantine silk fabrics. *CIBA Review, 75,* 2741–2767.

Heller, S. G. (2007). *Fashion in medieval France.* Rochester, NY: Brewer.

Herlihy, D. (1990). *Opera Muliebria: Women and work in medieval Europe.* Philadelphia, PA: Temple University Press.

Izbicki, T. M. (2005). Forbidden colors in the regulation of clerical dress from the Fourth Lateran Council (1215) to the time of Nicholas of Cusa (d. 1464). In R. Netherton & G. R. Owen-Crocker (Eds.), *Medieval clothing and textiles* (pp. 105–114). Woodbridge, UK: Boydell Press.

Jirousek, C. (2005). Ottoman influences in western dress. In S. Faroqhi & C. Neumann (Eds.), *Ottoman costumes: From textile to identity* (pp. 125–141). Istanbul, Turkey: Eren.

Rice, D. T. (1965). *The dawn of European civilization.* New York, NY: McGraw-Hill.

Rubens, A. (1967). *A history of Jewish costume.* New York, NY: Funk and Wagnalls.

Scott, M. (2007). *Medieval dress and fashion.* London, UK: British Library.

Snyder, J. (2002). From content to form: Court clothing in mid-twelfth-century northern French sculpture. In D. Koslin & J. E. Snyder (Eds.), *Encountering medieval textiles and dress* (pp. 85–101). New York, NY: Palgrave Macmillan.

Veblen, T. (1953). *The theory of the leisure class.* New York, NY: New American Library.

Waugh, C. F. (1999). "Well-cut through the body": Fitted clothing in twelfth century Europe. *Dress, 26*(1): 3–16.

Watt, J. C. Y., & Wardwell, A. E. (1997). *When silk was gold: Central Asian and Chinese textiles.* New York, NY: Metropolitan Museum of Art.

		14TH CENTURY	1300S	1347–1453	1348
FASHION AND TEXTILES		Tailors gain increased skill in cutting and sewing Fashion change becomes more evident	Heraldic devices show association with families, towns, and cities		
POLITICS AND CONFLICTS				France and England fight Hundred Years' War	
DECORATIVE AND FINE ARTS			Gothic styles in architecture		
ECONOMICS AND TRADE		Trade, commerce, and industry continue to revive			Black Death plague stifles economies
TECHNOLOGY AND IDEAS			Introduction of gunpowder and cannon to warfare		
RELIGION AND SOCIETY		Clergy dress according to their position as bishops, priests, monks, or nuns			

CHAPTER SIX

The Late Middle Ages

c. 1300–1500

15TH CENTURY	1453	1454	1492	1498

Mourning dress rituals, such as the wearing of dark colors to show grief, established

Large, rigid plates gradually replace chain mail armor

Ottoman Turks conquer Constantinople

Illuminated manuscripts richly depict life and dress

Columbus reaches America

Vasco da Gama, Portuguese explorer, reaches India

First record of printing with moveable type in Europe

The Late Middle Ages (1300–1500) in Europe were marked by a revival of trade, commerce, and industry that encouraged the growth of urban areas and populations. With the resulting increase in affluence, not only royalty and courtiers but also well-to-do townspeople could afford some luxuries. Textiles became an important trade commodity. Stirrings of interest in fashionable dress had appeared in the latter centuries of the Early Middle Ages, and as class distinctions became less rigid, more people were able to obtain and wear fashionable clothing. From this period on, fashion changed more and more frequently.

HISTORICAL BACKGROUND

As medieval monarchs successfully centralized their governments, the power of nobles and knights declined. Feudalism began to wane before the 14th century, because kings found new sources of revenue by taxing cities and towns. The income allowed them to hire knights who fought as long as they were paid. Monarchs learned that a paid army was more dependable than feudal nobles.

Changes in warfare sped the decline of the armored knight on horseback. In the Hundred Years' War, the English longbow decimated French knights. In the 15th century, the introduction of gunpowder and the cannon (Figure 6.1) gave an even greater advantage to the infantry over the armored knights on horseback; they also ended the security of medieval castles.

As kings brought law and order to their realms, the revival of trade, commerce, and industry that had begun in the 12th century continued. Although towns lost some independence as royal governments grew stronger, kings offered protection to cities because they were centers of business and an important source of taxes. Within the cities, commerce became more capitalistic, and the medieval guilds declined in importance. The merchant class became more influential by turning to new fields, particularly banking, which made them welcome by their rulers. For example, in France, Jacques Coeur (1395–1456), the son of a lowly artisan, made his fortune investing

FIGURE 6.1 Depiction of canon use in the Hundred Years' War between France and England. (Art Resource, NY)

in commerce and mining. He became treasurer to Charles VII (1403–1461), who later had him imprisoned and confiscated his wealth.

Instead of providing services, peasants paid rent. With these funds, the lord could hire landless peasants to work the land. The vast majority of the population consisted of peasants—farmers, day laborers, millers, bakers, cattle dealers, and domestic servants. In time of war they were the foot soldiers of the king.

As freemen they were also more mobile. Increased commercial activity in the towns drew people from the countryside in search of work and higher salaries. These new townspeople could, if they had the talent and the opportunity, move up in social status. As a result, the population of the rural areas declined after the middle of the 14th century, while some towns and cities continued to grow. The more populated city streets allowed for a quicker diffusion of fashion as inhabitants and visiting foreigners could examine and mimic the latest styles.

In the early years of the 14th century, urban populations also grew as peasants fled from a series of famines in the countryside. Heavy rainstorms and colder weather ruined the crops on which people and cattle depended. The result was catastrophe: famine and starvation.

A population already weakened by famine suffered another scourge, the Black Death, a plague that struck Europe in 1348 and repeatedly throughout the 14th and 15th centuries. As late as 1665 London was devastated by an outbreak of the plague. The Black Death, probably a combination of bubonic and pneumonic plagues, spread across Europe. The devastating disease killed a third of the population in the regions that it struck. The densely populated Italian cities suffered heavy losses (Figure 6.2). As a result of this depopulation, labor became scarce, affording new opportunities for lower class workers (Herlihy, 1974).

Wages rose sharply. Landlords and merchants had to grant concessions to peasants and workers. When they tried to restrict wages and raise rents, social unrest and popular insurrections followed, lasting throughout the century.

FIGURE 6.2 The plague devastated Europe. (© British Library/ HIP/Art Resource, NY)

MEDIEVAL SOCIAL STRUCTURE

Late medieval society can be divided into three classes: the nobility, the bourgeoisie, and the peasants, with clergy as a distinct and separate group (Figure 6.3). An early medieval bishop once said that society was divided into those who prayed, the clergy; those who fought, the nobles; and the rest of society, which labored (Nicholas, 1974).

The Nobility

If one were to judge from the painted miniatures, the life of the nobles was an endless round of entertainment: riding and hunting, feasting and

FIGURE 6.3 Contrast the more ornate garments of the bishop (right) with the simpler cut, colors, and rougher looking material worn by the monk (left). Bishops can be identified by the ceremonial miter or headgear worn. (Erich Lessing/Art Resource, NY; HIP/Art Resource, NY)

talking, music and dancing—and, of course, warfare. Intermittent fighting in France between the French and English marked the 1300s, as the Hundred Years' War continued off and on between 1337 and 1453.

Entertainment among the nobility provided a stage for the display of fashion. Wealthy noblemen and women dressed in rich silk brocades and velvets trimmed with fur. The Court of Burgundy was especially notable for luxurious dress during the 14th and 15th centuries. The kingdom of France did not then control all of the regions that are part of the present country of France. Powerful autonomous dukes, who sometimes allied themselves with and sometimes against France, governed regions such as Brittany to the northwest and Burgundy to the northeast.

The court of the dukes of Burgundy was renowned for its splendid costume. The garments worn by the dukes, their families, and members of the court have

been described at length in the chronicles of the period and painted by artists of the time. Some of the costumes of Philip the Bold, duke from 1363 to 1404, indicate the costliness of Burgundian dress. One of his doublets was described as scarlet, embroidered in pearls in a design of 40 lambs and swans. The lambs had little gold bells around their necks, and the swans held gold bells in their beaks (Wescher, 1946).

Even headwear could be quite extreme. An inventory made in 1420 of the clothing of Philip the Good mentions a silk hat with peacock feathers, flowers, and gold spangles. At the close of the 14th century, Burgundian women adopted a tall, exaggerated, steeple-shaped headdress style that some costume historians call a **hennin** (*hen'in*; Figure 6.4). The word *hennin* derives from an old French word meaning "to inconvenience," and certainly a tall, peaked hat a yard high must have been a considerable bother. Some authors believe the

FIGURE 6.4 Fifteenth-century wedding banquet. Bride, at center of table, wears traditional dress of royal women; the women who flank her wear tall headdresses, called *hennins*, and gowns typical of the late 1400s. Serving men in wide-shouldered jackets and hose wear long-pointed shoes, called *poulaines*. The man directing the serving, who is older and more conservative in his dress, wears a short houppelande. (Bridgeman-Giraudon/Art Resource, NY)

word *hennin* was not used as a fashion term but rather to poke fun at this extreme style. Sumptuary laws regulated the size of these hats. Princesses could wear steeple headdresses a yard in height, while noble ladies were permitted to wear hats no more than 24 inches. Jirousek (1995) suggested that the hennin may have been yet another element borrowed from the east. She pointed out similarities between tall Ottoman Turkish headdress for women and the steeple-shaped headdresses of Burgundy and France (Global Connections).

The dukes of Burgundy and their retinues traveled to other parts of Europe for royal weddings, funerals, councils, and other events. As a result, others copied the styles they affected. The travel also meant that Burgundian clothing was made from fabrics imported from all over Europe. Inventories list silk from Italy, wool from Flanders, and felt from Germany.

Much of the color and pageantry of costume of this period derived not only from the dress of royalty with its vivid colors and fanciful headdresses, but also from the garments of the dependent nobles and servants. Kings, dukes, and feudal lords established the practice of presenting robes or sets of clothing to men and women of their household. The French word for "to distribute" is *livraison*, and the items given became known as the *liveree* or, in English, **livery**. Eventually, the word *livery* came to mean special uniforms for servants; however, during the 14th and 15th centuries, not only servants but also court officials and ladies-in-waiting to queens or duchesses wore livery. Although subject to the wishes of the queen or duchess, a lady-in-waiting was not a servant but a well-born woman who lived and took part in the life of the court as part of the queen's retinue.

Global Connections

The Ottoman Empire captured Constantinople in 1453, destroying the Byzantine Empire. By the end of the 15th century, the Ottoman Turks commanded virtually all of the access points crucial to east-west trade (Inal, 2011). According to historian Jirousek, "European diplomatic relations with the Ottomans were a balancing act between military and mercantile interests" (1995, 23). Turkish fabrics, luxury goods, and raw materials were sought by the French, English, and Portuguese, among others. The Venetian government sent artist Gentile Bellini (c. 1435–1507) as part of a delegation to the court of Sultan Mehmet II, the ruler of Constantinople; first in 1444–1446, then in 1451–1481. This pen and ink drawing by Bellini records a young Turkish woman's dress, including a large pointed hat, similar to a hennin, worn over a turban from which hangs a veil.

Fashion information such as this drawn image was reproduced and copied widely in other works of art, as well as in costume albums. The Ottoman emphasis on headgear would continue to influence Europe fashion into the Renaissance. (© The Trustees of the British Museum/Art Resource, NY)

The garments that were distributed were decorated with the heraldic devices or special motifs and symbols associated with the noble or his family (Figure 6.5). The search for unique patterns led to the practice of sewing together sections of different-colored fabrics within one garment. Garments decorated in this way were called **mi-parti** (*me-partee*) or **parti-colored**. Some examples of parti-colored hose show as many as four different colors in a single pair. These divisions could reflect marriages among families and even represent colors of a particular city. Parti-colored effects were used in both men's and women's costume.

The Bourgeoisie

Merchants created a kind of middle class, not of the nobility and yet far wealthier than the peasant. Some of these men, such as the previously discussed Jacques Coeur, became rich and powerful and achieved high offices under kings whom they helped finance.

By far the larger numbers of merchants were men of more modest incomes who lived in the towns. They lived comfortably in houses furnished with well-crafted furniture, linen, and china. They lacked none of the necessities and had the resources to obtain some of the luxuries of the period.

The wife of the merchant supervised the household but did not do the housework herself. If she lived up to the standards of behavior for a woman of her class, she conducted herself discreetly and modestly, and her dress was free from extravagance. The elderly husband of a 15-year-old wife, referred to as "The Goodman of Paris," wrote her a book of instructions on how to conduct herself in every aspect of management of the home. He even included some recipes. Contemporary

FIGURE 6.5 Although this painting depicts figures from the first Crusade, the parti-colored garment on the man to the left and the houppelande and headpiece on the woman to the right firmly places this image in the 15th century. (Alfredo Dagli Orti/The Art Archive at Art Resource, NY)

Comments 6.1 presents his advice as to her dress and comportment when outdoors.

Not all merchants, however, agreed with this husband. Some merchants demonstrated their affluence through lavish dress for themselves and their wives. The passage of numerous sumptuary laws during this period testifies to the growing tendency of well-to-do burghers to imitate the nobility. Sumptuary laws sought to regulate who could wear certain fabrics, furs, colors, and trimmings. For example, one set of sumptuary laws from the time of Edward IV of England (c. 1450) was entitled "For the Outrageous and Excessive Apparel of Divers [different] People, against their Estate and Degree [status] to the Great Destruction and Impoverishment of All the Land." Sumptuary laws were often broken, however. According to the early 15th-century poet Christine de Pisan, people often dressed above their station in life, from the farm laborer's wife dressing as the wife of a craftsman, to a countess dressing as a queen (Dufresne, 1990).

The Peasant

Illustrated prayer books painted during the Middle Ages frequently depicted the rural peasant at work (Figure 6.6). Husbands and wives worked side by side on the land, planting, harvesting, and clipping the fleece from sheep. Women tended to their children and prepared simple food in a house of two or three rooms furnished with utilitarian tables, benches or stools, chests or cupboards, and beds.

The peasant wore everyday clothing that was plain, serviceable, and very much like that described for men of the earlier medieval period: a homespun tunic, belted at the waist, with stockings for cold weather, and a cloak. Wooden clogs or heavy boots (for muddy weather) and a hat to keep off the sun in summer or a hood to protect against the cold in winter completed his workday wardrobe. His wife wore a gown with a closely fitted bodice and a skirt with moderate fullness. Aprons protected the garments from dirt and muck. Skirts could be tucked into the belt, with an underneath chemise exposed, especially for field work where the long skirt hampered movement.

Although many peasants were poor and lived a hand-to-mouth existence, some were better off and some even reasonably affluent. The poorest, of course, clothed themselves only in coarse cloth that was either left undyed or dyed with readily available

Contemporary Comments 6.1

ADVICE ON DRESS

The "Goodman of Paris" (or menagier, *translated "householder"), a well-to-do older man, provided the following instructions on how to dress for his 15-year-old wife.*

Have a care, that you be honestly clad, without new devices and without too much or too little frippery. And before you leave your chamber and house, take care first that the collar of your shift [chemise], and of your blanchet, cotte, and surcote, do not hang out one over the other as happens with certain drunken, foolish, or witless women, who have no care for their honor, nor for the honesty of their estate or of their husbands, and who walk with roving eyes and heads horribly reared up like a lion, their hair straggling out of their wimples, and the collars of their shifts and cottes crumpled the one upon the other, and who walk mannishly and bear themselves uncouthly. . . . Therefore, fair sister, have a care that your hair, wimple, kerchief, and hood and all the rest of your attire be well arranged and decently ordered that none who see you can mock at you, but that all the others may find in you an example of fair and simple and decent array.

Power, E. (1968). *Medieval people*. New York, NY: Barnes and Noble, p. 102.

natural dyestuffs such as the blue dye, **woad**. For festive occasions, peasant dress reflected, somewhat, the fashionable lines of the wealthy.

FABRICS AND TAILORS

The technology of cloth manufacturing underwent no major changes, although the spinning wheel gradually replaced the distaff and spindle for the making of yarn. Earlier medieval trends in textile manufacturing continued to accelerate, as the **"putting out" system** became the normal way of completing textile business. A merchant became the middleman for textile workers: He sold fibers to the workers, bought back the finished cloth, sold the cloth to the fuller, then bought it back. The merchant arranged for dyeing and

FIGURE 6.6 Peasants harvesting grain while upper class men look on. Illumination from a book depicting agricultural techniques, French, c. 1470. (Detail: The Pierpont Morgan Library/ Art Resource, NY)

then sold the completed fabric to agents who sold it at trade fairs (Gies and Gies, 1994).

Tailors underwent a lengthy and rigorous apprenticeship to become skilled in the construction of clothing (Figure 6.7). Innovations such as the development of set-in sleeves, bias-cut hose, and piecing of fabric through gores, allowed for tighter fitting clothing. Cutting and sewing clothing in complex ways allowed for recognizable styles, which could be adopted and then discarded for the more fashionable looks. Makers increasingly used buttons (Newton, 1980), which made getting into and out of the tighter-fitting garments easier.

Different craftsmen made different items of dress: Tailors made garments, professional lingerie makers made wimples and veils, and bootmakers or shoemakers made boots or shoes. Rapid changes in dress extended to headdress, accessories, and decorative embellishments as new elements appeared and variations of existing styles increased (Netherton, 2005).

The variety of materials and colors was considerable. Fabrics were traded all over Europe and imported from Turkey and Palestine. Furs served as both trimmings and linings. One king of France, Philip the Tall (1294–1392), who was not extravagant, used 6,364 skins of gray squirrel in three months just to fur his own robes (Evans, 1969).

FIGURE 6.7 A tailor's shop in the late 14th century has colorful hats, hose, and fabric hanging over the rod in the back of the shop. The tailor in the center is examining a customer's sleeve. Two other workers sit and stitch garments. (Snark/Art Resource, NY)

SOURCES OF EVIDENCE ABOUT COSTUME

Art Sources

The variety of sources of information available to the costume historian for this period is considerably greater than for the earlier periods. Secular romances and religious works such as Bibles and prayer books were hand lettered and illustrated with vividly colored painted miniatures. These miniatures depicted scenes from the romances, from the Bible, or from church history in terms of everyday medieval life. Unfortunately, these two-dimensional art works often show only the front views of costumes. Artists may have also used clothing to denote the character of the person represented, such as dated clothing for the virtuous, high fashion for the sinful, and so on.

Stone sculpture on the façades of Gothic cathedrals, the tombs of the rich and high born, and painted wooden statues for churches show the three-dimensional form of costume (Figure 6.8). However, as Scott (1986) pointed out, it was not uncommon for tombs to have been made well after the lifetime of the deceased.

Extant garments and woven tapestries are another source of costume information. Unfortunately, only a few individual items of dress from the period have survived, such as a **pourpoint** (a sort of man's jacket) worn in the second half of the 14th century by a French

FIGURE 6.8 Gothic style entryway at Reims, France. (Photograph by Vincent R. Tortora)

nobleman, Charles of Blois, or a jacket worn by the Burgundian, Charles the Bold, around 1476.

Documentary Sources

In France and England, royal families kept annual inventories of gifts or purchases of clothing. These lists described the fabrics, including their costs, from which clothing was made. Historians can often precisely date the introduction of a style from these lists. Wills and wedding contracts provide clothing descriptions, as do moralist and cleric denouncements of both men and women's clothing.

A number of literary works survive from the 14th and 15th centuries (many of which are of limited use as they still await translation into modern English). They sometimes make reference to clothing and provide valuable information, especially about attitudes or customs related to clothing. Chaucer's *The Canterbury Tales* reveals detailed information about the dress of the upper, middle, and lower classes. Through descriptions of fabric, color, pattern, and adornments, each pilgrim's economic and social standing is communicated. For example, the Merchant is described thus: "Upon his heed a Flaundrish bever hat, His bootes clasped faire and fetisly" (1903, 4).

The invention of printing from moveable type in 1450 by Johann Gutenberg had far-reaching historical consequences. Heretofore, all books had to be hand lettered or hand printed in a laborious, expensive process. The new method of printing reduced substantially the cost of books, thus making them more readily available and consequently enabling more people to read. The invention laid the foundation for mass producing books, which increased the spread of fashion and other information (Figure 6.9).

Apparently, too, similar terms were applied to different items so the precise meanings of clothing names are still in doubt. Dating written material can also be a problem, because some authors borrowed liberally from original works written as much as a century and a half earlier (Scott, 1986).

FASHION CHANGE BECOMES EVIDENT

Many costume historians pinpoint the 14th century as the point at which fashion change begins. Although one can see instances in the Early Middle Ages when the affluent appear to be following fashion, by the close of the 15th century it is obvious that periodic changes in the predominant style are taking place and that those who can afford to do so are dressing according to the current mode. Details, noted Piponnier and Mane (1997), were in "a constant state of change, while big modifications of the silhouette took place only about every fifty years" (65).

COSTUME: 14TH CENTURY

For the first 40 years of the 14th century, styles for men continued to be much the same as those of the previous century. These were the chemise (see Figure 6.21, page

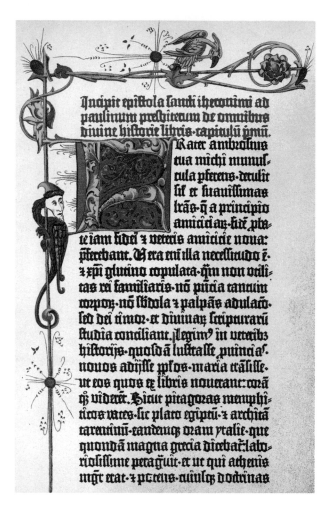

FIGURE 6.9 A page from the Gutenberg Bible. (© Ann Ronan Picture Library/HIP/Art Resource, NY)

166) and braies as undergarments and the cote (under tunic) worn with a surcote (outer tunic). Around 1340, styles for men changed markedly. Short skirts, always a part of peasant dress, returned to fashion for men of all classes. A number of new garments (pourpoints, cote-hardies, houppelandes) came into use, along with modifications of earlier forms.

Costume Components for Men

Garments

The **pourpoint** (*pour-pwant'*) was also called a **doublet** (*dub'-let*) or **gipon** (*jhi-pahn'*). This closely fitted, sleeveless garment with a padded front originated as military dress. After the turn of the century, ordinary soldiers wore padded garments alone as armor, as padding under armor, or over armor. Around 1340, men began wearing a sleeved version of the pourpoint for civilian dress, together with a pair of long hose.

Worn over the undershirt and cut to fit the body closely, the pourpoint closed down the front with laces or closely placed buttons. Strings with laces or ties ending in small metal tips or "points" were sewn to the underside of the pourpoint skirt. These points attached the hose to the pourpoint; thus the garment was *pour les points*, or "for the points."

The pourpoint neckline was round. Sleeves fitted the arm and fastened with buttons at the wrist (Figure 6.10). The pourpoint and other garments featured **set-in** (*sewn-in*) **sleeves**. Earlier tunics had been cut T-shaped, with sleeves as an extension of the body of the garment. To keep the underarm fullness from bunching up when worn under armor, sleeves had to be cut separately and sewn into the body of the tunic (Piponnier and Mane, 1997). These set-in sleeves made movement of the arm easier, an advantage in battle and in life. According to van Buren (2011),

FIGURE 6.10 Short doublet or pourpoint is depicted in a panel showing a detail of *The Passion of Christ* from Austria, Styria, c. 1400. The laces that close the doublet are visible on the second figure from left, who also wears parti-colored clothes. The hose of one man at the right have been undone, revealing his braies. His doublet is unbuttoned. (Diptych with the Passion of Christ, c. 1400. Austria, Styria, 15th century. Tempera and gold on wood oak; each wing: 45.7 x 27.0 cm. The Cleveland Museum of Art, Mr. and Mrs. William H. Marlatt Fund 1945.115)

because the pourpoint required less cloth than the former cote and surcote, it allowed in part for richer and more elaborate displays of expensive fabric.

Initially, pourpoints tended to be worn unbelted beneath another garment, but after about 1350 they were often the outermost garment and were belted. In the second half of the century, they become increasingly shorter, barely covering the hips. Some had sleeves extending as far as the knuckles. In English, the term *doublet* replaced the word *pourpoint* after 1400. Men who dressed conservatively continued to wear the surcote over a longer cote.

When worn over the pourpoint, the **cote-hardie** (*coat'-har'dee*) was shaped close to the body, was short in length, and was either sleeveless or had sleeves. The word *cote-hardie* illustrates the complexity of costume terminology both during the period and for modern dress historians. Evans (1969), a specialist in French medieval history, says that in France the cote-hardie was always a sleeved garment for outdoor wear that was first worn by the lower classes and later became a more elegant, often fur-trimmed or fur-lined, garment. Boucher (1987), a French costume historian, suggested that the term applied variously to the first short outer garments for men, to a gown, and to a surcote for men that was open in front and that buttoned at the sides. Cunnington and Cunnington (1952), who compiled a handbook of English medieval costume, identified the cote-hardie in England as a very specific garment that replaced the surcote for use over the pourpoint.

Cunnington and Cunnington (1952) provided quite a complete description of the English cote-hardie from the first half of the 1300s. It was fitted through the waist, where it buttoned; it then flared to a full skirt that was open at the front and, usually, knee length. The sleeves were apparently its major distinguishing feature. These ended at the elbow in front, while a short tongue or longer flap hung down in back. People commonly wore belts at hip level with the cote-hardie (Figure 6.11). Long belts had hanging ends, and short ones were made of metal plaques with an ornamental buckle. In the second half of the 14th century, buttons

FIGURE 6.11 Man on stilts wears a cote-hardie, and over his head a chaperon with a long liripipe hanging down the back. Manuscript pages were often decorated with playful figures in scenes from games or other aspects of life such as this one. (Detail: The Pierpont Morgan Library/ Art Resource, NY)

extended from neck to hem, instead of from neck to waist, and the length shortened. Hanging flaps at the elbows became longer and narrower.

The edges of garments, hanging sleeve flaps, and even hats were often cut into pointed or squared scallops called **dagging**. Dagging might even resemble foliage such as oak leaves. Materials for dagging included silk, fur, contrasting fabrics, and even leather trim (Figure 6.12). Moralist writers of the period, such as William Langland in *Piers Plowman* around 1378 associated dagging with frivolity when he spoke of those who "loved worldliness and ordered dagged clothes" (as cited in Friedman, 2013, 125).

French royal inventories first mentioned the houppelande (**hoop'land**) in 1359. This garment seems to have come to England slightly later. Apparently originating as a man's housecoat worn over the pourpoint, it was fitted over the shoulder before it widened below into deep, tubular folds or pleats, which were held in place by a belt (see Figure 6.12). The houppelande was constructed from four long

FIGURE 6.12 Solomon teaching a princely audience. Various forms of the houppelande, from the *houppelande à mi-jambe* (mid-calf) on the far left, versions with dagged sleeves in the middle, and enormous poke sleeves on the man in white. The man on the far right wears what appears to be a fur-lined huke. (The Pierpont Morgan Library/Art Resource, NY)

color. When the houppelande first appeared, sleeves were funnel shaped, with the upper edge ending at the wrist and the lower edge extending, in the most extreme versions, as far as the ground. Sleeve edges might also be finished in dagging or lined in contrasting color.

For outdoors people continued to wear the garnache, herigaut, and varied capes and cloaks. Several new forms appeared, including the **houce** or **housse** (*oose*). French accounts describe the houce as a wide-skirted overcoat with winged cape sleeves and two, flat, tongue-shaped lapels at the neck. It appears to be a French variation of the garnache, which also had tongue-shaped tabs (Figure 6.13). Another new form was the **corset** or round cape, which either buttoned on the right shoulder and left the right arm free, or closed at the center with a chain or ribbon. Round capes ranged from full length to mid-thigh. Some capes buttoned down the front. After mid-century, many short, shoulder-length capes were finished at the edge with dagging.

pieces sewn together at the sides, center front, and center back. Seams were sometimes left open at the bottom for a short distance to form vents. The style was especially suited to heavy fabrics such as velvet, satin, damasks, brocades, and wool fabrics. The houppelande is often depicted as fur trimmed.

Styles were either short, thigh length, or long (for ceremonial occasions). A mid-calf version **houppelande à mi-jambe** (*hoopland-ah-mee-zhamb*) appeared in the 1400s. Most versions had a high, standing collar that encircled the neck. Collar edges might be dagged, or the collar was lined in contrasting

FIGURE 6.13 Man at right wears a garnache, or houce, with two, flat, tongue-shaped lapels at the neck. Man at the left wears a cote-hardie with a chaperon. (Detail: The Pierpont Morgan Library/Art Resource, NY)

Hair and Headdress

Hair was cut moderately short, below the ears. Men's faces were most often clean shaven. In the first half of the century, hat styles seldom changed. Coifs and berets remained. The **chaperon** was a hooded shoulder cape with a hanging tail variously called a liripipe, cornet, or tippet (see Figure 6.11). This style and its many variations became very popular. New styles included a hat with a low, round crown and an elongated, pointed brim at the front and one with a high, domed crown and small, rolled or turned-up brim.

In the second half of the century, hat styles grew more varied and fanciful. Decorative brocades, colored hat bands, and trimmings of plumes ornamented some hats. Chaperones were transformed into turbanlike styles by varying the way they were worn. The face opening was placed around the head, the cape extended on one side and the liripipe on the other, and both of these could be draped or tied into various positions (Illustrated Table 6.1).

Footwear

Hose, either in colors that contrasted with the rest of the costume or in a different color for each leg (particolored), covered the legs (see Figure 6.10). Sometimes people wore footed hose with leather soles instead of shoes. Lower class men wore stockings that reached to the knee or just below the calf.

Shoes covered the foot entirely or were cut away, closing with a strap over the ankle. Wearing of the **poulaine** (*poo-lan'*) or **crackowe** (*crak'ow*), an elongated, exaggeratedly pointed-toed shoe, resumed toward the end of the century (Figure 6.14). The French name *poulaine* came from the word for Poland, and the English name *crackowe* came from the name of the capital city of Poland, Krakow. The passage quoted on page 134 in Chapter 5 describes its use in the 12th century. Although the toes of all shoes of this period were pointed, only nobles and the rich wore the extreme forms. As one writer put it, "The crackowe was a badge of rank; it was the characteristic of a man whose mode of life did not require him to perform physical labor" (Born, 1940, 1229). The French, English, Portuguese,

FIGURE 6.14 Leather poulaines, made 1370–1500. The toes could be stuffed with moss or wool to maintain their shape. (V&A Images, London/Art Resource, NY)

and Spaniards followed the style, but it never took hold in Italy. By 1410 poulaines were out of fashion, but the style returned later in the century.

Both fitted and loose styles of boots ranged from ankle length to calf length, or extended to the thighs for riding. Working-class men wore clogs when weather made streets muddy.

Accessories

In addition to belts such as those worn with the cote-hardie, some belts had suspended daggers or pouches for carrying valuables (Figure 6.15). Members of all classes now wore gloves, usually cuffed. More elaborate styles were embroidered.

Costume Components for Women

Garments

A woman wore multiple layers of clothing. Closest to the body was the linen undergarment, next came a fitted gown, and over that a second fitted gown was worn, usually richer in material and more decorative in design. On top of this, she layered a cloak or mantle. Similar garments took different names depending upon their place of origin. Changes in the first half of the 1300s were mostly confined to alterations of fit as the garments conformed closely to the body through the torso and flared out to a full skirt below (see Figure 6.15). The outer tunics or surcotes were made with or without sleeves.

By the second half of the century, women revealed their shoulders and necklines. A traditional form of

Illustrated Table 6.1

Late Middle Ages Accessories

Brooches, 15th century

Man's belt,
late 14th or early 15th century

Necklace, c. 1483

Purse, c. 1340

Purse, 15th century

Poulaine, or crakowes, 15th
century

Wooden clog worn with poulaine
to keep feet dry

Man's hat made
from draped hood,
14th century

Man's hat,
first half of 15th century

Sugarloaf hat,
second half of 15th century

Fillet worn over
coiled braids

FIGURE 6.15 The Butler Family at Mass, an English miniature, c. 1340, shows husband and wife in typically tight-fitting garments of this period with fur trimming. The man's belt holds a dagger. The prelate celebrating Mass wears religious dress of the period. (Photo Acquired by Henry Walters)

dress for French royal women had evolved. From this point on to the end of the Middle Ages this garment in painting or sculpture marked the wearer as a French queen or princess. Its major features were:

- **Gown**, fitting smoothly through the body with tight-fitting, long sleeves;
- **Surcote** (sideless), with a low décolletage (neckline), giving the appearance of straps across the shoulders, and a stiffened panel with a rounded lower edge— in French, the **plastron**, or *placard*—extended to the

hip where it joined a wide band encircling the hips to which the skirt was attached;
- **Skirt**, so long and so full that it had to be lifted when walking; and
- A vertical line of decorative brooches, referred to as **benzants** (jewel-like ornaments stamped from gold) placed on the front of the placard (Figure 6.16).

Sleeve styles on women's gowns changed throughout the century. In the early 1300s, sleeves of the outer tunics revealed the narrower, longer, under tunic sleeve. Around 1300, artists recorded slightly widened outer tunic sleeves that ended in a small point. Over time, these points grew longer, eventually forming **tippets**, or long, narrow sleeve extensions, often depicted in the white and gray patterning of miniver, a type of squirrel fur (Netherton, 2005).

Women also wore the houppelande and cotehardie. Adopted by women only after 1387, women's houppelandes reached their fullest development in the 1400s. These were often closed up to the neck, quite long, and belted beneath the bust. The English and Italian versions of the cote-hardie for women had a low, round neckline and sleeves ending at the elbow with a dangling lappet or sleeves with different colored linings (Figure 6.17).

Capes, cloaks, and the herigaut provided warmth. Fur linings were common for winter, although sumptuary laws attempted to regulate the type of fur that could be used for lining or trimming according to social status. For example, ermine and a fur resembling ermine, called **lettice**, were reserved for women of nobility, while the lower classes were allowed to use the fur of foxes, otters, and **conys** (small burrowing rodents). Royal women wore ceremonial mantles for state occasions, which were often either open or clasped across the front.

Hair and Headdress

Hairstyles and head coverings were initially wide rather than high. It was unusual for women's hair to be uncovered, as it was often hidden under a veil or held inside hair nets. If visible, hair was plaited, and either coiled around the ears (first half of the century)

FIGURE 6.16 Queen Isabelle of England at the center of a manuscript illumination of 1388 wears traditional dress of queens: a sideless surcote over a closely fitted cote. The bodice has a plastron, or placard, decorated with a vertical row of decorative brooches or benzants. To the left, King Richard II receives a copy of a manuscript of poet Froissart's chronicles from its author. King Charles VI of France, brother of Isabelle, greets her and Prince Edward, whom she holds by the hand. The child is dressed like an adult. The figure behind Queen Isabelle wears a long houppelande with extremely long sleeves. Other men in the illustration wear a variety of doublets and robes. (Detail: The Pierpont Morgan Library/Art Resource, NY)

or arranged parallel to the vertical direction of the face (see Figures 6.15 and 6.16).

The barbette with the fillet worn during the first part of the century gradually went out of use. The wimple continued in use somewhat longer, but by the end of the century only widows and members of religious orders wore it. A narrower fillet was worn over a net or, as nets were called, a **fret**.

Veils, often held in place by a fillet or chaplet, were not so closely wrapped as in earlier periods. One veil style featured a pleated section of the veil close to the face, which formed a frame for the top and both sides of the face. Fillets of metal, for royal ladies, in the form

FIGURE 6.17 Illuminated manuscript from c. 1400, Paris, of Solomon receiving the Queen of Sheba. The woman in green wears a sumptuous houppelande with ermine-lined sleeves; her attendants wear cote-hardies trimmed with lined sleeves. (© BnF, Dist. RMN-Grand Palais/Art Resource, NY)

of a small crown or coronet (see Figure 6.17), were important accessories with all kinds of veils. A French queen of 1372 owned 60 such chaplets according to her inventory. For travel and outdoor activity, women wore brimmed hats or hoods similar to men's.

Footwear

Stockings ended at the knee and were tied in place. Although women's shoes resembled men's, the toes of women's shoes were never elongated to the same extent and were mostly hidden underneath the long dresses.

Jewelry and Accessories

Specific types of jewelry included necklaces, bracelets, earrings, rings, decorative brooches, jeweled belts, buttons, and clasps for mantles (see Illustrated Table 6.1). Wealthy women also wore gloves.

Cosmetics and Grooming

Late in the 1300s it became fashionable to have a broad-looking, high forehead, achieved by plucking the hair growing around the face on the forehead as well as the eyebrows. Although not a common practice, some dyed their hair, especially to a blonde shade, and "face painting" was occasionally reported. Mouthwashes from mint and myrrh were used to treat bad breath and even gum disorders (Pointer, 2005). In the Contemporary Comments 6.2., an Italian writer, Sacchetti, complains about 14th-century fashions.

COSTUME: 15TH CENTURY

The styles of the 1400s described in the following section represent northern Europe, especially France and England. Italian styles of the 15th century are

Contemporary Comments 6.2

14TH-CENTURY FASHIONS

Fashions at the close of the 14th century are described by Sacchetti, an Italian writer.

And what more wretched, dangerous, and useless fashion ever existed than that of wearing such sleeves as they do, or great sacks as they might rather be called? They cannot raise a glass or take a mouthful without soiling both their sleeves, and the tablecloth by upsetting the glasses on the table. Likewise do many youths wear these immense sleeves, but still worse is it when even sucklings [infants] are dressed in them. The women wear hoods and cloaks. The young men for the most part go without cloaks and wear their hair long; they need but divest themselves of their breeches and they will then have left off everything they can, and truly these are so small that they could easily do without them. They put their legs into tight socks and upon their wrists they hang a yard of cloth; they put more cloth into the making of a glove than into a hood. . . . The Lord created our feet free, yet many persons are unable to walk on account of the long points of their shoes. He created legs with joints, but many have so stiffened them with strings and laces that they can scarcely sit down; their bodies are drawn in tightly, their arms are burdened with a train of cloth, their necks are squeezed into their hoods and their heads into a sort of nightcap, whereby all day they feel as though their heads were being sawn off. Truly there would be no end to describing the women's attire, considering the extravagance of their dress from their feet up to their heads, and how every day they are up on the roofs, some curling their hair, some smoothing it, and some bleaching it, so that often they die of the colds they catch!

Ross, J. B., & McLaughlin, M. M. (1977). *The portable medieval reader.* New York, NY: Penguin Books, pp. 168–169.

examined in Chapter 7, which deals with the Italian Renaissance that slowly spread northward.

Styles varied between France and England. These differences have been attributed not only to fewer rich fabrics in England but also to differences in social organization in these two countries. The French court and the nearby court of Burgundy provided a stage for the display of costume that was not equaled in England. Evans (1969) pointed out that England maintained a lower standard of luxury because the life of its upper classes was based on the castles of the countryside rather than the courts at Windsor or Westminster. English fashions were less impressive and changed less quickly.

Costume Components for Men

Garments

After the first decade of the century, the pourpoint, known in the 15th century as the doublet, was placed over the under shirt and beneath the jacket. It was short, barely reaching to the thighs and in some cases extending only a little below the waist. Often the sleeves and collars of doublets were the only sections visible. In such cases, these sections were made with decorative fabrics, while plain, less expensive fabrics were used for the invisible body of the garment. Detachable sleeves appeared at the close of the 15th century.

The hose, covering the lower part of the body, were exposed for almost their whole length. They were constructed in a new form, comparable to modern tights. Into the crotch of this garment, a pouch of fabric, called a **codpiece**, was sewn to accommodate the genitals. It tied shut with laces. Hose were laced to doublets by means of a series of small eyelets around the lower edge of the doublet and the upper edges of the hose. Points—laces made of leather with plain or decorated metal tips—connected the eyelets.

For the first two thirds of the 15th century, the houppelande continued to be an important garment for men. After mid-century it was called a gown, or robe, in England. The term appears often in the reign of Charles VII, who died in 1461, but does not appear in royal accounts after 1470 in France.

Houppelandes were fitted across the shoulders, and then from that point they were full. From 1410 to 1440, fullness was arranged all around the body with an equal number of pleats (often two) spaced at the front, back, and each side. After 1440, fullness was concentrated at front and back; garments were smooth at the sides. Although the houppelande closed down the front, the fastenings were generally not visible. The houppelandes in Figure 6.12 (page 157) represent a change from longer garments toward the shorter, mid-thigh variety (*houppelande à mi-jambe*; Figure 6.18).

Sleeve styles were either open at the end or closed at the cuff. Open styles included wide funnel-shaped

FIGURE 6.18 Men and women in a tapestry dated 1435–1440. Men's short versions of the houppelande show a variety of sleeve constructions including those with slits through which the arm could be placed, leaving the sleeve hanging behind. Women's gowns have V-shaped revers. Elaborately patterned fabrics are used for both men's and women's styles. (Image copyright © The Metropolitan Museum of Art. Image source: Art Resource, NY)

sleeves (stylish until c. 1450) and plain cylindrical sleeves, often lined in contrasting colored fabric and turned back at the wrist. Closed styles included "bagpipe" shapes (exceedingly popular after 1410) that widened from the shoulder to form a full, hanging pouch below a tight cuff. After 1445, small pleats gave increased height to sleeve caps. Sleeves narrowed somewhat, tapering to the wrist, and hanging sleeves featured either wide or tight-fitting wrists. The wearer placed his arm through an opening above the elbow. The rest of the sleeve then hung down behind the arm. Houppelandes worn in winter had fur linings. Decorations ranged from dagging to embroidery. Often the garments were constructed from colorful, woven, patterned fabrics.

During the early part of the 15th century, the cote-hardie was gradually replaced by the shorter houppelande or by an alternative style called a **jacket** (Figure 6.19). For the first part of the century in England the terms *jacket* and *cote-hardie* were used interchangeably; after 1450 the term *cote-hardie* was no longer used. In France, the term *pourpoint* was still applied to what the English called the jacket.

The 15th-century jacket was somewhat similar in function (though not in cut) to the modern suit jacket, although a man wore it with hose rather than trousers. Except for a cape or cloak, it was the outermost garment worn on the upper part of the body. The most popular lengths barely covered the hips. In other versions, skirts reached mid-thigh. Whereas short houppelandes went out of fashion, jackets continued to be important garments.

Jackets had vertical pleats at front and back, and shoulders were built up over pads to produce a broad, full sleeve cap. Usually collarless, the jacket typically had a rounded neck shaping to a shallow V shape at front and back, or it was cut with a deep V to the waist held together with lacings.

FIGURE 6.19 Men of all classes are depicted in this scene from a French manuscript of 1480. Fighting men at lower left seem to be wearing padded jackets. Criminals are executed in their chemises or undergarments. Fashionable gentlemen looking on wear robes and jackets cut in many styles. (Detail: The Pierpont Morgan Library/Art Resource, NY)

Jacket sleeve styles were numerous. Among the various sleeve types were those with shoulders that narrowed gradually to the wrists, full sleeves gathered to attach to small wrist bands, tube shapes with wide turned-back cuffs, and hanging sleeves. Toward the end of the century, the undersleeves of the doublet or shirt were visible through slashes in parts of the sleeves (see Figure 6.19).

Although similar in appearance to the short houppelande, the jacket was constructed differently. Jackets had a seam at the waist to join the top and the skirt sections, a feature that houppelandes lacked, and the jacket skirt flared out sharply from the hip.

Cloaks or full capes with hoods were the chief outdoor garment for working men. Upper class men favored the **huke** (*huque* in French). Like the cote and surcote, the huke originated as a covering for armor. It was shaped much like a tabard, as it closed over the shoulders and was open at the sides. In short versions, it had a slit at the front for ease when riding. Worn unbelted, belted, or with the belt passed across the front while the back hung free, hukes were more fashionable in the first half of the century than the second (Figure 6.20). Shoulder capes and a variety of other short capes that were about the same length as the jacket were also part of men's dress for outdoors.

Hair and Headdress

Hair was worn in a style frequently described by costume historians as the **bowl crop**, because it gives the appearance of an inverted bowl around the top of the head. Below the cut hair the neck was shaved. After mid-century, the shortness of the cut was modified somewhat, to be replaced after 1465 by longer styles, similar to what would now be called a **pageboy** cut. Faces were generally clean shaven.

The coif gradually disappeared except in the dress of clergy and in professions such as medicine. Caped hoods went out of style except for country folk, although the chaperone and liripipe inspired a number of the hats. The **sugar loaf** hat, named for its resemblance to the way sugar was produced and sold, was usually worn centered on top of the head (see

FIGURE 6.20 Jan Van Eyck's portrait of the Italian Arnolfini and his Flemish bride demonstrates Burgundian–Flemish fashions. Arnolfini wears a fur-lined huke with panels hanging front and back. Pattens lie on the floor in the far left of the painting. (© National Gallery, London/Art Resource, NY)

Figure 6.26 on page 170). Hats were made of fabric, straw, and fur.

Footwear

Most men preferred to cover their legs with hose. Joined hose predominated, although separate hose continued in use. Joined hose made with leather soles were worn both indoors and out. Often dyed to bright colors, many were parti-colored (see Figure 6.10, page 155).

Paintings may show hose as fitting the leg quite closely, but this depiction may have been an artistic convention, because hose of this period were made of woven cloth, usually wool, cut on the bias for greater stretch. They were seamed together up the back. Knitted hose did not take the place of woven-cloth stockings until the 16th century. Knitted stockings are listed in the records of the English city of Nottingham as early as 1519, and the oldest guild of stocking knitters was not founded until 1527 in Paris ("The Knitted Stocking," 1954). Lower class men wore knee or mid-calf length stockings.

Foot coverings were pointed, some with exaggerated or piked toes, and the length waxed and waned over the century. For the first ten years, while pointed in shape, they were relatively short; after mid-century, piked poulaines were revived, persisting in use until about 1480 when shoe forms became more rounded. Very long points were stuffed and stiffened; some were even rolled up. As in the 14th century, the extremes of this style were limited to the affluent. Shoes laced or buckled at the side to fit the foot closely.

Pattens were raised wooden platforms (or sometimes leather for the upper classes) that fastened over the shoe with a strap for protection during bad weather (see Illustrated Table 6.1).

For general wear, boots fit closely, ended at the calf, and closed with laces or buckles. Long, thigh-length boots with a turned-down cuff at the top, worn for riding in the first half of the century, became fashionable for general pedestrian wear in the second half.

Accessories

Accessories included jeweled collars, daggers, pouches or purses (see Illustrated Table 6.1), gloves, and decorative belts. In the first half of the 1400s, a man's belt was one of his most important possessions, and to deprive a man of his belt was a symbol of humiliation. In the second half of the century belts, became a less essential part of the costume. Manners books instructed men on proper grooming and behavior.

Costume Components for Women

Terminology becomes somewhat confusing as styles became more varied and the same garments were called different names in different countries. As

FIGURE 6.21 A rare depiction of woman and man clad in chemises survives in this detail from a tapestry of the third quarter of the 15th century. Woman's chemise is embroidered at the neck and armscye. Man's garment has embroidery at the armscye. (Detail: Image copyright © The Metropolitan Museum of Art. Image source: Art Resource, NY)

before, women tended to wear linen undergarments and one or two layers of outer garments.

Garments

The undermost garment for women was called a smock or a shift in English, *chemise* in French (Figure 6.21). In the Lengberg Castle, East Tyrol, Austria, researchers from the University of Innsbruck ("Medieval Lingerie Discovered," 2012) discovered four linen textiles that resembled the modern brassiere. According to the researchers, medieval written sources sometimes mention "bags for the breasts" or "shirts with bags." Radiocarbon dating suggests these garments date to the 15th century.

Women's houppelandes were always long and belted slightly above the anatomical waistline. They had soft, natural shoulder lines but otherwise were similar in cut to those of men. Collar styles on these garments included high-standing collars, usually open at the front to form a sort of winged effect (Figure 6.22), or flat, turned-down collars around a round or V-shaped neckline. Sleeve variations consisted of huge funnel shapes, lined in contrasting colors or fur, and reaching to the ground; bagpipe sleeves; plain tubular sleeves turned back at the end to show contrasting cuffs; or hanging sleeves, usually tubular in shape.

The English used the term *gown* when referring to women's dresses; the French called this garment a *cote* or *cotte*. In one style variation, two gowns were worn, one over the other. Gowns were worn with sideless surcotes. In England, where styles generally were less revealing than in France, women wore cote-hardies with hanging tippets or long, narrow fabric extensions. Upper class women in France appeared in gowns cut with low necks; closely fitted bodices that emphasized the protruding stomach, breasts, sloping shoulders; and full, long skirts (Figure 6.23). The pregnant look,

FIGURE 6.22 A houppelande of the 15th century seen from front and back. The pleating of the gown, the open hanging sleeves, and the broad belt are clearly seen in this tomb effigy in the French cathedral in Bourges, France. (Photographs by Vincent R. Tortora)

FIGURE 6.23 In this engagement scene, the bride wears the low-necked, closely fitted styles common in the period. The woman kneeling wears a cote-hardie with tippets of white fur trailing from short sleeves. Behind the bride and at far right, women wear more conservative forms of the houppelande. (© RMN-Grand Palais/Art Resource, NY)

FIGURE 6.24 The woman's gown style of about 1449 shows subtle variations in cut and fit when contrasted with styles of the second half of the century in Figure 6.25. The later styles have closely fitted sleeves and less fullness in the skirt. The clothing of the jeweler in its simplicity of cut and lack of ornamentation contrasts with the customer's more stylish, fur-trimmed jacket. (Image copyright © The Metropolitan Museum of Art. Image source: Art Resource, NY)

emphasized by posture and the holding of excess fabric to the belly, was common. Sleeves on dresses might be close fitting from shoulder to wrist; otherwise hanging sleeves were wide, full, and funnel shaped.

Gown styles evolved in the second half of the century. A soft, gathered fullness replaced rigid, tube-shaped pleats, which disappeared from women's dresses. The bodice developed a deep V, sometimes reaching all the way to the waist, and sometimes not so far. The edges of the V were turned back into **revers** (lapels that turned back to show the underside). The revers were generally lined in a contrasting color or in fur. The skirt was long and trained, usually so long that a woman had to lift it up in front to avoid treading on it as she walked. Often the skirt was bordered in the fabric of which the revers were made. The deepness of the V generally required that a modesty piece or filler be placed across the bodice. A wide, stiff belt encircled the waist.

In the earliest of these styles, the cut of the bodice was soft with fullness caught in by the belt (Figure 6.24). As the style evolved, the cut became more tailored and the bodice fitted the body more closely (Figure 6.25). When the V-shaped revers were set further out on the shoulders, women wore a transparent linen fabric piece pinned to the garment at the neckline, shoulders, and back to secure it in place. If one looks very closely at some of the Flemish portraits of the period, one can see that artists often gave a hint of this fabric and sometimes depicted the pins at the front of the bodices.

The **roc** was a loose-fitting gown. This style appears infrequently, seemingly most often in Flemish and German paintings. The bodice was cut with a round neckline that had a cascade of gathers, or pleats, at the very center of the front and back. Unbelted and made in soft fabric, the dress fell loose and unfitted to the ground. Sleeves were long and fitted, or short. When sleeves were short, the gown was worn over a long-sleeved under dress. Although this gown appears fairly frequently in northern European paintings, few

FIGURE 6.25 Women dressed in a variety of styles from the second half of the 15th century, including the full gown, the roc, that appears often in Flemish or German painting. Two of the figures have raised the skirts of their gowns so that the underdress in a contrasting fabric is visible. (Detail: The Pierpont Morgan Library/Art Resource, NY)

costume historians discuss it. Even the name, roc, may be another form of the general term **frock**.

Hooded cloaks were worn for bad weather. Open mantles, often worn over matching gowns and fastened with chains at the front, remained unchanged.

Hair and Headdress

Unmarried girls, brides, and queens at their coronations could bare their heads and show their hair. All other respectable adult women placed some covering over the head. High, smooth foreheads, achieved through plucking out the hair, remained popular; therefore, little or no hair was visible around the edges of the fanciful headdresses that became fashionable. When hair is visible in paintings, blond and red-haired women predominate.

For the first half of the century, headdresses were wide. Various structural forms were placed on the head including **cauls**, which were caplike netting that covered the head and extended at sides to cover and support two coils of hair at each side of the face. Either internally or externally supported, headdresses were often padded and could resemble double horns. Veils were often draped over the entire structure.

In the second half of the century, the headdress grew taller and more fanciful. Its size and shape ranged from a flat-topped, high-crowned, brimless hat that was four or five inches high to what came to be known as the hennin, which was an enormous cone-shaped, peaked hat that was as much as a yard high (Figure 6.26). This latter style was limited in use to France and Burgundy. Veils, ideally sheer

FIGURE 6.26 This fragment of an illuminated manuscript depicts headdress of men and women of the second half of the 15th century. Woman at center wears a tall, pointed hennin, woman at far right wears a bourrelet. Man at center of bottom row of figures wears a sugar loaf hat. (Detail: Snark/Art Resource, NY)

and gossamerlike, were pinned and draped over the headdresses.

Illustrated Table 6.2 depicts the various types of headdress and suggests the way in which headdresses may have evolved in the 15th century.

Footwear

Stockings ended at the knee and tied around the leg. Shoes fit the foot closely. Although toes were pointed and somewhat elongated, shoes for women never adopted the exaggeratedly piked cut characteristic of some men's shoes. In bad weather women wore wooden pattens (see Figure 6.20).

Accessories

Accessories consisted of jewelry, gloves, pouches or purses, and girdles (belts). With lower necklines, necklaces became more important (see Figures 6.4 and 6.24 and Illustrated Table 6.1).

COSTUME FOR CHILDREN: 14TH AND 15TH CENTURIES

What evidence is available shows that throughout the Middle Ages, children, except during infancy, were dressed in the same fashions as adults. The infant was swaddled, wrapped in bands of linen from head to foot. People believed that swaddling prevented deformity when the child grew older.

During the first four or five years, both boys and girls dressed in loose gowns. Those of royal children were of rich fabrics, elaborately trimmed. When children were old enough to leave the nursery and take part in the work or other activities of the family, they were dressed as miniature adults (see Figure 6.16).

Boys' tunics were generally somewhat shorter than those of adult men, except of course in periods when the male jacket became extremely short. Girls always wore long gowns.

Illustrated Table 6.2

Evolution and Styles of 15th-Century Headdress for Women

Caul: caplike netting covering head, extending at sides to cover and support two coils of hair at each side of face

Caul plus external supporter plus veil

Caul plus intricate treatment of veil

Caul with or without an internal supporter plus three pieces of veil

Internally supported caul plus bourrelet

Bourrelet: padded, crownlike roll worn on top of the head

Cone-shaped headdress

Internally supported bourrelet

Derived from information in Song, C. A., & Sibley, L. R. (1990). The vertical headdress of fifteenth century northern Europe. *Dress, The Journal of the Costume Society of America*, Vol. 16, 4–15.

The major difference in the dress of girls and women was in the hairdressing. Young girls went about with their hair uncovered until they married.

DRESS FOR RITES OF PASSAGE

Many societies assign particular kinds of dress for the important rites of passage. In western societies these rites are often associated with religious ceremonies, such as baptism, marriage, and funerals. The baptism of infants was the first rite most Christian children underwent. It appears from inventories that a special linen baptismal veil was used, though its precise nature is not clear. In the later centuries of the medieval period, the wealthy and high born were likely to wrap the newborn in fur-trimmed mantles. Piponnier and Mane (1997) noted that there was no special clothing associated with marriage; jewelry was more important, especially belts, rings, and brooches. In some regions red seems to have been a popular color for brides (see the bride in Figure 6.4, a depiction of a wedding banquet).

Special costume practices during mourning were not well established until the close of the 15th century, when the etiquette of mourning became more fixed and elaborate. By the mid-1300s, black (or what was referred to at the time as brunette or dark brown cloth) had become recognized in northern Europe as a symbol for grief. Previously a dark drab-colored garment worn with an enveloping dark hood placed over ordinary-colored clothing had been all that was required. The mourner did not have to give up color for a long period of time. A mother of the 1300s is cited as wearing black on the death of her son in the fall, but by the following spring she was dressing in colors again.

The dress of widows, however, was more fixed by tradition. After secular women gave up the wimple in the 1400s, it was traditional for widows to wear this veil. Bereaved wives also avoided bright hues, often wearing such shades as violet and gray for the rest of their lives.

It was not considered fitting for men to wear the short pourpoint or jacket during mourning. Robes had to be long and black. In France, members of both sexes wore the long, hooded cloak for mourning. Servants of great men were issued these black garments on the deaths of their masters.

COSTUME FOR SPECIALIZED OCCUPATIONS

Student Dress

Toward the close of the Middle Ages, certain items of dress that had once been part of fashionable dress became traditional for particular professions or categories of persons. During the 1400s students retained the cote and surcote after it had been abandoned for general wear. A variant of this long robe has been passed down over the intervening years and is still part of official academic dress, worn by students and faculty at graduation ceremonies.

Military Dress

During the 14th and 15th centuries, armor made from large, rigid plates gradually replaced the chain-mail armor characteristic of earlier medieval periods. The first step in this direction came with the development of solid metal defenses for the legs, elbows, and knees. By the third decade of the 14th century, soldiers had universally adopted these. Subsequently, solid armor for the trunk developed. This was first a cloth or leather garment lined with metal plates, called a **coat of plates**.

About 1350 when a knight put on his armor, he would first don a closely fitted shirt, braies, and hose. His arms and legs would be covered with metal protectors. Then he added a padded undercoat, called a **gambeson** (*gam'bee-sun*), and over this his hauberk (or the shorter coat of mail called the **haubergeon** (*ho'bear-zhun*). Next came a coat of plates, and over all went a surcote, often belted, and a sword belt. When going into action, he added his helmet, and a pair of metal gloves or gauntlets.

The coat of plates, actually a plate-lined, closely fitted surcote, opened in front and fastened with buckles. As Nickel (1991) noted,

> Before the development of plate armor, knights charged with their left (shield) side turned toward their enemies. Even after shields were abandoned, this practice continued; and impacts of lance and sword were expected to hit primarily on the knight's left side. To let these blows slide off, the left plate of the pair had to overlap the right. (15)

He concluded that the practice of buckling men's jackets left over right likely originated in the construction of this garment.

By 1400 the shape of the helmet had become more rounded. It still covered the entire face, but usually had a hinged visor: a face-guard that could be opened. Craftsmen skilled in making armor varied this construction and the shape of helmets according to their individual techniques. Local differences are also evident in sizes, shapes, and construction of all parts of the suit of armor (Figure 6.27).

The breast plate and back plate were constructed to protect these areas, and it was a logical step from this point to the complete suit of armor that could be constructed to protect all areas of the body. The armor was worn over a haubergeon until the second half of the 1400s, when the coat of mail was replaced by an arming coat, a padded coat made with mail in those areas not protected by the armor.

Until about 1420 a padded jacket, often sleeveless, was worn over the armor, but after this date "white" armor, or highly polished metal armor, was rarely covered except by a tabard or huke that served to identify the wearer by its colors or decoration.

The forms of armor that developed were many and were varied in their specific construction. For persons interested in further exploration of this topic several books about armor are available.

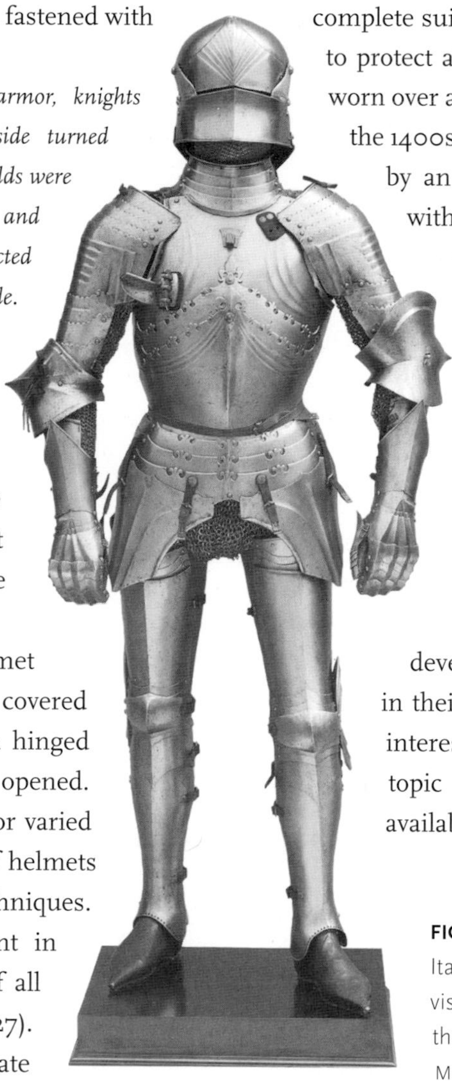

FIGURE 6.27 Complete suit of armor, Italian, 15th century. Mail protection is visible at those areas not covered by the plate armor. (Image copyright © The Metropolitan Museum of Art. Image source: Art Resource, NY)

Summary

Visual Summary

The accompanying Visual Summary shows the major style changes of the late medieval period. It is convenient to organize information so that it fits neatly into periods such as centuries or decades. Unfortunately, changes in the predominant styles in historic costume and the arts do not always fit into such convenient packages. Nor do stylistic changes come about with the same frequency in all periods. In order to help to clarify the changes of styles that come with increasing rapidity in subsequent chapters, going forward the visual summary tables at the end of each chapter will contain illustrations of the most typical garments of the period, together with a brief description of the major elements of styles and their duration.

Visual Summary Table

Garments from the Later Middle Ages

c. 1300–c. 1340
Man: cote and surcote, long except for military men.
Woman: long cote and surcote. Distinctions between men's and women's dress are minimal.

c. 1340–1400
Man: short, closely fitting garments (pourpoints, doublets), worn with hose. Long garments, such as the houppelande, still used for some occasions.
Woman: Long gowns, closely fitted to the body. Distinctions between men's and women's dress are pronounced.

c. 1340–1400
Women: Sideless surcotes over fitted gowns. Men: Cote-hardie an important garment for working men.

c. 1400–c. 1450
Man: short upper body garments (doublets; jackets) worn with hose. These continue to grow shorter, some ending at the waist.

c. 1400–1450
Houppelande made in full, mid-calf, and short lengths. Women now adopt houppelande. Cote-hardie no longer in fashion.

c. 1400–1500
Woman: Fitted gowns. Distinctions between men's and women's dress is clear. Specific details of styles keep changing.

c. 1450–1500
Women: V-neck gowns predominate, but fit becomes less full, bodice has closer fit. Wide belt. Overall styles do not change so much, but details of fit and cut change.

c. 1450–1500
Men: jacket, worn with hose, develops distinctive large shoulder. Long robes also have broad shoulders.

Themes

New costume forms for both men and women, and more distinctions between dress for men and dress for women highlight the theme of GENDER DIFFERENCES in clothing. At the beginning of the 14th century both men and women wore cotes and surcotes that, though different in fit, were not especially different in their basic construction. By the second half of the century men had adopted short styles: the pourpoint and hose. These styles came to men from military dress, an example of the theme of POLITICAL CONFLICT. When contrasted with women's long, flowing gowns, men's dress served to dramatize SOCIAL ROLE differences between the active life of men and the more passive lives of women. Many historians have pointed out that women of the Late Middle Ages had lost many of the economic and social privileges they had in the Early Middle Ages. Herlihy (1978) suggested that the loss of privileges was because the life expectancy of women increased in the 14th and 15th centuries. In the earlier periods, because many women died young, the value to society of a young woman of childbearing age was much greater.

An important theme of the Late Middle Ages was FASHION, as the 14th and 15th centuries were marked by increasingly rapid changes in styles. The increased emphasis on fashionable dress was seen in the accession to popularity for men of first the cote and surcote, then the cote-hardie or pourpoint, followed by the long and short houppelande, and finally giving way to the jacket (see Modern Influences). For women, comparable changes in fashion were demonstrated by the popularity of the gown and sideless surcote, the cote-hardie or fitted gown, the houppelande, and finally the high-belted fitted gown of the second half of the 1400s, together with a multitude of changes in headdress styles.

ECONOMIC CHANGES of the Late Middle Ages were in large part responsible for an increased interest in fashionable dress. Greater prosperity had brought fashionable clothing within the reach of an enlarging middle class, especially the merchant class. SOCIAL CLASS themes appear as the nobility, wanting to set themselves apart from the newly rich and lower classes, passed sumptuary laws to restrict luxurious dress, but historians tell us that these laws were generally ignored. Increased trade was one of the reasons for the greater prosperity of the period. Trade, with its concomitant CROSS-CULTURAL INFLUENCES, also brought a wide variety of fabrics from all over the world to the population centers of western Europe. The availability of these fabrics made possible the construction of colorful and elaborate garments characteristic of upper class dress of this period.

Ottoman influences continued to appear. Europeans traveled to the Ottoman Empire and Ottoman diplomats traveled to Europe, so the two regions experienced frequent contact. Jirousek (1995) pointed out the growing fashion for turbanlike headdress in Europe that began as another way

MODERN INFLUENCES

The fall/winter 2014 Tory Burch women's dress shows more similarity to men's than women's dress of the Late Middle Ages. With center-front buttons, mid-thigh length, scalloped sleeve hems, and a golden belt, this dress is reminiscent of men's cote-hardies of the late 14th century. The heraldic-inspired horse motif is also evocative of the medieval period.
(Giannoni/WWD/© Conde Nast)

of wearing the chaperon hood. In the Late Middle Ages parallels were seen between women's hornlike headdresses—including hennins of various heights—and Ottoman headgear.

Changes in textile manufacturing, an aspect of the theme of PRODUCTION AND ACQUISITION OF CLOTHING, led not only to greater prosperity for the textile trades but also to more variety in the raw materials of fashion. Tailors were gaining skill in cutting and sewing more and more sophisticated garments.

LEGACIES OF STYLES FROM THE LATE MIDDLE AGES

Revivals of earlier styles are sometimes intended to make a philosophical statement rather than to provide a precise reproduction of the earlier style. This is true of the attempt of several groups of artists of the second half of the 19th century to revive interest in medieval styles. These artists believed that craftsmanship of the medieval period was superior to that of the Victorian era. As part of their attempt to replicate what they viewed as superior design from an earlier period, they also created clothing which was very loosely based on medieval and Renaissance styles.

Fashion designers of the 20th century often turned to earlier historical periods for inspiration for their designs. One example of a late–20th-century style that can be compared to a medieval garment is tights worn as an outer garment, especially when paired with long sweaters or jackets. Hat designers of the 1940s based some designs on medieval hoods. Parti-colored designs, referred to as color blocking in the late 20th and 21st centuries, appear periodically in designers' collections.

REFERENCES

Born, W. (1940). The development of European footwear from the fall of Rome to the Renaissance. *CIBA Review, 34*, 1224–1229.

Boucher, F. (1987). *20,000 years of fashion*. London: Thames & Hudson.

Chaucer, G. (1903). *Canterbury Tales*. New York, NY: Thomas Y. Crowell & Co.

Cunnington, C. W., & P. Cunnington, P. (1952). *Handbook of medieval costume*. London: Faber and Faber.

Dufresne, L. R. (1990). A woman of excellent character: A case study of dress, reputation, and the changing costume of Christine de Pizan in the fifteenth century. *Dress, 17*, 105–119.

Evans, J. (1969). *Life in medieval France*. London: Phaidon.

Friedman, J. B. (2013). The iconography of dagged clothing and its reception by moralist writers. In R. Netherton & G. R. Owen-Crocker (Eds.), *Medieval clothing and textiles* (pp. 139–160). Woodbridge, UK: Boydell Press.

Gies, F., & Gies, J. (1994). *Cathedral, forge, and water wheel*. New York, NY: HarperCollins.

Herlihy, D. (1974). Ecological conditions and demographic change. In R. L. DeMolen (Ed.), *One thousand years: Western Europe in the Middle Ages* (pp.—3-43). Boston, MA: Houghton-Mifflin.

Herlihy, D. (1978). The natural history of medieval women. *Natural History, Mar.*, 56.

Inal, O. (2011). Women's fashions in transition: Ottoman borderlands and the Anglo–Ottoman exchange of costumes. *Journal of World History, 22*(2), 243–272.

Jirousek, C. (1995). More than oriental splendor: European and Ottoman headgear, 1380–1580. *Dress, 22*(1), 22–33.

Medieval lingerie discovered. (2012). *iPoint—University News*. Retrieved from *http://www.uibk.ac.at/ipoint/news/2012/buestenhalter-aus-dem-mittelalter.html.en*

Nicholas, D. (1974). Patterns of social mobility. In R. L. DeMolen (Ed.), *One thousand years: Western Europe in the middle ages* (pp. 45-104). Boston, MA: Houghton-Mifflin.

Nickel, H. (1991). Arms and armor from the permanent collection. *Metropolitan Museum of Art Bulletin, 49*(1).

Netherton, R. (2005). The tippet: Accessory after the fact? In R. Netherton & G. R. Owen-Crocker (Eds.), *Medieval clothing and textiles* (pp. 115–132). Woodbridge, UK: Boydell Press.

Newton, S. M. (1980). *Fashion in the age of the black prince: A study of the years 1340–1365*. Woodbridge, UK: Boydell Press.

Piponnier, F., & Mane, P. (1997). *Dress in the Middle Ages*. New Haven, CT: Yale University Press.

Pointer, S. (2005). *The artifice of beauty: A history and practical guide to perfume and cosmetics*. Charleston, SC: History Press.

Scott, M. (1986). *A visual history of costume: The fourteenth & fifteenth centuries*. London, UK: Batsford.

The knitted stocking. (1954). *CIBA Review, 106*, 3800.

Van Buren, A. H. (2011). *Illuminating fashion: Dress in the art of medieval France and the Netherlands, 1325–1515*. New York, NY: Morgan Library and Museum.

Wescher, H. (1946). Fashion and elegance at the Court of Burgundy. *CIBA Review, 51*, 1841–1848.

PART THREE

The Renaissance

Exciting cultural changes began in Italy c. mid-14th century when sculptors, painters, and writers began to identify with the ancient civilizations of Greece and Rome. These Italians believed that 1,000 years of darkness and ignorance separated the Roman era and their times. They believed that there had been a rebirth of classical arts and learning—a **Renaissance**—a term derived from the Italian word *renascere*, meaning "to be reborn." Modern historians in general do not consider that there was rebirth of the arts as such but rather that Europe underwent a chaotic change, a period of profound transition as medieval institutions crumbled and a new society and culture began to appear. The Renaissance was a time of transition from the medieval to a modern view of the world.

The Renaissance began around the middle of the 14th century in Italy and lasted until the end of the 16th century. Dates assigned to artistic and costume periods are, of necessity, arbitrary. In this book, the dates 1400–1600 are assigned to Renaissance style. Although this assignment is a useful device for separating one period from another, the intellectual and artistic trends leading to the first flowering of the Renaissance style in Italy actually appeared before 1400, during the Late Middle Ages. Not only do dress and artistic periods fail to fit into neat, clearly defined time periods, they also begin and end at different times in different parts of the world. While the rest of Europe was following a line of political, economic, and artistic development that was an extension of trends begun during the Middle Ages, a new perception of life had begun to emerge in Italy in the 15th century and from there spread to the rest of Europe.

Even during the medieval period, between c. 400 and 1300, Italy was in some ways different from the rest of Europe. Its ties with the Byzantine Empire were closer than those with northern Europe. Until the 11th century, northeastern Italy and Sicily were part of the Byzantine Empire. During the Middle Ages, urban centers in Italy remained more vigorous than those in most of northern Europe. Moreover, feudalism had relatively shallow roots in Italy because it flourished best in a more rural society. Italian feudal lords seldom exercised the independent powers of the great barons of France, England, and the Holy Roman Empire. Although Italian seaports declined to some extent during the Early Middle Ages, because of Italy's geographical position in the Mediterranean Sea, it continued to carry on overseas trade. Consequently, a more thriving economy allowed many Italians to enjoy a higher standard of living throughout the Early Middle Ages than did the men and women living in the more depressed northern lands. There, cities had declined, international trade had slowed to a trickle, and literacy was preserved only in the monasteries.

When the European economic revival began in the 11th century, Italy benefited first. By the 12th century, city-states with large seaports, such as Venice and Genoa, carried on a large volume of trade with the Middle East and with northern Europe. Crusaders bought provisions for their expeditions and sailed from Italian ports for the Middle East. In addition, improvements in ship construction allowed the Venetians and Genoese to carry more cargo and even to sail into the stormy Atlantic Ocean. The money generated by this trade enriched the merchants and rulers of these states. The Italian merchants became financiers and bankers as well as traders, chiefly in textiles.

Italy in the 12th and 13th centuries witnessed an intellectual ferment that radically altered philosophy, literature, and art in the 14th and 15th centuries. By the 15th century a fresh vitality in the arts had emerged. Medieval scholars continued to study and read Greek and Roman writings in order that they might know God. Medieval Christianity emphasized the spiritual need to prepare oneself for the next world. When Renaissance scholars turned to the writings of Greek and Roman philosophers, they focused on the humanistic aspect of classical thought, which emphasized the interests, achievements, and capabilities of human beings. From the spirituality of the Middle Ages, artists and scholars turned towards a more secular emphasis on humankind, each individual's abilities and place in the world. Even within the Roman Catholic Church, St. Francis of Assisi and his followers brought a new spirit of emphasis on human and earthly problems.

During the Middle Ages people thought of themselves as part of a social or religious group. In the Renaissance there was a strong sense of individualism, and Italians were not afraid of touting their individual talents. There was an emphasis on fully developing a person's potential whether painter, writer, scholar, or sculptor.

During the 14th and 15th centuries, the Renaissance was largely confined to Italy. The increasing growth of international trade throughout Europe and contacts between nations that came through warfare promoted the exchange of ideas. Students from northern Europe flocked to Italy to absorb the learning of the Renaissance and to carry it back to their countries. Kings and wealthy nobles brought to their lands Italian scholars and artists; many Italians were given prominent positions at northern courts and in the church. Consequently, during the 15th century the Renaissance in the arts and learning spread into northern Europe. There the Renaissance strongly influenced the emerging challenge to established religious dogma that would produce the Protestant Reformation.

The configuration of present-day Europe as a number of independent nations was gradually established during the Renaissance. During the medieval period strong nations with distinct national identities and strong hereditary monarchies such as France, England, and Spain had emerged. By the close of the Renaissance in 1600 the general outlines of European nations had begun to emerge. Germany and Italy were exceptions. In Germany the many separate states owed little allegiance to the Holy Roman Emperor. Italy also remained a set of independent city-states or territories, which were often under the domination of one or the other of the great European powers.

The styles that developed during the Renaissance in art, architecture, textiles, clothing, music, literature, and philosophy continue to influence western culture. The plays of Shakespeare and Christopher Marlowe are still performed, museums celebrate Renaissance paintings, Renaissance music is performed in concerts, and Renaissance textile designs are often reproduced in fabrics for drapery or upholstery or copied for wallpaper designs. Renaissance furniture and architectural styles have experienced revivals and will continue to do so. The term *Renaissance man* is still applied to the ideal of the cultured, learned person of many talents (Figure III.1).

Moreover, some of the discoveries and inventions of the Renaissance had a profound impact on the history of subsequent periods. In 1492 Christopher Columbus sailed west in search of India and stumbled upon the Americas instead. His discovery opened up new areas of the world for expansion and colonization by Europeans and shifted the center of European economic power away from Italy and the Mediterranean to the Atlantic. The geographic

FIGURE III.1 Made in Italy between 1560 and 1570, this box is richly decorated with embroidery and bobbin lace worked in silver-gilt thread. (V&A Images, London/Art Resource, NY)

discoveries opened up new opportunities to make fortunes. The Renaissance also saw a revolution in science, including Copernicus's theory that the earth revolved around the sun. The invention of printing from moveable type made written material more accessible, enabling more people to read and learn.

Although the Chinese, the Indians, the Greeks, the Arabs, the English, and the Germans all claim to have invented gunpowder, during the Renaissance it was used as a propellant in guns, first, and then in cannons, thus helping to end feudalism and begin a revolution in warfare.

		1300–1400	1304–1374	1400–1502	
FASHION AND TEXTILES		Middle Eastern style influences evident in fashionable women's headdresses		Renaissance portraits serve as an excellent source of information about dress	Black is recommended as appropriate for court dress by writers about proper behavior
POLITICS AND CONFLICTS				The Medici family rules Florence in war and peace	
DECORATIVE AND FINE ARTS		Giotto changes the course of painting with the introduction of human emotion into paintings		Fine arts flower under Medici patronage	
ECONOMICS AND TRADE				Venice a major port for trade with Asia	
TECHNOLOGY AND IDEAS			Life of Petrarch, Italian poet interested in the humanistic approach of the classics		Birth of Leonardo da Vinci, artist and inventor (1452)
RELIGION AND SOCIETY		Women rarely attain political power		Religious figures stress charity for the poor	

CHAPTER SEVEN

The Italian Renaissance

c. 1400–1600

1475–1493	1494–1500

Venetian women's dress differs from other Italian styles

Beginning in 1494, Northern Europeans struggle for control of large parts of Italy

Birth of Michelangelo (1475)

Columbus returns from the Americas, where precious metals for jewelry and coins are found (1493)

During the Italian Renaissance, Italian textile manufacturing skills produced elaborate silk fabrics traded throughout Europe

Italy had been the center of the Roman Empire. All around the Italians were imposing ruins, reminders of the grandeur of the Classical Period. Roman and Greek manuscripts had been copied and preserved in monasteries and churches. Interest in classical antiquity grew among the intellectual and artistic communities of the small city-states that were ruled by princes. These princes surrounded themselves with art they commissioned from leading artists such as Michelangelo and Raphael. Their courts provided a stage for the display of dress made from handsome textiles produced in the cloth industries of Italy. Renaissance art today provides an extensive record of the clothing of the Italian Renaissance.

HISTORICAL BACKGROUND

As lawyers and notaries in Italian city-states sought to justify the independence of these territories, they became interested in the writings of the Classical Period. Many early Renaissance writers, such as Petrarch, a gifted Italian poet and writer who lived from 1304 to 1374, were trained in the law. They embraced the humanistic approach of the classics, rejecting what they saw as a narrow, academic philosophy in the medieval universities. By the early years of the 15th century, a revival of interest in the classics in literature and the arts was under way (Gundersheimer, 1965).

The Political Organization in Renaissance Italy

At the time of the Renaissance, Italy was not a country but a geographic area made up of a number of small city-states, each one ruled by a powerful prince. These princes were sometimes members of ancient noble families, sometimes *condottieri* (hired military commanders who had taken over the reins of government in the states they were hired to defend), and sometimes members of wealthy merchant families who had achieved political, as well as financial, leadership.

Many of these princes were violent men, oppressive and cruel to their subjects. Others were more benevolent. Fortunately for the advancement of art, many rulers commissioned artwork as a way of displaying their wealth. They dressed lavishly in expensive clothing, and the artists who painted or sculpted their portraits depicted these garments in considerable detail.

Unlike France, Spain, and England, where people had unified under a single leader, these city-states often battled each other (Figure 7.1). This warfare resulted in the loss of large parts of Italy to other nations. From 1494 to 1549 the countryside was the scene of wars over the control of large segments of Italy by the northern powers. At the same time, the occupation of Italy by the northern countries helped to spread the Renaissance more quickly through the rest of Europe. The Northern Renaissance (the subject of Chapter 8) is generally dated from the beginning of the 16th century.

LIFE IN RENAISSANCE ITALY

The population of Renaissance Italy was divided among the aristocracy, the merchant class, artisans and artists, the town laborers, and the peasants of the countryside. Some families owned slaves from Mongolia, Turkey, or Russia. Most slaves were women who served as domestic help.

Men of aristocratic or noble families made up the ruling class in most Italian city-states. In some areas, however, merchants had gained great power and political control. These men generally sought to become more respectable by marrying into the noble families. In these families, sons inherited the family wealth. Even if she had no brothers, a girl received only a small portion of the family holdings while the bulk of the estate passed to her paternal uncle. Much of the family wealth had to be invested in equipping a marriageable daughter with a sufficiently large dowry to enable her to marry well. When a family had been blessed with too many daughters, some of them were

FIGURE 7.1 Leonardo da Vinci was not only one of the most famous artists of his day but was also hired by the rulers of Italian city-states and the King of France for his expertise in designing equipment for war. His notebooks show that he was studying the principles of flight that could be applied to manned flights. (© RMN-Grand Palais/Art Resource, NY)

packed off to convents where no dowry was required. A woman such as Caterina Sforza (c. 1463–1509), who ruled and defended the town of Forli against the her husband's assassins and later against other foes, was an exception and "existed outside of the general social framework of the Renaissance" (Gage, 1968, 179).

Even wealthy merchants were considered to be of lower status than the aristocracy in some towns, though not in Florence and Genoa where the ruling families had been merchants. Sons were educated to eventually take over their families' businesses, many of which were in some way related to the textile industry—weaving, dyeing, finishing, or trading cloth. Even bankers had first been traders in cloth.

Skilled artisans could do well and were more fortunate than unskilled laborers, who often had difficulty managing to feed and clothe themselves and their families. At the very bottom of the social scale were the peasants who farmed the land, working on a sharecropping basis with the landowner. Not only were they dependent on weather, but their lives were disrupted by the armies that constantly ravaged the countryside fighting for one city or another.

In spite of their economic difficulties, many people from lower levels of society tried to imitate the upper classes in their dress. Sumptuary laws, found in Italian cities where archives have survived, indicate that an enormous number of regulations regarding dress were passed during this period. One Renaissance author summarized the appropriate conduct for gentlemen: "Everyone should dress well, according to his age and his position in society. If he does not, it will be taken as a mark of contempt for other people" (Della Casa, as cited in Gage, 1968, 179). Sumptuary laws regulated the numbers of items of clothing an individual could acquire as well as the types of materials and ornamentation.

The head of a household had the responsibility for clothing the members of the household, which was usually made up of knights and squires committed to fight for him, pages, grooms, and valets. The mistress of the household had to supply the clothing for her lady attendants. The **guardaroba** (*gwar-da-ro'ba*) was a set of clothing made up of three garments: two layers of indoor clothing and a mantle for outdoors. (The term is comparable to the word *robe* in medieval French.) In middle-class Italian families, one new set of clothing was ordered each year. Discarded clothing was then passed along to the poor either by outright donation or by sale through secondhand clothing dealers (Birbari, 1975).

The Cloth Industries in Renaissance Italy

By the beginning of the Renaissance, Italian textiles were widely used throughout Europe. Wool and silk were the primary fabrics woven in Italy. Many of the

Italian wool fabrics were made from fiber imported from as far away as Britain, but the silk was cultivated locally. Silk, wool, cotton, and linen were used in Italian dress.

A description of the organization of the wool trade in the city of Prato around 1400 provides a brief overview of the production system for textiles. Entrepreneurs provided the capital and controlled the production. Washers and carders prepared the fiber for spinning. Those who spun the yarn prepared the yarn for the loom, and the weavers were almost all women working at home. Dyers were members of a cloth guild and subject to control by the entrepreneur, while the finishers who did the fulling, clipping, mending, and folding had their own workshops and tools and were more independent (Origo, 1957).

Although little documentary evidence exists, most scholars agree that the increase in the complexity of decoration of Italian silk fabrics of the 15th century indicates that improvements in silk-weaving looms must have been made at about this time.

Renaissance painters depicted many of these luxurious fabrics so realistically that one can identify them as satins, cut velvets, plain velvets, or brocades simply by looking at the pictures. These fabrics were especially suited to the almost sculptural lines of Italian Renaissance fashions. Birbiri's work (1975) stresses the luxuriousness of Italian textiles, seeing them as superior to textiles in the rest of Europe; see Figures 7.8 to 7.11 on pages 195–198.

Many of these fabrics copied Chinese, Indian, or Persian patterns and decorative motifs, a reflection of the close trading contacts between Italy and Asia. Some Renaissance painters are thought to have designed textiles; others sketched textile designs to incorporate into their paintings (Herald, 1981).

The Manufacture and Acquisition of Clothing

Those who were well-off ordered their clothing from tailors, who made garments for both men and women, or doublet makers, who made men's doublets. Tailoring skills had been refined during the 14th century once tailors had mastered the making of buttoned closures (Herald, 1981).

The less affluent might make their own clothing at home or purchase used clothing. There was apparently a large market in secondhand clothing, and such dealers were listed among the categories of tradesmen. Some ready-made garments may have been available. Some paintings show garments hanging in stalls in the street, but these may have been used clothing.

CROSS-CULTURAL INFLUENCES FROM THE MIDDLE EAST

The Ottoman Turks, conquerors of the Byzantine Empire in 1453, remained a military threat to Austria and eastern Europe until the end of the 17th century. The Turks controlled trade routes to Asia. They made treaties with Europeans to permit the safe passage of trading caravans, thereby making it possible for Italian merchants to pass to and from the Middle East and bring back goods and ideas. Probably the most obvious influences on fashion that emerged from these contacts were the aforementioned elaborate silk fabrics that likely originated as copies of silk fabrics imported from Asia. Castiglione, author of a book of advice about courtly behavior, reflected the presence of Turkish influences describing those who "clothe themselves like Turks" (as cited in St. Clair, 1973, 11).

One of the most important styles that seem to have originated in Turkish-dominated lands was the turbanlike hat styles that are often seen in portraits painted by many Italian Renaissance artists (see Figures 7.11 and 7.13, pages 198 and 200, and Global Connections).

SOURCES OF EVIDENCE ABOUT COSTUME

The Renaissance artist painted realistically, and this approach extended into the representation of clothing. Not only are the external folds and draping of the garment shown, but the artist also depicts gussets, eyelets for laces, and even the wrinkles on a pair of ill-fitting hose (see Figure 7.5, page 191).

Global Connections

The Middle Eastern turban, worn here by Sultan Mehmet II of the Ottoman Empire, has served as an inspiration to Euro-American dress for centuries. Women's beehivelike headdress appears in early Italian Renaissance art (see Figures 7.2 and 7.11, pages 189 and 198) and persists. Italian traders from ports such as Venice and Genoa traveled to Ottoman Empire ports where they must have seen the style that was an important element of Middle Eastern men's dress. Renaissance artists such as the Venetian painter of Mehmet II's portrait, Gentile Bellini, also traveled to the Middle East to paint Ottoman leaders. Once established as a popular headwear style, the turban reappeared from time to time and has become a classic. (© National Gallery, London/Art Resource, NY)

In addition to the pictorial and sculptural representations of costume, some actual items of dress remain. Written documents such as letters, diaries, and inventories of personal possessions shed some light on the quantity as well as the variety of garments commonly owned. The first books about costume were printed in the 16th century. Several books by Venetian authors depict authentic contemporary dress along with some historic and foreign costumes that scholars have found to be, at best, inaccurate and, at worst, imaginary. A passage that gives a contemporary comment on dress is reproduced on page 188 (Contemporary Comments 7.1).

Drawing conclusions about dress from the costumes on certain of the religious figures depicted by Renaissance artists requires caution. The Virgin Mary is almost always dressed more conservatively and less fashionably than other women. A veil usually covers her hair. Angels are frequently dressed in what appears to be a Renaissance version of the Greek chiton. Figures from classical mythology are garbed as the Renaissance artists believed ancient Greeks and Romans dressed. Furthermore, Newton (1975), in her extensive study of Renaissance theatrical costume, argued persuasively that figures such as the Magi (the Wise Men) in scenes of the Nativity are shown wearing the types of clothing worn by actors in religious pageants, rather than realistic costume of the time.

COSTUME: 1400–1600

Costume for Men: 1400–1450

Italian dress of the first half of the 15th century shared many characteristics of dress elsewhere in Europe around 1300 to 1500, a period when International Gothic styles influenced fine and applied arts

Contemporary Comments 7.1

APPROPRIATE ATTIRE FOR A RENAISSANCE COURT

In The Courtier, *a book published in 1528, the author Baldassare Castiglione instructs readers in appropriate attire for a Renaissance court and comments on the importance of dress in making an impression on others.*

I should prefer them not to be extreme in any way, as the French are sometimes in being over-ample and the Germans in being overscanty—but be as the one and the other style can be when corrected and given a better form by the Italians. Moreover, I prefer them always to tend a little more toward the grave and sober rather than the foppish. Hence, I think that black is more pleasing than any other color; and if not black, then at least some color on the dark side. I mean this of ordinary attire, for there is no doubt that bright and gay colors are more becoming on armor, and it is also more appropriate for gala dress to be trimmed, showy, and dashing; so too on public occasions, such as festivals, games, masquerades, and the like. For such garments, when they are so designed, have about them a certain liveliness and dash that accord very well with arms and sports. As for the rest, I would have our Courtier's dress show that sobriety which the Spanish nation so much observes, since external things often bear witness to inner things.

. . . [W]hat I think is important in the matter of dress, I wish our Courtier to be neat and dainty in his attire, and observe a certain modest elegance, yet not in a feminine or vain fashion. Nor would I have him more careful of one thing than of another, like many we see, who take such pains with their hair that they forget the rest; others attend to their teeth, others to their beard, others to their boots, others to their bonnets, others to their coifs; and thus it comes about that those slight touches of elegance seem borrowed by them, while all the rest, being entirely devoid of taste, is recognized as their very own. And such a manner I would advise our Courtier to avoid, and I would only add further that he ought to consider what appearance he wishes to have and what manner of man he wishes to be taken for, and dress accordingly; and see to it that his attire aid him to be so regarded even by those who do not hear him speak or see him do anything whatever.

I do not say . . . that by dress alone we are to make absolute judgments of the characters of men, or that men are not better known by their words and deeds than by their dress, but I do say that a man's attire is no slight index of the wearer's fancy, although sometimes it can be misleading. . . .

Castiglione, B. (1959/1528). *The book of the courtier* (C. S. Singleton, Trans). Garden City, NY: Anchor Books. pp. 121, 122–123.

including dress (Figure 7.2; see also Chapter 6). A few differences can be noted.

Many doublets worn with hose were knee length, not as short as in the north. Hukes were placed over doublets. Whether they were long or short, most houppelandes had either wide, funnel-shaped, or hanging sleeves. Although they were pointed, Italian shoe styles did not have the extreme piking seen in other parts of Europe. Hair was cut short, but the bowl cut does not seem to have been adopted in Italy.

Costume for Women: 1400–1450

Many houppelandes for women had imaginatively cut sleeves. Foreheads were bared and fashionably

FIGURE 7.2 Costume of men and women in Italy in the first half of the 15th century. Female figures at the lower left-hand corner of the painting are wearing houppelande-style gowns with long, full sleeves. The sleeves are lined in a contrasting fabric, and the edges of the sleeves are finished in dagging. They wear the high, round, beehive-shaped headdress favored by Italian women of the second quarter of the century. Just above and to the right are two men wearing knee-length jackets with full, hanging sleeves. Their footed hose are slightly piked. Men in fashionable dress in the rest of the picture wear variations of the same style in jackets and a variety of fashionable hats. Monks, priests, and nuns are dressed in typical religious garb. Angels wear slightly bloused outer tunics that derive from ancient Greek and Roman styles. (Image copyright © The Metropolitan Museum of Art. Image source: Art Resource, NY)

high, as in the rest of Europe, but Italian women covered their hair less completely than women elsewhere. A distinctive Italian women's headdress style of the second quarter of the century was a large, round, beehive-shaped hat (see Figure 7.2). These headcoverings were somewhat turbanlike, possibly a reflection of contacts with the Middle East.

About the beginning of the second half of the century, Italian dress and that of Northern Europe diverged, with distinct differences evident until the early 1500s. Neither the V-necked gown with wide revers nor the tall hennin, so often worn in France and Flanders, spread to Italy. The houppelande was supplanted by new and distinctly Italian styles, although even within the Italian styles regional variations were evident, especially in Venice.

Costume for Men: 1450–1500

The components of men's costume in Italy from 1450 to 1500 will not be new to readers. They are the same as those discussed for men in Chapter 6, pages 163–166, and include linen drawers, undershirts, doublets to which hose were attached, and outer jackets. The Italian word for men's shirts and women's chemises is the same: **camicia**. The plural form is camicie (*ca-mee'chay*). Italian versions of these garments show some stylistic differences from, as well as similarities to, those worn elsewhere at the same time.

Garments

Worn next to the skin as an undergarment, shirts were visible at the edges or openings of the outermost garments. Lower class men sometimes wore only shirts and underpants for hard labor (Figure 7.3). Shirts were made of coarse, heavy linen for lower class men, and finer, softer linen for upper class men. Sleeves and body were cut in one piece with gussets (small triangles of fabric) inset under the sleeve to permit ease of movement. Lengths ranged from between waist and hip to above the knees (Figure 7.4; see also Figure 7.3).

Doublets ended anywhere from the waist to below the hip. In longer lengths, doublets were sometimes

FIGURE 7.3 Workman. This laborer wears his jacket open and detached from his hose in order to allow him to move freely. Under his jacket one can see his camicia, and at the hip, under his camicia, one gets a slight glimpse of his short drawers. The loosened hose are rolled below the knee, and over the hose he wears shoes, probably leather, that come to the ankle. (Scala/Ministero per i Beni e le Attività culturali/ Art Resource, NY)

cut with a small skirt. Four seams (front, back, and both sides) allowed for a close fit (see Figures 7.3 and 7.4). Doublets (and jackets) often had a distinctive neckline finish that displayed the high level of skill of Italian tailors. At the front, the garments appear to have a collarless neckline. At the center of the back a deep U-shaped piece was cut out. Into the U-shaped opening was inserted a curved, U-shaped piece with a straight top edge. The results were a neck edge that stood away from the neck and a smooth unwrinkled back to the doublet from waist to neck without using darts or gathers. (The man at the far left of Figure 7.4 wears a garment with this design feature.)

Hose, which were tied to the doublet, were cut either as two separate pieces or seamed together at the crotch. Doublet and hose were worn by working men and soldiers. By the end of the century, fashionable young men began to wear the doublet and hose without an outer jacket. Most hose were still apparently made from woven fabrics and cut in the bias direction. Tight lacing of hose to the doublet helped attain a smooth fit but hampered physical activity. Renaissance painters frequently depict men involved in physical activity

FIGURE 7.4 A variety of different jacket, doublet, and sleeve styles. Figure on the left wears a dark red doublet with fitted sleeves under a jacket of green with hanging sleeves. The doublet sleeve is slit at the back seam, and the edges of the split are tied together with laces. A thin line of white from his camicia shows at the opening. The figure behind him wears a dark blue doublet with a sleeveless hukelike jacket that is belted. The sleeve of the doublet is full to the elbow, where it gathers to fit the tight lower portion of the sleeve, which closes with a row of small buttons. The man emerging from the well wears a jacket with a full sleeve gathered to fit the armscye then narrowing gradually to the wrist. The standing figure wears the hukelike jacket over a green doublet. His flat, round hat is typical of the period, as are the hairstyles of all men. (Scala/Ministero per i Beni e le Attività culturali/ Art Resource, NY)

with their laces untied and their hose hanging loosely at the back (see Figure 7.3).

Around mid-century, jackets fit smoothly through the torso. They had a flared skirt that attached at the waist and ended below the hip. In the last half of the century, jackets were usually fitted over the shoulders and upper chest, then fell in full pleats from a sort of yoke. Fullness was belted in at the waistline (Figure 7.5). Toward the end of the century, sleeveless jackets, looking much like hukes, were seamed at the shoulder and open under the arms. Full and pleated, this version was worn belted or unbelted (see the second man from the left in Figure 7.4).

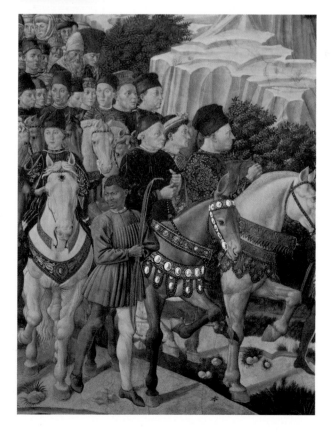

FIGURE 7.5 *Journey of the Magi* [detail], by Benozzo Gozzolo, c. 1460. Bowman in the entourage of the Medici princes wears a green, pleated jacket. His undershirt is visible at the neckline of his jacket, and his wrinkled hose are parti-colored. (Scala/Art Resource, NY)

Sleeve styles were among the distinctive aspects of Italian styles. Their construction could be quite complex. Sleeves tended to become more fitted in the second half of the century, and identifiable sleeve types seem to have evolved. Early in the century, sleeves were cut in two sections. One section was full and somewhat puffed from shoulder to elbow, and the other section was fitted from elbow to wrist (see Figures 7.3 and 7.4). Slightly later, one-piece sleeves were full at the shoulder and tapered gradually to the wrist (see Figure 7.4). Even later, sleeves narrowed for the length of the arm to fit smoothly. If sleeves were too tight to allow easy movement, one or more openings were left,

FIGURE 7.6 *Saint Anthony Distributing His Wealth to the Poor*, by Sassetta, second quarter of the 15th century. This painting contrasts the ragged, torn clothing of the poor, dressed in long gowns, with the fashionable, fur-trimmed costume of the saint. Children are dressed as the adults, except that the skirt of the boy's garment is short. (Image courtesy of The National Gallery of Art, Samuel H. Kress Collection. 1952)

through which the long, white shirt sleeve could be seen. To permit this ease of movement, seams were sometimes left open at various places closed with lacings), or a horizontal seam was left open at the back of the elbow (see Figure 7.4).

Sleeves could be fastened either by sewing them into the body of the doublet or jacket or by lacing them into the armhole. The fabric of the camicia was then pulled through the openings between the laces to form decorative puffs. The same sleeves might be removeable to serve as sleeves in more than one garment.

Hanging sleeves that were generally nonfunctional, purely decorative, and attached to the jacket appeared mostly in costume for ceremonial occasions. Jackets with hanging sleeves were worn over doublets so that the sleeves of the doublet were exposed (see Figure 7.4).

Ceremonial robes worn by state officials and lawyers were usually full-length gowns that were placed over doublet and hose, with the jacket as a third, outermost layer. Robes often had hanging sleeves.

For outdoor use and for warmth, men wore open and closed capes. These always covered the jacket completely, varying in length to correspond with the length of the jacket. Often they were trimmed in fur or lined in contrasting colors (Figure 7.6).

Hair and Headdress

Younger men cut their hair in medium to longer lengths that tapered gradually from below the ears in front to about the shoulders in the back. Hair might be straight or curly. Older men cut their hair shorter. Men were generally clean shaven.

A variety of hat styles are seen in paintings, including turbanlike styles, brimless pillbox styles, either soft or rigid high toques, and hats with soft crowns and upturned brims or round crowns and narrow brims (Illustrated Table 7.1).

Footwear

Pointed toes began to round off at the front toward the end of the 15th century. Leather-soled, footed hose were by far the most popular footwear for men. When

Illustrated Table 7.1

Italian Renaissance: Accessories

Turbanlike style, first
half of 15th century

Stiffened beretlike
hat, c. 1500

Soft skullcap
c. 1500

Black velvet hat and
brooch, second half
of 16th century

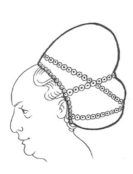

Beehive shape, first
half of 15th century

Veil covering hair,
c. 15th century

Turbanlike headdress,
c. 16th century

Ferroniere, c. 15th century

Necklace, c. 16th century

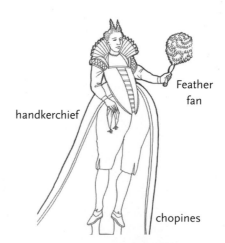

Feather
fan

handkerchief

chopines

Drawers and chopines,
c. 15th century

worn, shoes fitted closely and were cut high across the instep and below the anklebone. Boots, generally worn for outdoors in bad weather or for riding, tended to have turned-down cuffs and ended at mid-calf.

Costume for Women: 1450–1500

The most common combination of garments for women during the Italian Renaissance was a chemise worn as an undergarment beneath a dress and a second overdress on top. There are also a number of examples of women's dress in which only the chemise and an outer dress are worn.

Garments

The chemise, or camicia, was made of linen. The quality of the fabric of which it was made varied with the status of the wearer. The fullness of the cut related to the weight of the fabric; a fuller cut was used with sheerer fabrics. The camicia was floor length. Sleeves were generally long; some were cut in raglan style (i.e., seams running from below the arm at front and back

to the neck rather than being set into an armhole). In the last part of the century, large sections of the neckline of the camicia were displayed as an edging at the necklines of gowns, and fine embroidery, bindings, smocking, or edgings were added (see Figure 7.11, page 198). Although the camicia was an undergarment, peasant women are shown in some paintings wearing camicie to work in the fields, and apparently women wore the garment in the privacy of their own quarters during hot weather.

Lavish use of opulent fabrics for the dresses of upper class women gave garments of relatively straight cut a splendid appearance. By carefully manipulating the layers of camicia, dress, and overdress and choosing contrasting fabrics for each layer, rich decorative effects were achieved.

Dresses without an obvious overdress were usually straight from shoulder to hem with a smooth-fitting, yokelike construction over the shoulder, which opened into full pleats or gathers over the bustline. These full gowns were generally belted (Figure 7.7). Alternatively,

FIGURE 7.7 Italian women (c. 1450–1465) in Renaissance dresses made of richly colored fabric that may be velvet. Their headdresses are simpler than those in northern Europe. (Detail: Scala/Ministero per i Beni e le Attività culturali/Art Resource, NY)

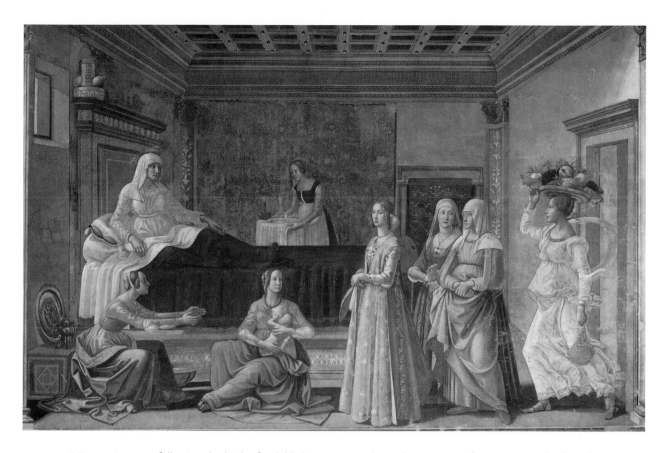

FIGURE 7.8 Domestic scene following the birth of a child shows women dressed in a variety of garments. To the far right are two women, one an older woman in a simple dress and mantle with a white veil over her head. To her left is a fashionable matron in a brocade outer gown worn over a gold gown, which can be seen at the neckline and at the end of the sleeves of the outer gown. The third figure to the left, a young woman, wears a fashionable under gown of blue brocade with red flowers. At the elbow of the sleeve and down the lower part of the arm her camicia is visible through the slits in the sleeve. Her sleeveless outer gown is of pink brocade and open at the sides. She carries a handkerchief. Her hair, which is uncovered, is of the fashionable blonde shade. Other women in the room all wear two-layered gowns except for the mother, whose camicia is visible at the neckline of her simple blue gown. The dress of the wet nurse, seated at the center, opens down the front so she can suckle the baby. The laces that close the dress of the seated figure at far left are visible under the arm. She, too, wears a split sleeve with her camicia bloused through below the elbow. Her mantle, the lining of which matches the sleeves of her under gown, has slipped off her shoulders and fallen to the ground. She wears a small, sheer cap denoting her status as a young matron. The figure at far right, as was the custom, is bringing fruit and wine as a gift from the city of Florence. (Detail: Scala/Art Resource, NY)

gowns could be made with a bodice section joined to a full gathered or pleated skirt. These dresses were usually closed by lacing up the front and also sometimes at the side (see woman at bottom left, Figure 7.8).

At mid-century, necklines were usually rounded but cut relatively high. Toward the end of the century, necklines tended to be lower, some more square than round, or with deep Vs held together by lacing that showed off the upper part of the chemise.

When two layers of dresses were obvious, underdresses were usually made with bodices and skirts joined together. They were fitted fairly closely and were visible at the neckline, sleeves, or under the arm of the outer dress. Outer dresses were often cut like a man's huke, that is, sleeveless, seamed at the shoulders, and open under the arm to display the underdress (see Figure 7.8).

Sleeve styles for women were similar to those for men. The most common forms were sleeves wider above the elbow and fitted below (see woman in background of Figure 7.8), closely fitted sleeves with openings to display the sleeves of the camicia (Figure 7.9), or hanging sleeves (see Figure 7.7).

Mantles or capes worn outdoors included both open and closed styles, often lined in contrasting fabric and sometimes matching the dresses with which they were worn. Some ladies wore a purely decorative cape fastened to the dress at the shoulder (but not covering the shoulder or upper arms) and extending into a long train.

Hair and Headdress

A major distinction is seen between Italian hairdressing and that of northern Europe. While northern European women covered the hair, Italian women arranged their hair elaborately, wearing a token head covering in the form of a small jeweled net set at the back of the head or a small sheer veil (see Figure 7.8). Young girls dressed their hair simply, curled into long tresses. Women placed a loose, curling tress on either side of the face and pulled the rest into a bun or a long braid or made more elaborate arrangements that combined braids, loops of hair, and curls (see Figure 7.9).

Footwear

Rarely seen in paintings, women's shoes appear to have been cut along the same lines as those of men.

Jewelry

Highly skilled jewelers created masterpieces from precious stones, pearls, gold, and silver. They made necklaces, earrings, brooches, and interesting hair ornaments. One of the latter that became especially popular was a chain or band of metal or pearls worn across the forehead with a jeweled decoration located over the center of the forehead. This chain was called a **ferroniere** (*fehr'ohn-yair*) (see Illustrated Table 7.1).

COSTUME: 16TH CENTURY

The distinctiveness of Italian dress persisted until about midway through the 16th century, after which, except for women's dress in Venice, styles became subject to Spanish and French influences as a result of the occupation of large areas of Italy by these two powers. Venice remained independent, and Venetians wore some unique styles.

FIGURE 7.9 *Bianca Maria Sforza*, by Ambrogio de Predis, c. 1493. The jeweled hair covering reveals more of the hair than was customary in northern Europe. The dark band that crosses her forehead is a ferroniere. Puffed areas of a white camicia show through the openings where the sleeve and the bodice lace together and at the back where the two sides of the closely fitted sleeve are laced together. A fine black line running from behind the neck to under the neckline probably marks the edge of the sheer fabric of the camicia, which is so fine that it seems to be transparent. (Image courtesy of the National Gallery of Art, Widener Collection)

Costume for Men

Garments

White linen camicie often had embroidered necklines and cuffs. Black work, a black-on-white Spanish embroidery, was especially popular (see Figure 8.13, page 220).

Over the camicia a man placed a closely fitted doublet that was sometimes worn without a jacket to create an extremely narrow silhouette. This style persisted only until shortly after the end of the first decade, after which men's doublets became fuller, though never so full as in France, England, or the German lands. Some had deep, square necklines to show off embroidered camicie. Decorative slashing, sometimes with puffs of contrasting fabric pulled through the slits, was more restrained than in other parts of Europe (contrast Figure 7.10 with Figure 8.6a, page 213). Some jackets had short sleeves, ending just below the shoulder line, which allowed a contrast between the jacket and the sleeve of the doublet

(Figure 7.10). Hose, which were attached to doublets, had a distinct, usually padded, codpiece.

The introduction of a codpiece into joined hose had been a practical solution to making the hose fit properly and to enable men to relieve themselves. But by 1500, the codpiece had grown to enormous proportions and had become a very obvious feature of men's clothing (see Figure 7.10). Vicary (1989) suggested that this feature may have been a response to an epidemic of syphilis in Europe that began about 1494 and spread rapidly. She noted that treatment of the disease required the use of medications that would have stained the clothing and that a padded codpiece would have provided protection. Because of the social stigma attached to this illness, almost universal adoption of the codpiece made it impossible to single out infected individuals. The codpiece disappeared in the later 16th century. Vicary suggested that as the population built up some level of immunity, the epidemic subsided.

Hair and Headdress

Men began to wear beards again.

Costume for Women

Garments

Camicie were sometimes cut high to show above the neckline of the gown (Figure 7.11). Sometimes this was just high enough to form a small border at the edge of the neckline. Camicie were often embroidered or otherwise decorated, and sometimes finished with a small neckline ruffle.

Silhouettes of dresses grew wider and fuller (see Figure 7.11). Bodices became more rigid, a reflection of the increasing Spanish influences on Italian styles. Square, wide, and low necklines predominated;

FIGURE 7.10 *Portrait of Lodovico Capponi*, by Agnolo Bronzino, middle of the 16th century. A row of buttons closes the closely fitted black jacket. The jacket sleeves end just below the shoulder, so that the slashed sleeves of the doublet are visible. At the wrists and around the neck, the edges of the camicia are visible. A prominent codpiece is seen at the top of the paned trunk hose. (Copyright The Frick Collection)

FIGURE 7.11 A *Young Woman and Her Little Boy*, by Agnolo Bronzino, c. 1540. The woman's decoratively embroidered camicia extends well beyond the neckline of her red brocade dress, and the ends of the camicia sleeve can be seen at her wrist. The turbanlike headdress was especially popular at this time. In her hand, she carries a pair of gloves, which at this period were often perfumed. (Image courtesy of The National Gallery of Art, Widener Collection)

sleeves widened. Often they had a full, wide puff at the top and were more closely fitted from above the elbow to the wrist. Many were decorated with puffs and slashes. Waistlines were straight in the early part of the century. Spanish-influenced V shapes in the front gradually began to appear as the century progressed.

Headdress

Turbans became quite fashionable (see Figure 7.11). The turban style derived from the Turkish headdress and reflected Italian trading contacts with the Turks of the Ottoman Empire.

REGIONAL DISTINCTIONS IN COSTUME FOR MEN AND WOMEN: 15TH AND 16TH CENTURIES

Although there were regional differences in Italy, basic clothing forms (i.e., layers worn, construction techniques, etc.) were similar. The clearest and most distinctive differences were evident in the costumes of Venice, particularly when compared with those of areas under Florentine influence.

Distinctive Venetian Costume for Women

Venetian women of the 15th century wore gowns with the waistline located just below the bosom. Fabrics appear to have been less heavy and rigid than in other regions. **Chopines** (*sho'peen*), very high platform-soled shoes, were worn throughout Italy and in northern Europe, but visitors to Venice reported that those worn in Venice were exceptionally high. Women bleached their hair to light blonde shades (Figure 7.12; see also Illustrated Table 7.1, page 193). Drawings of women also showed them wearing underdrawers, garments that were not common elsewhere in Europe until later centuries.

By the last half of the 16th century, Venetian gowns typically had normal waistlines in back, which dipped to a deep U shape in front. Women arranged their hair at the front above the forehead in little twin "horns." This style also appeared in some other parts of Europe, but it seems to have been most extreme in Venice. Chopines grew even taller.

The description of Venetian styles by a traveler who visited Venice in the 16th century is reprinted in Contemporary Comments 7.2 on page 199.

Distinctive Venetian Costume for Men

Venetian men of the 15th century wore garments with waistlines, V-shaped in front, located at the anatomical

Contemporary Comments 7.2

DRESS OF VENETIAN WOMEN

A Frenchman, Villemont, visiting Venice toward the close of the 16th century described the exaggerated forms of the styles worn by Venetian women:

They have their blond hair for the most part hanging nicely and arranged at the forehead in the shape of two horns half a foot high, without any iron mounting or any other thing to hold them up, unless it were the charming braiding which they do themselves. . . . They appear a foot taller than the men because they are mounted on patens of wood covered with leather, which are at least a foot high so that they are obliged to have a woman to aid them walk, and another to carry their train. . . . But the Romans, Milanese, Neapolitans, Florentines, Ferrarans and other ladies of Italy are more modest, for their patens are not so high, and also they do not bare their breasts.

Morse, H. K. (1934)]. *Elizabethan pageantry.* New York, NY: Studio Publication, p. 19

waist or slightly below at the back. Long outer tunics were preferred to jackets, although jackets were also worn.

By the 16th century, men's dress in Venice, like the styles for men elsewhere in Italy, was influenced by Spanish and French styles.

Venetian Dress for Officials

The Doge, the highest official in Venice, together with a hereditary ruling class of nobles, wore traditional long robes with wide sleeves. The wider the sleeve, the more important the rank. Colors varied according to rank and office. The Doge's headdress was worn over a coif and had something of the shape of a Phrygian bonnet, the point at the back stiffened and rigid (Figure 7.13). Venetian nobility did not give up these costumes until the 18th century.

FIGURE 7.12 Venetian women in a painting by Carpaccio wear typical high-waisted Venetian women's dresses. Notice the high-soled chopines visible just in front of the peacock. Their hair is of the fashionable blonde color. (Cameraphoto Arte, Venice/ Art Resource, NY)

FIGURE 7.13 The Doge of Venice, in the 1500s, is wearing the traditional headdress and golden brocade gown of the doge with a cape of ermine. He sits between two turbaned ambassadors from Persia. The turban influenced headwear in Italy during the Renaissance. See examples in Figures 7.2 and 7.11. (Cameraphoto Arte, Venice/Art Resource, NY)

COSTUME FOR CHILDREN DURING THE ITALIAN RENAISSANCE

The numerous paintings of the Madonna and infant Jesus confirm that once out of swaddling clothes, children started to wear clothing that was similar to that of adults. In some paintings the Christ child wears a camicia, in others a loose-fitting under tunic and an over tunic. Boys of nursery years wore skirts; older boys wore doublets, jackets, and hose. Little girls wore dresses similar to those of older women (Figure 7.14).

Summary

Themes

The history of Italian dress is marked throughout by the theme of CROSS-CULTURAL INFLUENCES, many of which resulted from POLITICAL CONFLICTS or POLITICAL ALLIANCES between the Italian city-states and France and Spain. In the first half of the 15th century, fashions were clearly shaped by the International Gothic style, and in the northwestern regions influences from

These costumes developed at a time when a new and independent spirit in the arts, literature, and philosophy was abroad in Italy. Moreover, ECONOMIC CHANGES brought powerful families, many of them merchants, to levels in the SOCIAL CLASS STRUCTURE where they could purchase luxurious clothing and accessories. Such materials were readily available through industries focused on the PRODUCTION OF TEXTILES, an important theme in Italian Renaissance dress.

The ARTS AND THEIR RELATION TO DRESS are notable because painters originated designs for textiles and for actual garments worn in pageants and theatrical presentations. The arts, too, made a most important contribution to costume history as A SOURCE OF INFORMATION ABOUT COSTUME. Depictions by artists show details of the actual construction of dress and of daily life as they portrayed individuals from a wide range of social classes (Figure 7.15).

CROSS-CULTURAL themes return to the fore in the 16th century when Italy was overpowered by the Spanish, the French, and the Austrians and the period of innovation in dress ended. Foreign influences came to dominate the Italian city-states. After 1500 fashions took on a more international cast. This was a result not only of the imposition of foreign rule on most parts of Italy, but also of the increasing movement among peoples and the improvements in COMMUNICATIONS that took place throughout Europe in the 16th century.

FIGURE 7.14 Renaissance patrons often commissioned paintings that depicted their families. Here members of the fashionably dressed Sforza family of Milano (c. 1490) kneel in worship before the Madonna, the Christ child, and saints who wear various forms of religious dress. Even an infant in swaddling clothes and cap is shown kneeling in prayer, an impossible position for a child so young. (Erich Lessing/Art Resource, NY)

LEGACY OF ITALIAN RENAISSANCE STYLES

The textile designs for which Italian Renaissance weavers were famous have had a lasting impact not only on clothing for luxury garments, but also on fabrics for interior design. Fortuny, a textile and fashion designer of the early 20th century, based many of his textile designs on these fabrics (see page 429).

Another area in which Renaissance designs frequently exert strong influence is that of jewelry. The ferroniere, often seen in Renaissance portraits, appeared again in the Romantic and Crinoline periods of the 19th century and occasionally in 21st-century fashion.

neighboring French and Burgundian regions were especially prominent.

Styles in Italy during the last half of the 15th century differed markedly from those of northern Europe. The distinctions were evident in the cut of clothing and in the types of fabrics used. Here, too, design motifs from East Asia can be seen in elaborate brocades, attractive cut velvets, and other sumptuously decorated textiles produced by Italian weavers, as well as in individual items of dress such as the turbanlike headdresses favored by Italian ladies.

FIGURE 7.15 Influences that artist Giotto had on Renaissance art were not confined to careful rendering of people's dress. He also painted human emotions and activities realistically, abandoning the more stylized art of earlier painters. (Detail: Alinari/Art Resource, NY)

The high platform shoes called chopines never again reached such dramatic heights, but platform soles in shoes returned (see Modern Influences). Their most notable revivals were during World War II, the 1960s, the 1990s, and the early 21st century.

REFERENCES

Birbari, E. (1975). *Dress in Italian painting 1460–1500.* London, UK: John Murray.

Gage, J. (1968). *Life in Italy at the time of the Medici.* New York, NY: Putnam.

Gundersheimer, W. L. (1965). *The Italian Renaissance.* Englewood Cliffs, NJ: Prentice-Hall.

Herald, J. (1981). *Renaissance dress in Italy 1400–1500.* Atlantic Highlands, NJ: Humanities Press.

Newton, S. M. (1975). *Renaissance theatre costume.* New York, NY: Theatre Arts Books.

Origo, I. (1957). *The merchant of Prato.* New York, NY: Knopf.

St. Clair, A. N. (1973). *The image of the Turk in Europe* [Exhibit catalog]. New York, NY: Metropolitan Museum of Art.

Vicary, G. Q. (1989). Visual art as social data: The Renaissance codpiece. *Cultural Anthropology, 4*(1), 3–25.

MODERN INFLUENCES

Venetian chopines with their very high platform soles can be seen as ancestors of these 2014 platform-soled shoes by Karwai Tang. (Karwei Tang/WireImage)

Visual Summary Table

Italian Renaissance

Man: 1400–1450
Doublet and hose

Woman: 1400–1450
Houppelandes and fitted gowns

Man: 1450–1500
Doublet under skirted
jacket and hose

Woman: 1450–1500
Gowns worn either as a single
layer or two layers

Man: (c. 1510) 1500–1550
Clothes grow wider, often
decorated with puffs and slashes

Woman: 1500–1550
Gowns are full, have puffed
sleeves; are decorated with
puffs and slashes

Man: 1550–1600
Silhouette widens, jackets
take on rigid shape, puffs
and slashes increase

Woman: late 1500s
Spanish influences appear in
more rigid bodices, V-shaped
waistlines

	1509	1517	1519	1520	1543	1547	1553	1556
FASHION AND TEXTILES			Spanish styles influence all Europe as Charles V is elected Holy Roman Emperor			Catherine de Medici, of France, brings Italian influences to French court		
POLITICS AND CONFLICTS	Henry VIII becomes king of England			Reign of Süleyman the Magnificent, Sultan of the Ottoman Empire, begins		Henry VIII dies and his son Edward becomes Edward VI		Charles V abdicates, dividing his territories
DECORATIVE AND FINE ARTS			Death of Leonardo da Vinci in France					
ECONOMICS AND TRADE					Portuguese sailors make first European contact with Japan			
TECHNOLOGY AND IDEAS					Nicholas Copernicus publishes *Revolution of the Heavenly Bodies*			
RELIGION AND SOCIETY		Martin Luther's debate with the Roman Catholic Church begins, and printing stimulates Protestant Reformation					Death of Edward VI brings Catholic Mary Tudor to the throne	

CHAPTER EIGHT

The Northern Renaissance

c. 1500–1600

1557	1558	1562–1598	1603

Queen Elizabeth I succeeds to the throne on death of Mary Tudor

Spanish lose control of the Dutch Provinces (1579)

Henry of Navarre becomes King Henry IV of France (1589)

Death of Elizabeth I of England

Death of Michelangelo (1564)

Shakespeare begins writing plays (1588)

Portuguese settlement in Macao establishes contact with Chinese

France wracked with religious strife

The spirit of the Renaissance in the arts and in philosophy gradually moved to northern Europe. Religious attitudes also changed as the Protestant Reformation spread among European nations. Explorations established routes by water to distant regions in Asia and reached the continents of North and South America, previously unknown to Europeans. Increased travel brought cross-cultural influences to dress in Europe, and the wealth that came from trade and conquest made courts a center for the display of changing fashions. Printed books became available, and some depicted the dress of far-off lands.

HISTORICAL BACKGROUND

By the beginning of the 16th century, northern Europe had experienced a gradual transition to participation in the new spirit of the Renaissance. Along with changes in arts and letters came profound changes in religious attitudes, which led some Christians to separate from the Roman Catholic Church. The Protestant Reformation, which began in the German states of the Holy Roman Empire, split Europe into two hostile religious camps.

At the beginning of the 16th century, the Hapsburg territories, the Low Countries, and Spain came under the rule of one man, the Emperor Charles V (1500–1558), who inherited from his grandparents a vast array of lands and claims. From his paternal grandfather, Emperor Maximilian, he inherited the Hapsburg lands, including Austria, and from his grandmother, Mary, the Burgundian lands, including the Low Countries. From his maternal grandparents, Ferdinand of Aragon and Isabella of Castile, he received Spain and the Spanish empire in America, as well as the kingdoms of Sicily, Naples, and Sardinia. In 1519, having inherited all of these lands and kingdoms, Charles V was elected Holy Roman Emperor and thus gained imperial rights over all of Germany and northern Italy. At the age of 19, he ruled over a larger territory than any ruler had ever attempted to govern.

So vast a territory made up of such a variety of peoples and lacking geographical unity was difficult to rule effectively. Moreover, the extent of Charles's empire meant that he was continually involved in wars with rival monarchs who feared a Hapsburg domination of Europe. Eventually, Charles found his burden so heavy that he abdicated. In 1556 he divided his territories between his brother Ferdinand (1503–1564), who received Austria and the Holy Roman Empire, and his son Philip (1527–1598), who inherited Spain, the Low Countries, and the New World.

Developments in Germany

German artists, rejecting the Gothic style of the medieval period, adopted Renaissance forms. Scholars turned toward an interest in science, philosophy, and morality. The artistic and intellectual ferment of the Renaissance in Germany coincided with an increasing dissatisfaction on the part of many people with certain practices within the Roman Catholic Church. The Germans objected to the Catholic practices of profiting financially from religion and corruption and to the moral laxity among some of the clergy and religious orders. The study of the Bible from original sources led to dissatisfaction with medieval Catholic theology. Growing nationalism rejected the political influence of the papacy. The printing press played a major role in the Reformation, because it became easier to publish and disseminate the arguments of the reformers, including the first translation of the New Testament into German. The secular spirit of the Renaissance was another factor.

Martin Luther (1483–1546), a priest and university professor, translated the Bible and became the spokesman and theorist for the dissenters. Luther had the essential support of local political leaders who saw in religious dissent an opportunity to break away from the control of Charles V, who was Catholic. The leaders also recognized the opportunity to confiscate the great wealth of the Christian church in Germany. Luther's argument with the Church began in 1517; it soon spread throughout much of Europe. And with it came war and revolution.

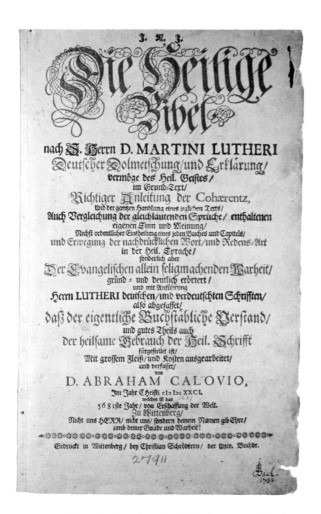

FIGURE 8.1 Martin Luther, founder of the Lutheran Church, nailed a list of his reasons for rebelling against the Roman Catholic Church on the door of a chapel. (bpk, Berlin/ Photographer Hermann Buresch/Art Resource, NY)

Developments in Spain

Areas of Spain, which had been under control of the Moors from northern Africa until late into the 15th century, were finally united in the late 1400s under Ferdinand and Isabella, the famous patrons of Columbus's voyage to the New World. Charles V inherited the Spanish throne in 1506.

Spain became incredibly wealthy from the influx of gold and silver from the exploitation of resources in the conquered American territories of Mexico and Peru. Spain dominated Europe as a result of Charles's political interests in so much of Europe and the wealth acquired from the Americas. The 16th century could

well be called the Golden Age of Spain. But the wealth proved a curse. There was so much gold that Spain suffered inflation. Charles spent his gold on expensive foreign wars; when the wealth was exhausted, nothing was left for the Spanish people.

The Reformation (see Figure 8.1) had little effect on Spain. Charles was a devout Catholic, and Spain was the most orthodox nation in Europe. Nevertheless, the Reformation prevented Charles from maintaining control over the Holy Roman Empire and preserving the unity of the Christian faith in Europe. The strain of attempting to maintain the empire led Charles V to abdicate the throne of Spain and the Low Countries in favor of his son, Philip II, a fervent Catholic who bore proudly the traditional title of the Spanish monarch, "The Most Catholic King." But Philip II antagonized the 17 prosperous provinces that made up the Low Countries. High taxes, the appointment of haughty Spanish administrators, Spanish troops stationed among them, and attempts to repress Protestantism made the people of the Low Countries resentful of Spanish rule. In 1568 revolution broke out, and by the end of the century, Philip had lost the seven northern provinces that formed the Dutch Republic, or Holland. Again Philip failed in 1588 when he dispatched the ill-fated armada of 130 ships to conquer England and restore that land to the Roman Catholic faith. His intervention in the French religious wars also failed. The increasing decline in Spanish political influence helped contribute to the end of the Golden Age of Spain.

Developments in England

The 16th century in England was divided between the great Tudor monarchs Henry VIII (1509–1547) and his second child Elizabeth I (1558–1603). Henry split with the Church of Rome over the Pope's refusal to permit him to divorce his Spanish queen, Katharine of Aragon, to whom he had been married for 18 years. Because Henry and Katharine had only one sickly daughter, Mary Tudor, Henry sought a divorce in order to remarry and father a male heir to preserve the Tudor line. Breaking with Rome, Henry established the national

FIGURE 8.2 Shakespeare's house in Stratford-upon-Avon. (© Paul Thompson/Corbis)

Church of England, but maintained the basic beliefs and practices of the Roman Catholic faith. During the short reign of his son Edward VI (1547–1553), the child of his third marriage, England became Protestant. Mary Tudor (1553–1558), who succeeded Edward, tried and failed to restore England to the Church of Rome. After Mary's death, Elizabeth became queen.

During Henry's reign, the Gothic style climaxed in England and the English Renaissance began. During the Elizabethan era, England enjoyed a literary Renaissance, chiefly in dramatic poetry. English theater was born thanks to dramatists such as William Shakespeare (see Figure 8.2), Christopher Marlowe, and Ben Jonson. Shakespeare surpassed his contemporaries with the vast range of his plays—comedies, topical dramas, histories, tragedies—and filled them with characters who became immortal. Elizabethan music profited from the genius of Thomas Tallis and William Byrd.

Both Henry and Elizabeth brought painters and sculptors to England from other parts of Europe to decorate their palaces. Elizabeth, who was well educated and enjoyed reading Latin verse, was praised in Edmund Spenser's great epic poem filled with national feeling, *The Faerie Queene*. She patronized the arts, thereby stimulating music and literary productions. The elaborate fashionable dress she wore was a strong influence on women's dress at the English court.

Developments in France

During the first half of the 16th century, the French Renaissance in the arts began under the monarch Francis I (1515–1547). He invited Italian artists and artisans—including Leonardo da Vinci and Benvenuto Cellini—to the French court to work. His son, Henry II, married an Italian, Catherine de Medici, who brought her Italian tailors and dressmakers, perfumers, cooks, and other craftsmen to France, where they found ample opportunity to employ their talents. Catherine's Italian perfumers are said to have started the French perfume industry.

After her husband's sudden death in 1559 and the death of her son Francis II in 1560, Catherine became the regent for her weak son, Charles IX, remaining the power behind the throne until 1588. In the reigns of Charles IX (1560–1574) and his brother Henry III (1574–1589), France was wracked by religious civil war as powerful Protestant and Catholic noble families struggled for political control. Catherine helped create a climate of revolt and political dissension for most of the rest of the century by throwing royal support behind the Catholic faction.

The accession of the Protestant Bourbon Henry IV (1589–1610) brought an end to religious persecution of the French Protestants. To appease the Roman Catholics who were in the majority, Henry IV converted to Roman Catholicism and settled the religious problem by issuing the Edict of Nantes guaranteeing freedom of conscience and full political rights to all Protestants. In the economic sphere, Henry encouraged French industry, and the cloth industries especially benefited. French linen rivaled that of Holland, and its silk-weaving industry challenged what had formerly been an Italian monopoly on the manufacture of silk.

FACTORS IN THE DISSEMINATION OF FASHION INFORMATION

One of the factors in the spread of fashion information from one part of Europe to another was the intermarriage of the royal families from different countries. These marriages were usually arranged to

TABLE 8.1 Royal Intermarriages during the 16th Century

ENGLAND AND SCOTLAND	FRANCE	SPAIN	AUSTRIA-GERMANY	ITALY
Henry VIII		Katharine of Aragon	Anne of Cleves	
	Henry II			Catherine de Medici
Mary, Queen of Scots	Francis II			
Mary I of England		Philip II		

cement alliances between two powers. The brides were sent from their own countries to their new homes equipped with a substantial dowry as well as a trousseau of the latest fashions and accompanied by a group of fashionably gowned ladies-in-waiting. Not surprisingly, the marriages contributed to the spread of fashions. Table 8.1 highlights the intermarriages between royal families during the 16th century and illustrates the cross-influences of styles that accompanied such weddings.

The intermarriage of members of royal families from one country with those of another was only one of the ways that fashion information could be spread from one locale to another. Other sources of fashion information included imported garments and fabrics, books dealing with costume, and travelers who brought back information about and examples of foreign styles. Peasants tended to use functional and simple clothing rather than fashionable dress, but among the upper classes a more or less internationalization of styles occurred in which the predominant silhouettes and features had substantial similarities. At the same time, distinctive local styles often traveled abroad, as this 16th-century poem attests (as cited in Chamberlin, 1969, p. 53.):

> *Behold a most accomplished cavalier,*
> *That the world's ape of Fashion doth appear.*
> *Walking the streets his humours to disclose,*
> *In the French doublet and the German hose,*

The muff, cloak, Spanish hat, Toledo blade,
Italian ruff, a shoe right Flemish made.

CROSS-CULTURAL INFLUENCES FROM THE MIDDLE EAST

In the early 1500s, Francis I of France found it politically expedient to make an alliance with Sultan Süleyman, leader of the Ottoman Turks. Although the Turks still menaced eastern Europe, other European powers interested in stimulating trade with Asia also made treaties. Style ideas brought back by diplomats, merchants, and travelers from the Middle East entered the European courts. The first illustrated travel book showing Middle Eastern scenes and styles appeared in 1486.

The Turks were viewed as fierce and exotic. Ballets, masques, and dramas featured Turkish characters (see Figure 8.3) but often portrayed them in a derogatory

FIGURE 8.3 Süleyman the Magnificent, with two attendants. (Bridgeman-Giraudon/Art Resource, NY)

manner. Nonetheless, their costume fascinated many in Europe, although direct influence on fashion appears to have been somewhat limited. In 1510 the English Earl of Essex appeared at a banquet dressed in what was described as "Turkish fashion." He wore long robes powdered with gold, a hat of crimson velvet with great rolls of gold (probably like a turban), and two scimitars (curved, Turkish-style swords; St. Clair, 1973). There is one portrait of Henry VIII of England dressed in what appears to be a Turkish robe, and some researchers believe the garment called the **ropa**, a loosely fitted overdress, derives from Middle Eastern styles (see Figure 8.14, page 221).

Changes in Textile Technology

Only a few advances in textile technology took place during the 16th century. A treadle-powered spinning wheel in combination with a device called a bobbin-and-flyer mechanism made spinning easier. Some sources credit Leonardo da Vinci with this invention; others say he simply sketched what he had seen in use. The device sped up the process of spinning by doing away with the need to stop to wind up the yarn after each length was spun. It was improved by a German inventor and came into use in the mid-1500s.

Hand knitting seems to have begun in Europe only after the 15th century. By the latter part of the 16th century, it was being used to make stockings. When an inventor, William Lee, sought a patent for a knitting machine for stockings in 1589 Queen Elizabeth refused the patent because she feared it would put the hand knitters out of business, so Lee took his invention to France where it was adopted (Derry and Williams, 1961). Knitting allowed for a closer fit of hose than woven materials.

Decorative Techniques of the 16th Century

New techniques for decorating fabrics became fashionable in the 16th century. Embroidered decorations were applied not only to outer garments but also to visible neck and sleeve edges of undergarments such as shirts and chemises (Figure 8.4; see also Figure 8.7). **Spanish work**, an especially

FIGURE 8.4 Woman's chemise from the late 16th century, probably from Venice. The white linen garment is embroidered with lavender floss silk and gold thread. Notice that the placement of embroidered designs on this chemise is similar to those on the neck and sleeves of the chemise in Figure 8.13. (Image copyright © The Metropolitan Museum of Art. Image source: Art Resource, NY)

fashionable embroidery, originated in Spain and spread throughout the rest of Europe. This embroidery consisted of delicate black silk figures worked on fine, white linen, often being applied to the neck band and wrists of men's shirts and women's chemises (see Figure 8.10).

A variety of Italian drawn and cutwork techniques were also employed. Threads were removed from the fabric and embroidery applied to the now open areas. Cutwork was created by embroidering designs on solid cloth, then cutting away sections of the cloth between the decorations. In another decorative technique called **filet** or **lacis**, the artisan embroidered patterns on a net background. Both cutwork and filet are considered the forerunners of lace.

Lace making probably began in Europe just before the beginning of the 16th century. **Lace** differs from either cutwork or filet in that it is constructed entirely from threads, dispensing with any backing fabric.

Two types of lace were made: **needlepoint lace**, which seems to have originated in Italy, and **bobbin lace**, which may have originated in the Low Countries. Needlepoint lace is made by embroidering over base threads arranged in a pattern, and connecting these base threads with a series of small intricate stitches. Bobbin lace, also called **pillow lace**, created a complex pattern by twisting or knotting together a series of threads held on bobbins. These laces could be made of any fine thread—linen or silk or cotton. During the last half of the 16th century lace was used almost universally to decorate both men's and women's garments (see Figures 8.10, 8.12, and 8.17).

SOURCES OF EVIDENCE FOR THE STUDY OF COSTUME

Art Sources

Art is the primary source of information about what people wore in the 15th century. Portraits, drawings, and tapestries abound, and from these one can gain a wealth of information about upper class dress. A number of books about costume were published; however, these tend to mix accurate and inaccurate drawings and must be approached with care.

Documentary Sources

Scholars can find many more inventories and other documentary records for the 1500s than for earlier periods. Such records can confirm or supplement evidence from portraits. Nevinson (1968), for example, compared the portrait of Prince Edward (see Figure 8.19) to royal household accounts of the time. He concluded that the portrait was a reasonably accurate representation of the Prince's clothing. He also noted that household accounts provided information about the undergarments and types of fabrics that was not clear in simply viewing the portrait.

Garments

Costume historians also have access to more garments surviving from the 16th century. The illustrations in this chapter include several examples. Such materials help enormously in learning about details of clothing construction and cut.

COSTUME FOR MEN: 16TH CENTURY

The speed with which styles changed continued to increase in the 16th century. Costume of men and women in this century can be said to have gone through three different phases. In each phase, styles differed markedly from the preceding phase. The general dates of these phases, however, are not the same for the dress of women and men. Moreover, styles of accessory items and underclothing did not necessarily vary as much as the overall silhouette did. For these reasons the summary of details of costume in this chapter is organized as follows: costume for all three phases will be discussed first for men, then for women, and finally accessory items for men and women will be given a century-long overview.

The three phases seen in men's styles can be summarized as consisting of an early phase in which a transition was made from medieval styles to the styles of the Renaissance (c. 1500–1515); a second phase concentrated in the second to the fourth decades of the century, in which strong German influence can be seen (c. 1515–1550); and a final phase in which Spanish influences predominated (1550–1600).

Throughout the century men wore an evolved form of the earlier braies, which the English tended to refer to as **drawers**.

1500–1515

Garments

Shirts, made of white linen, were cut full and gathered into a round or square neckline. The neckline was often decorated with embroidery or cutwork. Shirts had long, raglan sleeves.

Doublets and hose were laced together, the doublet being only waist length. Hose were seamed into one garment with a codpiece at the front (see discussion of the origin of the codpiece in Chapter 7, page 197). In one version the doublet (also called a **paltock** in

England) was cut with a deep V at the front, which sometimes had a filler (or **stomacher**) of contrasting color inserted under the V (Figure 8.5). Laces could be used to hold the open area together, and also to hold the sleeves in place. Following the Italian styles, sleeves of shirts were bloused through openings in the sleeves.

Jackets, sometimes worn over doublets and cut the same length, were like doublets in shaping. They were made either with or without sleeves. In England the term **jerkin** was used synonymously with the word *jacket* after 1500. Often it is difficult to make out from period illustrations whether men's outermost garments are doublets or jackets, especially after bases gained in popularity.

Bases were separate short skirts worn with a jacket or doublet for civil dress or over armor for military dress. Made from a series of lined and stiffened gores (wedge-shaped pieces), bases persisted in civilian dress until well into the mid-century, and over armor for even longer (see Figures 8.5 and 8.7). The term probably derives from the fact that this was the lower part, or the "base" of the jacket. The term seems to have been applied to this lower section of the garment and also to separate skirts that became popular in the early 16th century. The metal

skins of some suits of armor were made to simulate bases. It was not uncommon for armor to incorporate details of contemporary fashion for men.

Gowns or robes were long, full garments with huge funnel-shaped or large hanging sleeves that opened down the front. The front facings were made of contrasting fabric or fur and turned back to form wide, decorative revers. Younger and more fashionable men wore shorter gowns, ending below the hips. Gowns were worn over doublets or jackets (see Figure 8.5). This garment seems to have been distinctively northern European and had no precise counterpart in Italian styles. In a painting by the Italian artist Carpaccio, dated from the first part of the 16th century and set in Venice, titled *Reception of the English Ambassadors*, the ambassadors are clearly distinguishable by their robes.

Circular cloaks, open at the front and with a slit up the back to facilitate horseback riding were worn over doublets and hose for warmth outdoors.

1515–1550

Whereas the earlier styles had relatively slender silhouettes, the second phase emphasized fullness

FIGURE 8.5 *Lady with Three Suitors*, France, c. 1500. The two more visible suitors wear, respectively, a short jacket with wide lapels and a skirt, or bases, and a long robe. Both dress their hair in the predominant straight-cut style and wear French bonnets. Their shoes have broad, rounded toes. The lady wears a wide-sleeved gown with a typical square neckline. Her headdress is a coif with lappets hanging down on either side of the face. (A Lady with Three Suitors, c. 1500. France, 16th century. Pen and brown ink, brush and brown wash, with traces of black chalk; 23.0 x 19.3 cm. The Cleveland Museum of Art, John L. Severance Fund 1956.40)

in the construction of the costume with large, bulky, puffed areas. Garments were ornamented with decorative **slashings** or **panes** (narrow strips of fabric), under which contrasting linings were placed (see Figures 8.6a and 8.7).

According to one story, these slashes originated on the battlefield. A ragged but victorious Swiss army was said to have stuffed the colorful silk fabrics they had looted from the enemy camp under their badly torn clothes to keep warm. This impromptu fashion was supposedly picked up and imitated by the general population. Whether true or not, the Swiss and German soldiers' uniforms were indeed made with multicolored fabrics and decorated with a variety of cuts and slashes, panes, and layers. These same features were evident in men's costume almost everywhere, although German influences were more muted in Italy. Read (1951) suggested that these

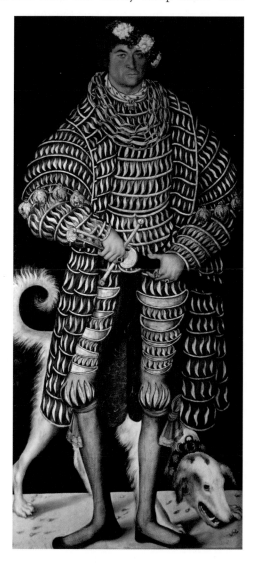

FIGURE 8.6 Henry, the German Duke of Saxony (a), and his wife Katarina of Mecklenburg (b) are dressed in typically German style of around about 1500. All of the duke's garments are ornamented with slashing. His wife's gown has sleeves made with a slashed puff at the elbow and cuffs that extend over her hand. Her large gold necklace and feathered hat are also typical of German women's dress. (Henry, Duke of Saxony (1473–1541), 1514 (oil on canvas), Cranach, Lucas, the Elder (1472–1553)/Gemaeldegalerie Alte Meister, Dresden, Germany/© Staatliche Kunstsammlungen Dresden/Bridgeman Images; bpk, Berlin/Gemaeldegalerie Alte Meister, Staatliche Kunstsammlungen, Dresden/Photographer Hans-Peter Klu/Art Resource, NY)

FIGURE 8.7 Henry VIII, king of England (1497–1543), is depicted wearing a doublet ornamented with slashes through which puffs of fabric are pulled. A prominent codpiece is visible at the front of the skirtlike bases. Over this is a fur-trimmed short robe. (Scala/Ministero per i Beni e le Attività culturali/ Art Resource, NY)

garments may have had a practical value as well, allowing men to lift and swing heavy weapons without placing too great a strain on the seams.

Garments

Shirts, doublets, and jackets continued much as before, with marked increases in the aforementioned slashed decoration. Instead of having separate bases, some doublets and jackets were cut with gored skirts. Some had no sleeves; some had wide U- or V-shaped necklines beneath which the wide neck, the doublet,

and part of the shirt were often visible. Bases were still worn with armor. Sleeves of the outermost garment were cut very full, often with a puff from armhole to elbow and a closer fit from elbow to wrist (see Figure 8.6a).

Men held up their hose by lacing them to the doublets. Some hose were divided into two sections: **upper stocks** and **nether stocks**, which were sewn together. Codpieces, the pouches of fabric for the genitals sewn at the front of the upper stocks, were sometimes padded for emphasis. Although upper stocks and nether stocks continued to be attached, upper stocks (also called **breeches**) eventually took on the appearance of a separate garment, and were cut somewhat fuller than the lower section. Style variations included long breeches, fitting the leg closely and ending at the knee, and breeches ending at the hip and more rounded. Any of these variations might be paned, with contrasting fabric placed beneath the panes.

Slight alterations in the cut and trim of gowns or robes made them wider. Wide revers extended into a wide collar. Sleeve types included those that were sleeveless but with wide, extremely deep armholes lined in contrasting fabric and turned back upon themselves to show off the lining. Other sleeves were either short, very full, puffed-and-slashed or paned sleeves (see Figure 8.7), or long, hanging sleeves.

1550–1600

By mid-century the width of the shoulders had narrowed somewhat and during the remainder of the century one can see gradual decreases in the width of the shoulders and gradual increases in the width of the hip area. By the beginning of the third phase a new combination of garments had evolved, and men no longer appeared in short jackets or longer skirted jackets and hose. Instead, the upper hose and nether hose had evolved into a large, padded breech (called **trunk hose**), which was joined to nether or lower stocks (Figure 8.8). Alternatively, separate breeches were worn with hose kept in place by garters. The codpiece gradually went out of style after mid-century.

FIGURE 8.8 *Prince Hercule-François, Duc d'Alençon*, 1572. The duke wears wide, somewhat melon-shaped, paned trunk hose with a codpiece. His jacket, with its high collar surrounded by a small ruff, has the fashionable peascod-belly shape, and finishes below the waistline in a row of pecadils. His hat is in the copotain (also spelled capotain) shape, decorated with a jeweled band and a plume. The short cape is fur lined. (Image courtesy of The National Gallery of Art, Samuel H. Kress Collection)

Garments

Around mid-century men displayed the small, square collar of the shirt at the neck edge of the doublet. Next, the collar of the shirt became a small ruffle, and in the final stage of evolution, the **ruff** developed as an individual item of costume, separate from the shirt. Very wide, often of lace, and stiffly starched, the ruff became one of the most characteristic features of costume during the second half of the 16th century and persisted into the first decades of the 17th century as well (see Contemporary Comments 8.1 and Figures 8.8 and 8.10).

The neck of the doublet was cut high, its shape and finish varied. A row of small, square flaps called **pecadils** was placed just below the waist (see Figure 8.8). Sleeves, though padded, followed the shape of the arm and narrowed as the century progressed until by 1600 sleeves were unpadded and closely fitted. Waistlines followed the natural waist at the back, but dipped to a point at the front, where padding emphasized the shape. By 1570 the amount of padding increased and the point at the front of the doublet became so pronounced that it was called a **peascod belly** as it resembled the puffed-out chest of a peacock (see Figures 8.8 and 8.10).

The jacket was similar in shape to the doublet, over which it was worn. It usually had short puffed sleeves or pecadils at the arm and no sleeve, thereby making the sleeve of the doublet the outermost sleeve.

Breeches were separate garments worn together with separate stockings. They included skintight versions, those wide at the top and tapering to the knee (called **Venetians**), and those wide and full throughout (called **open breeches**; Figures 8.9 and 8.10).

Trunk hose were made in several shapes. Melon-shaped trunk hose were usually paned, heavily padded, and ended at the hip or somewhat below. They were approximately the shape of a pumpkin (see Figure 8.8). Others sloped gradually from a narrow waist to fullness concentrated about mid-thigh, where they ended (see Figure 8.9). This type may have been called **gallygaskins** or **slops**. One form had limited use outside of very fashionable court circles. It was made of a short section, not much more than a pad around the hips, worn with very tight-fitting hose (see Figure 8.10). Boucher (n.d.) called them **culots**.

Trunk hose and, to a lesser extent, doublets were heavily padded with **bombast**, a stuffing made of wool, horsehair, short linen fibers called tow, or bran. Excessive use of bombast led one chronicler to suggest that a man was carrying the whole contents of his bed and his table linen as stuffing in his trunk hose. It was said that the English parliament house had to be enlarged to accommodate the bulky trunks of the members (Wescher, n.d.).

FIGURE 8.9 Close-up photograph (c. 1600) of slashed satin breeches shows how this garment was constructed. (V&A Images, London/Art Resource, NY)

Canions were extensions from the end of the trunk hose to the knees or slightly below that were either made in the same color or a contrasting color to trunk hose. Canions fastened to separate stockings at the bottom (see Figure 8.10).

Stockings were more often used with trunk hose and canions than the long, joined hose. Stockings and hose were either cut and sewn or knitted. References to knitting begin to appear around 1530.

After the middle of the century shorter and longer capes for outdoors largely replaced the aforementioned gowns. Short capes were cut very full, flaring out sharply from the shoulder.

COSTUME FOR WOMEN: 16TH CENTURY

During the classical and medieval periods, undergarments helped provide warmth and protected the skin from the garments worn closest to the body and the garments from being soiled by perspiration. By the 16th century there were changes in the function of undergarments—changes that had their beginnings in previous centuries but that became especially obvious during the 1500s.

Just when undergarments took on the function of shaping the body is not entirely clear. Ewing (1981)

FIGURE 8.10 Engraving of 1581 shows men who all wear peascod-belly–shaped doublets and neck ruffs. The man at left wears very full Venetian breeches, the men second from left and at the far right wear short trunks attached to full-length hose, and the man third from the left wears short trunks with canions. The engraver, de Bruyn D'Anvers, has identified them as Spanish. (Courtesy of Fairchild Publications, Inc.)

Contemporary Comments 8.1

PURITAN VIEW OF 16TH-CENTURY FASHION

Philip Stubbes, a Puritan writer of the Elizabethan period, published Anatomy of Abuses in England *in 1583. Included within a lengthy section in which he decries contemporary fashions is the following discussion of ruffs, an important part of the fashions of his time, and the variety of fabrics from which they could be made.*

Of ruffs worn by men, Stubbes says:

They have great and monstrous ruffs, made either of cambric, holland, lawn, or else of some other the finest cloth that can be got for money, whereof some be a quarter of a yard deep, yea some more, very few less; so that they stand a full quarter of a yard (and more) from their necks, hanging over their shoulder points instead of a veil. . . . The devil first . . . invented these great ruffs. . . . [The one arch or pillar whereby his kingdom of great ruffs is underpropped, is a certain kind of liquid matter which they call starch, wherein the devil has willed them to wash and dry their ruffs well, which, when they be dry, will then stand stiff and inflexible around their necks. The other pillar is a certain device of wires, created for the purpose, whipped over either with gold, thread, silver, or silk and this he [the devil] calls a support-asse, or underpropper. This is to be applied round their necks under the ruff, upon the outside of the band, to bear up the whole frame and body of the ruff from falling and hanging down.

Of women's ruffs, Stubbes says:

The women there use great ruffs and neckerchiefs of holland, lawn, cambric, and such cloth, as the greatest thread shall not be so big as the least hair that is: then lest they should fall down they are smeared and starched . . .; after that dried with great diligence, streaked, patted, and rubbed very nicely, and so applied to their goodly necks. [*Stubbes describes the styles of ruffs*] [T]hree or four degrees of minor ruffs [are] placed *gradatim*, step by step, one beneath another, and all under the master devil ruff. The skirts then, of these great ruffs are long and fall every way, pleated and crested full curiously. . . . Then, last of all, they are either clogged with gold, silver, or silk lace of stately price, wrought all over with needle work, speckled and sparkled here and there with the sun, the moon, the stars, and many other antiques, strange to behold. Some are wrought with open work down to the midst of the ruff and further, some so cloyed with pearled lace, and so pestered with other gewgaws as the ruff is the least part of itself. Sometimes they are pinned up to their ears, sometimes they are suffered to hang over their shoulders, like windmill sails fluttering in the wind, and thus every one pleaseth herself with her foolish devices.

Stubbes, P. (1877). *Phillip Stubbes's Anatomy of Abuses in England in Shakespeare's Youth A.D. 1583.* (F. J. Furnivall, Ed.). London, UK: New Shakespeare Society.

saw the forerunner of the corset in the tightly laced cote of the medieval period and cited evidence of a linen underbodice made from two layers of fabric stiffened with glue. By the 17th century this garment had taken on the name **stays** in English. Earlier it had been known as a **pair of bodys** as it was cut into two sections and fastened at the front and back with laces or tapes. This garment appears not only as an undergarment, but occasionally as an outer garment as well.

A few examples of steel or iron corsets dating from the 16th century can be found in museums.

These are regarded as either orthopedic garments or fanciful reconstructions made after this period. There is no evidence that these iron corsets were worn as fashionable dress. The stays that were worn seem to have followed the pattern described earlier: made of cloth, shaped as an under bodice and laced together at front, back, or both. The stiffening was provided by a **busk**, a device made from a long flat piece of wood or whalebone that was sewn into one or more casings provided in the stays. When gowns were constructed with a V-shaped section, called a *stomacher*, at the front of the bodice that extended to the waist or beyond, this removable busk could be placed in a sort of pocket sewn in the back of the stomacher.

The shaping and support of the outer garment is yet another function of undergarments, and was a particularly important element in women's clothing of the 1500s. Beginning with the verdugale, continuing with the bum roll, and culminating in the huge wheel farthingale, undergarments henceforth are important elements in the shape of western costume.

1500–1530

The first phase of women's costume was a transition from the styles of the medieval period.

Garments

The chemise continued to be the undermost garment. The gowns worn over the chemise were fairly plain; somber colors predominated. Bodices were fitted. Skirts were long and full, flaring gently from the waistline to the floor in the front and trailing into long trains at the back (see Figure 8.5).

Women wore either a single dress or two layers consisting of an outer and an under dress. If two dresses were worn, the outer skirt might be looped up in front to display the contrasting skirt of the under dress. Trains on outer gowns often had decorative underlinings. The train was buttoned or pinned to the waist at the back in order to show the lining fabric.

Most often dress necklines were square, with the edge of the chemise visible, or they might be cut with smaller or larger V-shaped openings at the front or at both front and back. Lacings held the V-shaped opening together.

Sleeve styles included smooth-fitting narrow sleeves with decorative cuffs, wide funnel shapes with contrasting linings, and hanging sleeves. When two layers were worn, the under dress usually had closely fitted sleeves and the outermost layer had large, full, funnel-shaped sleeves or hanging sleeves.

On ceremonial occasions, the open mantle fastened with a chain or braid at the front. For ordinary wear outdoors, women wore long, full cloaks.

Germany: 1530–1575

Although costume of the 16th century had become more international with styles from one country or another often predominating, regional differences continued to exist. This is particularly evident in German women's styles of the first half of the century (see Figure 8.6b).

During the second half of the century, German styles were subject to Spanish influence and lost much of their unique character. Styles of the first half of the 16th century had the following features. Softly gathered skirts were joined to closely fitted bodices that had low and square or rounded necklines. The neckline was usually filled in, most often by the chemise. Bodices were elaborately decorated or embroidered across the bosom. Sleeves were close fitting, with tight horizontal bands alternating with somewhat enlarged, puffed areas. The cuff extended into a point over the wrist. (This sleeve style does appear in other northern countries over the same period, but may itself derive from the Italian sleeves of the latter half of the 15th century in which the chemise puffed through openings in a tightly fitted sleeve.)

Hair was often held in a net, over which was placed a wide-brimmed hat trimmed with plumes. Gold chains, frequently worn along with a wide, jeweled "dog collar," were important status symbols.

Other Northern European Countries: 1530–1575

The second phase of costume for women outside of Germany was marked by Spanish influences (see

Figure 8.12), whereas men's styles of this period had been more directly influenced by German styles. Spanish influence was not evident in men's clothing until the second half of the century. One important aspect of the Spanish influence was a tendency to emphasize dark colors, especially black.

The changes in women's clothing after 1530 represent a gradual evolution in style, not a radical change.

Garments

Significant changes took place in the construction of dresses. Instead of an under dress and an outer dress, women wore a **petticoat** (an underskirt) and an overdress. The overall silhouette was rather like an hourglass. Bodices narrowed to a small waistline. Skirts gradually expanded to an inverted cone shape with an inverted V opening at the front (Figure 8.11).

Bodices and skirts of dresses were sewn together. The bodice narrowed and flattened, becoming quite rigid, and the waist dipped to an elongated V at the front. A rich, jeweled belt outlined the waistline, and from the dip in front its long end fell down the center front of the gown almost to the floor.

At first most necklines were square. Later more closed styles were preferred. Such dresses had closed necklines with standing, wing collars or necklines filled in by the chemise, which closed up to the throat and ended in a small ruffle (see Figure 8.13). Ruffs, of moderate size at this phase of their development, were worn with high, fitted collars (Figure 8.12).

The first of many changes in sleeves came early in the period when the previously described German and Italian style sleeves were adopted. Subsequently, others developed. Many sleeves were narrow at the shoulder and expanded to a huge, wide square cuff that turned back on itself. This cuff was often made of fur or of heavy brocade that matched the petticoat. A detachable, false sleeve, decorated with panes and slashes through which the linen of the chemise was visible might be sewn to the underside of the cuff, or, if the chemise was richly decorated, the sleeve of the chemise might be seen below the cuff (Figure 8.13; see also Figure 8.11).

FIGURE 8.11 Dress in the style that developed after the third decade of the 16th century. The ruffled cuff of the chemise is visible at the end of the sleeve. Large, detachable undersleeves match the fabric of the petticoat. The flared skirt was supported underneath by a hoop called a *verdugale* or *Spanish farthingale*. The painting by an unknown artist is of Queen Elizabeth I as a princess. (Album/Art Resource, NY)

Another style had a puff at the shoulder and a close-fitting, long extension of the sleeve to the wrist. Though worn elsewhere as well, this style was especially popular in France. A relatively simple style was full from shoulder to wrist where it was caught into a cuff. Some sleeves were remarkably complex, especially those worn at the Spanish court, as they utilized combinations of fitted, full, and hanging sleeves (see Figure 8.12).

Sleeve decorations included cutting and paning with decorative fabrics, and fastening the panes with

FIGURE 8.12 Stiffly rigid styles, often in black or white with elaborate embroidery and lace, were characteristic of the Spanish styles that influenced all of Europe in the 16th century (c. 1584). (Album/Art Resource, NY)

FIGURE 8.13 *Portrait of a Young Lady, Flemish*, c. 1535. The chemise, elaborately embroidered in black work, shows clearly at the neck and below the sleeves of the young lady's gown. Her sleeves, fitted at the shoulder, widen at the bottom. Her small coif is decorated with jewels. Her hair is enclosed in a dark, possibly velvet, hood at the back. (Image copyright © The Metropolitan Museum of Art. Image source: Art Resource, NY)

aiguillettes (small, jeweled metal points). Padded rolls of fabric were sometimes located at the joining of bodice and sleeve and these served to hide the laces fastening separate sleeves to bodices.

Skirts became more rigid. Many dresses were untrained and floor length. Although the petticoat was separate from the dress, its visibility through the inverted V at the front of the skirt made it an integral part of the ensemble. Petticoats were usually cut from rich, decorative fabric (often brocade or cut velvet).

The back of the petticoat was covered by the skirt of the dress, which made it possible to make the front of the petticoat of expensive fabric, and the invisible back of lighter weight, less-expensive fabric.

The flared, cone-shaped skirt required support to achieve the desired rigidity of line. A Spanish device called the **verdugale** (in Spanish, *verdugado*) or **Spanish farthingale** provided that support. The verdugale was a construction of whalebone, cane, or steel hoops graduated in size from the waist to the floor and sewn into a petticoat or underskirt. Formerly a visible part of the construction of traditional Spanish dress of the region of Catalonia, the hoops were at first sewn into the dress itself. English chroniclers report that Katharine of Aragon, the first wife of King Henry VIII, wore such a skirt in the early part of the century when she came to England from Spain; however, at that time it was noted as a foreign and atypical style.

FIGURE 8.14 *Portrait of Margaretta of Parma*, by Anthonis Mor van Dashorst, second half of the 16th century. This lady wears a Spanish-style, sleeveless ropa. Small ruffles, probably on her chemise, extend above the high collar and below the ends of her sleeves. Her coif dips slightly at the front. (The Philadelphia Museum of Art/Art Resource, NY)

The **ropa** was a garment of Spanish origin. It was an outer gown or surcote made either sleeveless or with one of several types of sleeve: a short puffed sleeve, or with a long sleeve, puffed at the top and fitted for the rest of the arm's length. The ropa fell from the shoulders, unbelted in an A-line to the floor. Some versions closed in front, but most were open to display the dress beneath. Some researchers have suggested that this garment originated with the Moors who had occupied Spain in the preceding centuries—it has the loose fit of a Middle Eastern caftan—and that it can be seen as another instance of Middle Eastern influences on European styles (Figure 8.14).

Costume Components: 1575–1600

The first changes in the last quarter of the century came in the shape of the skirt, which grew wider at the top (Figure 8.15). Instead of the cone-shaped Spanish farthingale, a padded roll was placed around the waist in order to give skirts greater width below the waist.

The English called these pads **bum rolls**, "bum" being English slang for buttocks. For better support of dresses than these rolls provided and to attain greater width, a modification of the farthingale was made. Instead of using graduated circles of whalebone, cane, or steel sewn into a canvas skirt, the circles were made the same diameter top to bottom. Steel or cane spokes fastened the topmost hoop to a waistband. It was called the **wheel**, **drum**, or **French farthingale** (Figures 8.15, 8.16, and 8.17).

This style was not used in Italy nor, to any great extent, in Spain at this period. Instead the older, hourglass shape of the Spanish farthingale with a slightly padded roll at the waist predominated. The wheel farthingale was essentially a northern European style. Even in northern Europe, some women continued to wear Spanish farthingales, or dresses widened slightly at the waist with bum rolls, or small wheel farthingales.

Dresses worn over wheel farthingales had enormous skirts that were either cut and sewn into one continuous piece all around, or open at the front or sides over a matching underskirt. A ruffle the width of the flat shelflike section of the farthingale was sometimes attached to the skirt. To avoid having the body appear disproportionately short in contrast with the width of the skirt, sleeves were made fuller and with very high sleeve caps. The stomacher at the front of the bodice was elongated, ending in a deep V at the waist. Additional height came from high-standing collars and dressing the hair high on the head.

Skirts of Spanish women of the late 16th and early 17th centuries often had a horizontal pleat going around the skirt. Explanations of its functions differ. It may have been placed there to allow enough fabric for the dress to be repaired if the skirt hem frayed, or it may have allowed the skirt to bend when the woman was seated, thereby modestly covering her legs (Reade, 1951).

Ruffs grew to enormous widths. Made of sheer linen or of lace, they had to be supported by a frame called the **supportasse** (see Figure 8.18) or by starching. Methods of constructing ruffs included gathering one edge of a band of fabric or lace to the size of the neck

FIGURE 8.15 *Princess Elizabeth (1596–1662), Later Queen of Bohemia*, ca. 1606, by Robert Peake (c. 1551–1619). The lady wears a wheel farthingale. The skirt of the farthingale opens at the front, but the petticoat beneath it is not visible. Around the waist is a ruffle the width of the farthingale. She wears a standing lace ruff at the neck. Her hair is dressed high with jeweled decorations. (Image copyright © The Metropolitan Museum of Art. Image source: Art Resource, NY)

to form a frill of deep folds or placing several layers of round lace pieces one over the other. Some ruffs were simply round, flat lace pieces without depth or folds, more like a wide collar. Open ruffs, almost a cross between a collar and a ruff, stood high behind the head and fastened in front into a wide, square neckline (see Figure 8.15). During the 18th and 19th centuries, revivals of this style were called **Medici collars** after the Medici queens of France, Catherine and Marie, in whose reigns this style was popular.

The **conch**, known in French as a *conque*, was a sheer, gauzelike veil so fine that in some portraits it can just barely be seen. It was cut the full length of the body from shoulder to floor and worn capelike over the shoulders. At the back of the neck it was attached to a winglike construction that stood up like a high collar behind the head. Some writers consider the conch to have had some significance as a widow's costume, and this may be true in France; however, in England it seems to have been more widely worn as a purely decorative element of dress by women, such as Queen Elizabeth, who were never widowed (see Figure 8.17).

COSTUME ACCESSORIES FOR MEN AND WOMEN: 16TH CENTURY

Changes in the styles of many accessories did not precisely parallel changes in overall silhouettes. Therefore the discussion of accessory items for men and women is not divided into phases, but extends across the entire century. See Illustrated Table 8.1 for depictions of some of the most widely worn accessory items.

Hair and Headdress for Men

At the beginning of the century men cut their hair straight across the back in a length anywhere from below the ears to the shoulder and combined this with a fringe of bangs across the forehead (see Figure 8.5). Among the fashionable hat styles was a pillboxlike shape with a turned-up brim. Some versions had decorative cutout sections in the brim. This hat was sometimes referred to as a **French bonnet** (see Figure 8.5). Men also wore a skullcap or hairnet holding the hair close to the head over which they placed a hat with a basin-shaped crown and wide brim, with the brim turned up at one point. Many hats were decorated with feathers.

After 1530 beards became fashionable, and the hair was cut short (see Figure 8.7). Hat styles included a moderately sized, flat-crowned hat with a small brim and a feather plume and beretlike styles with feather plumes (see Illustrated Table 8.1).

After mid-century men allowed their hair to grow longer; beards and mustaches remained popular (see Figure 8.10). Hats were made with increasingly high crowns, some with soft shapes, others with stiffer outlines. Brims tended to be narrow. The high-

FIGURE 8.16 Women in farthingales and men wearing jackets with wide ruffs, breeches, and hose participate in a ball at the court of the French king, Henri III, c. 1582. (© RMN-Grand Palais/Art Resource, NY)

FIGURE 8.17 *Portrait of a Lady*, c. 1600, by an unknown British painter. Over a farthingale-style dress, the lady wears a conch, a sheer headdress, and a cape edged in pearls. Her lace ruff is in the open style. In her right hand she holds a feathered fan. Her brocade dress is decorated with jeweled rosettes. (Image copyright © The Metropolitan Museum of Art. Image source: Art Resource, NY)

FIGURE 8.18 Drawing shows a ruff "underpropped with a supportasse," a frame that holds the ruff in place. (Courtesy of Fairchild Publications, Inc.)

crowned, narrow-brimmed hat was called a **copotain**, and this style remained popular until well into the 17th century (see Figure 8.8). Trimmings for hats included feathers, braid, and jewels.

Hair and Headdress for Women

The custom of having married and adult women cover the hair continued. One of the most important head coverings was the coif—a cap of white linen or more decorative fabric, usually with long lappets or short square (or pointed) extensions below the ears that covered the side of the face. Coif shapes ranged from round to heart-shaped or **gabled**, an English style

Illustrated Table 8.1

Northern Renaissance: Accessories

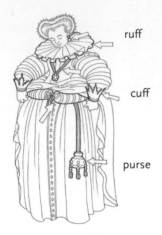

ruff

cuff

purse

Late 1500s. Woman with bum roll at waist, purse, lace ruff and cuffs, necklace and earrings

Feather fans, 16th century, and a square face shield

Elizabethan gloves

Women's headdress

English hood, 16th century

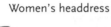

French hood, 16th century

German hat and hairnet, 16th century

Hat, late 1500s

Jeweled collar, King Henry VIII

Duckbilled shoes, first half 1500s

Small pins in king's hat

Undecorated cap of ordinary citizen

Early 1500s, Jeweled and feather-trimmed beret-style hat

shaped like a pointed arch (see Illustrated Table 8.1). Over the coif, women pinned a band about 40 inches long and 4 inches wide. The ends either hung down at either side of the face or were arranged in decorative folds. Some of these bands had hoods of semicircular fabric attached at the back. As the century progressed, the coif was set further back on the head, allowing more hair to show. Decorative overcaps might be placed on top of the coif, some trimmed with jewels or metallic netting (see Figures 8.11, 8.13, and 8.14).

In the last two thirds of the century, more hair was visible. The hair was combed back from the forehead, puffed up slightly around the face, then pulled into a coil at the back of the head. Local differences arose. The French combed the hair up, over small pads on either side to form a heart-shaped frame for the face. The English imitated the hair color of the queen, which was red, so that among ladies of the court red, auburn, and varying shades of blonde hair were fashionable. (Toward the end of her reign, Queen Elizabeth's hair had become so thin that she generally wore a red wig.) To balance the width of the wheel farthingale, women gained extra height by dressing the hair high and decorating it with jeweled ornaments (see Figures 8.15 and 8.17).

Hats popular toward the end of the century were generally small, with high crowns and narrow brims, and were trimmed with feathers (see Illustrated Table 8.1). Jeweled nets and caps were also worn.

Footwear

With a few exceptions, trends in styles of footwear were similar for men and for women. Often because they were more visible, men's styles tended to greater exaggeration. Square-toed shapes expanded as the period progressed, especially for men's shoes. By mid-century, when Mary I was queen of England, shoes had become so wide that a law was passed limiting the width to 6 inches. Decorations included slashing with puffs of fabric pulled through the openings. Costume historians of the 19th century called these shoes **duckbills**, because their shape resembled the bill of a duck (see Illustrated Table 8.1).

During the second half of the century, toes remained square, but width decreased and shoes conformed more closely to the shape of the foot. Shoes were also slashed at this time, but instead of puffs had a contrasting lining underneath that showed when the foot was bent.

Among the shoe styles worn by men and women were backless shoes called mules. Some shoes had a tongue and tied shut with laces (called **latchets**) that crossed the tongue from either side. High-heeled shoes for men and women first appeared sometime during the 1570s. The heels were about $1\frac{1}{2}$ inches high. Sometimes ribbon rosettes were placed at the front of the shoe or decorative stones were set into them.

Styles worn only by women included low-cut slippers with a strap across the ankle and chopines. These high, platform-soled shoes can be seen first in Italy, from where their use spread to other parts of Europe.

Boots were worn outdoors when riding horseback.

Jewelry

Although lavishly used by royalty and wealthy men and women during the first half of the century, jewelry use by men declined during the second half of the century. Men did not give up wearing jewelry but rather wore smaller quantities and more restrained pieces. Women continued to wear large quantities of extravagant jewels. Men wore wide, jeweled collars that were not a part of the garment but a separate circular piece made of ornamental plates joined together. Both men and women wore neck chains of gold or other precious metals that were wrapped several times around the neck. Women wore pendant necklaces.

Jeweled decorations were applied to almost any part of the costume. Men and women pinned brooches to hats, hoods, and other parts of the clothing. During the time when large, lacy ruffs were worn, some of which looked somewhat like spider webs, women wore jeweled pins made in the shape of spiders among the folds of the ruff. Aiguillettes (*ay'-gwe-laze*), small, jeweled points mounted on laces that served to hold panes or slashes together, were also placed on hats. Sleeve clasps, small jeweled pins, held paned segments of sleeves together (see Illustrated Table 8.1).

Earrings, seen in paintings of women, and occasionally of men, were popular in countries and periods when the hair or headdress did not cover the ears. Rings were worn everywhere. Bracelets were obscured by the large sleeves, and so were not much worn.

Some items of jewelry were worn exclusively by women. Women wore ferronieres in France, but this forehead ornament was not especially popular in England. Jeweled belts with long cords hanging down the front became popular for women after the second decade. On the cord were mounted such things as a jeweled tassel, a perfume holder (**pomander**), a purse, or a mirror.

Accessories

Both men and women carried purses, which were often suspended from belts. Middle and lower class persons used leather pouches. Purses of the wealthy were ornamented with embroidery, beading, metalwork, and jewels.

In their earliest form, fans were squares of embroidered fabric mounted on a stick. Later fans included ostrich or peacock feathers mounted on ornamental sticks and circular folding fans.

Both men and women carried handkerchiefs and wore gloves. Fashionable gloves often had decorated cuffs.

Women wore masks outdoors when riding to protect the complexion against the sun. Amateur performers in theatrical productions also used them, as did persons who wanted to remain disguised.

Cosmetics

Many cosmetics were made from potentially dangerous chemicals such as mercuric salts, which were used to whiten the complexion. Red coloring was applied to lips and cheeks. Perfumes were used. Puritans railed against these "evil practices," predicting that men and women would pay dearly for their concessions to vanity when they reached the afterworld. Philip Stubbes, writing in 1583, said,

> It must be granted that the dyeing and coloring of faces with artificial colors, and unnatural ointments is most offensive to God and derogatory to his Majesty. . . . And what are

FIGURE 8.19 *Portrait of Edward VI as a Child*, c. 1540, by Hans Holbein the Younger. The young prince is dressed in a miniature version of adult styles of the time, including an embroidered shirt that is visible at the neck and sleeves. Both his hat and sleeves are decorated with aiguillettes. Although the lower half of his garment is not visible, it is likely that at this early age the prince would have been wearing long skirts. (Image courtesy of The National Gallery of Art, Andrew Mellon Collection, 1937)

> they [artificial colors] else than the Devil's intentions, to entangle poor fools in the nets of perdition. (p. 66)

COSTUME FOR CHILDREN: 16TH CENTURY

The pattern of dressing children in the same kind of costume as their elders continued during the 16th century. Small children, both boys and girls, were dressed in skirts until they passed the age of 5 or 6, and then boys donned doublet and hose and whatever other garments were fashionable for men at the time. They did not escape even the large ruffs, which must have been especially awkward and ungainly for active children. Royal children wore elaborate, costly silks made into heavy velvets and brocades (Figure 8.19). Children of the poor and middle class dressed more simply, just as lower and middle class adults dressed more simply than the wealthy.

Patterns in social behavior can perhaps be related to developments in Spanish styles. Standards of social behavior and religious practice were rigorously enforced in Spain. At this same time, clothing style lines were stiff and rigid. Reade (1951) compared the use of Spanish undergarments that crated rigid silhouettes to the restraints imposed on society by the Spanish inquisition.

The theme of POLITICAL INFLUENCES emerges when the dress of monarchs such as Charles I and Catherine de Medici of France or Elizabeth I of England was imitated. This theme and its accompanying CROSS-CULTURAL INFLUENCES can be seen again as the rise and fall of fashion leadership parallel gains and losses of international prestige during the century. In the first half of the century fashion leadership came from Germany, Italy, and then, as Spain gained ascendency, chiefly from Spain in the second half. By the end of the century, Spanish fashion influence decreased just as Spanish political power was also waning.

LEGACY OF 16TH-CENTURY DRESS

A considerable number of details of costume that originated in the 16th century have become part of the repertory of fashion design in subsequent centuries. Some examples include the ruff (see Modern Influences) and the open, standing collar, later named the Medici collar. From the 16th century onward, an undergarment for supporting skirts appeared at least once in every century. The precise form of these garments is not the same in each instance, but once the basic idea that skirt shapes could be supported by a hoop or panniers was accepted, that idea was revived periodically (see Figure 10.17, page 285, and Illustrated Tables 13.1 and 17.1, pages 365 and 523).

REFERENCES

Boucher, F. (n.d.) *20,000 years of fashion*. New York, NY: Abrams.

Chamberlin, E. R. (1969). *Everyday life in Renaissance times*. New York, NY: Putnam.

Derry, T. K., & Williams, T. L. (1961). *A short history of technology*. New York, NY: Oxford University Press.

Ewing, E. (1981). *Dress and undress*. New York, NY: Drama Books.

Nevinson, J. L. (1968). Prince Edward's clothes. *Costume, 2*(1), p. 3–8.

Reade, B. (1951). *Costume of the western world: The dominance of Spain*. London, UK: Harrap.

St. Clair, A. N. (1973). *The image of the Turk in Europe* [Exhibit catalog]. New York, NY: Metropolitan Museum of Art.

Stubbes, P. (1877). *Phillip Stubbes's anatomy of abuses in England in Shakespeare's youth A.D. 1583* (F. J. Furnivall, Ed.). London, UK: New Shakespeare Society.

Wescher, H. (n.d.). Dress and fashion at the court of Queen Elizabeth. *CIBA Review, 78*, 2846.

MODERN INFLUENCES

Ruffs, major style features in Northern Europe in the 1500s, are sometimes revived, although rarely are they used to construct an entire blouse, as was done for the Givenchy haute couture collection in Spring/Summer of 2008.

(Catwalking/Getty Images)

PART FOUR

Baroque and Rococo

During the 17th century, Europe endured a crisis—a series of social and political upheavals involving civil war, revolts, peasant uprisings, and a rebellion against the nobility. This continent-wide crisis so shook the European nations that a form of stronger government—absolute monarchy—was needed to overcome it. By the 18th century, absolute monarchy was generally accepted everywhere in Europe except Great Britain, where the monarch's power had been limited as a result of the Glorious Revolution of 1688.

Nearly every year during the 18th century, there was either a war in progress or a rumor of an impending war. The wars between European powers became global, with the fighting spreading to India and North America. The century concluded in an era of revolution, beginning with the American Revolution and ending with the cataclysm of the French Revolution.

The Reformation had ended, but religious strife continued. Late in the 1500s, the Roman Catholic Church mounted a counterreformation, which halted the spread of Protestantism. In many areas, however, Protestantism was firmly established, and from this point on Catholics and Protestants coexisted more or less peaceably. France and Spain were the major Roman Catholic powers; Britain, northern Germany, Scandinavia, and Holland remained Protestant.

Religious toleration had been established in France in 1598 with the Edict of Nantes, which ended a series of religious wars. However, in 1685 Louis XIV revoked the Edict of Nantes and resumed the persecution of French Protestants. Many of these people, called *Huguenots*, fled from France to other European countries or to North America. Large numbers of them worked in the silk industry, and their exodus had drastic effects on the French economy.

In England, a branch of Protestantism appeared that opposed the Church of England and sought to cleanse it from Roman rituals. Nicknamed *Puritans*, members of this branch became the leading faction in opposing the Stuart kings of England. Eventually Puritans would settle in New England.

THE ARTS DURING THE BAROQUE AND ROCOCO PERIODS

The Baroque style, generally dated from the end of the 16th century to the middle of the 18th century, is the name given to the artistic style that developed during this period. The **Baroque style** emphasized lavish ornamentation, free and flowing lines, and flat and curved forms (Figure IV.1). It was massive rather than delicate. The patrons for this art form included the Catholic and Protestant churches, the aristocracy,

FIGURE IV.1 This commode by preeminent Baroque cabinetmaker André-Charles Boulle would have been appropriate for furnishing the palace of Versailles. (Image copyright © The Metropolitan Museum of Art. Image source: Art Resource, NY)

and the affluent bourgeoisie. Because the courts of Europe were the center for royal patronage, artists and artisans clustered around these centers.

Clothing styles were affected by these changes in the arts, and one can see in the lines of garments, particularly those of the first half of the 1600s, reflections of the Baroque emphasis on curvilinear forms. Squire (1974) spoke of artists who drew fashion plates in which they

> *caught the characteristic manner of bunching up the skirt when walking, to emphasize that exuberant ballooning drapery so beloved of artists like Bernini far away in Rome. Such a gesture was surely not accidental, but*

the unconscious spirit of an age working to achieve a recognizable style in every aspect of life. (86)

From about 1720 to 1770, the **rococo style** supplanted the Baroque. Rococo styles were smaller and more delicate in scale than the Baroque and marked by S- and C-curves, tracery, scrollwork, and fanciful adaptations of Chinese, classical, and even Gothic lines. Rococo found a reflection in the fashions of the times: in the curving lines of the hoop-supported skirts, the delicate lace and flower decorations of dresses, and the pastel shades favored by women as well as in men's waistcoats ornamented with delicate, rococo embroideries.

The final phase of the 18th century was marked by a revival of interest in classical styles. The neoclassical style was expressed in architecture, painting, sculpture, interior design, and furnishings during the second half of the 18th century. Its influence in costume was not as strongly felt until the Directoire period during the last decade of the 18th century.

EXPANDING TRADE WITH EAST ASIA

For centuries trade with Asia had involved commodities that were of small bulk but high value. The oldest and best known of the products were spices, particularly pepper, which seasoned the European diet. Silk and cotton also became invaluable commodities that found mass market appeal.

Although overland trade with the east had existed for centuries, the sea voyages of merchant shipping were not made until the late 15th and early 16th centuries when the Portuguese traveled around South Africa to India. The Portuguese established a colony in Macao and also were the first European contacts with Japan in 1542. A limited trade between Europe and Japan developed, but in the 1600s the Japanese government chose a policy of seclusion for its people and barred all foreigners from its shores. Although Japan was closed to trade, the European nations quickly began to compete for other lucrative commerce with east Asia.

Late in the 16th century, English merchants encountered stiff competition from the Dutch, who were on the verge of cornering the spice trade. English merchants were too weak to compete individually; consequently, they joined together to form the East India Company in 1599. The following year Queen Elizabeth I granted a charter to the East India Company that gave it a monopoly of English trade from the Cape of Good Hope (southernmost point in Africa) to the Straits of Magellan (southern South America). In 1608 the company set up their first "factory" at Surat. Located throughout the Indian subcontinent, factories were armed trading outposts with their own government and military establishments. In 1615 the East India Company brought its first cargo of cotton goods and indigo from India to England, thus producing a demand for cheap, washable fabrics for clothing and furnishings.

THE COTTON TRADE WITH INDIA

In Europe, cotton fabrics from India quickly became popular. Chintz was a particularly important fabric among the imports. **Chintz** in 17th-century India was a hand-painted or printed fabric that was sometimes glazed. Eastern designs, both realistic and imaginary, were fashionable, and these were among the designs produced on Indian chintz fabrics. First used as table and bed linens, chintz was much in demand as material for clothing by the latter half of the 17th century. Colorful printed calicos made of cotton also become popular in England. The term *calico* was first applied to fine-quality, printed cotton fabrics from Calcutta, India. Later the term came to be applied to a wide variety of colorful, printed cotton fabrics of all qualities.

Women paid exorbitant prices for very fine, lightweight, plain-weave muslin cottons from Bengal that became enormously popular in the late 18th and early 19th centuries. The softness and drapability of this fabric probably made a significant contribution to changes in the style of women's clothing that came about at the end of the 18th century. Indian trade in cotton goods grew in England in spite of a succession of parliamentary laws established to protect the domestic trade. The demand for cotton goods was so strong that smuggling and the evasion of laws was widespread.

In 1666, after the restoration of the monarchy, Charles II granted a new charter that gave the East India Company wide-ranging powers, including the rights to wage war and conclude peace, acquire territory, coin money, command fortresses, and administer troops. The company had, in effect, become a sovereign state. When the wars with France came in the 18th century, the company loaned money to the British government. In the Seven Years' War (1756–1763), the French, who still had a foothold in India, were defeated and obliged to withdraw. The East India Company reigned supreme.

THE INDUSTRIAL REVOLUTION

The Industrial Revolution began in England partly as a result of attempts to mechanize production of English cottons so that they would be more competitive with the cheaper imports from India, which were threatening English industry. The revolution's full impact on the textile industry was a significant factor influencing textiles of the 1700s.

Technological innovations and industrial capitalism developed together in the textile industry, largely as a result of the high cost of some of the innovative machinery. The spinning mule, the spinning jenny, and the Arkwright water-powered spinning frame had been developed by the end of the 18th century, and they provided the necessary speed in carding and spinning, but the mechanized loom was yet to come.

THE CONSUMER SOCIETY AND THE ACCELERATION OF FASHION CHANGE

Fashionable behavior had been evident in western Europe since the Middle Ages. But participation in the fashion process had been limited, for the most part, to an affluent elite consisting of royalty and their courts, the nobility, professionals, and wealthy merchants. McKendrick, Brewer, and Plumb (1982) argued convincingly that all of this changed in the 18th century in England when the consumer society was born.

The economic benefits of expanding consumer demand became evident with the widespread desire for the cheap cottons imported by the East India Company. Participants in the consumer revolution came from all levels of society where there was enough income to purchase nonessential goods. The English class structure, more compact and open than elsewhere in Europe; higher wages; the large proportion of the population living in the urban center of London; and the growth of an aggressive retailing industry facilitated increase in consumer demand. The desire to be "in fashion" was exploited by commercial interests.

Although McKendrick et al. focused on English society, it is safe to assume that similar patterns of behavior would have been transplanted to the American colonies. France maintained its leadership in innovating dress fashions, but it was not until after the French Revolution that fashion participation occurred at varying societal levels.

Among the results of the consumer revolution and increased commercialization of production were the increase in the speed of fashion change and a wider variety of styles. Writers of the 18th century testified their amazement at the rapidity with which new fashions were introduced. The great burst of growth in fashion terminology provides additional evidence of the proliferation of new styles.

To interest consumers in new styles, fashion information was communicated and advertised to a broader audience. Engraved drawings of fashions, many hand-colored, could be purchased. Fashion dolls, prepared by Parisian dressmakers, had existed since the 14th century, but these dolls had originally circulated only among the elite. In England by the 18th century, fashion dolls could be viewed for two shillings and rented, probably so that the costume could be more accurately copied, for seven shillings (McKendrick et al., 1982). An even less expensive variant on fashion dolls were cardboard dolls with wardrobes sold for a few pence each.

By the close of the 18th century, the commercialization of fashion was well established. Throughout western Europe and in North America, most of the population adopted fashionable dress and followed fashion trends. Notable exceptions were peasants who maintained regional folk dress, slaves who had no control over the provision of their own clothing, the abject poor, religious orders, and some religious sects.

REFERENCES

McKendrick, N., Brewer, J., & Plumb, J. H. (1982). *The birth of a consumer society: The commercialization of eighteenth century England*. Bloomington, IN: Indiana University Press.

Squire, G. (1974). *Dress and society: 1560–1970*. New York, NY: Viking Press.

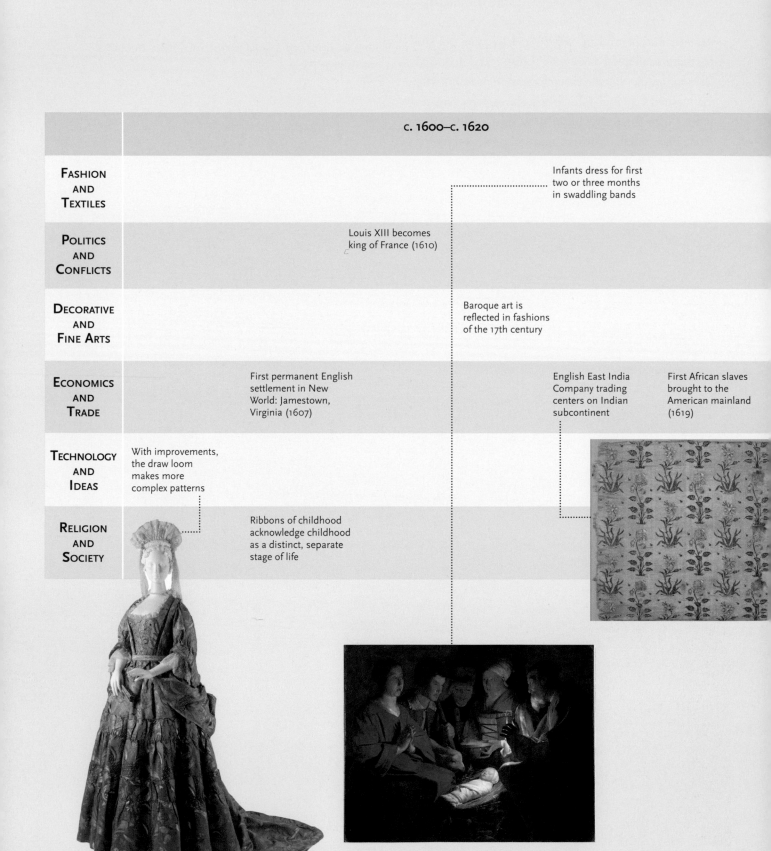

	c. 1600–c. 1620			
FASHION AND TEXTILES			Infants dress for first two or three months in swaddling bands	
POLITICS AND CONFLICTS	Louis XIII becomes king of France (1610)			
DECORATIVE AND FINE ARTS		Baroque art is reflected in fashions of the 17th century		
ECONOMICS AND TRADE	First permanent English settlement in New World: Jamestown, Virginia (1607)		English East India Company trading centers on Indian subcontinent	First African slaves brought to the American mainland (1619)
TECHNOLOGY AND IDEAS	With improvements, the draw loom makes more complex patterns			
RELIGION AND SOCIETY	Ribbons of childhood acknowledge childhood as a distinct, separate stage of life			

CHAPTER NINE

The Seventeenth Century

1600–1700

1620	1642–1660	1660	1669	1682	1685–1688	1689–1702

Louis XIV requires lavish dress at court

British civil war and republic

English monarchy reinstated

Louis XIV moves French court to Versailles

James II rules England

Ottoman Empire begins to disintegrate (1699)

Rembrandt dies

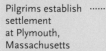

Pilgrims establish settlement at Plymouth, Massachusetts

William and Mary assent to Toleration Act, granting freedom of worship to Protestant dissenters

The ruling classes of the European powers in the 17th century (France, England, and Spain) originated and followed the fashions of this era. Other countries dominated the Italian peninsula, which remained divided into small political units. They, too, adopted prevailing fashions. Holland, now independent of Spain, was wealthy and prosperous with money enough to buy fashionable dress. The German princes, technically within the Holy Roman Empire, were sovereign powers, independent and free to make war or peace. The head of the Austrian Hapsburgs still had the title of Holy Roman Emperor, an illusionary honor. In reality, the Austrian Hapsburgs presided over only their hereditary lands in eastern Europe. As countries gained economic and political superiority, the fashions they favored tended to be the most widely followed.

Mannerist styles replaced Renaissance styles in the arts in the late 16th century. Mannerist art stressed realistic representation of religious themes, painted to appeal to the emotions of the beholder. The new style served as a bridge between the Renaissance and the Baroque styles. Italian artists of the 17th century led the artistic transition from Mannerism to the vigorous Baroque style that spread across the Alps into Northern Europe. The changes in art styles also influenced the form and ornamentation of dress styles.

Mannerist styles replaced Renaissance styles in the arts in the late 16th century. Mannerist art stressed realistic representation of religious themes to appeal to the emotions of the beholder. The new style served as a bridge between the Renaissance and the Baroque styles. Italian artists of the 17th century led the artistic transition from Mannerism to the vigorous Baroque style that spread across the Alps into Northern Europe.

HISTORICAL BACKGROUND

France

In France, the figure of Louis XIV dominated the Baroque period. Henry IV's young son became King Louis XIII after the assassination of Henry in 1610.

During a reign lasting until 1643, Louis XIII entrusted the government of France to Cardinal Richelieu, who sought to centralize authority in the monarchy and to raise France to a dominant position in Europe. After Richelieu's death in 1642, Cardinal Mazarin carried on his predecessor's work into the reign of Louis XIV, who succeeded his father on the throne in 1643 at the age of 5. At his death in 1715, after a reign of 72 years, Louis XIV's court had established a standard of grandeur to which other European monarchs would aspire but never equal (see Figure 9.1).

During his youth, some of the high-ranking nobility engaged in an open rebellion. This rebellion, called the *Fronde* (a Parisian child's game), was undertaken in an effort to ruin Cardinal Mazarin and to undermine absolute government. The life-threatening episode left a strong impression on young Louis. As an adult, he resolved to forestall rebellions by the nobility and to bring them to court where they could not endanger the security of France.

FIGURE 9.1 King Louis XIV in his royal robes. (© RMN-Grand Palais/Art Resource, NY)

Because the Fronde had also made Louis wary of the city mobs, he moved his court away from Paris. At great expense, he had an enormous palace constructed outside of Paris at the site of his father's hunting lodge. The Palace of Versailles became the symbol of the glory and the majesty of Louis XIV's reign, serving as a stage on which he played the role of an absolute monarch, the epitome of a divine-right king surrounded by fawning nobles.

When members of the nobility were out of favor with the king, they could not live close to the court, and instead were forced to live on their ancestral estates in the provinces. The king awarded salaried offices and pensions only to those living at court. By this tactic, Louis kept his nobles busy at court where he could keep an eye on them.

Noblemen at Versailles lived either at the palace in the royal apartments or in squalid lodgings. To maintain appearances at court, a nobleman needed an expensive, varied wardrobe and funds to spend on life at court. Nobles competed to participate in a complicated court ritual that included helping the king get up in the morning and prepare him for bed at night. Louis XIV kept the nobles so busy waiting on him and spending money that they had neither the time nor the funds to plot against him.

In 1589, Louis XIV's grandfather, Henry IV, had issued the Edict of Nantes, a political arrangement intended to bring peace between the warring Protestant minority, the Huguenots, and the Roman Catholic majority in France. Because the edict contravened Louis XIV's ideal of "one faith, one law, one king," his government gradually whittled away the rights enjoyed by the Huguenots. Louis formally revoked the Edict of Nantes in 1689, after which an estimated 200,000 Huguenots left France and settled in England, the Netherlands, Prussia, and even Boston and Charleston. Those exiled included many skilled artisans from the textile industries. Silk workers settled in Spitalfields, England, an important textile center. This influx of new labor stimulated this important English industry.

In his search for glory, Louis tried to dominate Europe through a series of wars. The European powers, reacting to his aggressions, formed alliances to thwart his ambitions. Louis's efforts at dominating Europe succeeded only in exhausting the nation and impoverishing the people. Despite his sins and errors, however, Louis XIV set the style for absolute monarchy, a style that was copied throughout Europe.

England

While the French king grew more powerful, the English monarchy across the channel was in difficulty. James VI of Scotland, cousin of Queen Elizabeth I, was crowned James I of Great Britain upon her death. The son of the ill-fated Mary Queen of Scots, James backed away from real confrontation with Parliament over issues of succession. A radical Protestant faction within the Church of England, the Puritans, grew during his reign. The Puritans wanted to purify the Church of England of the remnants of Roman Catholic ritual and practice. Some Puritans, known to American history as pilgrims, were sufficiently unhappy with James's religious policies that they fled to Holland, and from there in 1620 they sailed on the Mayflower to the New World.

James I's son, Charles I (1625–1649) believed that the monarch had a God-given right to the throne; inevitably, he and Parliament reached a showdown over money and religion. Charles antagonized the Puritans and other Englishmen by trying to compel religious conformity to the practices of the Church of England. He levied taxes without consent of Parliament. Civil war broke out in 1642, and by 1646 the king was a prisoner. In 1649 Charles I was beheaded, the monarchy was abolished, and a republic, called the Commonwealth, was proclaimed.

Oliver Cromwell, who commanded the army that defeated the royal forces, led the Commonwealth and later the Protectorate, a form of military dictatorship, until his death in 1659. In 1660, civil war threatened, and when no strong Puritan leader emerged, the British recalled the eldest son of Charles I, who had taken refuge in France at the court of Louis XIV.

The new monarch, Charles II, brought a taste for French styles and a bevy of royal mistresses to the court. A witty, shrewd politician, Charles schemed, plotted, and bribed to gain absolute power. With victory almost assured, he died suddenly in 1685 leaving no legitimate children. His brother James II succeeded to the throne.

James II, a Roman Catholic and an incompetent politician, pursued policies that frightened all political factions. The birth of a son who would be raised in the Roman Catholic faith led leaders of English political parties to invite William of Orange to come over from Holland to help end the reign of James II. James was allowed to escape to France in 1688.

William and his wife Mary, the Protestant daughter of James II, accepted the throne offered them by Parliament. During their reign (1689–1702), Parliament limited the power of the monarch and protected the rights of individuals, granting freedom of worship to Protestant dissenters but not to Roman Catholics. Nevertheless, religious persecution ended for English men and women.

SOCIAL LIFE DURING THE 17TH CENTURY

Dress is often used to communicate social status in both obvious and subtle ways. In a society in which social classes are well defined, customs relating to dress are frequently a visible symbol of one's rank.

The French Court
Courtiers at Versailles lodged either in the palace, in their own houses nearby, or in Paris. Except for the quarters of the royal family, court housing accommodations were neither spacious nor luxurious. Those of sufficient rank attended to the king when he arose in the morning. (The king lived most of his life in public, including dressing in the morning.) He donned his breeches, then was handed his shirt by the highest ranking person present. Washing consisted of rubbing his face with cotton soaked in diluted, scented alcohol. Because washing in water was considered dangerous, bathing was rare. The rest of his day was just as ritualized. Court etiquette prescribed the

activities of each and every person. Rules dictated the length of the trains of noble ladies' dresses: For the queen, it was 11 ells long (1 ell equaled about 45 inches); the king's daughter, 9; his granddaughter, 7; a princess (related but not a direct descendant of the king), 5; and a duchess, 3 (Levron, 1968).

Clothing was one of the major items of expense for courtiers. One writer of the period, St. Simon, wrote of spending 800 *louis d'or* for clothes for himself and his wife for the wedding of the duke of Burgundy. One louis d'or equals about $5.00 today, so St. Simon must have spent around $4,000 for costumes for this one occasion. Obviously not all clothing was so luxurious, nor should it be assumed that this figure was the cost of one or two items of clothing. The festivities of an elaborate wedding would have required many different changes of clothing.

The English Aristocracy
In England during the reign of Charles I, the court was less important than it was to become under his son, Charles II. In the first half of the 17th century, England was largely rural, and many aristocrats lived on country estates. Members of Parliament who lived in the country went to London for parliamentary sessions, returning home when Parliament ended. Others lived in houses in London or in towns. Life continued to center in the rural areas after the end of the English Civil War and during the Commonwealth. When Charles II ascended the throne, the social life of the upper classes centered more at court, making London society fashion leaders.

The Dutch Upper Classes
Dutch interests in trade made for a prosperous middle class. The number of items of clothing owned by some individuals is remarkable. For example, a dowry of the daughter from a wealthy Amsterdam family was said to include 150 chemises and 50 scarves. Reports assigned one upper class widow of the first half of the century 32 different ruffs, and the inventory of the wardrobe of the mayor of one town listed 40 pairs of drawers, 150 shirts, 150 collars, 154 pairs of ruffled

cuffs, 60 hats, 92 nightcaps, 20 dressing gowns (worn as informal attire during the day), a dozen nightgowns, and 35 pairs of gloves (Zumthor, 1963).

The North American Colonists

Among the early Puritan settlers of New England, one might expect to find a population with little interest in fashion, living under somewhat primitive conditions. The earliest settlers in New England did live in temporary structures under difficult conditions, but these structures were gone by 1660, replaced by more permanent houses. Wills of the period reveal that some houses were well equipped while others had more frugal belongings.

An invoice of English goods shipped to New England around 1690 included many fashionable accessories and fabrics for making suits and dresses. Cargo lists included felt and castor (beaver) hats for men and boys, hair powder, looking glasses, periwigs, wool hose, lace, girdles (belts), caps, fringe, cornette and fontange wires (supports for fashionable headdresses). Also listed as a wide range of fabrics, including "worsted fancies," "striped silk crepes," "silk fancies," "camblett" (or camlet, a wool fabric), as well as more mundane fabrics such as kerseys (a coarse, rib-weave, woolen cloth) in brown, gray, and drab; linsey-woolsey (a linen and wool fabric); and cottons in shades of white, red, blue, and yellow. One well-to-do woman was sent a feather fan with a silver handle and "two tortoise fans, 200 needles, 5 yards of calico, silver gimp, blank sarindin (a white fabric), a cloak, a damson leather skin, and two women's ivory knives" (Dow, 1925).

Religious and secular leaders did not always approve of such "fancies." Some communities passed sumptuary laws including provisions that neither men nor women "should wear clothing with more than one slash on each sleeve and another on the back" (Dow, 1925). Cutwork, embroidery, needlework caps, **bands** (*lace collars*), and **head rails** (*scarves*) were among the items prohibited, as were ruffs; beaver hats; and shoulder-length, curled hair. One minister disinherited his nephew because he wore his hair fashionably long. These laws were more likely ignored than observed. Captain George Corwin, a merchant of Salem, Massachusetts, included in his large wardrobe a cloth coat trimmed with silver lace, a velvet coat, and such accessories as golden-topped gloves, embroidered and fringed gloves, a silver hat band, and a silverheaded cane (Dow, 1925).

SOME DISTINCTIVE COSTUME TRADITIONS

In spite of a trend toward greater international style, some distinctive costume traditions did develop. The clothing of English Puritans reflected their spiritual and political values. Distinctive Spanish styles probably resulted from conservatism and resistance to change.

Puritan Costume

Historians of the civil strife between the Puritans and Cavaliers (or Royalists) in England often imply that these two parties wore styles of garments that separated one group from the other. In reality, the Puritans followed styles similar to the rest of the population. Distinctions between these factions were chiefly those of degree. Puritans' objections centered on excesses of dress and wearing clothes more stylish than appropriate to one's station. However, Cavaliers and their ladies stressed lavishly decorated costumes in vivid colors.

Puritan dress is often described as "sad colored," generally understood as drab. Wealthy Puritans wore clothing of fine quality albeit more restrained in decoration and color than those of their Cavalier neighbors. Soldiers who followed the Puritan cause cut their hair shorter and avoided the elaborate curls of the Cavaliers, thereby earning the nickname "Roundheads."

Cavalier or Royalist sympathizers tended to wear broad-brimmed, flat-crowned hats trimmed with plumes, while the Puritans favored high-crowned, narrower brimmed copotains, but neither faction followed this pattern slavishly. Puritan women and

Cavalier women alike wore aprons for every day, but the Puritans' aprons were less ornate as a rule.

The Puritan settlers in New England brought with them the styles current in England at the time of their sailing, 1620. Like their English counterparts, the New England clergy stressed restrained and simple styles. In spite of the clergy's admonishments and the time for fashion information to travel across the Atlantic, these colonists tried to keep up with the major developments in European fashions (Figure 9.2).

Spanish Costume

Although Spain had been the major fashion leader of western Europe during the latter half of the 16th century, by the beginning of the 17th century

FIGURE 9.2 *Mrs. Elizabeth Freake and Baby Mary*, by an unidentified artist, c. 1674. These Massachusetts settlers dressed for their portraits in light and bright colors, contrary to the stereotype of the drab and dark-colored dress of the Puritans. (Worcester Art Museum (MA), Gift of Mr. and Mrs. Albert W. Rice, 1963.134)

Spanish styles were beginning to lag behind those of other countries. The Spanish were generally more conservative than other nations, and this conservatism prolonged styles such as the ruff and the Spanish farthingale, or **verdugado** (*vair-du-ga'do*), even after the rest of Europe abandoned them.

Even the Spanish **mantilla** (*man-teel'ya*), the veil covering the hair that is now associated with traditional Spanish costume, is a smaller version of the mantle worn by women during the medieval period and carried over into later times. Custom was strong in Spain and tradition regulated the length of this veil according to the status of the woman as widow, married woman, or unmarried girl. In some regions, an unmarried girl was expected to cover her face when outside of the house. This practice may have been borrowed from the Moors who occupied Spain for such a long time during the Middle Ages.

A notable Spanish costume practice of the 17th century is the belated adoption of a style somewhat similar to the wide French farthingale. Obsolete in the rest of Europe after the second decade of the 17th century, wealthy Spanish women took up the style only around the mid-1600s. The Spanish called the style the **guardinfante** (*gward-in-fahn'tay*; Figure 9.3). The skirt was more oval than the French farthingale, with greater width from side to side. The bodice had a long, wide **basque** (*bask*; an extension of the bodice below the waistline) that extended down over the top of the wide skirt. The bodice shoulderline was usually horizontal and is similar to necklines of costumes then being worn in the rest of Europe (see Figure 9.15, page 255). Sleeves were full and slashed to show contrasting underlinings and generally ended in fitted cuffs. With these dresses women wore high chopines with wooden or cork soles that helped to elongate the figure somewhat to compensate for the width of the guardinfante. Not all Spanish women wore these excessively wide skirts, which were a feature of court dress. Reade (1951) saw the difficulty of performing daily tasks while wearing the garment as a way to distinguish upper from lower classes. Less affluent women often placed pads around their waists to create slightly wider skirts.

Spanish men's styles also changed slowly. They retained the ruff and trunk hose somewhat longer than men in the rest of Europe. However, men's styles were never so extreme in their regional differences as women's. By 1700, the Spanish had re-entered the mainstream of European fashion.

PRODUCTION AND ACQUISITION OF TEXTILES AND CLOTHING

Gradual improvements in machinery were made. Elaborately figured silk fabrics were woven on a **draw loom**, which required a small boy or girl to sit on top and manually raise and lower sets of yarns according to instructions from the weaver in order to create a pattern. The draw loom may have been invented in China. By the Late Middle Ages it was in use in Italy and by 1600 was being used whenever complicated patterns in silk fabrics were being woven. As a result, figured silk fabrics were readily available and quite popular throughout the century.

Siamese ambassadors wore sumptuous garments when visiting the court of Louis XIV in 1684, and these garments are said to have inspired imitations called *siamoises*, which were made of cotton with colorful silk stripes (Montgomery, 1984). In the last decades of the 17th century, fine English woolens somewhat eclipsed the popularity of silks, a vogue extending as far as Egypt (Braudel, 1982).

For the upper classes, a hired professional tailor made clothing; for the lower classes, women of the family did the work. Most professional tailors were male, although women frequently did ornamental and fine hand sewing. Women began to move into this profession after 1675. A group of French women seamstresses applied for the right to form a guild of female tailors for making women's clothes. The application was approved. Hollander (1994, 67) believed that as a result,

> A difference in the way clothes were conceived and made for the two sexes came into existence for the first time, a separation that profoundly affected both the character and reputation of fashion for the next two centuries, and that still survives.

FIGURE 9.3 *The Infanta Maria Margarita (1651–1673) in Pink* (oil on canvas), by Diego Rodriguez de Silva y Velazquez (1599–1660). Princess dressed in the Spanish court style called the guardinfante. (The Infanta Margarita of Austria, c.1665 (oil on canvas), Mazo, Juan Bautista Martinez del (1612-67)/Prado, Madrid, Spain/Bridgeman Images)

SOURCES OF EVIDENCE OF HISTORIC COSTUME

Although more garments survive from the 17th century than from earlier periods, works of art make up the largest part of sources of information about costume in the 17th century. These works include painted portraits and drawings of actual individuals and paintings and drawings of scenes of everyday life.

Hand-colored fashion plates began to be produced in Paris in the late 17th century (and on into the 18th century). These were accompanied by brief written descriptions. Cumming (1985, 14) cautioned that these plates were "more akin to modern fashion photographs in glossy magazines than to styles of dress which were generally worn," produced as they apparently were in consultation with tailors, seamstresses, and milliners. As for verbal descriptions, they are often hard to interpret. Words were coined, and specialized fashion terms proliferated.

Marshall (1981) evaluated 17th-century Scottish portraits and found that they could be valuable sources of information. She pointed out, however, that some examples are misleading because some artists invented garments, some portraits were painted after the death of the subject and were dressed in clothing of later dates, and some examples are of persons long dead and dressed in purely imaginary garments.

Cumming (1985) listed questions that should be asked when looking, for example, at a painting from the mid-1600s:

> Are the figures depicted in it fashionable city dwellers or provincial conservatives? Are they elderly, wearing a style once fashionable which they cling to for sentimental reasons, or have they adopted a current fashion . . . ? Are they young, rich, experimental? Are they from the lower orders in society, or do they practice a profession which dictates a certain style of dress which overlays or distorts a contemporary fashion? Or are they subscribing to an artistic and social admiration for a form of stylized dress, perhaps pseudo-Classical or "antique" or pastoral, which they and/or their chosen artist wish to translate into timeless fashion . . . ? (12)

Works by great artists may often be less useful than those of lesser artists. We know, for example, that Rembrandt collected Near Eastern paraphernalia that he used to dress the subjects of his paintings (Jansen, 1991). It is rare to find a Rembrandt portrait that is useful in illustrating costume (Figure 9.4).

Sometimes figures in the background of a painting may be quite useful. "From such representations one may learn how bodies in their clothes not only were supposed to look, or were conceived by the privileged eyes of artists, but undoubtedly how they actually did look in the eyes of the epoch" (Hollander, 1978, 319).

FIGURE 9.4 Rembrandt's portraits are not always an ideal tool for the study of dress history as he enjoyed dressing some of his subjects in fancy or imaginative dress. (© RMN-Grand Palais/ Art Resource, NY)

COSTUME FOR MEN: 17TH CENTURY

Men's costume in the first two decades of the century retained the major elements characteristic of costume of the latter part of the 1500s. In these two decades major elements of costume were the shirt, the doublet, the jacket or jerkin, and trunk hose or knee-length breeches, called *Venetians*. Trunk hose became baggy and full, extending to the knees. By the close of the third decade, however, a different style had emerged, the first of three fairly distinct phases in men's clothing styles.

A number of variants in the style of and the terminology used to describe garments that covered men's bodies below the waist developed in the 17th and subsequent centuries. Table 9.1 summarizes these developments.

TABLE 9.1 Terms Describing Men's Trouser-type Garments: 16th Century to 19th Century

TERMS	ORIGINS OF TERMS	DATES IN USE	DESCRIPTION
breeches	probably derived from term *braies*	beginning about 1570; by the 1620s breeches replaced trunk-hose in England	made with seams on outside and inside of each leg, hung from waist, and had varying degrees of fullness; the term continues in use until the present but shape and cut have varied over time (for example, see Figures 9.3 and 10.6, page 275)
slopp (also spelled sloppe)	seems to originate with the Dutch; eventually the meaning changes and the term is applied to any ready-made clothing	from 16th century to 19th century	seems to apply to breeches that appear wide at the knees; the Dutch were said generally to wear wider breeches (see Figure 8.6, page 213)
petticoat breeches or rhinegraves	had a skirtlike shape, hence the name "petticoat" breeches	c. 1658–1680	wide, bifurcated garment that has the appearance of a skirt (see Figure 9.5)
trowsers or trousers	origin uncertain; appears to derive from an Irish term for garment similar to breeches	in 17th century as sailors' clothing, possibly over breeches as a protective garment in America in the 18th century; from c. 1800 to the present for fashionable dress	initially cut as short as the knee and full for sailors; later long but fairly full; in 18th century, generally a workingman's garment, long and fairly loose; by 19th century, has come to have the modern meaning of a generic bifurcated garment (see Figure 11.9, page 317)
pantaloon	derives from the name of St. Pantaleon, from Venice, and is named after an Italian comic character called Pantalone who always appeared dressed in ankle-length breeches or "trowsers"	for civilian dress, late 18th century; used earlier for military dress	garment cut from waist to ankle in one piece; at various times was cut to fit either close to the leg or fuller; by the 19th century, the terms *pantaloons* and *trousers* were sometimes used interchangeably
pants	shortened form of the word *pantaloons*, which is used mostly in the United States	19th century and after	in modern usage is used interchangeably with trousers
overalls	derives from practice of wearing this garment to cover or protect other garments	c. 18th century and after	worn as outer layer over a second garment; trousers also were sometimes used as protective outer garment and in early usage, distinction between overalls and trousers is not clear; eventually a bib was added; bib and overalls came to be work clothing
sherryvallies	probably derived from Polish *szarawary*, a term for a similar garment	during the American Revolution, c. 1776 to about 1830	a legcovering generally worn by horseback riders over trousers or pantaloons that buttoned up on the outside of the leg
knickerbockers, more often shortened to knickers	derived from the name of the pretended author of Washington Irving's *History of New York*; the term came into usage to describe the descendants of the original Dutch settlers of New York, and was applied to full, loose-fitting breeches, gathered at the knee, which looked like the garments in the illustrations in the aforementioned book	term originates in the mid-19th century and has been used ever since	breeches, full and loose, and gathered into a band at the knee; a garment for sports in the 19th century, and until the 1940s; also worn by preadolescent boys; this style is revived occasionally and is also worn for cross-country skiing (see Figure 15.21, page 446)

Information derived from Murray, A. 1976. "From Breeches to Sherryvallies." *Dress*, Vol. 2, No. 1, p. 17.

1625–1650

Garments

Now less an undergarment and more an integral part of the whole costume, the shirt was cut very full, was made of white linen, and had a flat collar (**falling band**) that replaced the ruff. Sleeve cuffs and collars were often of lace or decorated with cutwork embroidery.

The doublet was worn over the shirt and tied (laced) to breeches. Evolving forms, all with the waistline set somewhat above the anatomical waistline, included a short tabbed extension below the waist, which was the earliest form, carried over from the previous century. The new style had a skirtlike extension reaching to the hip (Figures 9.5 and 9.6). Some doublets had panes or slits through which the shirt or a colored lining was visible (see Figure 9.5).

Breeches, cut full throughout or cut more closely and tapering gradually to the knee, began at the waist

and extended to the knee. The lower edges might be decorated with ribbons and lace (see Figures 9.5 and 9.6).

For outdoors, men wore capes and cloaks, which often had wide collars. One type of cape was convertible into a coat. Larger, more enveloping cloaks were worn over both shoulders, while circular capes, which hung over one shoulder, were often secured with a cord that passed under the wide collar (see Figure 9.6). In France, such capes were called **Balagny** (*bal-ahn'yee*) cloaks, after a popular military hero. **Cassocks** or the French **casaques** (*ka-zaks'*) were coats cut with wide, full sleeves that were wide throughout the body and ended at the thigh or below.

Hair and Headdress

Most men wore their hair long and curling. Beards were trimmed to a point; moustaches were large and curled. French and English men of fashion grew one lock of hair (a **love lock**) longer than the rest (see Figure 9.5). Large-brimmed hats had full feather plumes (see Figures 9.5 and 9.6).

Footwear

Both shoes and boots had high heels and **straight soles**, without shaping for left or right feet. Prior to the appearance of high heels, shoes were shaped for either right or left feet. It appears that when shoes began to have high heels, shoemakers found it too difficult to make both high heels and shaped soles, and so straights were made until the early 19th century when shoes might be, once again, shaped to fit each foot (Swann, 1991).

FIGURE 9.5 Painting of Henri, Duc de Guise, by Van Dyck. The duke wears a doublet over a white shirt, which can be seen at the front of his doublet and through the slashes in its sleeves. His collar, a falling band, and cuffs are decorated with lace and embroidery. His breeches extend below the knee and are decorated with lace where they meet his high boots. One lock of his hair is grown longer than the rest, tied with a ribbon and called a "love lock." He carries a wide-brimmed, plumed hat and a cloak over his arm. (Image courtesy of The National Gallery of Art, Gift of Cornelius Vanderbilt Whitney, 1947)

FIGURE 9.6 *The Ball*, by Abraham Bosse, depicts fashionable men and women of the third and fourth decades of the 17th century. Note the coat worn over the shoulder in the manner of a cape by the gentleman in the right foreground. (Detail: Image copyright © The Metropolitan Museum of Art. Image source: Art Resource, NY)

Some boots and shoes had **slap soles**, a flat sole attached only at the front, not at the heel. These soles "slapped" the ground as the wearer walked. These were intended to keep the heel of the shoe or boot from sinking into soft ground (Illustrated Table 9.1; see also the man in the foreground of Figure 9.6).

The most important items of footwear were boots extending to the knee, where they met the breeches (see Figure 9.5), and shoes with large, open sides and extensions (called **latchets**) that tied across the instep. Until the 1630s toes were rounded; afterward, toes were more square with very large rosettes and ribbon decorations over a high square tongue (see Figure 9.6). Hose or stockings were knee-length and worn under shoes or boots.

1650–1680

Garments

Changes in the doublet caused shirts to become more visible and more important. Collars or bands were either a part of the shirt or a separate piece. These enlarged at the front to form a biblike, often lace-trimmed, construction. After 1665, a long linen tie served as an alternative to the collar.

The doublet shortened, ending several inches above the waist. It was straight and unfitted through

Illustrated Table 9.1

17th-Century Accessories

Falling band, man's collar,
first half of the 1600s

Lace cravat, c. 1640

Cavalier-style man's hat,
c. 1640

Copotain-style hat,
c. 1650

Boot with slap sole,
c. first half of the 1600s

Jackboot, 17th century

Mule-style shoe, called a
pantofle, 17th century

Fontange or commode
headdress, c. 1680

Child's protective head
covering called a pudding,
17th century

Fan, 17th century

Woman's mask for outdoors,
worn with hood, c. 1640

FIGURE 9.7 Man dressed in the style (popular between 1650 and 1680) called petticoat breeches or rhinegraves, a divided skirt cut so full that it has the appearance of a skirt. His short jacket allows a large expanse of his white shirt to show. Over this he wears a cape. (The New York Public Library/Art Resource, NY)

FIGURE 9.8 *A Game of Skittles* [detail], by Pieter de Hooch, copyist. Dutch men, c. 1665, wear petticoat breeches with waist-length jackets over white shirts. The man at the right has a pair of canons, a wide ruffle, at his knees. A notable aspect of the woman's dress is the large, square, white linen collar. (Unidentified Artist, GAME OF SKITTLES, Circa 1660s, oil on canvas, Cincinnati Art Museum, Gift of Mary Hanna, 1950.19)

the body. Although its sleeves ended at the elbow, there were also some sleeveless forms (Figures 9.7 and 9.8).

Knee-length breeches were either short and straight or full and drawn in to tie at the knee. An alternative form was made in a style called **petticoat breeches** or **rhinegraves**. These breeches were actually a divided skirt, rather like a modern culotte, that was cut so full that it gave the appearance of a short skirt (see Figure 9.7). The origin of these breeches, popular from about 1650 to 1675, is uncertain, but the name *rhinegraves* would indicate that they may have originated in Germany. Full, wide ruffles attached at the bottom of breeches were called **canons**.

The Vest

The origin of the prototype that eventually evolved into the three-piece suit is thought to be a garment that was introduced to the English court by Charles II in 1666 (Kuchta, 1990). The actual costume consisted of below-the-knee–length coat and what we would call a vest or a waistcoat of the same length worn over narrow breeches. (Petticoat breeches, the predominant style of the time, were too full to fit beneath the vest and coat.)

Called by contemporaries a **vest**, a term used in describing some Persian garments of a similar cut, it is thought to have Eastern antecedents. The king, contrary to a promise he made never to change from

FIGURE 9.9 Man's long vest worn under an outer coat that is just slightly longer and breeches, which are almost invisible. The long vest probably derives from the style introduced by Charles II in 1666, and this three-piece outfit is considered to be the forerunner of the modern three-piece suit. (The New York Public Library/Art Resource, NY)

this style, did not wear this type of garment for the rest of his life. The basic pattern of a long coat and a long vest underneath worn over a shirt and breeches did, however, become the basic components of men's dress not only in England but also in France by around 1680. Contemporary Comments 9.1 reproduces reactions to and comments about the king's vest (see also Figure 9.9 and Global Connections).

Outdoor Garments

Outdoor garments included cloaks or capes and coats that were cut full, some versions ending at the knee and obscuring the costume beneath.

Hair and Headdress

Some men shaved their heads and wore long, curling wigs. Others dressed their own hair in long, curling styles. In England, alternative hat styles demonstrated

the wearer's political affiliations. A wide-brimmed, low-crowned, feather-trimmed hat was associated with Cavaliers or supporters of the British royal family. High-crowned, small-brimmed copotains were associated with supporters of the Puritan faction, opposed to the King. Men wore hats indoors and out and in church (see Illustrated Table 9.1, page 248).

Footwear

Shoes had elaborate rosette, ribbon, and buckle trimmings. Shoes were preferred to boots for fashionable dress, and boots were worn for riding and in bad weather. The term **galosh** (or golosh) appears in contemporary records. Swann (1991) defined it as a flat-soled overshoe with a toe cap for keeping it in place. Although Swann noted the use of red-heeled and soled shoes as early as 1614 and spoke of them for court wear in England in the 1640s, Louis XIV is often credited with originating the style during his reign. Whatever the origin, this style was very popular in court circles in France and England for the remainder of the century and on into the 18th century.

1680–1710

Garments

Shirts were little changed from the forms worn earlier in the century. **Cravats**, long, narrow, scarflike pieces separate from the shirt were worn instead of collars (Figure 9.9). Of one "dandy," with an excessively long cravat it was said, "his cravat reached down to his middle and had stuff enough in it to make a sail for a barge" (Edwards and Ramsey 1968, 448).

Knee-length coats replaced doublets as outer garments. Called **surtouts** (*sur-tu'*) or **justacorps** (*jewst-a-cor'*) by the French and cassocks by the English, such garments had fitted straight sleeves with turned back cuffs, and buttoned down the front. They completely covered the breeches and waistcoat (Figure 9.10).

By the late 17th century the terms *vest* and **waistcoat** were being used interchangeably. These garments were cut along the same lines as outer coats, but slightly shorter and less full. Before 1700 most were sleeved; later some were made without sleeves. These

Contemporary Comments 9.1

CHARLES II OF ENGLAND'S VEST

Comments about Charles II of England's introduction of a new style of men's dress to the English court, from Samuel Pepys's 1666 diary.

October 8th.

The King hath yesterday in Council declared his resolution of setting a fashion for clothes, which he will never alter. It will be a vest, I know not well how; but it is to teach the nobility thrift and will do good.

October 13th.

To White Hall, and there the Duke of York . . . was just come in from hunting. So I stood and saw him dress himself and try on his vest, which is the King's new fashion, and will be in it for good and all on Monday next, and the whole Court: it is a fashion the King says he will never change.

October 15.

This day the King begins to put on his vest, and I did see several persons of the House of Lords and Commons too, great courtiers, who are in it; being a long cassocke close to the body, of black cloth and pinked [cut] with white silk under it, and a coat over it, and the legs ruffled with a black riband like a pigeon's leg; and upon the whole I wish the King may keep it, for it is a very fine and handsome garment.

Pepys, S. (n.d.). *Diary and correspondence of Samuel Pepys, F.R.S.: Secretary to the admirality in the reigns of Charles II and James II* (Vol. 2). New York, NY: National Library Company, pp. 467, 471, 473.

From John Evelyn's 1666 diary.

October 18.

To Court. It being the first time his Majesty put himself solemnly into the Eastern fashion of vest, changing doublet, stiff collar, bands, and cloak into a comely dress after the Persian mode, with girdle or straps, and shoe strings and garters into buckles, of which some were set with precious stones, resolving never to alter it, and to leave the French mode, which had hitherto obtained to our great expense and reproach. Upon which various courtiers and gentlemen gave his Majesty gold by way of wager that he would not persist in this resolution [i.e., to wear only this costume henceforth]. I had sometime before presented an invective against that unconstancy, and our so much affecting the French fashion, to his Majesty, in which I took occasion to describe the comeliness and usefulness of the Persian clothing, in the very same manner his Majesty now clad himself. This pamphlet I entitled "Tyrranus, or the Mode," and gave it to the King to read. I do not impute to this discourse the change which soon happened, but it was an identity [coincidence] that I could not but take notice of.

October 30th.

To London to our office, and now had I on the vest and surcoat and tunic as 'twas called, after his Majesty had brought the whole Court to it. It was a comely and manly habit, too good to hold, it being impossible for us in good earnest to leave the Monsieurs' vanities [i.e., the French styles] long.

De Beer (Ed.). (1955). *The diary of John Evelyn, Vol. 3: Kalendarium, 1650–1672.* New York, NY: Oxford University Press.

Global Connections

This garment, known as "the King's vest," was said to have been a gift from a Persian ruler to King Charles II of England (1660–1685). Gifts of clothing from one monarch to another were common and appropriate. This coat, made of silk embroidered with plants, flowers, and animals, is identified as belonging to 17th-century Persian king Shah Jehan (1628–1658). If a coat similar to this was part of that gift, this garment can be viewed as an ancestor of one of the elements of the modern three-piece suit, a style that evolved from the garments so well received by King Charles II in 1666. (Visual Arts Library/Art Resource, NY)

FIGURE 9.10 Costume made for the wedding of Sir Thomas Isham in 1681. Men's outer coats had lengthened to the extent that they hid the knee-breeches beneath. (V&A Images, London/Art Resource, NY)

coats and waistcoats can be seen as developing from the vest introduced by Charles II of England.

Cut with less fullness than in earlier periods, breeches ended at the knee.

Hair and Headdress

Wigs grew larger, the hair built up somewhat on the top of the head. Some wigs were dusted with powder to make them white, but most were worn in natural colors.

Hats were somewhat superfluous, given the large scale of wigs and were more often carried under the arm than worn. Flat hats with brims turned or "cocked" up at one or more points were often seen, especially one with the brim turned up at three points to form a triangle. Nineteenth-century writers called this a **tricorne**; however, that term does not appear in the 17th and 18th centuries.

Footwear

Styles were similar to those from earlier in the century. Shoes were preferred over boots for general

FIGURE 9.11 *Portrait of a Genoese Noblewoman, an Italian Marquise,* painted by Van Dyck. Costume is characteristic of Spain and the Low Countries in the first several decades of the 1600s. (Copyright The Frick Collection)

FIGURE 9.12 The artist Peter Paul Rubens painted his wife in her wedding dress, 1630. The large virago sleeves are a focal point of this dress, and the fabric of the under dress is a brocade of gold on white. (bpk, Berlin/Alte Pinakothek, Bayerische Staatsgemaeldesammlungen, Munich, Germany/Art Resource, NY)

wear. Shoe buckles, which could be quite costly, were made to transfer from one pair of shoes to another. High, rigid boots made of heavy leather and called **jack boots** were worn for horseback riding in the latter 1600s (see Illustrated Table 9.1, page 248). Knee-length stockings, also called hose, were worn with knee breeches.

COSTUME FOR WOMEN: 17TH CENTURY

The wheel farthingale retained its hold on fashion in the first years of the 17th century. Gradually, however, the farthingale flattened in front and the whole line of the costume grew softer. Necklines were low and rounded. In Spain and Holland the stomacher of the dress elongated into a rigidly boned U-shape. The sides of the gown remained wide and full. Sleeves

were multilayered with fitted sleeves under hanging sleeves, and the ruff became even more enormous (Figure 9.11).

Although the farthingale lingered on at the Spanish court, it went out of style elsewhere in Europe, and the transition to a new style was complete by about the end of the third decade.

1630–1660

Garments

The undermost garment continued to be the white linen chemise. Generally, gowns were made with bodices and skirts seamed together at the waist, which was slightly elevated. Gowns, open at center front, served as one of several layers. The outer layer was worn over an under bodice, a boned, stiffened garment like a corset that had a long, U-shaped stomacher at the front and this filled in the upper part of the gown (Figure 9.12).

FIGURE 9.13 *Lady with Mask and Muff*, by Wenceslaus Hollar (Bohemian, active in London, 1607–1677). Woman, c. 1645, with her outer skirt (*modeste*) raised to reveal her underskirt (*secret*). She carries a popular accessory, a large fur muff, and wears a mask. (Wenceslaus Hollar, Bohemian, active in London, 1607–1677. Lady with Mask and Muff, from Ornatus Muliebris Anglicanus (The Severall Habits of English Women), 1640 Etching Plate: 134 x 70 mm (5 ¹/₄ x 2 ³/₄ in.) The Fine Arts Museums of San Francisco, Achenbach Foundation for Graphic Arts, 1963.30.17838)

Skirts were separate garments worn under gowns, visible at the front when gowns were open or seen when the outer skirts were carried looped up over the arm. Even when the skirts of outer gowns were closed in front, a second layer or underskirt was worn. The French called the outer layer the **modeste** (*mow-dest'*) and the under layer the **secret** (*sek-ray'*; Figure 9.13).

Jackets could be worn in combination with skirts instead of gowns. These bodices had short tabs (*basques*) extending below the waist. Jackets worn at home were often quilted, looser in fit than fashionable dress and without elaborate sleeve constructions (Figure 9.14).

Writers of the period refer to stylish sleeves that were paned and tied into a series of puffs as **virago sleeves** (see Figure 9.12).

Necklines tended to be low; some were V-shaped, some square, and others horizontal in shape. Stiff ruffs had been replaced by falling ruffs, which were gathered collars that sloped from neck to shoulder, or wide collars tied under the chin with strings. Also seen were large neckerchiefs. Horizontal necklines were often edged with a wide, flat collar that in present-day fashion terms would be called a *bertha* (see Figure 9.2, page 242).

Capes, cut full, with flat, turned-down collars, and occasionally fur lined, were worn outdoors.

Hair and Headdress

Ladies parted their hair behind the ears and drew the back hair into a roll or chignon at the back of the head. The front hair was arranged in curled locks around the face. Although hats were worn indoors and out, women also went bareheaded. Styles included wide-brimmed, cavalier-style hats (see Figure 9.14) and copotains, which were frequently worn over a white, close-fitting small cap or coif. Figure 9.2 depicts a

FIGURE 9.14 *Queen Henrietta Maria with Sir Jeffrey Hudson*, by Van Dyck. The tabs of the jacket in the style of 1625–1660 can be seen where they extend below the waistline. (Image courtesy of The National Gallery of Art, Washington, 1633, Samuel H. Kress Collection)

FIGURE 9.15 *The Intruder,* by Gabriel Metsu. The lady at the center of the picture is partially undressed. Her braid-decorated outer skirt is draped across the chair in the foreground, as is her characteristically Dutch, velvet, fur-trimmed outer jacket. On her head is a linen nightcap. She has just taken off her backless shoes, which are on the floor. The woman seated by the window wears a jacket similar to the one on the chair. (Image courtesy of the National Gallery of Art, Andrew W. Mellon Collection)

square of fabric tied under the chin or sewn or pinned to form a cap. Hoods provided head coverings for outdoors (see Illustrated Table 9.1, page 248).

Footwear

Shoes were similar in shape to those described for men. For bad weather, clogs with toe caps, instep straps, no heels, and wooden soles protected the shoes and raised them out of the wet streets.

1660–1680

Garments

As undergarments, women wore chemises and under petticoats (not to be confused with visible, decorative, outer petticoats or skirts). Drawers, which had been worn by women for some time on the continent, were not yet worn in England. Chemises usually showed slightly at the neckline and the edge of sleeves.

The silhouette and shaping of women's gowns changed somewhat. Bodices lengthened and narrowed, becoming long-waisted and more slender with an extended V-shaped point at the front. Heavy satin fabrics seem to have been fashionable for formal dresses. Pastel colors predominate in paintings, but actual fabrics of the period are also brightly colored (Figure 9.15).

Frequently edged by a wide lace collar or band of linen called a **whisk**, necks tended to be low, wide, and horizontal or oval in shape (see Figure 9.15). Most sleeves were set low on the shoulder, opening into a full puff that ended below the elbow. Some skirts fell straight to the floor and were closed all round, and others were split at the front and pulled back into puffs or looped up over the hips. Decorations for gowns often consisted of a row of ruffles down the front or lines of jeweled decoration or braid placed on top of seam construction lines.

FIGURE 9.16 *Portrait of a Woman*, c. 1663, by Gerard ter Borch, Dutch, 1917–1681. Dutch woman from after 1660. Her open overskirt displays the decorative underskirt beneath. The panel of ribbons at the front is a typical feature of many women's costumes of this period. (Portrait of a Woman, c. 1665. Gerard Terborch II (Dutch, 1617-1681). Oil on canvas; 63.3 x 52.7 cm. The Cleveland Museum of Art, The Elisabeth Severance Prentiss Collection 1944.93)

1680–1700

Garments

Undergarments continued to be much as they had been in the preceding 20 years.

Styles of gowns evolved. Necklines revealed less bosom and became more square. This may have been as a result of the influence of Madame de Maintenon, a conservative widow whom King Louis XIV of France is believed to have married secretly in 1684.

Corsets were now visible at the front of the bodice. They were heavily decorated, ending in a pronounced V at the waist. Separate stomachers could be tied or pinned to the front of the corset to vary the appearance of a dress (see Figure 10.15, page 283).

Skirts composed of several layers were often so heavy that they required additional support from whalebone, metal, or basketwork supports. Overskirts were generally split at the front and looped up in complex drapery with a long, back train. The underskirt, which could be seen through the split overskirt, was ornamented with embroidery, ruffles, pleated edgings, and other trimmings (Figures 9.16 and 9.17).

A new construction for women's dresses appeared. Instead of cutting the bodice and skirt as separate pieces that were sewn together, bodice and skirt were cut in one length from shoulder to hem. The shaping of this garment, called a **mantua** (*man-too-a'*) or **manteau** (*man-toe'*), is thought to derive from the construction of Middle Eastern robes that were imported into Europe. The resulting garment,

FIGURE 9.17 The draped overskirt of a seated woman, c. 1684, is open in front to show a lavender skirt with ornamental trimming along the hem. Her ribbon-trimmed stomacher matches the skirt. On her head is a tall lace fontange headdress. (Detail: © RMN-Grand Palais/Art Resource, NY)

however, was quite different from its supposed ancestor. Full in both back and front, the garment was worn over a corset and an underskirt. For casual wear it was loose (the style is thought to have originated to provide a less confining costume for women), but for more formal wear it was pleated to fit the body at front and back and belted. Front skirt edges were sometimes pulled to the back and fastened to form a draped effect (Figure 9.18).

For outdoors, capes in shorter or longer lengths still predominated. Coats, cut like men's cassocks, were worn for riding or walking. Long, broad scarves were placed around the shoulders, as were lappets or short, waist-length capes.

Hair and Headdress

Hair was built up high, on top of the head, with long curling locks at the back and sides. On top of the hair women placed a device made of a series of ruffles held in place with wire supports and known as the **fontange** (*fone-tanj'*) in France and the **commode** in England and the American colonies. The first version of this headdress, which evolved over a period of about 30 years, was a small bow tying up the hair in front. Its final form was an elaborate, tall structure of three or four lace tiers in front and a cascade of ruffles and bows in the back (see Illustrated Table 9.1, page 248, and Figure 9.17). It is said that the fontange was named after one of Louis XIV's mistresses. She supposedly emerged from the woods during a royal hunt in a somewhat disheveled state, probably as the result of an amorous encounter with the King. Using her lace garter to tie up her hair, she is supposed to have begun this fashion (see Contemporary Comments 9.2).

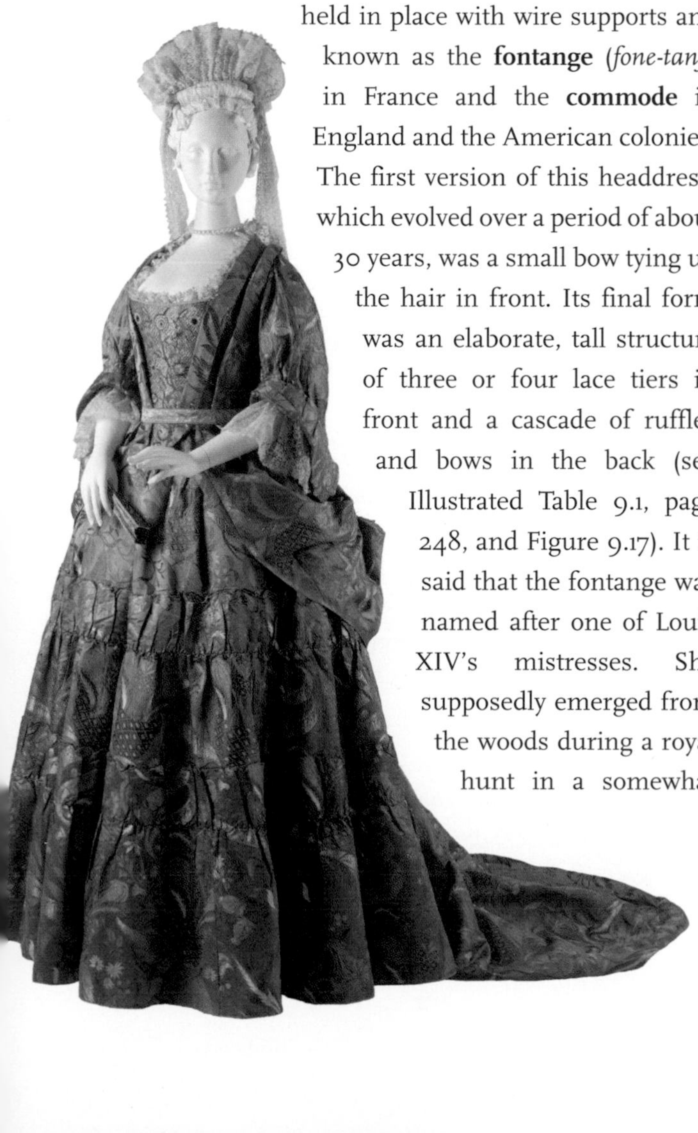

Footwear

Shapes changed, as shoes became more pointed at the front, and heels became higher and narrower. Shoemakers used brocades and decorated leathers for fashionable shoes. Although men used buckles to close shoes, women tended to use ties because the buckles were likely to catch on dresses or petticoats.

Pantofles (*pan-toff'ahl*) were heel-less slippers or mules that, though worn throughout the century, became especially fashionable toward the end of the period (see Illustrated Table 9.1, page 248). The word *pantofle* derives from the Greek word *pantophellos*, which means "cork." Apparently, the earliest versions of these backless slippers were made with cork soles and were used as overshoes. By the 17th century they were made with leather soles and worn indoors as well.

Knitted both by machine and by hand from wool or silk, some stockings had knitted or embroidered decorations.

Costume for Men and Women: 17th Century

Accessories

Accessories of dress, use of cosmetics, and grooming practices are not easily separated into the same time periods as clothing. Also, both men and women used many of these items. For these reasons the following section summarizes the major trends in accessories, jewelry, cosmetics, and grooming during the 17th century for both men and women (see Illustrated Table 9.1, page 248).

FIGURE 9.18 Mantua and petticoat of silk damask brocaded with gold thread, c. 1708. Improvements in the draw loom made it possible for Europeans to imitate complex Asian designs like this one. (Image copyright © The Metropolitan Museum of Art. Image source: Art Resource, NY)

Contemporary Comments 9.2

THE RISE AND FALL OF THE FONTANGE

The following series of quotations from letters written at the French court and from the English newspaper The Spectator *provide a contemporary account of the rise and fall of the headdress called the fontange in France and the commode in England.*

Versailles to June 1687. It doesn't surprise me to hear that you are wearing coiffures of ribbon—everyone here does, from little girls to old ladies of eighty, the difference being that young people wear bright colours and old ones dark shades or black. The reason I don't wear them is that I can't bear anything on my head during the day, and at night I find the rustling of the ribbons too noisy; I should never get any sleep, so I have given this fashion a miss.

Versailles 26 January 1688. . . . No one at court wears a fichu. The coiffures grow taller and taller every day. The King told us at dinner today that a fellow by the name of Allart, who used to do people's hair here, has dressed all the ladies of London so tall that they can't get into their sedan-chairs, and have been obliged to have them heightened in order to follow the French fashion.

Versailles 11 December 1695. We don't dress our hair so very high now, still high but not so high as before. The headdresses are now worn bent forward and not so straight up as they used to be. It isn't true that a tax has been put on the coiffure, someone must have invented that tale as a joke.

Forster, E. (Trans.). (1984). *A woman's life at the court of the Sun King. Letters of Liselotte von der Pfalz, Elizabeth Charlotte, Duchesse d'Orléans, 1652–1722.* Baltimore, MD: Johns Hopkins University Press, pp. 47, 48, 71.

The Spectator, *an English daily periodical, remarked on the abandonment of the style:*

Friday, June 22, 1711. There is not so variable a thing in Nature as a Lady's Head-dress: Within my own Memory I have known it rise and fall above thirty Degrees. About ten Years ago it shot up to a very great Height, insomuch that the Female Part of our Species were much taller than the Men. . . . At present the whole Sex is in manner dwarfed and shrunk into a race of Beauties that seems almost another Species. I remember several ladies, who were once very near seven Foot high, that at present want some inches of five. . . .

Apparently the style changed first in England. St. Simon, in his Memoires of the Court of Louis XIV, *describes the reaction of the English Duchess of Shrewsbury to the style in his memoirs for the year 1713 (St. Simon wrote his memoirs between 1739 and 1751 based on notes taken at the time of which he wrote).*

[I]t was not long before she had pronounced the ladies' style of hairdressing to be perfectly ridiculous—as indeed it was, for they then wore erections of wire, ribbons, and false hair, supplemented with all manner of gewgaws, rising to a height of more than two feet. When they moved, the entire edifice trembled and the discomfort was extreme. The King, so autocratic in small details, detested this fashion, but despite his wishes it continued to be worn for more than a decade.

What the monarch could not command, the taste and example of an eccentric old foreigner achieved with surprising speed. From those exaggerated heights the ladies suddenly descended to an extremity of flatness, and the new style, so much simpler, more practical, and infinitely more becoming, has lasted to the present day.

Norton, L. (Ed. & Trans.). (1984). *Historical memoirs of the Duc de Saint-Simon. Vol. II, 1710–1715* (Shortened version). New York, NY: McGraw-Hill, p. 284.

Among the more widely used accessories were:

- gloves for both men and women, sometimes scented with perfume;

- handkerchiefs and purses, carried by men and women;

- purses made of beaded leather or embroidered;

- fans for women, made of feathers or of the folding type;

- muffs made of silk, velvet, or satin; fur; or fur-trimmed fabrics and carried by ladies;

- face masks, worn by ladies who wanted to protect their faces against the weather or to engage in flirtations without being recognized; and

- aprons, worn to protect the garment beneath as women went about their household tasks (practical cotton or linen varieties) and as an attractive accessory to fashionable dress (decorative ones made of silk or lace and lavishly embroidered).

Jewelry

Men wore neck chains, pendants, lockets, rings, and, in the first part of the century, earrings. Women wore necklaces, bracelets, earrings, and rings. They also placed mirrors and **pomander balls** around their waists on chains. Pomander balls were small balls of perfume enclosed in decorated, perforated boxes that might be shaped like an apple. The French word *pomme*, from which the word *pomander* derives, means "apple."

Cosmetics and Grooming

Women and some men used cosmetics. Perfume was applied to the person and to articles of clothing. Lead combs were used to darken the eyebrows; paint, and powder, to tint the face. Some women colored their lips and fingernails red. Cunnington and Cunnington (1972) reported that artificial eyebrows made of mouse skins were mentioned by contemporary satirists.

Patches, small fabric shapes, were glued to the face to cover imperfections or skin blemishes. Ladies wore night masks to protect and soften the skin, and to remove wrinkles. From 1660 to 1700 some women placed **plumpers**, small balls of wax, in the cheeks to give the face a fashionably rounded shape.

COSTUME FOR CHILDREN: 17TH CENTURY

Many costume historians note that the first changes in clothing for children that reflect changes in attitudes toward them took place in the late 1700s. Aries (1962), in a social history of the family and childhood, disagreed, arguing that the first important changes in costume for children came as early as the beginning of the 16th century. He identified well-established changes that had become common practice during the 17th century, at least for upper class children (Aries, 1962).

For many centuries, once children were released from their swaddling clothes, they dressed in the same styles as the adults of their region and class. Starting the 16th century, this changed for small boys, but not for girls. The nursery-age boy dressed not in the clothing of his elders but in the same dress as his sisters, who dressed like small women. Later the boy dressed in a long robe that buttoned or fastened down the front. As a result, the sequence of costumes worn by boys was, first, swaddling clothes, , then a skirt, a robe, and an apron. About age 3 or 4 years, the boy donned the long robe, and at 6 or 7 he was first dressed in adult male styles. Louis XIII received his first doublet and breeches at age 7. In England the occasion on which a young boy was presented with his first pair of breeches was called his "breeching" and was an occasion for celebration by all of the family and their friends.

Aries (1962) pointed out that the distinctive item of costume for small boys was the robe, which was not worn by adults or by girls. Here, he said, was a clear example of a costume exclusively for a child, and it had its origins in costume of the past. During the High Middle Ages men wore long robes. When these robes went out of general use, replaced by shorter jackets, they continued to be used by priests, certain professions, and by children in upper class families. This was not a universal practice in western Europe. Children in Renaissance Italy seem not to have followed it, but French, German, and English children did.

FIGURE 9.19 *Dutch Family Portrait*, c. 1664, by Jacob Ochterveldt. Toddler, probably a boy, standing beside his mother, wears a padded protective cap called a pudding and a pinafore over a long skirt. Kneeling girl has wide "ribbons of childhood" attached to the back of her dress. Standing, older boy wears petticoat breeches of the type worn by adult men of the period. Girl child being carried wears a dress cut in adult woman's style and a white cap. (Wadsworth Atheneum Museum of Art/Art Resource, NY)

portraits of the time both leading strings and these ribbons are depicted. Leading strings were narrow, ropelike in construction, compared with the flat **ribbons of childhood**. Instead, he argued convincingly, they were probably a stylized or atrophied form of the hanging sleeves that were part of the medieval costume (Figures 9.19 and 9.20).

Of the origins of these archaic styles for children, Aries (1962) said it was obviously out of the question to invent a costume for them, yet it was felt necessary to separate them in a visible manner by means of their dress. Their dress derived from a tradition previously maintained in certain classes, but which adults no longer wore. The adoption of a special costume for children, which became generalized throughout the upper classes from the end of the 16th century, corresponded with the beginnings of the idea of childhood as a separate stage of life.

Other vestiges of earlier styles were also preserved in children's dress. The infants' cap worn by children is almost identical to the medieval coif. Attached to the shoulders of the robes for boys and dresses for girls was a broad ribbon of fabric that hung down the back. Many writers identify these ribbons as **leading strings**, small strings used to help hold the child upright when he or she learned to walk and retained for another two years or so to help control the child's movements. Aries (1962) disagreed, pointing out that in many

FIGURE 9.20 Front and back views of a dress for a boy or a girl from after 1690 that has "ribbons of childhood" behind the sleeves. (Division of Home And Community Life, National Museum of American History, Smithsonian Institution)

Costume Components for Children

Layette

For an infant in the 17th century, a layette would have consisted of swaddling bands, bibs, caps (also called **biggins**), shirts, mittens and sleeves, and what the English called **tailclouts**, or **nappies**, and Americans would call **diapers**. This latter term derives from "diaper weave," the construction of linen cloth made in a dense checked pattern. This cloth was often used as nappies and usually made from unbleached linen. One Englishwoman, Lady Anne Clifford, used her husband's old shirts (Kevill-Davies, 1991).

Swaddling Bands

Infants were swaddled for the first 2 or 3 months, tightly wrapped in bands of linen that inhibited movement (see Figure 9.21). When these bands were

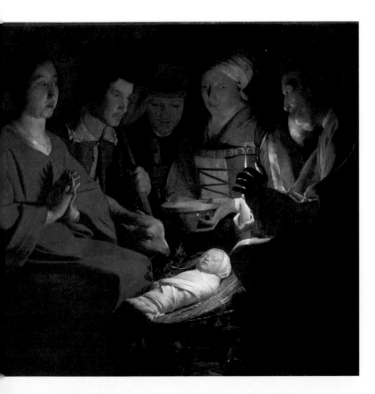

FIGURE 9.21 In a painting by Georges de La Tour, a 17th-century newborn infant is wrapped in swaddling bands. (Erich Lessing/Art Resource, NY)

removed, they were replaced by thick corded or quilted material that was tied tightly around the body. These pieces called **stays**, **staybands**, or **rollers** were probably intended to prevent umbilical hernias or to promote an upright posture.

Christenings

The christening was the major occasion in the baby's first year of life. Christening robes and accessories differed little from those of later centuries. Charles I of England's christening clothes, which have been preserved, consisted of undershirts open at the front and closed by small crossed tabs, binders for the stomach, bibs, a small cap, and a long, embroidered christening gown.

Gowns

Infants unable to walk were dressed in long gowns called **carrying frocks**. Children old enough to walk wore shorter dresses, or **going frocks**. During the 17th century aprons or pinafores replaced bibs. The term **pinafore** derived from the practice of pinning this garment to the front or forepart of the gown. Sometimes a handkerchief, called a **muckinder**, was pinned to the front of the dress for extra protection (Kevill-Davies, 1991; see Figure 9.19).

To protect the head, toddlers who might fall while learning to walk and wore a special padded cap, called a **pudding** (see Illustrated Table 9.1, page 248).

Another form of dress for young boys can be observed in a few 17th-century portraits. Almost a compromise between the dress of adult and child, boys ages 5 to 7 sometimes wore the waistcoat of the first half of the century with a long, full, gathered skirt.

Coral Teething Rings or Necklaces

Paintings often depicted small pieces of coral mounted in silver or gold and suspended around the necks of infants and very young children. From as early as the Roman era, coral has been thought to have magical power to ward off evil. It also provided a cool, hard surface for babies to bite on to relieve the pain of teething.

FIGURE 9.22 During the 17th century, English East India Company trading centered on the Indian subcontinent. (Image copyright © The Metropolitan Museum of Art. Image source: Art Resource, NY)

Summary

Themes

Costume displays the themes of POLITICS AND POLITICAL CONFLICT throughout the 17th century. Differences between the dress of the Cavaliers and the Roundheads in the second half of the century in England accompanied the POLITICAL CONFLICT between those who supported King Charles I and those who opposed him. Louis XIV of France centralized the power of government and focused attention on the court at Versailles as a stage on which to display fashion. Courtiers who had to spend vast sums of money keeping up with the latest styles had little time and few resources for plotting against the government. Charles II of England sought asylum in France during the English Civil War. He observed the latest French fashions while there, and when he returned to claim the throne of England, French court styles became a major influence on English styles.

SOCIAL CLASS STRUCTURE, another theme, is intimately related to French court dress. Social rank determined such specific aspects of dress as the length of women's trains. In England and Spain SOCIAL VALUES were expressed through dress. The English Puritans avoided lavish sartorial display, and Spanish traditionalism and rigid social conventions contributed to the social distinctions evident in the dress of upper and lower classes.

ECONOMIC EVENTS that had an impact on styles include the expansion of trade with the Middle East and East Asia. Both the famous vest of Charles II of England and the mantua gown of the late 1600s probably originated in the Middle East, providing examples of CROSS-CULTURAL INFLUENCES that stemmed from trade (see Figure 9.22).

The new TECHNOLOGY of printing facilitated the spread of fashion both at home and abroad. Styles

Visual Summary Table

Baroque

Man: 1600–1620

Short, wide trunk hose worn with doublet, jacket, or jerkin.

Man: 1625–1650

Shirt, doublet, ending with tabs or skirtike section below the waist, worn with knee breeches.

Man: 1650–1680

Shirt, waist-length doublet, and knee-length breeches cut to look like a skirt or straight or full and drawn in to knee.

Man: 1680–1710

Shirt, a knee-length vest, and a knee-length outer coat that hid knee-length breeches.

Woman: 1600–1630

Skirt flat in front, sides wide and full. Bodice has elongated U-shaped stomacher and complex sleeves.

Woman: 1630–1660

Low-necked bodice with puffed and paned sleeves has U-shaped stomacher and slightly elevated waist. Open front of skirt shows underskirt.

Woman: 1660–1680

Elongated bodice has V-shaped point at the bottom of the front. Skirts are either closed or open at front to show underskirt.

Woman: 1680–1900

Bodice front opens showing decorative stomacher. Trained and heavy skirts need support. New cut is called a mantua.

changed more easily because of the expansion of this MEDIUM OF COMMUNICATION that made printed descriptions and drawings of fashionable dress readily available.

At the same time, regional differences in dress persisted. Clothing worn at the court of Spain, which clung to the styles of the late 16th century for more than 50 years, is the most obvious example of localized dress, but styles that were preferred by and associated with the Italians, the Dutch, the French, and the English can also be identified.

The costume historian finds the theme of SOURCES OF INFORMATION ABOUT COSTUME particularly worthy of note in the 17th century. The many portraits and drawings not only of the well-to-do but also of everyday life among the lower classes are supplemented by the aforementioned printed materials that touched on current fashion. Also, greater numbers of actual garments remain in museums, particularly in England.

All periods evidence the theme of RELATIONSHIPS BETWEEN COSTUME AND DEVELOPMENTS IN THE FINE AND APPLIED ARTS. These relationships are relatively easy to see in 17th-century architecture, sculpture, painting, and textiles. The baroque style—with its larger scale, flowing lines, ornamentation, and proportions in the fine and applied arts, including fashionable dress—is remarkably similar.

LEGACIES OF 17TH-CENTURY STYLES

Portraits painted in the 17th century, especially those painted by Anthony Van Dyck, exercised a considerable influence on styles of the 18th century. To what extent these revivals were limited to fancy dress for masquerades or worn by sitters when they had their portraits painted is not entirely clear.

Oscar Wilde, the English poet and playwright, adopted a style of dress in the 1880s that included knee breeches, a wide collar, and long curling hair that he said was based on Cavalier men's dress. Although

adults other than those in Wilde's aesthetic circle never adopted these styles, they were used as the basis of a style for boys called "Little Lord Fauntleroy" suits, a name derived from the popular children's book of the same name (see Figure 14.23, page 411).

Neckwear of the 17th century often appears in later centuries. Ruffs, standing lace collars, and wide lace collars (see Modern Influences) can be found throughout the 19th century and on into the early 20th century (see Figures 14.15a, page 404, and 14.17, page 405).

REFERENCES

Aries, P. (1962). *Centuries of childhood: A social history of family life*. New York, NY: Knopf.

Braudel, F. (1982). *The wheels of commerce*. New York, NY: Harper & Row.

Cumming, V. 1985. *A visual history of costume: The 17th century*. New York, NY: Drama Books.

Cunnington, C. W., & Cunnington, P. (1972). *Handbook of English costume in the seventeenth century*. London, UK: Faber and Faber.

Dow, G. F. (1925). *Domestic life in New England in the seventeenth century* [Lecture]. Opening of the American Wing of the Metropolitan Museum of Art. New York, NY.

MODERN INFLUENCES

John Galliano, in this design for Dior's haute couture collection of 2009, acknowledged as his inspiration the paintings of Vermeer and the fashionable 17th-century creamy white collars and cuffs worn by fashionable Flemish women. (Jacques Brinon/AP Images)

Edwards, R., & Ramsey, L. (Eds.). (1968). *The connoisseur & complete period guides*. New York, NY: Bonanza.

Hollander, A. (1978). *Seeing through clothes*. New York, NY: Viking Press.

Hollander, A. (1994). *Sex and suits*. New York, NY: Knopf.

Jansen, H. W. (1991). *History of art* (4th ed.). New York, NY: Abrams.

Kevill-Davies, S. (1991). *Yesterday's children*. Woodbridge, UK: Antique Collector's Club.

Kuchta, D. M. (1990). "Graceful, virile and useful;" The origins of the three-piece suit." *Dress, 17*, 118–126.

Levron, J. (1968). *Daily life at Versailles in the 17th and 18th centuries*. New York, NY: Macmillan.

Marshall, R. K. (1981). Scottish portraits as a source for the costume historian. *Costume, 15*, p. 67.

Montgomery, F. (1984). *Textiles in America, 1650–1870*. New York, NY: Norton.

Reade, B. (1951). *Costume of the western world: The dominance of Spain*. London: Harrap.

Swann, J. (1991). *Shoes*. London, UK: Batsford.

Zumthor, P. (1963). *Daily life in Rembrandt's Holland*. New York, NY: Macmillan.

	1714–1820	1715	1733	c. 1720– c. 1770	c. 1770– MID-1800s	1745	1748	1756
FASHION AND TEXTILES						Madame de Pompadour becomes mistress of King Louis XV and influences arts and fashions of the French court		
POLITICS AND CONFLICTS		Death of Louis XIV; Louis XV, his great-grandson, becomes king						
DECORATIVE AND FINE ARTS	Georgian Period in England			Rococo styles predominate	Neoclassical styles predominate		Discovery of Roman ruins at Pompeii and excavations at Herculaneum helps stimulate Neoclassical revival	Birth of Mozart
ECONOMICS AND TRADE								
TECHNOLOGY AND IDEAS			John Kay patents the flying shuttle					
RELIGION AND SOCIETY	British social classes mingle at spas, amusement parks, and the theater							

CHAPTER TEN

The Eighteenth Century

1700–1790

1764	1769	1774	1776	1778	1789

Death of Louis XV; Louis XVI, his grandson, becomes king

American Revolution

French Revolution

Competition from Indian textile imports stimulates advances in textile technology

James Hargreaves invents spinning jenny

Richard Arkwright develops the spinning machine; James Watt patents the steam engine

Voltaire, Enlightenment writer, philosopher, and historian, dies

Failure to observe court etiquette makes Queen Marie Antoinette unpopular with nobles

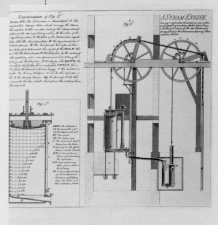

Under Louis XIV, the French court of the 17th century had become a powerful influence on the arts and fashions, and this dominance continued into the 18th century under Louis XV. The more delicate, curvilinear forms of the rococo replaced the baroque style in the last half of the century (see Figure 10.1). These forms, in turn, were followed by a revival of classical influences in the neoclassical period. International trade brought Asian influences to European dress where they appeared in silks from China (see Global Connections, page 280) and cottons from India. Advances in textile technology foreshadowed the Industrial Revolution, while the successful conclusion of the American Revolution separated the United States from Great Britain.

HISTORICAL BACKGROUND

Upon the death of Louis XIV in 1715, his great-grandson, Louis XV, became king of France at the age of 5. During the time that the king was too young to reign alone, a period called the Regency (1715–1723), baroque art styles that had dominated in the previous century underwent a gradual change. The new style lines were less massive, the curves were more slender and delicate, and an emphasis on asymmetrical balance gained importance. This new, rococo, style reached its height during the reign of Louis XV.

King Louis XV lacked the intelligence and the common sense needed for the task of governing. Lazy, egotistical, and bored by affairs of state, he sought entertainment through hunting. His other great passion was women. Madame de Pompadour, who encouraged authors and helped artists, while also serving as the king's political adviser, was the most famous and influential of his mistresses.

France engaged in costly wars during much of Louis XV's reign. These conflicts brought little but defeat and debts. Louis's half-hearted efforts never succeeded in solving the nation's mounting fiscal crisis. The lifestyle enjoyed at his lavish court contrasted sharply with the lives of the ordinary citizens. Louis XV died in 1774, more hated and despised than any other French king for many generations.

Despite its lamentable condition of finances, France dominated the culture of western Europe. France set the style in fashion, literature, decorative arts, and in philosophy. French had become the international language of Europe, preferred by royalty and aristocracy.

Louis XV's grandson and successor, Louis XVI, was a well-meaning and pious king. As a hobby he made and repaired locks. He also enjoyed hunting. But he was unfit for the heavy task that confronted him. His wife, an attractive but immature 14-year-old Austrian princess, Marie Antoinette, had an intense dislike for the customs and etiquette of the French court (see Figure 10.2). Her unpopularity with both the older nobles and the people did little to support the monarchy.

FIGURE 10.1 One of the prominent British furniture makers of the Georgian Period was Thomas Chippendale, and his very fashionable chair styles were well known through his catalog. (Image copyright © The Metropolitan Museum of Art. Image source: Art Resource, NY)

At the same time, Enlightenment writers, called *philosophes*, believed that the application of reason and science would create a better world. They used the press to unleash a wave of criticism aimed at the abuses in French society and government. The success of the French-supported American Revolution encouraged Frenchmen who wanted to reform government and society. Their opportunity came in 1789 when the bankruptcy of the French government led to a gathering that declared itself a National Assembly; its members abolished feudalism and began to write a constitution. France was undergoing a revolution. Defeats suffered in war with Austria and Prussia allowed radicals to take over the revolution. They ended the monarchy and in 1793 executed the king and queen. The old regime was abolished.

The Arts

Mid-century changes in philosophy brought related changes in styles of art. A neoclassical revival replaced rococo styles after excavations in Italy, in 1719 and 1748, uncovered the ruins of two Roman cities, Pompeii and Herculaneum, that had been destroyed in 79 CE by the eruption of Mt. Vesuvius near Naples. The discovery of these remains fueled a revived interest in classical antiquity. Although neoclassical style influences on women's dress did not appear until near the close of the century, neoclassical styles in art and architecture were evident from mid-century onward.

For the first half of the 18th century, the influence of the French court styles was also felt throughout Europe. In Prussia, Frederick the Great (1740–1786) patterned his court and architecture on those of the French court. Empress Maria Theresa of Austria, mother of Marie Antoinette, maintained loose links with France. The great-grandson of Louis XIV, Philip V, became Spain's first Bourbon king in 1700, which tied Spain to France. France and then Austria dominated

the Italian peninsula. Only the Venetian Republic remained independent until, at the end of the 18th century, it was handed over to Austria by Napoleon.

In England, the Georgian era had begun. Except for a short period at the beginning of the century when Queen Anne (daughter of James II) reigned, kings of German extraction—George I, George II, and George III—ruled England. English ideas exerted strong influence on France in the late 18th century, especially in reforms to the government and civil rights. English influences extended to fashions as well. A veritable Anglomania took hold in the 1780s.

18TH-CENTURY FRENCH SOCIETY

Versailles was abandoned during the minority of Louis XV, and the center of the French administration was moved to nearby Paris. After Louis came of age in 1723 at age 13, he returned to Versailles, and the palace was again the center of royal life. Madame de Pompadour,

FIGURE 10.2 The young queen Marie Antoinette had little time for French court customs and preferred to spend her time in social activities such as hunting that took her away from a court she considered rigid and stuffy. (Detail: © RMN-Grand Palais/Art Resource, NY)

an official mistress of King Louis XV, was a major influence on styles in costume and the arts during his reign. Her patronage assured artists and artisans of success. In return, they named styles in such diverse areas as fans, hairdos, dresses, dishes, sofas, beds, chairs, ribbons, and the rose pattern of her favorite porcelain after her (Durant and Durant, 1965).

The court became somewhat less important during the reign of Louis XVI, in large part because Queen Marie Antoinette found the French court etiquette stifling. Ceremony required that when the queen arose in the morning, one person handed her the chemise and another person, her petticoat and dress, but if a person of higher rank entered the room, the task had to be turned over to her. The queen changed this procedure after one cold winter day on which the following incident (described by her attendant) took place:

> ... the Queen, quite undressed, was about to slip on her chemise. I was holding it unfolded. The Lady-in-waiting entered, hastened to remove her gloves and took the chemise. Someone scratched at the door, which was opened; it was the Duchesse de Chartres. She had removed her gloves and came to take the chemise, but the lady-in-waiting handed it, not to her, but to me. I gave it to the Duchesse. Someone else scratched at the door: it was the Comptesse de Provence; the Duchesse de Chartres passed her the chemise. The Queen had folded her arms over her bosom and looked cold. Madame [the Comptesse] saw her strained attitude, just dropped her handkerchief, kept on her gloves and while passing the chemise over the Queen's head, ruffled her hair. (Levron, 1968, 194)

The queen abandoned traditional court etiquette, adding to the strains between the royal family and the older, more conservative nobility. Furthermore, the queen was extravagant at a time when the economy of France was in difficulty. She spent a great deal on jewelry, ordered on average 150 dresses a year, and spent the equivalent of about $40,000 on clothes. One year, she sent a lock of hair to Lyons, a city in the south of France where the silk industry was located, in order to be sure that fabric for a dress was dyed precisely the right color to match her ash blonde hair (Levron,

1968). Contemporary Comments 10.1 describes the costume required for presentation at court.

For a time Marie Antoinette abandoned the palace at Versailles for life at the Petit Trianon, a small chateau on the grounds of the palace. In this simulated country farmhouse she and her court favorites played at being "country folk" and started a fashion for peasant-style dresses and hats. The importance of the queen's lifestyle as a cause of the French Revolution is often overemphasized, but it is true that her lack of popularity with both the old nobility and the people were factors in the decline of support for the monarchy.

18TH-CENTURY ENGLISH SOCIETY

English society was less centered on the court than that of France. London was the center of fashionable life, but small towns and country estates also had their own social class structure and took an interest in fashionable dress. The apprenticeships available to young men of the provinces reveal the diversity of occupations related to clothing and fashion: clothiers, collar makers, cordwainers (shoemakers), glovers, lace makers, linen drapers, mantua makers (dressmakers), peruke (wig) makers, tailors, weavers, wool combers, wool winders, and woolen drapers (Marshall, 1969).

Fashionable clothing was divided into categories according to the time of day the costume was worn or the sort of occasion for which it was appropriate. A man divided his garments among *undress*, or lounging clothes; *dress*, slightly more formal outfits for daytime or evening wear; and *full dress*—the most formal evening dress. His *nightgown* was not a sleeping garment in the modern sense, but a dressing gown, or informal robe, worn indoors. He also had a *powdering jacket*, worn to keep the powder off his clothing while having his wig powdered.

A woman wore clothing around the house known as her *undress*, *half dress*, or *morning dress*. A riding costume or a tailor-made costume was called a *habit*. Her *coat* was not for outdoors but was her petticoat. The garment we call a coat today, she would have called a *greatcoat*. She never called a dress a *frock*, because that

Contemporary Comments 10.1

COSTUME FOR PRESENTATION AT COURT

In her memoirs Madame de la Tour du Pin, a member of the French nobility, describes her costume for presentation at court in 1787.

I was presented on Sunday morning, after Mass. I was "en grand corps," that is to say, wearing a special bodice without shoulders, laced at the back, but narrow enough for the lacings, four inches wide at the bottom, to show a chemise of the finest lawn [fabric] through which it could easily be seen if the wearer's skin was not white. This chemise had sleeves, but they were only three inches deep and the shoulders were uncovered. From the top of the arm to the elbow fell three or four flounces of blonde lace. The throat was bare. Mine was partly covered by the seven or eight rows of large diamonds which the Queen [Marie Antoinette] had kindly lent me. The front of the bodice was as if laced with rows of diamonds and on my head were more diamonds, some in clusters and some in aigrets [feathers].

The gown itself was very lovely. On account of my half-mourning, it was all in white and the entire skirt was embroidered with pearls and silver.

Harcourt, F. (Trans.) (1971). *Memoirs of Madame de la Tour du Pin: Laughing and dancing our way to the precipice.* New York, NY: McCall, p. 69.

term was applied to a type of man's coat (*frock coat*) or to children's dresses. Although by the end of the century she was wearing what the 19th-century fashion magazines would call a bustle, she called it a *false rump*.

The man of means got up late, ate breakfast, and (wearing his nightgown) received his friends at home. In the afternoon he went out to a popular spot or to the shops, and then on to dinner; after dinner, he went to a play or coffee house. During the summer he might go to a spa, a fashionable resort, to take the curative waters for real or imagined ailments. A man who paid a great deal of attention to his dress was called a *beau*, a *coxcomb*, or a *fop*. Men who adopted French and Italian-inspired fashions during the last half of the century were called **macaronis**. This name derived from the Macaroni Club, formed by young men who affected an interest in continental culture and who were noted for their brightly colored silks, lace-trimmed coats in the latest silhouette, and

fashionable wigs and hats. When the English sang of Yankee Doodle Dandy who "stuck a feather in his hat and called it macaroni," they were commenting on his attempt to appear fashionable.

Fashionable ladies spent their mornings in bed, where they reclined while receiving guests. The late-rising lady required several hours to dress. She either visited friends or drank tea in the afternoon. Dinner was taken about 4 p.m., and she spent evenings card playing and dancing.

Wealthy aristocrats and the middle class, a growing segment of English society, kept up with fashion. They traveled to spas for vacations and to many other places where the middle-class lady or gentleman could observe the most recent styles in dress and home furnishings. Social classes mingled at outdoor amusement parks and the theater. Nor was it uncommon for the rich daughters of merchants to marry into upper class families.

THE AMERICAN COLONIES IN THE 18TH CENTURY

Americans living in towns and nearby areas imported British goods and followed European fashions, many of which originated in Paris. Some clothes were imported; others were made in the colonies by copying styles shown on fashion plates or on the fashion dolls (called **fashion babies**) made in Paris.

American Quakers, like their English counterparts, dressed somewhat differently from the rest of the population. Quaker men wore plain hats and no wigs. Women wore simply shaped hats, which were later replaced by unadorned bonnets. By the end of the 18th century, some Quakers were giving up their distinctive dress.

Working-class dress was designed for convenience. Women wore a chemise and over this a petticoat skirt and a hip-length garment called a **short gown**, which was like a jacket or an overblouse. They added a serviceable apron and a kerchief at the neck, together with some kind of a cap covering the hair (Figure 10.3).

Farmers and artisans wore loose smocks over breeches made of coarse linen for summer and wool in winter. These garments pulled over the head and tied at the neck with strings. Laborers often placed a leather apron over the smock. On the frontier men adopted a costume derived, in part, from Native American styles. A loose smock, or a shirt made of fringed deerskin, or coarse homespun decorated with fringes covered the upper body. Native-American–style deerskin leggings were worn for traveling through wooded regions. Closely fitt caps of coonskin, fox, bear, or squirrel often had a long, hanging tail sewn to the back.

PRODUCTION AND ACQUISITION OF CLOTHING AND TEXTILES

Any item of dress made from textiles must go through a number of processes. Textile fibers in the 18th century would have been obtained from plants (cotton or linen) or animals (wool or silk). Once the fiber was obtained, it had to be spun into a yarn so it could be

FIGURE 10.3 Short gown, a sort of overblouse worn with a petticoat, now more likely to be called a skirt, is typical of what working class and enslaved women would have worn as everyday dress in the late 18th and early 19th centuries. (Courtesy of the Colonial Williamsburg Foundation)

woven into cloth. Where and how each of these steps was carried out differed depending on the natural resources and technologies available and the skills of the laborers (see Figure 10.4).

Advances in Textile Technology

Textile-manufacturing technology advanced rapidly in the 18th century. Increases in weaving speed meant that the weaver consumed yarn more rapidly. Inventors

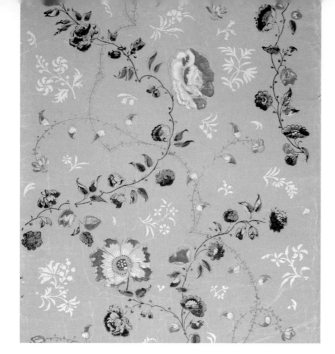

FIGURE 10.4 Imported high-quality and low-cost cotton textiles printed in rococo designs were enormously fashionable. The negative effects on European textile industry stimulated the inventions of the Industrial Revolution that would lead to mechanization and lower costs for textiles. Textiles and wallpaper were printed in similar patterns. (Wallpaper design with scattered flowers, English School (18th century)/Deutsches Tapetenmuseum, Kassel, Germany/© Museumslandschaft Hessen Kassel/Gabriele Boessert/Bridgeman Images)

searching for faster spinning methods produced a number of mechanized spinning devices. Steam (see Figure 10.5) and waterpower were being used to run this new machinery by 1800. Cotton benefited most from these advances, so cotton fabrics became available at much lower prices than heretofore. This pricing stimulated the use of cotton fabrics. In the 19th century these advances would extend to spinning other fibers.

Home versus Factory Production of Cloth

European mills produced textiles with elaborate and sophisticated patterns. The American colonies were an important market for English manufacturers who sold handsome fabrics to well-to-do colonists and poor-quality, cheap cloth to those less well off. Although the British had banned the import of Asian fabrics in order to protect their home industries, powerful British trading companies were not prohibited from selling Asian goods to the colonies. American colonists were, however, forbidden to buy French textiles. After the

Americans became independent of Britain, these restrictions were lifted.

Most of the poorer families living in American rural areas or small towns produced their own textiles, especially those made of linen or wool. Professional weavers also produced cloth. Some traveled from home to home to weave; others had their own shops.

Clothing Manufacturing and Sale

The practice of having male tailors make men's suits and coats and women make dresses for women was well established. By the 18th century affluent individuals had their clothing made for them by skilled professionals. The skills of women working at home making much of the clothing for those of ordinary means were probably limited. As Kidwell and Christman (1974, 27) wrote of the 18th-century American housewife,

FIGURE 10.5 The steam engine provided the power needed for the new mechanized devices used to manufacture textiles. (Detail: bpk, Berlin/Photographer Hermann Buresch/Art Resource, NY)

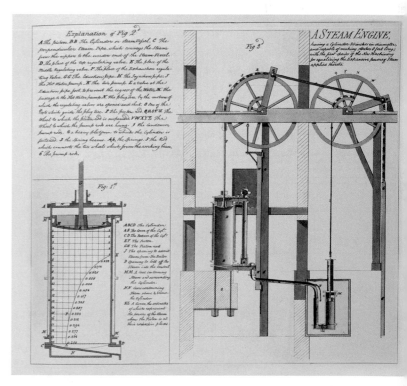

Although she might sew a fine seam, she was ignorant of the variety of stitches as they were employed by the trained tailor. Her mandate was not to create fashionable shapes out of unfashionable figures, but merely to be sure that her family was clothed against the elements. Homemade clothing must have looked homemade.

Ready-made clothing, though in limited quantities, had always been and was still available.

Among the poor, simply keeping dressed was a problem. In the country, women could spin wool and weave or knit garments, but in town clothing had to be purchased at high prices. W. H. Hutton's autobiography described how it took him 2 years to save enough money to purchase a good suit of clothes. Unfortunately, the suit was stolen, and it took him another 5 years to save for a replacement. Theft of clothing was common. Some thieves were even so enterprising as to cut holes in the backs of carriages through which they grasped a passenger's wig and whisked it away (Marshall, 1969).

The poor purchased clothing from dealers who obtained secondhand clothes from the servants of good families, to whom castoff clothing was routinely given, or from thieves. In some towns, "breeches clubs" were formed in which each member contributed a small amount to a common fund. When the fund was large enough, a name was drawn and that person received a pair of breeches. The club continued to function until a pair had been obtained by every member.

INFLUENCES ON COSTUME IN THE 18TH CENTURY

Styles of the 18th century, like those of the 17th century, reflected the increasing European trade with East Asia. Specific clothing items that originated abroad, such as men's dressing gowns and the mantua cut for women's dresses, were relatively rare, but Eastern textiles were very important. Asian silk brocades and damasks; Indian chintz, calico, and muslin fabrics; and European copies of these fabrics were made into handsome garments.

During the last quarter of the century English styles for both men and women had a significant impact on Parisian fashion. In women's clothes, **Anglomania** (a French fad for things English) became evident in a vogue for simpler styles, for English riding habits, and for coat-dresses derived from English men's riding coats, which were called **redingotes**. Frenchmen copied Englishmen's tailoring, and, except for court functions, wore simpler, undecorated suits and affected a more casual mode of dress. Mercier, in Contemporary Comments 10.2, page 275, pokes fun at Anglomania and at current French excesses in dress.

SOURCES OF INFORMATION ABOUT COSTUME

Museum collections include many more garments dating from this period. For the most part these are upper class clothes.

Eighteenth-century portraits are excellent sources of information, unless the artist felt a portrait demanded timeless rather than fashionable dress. One of the most prominent English portraitists, Sir Joshua Reynolds, "despised fashion" and "exhorted young artists to rise above it," advising young artists to "change the dress from a contemporary fashion to one more permanent, which has annexed to it no ideas of meanness from its being familiar to us." He urged artists to "disregard all local and temporary ornaments, and look only on those general habits which are everywhere and always the same. . . ." (Reynolds, 1891, 171 ff).

Some English portraits of the 18th century also reflected the interest of fashionable people in masquerades. The portraits of Van Dyck were one popular source of inspiration for masquerade costume, and some individuals had their portraits painted in these 17th-century–inspired styles.

Costume for Men: 18th Century

Underdrawers, a shirt, waistcoat, an outer coat, knee-length breeches, hose, and shoes were the major elements of men's costume. Hats and wigs were added on appropriate occasions, along with other accessories and outdoor wear. Although the elements remained constant throughout the century, the lines of styles

Contemporary Comments 10.2

ANGLOMANIA IN FRANCE

Louis-Sébastien Mercier, slightly tongue-in-cheek, exhorts his fellow countrymen to abandon English styles and return to those that are French.

Just now English clothing is all the wear. Rich man's son, sprig of nobility, counter-jumper—you see them dressed all alike in the long coat, cut close, thick stockings, puffed stock; with hats on their heads and a riding-switch in their hands. Not one of the gentlemen thus attired, however, has ever crossed the Channel or can speak one word of English. . . . No, no, my young friend. Dress French again, wear your laces, your embroidered waistcoats, your laced coats; powder your hair to the newest tune; keep your hat under your arm, in that place which nature, in Paris at any rate, designed for it, and wear your two watches, with concomitant fobs, both at once.

Shopkeepers hang out signs—"English Spoken Here." The lemonade-sellers even have succumbed to the lure of punch [an English drink], and write the word on their windows. English coats, with their triple capes, envelop our young exquisites. Small boys wear their hair cut round, uncurled and without powder. Older men walk with the English gait, a trifle round-shouldered. Our women take their headgear from London. The racecourse at Vincennes is copied from that at Newmarket. Finally, we have Shakespeare on our stage, rhymed, it is true, by M. Ducis [a French poet], but impressive nevertheless.

Mercier, L.-S. (1933). *The waiting city: Paris 1782–88.* H. Simpson (Trans.). Philadelphia, PA: Lippincott, p. 29–30.

of costume elements were different in the first and second half of the century.

The underwear worn next to the body remained much the same for most of the 18th century. Shirts were considered to be part of "underclothing."

Garments

Drawers, which were worn next to the skin beneath the breeches, were the functional equivalent of modern undershorts or medieval braies. They closed at the waist with drawstrings or buttons, were made of white linen, cotton, or wool, and ended at the knee (Figure 10.6).

FIGURE 10.6 Undergarment of the 18th century from England, made of flannel for warmth. (Courtesy of the Colonial Williamsburg Foundation)

Shirts were cut much like those of preceding centuries with a ruffled frill at the front of the neck and the end of the sleeves. Collars and cravats were generally made of white cotton or linen. During the first half of century, collars were gathered to a neckband. Neck cloths or cravats wound around the neck and knotted under the chin, concealing the collar. Neckbands lengthened, in the second half of the century, evolving into a collar that was sewn to the shirt. The **steinkirk** was a cravat in which the tie pulled through the buttonhole and twisted loosely. Soldiers supposedly twisted their cravats loosely around the neck during a battle in 1692. Evidence, however, indicates that the style originated several years before the battle for which it was supposed to have been named.

Some men wore a second waistcoat either over or under the shirt during cold weather. Sometimes waistcoats worn over the shirt were made with a visible collar. Others that were strictly utilitarian garments to provide warmth were hidden from view.

Up to Mid-18th Century

Classification as either "dress" or "full dress" depended on the degree of formality of the item. Dress coats, breeches, and waistcoats were usually made from less decorative fabrics; full-dress garments were made from elaborate brocades and trimmed with handsome embroidery and lace.

By 1700, extra fullness was added to the straighter cut that had been characteristic of the 1680s. Coats were knee length and until about 1720 buttoned to the hem. After 1720, they only closed to the waist (Figure 10.7; see also Figure 10.8). Buckram stiffening held out the full skirts of coats. Side seams were usually left open from below the waist to accommodate swords. Pockets were usually positioned at hip level, and pocket flaps had scalloped edges.

Until the 1730s most sleeves ended in large, full, attached cuffs that either closed all around or were open at the back. Cuffs that reached to the elbow were called **boot cuffs**. An alternative style had no cuffs and was slit at the back to expose the sleeve ruffle.

FIGURE 10.7 Silk ditto suit, first half of the 18th century, showing the cuff construction of the sleeve and long waistcoat, characteristic of the first half of the century. (V&A Images, London/Art Resource, NY)

Waistcoats followed the lines of outer coats, ending close to the knee. They were made either with or without sleeves and usually matched the outer coat in color and fabric. At home, as casual wear, or as undress, men wore sleeveless waistcoats over shirts without outer coats.

The cut of breeches was moderately full. The seat was cut very full and gathered to a waistband that rode, loosely fitted, below the waist. Breeches ended at the knee, often being just barely visible when the coat was closed. They closed at the front with buttons or, after

FIGURE 10.8 Three gentlemen in a country scene are dressed in informal frock coats. The figure at the right holds a three-cornered hat in his hand and wears what appear to be knee-length spatterdashers, or gaiters, over his shoes. (Image copyright © The Metropolitan Museum of Art. Image source: Art Resource, NY)

1730, with a **fall**, a square, central flap that buttoned to the waistline (see Figure 10.10, page 278).

Frock coats were cut looser and shorter than dress coats and they had flat, turned-down collars. After 1730, frock coats were considered suitable for country wear and after 1770, they were accepted for more formal wear as well. They were not embroidered and usually were made from such fabrics as serge, plush, or sturdy woven cloth (Figure 10.8).

The origin of the term *frock coat*, like the origins of so many costume terms, is not entirely clear. Before being applied to the coat style described earlier, the word *frock* had been applied to several other garments—among these a woman's undergarment, a priest's gown, a child's dress, and a loose-fitting riding coat. A garment worn by Spanish shepherds that was a loosely fitted, washable linen outer garment seems to have traveled to England by way of the Spanish Netherlands. In England it was adopted by laborers and farmers and called a smock frock (DeMarly, 1986). The **smock frock** (later called a **smock**) continued in use for English agricultural workers up until the 19th century, when it was frequently decorated with

a type of embroidery that is now called **smocking**. Given that most other garments to which the term *frock* was applied were loosely fitted, it may be that the designation *frock coat* came about because of the looser fit of this garment.

Suit and coat fabrics for daytime or less formal evenings included plain, woven wool, plush, velvet, and silks including satin trimmed with lace, braid, or fur. Full-dress clothing was usually made of cloth of gold or silver, brocade, flowered velvet, or embroidered materials. Breeches utilized sturdy woven cloth, plush, or serge for casual wear; silk satin or velvet for evening; and leather, especially buckskin, for riding. Coats did not necessarily match breeches or waistcoats. When all three items were made of the same fabric, the suit was called a **ditto suit**. Cunningham (1984) noted that this term was first encountered after 1750, although such suits were seen earlier (see Figure 10.7).

Changes after the Mid-18th Century

In the second part of the century fullness of coats decreased, side pleats were eliminated, and the front of the coat curved toward the side. By 1760 a narrow,

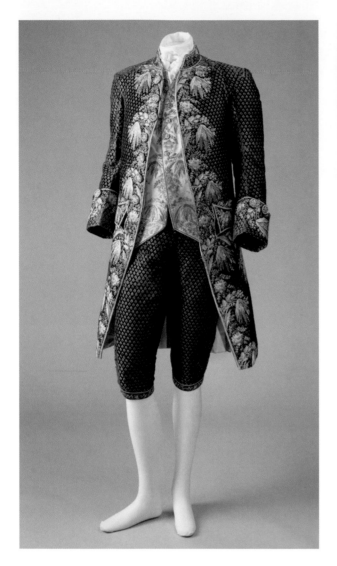

FIGURE 10.9 The shorter waistcoat style and standing collar characteristic of the second half of the century are visible in this suit. (Image copyright © The Metropolitan Museum of Art. Image source: Art Resource, NY)

stand-up collar appeared. The silhouette narrowed, as did sleeves, which were longer and generally cuffed (Figure 10.9).

Now sleeveless and shorter, waistcoats were both single and double breasted. Because coats were worn open, the waistcoat fabric became a center of attention and more brocades, or elaborately embroidered silks, were used. Breeches fit more closely. The fall or flap closing predominated (Figure 10.10).

After 1730 cravats tended to be replaced by **stocks**, a linen square folded to form a high neckband that

FIGURE 10.10 Man's knee-breeches, c. 1780–1790. The front closing is of the type called fall or flap. (Division of Home And Community Life, National Museum of American History, Smithsonian Institution)

was stiffened with buckram, and fastened behind the neck. Often a length of black ribbon tied in a bow at the front was worn over the stock.

Until mid-century, capes or cloaks for outdoors were cut full and gathered at the neck under a flat collar. After mid-century, full, wide-skirted greatcoats (**surtouts**) ended below the knee. Coat sleeves were generally cuffed. Some coats had as many as three broad, falling, capelike collars, each shorter than the one below.

Comfortable loosely fitted garments, variously known as nightgowns, morning gowns, dressing gowns, **Indian gowns**, or **banyans** (*ban'-yan*), were worn throughout the century as casual or undress at home. In a detailed study Cunningham (1984) identified several variations. A loose, full kimono style was more widely worn in the early part of the century (see Figure 10.24, page 292). Another type was more form fitting, similar to a man's coat, with set-in sleeves (Figure 10.11). Each of these basic styles could have additional variations. Fabrics preferred for banyans included cotton calicos; silk damasks, brocades, velvets, taffetas, or satins; and wool worsteds and calamancos (glazed, wool worsted fabric with raised stripes of the same color).

Writings of the period indicate these garments were worn outdoors as well as at home. Many men had their

FIGURE 10.11 Three banyans and nightcaps. From left to right: Printed cotton chintz, 1770–1790, made in Britain of East Indian fabric worn, with nightcap of embroidered linen decorated with lace; silk-brocaded banyan and matching waistcoat, c. 1760, and cotton-embroidered cap; block-printed cotton banyan and white linen cap. (Courtesy of the Colonial Williamsburg Foundation)

portraits painted in these handsome garments. They appear to derive from full, loose Asian garments, and several of the names given to them (e.g., Indian gown, banyan) reflect these origins. They are yet another example of the strong Asian and Middle Eastern influences on fashions of the 18th century.

Hair and Headdress

Most men who could afford them wore wigs. Styles varied. Until the 1730s, long, **full-bottomed wigs**, such as those of the 1600s, were favored, although fullness gradually shifted to the back (Figure 10.12). Brushing the hair straight back from the forehead and into a slightly elevated roll began in the 1730s. This style was

FIGURE 10.12 Men and women in the dress of the early 18th century. Men wear "full-bottomed" wigs. Although white wedding dresses were not yet customary, this bride of 1729 wears cream satin and gold. (Detail: Image copyright © The Metropolitan Museum of Art. Image source: Art Resource, NY)

Global Connections

This banyan is a true example of global connections: a man's garment from the 18th century worn in Holland, made of silk from China to satisfy European's desire for fabrics with rococo ornamentation, and in a style that probably originated as a cut similar to those that are much like the depictions of garments worn by men in Middle Eastern regions. In the 18th century Chinese weavers used sophisticated draw looms to create figured textiles in patterns that European trade companies knew their European customers would want. (Digital Image © 2007 Museum Associates/LACMA; Licensed by Art Resource, NY)

called in French **toupee** (*too-pay'*) or in English **foretop** (Figure 10.13). Hair was dressed higher after 1750 and wider in the 1780s, paralleling women's hairstyles.

Other popular styles included wigs with **queues** (a lock or pigtail at the back), and **club wigs**, or **catogans** (*ka-toe'gan*), in which queues were doubled up on themselves and tied at the middle to form a loop of hair (see Figure 10.14).

Colors varied, but powdered wigs were preferred for formal dress. Wigs were made of human hair, horsehair, or goat hair (see Illustrated Table 10.1, page 282).

The widespread use of wigs made hats less important. The three-cornered hat was the most common style. Others were a large flat hat called **chapeau bras** (*shap'-po-brah*) that was carried under

FIGURE 10.13 Satirical drawing of 1777 pokes fun at the tight lacing of corsets and the hairstyles of that period. (Division of Home And Community Life, National Museum of American History, Smithsonian Institution)

FIGURE 10.14 Wolfgang Amadeus Mozart was a musical child prodigy who performed in the courts of Europe. Although still a child, his dress for such performances was adult attire, even including wearing his hair in a fashionable queue. (Scala/Art Resource, NY)

the arm rather than being worn. Two-cornered hats appeared about 1780. In the 19th century, three-cornered hats were named **tricornes**, and two-cornered hats, **bicornes**, by costume historians. Three-cornered hats and jockey caps were worn for riding and, after the 1770s, the hats that would be called top hats today were worn for riding and called *round hats* (see Illustrated Table 10.1, page 282).

Men wore caps at home instead of wigs. Two of the styles most frequently depicted were a cap with round crown and flat, turned-up brim that fit close against the crown (see Figure 10.11) or one with a shapeless crown and rolled brim, somewhat turbanlike.

Footwear

Stockings were long, ending above the knee. Men of the 1770s and later who wanted their calves to be fashionably shaped might wear "artificial calves," padding strapped to hose or strapped to the leg.

Shoes had square toes, high square heels, and large square tongues until 1720. Later shapes were rounder, and the heels not so high. Young men of the late 18th century nicknamed older, more conventional and conservative men "square toes," using the phrase in much the same way as young people today might use the term *square* (Swann, 1982).

Decorative buckles were placed at the base of shoe tongues. Red heels were favored for court dress and for fashionable men before 1750 and after 1770. Slippers and dress shoes had low heels and flat soles (see Illustrated Table 10.1, page 282).

When sturdy shoes were worn outdoors, men could add **spatterdashers** (also called **spats**, or gaiters). These were separate protective coverings that extended from the top of the shoe to some point below the knee, in order to protect the legs (see Figure 10.8).

Various sizes and shapes of boots were worn for riding, traveling, and hunting, as well as worn by the military. Boots, not designed to be worn indoors, tended to be sturdy and practical. Jackboots made of rigid, stiff leather were knee length and protected the legs of horseback riders. Boots of softer leather and shorter lengths were also adopted, some copied from jockeys' boots and others from military styles.

Accessories and Jewelry

Men used such accessories as muffs, walking sticks, watches, pocketbooks, and decorated snuff boxes for carrying powdered tobacco, which was inhaled. They wore rings, sometimes brooches, and jeweled shoe buckles (see Illustrated Table 10.1, page 282).

Cosmetics and Grooming

Men used powder and perfume. Most were clean shaven.

Costume for Women:
18th Century

A variety of supporting undergarments determined the shape of women's costume during the 18th century. The silhouette described in Chapter 9 of a long slender bodice and a skirt with back fullness

Illustrated Table 10.1

18th-Century Accessories

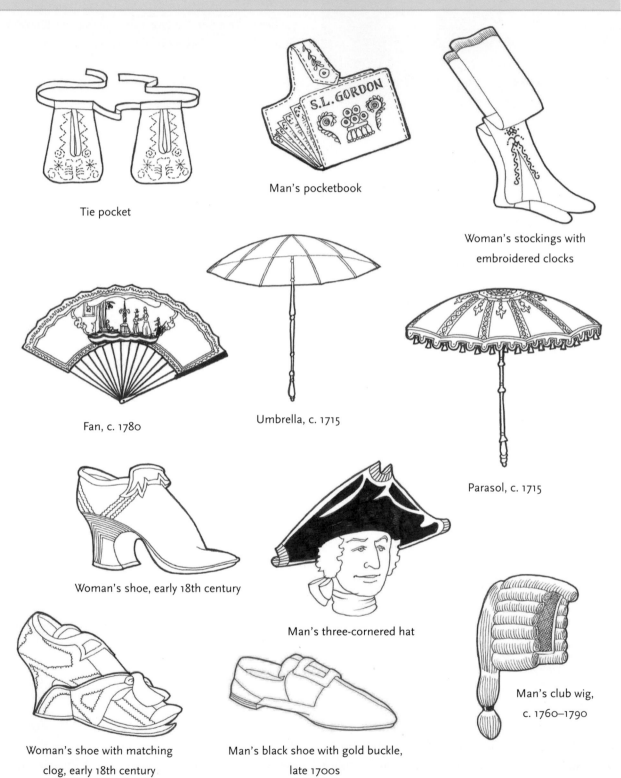

Tie pocket

Man's pocketbook

Woman's stockings with embroidered clocks

Fan, c. 1780

Umbrella, c. 1715

Parasol, c. 1715

Woman's shoe, early 18th century

Man's three-cornered hat

Man's club wig, c. 1760–1790

Woman's shoe with matching clog, early 18th century

Man's black shoe with gold buckle, late 1700s

continued until about 1720 (see Figure 10.12). Wide hoops were used first in England about 1720 and slightly later in France. From the end of the second decade until about 1770–1780, hoops were a part of everyday costume.

The French called these hoops **paniers** (*pahn-yay'*), which means "basket." Some hoops did produce the visual effect of perching a basket on either hip; however, the term was derived from the fact that both baskets and paniers might be made of wicker. In England, they were more likely to be called **hoops** (see Figure 10.17b).

The extreme width of their skirts forced ladies to enter rooms sideways. Small railings were built around the edges of table tops and other furniture to prevent the sweeping of teacups and *objets d'art* from the tables to the floor. Some paniers were hinged so that they could be folded up under the arms when necessary for mobility.

Caricatures and contemporary literary sources are full of gibes at ladies for wearing such an "outrageous" style. Cunnington and Cunnington reprint these observations:

- *The Spectator* of 1711: "the hoop petticoat is made use of to keep us [i.e., the male sex] at a distance."
- *The Weekly Journal*, in 1717, appealed to women to "find one tolerable convenience in these machines."
- *The Salisbury Journal* noted that the swaying hoops revealed ankles and legs, scolding ladies whom they accused of making their petticoats short so "that a hoop eight yards wide may indecently show how your garters are ty'd."

Between 1720 and 1780, the shape of the hoop varied, thereby causing changes in the silhouette of the garments it supported. Although all classes adopted hoops, not every woman wore hoops. Between 1770 and 1780, as part of the focus on less formal English styles, hip pads and bustles supplanted hoops as

support garments. The French, however, continued to wear the hoop-supported robe à la Française (see Figure 10.17a) for ceremonial occasions even after the French Revolution. Even when hoops were entirely out of style, they were preserved in the required formal dress at the English court.

Undergarments

As undergarments women wore chemises, under petticoats, and the aforementioned hoops. Drawers were not yet universally worn. Chemises, which were worn next to the body, were knee length and cut full, with wide necklines edged with lace. This lace often showed at the neckline of the outer dress. Chemise sleeves were full, to the elbow, but not visible.

Placed over the chemise but under the hoop, under petticoats were fairly straight garments made of fabrics including **cambric** (a plain-weave, fine, white linen fabric), **dimity** (usually of cotton with a woven lengthwise cord or figure, **flannel** (a soft wool with a napped surface), or calico (colorful, Indian, printed cotton.) In winter petticoats were often quilted for warmth.

Corsets, commonly called **stays**, were made of coarse fabric unless they were intended to be a visible part of the costume, in which case they were covered at least in front by dress fabric. Both the front and back were boned. Most laced up the back, although some laced at the front and back, and for stout and pregnant women, side lacings were sometimes added (see Figure 10.13). Some had fronts constructed to allow the insertion of a decorative, V-shaped stomacher (Figure 10.15).

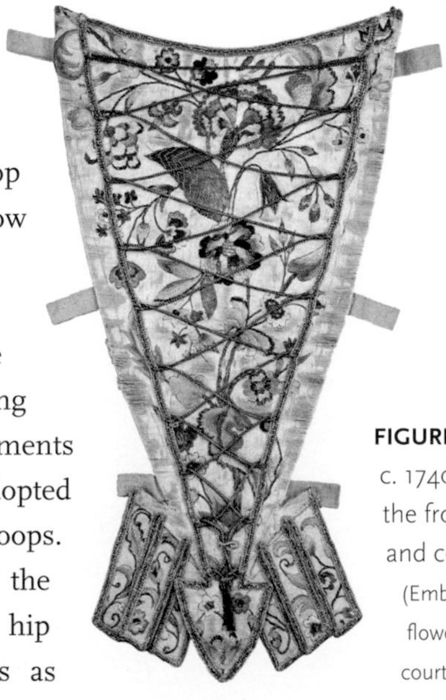

FIGURE 10.15 Embroidered silk-satin stomacher, c. 1740. These elaborately decorated fillers for the front of 18th-century dresses were removable and could be worn with different garments.
(Embroidered ivory silk satin stomacher with polychrome flowers and gilt cord lacing; English, ca. 1740; image courtesy of Cora Ginsburg LLC)

The term **jumps** was applied to loose, unboned bodices worn at home to provide relief from tight corseting.

The hoop that shaped the skirt had a construction that was similar to that of the farthingale of the 16th century. From around 1710, they were cone shaped and made of circles of whalebone sewn into petticoats of sturdy fabric, each hoop increasing in size as it moved nearer the floor. In the 1720s the shape became rounded like a dome; in the 1730s the favored shape was narrower from front to back and wider from side to side; and by the 1740s extreme widths were reached. Some hoops reached a width of 2 3/4 yards; these wide styles remained until the 1760s.

The earliest hoops were made of whalebone. As the style persisted, the materials used expanded to include metal hoops and wicker basketlike shapes, one worn over each hip. Some metal or whalebone hoops were sewn into a petticoat while others were made as a frame held together with tapes and tied around the waist (see Figure 10.17b). Some dress bodices were so heavily boned as to make stays superfluous, in which case they were not worn.

1715–1730

Outer Garments

Gowns and two-piece garments were constructed to be either open or closed at center front. Gowns could be either loose or fitted. **Sacque** (*sahk*), **robe battante** (*ba-tahnt'*), **robe volante** (*vo-lahnt'*), and **innocente** (*in-no-sahnt'*) are all names for a gown that was unbelted, loose from the shoulder to floor. Made with pleats at the back and at the shoulder in front, sacques were worn over a dome-shaped hoop and might either have a closed front or be worn open over a corset and petticoat (Figure 10.16). From the time of the death of Louis XIV until Louis XV reached adulthood, rigid court etiquette relaxed somewhat. The loose-fitting gown is sometimes cited as evidence of this lack of formality.

Other important styles included the **pet en l'air** (*pet'-ahn-lair*), and a **mantua-style** gown. The former was a short, hip-length version worn with a separate, gathered skirt, and the latter was cut in one piece from shoulder to hem and fitted to the body in front and back. These gowns were more popular in England

FIGURE 10.16 Women of 1831 in gowns of various styles. The two seated women wear loose-fitting sacque dresses. The woman standing with her back to the viewer appears to be wearing a *robe à la Française*. (bpk, Berlin/Charlottenburg Castle, Preussische Schloesser und Gaerten, Berlin/Photographer Jorg P. Anders/Art Resource, NY)

than in France. Many were open in front with the petticoat visible. Sometimes petticoats were quilted.

Hair and Headdress

See Illustrated Table 10.2, page 286, for some examples of hairstyles and headdresses in the 18th century.

Fairly simple hairstyles replaced the fontange styles, which went out of fashion about 1710. Waved loosely around the face, the hair was twisted into a small roll or bun worn at the top of the head, toward the back, An alternative had the hair arranged around the face in ringlets or waves. Women, like men, might powder their hair for formal occasions.

Hats were worn indoors and outdoors. Women wore **pinners** indoors. These were circular caps with single or double frills around the edge that were placed flat on the head. **Mob caps** were also for household use. These had high, puffed-out crowns at the back of the cap and wide, flat borders that encircled the face. Lace trimming was much used. Long lace or fabric streamers (lappets) hung from the edge or tied under the chin. White indoor caps might also be worn outdoors, under other hats. Outdoors, women covered their heads with hoods or wore small straw or silk hats with narrow brims and narrow ribbon band trimmings.

1730–1760

Garments

Two new styles replaced the loose sacque. The *robe à la Française* (*frahn-says'*) had a full, pleated cut at the back and a fitted front (Figure 10.17a). The *robe à l'Anglaise* (*lahn-glays'*) had a close fit in the front and at the back (Figure 10.18). The *robe à la Française* was more popular in France, and *à l'Anglaise*, in England, though both styles were worn in both countries and in America. The term **Watteau back** (*wat-tow'*) came to be attached to the loose-fitting, pleated-back *robe à la Française* in the 19th century when similar styles were revived. The term *Watteau back* was not used in the 18th century. Watteau was an 18th-century painter who often depicted women wearing such gowns.

a

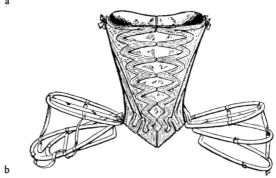

b

FIGURE 10.17 Robes à la Française of the mid-18th century (a), made of flowered silk. (Image copyright © The Metropolitan Museum of Art. Image source: Art Resource, NY) The wide skirts of the dresses are supported by a frame called panniers (b), depicted in this drawing. (Courtesy of Fairchild Publications, Inc.)

Most gowns had open bodices and skirts that allowed the display of decorative stomachers and petticoats (see Figure 10.15). The stomacher, a triangular piece, had tabs on the sides and was pinned either to the bodice or to the stays. Embroidery ornamented

Illustrated Table 10.2

Typical Women's Hairstyles and Headdress in the 18th Century

Hairstyle of the first decade of the 18th century[1]

Hairstyle and indoor cap of about 1725[1]

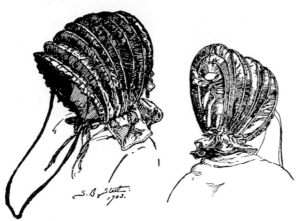

Calash, a folding hood of about 1765

Tall headdress popular after about 1775[2]

c. 1789: hair dressed *à la hedgehog*[3]

Late-18th-century hairstyle and hat[3]

[1] Bayerische Staatsbibliothek München

[2] Author's collection of fashion plates.

[3] New York Public Library/Art Resource, NY

some stomachers; others were covered with ribbons (**eschelles**, *eh-shell'*) or masses of artificial flowers or lace. Formal gowns and their petticoats were usually made from the same fabric, thereby giving them the appearance of being a single garment. The extremely wide skirts effectively showed off the elaborately patterned fabrics used for full dress. Contemporary Comments 10.3 describes the decorative fabrics worn in English court circles in the 1730s.

The necklines of these gowns were usually low and square or oval in shape. Sleeves ended below the elbow, finishing in one or more ruffles (called **engageants** (*on-gaj-ahnt'*).

When garments consisted of separate tops worn over petticoats or skirts, the skirts were full, supported by paniers. Fashionable tops included the short sacque or *pet en l'air* and a jacket (in French, **casaquin**, pronounced *cas-ah-can'*) that was fitted through the bodice and flared out below the waist almost to the knee. Sleeves were tight, with a small, turned-back cuff.

Hair and Headdress

Hairstyles began to change by 1750 when hair was combed back from the face, smooth and high on top in toupee fashion, then arranged in a bun at the top of the head or a plait at the back. Another style was achieved by close, tight curls called **tête de mouton** (*tet-duh-moo-tahn'*), which in English means "sheep's head." The curls resembled the curly pelts of sheep.

The caps worn indoors remained much the same. For outdoors women wore either large flat straw hats with low crowns and wide brims, called **bergere** (*bear-jere'*) or **shepherdess hats**, that tied under or over the brim; three-cornered hats; or, for riding, jockey caps of black velvet with a peak at the front.

1760–1790

Garments

After 1770, the *robe à la Française* was modified, as paniers were replaced by hip pads. Excess fabric was pulled through pocket slits in such a way that the

FIGURE 10.18 *Young Woman with Servant*, Stephen Slaughter; English, 1697–1765. Standing woman wears a *robe à l'Anglaise*, which is fitted close to the waist at front and back. Seated woman wears a bergere or shepherdess hat. Her stomacher is covered with the ribbons called *eschelles*. (Wadsworth Atheneum Museum of Art/Art Resource, NY)

bunched fabric hung through the pocket to form a drapery. By 1780 the *robe à la Française* was no longer fashionable. The *robe à l'Anglaise*, with slight modifications in waistline placement and a fuller bodice, continued to be worn into the 1780s (see Figure 10.18). Skirt fullness swung from sides to back in the late 1770s, and a false rump pad, tied at the back of the waist, supported the fullness. Contemporary references indicate **false rumps** were filled with cork or other light cushioning materials. The *London*

Contemporary Comments 10.3

ELABORATE ENGLISH FASHIONS OF 1738–1739

The contemporary description by Mary Granville of clothing worn in English court circles in the years of 1738 and 1739 provides a glimpse of the lavishness of English upper class costume during this period. In her letter to her sister of January 23, 1738–1739, she wrote,

I never saw so much finery without any mixture of trumpery in my life. Lady Huntington's, as the most extraordinary I must describe first:—her petticoat was black velvet embroidered with chenille, the pattern a large stone vase filled with ramping flowers that spread almost over a breadth of the petticoat from the bottom to the top; between each vase of flowers was a pattern of gold shells, and foliage embossed and most heavily rich; the gown was white satin embroidered also with chenille mixt with gold ornaments, no vases on the sleeve, but two or three on the tail; it was a most labored piece of finery, the pattern much properer for a stucco staircase than the apparel of a lady—a mere shadow that tottered under every step she took under the load. . . .

In another letter to her sister of January 22, 1739–40

. . . Lady Dysart was in a scarlet damask gown. Facings [trimmings] and robings [bands of decoration] embroidered with gold and colours, her petticoat white satin, all covered with embroidery of the same sort, very fine and handsome. . . . The Princess's clothes were white satin the petticoat, robings, and facings covered with a rich gold net, and upon that flowers in their natural colours embroidered, her head crowned with jewels and her behavior, (as it always is,) affable and obliging to everybody. . . . The Duchess of Bedford's petticoat was green padusoy [peau de soie], embroidered very richly with gold and silver and a few colours; the pattern was festoons of shells, coral, corn, corn-flowers, and sea weeds; everything in different works of gold and silver except the flowers and coral, the body of the gown white satin, with a mosaic pattern of gold facings, robings and train the same of the petticoat; there was an abundance of embroidery, and many people in gowns and petticoats of different colours. The men were as fine as the ladies. . . . My Lord Baltimore was in light brown and silver, his coat lined quite throughout with ermine.

Delany, M. (1861). *The autobiography and correspondence of Mary Granville, Mrs. Delany* (Vol. 2). London, UK: Bentley.

Magazine of 1777 issued this warning to prospective bridegrooms:

> Let her gown be tuck'd up to the hips on each side
> Shoes too high for to walk or to jump;
> And to deck the sweet creature complete for a bride
> Let the cork-cutter cut her a rump.
> Thus finish'd in taste, while on Chloe you gaze
> You may take the dear charmer for life;
> But never undress her—for out of her stays,
> You'll find you have lost half your wife.

In the late 1770s and 1780s some skirts shortened, revealing the leg above the ankle (Figure 10.19). The many gown styles include the **polonaise** (po-lohn-ays') (fashionable from about 1770–1785), which was an overdress and petticoat in which the overskirt was puffed and looped by means of tapes and rings sewn into the skirt. A hoop or bustle supported the skirt (see Figure 10.17b). In subsequent periods the term *polonaise* will be used very broadly to refer to any overskirt that is puffed or draped over an under layer. Other gowns

FIGURE 10.19 Silk brocades with flower patterns in pastel and light colors were among the more widely used fabrics for women's dresses in the 18th century (England, 1775–1785). The puffed and looped overskirt was called a *polonaise*. (INFORMAL DRESS AND PETTICOAT, 1775-1785, silk taffeta, Cincinnati Art Museum, John J. Emery Endowment. 1986.1029a-b)

that were seen frequently were closed or **round gowns**, that is, gowns closed all the way down the front. **Redingote dresses** resembled buttoned greatcoats or English riding coats with wide lapels or revers at the neck. The **chemise à la reine** (*chem-eze'ah-la-rehn*) was a white muslin gown that resembled the chemise undergarment of the period, but, unlike the chemise, had a waistline and a soft, fully gathered skirt. This garment, made of very costly muslin imported from India, was a forerunner of styles of the beginning of the 19th century (Figure 10.20).

Fashionable two-piece garments included skirts worn with a long, fitted jacket, the **caraçao** (*kara-sow'*) bodice. Similar in style to the aforementioned casaquin in cut and to jackets based on English men's riding dress, the caraçao (Figure 10.21) was worn with men's hats.

Hair and Headdress

Hairstyles expanded to extreme sizes (Figure 10.22). See Illustrated Table 10.2, page 286, for some examples of hairstyles and headdress in the 18th century.

In the 1760s hair was dressed higher and frizzed around the face. This changed to an arrangement of sausage curls worn flat against the head, running

FIGURE 10.20 Antoine-Laurent Lavoisier and his wife, 1788, by Jacques-Louis David. Madame Lavoisier wears a muslin dress of the *chemise à la reine* style. Her hair is dressed *à la herisson*, or in the "hedgehog" fashion. (Detail: Image copyright © The Metropolitan Museum of Art. Image source: Art Resource, NY)

from ear to ear. In the 1770s, maximum size was reached when towering structures were supplemented by feathers, jewels, ribbons, and seemingly almost anything a lady could perch on top of her head (see Illustrated Table 10.2, page 286). In 1768 *London Magazine* was talking about hairstyles raised "a foot high and tower-wise." In the 1780s height diminished, but fullness was retained in the **hedgehog fashion**, with hair curled, full and wide around the face and long locks hanging at the back (see Figure 10.20).

For indoors, small day caps were discarded when hairstyles grew to exaggerated sizes, although some mob caps were enlarged to accommodate high hairstyles. For outdoors, hoods were made large enough to cover the hair. These included **calashes** or **caleches** (*cal-eshes'*), which were made of a series of semi-hoops sewn into the hood at intervals. These hoops supported the hood without crushing the

FIGURE 10.21 Yellow satin caraçao jacket and matching petticoat, c. 1775. At this time the word petticoat could refer to either an outer garment or an under layer. (Image copyright © The Metropolitan Museum of Art. Image source: Art Resource, NY)

hair, and folded flat when not in use. Other hats perched on top of the tall headdress. Women set enormous hat structures with great quantities of lace, ribbons, feathers, and flowers flat on the head or at an angle when the flatter hedgehog hairstyle developed (see Illustrated Table 10.2, page 286).

FIGURE 10.22 The American Revolution, financed in part by France, provided cartoonists an opportunity to caricature the French fashion in enormous coiffures while showing support for the Americans. (Art Resource/Art Resource, NY)

Other Costume Components: The 18th Century

Outdoor Garments

Cloaks were cut full, to fit over wide skirts. These varied in length, some being full length and others ending at the waist or hip. Some were hooded. Fabrics included velvet and wool, with fur trims for cold weather and silk or other lightweight fabrics for warm weather (Figure 10.23). Overcoats, cut like a man's greatcoat, though more closely fitted, were used in the last two decades after the style for hoops had passed.

Other outdoor garments included large scarves, shawls, and wraps, with or without sleeves that covered the upper part of the body or smaller shawls and short capes covering the shoulders and upper arms. Narrow fur or feather pieces, like a modern-day stole but called **tippets**, were worn around the shoulders.

Footwear

Made of such fabrics as cotton, wool, or silk knits, stockings extended to the knee and were held in place with garters.

Shoes had pointed toes, high heels, tongues, and side pieces called **latchets** that fastened over the instep. Backless slippers (**mules**) were popular. In the late 1880s Chinese influences were evident in slippers with small, low heels and turned-up toes that were held on the foot by a drawstring in a casing around the top of the shoe. Such Asian influences are evident in all the decorative arts of the 18th century, although in clothing they are most evident in men's dressing gowns and in fabric decoration.

Clogs or **pattens**, overshoes that protect against wet and muddy surfaces, were made of matching or other fabrics and had sturdy leather soles, built-up arches, and latchets that tied across the instep to hold the clog in place. Country people wore wooden clogs or metal pattens to raise the shoe out of the mud (see Illustrated Table 10.1, page 282, for examples of footwear).

FIGURE 10.23 Silk satin cloak of the 18th century. A brown fur muff keeps the wearer's hands warm. (V&A Images, London/Art Resource, NY)

Accessories

See Illustrated Table 10.1, page 282, for examples of some types of 18th-century accessories. Items for covering the hands included gloves, mittens, and muffs. Gloves usually extended to the elbow. Mittens were gloves without thumb and finger coverings. Muffs, small until the 1770s after which they enlarged, were most often made of feathers, fabric, or fur and often had matching tippets.

Pockets were not yet sewn into dresses. Instead they were bags sewn onto a ribbon, tied around the waist, and reached through a slit in the skirt. After 1760, some women carried small bags in addition to pockets.

Other accessories included folding fans of various sizes and shapes, parasols, and black masks mounted on sticks that were held up before the face to cover the full or half face. These masks were often worn to balls.

Jewelry

Among the more commonly used items of jewelry were necklaces, often with matching earrings, gold watches worn around the neck, jeweled hair pins and hair ornaments, and jeweled buckles for shoes. Among the popular necklaces were rows of pearls, chains, lockets, pendants, and crosses.

Cosmetics and Grooming

Lips, cheeks, and fingernails could be colored red with rouge. Eyebrows were shaped with scissors, or by plucking, and blackened with combs of soft lead. Patches and plumpers (noted in the 17th century) continued in use. Perfumes were used, as were creams. Creams smeared on bands of cloth and wrapped around the head, were worn at night to remove wrinkles. In place of soap, women used **wash balls**—a combination of rice powder, flour, starch, white lead, and orris root. The lead was probably injurious to the skin.

COSTUMES FOR ACTIVE SPORTS FOR MEN AND WOMEN: THE 18TH CENTURY

Instead of special riding or hunting dress men wore frock coats, breeches (preferably of buckskin), and high boots. Toward the end of the 18th century, the first top hats developed as part of men's riding costume.

Women adapted everyday styles worn by men for their riding costume, which consisted of a shirt, waistcoat, outer coat, and skirt. Coat and waistcoat reached almost to the knees until after mid-century, when they were shortened and became fuller and more flared. By the end of the 18th century, a variation modeled on men's greatcoats appeared. Women wore three-cornered hats; black velvet jockey caps; and high-crowned, narrow-brimmed hats for riding.

Both men and women were bathing in the sea in England by the 18th century, and written evidence together with engravings indicates that nude bathing took place in segregated areas. At most resorts, however, a special costume was worn. Cunnington and Mansfield (1969) described this garment as jackets and petticoats of brown linen or long, loose sacks of flannel. Sea bathing was not popular in America until after 1800, but bathing at spas and springs was considered beneficial to health. An existing blue-and-white–checked bathing gown is said to have belonged to Martha Washington. Its cut is similar to that of a chemise, although the sleeves are narrower and the neck higher. Lead disks are wrapped in linen and attached to the gown near the hem, which probably served to keep the gown in place when the bather entered the water (Kidwell, 1968).

Men and, more rarely, women played tennis; in England they played golf and cricket as well. They

FIGURE 10.24 Informal family group at home. The child wears a dress in the style *à l'Anglaise*. The mother, in a combing jacket, has not yet had her hair arranged. The father, in a banyan with a matching waistcoat, is already wearing his powdered wig. (Image courtesy of The National Gallery of Art, Samuel H. Kress Collection)

skated, too, but no special costume had been developed for these activities.

COSTUME FOR CHILDREN: THE 18TH CENTURY

First Half of the 18th Century

Babies were wrapped in swaddling clothes. After infancy to age 6 or 7, both boys and girls wore skirts. After age 6 or 7 both boys and girls wore adult styles (Figure 10.24), although the ribbons of childhood were still appearing on young and even adolescent girls' dresses until about 1770.

Some children were sent away to boarding schools, and some ran away from school. Accounts of runaway children provide some descriptions of how children were dressed. One boy, age 11 or 12, was wearing a "sad color kersey coat trim'd with flat new gilded brass buttons, a whitish callamanca [glazed fabric with same color raised stripe] waistcoat with round silver buttons, silver edging to his hat, rolled white worsted stock. Sad color [any dull color] sagathy [lightweight serge] stuff [fabric] britches with silver plate buttons" (Ashton, 1929, 50).

Second Half of the 18th Century

Styles, especially for children, differed from either previous or contemporary adult dress. Jean-Jacques Rousseau, a French philosopher, is often given credit for inspiring this change. His writings stressed the importance of modifying current clothing practices in the direction of greater freedom for children, but Macquoid (1925) pointed out that changes in English styles for children had already begun to take place before the publication in 1760 of *Emile*. Macquoid noted that portraits of little girls in sacques after 1720 are very rare, in spite of their popularity for wear among adult women, and that boys were dressed in straighter, less-full coats than their elders. Moore (1953) suggested that paintings by the artist Joshua Reynolds may have helped spread styles from England to the continent, because he liked to paint children in unadorned costume or in costumes from his own stock of clothes, which were not necessarily part of actual street dress.

The import of muslin from India may also have had an impact on children's dress. This sheer white fabric was at first very expensive, and artists enjoyed painting wealthy children dressed in the soft folds of the fabric (Figure 10.25).

But even if the less restrictive styles for children were not a result of Rousseau's philosophy of child rearing, his recommendations must have lent this trend considerable support. His counsel was quite revolutionary in the light of previous practices. Summarized briefly, the guidelines he laid down for children's dress included:

1. For infants, "[n]o caps, no bandages, no swaddling clothes." Instead he recommended loose and flowing flannel wrappers that were neither too heavy to check the child's movements nor too warm to prevent feeling the air.
2. For older children, nothing to cramp or hinder the movement of the limbs of the growing child: no tight, closely fitting clothes, no belts.
3. Keep children in frocks (skirts) as long as possible.
4. Dress children in bright colors. He said, "Children like the bright colors best, and they suit them better too."
5. "[T]he plainest and most comfortable clothes, those which leave him most liberty" (Rousseau, 1933, pp. 27, 91, 92).

Although clothing for children did not reach the ideal recommended by Rousseau, it did improve significantly during the second half of the century. One of Rousseau's strongest statements was about the detrimental effects of swaddling infants. Whether a result of his influence or not, the practice was, at least in England and the United States, pretty well given up by the end of the century.

The usual clothes for toddlers up to age 6 or 7 were dresses or robes. After 1780 boys older than 7 or 8 wore long straight trousers, a white shirt with a wide collar that finished in a ruffled edge, and, over the shirt, a jacket that was either a shorter, simplified

FIGURE 10.25 Children, late 18th century. Girls are dressed in white muslin dresses; the boy wears a skeleton suit. (Image copyright © The Metropolitan Museum of Art. Image source: Art Resource, NY)

version of those of adults or cut to the waist and double-breasted. This costume was called a **skeleton suit** (see Figure 10.25).

Just how boys came to wear trousers is not clear. In the adult world trousers were worn in the 17th and 18th centuries by Italian comic actors and by city laborers in the 18th century. English sailors seem to have been the first Englishmen to wear long trousers. Moore (1953) suggested that they may have been used for young boys first as a way of copying the sailor's costume.

Girls wore simple straight dresses, often of white muslin. Dresses tended to have slightly elevated waistlines (see Figure 10.25). Outdoors, girls wore long or short cloaks. Small, white linen mob caps were worn indoors and out. Some small girls appear in portraits in large, decorative hats, similar to those of adult women, but this may have been the artist's choice and not common practice. After age 11 or 12 boys and girls assumed adult dress.

Summary

Themes

The themes of SOCIAL LIFE, SOCIAL CLASS STRUCTURE, and SOCIAL ROLES stand out clearly against the background of 18th-century dress. Costume history before the 19th century generally focuses on the clothing of the well-to-do. Pictorial evidence as well as the clothing that is preserved in museums leads to this upper class bias. As can be seen from Figure 10.3 (page 272), clothing of less affluent people and servants was simple and practical, with some general reflection of the lines of fashionable dress. These differences in style also served to reinforce the class distinctions that permeated society. The fairly decorative dress of servants of the nobility was a statement of a sort of reflected glory, as if the status of the master would be diminished if his servant were inadequately attired.

Related to the theme of ECONOMICS is Thorstein Veblen's *Theory of the Leisure Classes* (1936), which can easily be applied to the styles of the 18th century. His view was that clothing can be a means of showing one's wealth through the owning and display of valuable objects (conspicuous consumption) and through demonstrating that one does not need to work (conspicuous leisure). The lavishness of 18th-century clothing illustrates the principle of conspicuous consumption. Conspicuous leisure is evident in the inconvenience of the tall headdresses and wide paniers, because the wearers could not possibly be accused of doing any productive work.

It is rarely possible to point to clear, unambiguous parallels between costume and current events, but it is tempting to see the variability of styles, the extremes of size and shape, and the lavishness of decoration as evidence of a frantic attempt on the part of the French nobility to escape the POLITICAL CONFLICTS that would shortly lead to the bloody French Revolution.

If such analogies were so clear cut, however, then one would expect to see quite different styles in America following 1776, and yet women in America also powdered their hair and donned paniers. However, American styles were less extreme and lagged a little behind those of the European courts.

The themes of INTERNATIONAL TRADE and CROSS-CULTURAL INFLUENCES on costume appear not only in the styles of some shoes and in men's robes or dressing gowns, but also in the use of Indian chintzes, muslins, and in the Asian designs of woven brocades and damasks. Fringed buckskin clothes for American men demonstrate that Native American dress was influencing the American settlers. TECHNOLOGY, another recurring topic, is important as advances within the textile industry served to expand textile availability and led to lower fabric costs.

SOCIAL ATTITUDES toward children, shaped by the writings of Rousseau, seem to have been changing at about the same time that clothing for children changed. Greater freedom in both child-rearing methods and in clothing for children shows interesting parallels.

Challenges to SOCIAL NORMS were expressed through clothing as well. Quaker men avoided wearing fashionable wigs, and both men and women of the Quaker faith wore subdued colors without elaborate embellishments.

Clearly a major role of clothing was the establishment of SOCIOECONOMIC STATUS. Although advances in the technology for manufacturing cloth were beginning to have an impact on the availability of fine fabrics, the enormous amount of hand labor required to make both men's and women's clothing

Visual Summary Table

Rococo

Man: 1700 to c. 1750

Shirt, waistcoat and coat, ending just below the knee, with full skirts; knee-length rather full breeches.

Man: c. 1750–1800

The line narrows. Shirt under shorter waistcoat; slender coats, worn open, angle toward the side. Narrower breeches are knee-length.

Woman: 1700–1715

Continuation of styles of 1680–1700.

Woman: 1715–1730

Gowns either full from shoulder to floor or fitted. Hoops hold out wide skirts.

Woman: 1730–1760

Open bodices have decorative stomachers. Skirts grow very wide. Gowns with full backs called *à la Francaise;* if fitted in back *à l'Anglaise.*

Woman: 1760–1790

Hoops replaced by hip pads to support skirts, which are less wide. Skirt fullness gradually swings toward back.

shows not only the wealth of the owner but also the ready availability of low-paid men and women who spent hours in sewing and embroidering these garments.

The French Revolution in 1795 marked the end of the *Ancien Régime*, a way of life in which the aristocracy was separated from the rest of the population. It has long been held that radical changes in costume accompanied the political upheavals of the Revolution, mirroring the contrasts between pre-Revolutionary and post-Revolutionary eras. Steele has argued that these changes were already underway before the Revolution, and that the "roots of the change in fashion precede the great event" (Steele, 1988, 40).

Both points of view (that the end of the 18th century saw revolutionary fashion changes paralleling the revolutionary political changes or that these fashion changes had their roots in earlier style changes) can be seen as analogous to the sociopolitical developments of the 18th century. The Revolution brought an abrupt and violent end to one regime, but the roots of the Revolution, like the roots of fashion change, preceded the great event.

LEGACIES OF 18TH-CENTURY DRESS

Pompadour, polonaise, Watteau back, tricorne, and *bicorne* are all names assigned to costume items of the 18th century long after that century had passed. That these terms have continued in use today is evidence of costume survival. The hairstyle worn by Madame de Pompadour has entered the repertoire of hairdressing, and was especially notable in the Edwardian period (1900–1910; (see Illustrated Table 15.2, page 436) and during the late 1930s and World War II. The Watteau back, the construction of the back of the *robe à la Française*, has appeared in dressing gowns in a number of subsequent periods. The polonaise had

extensive revival in the crinoline and bustle periods and has been used in wedding and ball gowns, though sometimes the overskirt is simulated rather than being a second layer (see Modern Influences). Although men gave up tricorne and bicorne hats after the early 19th century, women's hat designers have continued to employ these forms.

REFERENCES

Ashton, J. (1929). *Social life in the reign of Queen Anne.* New York, NY: Scribners.

Cunningham, P. (1984). Eighteenth century nightgowns: The gentleman's robe in art and fashion. *Dress, Journal of the Costume Society of America, 10,* 2–11.

Cunnington, C. W. & Cunnington, P. (1957). *Handbook of English costume in the eighteenth century.* London, UK: Faber and Faber.

Cunnington, P. & Mansfield, A. (1969). *English costume for sports and outdoor recreation.* New York, NY: Barnes and Noble.

DeMarly, D. (1986). *Working Dress: A history of occupational clothing.* New York, NY: Holmes and Meier.

Durant, W., & Durant, A. (1965). *The age of Voltaire.* New York, NY: Simon and Schuster.

MODERN INFLUENCES

Designer John Galliano for Christian Dior's couture collection of Spring/Summer 1998, apparently inspired by the wide-skirted, elaborately ornamented gowns of the 1700s, created the appearance of a skirt held out by paniers.

(Detail: Image copyright © The Metropolitan Museum of Art. Image source: Art Resource, NY)

Kidwell, C. B. (1968). *Women's bathing and swimming costume in the United States*. Washington, DC: Smithsonian Institution Press.

Kidwell, C., & Christman, M. (1974). *Suiting everyone: The democratization of clothing in America*. Washington, DC: Smithsonian Institution Press.

Levron, J. (1968). *Daily life at Versailles in the 17th and 18th centuries*. New York, NY: Macmillan.

Macquoid, P. (1925). *Four hundred years of children's costume from the great masters, 1400–1800*. London, UK: Medici Society.

Marshall, D. (1969). *English people in the 18th century*. London, UK: Longmans.

Moore, D. L. (1953). *The child in fashion*. London, UK: Batsford.

Reynolds, J. (1891). *Sir Joshua Reynolds' discourses*. Chicago, IL: McClurg.

Rousseau, J. J. (1933). *Emile*. London, UK: J. M. Dent.

Steele, V. (1988). *Paris fashion: A cultural history*. New York, NY: Oxford University Press.

Swann, J. (1982). *Shoes*. London, UK: Batsford.

Veblen, T. (1936). *Theory of the leisure class*. New York, NY: Viking.

PART FIVE

The Nineteenth Century

The 19th century was a time of great, kaleidoscopic growth and change in both Europe and the United States, with resulting changes in dress.

FRANCE

The French Revolution of 1789 and the French Republic shortly gave way to the First Empire, founded by Napoleon Bonaparte. He reestablished a court and made Paris the center of power and fashion. After his overthrow, the Bourbon monarchy was restored under Louis XVIII in 1814. For the remainder of the century, France experienced changing governments: two monarchies (King Charles X, 1824–1830, and King Louis Philippe, 1830–1848); a republic, the Second Empire, with Louis Bonaparte as president, who then became Napoleon III; and another republic after 1870, the Third Republic, which lasted through the remainder of the 19th century.

ENGLAND

In Great Britain, the prince regent governed for his father, the mentally unstable King George III. The prince gathered around him a fashionable circle of men and women who set the styles for the upper classes. After the king's death in 1830, William IV succeeded him, and he in turn was followed by a niece, Victoria, who came to the throne in 1837 at the age of 18. She ruled Great Britain and the British Empire until her death in 1901. Through her personality, she helped restore the popularity of the monarchy. So strong was her influence that her name has often been used to describe the greater part of the 19th century—the Victorian Age.

ITALY AND AUSTRIA

In the mid-19th century, the forces of nationalism altered the map of Europe. For centuries Italy had been controlled by stronger powers. Revolutionary movements to establish a republic failed. However, in an alliance with Napoleon III of France, Piedmont, the only genuinely independent Italian state, defeated Austria and established an independent Italy in the north in 1859. A military expedition under Giuseppe Garibaldi conquered southern Italy. By 1861, the unification of Italy was complete, except for Venice and Rome, and Victor Emmanuel became the first king of Italy.

In central Europe, Austria dominated the German states until defeated by Prussia in 1866 in a short war. In 1870, after defeating France, Prussia united the German states in the German Empire.

THE UNITED STATES

The 19th century in the United States was the era of westward expansion as new territories were added. In 1800 the country was composed of 16 states, all east of the Mississippi River. After a bloody Civil War (1861–1865), a united nation of 45 states stretched from the Atlantic Ocean to the Pacific. The expanding nation, which offered vast opportunities for a new life, attracted millions of immigrants, primarily from Europe.

IMMIGRATION

Between 1865 and 1930, 33 million immigrants came to the United States, bringing a unique cultural heritage and making possible the great westward expansion. After the Civil War, the largest number of immigrants came from northern and western Europe. By the 1870s immigrants came from the Austro-Hungarian empire, Italy, and Russia. Later, immigrants from southern and eastern Europe including Jews, Poles, and Italians, settled in the towns and cities of the east, many of whom worked as unskilled laborers in mines, mills, and factories.

Most of these immigrants gave up their loyalties to their native lands and took on the customs and ways of their new homeland, including language. Soon the immigrants were making a major contribution to American life. Among them were Alexander Graham Bell, inventor of the telephone; Andrew Carnegie, financier; and Joseph Pulitzer, newspaper publisher.

CLOTHING OF INDIGENOUS PEOPLES

When the Europeans arrived, Native Americans acquired new textiles, garments, and decorative materials such as beads and ribbons and incorporated these into their dress. At the same time, European settlers found some of the clothing worn by indigenous people practical for the climate and geography of a world new to them, and they in turn adapted elements of Native American dress.

Although the indigenous inhabitants of the Hawaiian Islands had been in contact with western traders and familiar with western textiles since 1778, the arrival of American Congregationalist missionaries in 1820 had a long-lasting impact on clothing worn by the islanders. Based on the Empire styles, the Hawaiians adopted full-length, loose-fitting dresses that fell from a yoke with a high neck and long sleeves (Figure V.1). This garment, called a **holoku**, became a traditional part of Hawaiian dress. In 1820, the missionaries also gave Hawaiian women chemises, which became known as **mu'umu'u** (meaning *cut off*). They were worn for swimming and sleeping, and later for street wear (Arthur, 2010).

FIGURE V.1 Princess Kaiulani of Hawaii photographed in the 1890s wearing a holoku, a traditional Hawaiian costume that derives from Empire-style dresses worn by American missionaries in Hawaii around 1820. (Courtesy of Hawaii State Archives)

INDUSTRIALIZATION

The Industrial Revolution, which had begun in the preceding century, accelerated during the 19th century, resulting in increased production of goods at lower prices. Though work was often harsh and cruel, for many it ultimately provided a higher standard of living.

The Industrial Revolution produced a factory system that demanded the migration of people from rural areas to towns and cities unprepared to receive them. Industrial changes produced squalor and misery for many workers who were required to work long hours under unsafe conditions for low pay.

The factory laborers who were most abused were the women, the children, and the unskilled. Even those who worked at home were subjected to exploitation. In one such swindle, employers refused to pay workers, claiming that their sewing was not good enough, only to then press, sort, and package for sale the supposedly ruined garments (Hapke, 2004).

For the industrial capitalists, however, industrialization brought wealth and luxury. The early Victorian period in England also saw the middle class achieve greater numbers and a more important place in society.

TEXTILES FROM INDIA

The importation of fine linen muslins from India, first seen in the soft chemise dresses of the late 18th century, continued. White muslin, sometimes printed or embroidered, was used extensively in the first two decades of the 1800s. Imported fabrics of this sort were very costly, and soon European manufacturers were producing cheaper imitations. The **Kashmir shawl** is a particularly good illustration of this production process.

Indian men wore shawls made from the soft hair of the cashmere goat woven in Kashmir, a northern province on the Indian subcontinent. Beginning in the late 1600s, these shawls incorporated a decorative motif thought to derive from the *boteh*, a stylized representation of the growing shoot of the date palm.

The rapid growth of interest in the style, in spite of its enormously high cost, led European manufacturers to begin imitating the design of these shawls, not in cashmere but in less costly and rougher wools and in silk. The traditional design and name of the garment also underwent changes.

The Scottish town of Paisley began producing large quantities of shawls. So closely was the motif (by now the shape of a pine cone rather than the traditional stylized palm) associated with the textile mills of Paisley that the design came to be known as **paisley**, and the shawls themselves were often called **paisley shawls**, even if they were not manufactured in the Paisley mills (see Figure 12.14).

The fashion for Kashmir or paisley shawls continued for almost 100 years. The most fashionable shapes, decorations, and preferences for colors changed from time to time, but the basic style had a long life during the 19th century.

RESUMPTION OF TRADE WITH JAPAN

By the 19th century Russia, Britain, and the United States were keenly interested in trade with Japan. The U.S. Navy forced Japan to end its policy of seclusion. Japan signed treaties and opened ports to the American, and then British, Russian, and Dutch governments. Soon foreign merchants set up business concerns in Japanese port cities.

One of the first Japanese industries to profit from the opening of trade was the silk industry. Japan adopted western industrial techniques on a large scale and produced more uniform and superior silk thread than other Asian competitors. As a result, Japan soon had the major portion of the silk market in Europe and the United States and by the end of the 19th century textiles dominated Japanese exports.

In the second half of the 19th century Japanese art had an immediate and major impact on European fine and decorative arts. Artists often posed their subjects in Japanese kimonos and fans (Figure V.2). It was not until the early 20th century, however, that Asian garments can be seen to exert

FIGURE V.2 Impressionist artists such as Auguste Renoir often painted portraits of their subjects dressed in Japanese kimonos. This 1882 painting shows Madame Heriot in a Japanese kimono worn over a dress of the style of the 1880s. (Madame Heriot, 1882 (oil on canvas), Renoir, Pierre Auguste (1841-1919)/ Hamburger Kunsthalle, Hamburg, Germany/ Bridgeman Images)

major influences on the cut and styling of women's garments in the west.

DRESS REFORM FOR WOMEN

Mid-19th-century feminists, who viewed the constitutional disenfranchisement of women as political oppression, began to view popular fashions as repressive as well. Several efforts at dress reform were mounted. The first of these was attempted by the suffragists between 1851 and 1854. The bloomer costume, with a full-skirted, short dress placed over trousers, gained few adherents. However, similar styles were retained for athletic activities for women, as evident in clothing for physical education, added to the curriculum at Vassar College in 1865, and in bathing dress (Cunningham, 1993).

Although feminists abandoned the bloomer dress, they did not stop their belief in the need for dress reform. Emphasis on change of underwear styles focused on the dangers of tight corseting and the ill effects of the weight of too much heavy underwear.

Beginning with the pre-Raphaelite artists in the 1860s, continuing into Aesthetic dress of the 1870s and 1880s, and the "rational–artistic dress" of the Arts and Crafts movement near the turn of the century, dress reformers viewed Aesthetic or artistic dress, with its looser fit, diminished draperies, and less restrictive corseting, as healthier than fashionable dress (Cunningham, 1993).

CHANGES IN CLOTHING FOR MEN

Although they had different characteristics, the clothing styles of men and women up to about the French Revolution were equally grand and elaborate. With changes in occupations for men that stemmed from the Industrial Revolution, this changed.

The essence of fine clothing for men was in the cut and tailoring, rather than in ornamentation. The variety of choices decreased and decoration diminished. It would be a mistake, however, to assume that fashion change disappeared from men's clothing style. Though these style changes became less obvious, they continued to evolve. By contrast, changes in women's dress were more dramatic and flamboyant. We see this legacy today in the predominance of women's fashion over men's in the media and through the remaining chapters of this book.

REFERENCES

Arthur, L. (2010). Hawaiian dress prior to 1898. *Encyclopedia of world dress and fashion* (Vol. 8). Oxford, UK: Berg.

Cunningham, P. (1993). Healthful, artistic, and correct dress. *With grace and favor: Victorian and Edwardian fashions in America* (pp. 14–25). Cincinnati, OH: Cincinnati Art Museum.

Hapke, L. (2004). *Sweatshop: The history of an American idea.* Piscataway Township, New Jersey: Rutgers University Press.

	1789	1792	1793	1793–1794	1795
FASHION AND TEXTILES					Extreme fashions appear at the end of the French Revolution
POLITICS AND CONFLICTS	Declaration of the Rights of Man	Abolition of the French monarchy		Reign of Terror in France	
DECORATIVE AND FINE ARTS	Neoclassical styles influence fine and applied arts				
ECONOMICS AND TRADE		Industrial Revolution technologies aid European textile industries			
TECHNOLOGY AND IDEAS			Eli Whitney invents the cotton gin for separating cotton fiber from seeds		
RELIGION AND SOCIETY					

CHAPTER ELEVEN

The Directoire Period and the Empire Period

1790–1820

1803–1804		1811–1820

Josephine favors costly Indian shawls

Men are more likely to wear trousers than breeches

Napoleon and Josephine crowned emperor and empress (1804)

Prince of Wales named regent to act for his father, the ailing George III

English and Prussians defeat Napoleon at Waterloo (1815)

In England, Regency architecture is marked by formality, symmetry, liberal use of classical columns

Louisiana Purchase of 1803 opens western lands to American settlers

Slavery abolished north of the Mason-Dixon Line

Publication of *Pride and Prejudice*, Jane Austen's novel depicting English society (1813)

LET IT BE WRITTEN SO IT CAN BE READ.—From the *Herald* (New York).

During much of the period from 1790 to 1820, Napoleon Bonaparte ruled France as emperor. The influence of the neoclassical period on architecture and the fine and decorative arts extended into the 19th century, and the dress of classical antiquity was an obvious influence on fashions and the arts (Figure 11.1). Men's dress changed radically after the French Revolution. Simple and somber dark suits made up of jackets, vests, and trousers replaced elaborate brocade and embroidered satin suits, waistcoats, and knee breeches. Another revolution, the Industrial Revolution, with its technological advances brought significant changes to the production of textiles.

HISTORICAL BACKGROUND

The Directoire period (c. 1790–1800) includes the French Revolution and the establishment of the Directory (in French, *Directoire*), a government by a five-man executive body. The Empire period followed, coinciding generally with the period during which Napoleon Bonaparte was head of state in France. Indeed, the name of the period derives from the name of his era, the Napoleonic empire.

FIGURE 11.1 Neoclassical styles from the Regency period in England included homes designed by the Adams brothers, noted architects. (© Vanni Archive/Art Resource, NY)

France: The Revolution and the Directory

Social, political, and economic grievances, including high unemployment and high prices, along with a bankrupt government, made France ripe for revolution. Peasants bore the heaviest load of unjust taxation, but leadership of the revolution belonged to the urban bourgeoisie. They resented the nobility for monopolizing high offices in government, church, and the armed forces.

Louis XVI, unable to solve the national financial crisis, summoned the Estates General. This representative assembly of French citizens met in 1789 for the first time in more than a century and a half. Each estate was assigned a specific mode of dress and the grand master of ceremonies sent instructions to participants as to the dress to be worn for the meeting. The clergy, also called the *first estate*, were to wear the various forms of dress that were traditional for their ecclesiastical positions. The second estate, the aristocrats, wore black silk coats and waistcoats trimmed with gold braid, black silk breeches, white stockings, lace cravats, hats with feathers of the Order of St. Esprit (a special order open only to the nobility), and black silk cloaks. They also carried swords. The third estate (the largest group of deputies composed of individuals ranging from upper middle class to peasants) were instructed to dress simply, in suits of black cloth (not silk), short black silk capes, black stockings, plain muslin cravats, and black, three-cornered hats. They were not permitted to wear swords, as this right was limited to "gentlemen." Third-estate members objected to these dress regulations, many refusing to comply, and when the estates convened on October 15, the dress regulations were abolished (Ribero, 1988).

The Estates General proclaimed itself a National Assembly and began to reform France by abolishing feudalism, adopting the Declaration of the Rights of Man and of the Citizen, and drafting the first written constitution in French history. In 1792, war broke out with Austria and Prussia. Parisian rioters, frightened by the defeats on the battlefield, overthrew the monarchy and established the first French republic.

The king was tried and executed in 1793. The radical Jacobins brought forth the Reign of Terror (1793–1794) in an effort to save the nation from defeat. Although they saved France, the Jacobins were overthrown in 1794, and a new government established. The Directoire (*dye-rec-twar'*), composed of five men, ruled France for the next 5 years.

The silhouette of fashions for women during the revolution did not change radically from those of the pre-Revolutionary period. Styles had already been simplified. English-influenced styles were popular. Neckcloths, similar to those worn by peasants and working class women, became popular. Citizens declared their revolutionary ardor by displaying the revolutionary colors—red, white, and blue. These fashionable colors appeared often in dresses. Both clothing and hats often had red, white, and blue flowers or ribbons. Beginning September 21, 1793, wearing a tricolor ribbon cockade was mandatory.

Men's costumes took on a number of symbolic meanings. The most obvious and most visible symbols of the Revolution were the **bonnet rouge** (*buhn-ay' ruhze*), or the red cap of liberty, and the costume of the **sans culottes** (*sahn koo-lot'*). Ribeiro (1988) noted, "It is easier to define what the sans culottes wore than what they were, the vocal element of the working classes with, from the summer of 1792, hitherto unheard-of access to power at the highest levels."

Culotte was the French word for "knee breeches." For many generations, men of the laboring classes wore trousers, while the nobility and the more affluent wore knee breeches. Working class men, who supported the Revolution, wore trousers—hence the name "sans culottes," meaning *without knee breeches*. Other elements of sans culotte dress included the **carmagnole** (*kar-man-yole'*), a short woolen or cloth jacket of a dark color. It was hip length with fullness at the back, cut rather like a smock. Trousers were made of the same material, or of red, white, and blue striped drill. Added to this outfit was a red waistcoat and wooden shoes called *clogs*, or sabots, and a soft, red, woolen peasant's cap (the bonnet rouge; Figure 11.2).

Though its origins have been debated, the bonnet rouge became synonymous with the Revolution. Ribero (1988), in a footnote to her excellent and detailed study, *Fashion in the French Revolution*, cited a French source of 1796 stating that the cap had Roman origins. The revolutionaries apparently believed the cap had been worn in Greece and Rome as a "symbol of freedom and a rallying cry for all those who hated despotism" (140–141). Ribero offered an alternative explanation: "In the Middle Ages a similarly shaped cap was worn to celebrate the end of apprenticeship, and by the sixteenth century there are a few references to it as a general item of working-class/peasant dress in France" (85). Whatever its origins, the cap became a widely used symbol. Jacobin radicals donned the bonnet rouge at their political meetings.

Fashionable men gave up knee breeches for long, tight-fitting, ankle-length trousers called *pantaloons*, which they chose to avoid being mistaken for the now very unpopular nobility. At the same time these pantaloons bore little resemblance to the baggy, loose-fitting trousers of the sans culottes.

The passions aroused during the Revolution began to cool when the Reign of Terror ended and the Directoire was established. At this point the silhouette of French women's dresses changed radically. A new style, elements of which are thought to have appeared first in England, became fashionable. Based on ancient Greek forms and cut with little or no sleeve; a low, round neckline; and a high waist, the dress fell straight to the floor. Soft, clinging fabrics such as muslin or linen were employed. Many were sheer and under these dresses some women wore little underwear, aside from the chemise, and no corseting. Others quite boldly wore pink tights to give the illusion of flesh.

Steele (1988) saw the antecedents of this style in the muslin chemise dresses worn by aristocratic women before the French Revolution, in the neoclassical revivals in the decorative and fine arts, and in the interest in the philosophy and politics of the ancient Greeks and Romans. Men's dress was similar in its basic aspects to that from before the Revolution: a fitted

FIGURE 11.2 A crowd gathered at the planting of the tree of liberty at a celebration in France in 1789 includes (from left to right) military men; municipal officials, wearing the revolutionary colors; men in the typical garb of the revolutionaries, including the red cap of liberty, the carmagnole jacket, and trousers; and women wearing ribbons of the revolutionary colors. (*The Planting of a Tree of Liberty*, c. 1789 [gouache on paper], Lesueur Brothers, [18th century]/Musee de la Ville de Paris, Musee Carnavalet, Paris, France/Giraudon/Bridgeman Images)

coat, a waistcoat, and knee breeches. Extremists in fashion were assigned nicknames. The **Merveilleuses** (*mere-vay-use'*), or the *marvelous ones*, were women who affected the most extreme of the Directoire styles, with long flowing trains, the sheerest of fabrics, necklines cut in some extreme cases to the waistline, and huge, exaggerated jockeylike caps. The men, known as **Incroyables** (*ahn-kroy-ab-luh'*), or *incredibles*, wore waistcoats of loose fit at the shoulders, excessively tight breeches, and cravats (*neckties*) and collars that covered so much of their chins that one wonders if they could be heard or understood when they spoke. Both men and women affected a shaggy, unkempt hairdress (Figure 11.3).

France: The Empire

The French Revolution had opened careers to young men of talent. Napoleon Bonaparte, from the French island Corsica—a second lieutenant in artillery in 1789 and a brigadier general by 1795—saved the Directoire from a mob with a "whiff of grapeshot." Promoted to major general, his victories over the Austrians in Italy (1796–1797) and his victories in Egypt against the British and the Turks (1798–1799) made him the hero of Paris.

The Directoire governed ineffectively. After initial successes, the European war again went badly, giving conspirators the opportunity to join with Napoleon in staging a coup in 1799 to overthrow the Directoire

FIGURE 11.3 The extreme fashions adopted by the so-called Incroyables (men) and the Merveilleuses (women) included these exaggerated fashions and hairstyles. (*Incroyable et Merveilleuse in Paris*, 1797 [oil on canvas], Boilly, Louis Leopold [1761–1845] [attr. to]/Private Collection/Archives Charmet/ Bridgeman Images)

because they feared another Terror. An executive group consisting of Napoleon and two other consuls took power. Napoleon, as first consul, was able to consolidate his power and was crowned emperor of the French in 1804 (Figure 11.4). In the next 10 years, Napoleon instituted legal and educational reforms and reorganized the government to make it more efficient, competent, and honest. Napoleon extended his control over Europe, defeating all but Great Britain. In 1812, his armies marched to Moscow, but the tsar refused to surrender. With winter coming, Napoleon had to retreat. Harassed by Russian troops, the retreatants were defeated. It was the beginning of the end for Napoleon. In 1814 he abdicated and was exiled to the Island of Elba.

After the establishment of the Empire period, the basic style lines that had been worn by both men and women during the Directoire continued, but the extremes of nudity and the styles of the Merveilleuse and Incroyable disappeared; Napoleon was somewhat conservative and considered the more extreme styles immoral. The emperor attempted to recreate the elegance of the old regime. His court provided a stage for the display of fashions. More elaborate fabrics and styles began to appear as Napoleon tried to encourage French industry by stimulating the demand for French goods. He restricted the importation of fabrics from abroad, particularly muslin and printed cottons from India. Shawls from India were a popular fashion item, but Napoleon ended their importation and ordered that they be copied in France. (His first wife, Josephine, however, continued to have her own shawls imported without his knowledge.) She must have helped stimulate French industry almost single-handedly, because an inventory of her wardrobe in 1809 included 666 winter dresses, 230 summer

FIGURE 11.4 Empress Josephine was a fashion leader. Her coronation regalia featured the fashionable Empire line together with an elaborate gold-embroidered velvet train and a jeweled coronet. (Erich Lessing/Art Resource, NY)

dresses, and 60 cashmere shawls (Knapton, 1963, 282) (Figure 11.5).

Napoleon himself had an extensive wardrobe. See Contemporary Comments 11.1 for his letter instructing one of his staff about the items he wished to have ordered.

England

In England, King George III reigned from 1738 to 1820. A pious, virtuous man who enjoyed the simple life, he presided over the loss of the American colonies in 1776. Victim of a hereditary disease, porphyria, that periodically incapacitated him, he could no longer rule by 1810; the Prince of Wales had to be named as regent to act for him. During the Regency period (1811–1820), the English court and fashionable society were organized around the Prince Regent, who had an eye for the ladies; the pursuit of pleasure was possibly his most active pastime. His cleverness and gracious manners gave him the informal title "the first gentleman of Europe." As a result, the court became the center of fashion in England.

For the greater part of the period the English remained at war with France. The defeat of the French fleet at Trafalgar in 1805 ended British fears of French invasion. Peace came with the defeat of Napoleon at Waterloo in 1815.

At the beginning of the Empire period, English and French women's dress styles diverged. While the French were narrowing the silhouette as it fell from the elevated Empire waist, the English placed a padded roll under the waistline to create a fuller, rounded line to the skirt. These differences may have developed because war restricted trade and dissemination of ideas. After about a year or two, the English line narrowed and became like that of the French.

The United States

The continuing expansion of the American frontier brought Native American and European populations into frequent contact. Many Native Americans added goods such as glass beads gained in trade to their apparel. European settlers also adapted some items of Native American dress, a further example of the

FIGURE 11.5 Empress Josephine is shown in the typical dress of the early 1800s. She reclines with one of the imported Indian shawls of which she was so fond. (Erich Lessing/Art Resource, NY)

process of cultural authentication (Figure 11.6; see also Global Connections, page 313).

Some of these interchanges produced garments that have persisted in use for long periods of time. For example, the Europeans traded blankets bordered with colored bands (so-called *Indian blankets*). Native Americans in Canada appear to have cut these blankets

FIGURE 11.6 After acquiring the western territories and its impressive mountains through the Louisiana Purchase, the United States warned other countries to end colonization in North America in the Monroe Doctrine. (© Bettmann/CORBIS)

into coats, placing the colored borders at the bottom of the coat. Rural settlers and the Canadian military adopted these coats, cutting them along the lines of fashionable dress of this and subsequent periods. Over time, these warm, hooded coats were adopted for outdoor sports in Canada and the United States. Their descendants can still be found today (Beaudoin-Ross, 1980).

The footwear of Native Americans, boots and moccasins, were also adopted by settlers (see Global Connections). Canadian settlers in French-speaking Canada found the soft deer and moose skins used by native people for these shoes too fragile for daily use and wear. Instead, those settlers constructed them from the sturdier hides of farm animals (Beaudoin-Ross, 1980).

Most dress styles in the United States paralleled those of Europe. Imported fashion engravings provided information about current fashions in Paris and London.

THE ARTS AND COSTUME STYLES OF THE PERIOD

Interest in the arts of classical antiquity that had begun in the second half of the 18th century continued and even accelerated during the Empire period.

LET IT BE WRITTEN SO IT CAN BE READ.—From the *Herald* (New York).

Contemporary Comments 11.1

NAPOLEON'S WARDROBE

In August 1811, Napoleon wrote to General Duroc, the grand marshall of the palace, about his wardrobe, providing a complete list of the items he wished to have ordered.

Inform Count Rémusat that he is to have nothing more to do with my Wardrobe, and that I have deprived him of the title of Master of the Wardrobe. You are to carry on his functions until I find a substitute for him. . . .

Have an inventory made of my things: see that they are there, and check them off. . . . See that the tailor arranges to send in no bad work, and not to exceed his estimates. Whenever any new clothes are delivered, bring them to me yourself, so that I may see whether they fit me properly: if they do, I will have them. Regularise all this, so that, when I appoint a Master of the Wardrobe, he will find his duties cut and dried. . . .

Estimate for the Emperor's Wardrobe

Uniforms and Greatcoats

1 Grenadier's tail coat on January 1st with epaulettes, etc.

1 Chasseur's tail coat on April 1st with epaulettes, etc.

1 Grenadier's tail coat on July 1st with epaulettes, etc.

1 Chausseur's tail coat on October 17, with epaulettes, etc. (Each tail coat will have to last 3 years.)

2 Hunting coats: one for riding, in the Saint-Hubert style, the other for shooting, on August 1st. (These coats will have to last 3 years.)

1 Civilian coat on November 1st (to last 3 years.)

2 Frock coats: one grey, and the other another color. (They will be supplied on October 1st every year and will have to last 3 years.)

Waistcoats and Breeches

48 pairs of breeches and white waistcoats at 80 francs (They are to be supplied every week, and must last 3 years.)

Dressing Gowns, Pantaloons, and Vests

2 dressing gowns, one quilted, on May 1st and one of swans-down, on October 1st.

2 pairs of pantaloons, one quilted and one of wool, supplied in the same way. (The dressing gowns and pantaloons will have to last 3 years.)

48 flannel vests (one a week) at 30 francs. (The vests will have to last 3 years.)

Body Linen

4 dozen shirts (a dozen a week)

4 dozen handkerchiefs (a dozen a week)

2 dozen cravats (one a fortnight [two weeks])

1 dozen black collars (once a month) which must last a year.

2 dozen towels (a dozen a fortnight)

6 Madras night caps (one every 2 months) to last 3 years

2 dozen pairs of silk stockings at 18 francs (one pair a fortnight)

2 dozen pairs of socks (one pair a fortnight) (All this linen, except the black collar and night caps will have to last 6 years.)

Footwear

24 pairs of shoes (one pair a fortnight, which must last 2 years)

6 pairs of boots, to last 2 years

Headwear

4 hats a year, supplied with the tail coats

Miscellaneous

Scents slimming mixture, eau de Cologne, etc.

Washing the linen and silk stockings

Various expenses. (Nothing to be spent without His Majesty's approval.)

Reprinted from Thompson, J. M. (1934). *Napoleon self-revealed.* Oxford, UK: Blackwell.

Global Connections

North American native dress was both decorative and practical. Deerskin provided protection for passing through woodlands and was more flexible than stiff leather. Tribal people ornamented their deerskin garments with porcupine quills colored with natural materials. When Europeans provided colored glass beads as trade goods, native people quickly became skilled in adding these ornaments to their comfortable moccasins (an anglicized form of an Algonquian word for shoes or footwear). Moccasin-style shoes have become a classic shoe style and are used worldwide today. (The Colonial Williamsburg Foundation. Museum Purchase)

The military campaigns of Napoleon in Italy, where Roman ruins abounded, and political emphasis on the revival of the republican ideals of ancient Greece and Rome contributed to this interest. French artists depicted events in ancient history on huge canvasses, architecture emphasized classic styles, and, when Napoleon took artists who sketched the ruins of Egyptian civilization with his army, a number of Egyptian influences began to find their way into furniture and design.

Philosophers, lawyers, and political leaders found ancient texts to be important sources from which to develop their thinking. The world of classical antiquity inspired revivals in the arts that had parallels in the revival of many classical elements in the new costume style for women. Women's dress was an interpretation of the styles worn by Greek women in the Golden Age. Remains of statues and Greek vase painting illustrated these earlier styles. The color of Greek and Roman

statues had been bleached away over the centuries since their creation, leaving them completely white and leading to the incorrect assumption that classical costume had been white.

Empire styles flowered suddenly. When images of these new styles are placed beside images from the pre-Revolutionary period (compare Figures 10.19, page 289, and 11.5, page 311), the differences are obvious and, to many costume historians, revolutionary. Ribeiro (1988) took a somewhat different view. "In some respects, it [the Revolution] acted as a catalyst for styles already in the pipeline, but which were pushed to the forefront by the impact of politics" (140). It is not far-fetched to see in these styles a visible symbol of the political ideals of the period in which they flowered. Their obvious inspiration came from Greek and Roman styles. They were visible evidence of the ascendancy of a political ideal, an ideal that the population believed had originated in classical antiquity.

THE REVOLUTION IN MEN'S CLOTHES

Men's clothing underwent more subtle changes, but more lasting than those in women's dress. Although neither the components of men's dress (coat, waistcoat, breeches, or, later, trousers) nor the silhouette were radically altered, gone were the colors, the lavish embroideries, and the luxurious fabrics. Ribeiro (1988) effectively summarized the impact of the political revolution on men's dress.

> For most of the eighteenth century there was a sartorial harmony in the dress of men and women; they were united in their love of colour, elegant design and luxurious materials. One of the results of the French Revolution was to divide the sexes in terms of their clothing. Men's dress becomes plain in design and sober in colour; it is unadorned with decoration. It symbolizes gravitas and an indifference to luxury—essential elements of republican austerity; its virtual uniformity emphasizes the revolutionary ideal of equality (141).

England led the change to more sober attire for men. British dress had been for some time less formal and more egalitarian or classless. English tailors for men had a fine reputation. During the Regency period in England George "Beau" Brummel, a favorite companion of the Prince Regent, became an arbiter of men's styles. Brummel was famous for his impeccable dress. He wore beautifully tailored coats, the linen of his shirts and cravats was immaculate, and he personified the Regency **dandy**, a fashionable man who dressed well, circulated in the best society, and was always ready with a witty comment. Beau Brummel set the fashions until he fell out of favor with the prince.

PRODUCTION AND ACQUISITION OF CLOTHING AND TEXTILES

The growth of the textile industry accelerated as the Industrial Revolution continued. The cotton gin (patented 1794) had an enormous impact on cotton production in the American south (Figure 11.7). The annual output of raw cotton rose from 2 million to 85

FIGURE 11.7 The cotton gin automated the separation of cotton fiber from cotton seeds, thereby speeding up the manufacture of cotton textiles. (© Bettmann/CORBIS)

million pounds within 16 years (Cipolla and Birdsall, 1979). Prices dropped with this increased supply of cotton. Adoption of water or steam to power textile mills helped make cotton both affordable and available.

Joseph Marie Jacquard, a Frenchman, developed a type of mechanized loom for weaving patterned fabrics. In 1801, Jacquard's machine provided a means of automatically raising and lowering yarns that formed the pattern. More than 10,000 of these looms were sold within the next ten years (Cipolla and Birdsall, 1979).

Most women's clothing, as before, was made at home or by seamstresses. Tailors of the 1820s were beginning to produce men's clothing that was ready-made as well as custom-made. From an 1827 advertisement, Kidwell and Christman (1974) quoted a description of T. S. Whitmarsh of Boston, who "keeps constantly for Sale, from 5 to 10,000 Fashionable ready-made Garments, comprising every article of apparel to a Gentleman's Wardrobe" (47).

SOURCES OF INFORMATION ABOUT COSTUME

A substantial quantity of actual garments from the Empire period is available for study. When using this material, however, some care must be taken. As

Newton (1975) cautioned, "Surviving clothes in our museums are those which were saved in the past because their condition was too good for them to have been thrown away; they are not the most representative nor the most interesting of their period" (24).

Individual garments provide detailed information about construction and fabrics, but they rarely furnish insights into just how individuals were supposed to look when fully dressed. Garments were placed over undergarments and were combined with accessories, headdress, and grooming to create a total look. Other sources, such as paintings, drawings, or fashion plates, provide this information.

DIRECTOIRE AND EMPIRE PERIODS

Costume Components for Women

Men could no longer compete with women in the arena of fashion. Women's clothing, in comparison to that of men, was more complicated and more subject to change.

Garments

Very fashionable French women ceased wearing corsets during the Directoire period (c. 1795–1800) and wore, at most, a lightweight chemise as underclothing. The average woman, however, did not give up her corset but placed it over the chemise, which was made of cotton or linen and worn next to the body. Cut full and straight from the neck to the knees, the chemise had short, set-in sleeves with a gusset under the arm and a low, square neck. Corsets, more commonly known as stays, were cut in a straight line without waistline indentation and pushed the breasts up and out. The use of false bosoms is noted; these were made of wax or cotton. One disgruntled lover lamented in an 1800 English periodical, *The Oracle*:

> My Delia's heart I find so hard, I would she were *forgotten!*
>
> For how can hearts be *adamant* when all the breast—
> is cotton? *(Cunnington and Cunnington, 1979, 367)*

Although drawers were new to England and the American colonies, continental European women seem to have worn cotton or linen drawers much earlier. From the Empire period on, drawers became a basic part of women's underclothing. Unlike modern underpants, they were usually open through the crotch area, an important convenience when women wearing long, bulky skirts needed to relieve themselves.

Some women placed petticoats over their chemises. Poor women and African slaves in the Americas often wore petticoats in combination with short gowns as street clothing (see Figure 10.3, page 272). The skirts of dresses remained narrow, and undergarments were cut fairly straight. As skirts widened toward the end of the Empire period, both the chemise and petticoat gained in breadth.

Pantalettes, straight, white drawers trimmed with rows of lace or tucks at the hem, became fashionable for a short time around 1809. This fashion did not continue for adult women. Young girls wore them throughout this and subsequent periods.

During the closing years of the period women placed bustlelike padded rolls at the back of the waistline beneath dresses. The peculiar forward slant that resulted was known as the *Grecian bend*.

With a waistline placement just under the bosom, dresses had a tubular shape. Skirts reached to the floor. Supple and lightweight fabrics had to be used to achieve the straight line and incorporate the gathered fullness. A small concentration of gathered fabric at the back of the skirt was a vestige of the back fullness characteristic of the last part of the 1700s. Dresses were either trained or untrained until about 1812 when skirts shortened, eliminating trains.

Some dresses opened at the front to display an elaborate, decorated petticoat, which was not an undergarment but a visible underskirt. This style was often worn for evening. Daytime or evening dresses that did not open at the front to show a petticoat were called **round gowns** (Figure 11.8). Tunic dresses had an underdress placed beneath a loose, shorter (ranging from hip to ankle) tunic, or outer dress.

The apron, or **high stomacher dress**, had a complex construction in which the bodice was sewn to the skirt at the back only. Side front seams were left open to

FIGURE 11.8 Printed cotton round gown of 1800. (Division of Home And Community Life, National Museum of American History, Smithsonian Institution)

several inches below the waist, and a band or string was located at the front of the skirt's waist. A woman slipped the garment over her head, put her arms into the sleeves, and then tied the waist string around the back like an apron. The bodice often had a pair of under flaps that pinned across the chest, supporting the bust. The outer bodice closed in front by wrapping it across the bosom like a shawl, lacing it up the front over a short undershirt (called a **habit shirt**), or buttoning it down the front.

Low-cut necklines on the aforementioned dresses were either round or square. Higher necklines often finished in a small ruff, or ruffle, or with a drawstring that tied around the neck.

The most common types of sleeve styles on these dresses were short, puffed, or fitted (see Figures 11.3 and 11.5). Sometimes, these short sleeves were covered by sheer oversleeves. Long sleeves were either fitted or full. Some full, long sleeves were tied into sections of short puffs (see Figure 11.14), and others had a single puff at the shoulder with the rest of the sleeve fitted to the arm (see Figure 11.4).

Lightweight cotton and linen muslins and soft silks served these styles best. Plain, white, undecorated Grecian-style gowns were fashionable in the Directoire period. With the coming of the Empire period, pastel shades or white with a variety of delicate embroideries were used more often.

Outdoor Garments

Shawls, stoles, cloaks, and capes were worn over dresses when outdoors. Shawls or stoles were square or oblong in shape. These provided relatively little protection in winter. A flu epidemic during the Directoire period gained the nickname "muslin fever"

because of the practice of wearing lightweight muslin dresses with so little covering over them. The terms *mantle, cloak,* and *cape* were used interchangeably.

The **spencer** was a short jacket (worn by both men and women) that ended at the waistline for men and just under the bosom for women. Made with sleeves or sleeveless, the color usually contrasted with the rest of the costume. Spencers were worn indoors as well as out (Figure 11.9). At least three different stories explain how the spencer came into being. In the first anecdote, Lord Spencer is supposed to have made a bet with a friend that he could start a new fashion within 2 weeks. The bet was taken. On the spot, Lord Spencer cut off his coattails and, by starting a new fashion, won his bet. Another version relates how Lord Spencer was standing too close to an open fire at a party, and his coattails caught on fire. After the fire was extinguished, Lord Spencer cut off the singed coattails, thereby beginning a new fashion. The final version has the same Lord Spencer being thrown by his horse. In the accident his coattails were torn off. Because he did not want to leave the races, he simply went about wearing the shortened coat. One of these stories—or none—may be true.

The **pelisse** was similar to a modern coat that was full length and followed the typical Empire period silhouette. For winter, especially when made of silk or cotton, pelisses had warm linings (Figure 11.10).

Hair and Headdress

See Illustrated Table 11.1 for depictions of some hairstyles and headdress of the Empire period.

Greek sculpture provided the inspiration for hairstyles in which the hair was combed back from the face and gathered in ringlets or coils at the back of the head while the hair around the face was arranged in soft curls. Other modes included a short, curly style called *à la victime* or *à la Titus*. The former term was a reference to the short haircuts given to victims about to be guillotined during the French Revolution; the latter, to short hair depicted on Roman statues of men.

Hat styles included jockey caps, especially for riding. Riding was one of the few sports in which women could participate. Turbans were especially fashionable after Napoleon's invasion of Egypt. Influences from ancient Greece and Rome were evident in small fabric hats similar to military helmets of classic antiquity.

Bonnets had fabric or straw crowns. Brims were wide. **Toques** were high, brimless hats, and **gypsy hats**, with a low crown and a moderately wide brim, were worn with ribbon tied over the outside of the brim and under the chin. Mature women wore small muslin or lace caps, called **day caps**, indoors. Hats were worn not only outdoors but also for evening events, such as the theater or balls.

Footwear

Shoes in colors matching dresses or pelisses were usually made of leather, velvet, or satin. They had no heels. With the return of flat shoes, soles of some shoes were once again shaped to fit right and left feet. Some slippers had crisscross lacings that ran up the leg to below the knee (Illustrated Table 11.2).

Short boots reached to the calf. Boots closed at the sides with laces or buttons or at the back with laces. For bad weather women wore pattens, small platforms of wood or steel that fastened over shoes.

Accessories

See Illustrated Table 11.2 for depictions of some accessories of this period.

Gloves were made of leather, silk, or net. Long gloves, ending on the upper arm or above the elbow, were worn with short-sleeved dresses.

FIGURE 11.9 Man's tailcoat and woman's short jacket called a *spencer*, c. 1815. (HIP/Art Resource, NY. Eileen Tweedy/The Art Archive at Art Resource, NY)

FIGURE 11.10 The preferred garment for outdoors during the Empire period was a pelisse, which was often padded for warmth and, like dresses, was made with a high Empire waistline. Large fur muffs kept ladies' hands warm, and the preferred hat style was a poke bonnet. (© Mary Evans Picture Library)

Illustrated Table 11.1

Typical Women's Hairstyles and Headdress in the Empire Period

Haircut *à la victime*
or *à la Titus*[1]

Hairstyles and hats of 1802[2]

Head coverings of 1806[2]

Bonnets

Indoor day caps

Turbans

[1] *Le Journal de Dames et des Modes*, c. 1801.

[2] Bayerische Staatsbibliothek München.

Illustrated Table 11.2

Empire Period: Accessories

Bicorne folding hat,
c. 1800

Woman's reticule,
c. 1800–1820

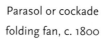

Parasol or cockade
folding fan, c. 1800

Man, c. 1800.
Carrying an umbrella,
wearing a top hat, a cravat
at his neck, and spats to
cover his stockings.

Woman, c. 1818.
Wearing an oblong shawl,
a bracelet above the elbow-
length gloves, a jeweled
necklace, and flat-soled
black shoes.

Roman-influenced
Directoire Period sandals

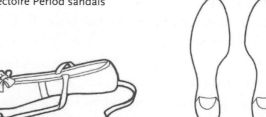

Large muff,
c. 1810–1820

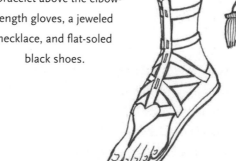

Satin slippers,
c. 1800–1820

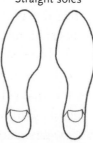

Straight soles

Soles for right
and left feet

Reticules or indispensibles were small handbags, often with a drawstring at the top. In earlier periods, when skirts were full, pockets were placed under the skirt for carrying small personal objects. The narrow silhouette of the Empire period made such pockets impractical, so the reticule replaced the pocket. Some found the device amusing and took to calling it a *ridicule*.

Other hand-carried accessories included large muffs, often of fur, swansdown, or fabric; parasols, moderate to small in size, some of which were pagoda shaped; fans; and decorative handkerchiefs.

Jewelry

Popular jewelry items were necklaces, earrings, rings, small watches that pinned to the dress, and brooches, some of which served the function of closing the dress. Bracelets were worn high on the arm in imitation of those on Greek and Roman statues and vases.

COSTUME COMPONENTS FOR MEN

Garments

Drawers, usually made of linen or cotton, were similar to those of the 1700s. Cotton or linen full-cut shirts had high, standing collars that reached to the cheek. The shirt front was generally pleated or ruffled. Around the shirt's neck, men wrapped **cravats** (large squares of fabric folded, wrapped several times around the neck, and tied in front) or **stocks** (stiffened neck bands that buckled or tied behind the neck; Figure 11.11).

A coat, a waistcoat (worn beneath the coat), and either breeches or trousers made up the suit. Clothing for "dress" (formal occasions) and "undress" (less formal occasions) usually differed only in color or quality of fabric, buttons, and accessories. Rarely were the three parts of the suit the same color; generally, they contrasted. Colors were light or dark, bright or subdued. Wool was used in a variety of weights and qualities. For formal occasions and especially at the French or English courts, lavishly decorated velvets and silk fabrics were suitable.

Coat fronts generally ended at the waist, either curving gradually back from the waist into two tails that

FIGURE 11.11 Men's dress in the 19th century lost much of its color. As a result, neckwear took on more importance, showing off stiffly starched, white collars and carefully tied black cravats. Former slaves, both men and women freed in northern states after 1804, adopted fashionable dress. (Image courtesy of National Gallery of Art)

ended slightly above the knee, or with a cut-in, a rounded or square space at the front where no skirt was attached. The tails began where the cut-in ended (Figures 11.12 and 11.13). Coat collars generally had a notch where the collar joined the lapel. Some coats had velvet facings applied. Closings were both single and double breasted. Pockets were located in the pleats of the coattails or at the waist. Some coats had false pocket flaps.

Only the front of the sleeveless waistcoat was visible when a coat was worn; therefore, the back was made of plain cotton or linen fabric or the waistcoat's lining fabric. Collars generally stood upright. Some were cut so that the upper and lower edges formed a steplike structure; that is, they were "stepped." About 2 inches of waistcoat were visible at the bottom of the coat when it was closed, and only a small edge of the waistcoat was visible at the open neck of the coat (see Figure 11.13). Several waistcoats worn one over the other provided more warmth.

FIGURE 11.12 Men and a woman of 1809. The man at the left wears a tailcoat with knee breeches. His white waistcoat is not visible at the bottom of his jacket but can be seen at the neckline of his jacket. He has a white cravat around his neck. On his head is a bicorne, or two-cornered hat. The man at center wears a similar jacket and holds a top hat in his hand. He is wearing trousers that are covered by his boots. The woman holds an unopened parasol in her hand and wears a typical Empire line white dress. (Full and Half Full Dresses for April, illustration from 'Le Beau Monde or, Literary and Fashionable Magazine,' 1809 (coloured engraving), English School (19th century)/Private Collection/Bridgeman Images)

Until about 1807 breeches were worn extensively. Breeches ended at the knee; trousers extended to the ankle (see Figure 11.13). **Pantaloons** at this period were generally defined as fitting the leg more closely than trousers, which were made in closely fitted, moderately full, or very full styles. The extremely full trousers were based on the dress of Russian soldiers, and fashion publications called them **cossacks**. Tight pantaloons or trousers had an instep strap to keep them from riding up the leg. Trousers had been introduced for fashionable wear during the French Revolution but were discarded again by fashion leaders immediately following the Revolution. After 1807 they returned as acceptable fashions.

Outdoor Garments

Overcoats or great coats worn for cold weather were very full, single or double breasted, knee or full length. Coats had collars and lapels. Some had one or more capes at the shoulder. Cloaks were no longer fashionable but were sometimes worn for travel.

Spencers were worn by men as well as by women, but for men they took the place of the coat with a suit.

Dressing Gown, or Banyan

The dressing gown, or banyan, was usually ankle length, cut with a full, flared skirt and made in fabrics such as decorative damasks or brocades of wool, cotton, or silk. Some had matching waistcoats. According to Coleman (1975, 6), "in the eighteenth and early nineteenth centuries this outfit was not confined to 'at home' wear as its descendant, the robe or dressing gown, is today. It was accepted for street and office wear."

Hair and Headdress

Men cut their hair short. Faces were clean shaven, although side whiskers were somewhat long.

The predominant hat style was the **top hat**. These hats had either taller or shorter crowns and medium-sized brims that rolled up slightly at the sides and dipped in front and back. The **bicorne** was a two-pointed hat worn either with the points from front to back or from side to side. When worn for evening and carried flattened, under the

FIGURE 11.13 Blue tailcoat and trousers, which by 1820 were more widely worn than knee breeches. The trousers are held in place by a strap under the shoe. Around the neck is a black cravat. (Image copyright © The Metropolitan Museum of Art. Image source: Art Resource, NY)

arm, the two-pointed hat was called a **chapeau bras** (a French phrase meaning *hat for the arm*). Hats were made from silk, wool felt, or beaver (felted beaver fur mixed with wool; see Illustrated Table 11.2).

Footwear

Early in the period shoes closed with decorative buckles. A tie closing at the front gradually supplanted buckles. Shoes had low, round heels and rounded toes. The French Revolution may have helped to end the fashion for buckles, as one of the revolutionary slogans was "down with the aristocratic shoe buckle" (Swann, 1982, 29).

Many boot styles were named for military heroes or well-known army units (e.g., napoleons, wellingtons, bluchers, cossacks, and Hessian boots). True military boots were high in front, covering the knees, and scooped down behind the knee in back so that the knee could bend easily. Other boot styles had turned-down tops with contrasting linings. Shorter boots were worn over closely fitted trousers.

Accessories

Gloves were short and made of cotton or leather. Hand-carried accessories included canes and **quizzing glasses**, magnifying glasses mounted on a handle and worn around the neck. Some authors claim that the fad for quizzing glasses led some dandies to have their optic nerves surgically loosened in order to justify the acquisition of a glass, but this is undoubtedly an example of the exaggerated claims often made for the impact of fad or fashion.

Jewelry

Men's jewelry was limited, consisting mostly of rings and decorative watch fobs. Occasionally decorative brooches appeared on shirts or neck cloths.

Cosmetics

Some very fashion-conscious men used rouge to heighten their color, bleached their hands to whiten them, and used substantial quantities of eau de cologne.

COSTUME FOR CHILDREN: THE EMPIRE PERIOD

Costume Components for Girls

Garments

Dresses were cut along the same lines as those of adult women but shorter for both little girls and young adolescents. Girls wore pantalettes under dresses and shawls and pelisses outdoors (Figure 11.14).

Hair and Headdress

Although small girls wore simple, natural styles, adolescents adopted fashionable adult styles, particularly Grecian styles. The most popular hat styles were bonnets.

Footwear

Girls wore slippers or soft boots made of leather or fabric.

Costume Components for Boys

Garments

From infancy to about 4 or 5, boys wore dresses with skirts similar to those of little girls, although generally slightly shorter. By age 4 or 5, they usually wore trousers under skirts. After age 6 or 7, boys donned skeleton suits consisting of a loose shirt with a wide, frilled collar and high-waisted, ankle-length trousers that were generally buttoned to the shirt. This style was very popular for young boys. After age 11 or 12, boys dressed much the same as men. For cold weather boys wore overcoats.

Hair and Headdress

Boys' hair was either long or short.

Footwear

Either slippers or soft boots were usually worn.

FIGURE 11.14 A large family, in which the changes in children's clothing according to age can be seen. The youngest child, a boy, wears a dress; a slightly older boy wears a long jacket over trousers. Younger girls wear shorter skirts with pantalettes; older girls wear dresses of typical Empire style, but of slightly shorter length than their mother, whose gown reaches to the floor. (Owned by National Gallery of Denmark, SMK Photo)

Summary

Themes

At the beginning of the years covered in this chapter, the themes of POLITICS and POLITICAL CONFLICT were expressed through dress in France when, as the French Revolution accelerated, clothing was used to make obvious political statements. The revolutionaries traded their aristocratic knee breeches for trousers and donned the "red hat of liberty," while women ornamented their dresses with revolutionary colors. The revival of classical Greek and Roman styles in women's dresses during the Directoire paralleled the interest in the political ideals of the Greek and Roman republics.

Intertwined with the political overtones of dress is the theme of RELATIONSHIPS BETWEEN COSTUME AND DEVELOPMENTS IN THE FINE AND APPLIED ARTS. Classical revivals, which had begun in the late 18th century, continued to influence not only dress but also architecture, interior design, furnishings, and the fine arts.

The soft, white muslins suitable for classical revival styles were also related to the themes of TRADE and CROSS-CULTURAL contacts that, in turn, interacted with TECHNOLOGY and the PRODUCTION AND ACQUISITION OF TEXTILES AND APPAREL. Cotton fabrics brought to Europe from India during the 18th century were by the early 19th century imitated by European and American manufacturers, thanks to the technological advances of the Industrial Revolution.

Yet another theme important in dress in this and subsequent periods was that of GENDER DIFFERENCES. Dress reflected changes in SOCIAL ROLES of men and women after the Industrial Revolution. Clothing for men and women during the Directoire and Empire periods contrasts with the styles of the preceding century. For men the acceptance of trousers in place of knee breeches represented the triumph of a style that had once been associated with working class men. Moreover, the accepted styles for men for the rest of the 19th century and on into the 20th century

Visual Summary Table

Directoire and Empire Period

Man: 1790 to c. 1807
Shirts, under waist-length waistcoats. Over these, tailcoats, worn with knee breeches or trousers.

Man: c. 1807–1820
Men more likely to wear trousers than knee breeches. Otherwise, little change.

Woman: 1790–1800
Elevated waistline, soft gathered skirt with narrower silhouette. Sleeves tend to be short; necklines low.

Woman: 1816
Sleeve variations and necklines appear and gradual widening of skirt hem and rising of waistlines as the period progresses.

continued to utilize the more somber colors and plainer fabrics that had become acceptable for upper class men in these first two decades. By comparison with men's costume, women's dress utilized more decorative fabrics, a greater variety of colors, and varying style details. This trend continued in subsequent periods.

LEGACIES OF EMPIRE STYLE COSTUME

Subsequent revivals of Empire styles for women are, in a sense, a revival of a revival. The inspiration for the Empire style lay in the styles of classical antiquity. However, with time and the evolution of fashion, these styles developed very distinct characteristics of their own. The so-called Empire waistline for women's dresses was revived around 1910 (see Figure 15.14, page 438) and again just before 1960 (see Figure 17.18, page 530). In 1996, with the popularity of films based on the novels of Jane Austen (published 1811–1818), designers were once again reviving Empire period styles. Contemporary designers keep the Empire waistline as one of their options for style choices (see Modern Influences).

In the Hawaiian Islands, the Empire period dress of the first American missionaries was transformed into the holoku. This garment, still worn in Hawaii, is a direct descendant of Empire period styles (see Figure V.1).

REFERENCES

Beaudoin-Ross, J. (1980). A la Canadienne: Some aspects of 19th century habitant dress. *Dress, Vol. 6*, 71–82.

Cipolla, C., & Birdsall, D. (1979). *The technology of man.* New York, NY: Holt, Rinehart and Winston.

Coleman, E. A. (1975). *Of men only, a review of men's and boy's fashion, 1750–1975.* New York, NY: The Brooklyn Museum.

Cunnington, C. W., and Cunnington, P. (1979). *Handbook of English costume in the 19th century.* Boston, MA: Plays Inc.

Kidwell, C., & Christman, M. (1974). *Suiting everyone: The democratization of clothing in America.* Washington, DC: Smithsonian Institution Press.

Knapton, E. J. (1963). *Empress Josephine.* New York, NY: Harvard University Press.

Newton, S. M. (1975). *Renaissance theatre costume and the sense of the historic past.* London, UK: Rapp and Whitney.

Ribeiro, A. (1988). *Fashion in the French revolution.* London, UK: B. T. Batsford.

Steele, V. (1988). *Paris fashions: A cultural history.* New York, NY: Oxford University Press.

Swann, J. (1982). *Shoes.* London, UK: B. T. Batsford.

MODERN INFLUENCES

Contemporary fashion designers frequently incorporate the empire waistline into their designs, as in this sequin-studded dress where the raised waistline is marked by a change in color just under the bust. (Mitra/WWD/© Conde Nast)

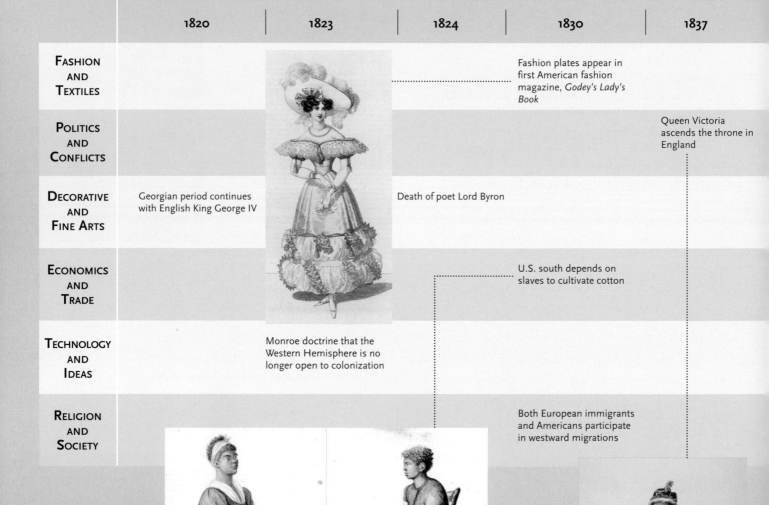

	1820	1823	1824	1830	1837
FASHION AND TEXTILES				Fashion plates appear in first American fashion magazine, *Godey's Lady's Book*	
POLITICS AND CONFLICTS					Queen Victoria ascends the throne in England
DECORATIVE AND FINE ARTS	Georgian period continues with English King George IV		Death of poet Lord Byron		
ECONOMICS AND TRADE				U.S. south depends on slaves to cultivate cotton	
TECHNOLOGY AND IDEAS		Monroe doctrine that the Western Hemisphere is no longer open to colonization			
RELIGION AND SOCIETY				Both European immigrants and Americans participate in westward migrations	

CHAPTER TWELVE

The Romantic Period

1820–1850

1839	1840	1845	1846	1848	1849

Paisley shawls a fashionable garment for outdoors

Wedding of Queen Victoria to Prince Albert

U.S. annexes Texas

Revolution in France; Louis Napoleon elected president of France

Victorians favor ornate furniture, such as this lacquered and inlaid tilt-top table

California Gold Rush

Louis Daguerre makes world's first photographic images

Elias Howe invents the lock stitch sewing machine

Declaration of the Rights of Women, Seneca Falls, NY, proposes vote for women

The term *Romantic* is applied to the literature, music, graphic arts, and the dress of c. 1820–1840. Expression of emotion, sentiment, and feeling were primary. Revivals of fashions in dress, interior design, and architecture from earlier periods reflected an emphasis on and interest in past history (Figure 12.1). Fashion information was readily available from women's magazines including depictions of current fashions in hand-colored engravings. Mass production of lace on sophisticated textile equipment made this decorative fabric inexpensive and easily available. Men could buy some types of ready-made, but most women's clothing was still made by seamstresses or at home.

HISTORICAL BACKGROUND

In its emphasis on sentiment and feeling, Romanticism represented a reaction against the formal classical styles of the 17th and 18th centuries. Romantics rejected the classical insistence on rules governing creative work. Content was more important than form; rules could be broken. Romantic writers assumed that "empirical science and philosophy were inadequate as a means of answering all the most important questions concerning human life" (Harris, 1969, 19). Romantic artists appealed to the emotions.

Romanticists rebelled against restrictions on artistic expression. Artists and writers expressed their feelings in any form that pleased the senses. Imagination was more important than reason.

Romantics ignored social conventions, including marriage; they resorted to tears and violent emotions; they loved and hated fiercely. A true Romantic heroine fainted easily because of inner spiritual turmoil. Romantic men had beards, long hair, and unusual clothing. English poets such as Lord Byron, Shelley, and Keats were nonconformist in their lifestyles, as well as in their poetry.

Romantics preferred other times and places. They loved the Middle Ages. The Romantic movement invented the historical novel. Sir Walter Scott wrote popular historical novels, such as *Ivanhoe*. Alexander

FIGURE 12.1 Victorian furniture, such as this tilt-top table ornamented with inlaid mother-of-pearl and lacquered papier-mache and with lines not unlike those of the rococo period, reflected Romantic artists' interest in past historical periods. (bpk, Berlin/Kunstgewerbemuseum/Art Resource, NY)

Dumas the Elder wrote swashbuckling historical novels, such as *The Three Musketeers* and *The Count of Monte Cristo*. Events from the past or eastern and Mediterranean scenes of violent action often were subjects of Romantic paintings; artists painted moonlit ruins, ghosts, and mysterious forms. Tales such as Mary Wollstonecraft Shelley's *Frankenstein* exemplified the Romantic love of the unusual and fantastic.

After 1820, elements related to Romanticism in the arts began to appear in women's dress with historical antecedents. Neck ruffs, the ferroniere (a chain with a jewel worn at the center of the forehead), or sleeve styles from earlier costume periods appeared again. Men and women dressed as figures from the past at costume balls. The leading Romantic poet, Lord Byron, had an interest in exotic costume, and as a result some styles or names of styles in men's dress were named for him. Fashionable colors were given romantic names such as "dust of ruins" or "Egyptian earth." Romanticism declined in France after the revolution of 1848–1849.

England

The Romantic movement was played out against the following political background. In England, the Prince Regent, who had ruled for his incapacitated father since 1810, finally became King George IV in 1820. The scandals surrounding his marital life made him unpopular. William IV, an eccentric old sailor with little political sense, succeeded his brother on the throne in 1830. When William died without an heir in 1837, his 18-year-old niece Victoria became queen (Figure 12.2). Victoria ruled until 1901 and gave her name to an age, the Victorian era. She restored the prestige of the monarchy, recapturing for it the respect and admiration of the English people.

France

The Bourbon monarchy was restored in France after the fall of Napoleon. Louis XVIII, brother of the executed Louis XVI, became king and granted the nation a written constitution. The restoration of the Bourbons contributed (along with the historicism of the Romantic writers) to the revival of styles from earlier monarchical periods and to an interest in costume balls.

In 1824, Louis's brother succeeded him as Charles X. A king lacking in common sense, he attempted to restore royal absolutism, which led to revolution in July 1830. The revolution was led by an alliance of enthusiastic supporters of the rebellious spirit of Romanticism. They expressed their rebellion through political actions and by wearing working class clothes. These were deliberately different from those of fashionable men. They also rejected stiff collars and neckcloths.

After 3 days of fighting the rebels, Charles X abdicated in favor of his grandson. The Parisians wanted no more of the Bourbon dynasty but were unsuccessful in finding a leader until Louis Napoleon, who was the nephew of Napoleon Bonaparte and a member of the French national assembly, was elected president. Through political maneuvering, Louis Napoleon succeeded in having the Second Republic become the Second Empire in 1852. Meanwhile,

FIGURE 12.2 When Victoria was crowned queen in 1837, mementos such as this statuette depicting the young queen were available as souvenirs of the occasion. (V&A Images, London/Art Resource, NY)

the revolution in France had led to a tidal wave of revolution that swept over Austria, the German states, and Italy.

The United States

In the United States during the same period, westward expansion had begun. Texas was annexed in 1845, and after a war with Mexico, New Mexico and California were ceded to the United States. The Oregon territory was also acquired, giving the U.S. government control over virtually all of the territory now part of the continental United States.

By the mid-19th century, the cultivation of cotton dominated the economy of the southern states. Cotton brought high financial returns. With cotton so important to the southern economy, slavery flourished. Because of cotton, the south was identified with slavery, a condition that separated the south from the north.

By 1840 almost half of the population in Louisiana and Alabama and more than half the population in Mississippi were slaves. According to the census of 1860, there were 3,521,111 slaves in the southern states and 429,401 in the border states (Delaware, Maryland, Kentucky, and Missouri). However, nearly three fourths of the families in the south owned no slaves, and the great majority of slaveholders possessed only a few slaves.

Slaves worked not only in the fields tending the cotton crop but also as skilled artisans and in textile mills, mines, and tobacco factories. Slaveholders received a good return from their investment in slaves.

Slavery did not exist without challenge. Abolitionists vehemently opposed slavery. Local abolitionist societies became the basis for a movement with a membership of two million members by 1840. They opposed slavery, denying the validity of any law that recognized slavery as an institution, and they dwelt on the cruelties of slavery. Eventually abolitionists convinced many northerners that slavery was immoral and consequently could not be accepted as a permanent institution in the United States.

The abolitionists tried to use moral persuasion and political influence to end slavery. Although they did not favor the use of force to end slavery, their efforts in publicizing the evils of slavery helped prepare northerners for the terrible struggle that divided the country when the Civil War came in 1861. There were also abolitionists who fought for women's rights (Figure 12.3).

In the Monroe Doctrine of 1823, the United States had also given notice to the European powers

FIGURE 12.3 Elizabeth Cady Stanton and Susan B. Anthony led the Seneca Falls, New York, convention that published the Declaration of the Rights of Women, which proposed granting women the right to vote in 1848. (National Portrait Gallery, Smithsonian Institution/Art Resource, NY)

that the western hemisphere was no longer open to colonization. But although Americans were becoming politically independent of Europe, American people continued to follow the fashions in dress that originated abroad.

WOMEN'S SOCIAL ROLES AND CLOTHING STYLES

Romantic poets often emphasized the maiden who died for love or the one whose hard-heartedness caused despair in her lover. According to one analysis of women's attitudes in the 19th century, it was distinctly unstylish to appear to be in good health. Circles under the eyes were cultivated, and rice powder was liberally applied to produce a pale look. The middle-class woman was expected, furthermore, to be a perfect lady (Cunnington, 1935).

With industrialization and location of business in workplaces away from home, women's roles were increasingly confined to the home. Affluent women were severely limited in their activities. The home was the center of entertainment, and well-to-do women served as hostesses for their husbands. For this role, they required a substantial wardrobe of fashionable clothes. They supervised the servants, who did all of the household tasks. Women who dressed in the most stylish gowns of the 1830s and 1840s, when sleeves were set low on the shoulder, would not have been able to raise their arms above their heads and were virtually incapable of performing any physical labor. Accomplishments such as sewing, embroidering, modeling in wax, sketching, painting on glass or china, or decorating other functional objects were encouraged. Affluent women had seamstresses who would come to the home to make the more complicated garments.

Women from working class families and rural areas, and women pioneers, however, did toil at a wide variety of tasks. Their garments were less hampering, more practical in form, and made from less expensive fabrics. Even so, their dresses followed the basic style lines and silhouette of the period (see Figure 12.8). Farm and pioneer women transformed the fashionable bonnet of the Romantic period into a sunbonnet, a practical covering to protect the face and head from the hot sun.

MANUFACTURE AND ACQUISITION OF CLOTHING AND TEXTILES

The advances in the technology for producing woven textiles were now well established. Machines for producing lace had been gradually growing more sophisticated. By about 1840, most of the traditional handmade lace patterns could be made by machine in both narrow and wide widths, making lace trimmings and fabrics available at relatively low cost. Another advance in the 1840s was the development of a power-driven knitting frame that could make seamless hosiery.

The variety and types of ready-made clothing available for men continued to expand; however, women could buy few ready-made garments other than corsets and cloaks.

SOURCES OF EVIDENCE ABOUT COSTUME

A major source of fashion information was women's magazines, which carried a number of features about current styles. Introduced in Europe in the late 18th century, these periodicals included hand-colored prints showing the latest styles, together with a printed description. The major American fashion magazines of the 19th century, *Godey's Lady's Book* and *Peterson's Magazine*, began publication in 1830 and 1842, respectively. From the 1830s up to the present time, fashion magazines have served as an excellent primary source of information about what has been considered the newest fashion.

Descriptions of plates in both English and American magazines usually emphasized that they were the "latest Paris fashions." Descriptions were heavily larded with French phrases and French names for garments or fabrics.

In using fashion plates as sources of fashion information, the historian must remember that a fashion plate represented the *proposed* style, and this style may not always have found its way into mainstream fashion. Also, fashion plates were made by tinting an engraved picture with water colors. The representation that resulted was quite different from that produced by the painter working in oils. The result provided much less information about the texture and even the type of fabric than a painting might have provided.

The colors of fashion plates may be misleading. Fashion plate descriptions sometimes describe colors different from those shown on the plate. Individuals hired to hand tint these plates may have run out of one color and substituted another.

The 1840s also marked the beginning of photographic portraiture. Louis Daguerre of France perfected his photographic process (Figure 12.4), and it immediately became fashionable for individuals to sit for their daguerreotypes. These pictures not only provide a record of styles actually being worn but also allow comparison of the idealized fashion plates

FIGURE 12.4 Not only did the photographs of individuals and families in their "best dress" provide mementos of personal celebrations, but pictures of the United States Capitol, which had opened in November 1800, made nice souvenirs for visitors. (© Bettmann/CORBIS)

and artists' painted portraits with real clothing. Since 1849 on, when the process became established in the United States, there has been a wealth of photographic material documenting costumes.

Items from between 1820 and 1850 in historic costume collections are more plentiful than those from earlier periods, although the largest number of garments tends to be wedding dresses, ball gowns, and other special clothing. Everyday dresses and men's and children's costumes are rarely represented in quantity in collections.

COSTUME: THE ROMANTIC PERIOD, 1820–1850

Costume Components for Women: 1820–1835

The period between 1820 and 1825 was one of transition between the Empire styles and the newer Romantic mode. A change in the location of the waistline took place gradually. By 1825, the waistline had moved downward from just under the bust to several inches above the anatomical location of the waist (Figure 12.5). Along with the changes in waistline placement,

women's dresses had, by 1825, developed large sleeves, which continued to grow larger, and gored skirts, which were widening and becoming gradually shorter (Figure 12.6).

Garments

Women's undergarments included chemises, drawers, stays, and petticoats. Chemises were wide, about knee length, and usually had short sleeves (Figure 12.7). No substantive changes took place in the construction of women's drawers. Women of all social classes were increasingly likely to wear them. As dress silhouettes placed greater emphasis on a small waist, stays were shortened and laced tightly to pull in the waist. Multiple layers of petticoats supported the ever-wider skirts of dresses. **Bustles**, which were small down- or cotton-filled pads that tied on around the waist at the back, held out skirts in back (see Figure 12.7).

Dresses were frequently identified in fashion magazines according to the time of day or the activity for which they were intended. As a result, fashion plates generally carried captions such as "morning dress," "day dress," "walking" or "promenade dress," "carriage

FIGURE 12.5 Dress for evening in 1823 shows the elements of the transition that is taking place from Empire to early Romantic styles. The waistline has moved to a somewhat lower placement, the skirt is more bell-shaped and ornamented around the hem, and the sleeves are beginning to be somewhat larger. (Reprinted from *Ackerman's Repository of the Arts* with permission by Dover Publications, Inc.)

FIGURE 12.6 Woman's printed cotton dress of c. 1830–1835 has demi-gigot sleeves. (V&A Images, London/Art Resource, NY)

FIGURE 12.7 Caricature of 1831 shows the down-filled hip pad, called a *bustle*, that was worn under full-skirted dresses. Other garments depicted include a corset, worn over a chemise. The sleeves of the chemise are puffed and stiffened to support the large sleeves of dresses of the period. Several layers of petticoats are visible. The lady is tucking a handkerchief into a pocket suspended from the waist. These pockets were reached through openings in the skirt seams. (Division of Home And Community Life, National Museum of American History, Smithsonian Institution) dress," "dinner dress," or "evening" or "ball dress." **Morning dresses** were generally the most informal, often being made of lingerie-type fabrics such as white cotton or fine linen with lace or ruffled trimmings. **Day dresses**, **promenade** or **walking dresses**, and **carriage dresses** are often indistinguishable one from the other, especially in summer.

Daytime dresses with their lower waistlines, wide sleeves, and full skirts fastened either in front or in back. They were not trained. Necklines varied, with many being V-shaped. Others were high, ending at the throat, and finished off with a small collar or ruff. Draped necklines had crossover folds arranged in various ways. Open necklines might have white linen or cotton fillers.

In the 1820s and 1830s, many bodices had wide, V-shaped revers extending from shoulder to waist in front and back. Wide, capelike collars in matching colors or whitework also were popular.

Sleeves were exceptionally diverse. Fashion periodicals gave many different names to the styles they showed. The following are the major varieties identified by Cunnington and Cunnington (1970):

- puffed at the shoulder then attached to a long sleeve, which was fitted to the wrist. Others consisted of a small puff covered by a sheer oversleeve. Decorative epaulettes—**mancherons** (*mahn-sher-ohng'*)—were sometimes placed at the shoulder.
- **Marie sleeve**: full to the wrist, but tied in at intervals with ribbons or bands (Figure 12.8).
- **demi-gigot** (*demi-ghe-go'*): full from shoulder to elbow, then fitted from elbow to wrist, often with an extension over the wrist (see Figure 12.6).
- **gigot** (*ghe-go'*), also called **leg-of-mutton sleeves**: full at the shoulder, gradually decreasing in size to the wrist where they ended in a fitted cuff (see Figure 12.11).
- **imbecile** or **idiot sleeves**: extremely full from shoulder to wrist, where they gathered into a fitted cuff (Figure 12.9). The name *imbecile* derived from the fact that its construction was similar to that of sleeves used on garments for confining mad persons—a sort of strait jacket of the period.

Waistlines remained straight, with buckled belts or sashes at the waist, until about 1833 after which V-shaped points were used at the front of the waistline. Skirt lengths changed gradually. At first long, ending at the top of the foot, they shortened about 1828. From the end of the 1820s until about 1836, skirts were ankle length or slightly shorter, and then in 1836 they lengthened again, stopping at the instep. From about 1821 to 1828, skirts were fitted through the hips with gores, gradually flaring out to ever-greater fullness at the hem (see Figure 12.5). After 1828, skirts were fuller

FIGURE 12.8 One of the popular sleeve styles of the Romantic period was the Marie sleeve, made with puffs formed by using ribbons or bands to pull a full sleeve close to the arm. (V&A Images, London/Art Resource, NY)

FIGURE 12.9 A pelisse with the enormous sleeves that were called *imbecile sleeves* because they were similar to the sleeves used for confining the mentally ill who became violent. (Photograph by Vincent R. Tortora)

FIGURE 12.10 Evening dress of c. 1830–1835 was generally short enough to reveal the foot and the ankle and often had large padded trim around the hem, a belt at the waistline, and an off-the-shoulder neckline edged in a lace or ruffled bertha. Elaborately curled hairstyles and large hats with feathers, ribbons, or other trimmings were worn in the evening. (University of Washington Libraries, Special Collections, UW28379z)

through the hips, and this fullness was gathered or pleated into the waist (see Figure 12.6).

Pelisse-robe was a name given to a dress for daytime that was adapted from the pelisse that was worn outdoors. A sort of coatdress, it closed down the front with buttons, ribbon ties, or, sometimes, hidden hooks and eyes.

The most popular fabrics for daytime dresses included muslins, printed cottons, challis, merinos (wool), and batistes.

Dresses for evening differed from daytime dresses in details but not in basic silhouette. Necklines were lower, sleeves were shorter, and skirts were shorter. In the 1820s necklines tended to be square, round, or elliptical; in the late 1820s and 1830s, they were more likely to be off-the-shoulder (Figure 12.10). Fabrics for evening dresses included silk satins or softer gauzes and organdy held out by full petticoats.

Accessory Garments for Dresses

A number of separate garments were used as accessories to dresses. By varying these, the same dress could be given different appearances.

Fillers, also called **chemisettes** (*shem-eze-zet'*) or **tuckers**, raised the necklines of daytime dresses. They were separate from the dress and could be worn with different bodices. Wide, capelike collars that extended over the shoulders and down across the bosom, called **pelerines** (*pel-er-eens'*), were especially popular (Figure 12.11). A variant of the pelerine, the **fichu pelerine** (*fee-shu' pel-er-een*) had two wide panels,

FIGURE 12.11 Both the pelisse and the dress are made in colors that fashion commentators of the period called "amber," "apricot," or "citron." The white embroidered pelerine is a typical feature of dresses of the period, and its shape is echoed in the collar of the pelisse. The yellow dress has gigot, or leg-of-mutton, sleeves. (DAY COAT, 1830, silk brocade, velvet, Cincinnati Art Museum, Gift of Mrs. Chase H. Davis, 1957.513)

or lappets, extending down the front of the dress and passed under the belt.

Other popular accessories were the **santon** (*sahn-tohn'*), a silk cravat worn over a ruff, and the **canezou** (*can-eh-zoo'*). In some fashion plates, the canezou appears as a small, sleeveless spencer worn over a bodice, and in others, as a garment synonymous with the pelerine.

Hair and Headdress

See Illustrated Table 12.1 for some examples of hairstyles and head coverings for the Romantic period.

Generally, women parted their hair at the center front. In the early 1820s, hair around the forehead and temples was arranged in tight curls, and the back was pulled into a knot, bun, or (for evening) ringlets. After 1824, elaborate loops or plaits of false hair were added. The style called *à la Chinoise* (*ah la shen-wahs'*) of about 1829 was created by pulling back and side hair into a knot at the top of the head, while hair at forehead and temples was arranged in curls.

Day caps were worn indoors by adult women. These caps were made of white cotton, linen, or silk and often had lace or ribbon trimming. Hats were usually large brimmed with high, round crowns and large feather and lace decorations. Others were bonnet styles that framed the face and tied under the chin. One bonnet, the **capote**, had a soft fabric crown and a stiff brim.

Many hair ornaments were used, and these included jewels, tortoise shell combs, ribbons, flowers, and feathers. For evening, hair ornaments were favored over hats, although berets and turbans were also worn.

Costume Components for Women: 1836–1850

Dresses

The silhouette of dresses gradually became more subdued. The change in sleeve shaping has been compared to a balloon that started to deflate. Although fullness in the sleeves did not entirely disappear, it moved lower on the arm until about 1840 when sleeves became narrower and more closely fitted. At the same time, skirts lengthened. The result was a subtle change in the feeling of the costume from one of lightness to one of a heavier, almost drooping quality (Figures 12.12 and 12.13). Bodices generally ended at the waist, which was likely to come to a point at the front and to close with hooks, buttons, or laces down the front or back. Although dresses were predominantly one piece, there were also some two-piece jacket and skirt styles. Some front-buttoning jacket bodices had short basques (extensions of the bodice below the waist). One popular style was the **gilet corsage** (*jhe-lay kor-sajhe'*), made in imitation of a man's waistcoat. French

Illustrated Table 12.1

Examples of Women's Hairstyles and Headdress: 1820–1850

Turban, 1825

Hat, 1825

Hairstyle *à la Chinoise*, c. 1830

Front view of bonnet, 1834

Back view of bonnet, 1834

Hairstyle, 1839

Bonnet with veil over it, 1848

Bonnet, 1848

period was made with a row of vertical pleats at the shoulder that released into a soft, full sleeve gathered to a fitted cuff at the wrist, was popular until about 1840. The **sleeve en bouffant** (*ahn boo-fahn'*) or **en sabot** (*ahn sah-bow'*) alternated places of tightness with puffed-out expansions. A variation of this construction, the **Victoria**, had a puff at the elbow. There were also tight sleeves with decorative frills above the elbow, those with short oversleeves, and others with epaulettes at the shoulder. A new style, seen early in the 1840s, fitted at the shoulder and widened about halfway between the elbow and wrist into a funnel or bell shape. White lace- or embroidery-trimmed cotton or linen undersleeves were sewn into the wide, open end of the sleeve and could be removed for laundering.

The shape of skirts (whether attached to bodices or separate) was full, and that fullness was gathered into the waist. Innovations in skirt constructions dating from about 1840 included edging skirt hems with braid to prevent wear and sewing pockets into skirts.

FIGURE 12.12 On the left is a daytime dress of the 1840s made of barege, a fabric made from a blending of silk and wool fiber. Contrast the more elaborate fabric and garment details of this garment with the one on the right, an everyday dress belonging to a woman of more modest means, which is made of cotton fabric and worn with an embroidered apron. (Division of Home And Community Life, National Museum of American History, Smithsonian Institution)

terms appear frequently in descriptions of fashions on fashion plates or in women's magazines. *Gilet* is French for "waistcoat," and *corsage* means "bodice."

Most sleeves were set low, off the shoulder after 1838. Cunnington and Cunnington (1970) identified several sleeve constructions and their fashion names. The **bishop sleeve**, which at this

FIGURE 12.13 The marked contrast between the cut and lines of women's dresses is visible when comparing the dress on the left from 1837 and the dress on the right from 1842. (Image copyright © The Metropolitan Museum of Art. Image source: Art Resource, NY)

Prior to this time, pockets were made separately from dresses and tied around the waist; they were reached through slits in the skirts.

Trimmings included **ruchings** (*roo'shings*)—pleated or gathered strips of fabric—flounces, scallops, and cordings. Many fashion plates show skirts with one, two, or multiple rows of flounces for the entire length of the skirt. The styles depicted on fashion plates are not necessarily representative of the styles worn by ordinary women. For example, although fashion magazines of the 1840s show skirt decorations arranged in a vertical panel at the front or horizontally around the skirt, most extant examples of costumes in collections lack such trims.

The silhouette of evening dresses was similar to that of daytime dresses. Evening dresses were most often made with off-the-shoulder necklines that extended straight across or **en coeur** (*ahn kour*), made with a dip at the center. Many had **berthas**, wide, deep collars following the neckline.

Some gowns had overskirts that were open at the front or puffed up. Silks, especially moiré, organdy, and velvet, were used. Trimmings were more extensive on evening dresses, with lace, ribbon, and artificial flowers being the most popular (Figure 12.14).

Hair and Headdress

See Illustrated Table 12.1 for some examples of hairstyles and headdresses for the Romantic period. Parted in the middle, the hair was pulled smoothly to the temples where it was arranged in hanging, sausage-shaped curls or in plaits or with a loop of hair encircling the ears. At the back, hair was pulled into a bun, or chignon.

Adult women continued to wear small white cotton or linen caps indoors. Some had long, hanging lappets. The predominant hat shape was the bonnet, and both utilitarian and decorative types were worn, including sunbonnets to keep the sun from the faces of women who worked outdoors. These were made of quilted cotton or linen with a **bavolet** (*bah-vo-lay'*) or ruffle at the back of the neck to keep the sun off the neck. Fashionable bonnets were often worn with

FIGURE 12.14 Evening dress of 1845 has a neckline *en coeur* (with a dip at the center) and is edged with a large lace bertha. Two wide lace flounces are applied to the skirt of this satin gown. By this time the technology had been developed to make lace by machine as well as by hand. (© RMN-Grand Palais/Art Resource, NY)

bonnet veils attached to the base of the crown, the veil worn either hanging over the brim or thrown back over the crown.

Fashionable bonnet styles included **drawn bonnets**, made from concentric circles of metal, whalebone, or cane and covered in silk; capotes (with soft crowns and rigid brims), and small bonnets that framed the face. For evening, hair decorations were preferred over hats.

Costume Components for Women: 1820–1850

Although women's dress silhouettes showed major differences during the years 1820–1836 and 1836–1850, differences in other costume components were less complex and less marked. Therefore, components such as outdoor garments, footwear, and accessories can be discussed for the entire period from 1820 to 1850. See Illustrated Table 12.2 (page 341) for examples of commonly worn accessories.

Outdoor Garments

The pelisse followed the general lines of dress and sleeve styles until the mid-1830s (see Figure 12.13) when it was replaced by a variety of shawls and mantles worn outdoors during the day or in the evening. Paisley shawls, woven on Jacquard looms, used designs first seen in Europe on costly Kashmir shawls imported from India (see Global Connections). Once the less expensive machine-woven shawls were available, they were often worn. Until about 1836, full-length mantles predominated; later they shortened. Evening styles were made in more luxurious, decorative fabrics such as velvet or satin and trimmed with braid.

Fashion terminology for mantles proliferates. Some of the more commonly seen terms in ladies' magazines include:

- **mantle** or **shawl-mantle**: a short garment rather like a hybrid between a shawl and a short mantle with points hanging down at either side of the front;
- **pelerine-mantle**: with a deep cape, coming well over the elbows and having long, broad front lappets worn over, not under, a belt;
- **burnous**: a large mantle of about three-quarter length with a hood, the name and style deriving from a similar garment worn by Arabs who lived in the Middle Eastern deserts;
- **paletot** (*pal-to'*): about knee length and having three capes and slits for the arms; and
- **pardessus** (*par-duh-sue'*): a term applied to any of a number of garments for outdoor wear that had a defined waistline and sleeves and were from one half to three quarters in length.

Footwear

Generally, stockings were knitted of cotton or silk or worsted wool. For evening in the 1830s and 1840s, black silk stockings were fashionable.

Most shoes were of the slipper type. Toes became somewhat square after the late 1820s (see Illustrated

Global Connections

This fabric for a 19th-century cashmere shawl would have been hand woven in India for an important man. Imported by a European trading company, its cost would have been very high. In Europe or North America it would have been worn by a woman as an outdoor garment convenient for wearing over a wide skirt. The border design, the boteh, was imitated by weavers in Paisley, Scotland, where much less expensive "paisley shawls" were manufactured on Jacquard looms. The town's name is now applied to the classic design known as *paisley*. After shawls were no longer fashionable, they might have been recut into another garment. (V&A Images, London/Art Resource, NY)

Illustrated Table 12.2

Romantic Period: Accessories

Small beaded handbag,
c. 1820–1840

Variously shaped
men's top hats
c. 1830–1840

Woman's chatelaine, an
ornamental cluster of
small tools worn hanging
from the waist

Women's gloves,
c. 1830s and 1840s
(a) Fingerless glove called a mitt
or mitten, made of black silk net
(b) Short kid glove

Cravat that wraps
around neck and
ties in front with a bow,
c. 1830

Parasol, c. 1830s

Women's shoes of the 1840s:
(a) Flat heel with a squared toe
(b) Low-heeled laced boot
(c) Boot with an elastic inset gusset
    Boot with an elastic inset gusset,
    also called a congress boot.

Table 12.2). Very small heels were applied in the late 1840s. Black satin slippers seem to have predominated for evening until about 1840, when ribbon sandals and white satin evening boots appeared.

In cold weather women wore leather shoes or boots with cloth gaiters (a covering for the upper part of the shoe and the ankle) in colors matching that of the shoe. Rubber **galoshes** or overshoes were introduced in the late 1840s.

Accessories

Gloves were worn for both daytime and evenings. Daytime gloves were short and made of cotton, silk, or kid. Evening gloves were long until the second half of the 1830s, after which they were shortened. Gloves, cut to cover the palm and back of the hand but not the fingers, were called **mittens** or **mitts**.

Hand-carried accessories included reticules, handbags, purses, fans, muffs, and parasols. When hats were very large (1820s and 1830s), parasols were often carried unopened. Parasols of the 1840s were small and included **carriage parasols** with folding handles.

Jewelry

In the 1820s and 1830s, women wore gold chains with lockets, scent bottles, or crosses attached. **Chatelaines** (*shat'-te-lehns*) were ornamental chains worn at the waist from which were suspended useful items such as scissors, thimbles, button hooks, and penknives. Other items in wide use were brooches, bracelets, armlets, and drop earrings.

In the 1830s a narrow tress of hair or piece of velvet ribbon was used to suspend a cross or heart of pearls around the neck (called a **Jeanette**). By the 1840s, less jewelry was being worn. Watches were suspended around the neck or placed in a pocket made in the skirt waistband.

Cosmetics and Grooming

Rice powder was used to achieve a pale and wan appearance, but obvious rouge or other kinds of face paint were not considered proper.

Costume Components for Men: 1820–1840

Although men's clothing had become more subdued in color and ornamentation, there were subtle details in cut and style that marked the dress of men who wanted to be fashionable. The variety of fashion terms applied to items of men's wardrobes, as well as for women's, increased substantially.

Garments

No major changes took place in the kinds of undergarments being worn. Some men used corsets and padding to achieve a fashionable silhouette (Figure 12.15).

Shirts were cut with deep collars, long enough to fold over a cravat or neckcloth wrapped around the neck. Daytime shirts had tucked insets at the front; insets for evening shirts were frilled. Sleeves were cuffed, closing with buttons or studs. With these shirts men wore either stocks (wide, often black, shaped neckpieces fastening at the back) or cravats

FIGURE 12.15 Caricature of 1822 depicts the artificial assistance required by some men to achieve a fashionable silhouette: pads at the shoulder, chest, hip, and calf; and a tight corset. (*Monsieur Belle Taille*) (Division of Home And Community Life, National Museum of American History, Smithsonian Institution)

(square cloths folded diagonally into long strips and tied around the neck, finishing in a bow or knot; see Illustrated Table 12.2 and Figure 11.11, page 320).

Coat, waistcoat, and trousers were the components of a suit. Tailcoats and frock coats were the most common types of coats (Figures 12.16 and 12.17). Variations of the frock coat included "military" frock coats that were worn by civilians but with evident military influences. They had a rolled or standing collar and no lapel. Riding coats had exceptionally large collars and lapels.

At least one, sometimes more, waistcoats were worn under the outer or suit coat. These were arranged so as to show only at the edge of the outer coat. Waistcoats were sleeveless and had either straight, standing collars or small, rolled collars without a notch between the collar and lapel. The roll of the collar extended as far as

the second or third waistcoat button. Both single- and double-breasted waistcoats were worn, although in the 1820s single-breasted styles predominated for daytime wear. Evening waistcoats were white or black, and often made of velvet (see Figure 12.17). The ultrafashionable English "dandies" of the 1820s wore waistcoats in colors contrasting with dark, evening dress suits.

The terms trousers and pantaloons were used interchangeably. Most were close fitting, with an ankle strap or slit that laced to fit the ankle (see Figures 12.16 and 12.17). In the 1820s it was fashionable to use a different color, or at the least a different shade of the same color, for each part of the costume.

Costume Components for Men: 1840–1850

The components of a suit (coat, waistcoat, and trousers) underwent some changes. Coat styles were

FIGURE 12.16 Left to right: Boy in tunic suit. The jacket has large demi-gigot sleeves and is worn over contrasting trousers. Man in frock coat, top hat, and trousers. Man dressed in riding coat, knee-breeches, and boots. (Photograph by Vincent R. Tortora)

FIGURE 12.17 Of all the items of menswear, waistcoats were most likely to provide touches of brightness. Man at left wears an opera cloak over his evening clothes and carries a chapeau bras. Man at right wears a frock coat and carries a top hat. (1834, Italian fashion plate.) (Photograph by Vincent R. Tortora)

usually either of the tailcoat or frock coat types. The tailcoat was either single or double breasted. Double-breasted coats had large lapels; single-breasted styles had smaller lapels. Collars were cut high behind the neck, with the rolled collar joined to a lapel to form either a V-shaped or M-shaped notch.

Until 1832 coat sleeves were cut full through the armscye and gathered into the armhole opening, which made a full puff at the joining. In the 1840s this gathering disappeared, and sleeves fit into the armhole more smoothly. The most fashionable of men's coats had padding in the shoulder and chest areas, the width helping to emphasize a narrow, sometimes corseted, waist. This heavy padding disappeared after about 1837.

A more casual garment than tailcoats, frock coats fit the torso. Its collar, lapel, sleeve construction, and chest and shoulder padding were as described previously, but at the waist a frock coat had a skirt flared out all around ending at about knee level. (After c. 1830, the skirts were somewhat shorter.) After 1830, frock coats were more generally worn during the day, while tailcoats were more often used for evening dress. Frock coats were preferred for "undress" or casual wear. Coats became longer waisted, skirts narrower and shorter, and sleeves fitted into armholes without gathers.

New coat styles included a riding, or **Newmarket**, coat, which differed from the tailcoat in that the coat sloped gradually to the back from well above the waist, rather than having a squared, open area at the front. Jacket styles were single breasted, with or without a seam at the waist. Jackets had side pleats and no back vent. The front closing was fairly straight, curved back slightly below the waist to stand open. Collars and lapels were small, and pockets were placed low, with or without flaps.

Waistcoats lengthened and developed a point at the front (called a **Hussar front** or **beak**). Lapels narrowed and were less curved. By the end of the 1840s, however, lapels grew wider again and were sometimes worn turned over the edge of coat collars and lapels. Wedding waistcoats were white or cream colored; evening waistcoats were made of silk, satin, velvet, and cashmere.

By 1840, breeches were limited to sportswear and ceremonial full dress and trousers were for daily wear. The name **trousers** gradually superseded the term *pantaloons*. Fly-front closures were replacing fall closures for trousers.

Made of vivid colors, dressing gowns were worn at home, especially in the mornings. The cut did not change markedly from styles of the Empire period (Figure 12.18).

Costume Components for Men: 1820–1850

Outdoor Garments

After the 1820s, the spencer went out of fashion but many other garments were quite similar to those of the Empire period and included:

FIGURE 12.18 Paisley-patterned fabrics were widely used in the 19th century, and the garments that were made from them ranged from women's paisley shawls to men's dressing gowns; this one is from c. 1845. (Image courtesy of National Gallery of Art, Given in memory of the Reverend William Lawrence by his children)

- **greatcoats**: a general term for overcoats (Figure 12.19). With and without lapels, coats could be single or double breasted, they were often as long as to the ankle, and their collars had a deep roll.
- **box coats**: large, loose greatcoats with one or more capes at the shoulder. (In the 1840s, this coat was likely to be called a **curricle coat**.)

Some new terminology developed.
- **paletot**: a term first used in the 1830s. The styles to which the term was applied vary over time. At this period it appears to have been a short greatcoat, either single or double breasted, with a small flat collar and lapels. Sometimes it had a waist seam, sometimes not.
- **Chesterfield**: Named after the Sixth Earl of Chesterfield, who was influential in English social life in the 1830s and 1840s, this term is used first in the 1840s and then applied to a coat with either a single- or double-breasted closing, although the double-breasted closing has since been more closely associated with this term. The coat had no waistline seam, a short vent in the back, no side pleats, and often a velvet collar.
- **mackintosh**: a waterproof coat made of rubber and cut like a short, loose overcoat. This new garment was named after its inventor, Charles Mackintosh. Waterproof cloaks and paletots are also mentioned. These early mackintoshes did not meet with universal approval. The Cunningtons (1970) noted that the rubber coating that made the mackintosh waterproof had such an offensive smell, that wearers sometimes might not be permitted to ride on buses.

Cloaks were especially used for evening dress (see Figure 12.17). Cut with gores and fitting smoothly at

FIGURE 12.19 Overcoat of the 1830s. Note fullness in sleeve cap and close fit through the body, characteristics that disappeared in the 1840s. (Division of Home And Community Life, National Museum of American History, Smithsonian Institution)

the neck and shoulder, capes had both large flat collars and semi-standing collars. Some had multiple capes at the shoulders. Late in the period, evening cloaks became more elaborate, many with large sleeves with slits in front that allowed the sleeve to hang behind the arm like a medieval hanging sleeve. Lengths varied. In the late 1830s and the 1840s, a short, round, full, so-called Spanish cape lined in silk of a contrasting collar was worn for evening.

Hair and Headdress

Most men wore their hair in loose curls or loosely waved, short to moderate in length, and cut short at the back. Beards, beginning with a small fringe of whiskers, returned to fashion around 1825, and gradually grew to larger proportions.

The **top hat** was the predominant headwear style for day and evening. Different names were applied to top hats, based on subtle differences in shape. The crown was a cylinder of varying height and shape, ranging from those that looked like inverted pots to tubes with a slight outward curve at the top. Brims were small, sometimes turned up at the side. The **gibus hat**, a collapsible top hat for evening named for its inventor, was fitted with a spring so that the hat could be folded flat and carried under the arm. **Derby hats** (in the United States) or **bowlers** (in England) began to be worn at the close of the period. These hats had stiff, round, bowl-shaped crowns with narrow brims. Caps were favored for sports (see Illustrated Table 12.2).

Footwear

Most stockings were knitted from worsted, cotton, or silk. Shoes had square toes and low heels. Shoes lacing up the front through three or four eyelets came into use in the 1830s. Formal footwear was open over the instep and tied shut with a ribbon bow. Boots were important for riding. The first rubber soles for shoes were made about 1832. By the 1840s rubber overshoes, galoshes, and elastic-sided shoes were available.

Bedroom slippers were worn at home. Women's magazines frequently included patterns for making needlepoint slippers as a gift for gentlemen.

Gaiters made of sturdy cloth and added to shoes for bad weather or for hunting were called spatterdashers, or spats. Those worn for sports ended below the knee; those for every day were ankle length. Elastic gaiters were invented in the 1840s.

Accessories

The most important accessories for men were gloves, usually made of doeskin or kid leather, worsted wool, or cotton for daytime; and of silk or kid for evening. Men who took snuff (a tobacco that was inhaled) carried pocket handkerchiefs because inhaling snuff caused sneezing. Canes and umbrellas were used for rainy weather.

Jewelry

Men wore little jewelry other than such items as cravat pins, brooches worn on shirt fronts, watches, jeweled shirt buttons and studs, and decorative gold watch chains and watches.

COSTUME FOR CHILDREN

Children of the late 18th century through the Empire period seem to have escaped from wearing uncomfortable, burdensome clothing—thanks to the relative simplicity of adult women's clothing and the tendency to dress children in less constricting styles than in adult styles. During the Romantic period, the clothes for children reverted to some extent to less comfortable clothes based on adult fashions.

Both boys' and girls' costumes in fashion plates of the period are curiously like fashion plates of adult styles. When narrow waists for both men and women were emphasized in the drawings, the children were likewise given abnormally small waists. During the time that women's sleeves ballooned out to enormous proportions, little girls and little boys were depicted in the awkward, large sleeves (Figures 12.20 and 12.21; see also Figure 12.16).

Costume Components for Girls

Girls' dresses were like those of women, but shorter and with low necklines and short sleeves. White, lace-trimmed drawers, or **leglets**, a sort of half-pantalette that tied around the leg, were worn under dresses.

Some kind of hat, bonnet, or starched lingerie cap was worn outdoors.

FIGURE 12.20 Small girl wears a dress similar to adult women's dresses of the early 1830s with very large sleeves. She wears a coral necklace. Children were often given coral jewelry and teething rings, because coral was thought to bring good fortune to the wearer. Her pantalettes are visible at the bottom of her skirt. (*Girl in Red Dress with Cat and Dog*, Ammi Phillips (1788–1865) Vicinity of Amenia, New York 1830–1835. Oil on canvas 30 x 25". Collection American Folk Art Museum, New York. Gift of Ralph Esmerian, 2001.37.1 Photo by John Parnelll)

FIGURE 12.21 By 1839 styles had changed for both adults and children, and their styles were similar, again, to adult women, with sleeve fullness now concentrated low on the arm. The child at far left in green is probably a young boy, because he wears a darker colored dress and holds a hammer in his hand. His hair is also shorter than any of his sisters. (Image copyright © The Metropolitan Museum of Art. Image source: Art Resource, NY)

Costume Components for Boys

Until age 5 or 6 most boys were dressed in skirts, after which they were put into trousers. Boys, like men, wore suits. The skeleton suit, a carryover from the Empire period, was worn until about 1830. The **Eton suit** consisted of a short, single-breasted jacket, ending at the waist. The front was cut square, the lapels wide with a turned-down collar. The suit was completed with a necktie, vest or waistcoat, and trousers. This style derived from the schoolboy clothing worn at Eton School in England. This suit, with minor variations, remained a basic style for young boys for the rest of the century.

The **tunic suit** consisted of a jacket, fitted to the waist where it attached to a full, gathered, or pleated skirt that ended at the knee. It buttoned down the front and often had a wide belt. Usually worn with trousers (see Figure 12.16), some versions for small boys ages 3 to 6 combined the tunic jacket with frilled, white drawers.

Jackets, in combination with trousers, were cut like those of adult men. Boys did not wear frock or dress coats, however.

Footwear for Boys and Girls

Both boys and girls wore ankle-high boots. Slippers were more often seen on girls than on boys. Both boys and girls wore white cotton stockings.

CLOTHING FOR SLAVES IN NORTH AMERICA

Recent scholarly interest in clothing of the enslaved has provided some insights into the dress of slaves in the decades before the Civil War. Few depictions of slaves exist. Those that do often reflect the bias for or against slavery of the individual who created the picture. Several garments that may have been worn by slaves have been preserved and studied (Tandberg, 1980).

Newspaper notices for runaway slaves described what they had been wearing in detail (see Contemporary Comments 12.1). Oral histories were taken in the 1930s from former slaves. Some former slaves, slave owners, and visitors to the south kept diaries and journals. Extant plantation inventories and financial records list purchases of cloth or clothing for slaves. From these various sources, researchers have gleaned some information, and more is certain to be added as research proceeds.

Warner and Parker (1990), describing North Carolina practices, reported that most owners issued two outfits of clothing a year to slaves. One outfit was for the warm months, and one for the cold. This usually amounted to an allotment of materials to make the clothes. One plantation owner entered these amounts into his diary for the winter: "six yards of woolen cloth, six yards of cotton drilling [which later became a fabric used for summer uniforms for the army and navy],

a needle, a skein of thread, and 1/2 dozen buttons." Information collected from former slaves, however, indicates this practice was not universal. As Thomas H. Jones, an enslaved man from North Carolina reported,

Once a year [the master] distributed clothing to his slaves. . . . The slaves were obliged to make up their own clothes, after the severe labor of the plantation had been performed. Any other clothing, beyond this yearly supply, which they might need, the slaves were compelled to get by extra work, or do without. (as cited in Foster, 1997)

Fabrics were coarse and harsh, either homespun or purchased from manufacturers in Rhode Island and Europe who provided the "cheapest, meanest cloth for slave purposes" (P. C. Warner, personal communication, 1993). The name **negro cloth** was given to a coarse, white homespun used for slaves in the West Indies and the American south.

House slaves were dressed more fashionably (see Figure 12.22a and b), perhaps even in hand-me-downs from white owners.

No attention was wasted on the niceties of style for field hand clothing. Fabrics were generally not dyed, unless the wearers themselves were able to dye the

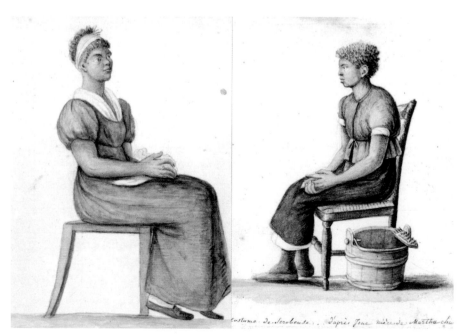

FIGURE 12.22 Drawings of enslaved women from c. 1807–1822 show how individuals were given different kinds of clothing depending on their status in the household. The cook (a) on the left wears a simple but fashionable dress. The scrubwoman (b) on the right wears a short gown and skirt, the kind of clothing worn by laboring women. (http://www.nyhistory.org Photography © New York Historical Society)

Contemporary Comments 12.1

CLOTHING OF RUNAWAY SLAVES

Antebellum period descriptions of clothing worn by African Americans, whether slaves or free, are rare. One place that contemporary records of their clothing is to be found is in newspapers. Owners of runaway slaves or prison officials who had arrested individuals suspected of being escaped slaves placed notices in local newspapers. Such listings generally included a description of the clothing they wore.

The Globe, a semiweekly newspaper in Washington, D.C., regularly printed notices of apprehended slaves. The following reprint is one such notice, to provide the flavor of the context in which the clothing descriptions appeared.

October 12, 1831.

NOTICE

Was committed to the prison of Washing County, D.C., on the 17th of September, 1831, as a runaway Negroman, who calls himself Jacob Johnson: he is 5 feet 5 inches high, had on when committed a bang-up roundabout[1] and pantaloons: he says he is a free man; he is very light complected, and has a black mole on the right side of his nose; he has a very heavy black beard on his upper lip and chin; he has a very large square-looking face, a pleasant look when spoken to, he is about 37 years of age. The owner or owners of the above described negroman are requested to come forward and prove him and take him away or he will be sold for his prison and other expenses, as the law directs.

A number of descriptions quoted from other similar notices in The Globe *are listed below:*

July 16, 1831:
". . . had on when committed, an old drab peacoat, and dark colored pantaloons."

August 10, 1831:
"She had on when committed, a light colored calico dress."

September 14, 1831:
"Had on when committed a Grey Virginia Cassimere[2] coatee, a pair of Black Ratinett[3] Pantaloons and an old Fur Hat."

September 21, 1831:
". . . had on, when committed, linen pantaloons, domestic roundabout and vest, black hat, very much worn."

October 26, 1831:
"His clothing were cassinet[4] coat and cordury [sic] pantaloons—hat and shoes."

"Her clothing consisted of a striped cotton frock, bonnet, shoes and stockings."

"His clothing when committed were cassinet coatee, and pantaloons, palm leaf hat—and wears rings in his ears."

November 12, 1831:
". . . had on when committed a striped linsey dress and check apron."

The Georgia Advertiser *of Augusta, Georgia, dated March 2, 1822, carried an advertisement for two "runaway slaves" who were described as wearing:*

Of the first person it was said, " . . . and wore away a blue broadcloth coat, with covered buttons, black cloth waistcoat, and blue jeans pantaloons." The second person wore "blue broadcloth coat, yellow striped waistcoat, and black cassimere pantaloons."

1. A roundabout is a jacket.
2. Cassimere was a wool cloth, of medium weight with a twill weave.
3. A cheap, coarse worsted wool cloth.
4. A modified form of cassimere, sometimes also called "negro cloth."

FIGURE 12.23 Men and women who have just been freed from slavery during the U.S. Civil War. The women are dressed in similar simple, unornamented one-piece cotton dresses of a cut that predominated between between 1848 and 1865. All wear headcloths. The men's dress varies from suits to shirts and trousers, sometimes worn with vests. (Collection of the J. Paul Getty Museum, Los Angeles, California, Henry P. Moore, "Slaves of General Thomas F. Drayton," 1862)

fabric with natural dyestuffs. Slave accounts speak of dyeing with materials such as indigo, which had to be purchased, tree bark, poison ivy, sumac, and other plants (Foster, 1997).

Tandberg (1980) described the dress of slave women as being of two types. One consisted of a frock or robe with a simple, sleeveless and collarless bodice joined to a skirt. If the bodice had sleeves, they were short and set into loose armscyes. The neck was V-shaped; skirt lengths ranged from below the knee to the top of the foot. The other type had a semi-fitted bodice with a round neckline (sometimes with an attached collar); long, loose sleeves; and a gathered skirt. Some pictures show a shortened version of this frock worn over a skirt, and quite similar to short gowns (see Figure 12.22b).

Enslaved males wore loose-fitting shirts, cut to require as little sewing as possible, over loose pantaloons or short breeches. Children wore a sort of long shirt. At least one diary entry indicated that little girls may sometimes have been given dresses, and some examples of boys' pantaloons and sleeveless shirts have been preserved at one Mississippi plantation (Tandberg, 1980).

Whenever possible, slaves decorated their clothing items and tried to personalize them. Baumgarten (1992) noted that they did this by trimming and dyeing clothing in an individualistic style, by making some of their own clothing, and by purchasing extra clothing or accessories with money earned through tips and sale of farm produce that they grew. Clearly, attempts were made to conform to current fashion. Reports from formerly enslaved men and women tell of the ways women attempted to conform to fashion when hoopskirts became fashionable in the late 1850s. Some apparently made hoops from grapevines or flexible, thin tree limbs, or used stiff paper to support skirts (Foster, 1997).

Even so, active and free participation in the fashion process was not possible for slaves. Their clothing generally served to mark their status (see Figure 12.23). Escape to the north, especially to Canada, could bring freedom. Runaway slaves knew that they must dress like freed slaves in order to avoid capture. For this reason, they often took more fashionable clothing to wear or to sell on their journey. Once free, they dressed as did other Americans (see Figure 11.11, page 320).

Summary

Themes

The theme of RELATIONSHIPS BETWEEN COSTUME AND DEVELOPMENTS IN THE FINE AND APPLIED ARTS continued to be evident as classical styles gave way to those of the Romantic movement. Literary works, as well as the visual arts, contributed to a broad interest in and REVIVAL of styles from the past. POLITICS also contributed to this interest in the past. The French monarchy had been restored and the population, at least for a time, glorified past monarchs such as 17th century's Henry IV. Costume recalled history with such features as hanging sleeves, neck ruffs, and standing lace collars.

Toward the end of this period, a new MEDIUM OF COMMUNICATION, photography, proliferated, adding to the variety of SOURCES OF INFORMATION ABOUT COSTUME. The number of publications for women that carried fashion news and hand-colored fashion plates also increased.

It is clear from these plates that the Romantic period was one of evolution, which brings in another persistent theme, FASHION. For women this evolution can be seen in the gradual shift of the waistline from the Empire placement to a lower position, slightly above the natural, anatomical waist, and finally to the natural position by the close of the period. Sleeves, too, evolved year by year, first enlarging gradually until they reached maximum dimensions, then collapsing with the fullness moving gradually down the arm (see Modern Influences). Hemlines shortened gradually, then lengthened just as gradually.

In men's styles there were echoes of the changes in women's styles and an evolutionary development. The sleeves of men's coats grew larger, then smaller again. The skirts of frock coats widened, then narrowed. At the same time the GENDER DIFFERENCES that had been established at the beginning of the century continued: subdued colors and styles for men and more fanciful styles for women.

By the end of the period a new fashionable look had been established that was a marked contrast to that seen in the early years of the 1820s. This new style can also be seen as a reflection of the theme of PATTERNS OF SOCIAL BEHAVIOR. In Cunnington's (1935) view women had to be, above all, genteel, as Squire (1974) put it, "the bounce was gone, replaced by a sensitive fragility" (159).

LEGACIES OF ROMANTIC PERIOD COSTUME STYLES

Romantic period styles in women's dress incorporated a number of elements from earlier periods. Even so, a few distinctive elements from this period appeared again later in the century. The leg-of-mutton sleeve

MODERN INFLUENCES

This Alexander McQueen gown from the fall of 2013 uses a very large puffed sleeve similar to those incorporated in Romantic period dresses that could have provided the inspiration for this detail. McQueen has set this sleeve so as to bare the shoulder, a detail that would have been unacceptable in the more conservative Romantic era.
(Giannoni/WWD/© Conde Nast)

Visual Summary Table

Romantic Period

Man: 1820–1840

Shirt, waist-length waistcoat, and
trousers, worn with a frock coat or
tailcoat, possibly made with nipped-in
waistline and slightly puffed sleeve cap.

Man: 1840–1850

Shirt, waistcoat, and trousers, worn
with tailcoats for dress and frock
coats for everyday. Skirt of coat
narrows slightly; waistline falls.

Woman: 1820–1835

Waistline closer to anatomical waist,
skirts wider and short enough
that ankles may show. Sleeves
may be very large.

Woman: 1836–1850

Full, less buoyant-appearing skirts
lengthen to floor. Waistline at anatomical
waist. Dropped shoulder line
for narrower sleeves.

made its first appearance in the early Romantic period. It was revived in the 1890s, although its shape was not precisely the same as it was in the 1830s (see Figure 14.15, page 404). Many wedding dresses of the late 1980s also utilized large, leg-of-mutton style sleeves.

The bertha, a neckline style of the 1840s, continued in use into the 1850s and 1860s, then disappeared. It was revived again in the 1940s and 1950s, especially for evening wear.

REFERENCES

Baumgarten, L. (1992). Personal expression in slaves' clothing and appearance before 1830. *Costume Society of America: Symposium Abstracts*, May 22–30, San Antonio, TX, p. 17.

Cunnington, C. W. (1935). *Feminine attitudes in the 19th century*. London, UK: Heinemann.

Cunnington, C. W. & Cunnington, P. (1970). *Handbook of English costume in the 19th century*. London, UK: Faber and Faber.

Foster, H. B. (1997). *New raiments of self: African American clothing in the antebellum south*. New York, NY: Berg.

Harris, R. W. (1969). *Romanticism and the social order*. New York, NY: Barnes and Noble.

Squire, G. (1974). *Dress and society*. New York, NY: Viking.

Tandberg, G. G. (1980). Field hand clothing in Louisiana and Mississippi during the ante-bellum period. *Dress, 5,* 90.

Warner, P. C. & Parker, D. (1990). Slave clothing and textiles in North Carolina, 1775–1835. In B. M. Starke, L. O. Holloman, & B. Nordquist (Eds.), *African American dress and adornment: A cultural perspective*. Dubuque, IA: Kendall/Hunt.

	1849	1850–1870	1851	1852	1857
FASHION AND TEXTILES	Gold discovered at Sutter's Mill sparks California Gold Rush and Levi's blue jeans				Hoopskirt, or *cage crinoline*, is introduced
POLITICS AND CONFLICTS				Emperor Napoleon III and his wife Empress Eugenie lead the Second French Empire, 1852–1870	
DECORATIVE AND FINE ARTS		Decorative styles of earlier periods revived during Victorian era			
ECONOMICS AND TRADE			Isaac M. Singer successfully markets his sewing machine		
TECHNOLOGY AND IDEAS		Improvements in technology for working with metals make the mass production of hoopskirts possible			
RELIGION AND SOCIETY					

The Crinoline Period

1850–1870

| 1858 | 1859 | 1861 | 1861–1865 | 1862 | 1863 | 1867 | 1869 |

Charles Worth opens couture establishment in Paris

U.S. Civil War

The United States purchases Alaska from Russia

Ebenezer Butterick patents the first sized, paper patterns for clothing

Transcontinental railroad completed

Charles Darwin publishes his theory of evolution

Fashionable red garibaldi shirts celebrate reunification of Italy

Congress passes the Morill Act, establishing land-grant colleges

Emancipation Proclamation ends slavery in the United States

PETERSON'S MAGAZINE, MARCH, 1862.

GARIBALDI DRESSES.

This period is named for the cage crinoline, a device for holding out women's skirts. Women's rights advocates encouraged dress reform and joined abolitionists in working to end slavery in the United States. The U.S. Civil War divided the country. Sewing machines proved a boon to the manufacturing of military uniforms and after the war replaced the laborious hand-sewing of garments. The House of Worth, the first French couture house, opened its doors in 1858, and blue denim trousers, known as *Levi's*, were popular as durable pants for men during the California Gold Rush. The technological advances in photography provided a permanent record of contemporary styles.

HISTORICAL BACKGROUND

The increasing width of women's skirts had been leading to the use of multiple layers of stiffened petticoats. In September 1856 the editor of *Peterson's Magazine* hailed the revival of the 18th-century hoopskirts as a means of holding out these voluminous skirts:

> There can be no doubt that, so long as wide and expanded skirts are to be worn, it is altogether healthier to puff them out with a light hoop than with half-a-dozen starched cambric petticoats as has been the practice until lately. Physicians are now agreed that a fertile source of bad health with females is the enormous weight of skirts previously worn. The hoop avoids that evil entirely. It also, if properly adjusted, gives a lighter and more graceful appearance to the skirt.

WORTH AND THE PARIS COUTURE

The person who invented the hoopskirt—or rather who chose to revive it, for it had been used in much the same form in the early 1700s and 1500s—is unknown. Many sources have given the credit to Charles Frederick Worth, but there is no evidence for this attribution. Charles Worth was an Englishman who could claim to be the founder of the French couture. With only 117 francs and unable to speak a word of French, he came to Paris to work in the fabric houses. While an employee of the Maison Gagelin, he began to have his attractive French wife wear dresses he had designed. Soon customers began to request that similar designs be made for them. Worth set up his own establishment in 1858. Seeking the patronage of influential women, he presented his designs to Princess Pauline von Metternich. As the wife of the Austrian ambassador, she appeared at the court of Emperor Louis Napoleon III as a leader of Paris fashion. The success of the gowns Worth made for the princess helped him to win the favor of Empress Eugénie, and soon all of fashionable Paris patronized his salon (Figure 13.1).

Worth dressed the most respectable, as well as the most notorious, women of the world. His clients ranged from Queen Victoria to Cora Pearl, a well-known courtesan. He sold designs wholesale for adaptation by foreign dressmakers and stores. A unique aspect of Worth's talent was his engineering. He designed clothes so that each part would fit interchangeably with another. For example, each sleeve could fit any number of different bodices, and bodices could fit any number of skirts.

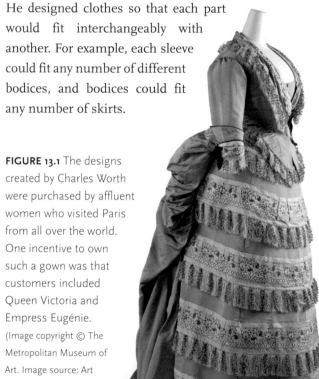

FIGURE 13.1 The designs created by Charles Worth were purchased by affluent women who visited Paris from all over the world. One incentive to own such a gown was that customers included Queen Victoria and Empress Eugénie. (Image copyright © The Metropolitan Museum of Art. Image source: Art Resource, NY)

Worth worked as a couturier until the 1880s; his sons continued the business after his retirement. The number of couturiers had expanded since their father had opened his salon. Worth's sons structured the couture into the **Chambre Syndicale de la Couture Parisienne**, an organization of couturiers that continues to this day. After declining in importance in the 1920s and 1930s, the house of Worth closed after World War II, although a perfume bearing the name of Worth is still sold.

England

The ideal woman for the British was a virtuous wife and mother. They found the perfect example in their young queen, Victoria. In 1840 she married a German prince, Albert, and became the model of sedate, respectable motherhood. She brought to the throne a sense of a loving family, something lacking among British monarchs who preceded her.

In mid-century, Britain enjoyed prosperity marked by increasing imports and exports, expanding production of iron and steel, and industrial growth. Other nations not only envied Britain's industry but also tried to emulate its success. Nothing symbolized the well-being of Britain so much as the Great Exhibition of 1851, held in a specially designed great glass building in Hyde Park where more than 7,000 British exhibitors demonstrated their products as evidence of Victorian progress. Some of these products were reminders of the past: Architectural and furnishing styles often revived earlier historic periods (Figure 13.2).

France

Worth had helped Paris become the fashion center of Europe as it recovered from violent revolutions in 1830 and again in 1848. The Second Republic, proclaimed after King Louis Philippe had abdicated in 1848, enjoyed a short life. The French president, Louis Napoleon, nephew of Napoleon Bonaparte, staged a coup d'état and assumed the title of Emperor Napoleon III. In 1852, following a carefully staged election that approved a Second Empire, France

FIGURE 13.2 One of the important furniture styles of the Victorian period was based on designs inspired by the Gothic period styles of the Middle Ages. (© Elizabeth A. Whiting; Elizabeth Whiting & Associates/CORBIS)

regained the leadership of Europe, and Paris again became a world capital. Empress Eugénie presided over Parisian social life centered in the Tuileries Palace. Kings, princes, princesses, statesmen, and their ladies appeared bejeweled and dressed in the best of Paris fashion. Masked balls, the rage again, offered ladies opportunities to display fanciful gowns.

Although his glittering court was the most brilliant and colorful since the old monarchy, Louis Napoleon was himself a man of conservative and simple tastes. In the morning he dressed in a dark blue coat, a waistcoat, and gray trousers. The ribbons of the Legion of Honor and a military medal were the only symbols of authority that he wore. For concerts and official dinners in the evening, he wore the typical evening dress of the period: a tailcoat with black knee breeches and silk stockings. For really gala events he dressed in a general's uniform with his tunic covered with orders and crosses.

His wife, Eugénie de Montijo, a Spanish countess who was much younger than he, was quite beautiful (Figure 13.3). Although she dressed lavishly for state occasions, Eugénie really had little interest in clothes. Actually she was reluctant to adopt new fashions even after they had become popular. At home she wore a plain black dress. Eugénie followed fashion; she was not a fashion setter.

Nevertheless, the arrangements for the storage of her wardrobe were formidable. Her dressing room was located directly beneath a group of rooms in which wardrobes with sliding panels were located. Here her clothing was arranged in perfect order. Four dressmaker forms with the exact measurements of the empress served a twofold purpose. First, they made it unnecessary for Eugénie to try on her clothes too often when they were being made. Second, when her costume for the day had been selected, the form was dressed and, complete with all parts of the costume, was lowered by elevator through an opening in the ceiling of her dressing room.

To be a guest at the court or one of the royal residences required a considerable wardrobe. A visiting American socialite described her wardrobe for a week-long royal visit: "I was obliged to have about twenty dresses, eight day costumes (counting my traveling suit), the green cloth dresses for the hunt, which I was told was absolutely necessary, seven ball dresses, five gowns for tea" (Hegermann-Lindencrone, 1912, 60).

Napoleon III did much for the economic life of the empire, including the rebuilding of Paris. His foreign adventures led to his downfall, and in the 1860s his fortunes began to decline. After Prussia defeated France in 1870, the emperor abdicated and fled to Britain, where he spent the remainder of his life in exile with Eugénie and their son. The Second Empire vanished, to be replaced by the more somber Third Republic. Paris, however, never conceded its position as the fashion center of Europe.

FIGURE 13.3 Empress Eugénie was surrounded by beautiful ladies in waiting. She and her court attendants dressed in the latest fashions, many of which were designed by Charles Worth, who is considered to have been the first Parisian couturier. (Erich Lessing/Art Resource, NY)

The United States

The crinoline period coincided with the U.S. Civil War. Americans numbered about 23 million, and a little more than half lived west of the Allegheny Mountains. Twelve percent of the population was foreign born. In 1850 there were 141 cities of more than 8,000 residents, containing 16 percent of the population.

Thanks to the Industrial Revolution, the annual output of mills and factories had surpassed the value of agricultural products. Manufacturing was concentrated in the northeastern states. The nation was bound together by a network of turnpikes, rivers, canals, and railroads, and by 1870 east and west were connected by a transcontinental railroad.

Although education remained predominantly private, the foundations of public school education had been laid. In 1862, Congress passed the Morill Act establishing the land-grant system of higher education. The new colleges were intended to emphasize a more practical education in agriculture and industry. In addition, they were coeducational, preparing women in "domestic sciences," later known as home economics.

The women's rights movement had begun and would get increased impetus through an alliance of this movement with the antislavery and temperance (antialcohol) movements. Women still lived under many legal and social restrictions. They had no legal control over property; they lacked the vote; and as late as 1850, some states allowed a husband to beat his wife with a "reasonable instrument."

Religion had a strong influence in antebellum America; some forms of religious expression were allied with an interest in utopian societies, some of which had their own form of dress. Women of the Oneida Community in New York wore a bodice, loose trousers, and a skirt ending slightly above the knees, dress that was similar to the bloomer costume (see pages 361–363).

The Gold Rush and the Origins of Levi's

The discovery of gold at Sutter's Mill in California in 1848 brought more than 40,000 prospectors to California within the next 2 years. Entrepreneurs who saw potential markets for selling products the miners would need arrived along with them. The garment called **Levi's** was one of these products. The miners complained that their pants didn't last long under the rough work of mining and that the pockets ripped out. Tailor Jacob Davis secured the pockets with rivets, and his blue denim pants sold well. When Davis didn't want to pay to patent the design, Levi Strauss, owner of a fabric supply house, patented the design for Davis. Strauss supplied the denim. Miners liked the pants, telling others about "those pants that Levi made for us," and thus the term *Levi's*, often used synonymously with **blue jeans**, was born (Ratner, 1975, 1). The generic term *blue jeans*, eventually shortened to *jeans*, derives from the color and name of the fabric of which these work pants were made. Jean is a heavy twill-weave cotton fabric, very much like denim, and indigo-blue dye produced dark blue, a color with good fastness (durability of the color).

The firm established by Levi Strauss flourished. Blue jeans became a basic item of work clothing for farmers, cowboys, and laborers. The features now associated with the trademarked Levi's- were gradually added: ,a double arc design stitched on the back pockets with orange thread in 1873, a leather patch with two horse brands in 1886, belt loops in 1922, a red tab trademark on back pockets in 1936, and concealed back pocket rivets in 1937. Zippers were added to some styles in 1954. From their beginnings in 1850 up to the present day, Levi's have remained an important costume component (Sullivan, 2006).

The Civil War and Dress

National divisions over slavery came to a head in the war between the north and south, the bloodiest conflict in American history. The Civil War had profound and far-reaching effects on American society, the political system, and the economy. The conflict halted secession and ended slavery. It strengthened the central government at the expense of the states, which were no longer members of a voluntary confederation but now belonged to a nation. The Civil War also accelerated the spread of mechanization and the factory system. The number of sewing machines doubled between 1860 and 1865. The production of shoes increased during the war with the development of machines to sew the uppers to the soles.

The war had little direct influence on the continuity of western fashions that were being set abroad, but women living in the beleaguered south were forced to rely on their ingenuity to keep up with fashion. Because the Union fleet was blockading southern ports, the importation of foreign goods ceased. Moreover, the major manufacturers of textiles were located in the north so that even domestically produced goods were unavailable. In addition, fashion magazines were printed in northern cities such as Philadelphia and Boston.

For one southern woman the first year of the war presented little difficulty because "most of us had on hand a large supply of clothing." But southern women continued the practice of giving away clothing they had tired of only to regret it later, wondering how they "could ever been so foolish as to give away anything so little worn." They were grateful for the popularity of skirts and blouses, which could be made from scarves, aprons, or shawls; and for tight sleeves, which could be cut down from the wide ones so popular in preceding years.

Women had to patch their clothes and piece them with scraps cut from worn-out clothes. Inflation also took its toll. Milliners paid $150 in Confederate dollars for an old velvet bonnet that they then renovated and sold for $500. In the final year of the war, $1,000 was not considered an unreasonable price for a hat (Hay, 1866).

An extended excerpt from a southern woman's account of the problems southern women encountered with their clothing as a result of the northern blockade of southern ports is reprinted in Contemporary Comments 13.1.

PRODUCTION OF CLOTHING: THE SEWING MACHINE

The first patents on the sewing machine were taken out in the 1840s. Public response to the new device was not overwhelming because the cost was relatively high, at least $100. In 1857, James Gibbs, a Virginia farmhand, devised a simpler, less expensive type of sewing machine that he marketed for about $50. Elias Howe patented a sewing machine in 1845 and 1846, but it was Isaac Singer, mechanic, unemployed actor, and inventor who developed one of the most successful sewing machines. Singer's sewing machines became one of the first domestic appliances manufactured on a production-line basis using interchangeable parts. Consequently, the Singer sewing machines could be produced in quantities sufficient to reduce the price substantially.

Singer also pioneered innovative sales methods. He displayed his sewing machines in elaborate showrooms where pretty young ladies not only demonstrated the sewing machines but also taught purchasers how to operate them. Singer sold his machines to seamstresses on the installment plan: $5 down and the remainder, with interest, in monthly installments. To interest respectable ladies in purchasing sewing machines, Singer sold his machines at half price to church-connected sewing societies in the hope that each member would soon want to own her own sewing machine. The company also allowed $50 credit on an old sewing machine when a customer purchased a new one.

But it was the Civil War that demonstrated the usefulness of the sewing machine. The war generated an immediate and enormous demand for ready-to-wear uniforms: The Union army wore out over a million and a half uniforms a year. Such quantities could be supplied only by using sewing machines. Although Howe eventually won a patent infringement lawsuit against Singer, Singer's superior sales techniques and promotional skills made him more successful.

During the war, the Union army collected statistics on the form and build of American males. These statistics were useful to manufacturers of civilian clothing in developing the ready-to-wear clothing industry after the Civil War. The sewing machine became a vital factor in the development of the ready-to-wear industry. Without the sewing machine, it would have been impossible to produce sufficient quantities of clothing to meet the needs of the growing American population (see Figure 13.4).

Contemporary Comments 13.1

REBEL DRESS DURING THE CIVIL WAR

After the end of the Civil War, Godey's Lady's Book *printed the following description of wartime dress: "Dress under Difficulties; or, Passages from the Blockade Experience of Rebel Women" by southern writer Elzey Hay.*

We managed pretty well during the first year of the war, for although we were too "patriotic," as we called it, to buy any "new Yankee goods," most of us had on hand a large supply of clothing. Planters were rich men in those days; and their wives and daughters always had more clothes than they could wear out. . . . Before the blockade was raised all learned to wear every garment to the very last rag that would hang on our backs. . . . [T]here began to be, however, a marked change in our style of dress. Instead of kid gloves, we wore silk or lace mitts; we had no fresh new ribbons; our summer dresses were no longer trimmed with rich Valenciennes lace, and our hats and bonnets were those of the last season "done over." In a word, we began to grow seedy. . . .

. . . We knew very little of the modes in the outer world. Now and then a Godey or a Bon Ton [fashion magazines] would find its way through the blockade, and create a greater sensation than the last battle . . . I remember walking three miles once to see a number of the Lady's Book only six months old.

. . . The blessed Garibaldi [blouse] came in, which must have been invented expressly for poor blockaded mortals, whose skirts had outlasted their natural bodies [bodices]. . . . Black silk was the favorite material for piecing out old clothes, because it suited everything. . . . An old black silk skirt with nine flounces was a treasure in our family for nearly two years, and when that store was exhausted, we fell back on the cover of a worn-out silk umbrella. The finest traveling dress I had during the war, was a brown alpaca turned wrong side out, upside down, and trimmed with quillings made of that same umbrella cover. I will venture to say that no umbrella ever served so many purposes or was so thoroughly used up before. The whalebones served to stiffen corsets and the waist of a homespun dress, and the handle was given to a wounded soldier for a walking stick.

Hay, E. (1866). Dress under difficulties; or, passages from the blockade experience of rebel women. *Godey's Lady's Book*, July, 32.

Seamstresses, particularly those hired by clothing manufacturers to do piecework in their homes, soon saw the benefits of the increased speed of the sewing machine. The first major savings in time were in simple items: men's shirts, aprons, calico dresses. These were the first items to be mass produced.

Sewing machines were used in the production of men's and boys' suits and overcoats. In the 1860s, a first-rate overcoat that required 6 days of steady sewing by hand could be finished in 3 days with the help of the sewing machine.

By using sewing machines instead of hand sewing, manufacturers could produce ready-made women's cloaks and the hoopskirt cheaply and in quantity. Attachments for sewing machines made the addition of braiding, tucking, and pleating to fabrics easy, and the use of these trimmings increased.

EARLY ATTEMPTS AT DRESS REFORM: THE "BLOOMER" COSTUME

The increasing numbers of petticoats required to support the skirts of the late 1840s were uncomfortable and hindered easy movement. A group of American feminists combined their interest in women's rights with a desire to reform dress that they saw as

FIGURE 13.4 The sewing machine proved its value in increasing the speed with which uniforms for Union soldiers could be produced and in lightening the workload of women making clothing for their families. (Ann Ronan Picture Library/HIP/ Art Resource, NY)

The bloomer costume consisted of a pair of full trousers gathered in at the ankle, over which a dress with a knee-length skirt was placed. The style was not limited to the United States but was also seen in Germany, England, the Netherlands, and Sweden. English cartoonists had great fun caricaturing the style in the humor magazine *Punch.*

Few women outside the feminist movement took up bloomers. The ridicule it provoked led some feminists to conclude that emphasizing the costume was counterproductive. When the hoopskirt became fashionable, Mrs. Bloomer found the cage crinoline a "comfortable and practical garment," and she and others willingly discarded the bloomer costume. The cut of the trousers, however, retained the name **bloomers**. Some women's undergarments had a similar cut and

confining and impractical. According to Lucy Stone, a leader of the movement, "Women are in bondage; their clothes are a great hindrance to their engaging in any business which will make them pecuniarily [financially] independent" (Harper, 1898).

Elizabeth Smith Miller had seen women in health sanitariums in Europe wearing short skirts over **Turkish trousers**. (Turkish trousers had full legs that were gathered to fit tightly at the ankle). She adopted the style, wearing it on a visit to her cousin, the feminist leader Elizabeth Cady Stanton. Stanton, Stone, Susan B. Anthony, and Amelia Bloomer all adopted the style. Even though Bloomer did not originate the style, it was named after her. She endorsed it, wrote favorably about it in 1851 in a journal she edited, and wore it for lectures (Figure 13.5).

FIGURE 13.5 Amelia Bloomer wearing the so-called "bloomer costume." The contemporary drawing is based on a daguerreotype of Bloomer. (The New York Public Library/Art Resource, NY)

were nicknamed *bloomers*. The term is now applied to any full pants gathered in at the bottom.

GYMNASTICS FOR WOMEN

The bloomer costume had a short life as fashionable dress, but it did survive in athletic costume for women. An exceptionally successful book of the 1860s titled the *New Gymnastics for Men, Women and Children* endorsed an exercise outfit for women consisting of Turkish trousers with shorter skirts.

Women's seminaries or colleges of the period included calisthenics or some type of exercise program. In 1863, Mount Holyoke College adopted the overskirt and Turkish trouser as appropriate dress for physical education. Vassar College also adopted a similar style (Warner, 1993).

Examples of bathing dress in some historic costume collections also appear to be modeled on the bloomer styles. Warner (1993) noted that *bloomer* was not a word used in describing these outfits at that time. Even in subsequent decades of the 19th century the term *Turkish trousers* was apparently preferred over the rejected *bloomers*.

SOURCES OF EVIDENCE ABOUT COSTUME

Many costume collections have substantial numbers of garments dating from this period. Women's magazines regularly printed hand-colored fashion plates and their descriptions. As a result, the fashion historian can find a wealth of detailed information about fashions from this period.

The practice of photography was so widespread that it was the rare family that had not immortalized its members in photos (Figure 13.6). The *carte de visite* and other portrait photographs (in black and white only) show how thousands of people wanted to be seen. However, they do not show undergarments or how people dressed for outdoors in winter or workday clothing. Some of these gaps can be filled in by nonportrait photography, but the record is not complete.

FIGURE 13.6 Woman of c. 1866 wears a one-piece dress with jacket-type sleeves. The wide braid-trimmed skirt is pleated into a narrow waist. Skirt fullness is supported by a hoop beneath. Her hair is dressed typically, parted in the middle and apparently held in a net. Her husband wears a frock coat. His watch chain is visible at the front of his vest. His shoes have rather high heels. The photograph was taken on the couple's wedding day. (Courtesy of Washington State Historical Society)

Even with the rising popularity of photography, portraits and other paintings also continue to be an important source for the 19th century, especially because they provide a record of color in clothing. Foster (1984) noted the usefulness of genre or modern-life paintings, although she observed that working class individuals are not often depicted and that if poor people appear, they may have been "cleaned up."

COSTUME FOR MEN AND WOMEN: THE CRINOLINE PERIOD

The basic silhouette of women's costume (and also, therefore, of children up to age 5 or 6 and girls older than 6) fit closely through the bodice to the waist then immediately widened into a full round or dome shape. Armhole seams were placed below the natural shoulder on the upper part of the arm (see Figure 13.9c and d, page 367).

Fabrics used are fairly crisp, with enough body to enhance the fullness of the skirt, even though a hoop supports it. Among the silks used for better dresses, a great many were taffetas, particularly plaid and striped patterns (Figure 13.7) and **shot**, or iridescent, fabrics, created by weaving one color in the warp yarns and another in the weft yarns. Washable cotton or linen was used for everyday clothing (very little of which has been preserved), for underwear, and for much of the clothing for children. Wool fabrics appeared in everyday and dressier clothing for women and suits for men. Outerwear for men, women, and children was usually made of wool. Also seen was an attractive silk and wool blended fabric, relatively sheer, crisp and lightweight, called **barege**.

The first synthetic coal tar dyes were synthesized in 1856. A vivid magenta shade, called *mauve*, was the first dye to be made, but the development of other colors followed rapidly. This technological advance increased not only the range of colored fabrics readily available but also their intensity (see Figure 13.7).

FIGURE 13.7 The silhouette of crinoline period styles was achieved through the use of the hoop. Some of the more vivid colors in fabrics and trimmings were often due to the growing use of coal tar dyes, first synthesized in 1856. (EVENING DRESS, 1856-1858, silk; Cincinnati Art Museum, Gift of Mrs. Jesse Whitley, 1964.281a-b)

Although knowledge of silhouette and costume detail is useful in dating historic costume, clues as to dates can sometimes be found within the garment itself. For example, men's waistcoats or trousers in this period and later may have buckles that were used to adjust their fit. Some of these buckles contain a patent number and even the date of the patent. Other closures such as hooks and eyes, snaps, and some buttons are marked with patent numbers. Armed with the patent numbers, a researcher can ascertain the dates of patents and the earliest a garment could have been created.

Costume Components for Women

Garments

As undergarments, a woman wore a chemise and drawers under a corset and a hoop. She placed a petticoat on top of the hoop. Undergarments were made of cotton or linen (see Illustrated Table 13.1, page 365). The chemise was a short-sleeved, knee-length garment, short and full without much decoration. Drawers were knee length and trimmed at edges with tucking, lace, or embroidery. The crotch was left open and unseamed. In winter some women wore colored flannel drawers for warmth.

A **camisole** or **corset cover** was placed over the corset. This waist-length garment was shaped to the figure, had short sleeves, and buttoned down the front. Instead of using as much whalebone as previously used, corsets were shaped with gores of fabric and inset gussets of elastic. After the introduction of the crinoline, corsets shorted, as there was no need to confine the hips. When the crinoline declined in size, corsets became tighter. Reference to "stays" declined; the term *corset* was more widely used.

Illustrated Table 13.1

Selected Undergarments for Women, Men, and Children: 1850–1870

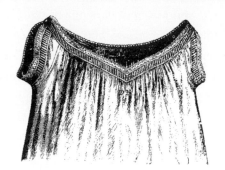

Woman's chemise, 1870[1]

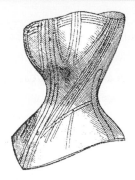

Woman's corset, front and back views, 1862[2]

Woman's corset cover, 1864[2]

Woman's knitted wool under petticoat, 1864[2]

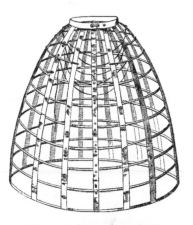

Woman's hoopskirt, 1858[2]

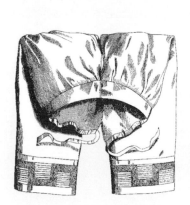

Woman's drawers, 1862[2]

Bodice and drawers for a boy, age 3 or 4, 1869[2]

Man's shirt, 1870[1]

Man's drawers, 1869[2]

[1] *Harper's Bazaar,* 1870, reprinted in Schroeder, J. S. 1971. *The Wonderful World of Ladies Fashion.* Northfield, IL: Digest Books.

[2] Blum, S., ed. 1985. *Fashions and Costumes from Godey's Lady's Book.* New York: Dover.

A series of either whalebone or steel (only after 1857) hoops were sewn onto tapes or into a fabric skirt to make a hoopskirt or *cage crinoline*, as it was called (Figure 13.8). Shapes varied with changes in the fashionable silhouette, which was round in the 1850s and flatter in front and fuller at the back in the 1860s. A single petticoat decorated with lace, embroidery, or small tucks was placed over the hoop. Additional layers of flannel or quilted petticoats could be worn in winter for warmth.

Daytime dresses (Figure 13.9) were either one piece, with bodice and skirt seamed together at the waist; princess style without a waistline seam; or, increasingly, two pieces with matching but separate bodices and skirts. Bodice shaping was often achieved through curved seams in back and darts in front. Armholes were placed low on the arm, below the natural shoulderline in a so-called "dropped" shoulder. Silk or wool garment bodices were usually lined with cotton or linen fabric and occasionally had some whalebone pieces stitched to seams.

Separate bodices worn for daytime generally ended at the waist and fastened up the back or front with buttons or hooks and eyes. Some were cut like a jacket and had extensions of the bodice called **basques**, which flared out below the waist. Before 1860, basques were generally formed by cutting the bodice longer than the waist. Later they were often made by sewing separate pieces to the bodice at the waist. Some extended about 6 inches below the waist and were even all around; others were short in front, long in back.

Necklines were high, without attached collars, and usually finished in bias piping. Removable, washable collars and cuffs were usually worn with daytime dresses (see Figure 13.9). Many sleeves were open at the end and were worn with removable lace or muslin undersleeves (called in French and in some fashion magazines **engageantes**, pronounced *ahn-gahj'eh-ahnts*). Photographs and fashion plates often depict a variety of sleeve styles. Bell-shaped sleeves, which were narrow at the shoulder and gradually widened, ended between elbow and wrist (see Figure 13.9a). **Pagoda sleeves** were narrow at the shoulder and expanded abruptly to a wide mouth at the end. They were sometimes shorter in front, longer in back. Some sleeves consisted of double ruffles, the second ruffle ending about three quarters of the way down the arm. In the 1860s, sleeves were frequently closed

a

b

FIGURE 13.8 Cartoonists found the hoop an irresistible target. Drawing (a) shows a harried husband of 1858 being asked by his wife's maid if he can find room for her hoop in his suitcase. In drawing (b), the hazards of public transportation for hoop-wearing ladies are noted. (The New York Public Library/Art Resource, NY)

FIGURE 13.9 *Carte de visite*–type photographs from the crinoline period. The first two figures, (a) and (b) upper left, wear open sleeves with engageants. The woman on the left wears her hair in a chenille snood, the one on the right has on a small lingerie cap. The young woman (c) at upper right has sleeves of the jacket type, which are decorated at the top with epaulettes. The outlines of the hoops underneath their skirts can be seen clearly in the photographs of the woman (d) and child at lower left (e). The woman on the right (f) wears her hair in sausage curls, or ringlets, around her face. On her head is a small cap with hanging ribbon lappets. All of the figures part their hair in the center. All except the little girl wear detachable white collars. (Photographs from the author's collection)

at the end (see Figure 13.9d and e). Variations of closed sleeves included sleeves pleated into the armhole with released fullness gathered into a wristband; sleeves closely fitted to the wrist with epaulettes at the armhole; or sleeves made up of a series of puffs from shoulder to wrist. Jacket-type sleeves were made like a man's coat sleeve, with an inner seam under the arm and an outer seam down the back of the arm. These sleeves had no gathers at the shoulder and were relatively fitted for the length of the arm (see Figure 13.6).

Separate blouses were worn with skirts. These generally had high necks and the aforementioned closed sleeves. The red **garibaldi** (*gar-ee-bal'dee*) blouse was especially popular in the 1860s (Figure 13.10). Red shirts worn by Italian soldiers who fought to unify Italy under General Giuseppe Garibaldi inspired the fashionable blouses.

Skirts widened throughout the 1850s and into the 1860s (some were 12 to 15 feet in circumference). In the early 1850s, skirts were dome shaped. In the 1860s, they were more pyramid shaped with fullness toward the back. By the late 1860s, there was less fullness at the waist, skirts were gored instead of gathered, and the waistline was located somewhat above the natural anatomical placement (see Figure 13.13). Skirts were usually lined completely, halfway, or with a band of lining around the underside of the hem to keep the skirt from being soiled. Braid placed at the hem edge helped reinforce it and keep it from fraying as it touched the ground. Some skirts were plain and undecorated. Others consisted of two or more flounces sewn onto an underskirt. A similar effect could be achieved by layering skirts, with each layer being cut shorter than the last to form a flounce. Decorative skirts were made of rows of narrow frills or of double skirts on which the outer skirt layer was puffed or looped up.

The **princess dress** was a new, one-piece style that was cut without a waistline seam. Long gored sections, extending from the shoulder to the floor, were shaped to fit at the waist through the curved cut of the sections.

To protect garments or to vary their appearance, women wore accessory garments such as washable aprons. Elaborately embroidered silk aprons were worn for decoration, not practicality. The aforementioned separate collars and undersleeves were generally white and washable and trimmed in lace or embroidered. **Fichus** appear in pictures worn crisscrossed and tied in back. **Canezou** is a fashion term applied to a variety of accessories including fichus, muslin jackets worn over bodices, and chemisette neck fillers. The term *canezou* seems to have gone out of use after this period.

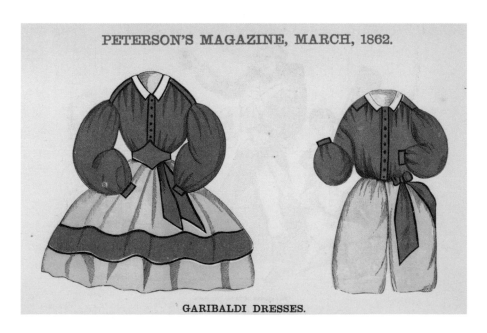

PETERSON'S MAGAZINE, MARCH, 1862.

GARIBALDI DRESSES.

FIGURE 13.10 Red cotton garibaldi blouses were named after the popular Italian General Giuseppe Garibaldi, who wore a similar red shirt as part of his uniform in the military campaign to unite Italy. These blouses were worn by women, girls, and boys. (The New York Public Library/Art Resource, NY)

Differences in dresses worn for evening from dresses worn for daytime were seen mostly in the cut of the neck, sleeves, types of fabrics used, and elaborateness of decoration. Frequently two-piece, some evening dresses were made in the princess style.

Most evening dresses had off-the-shoulder necklines, either straight across or with a dip at the center (*en coeur*), and often with a wide bertha trim (a folded band of fabric around the neckline; Figure 13.11). Sleeves were short, straight, and often obscured by the bertha. In the late 1860s, some sleeveless dresses had shoulder straps or ribbons tied over the shoulders. Double skirts might have decorative effects created by looping or puffing up the outer layer. Skirts were trimmed with artificial flowers, ribbons, rosettes, or lace. The silhouette of evening dresses of the latter years of the 1860s, like that of daytime dresses, fit more closely through the waistline, which moved higher, and skirt fullness swung toward the back (see Figure 13.13).

Outdoor Garments

Outdoors, women wore either sleeved, unfitted coats of varying lengths; sleeved, fitted coats of varying lengths; or sleeveless loose capes, cloaks, and shawls (Figures 13.12a and b).

The tendency of fashion magazines to assign names to each of a number of different styles tends to confuse terminology. The following are some of the names reported by Cunnington and Cunnington (1970) for these garments:

- **pardessus**: sleeved outdoor garment;
- **paletot**: sleeved outdoor garment that fitted the figure;
- **pelisse-mantle**: double-breasted, sleeved, unfitted coat with wide, flat collar and wide, reversed cuffs;
- **mantle**: three-quarter–length coat, fitted to waist in front, full at the back, with either long loose sleeves or full, shawl-like sleeves cut as part of the mantle;
- **shawl-mantle**: loose cloak, reaching almost to the skirt hem;
- **talma-mantle**: full cloak with tasseled hood or flat collar;

FIGURE 13.11 Evening dresses of the 1850s were similar to those of the late 1840s. In this portrait (c. 1851–1853) by the French artist Ingres, the sitter wears a gown made of lustrous silk satin and lace. The jewelry she wears and her hairstyle are typical of this period. Her skirt is held out by petticoats, as the hoopskirt has not yet been developed. (Detail: Image copyright © The Metropolitan Museum of Art. Image source: Art Resource, NY)

- **rotonde**: shorter version of the talma-mantle;
- **burnous**: hooded cape; and
- **Zouave** (*zoo-ahv'*): short, collarless jacket, trimmed with braid and often worn over a garibaldi shirt (see Figures 13.10 and 13.13a). Zouave jackets derived from the uniforms of Algerian troops that fought as part of the French army. During the U.S. Civil War, a regiment called the Zouaves fought for the North and adopted, in part, the costume of the French Zouaves.

Hair and Headdress

See Illustrated Table 13.2 for examples of hairstyles and head coverings for the crinoline period.

a

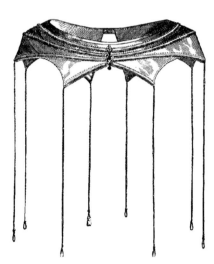

b

FIGURE 13.12 Outdoor garments (a) from 1863. On the right, a full, plaid mantle trimmed with cording and tassels, worn over a dress with a skirt having a band of matching plaid around the hem. On the left, a coat of the pardessus type, closed with frogs. The skirt under the jacket is raised from the ground by means of a **porte jupe**, or **dress elevator** (b), which was placed under the skirt and fastened to the hem of the skirt with loops that enclose buttons. A tab at the front of the elevator pulled to raise the device in much the same way that one would raise a modern-day Venetian blind. (The New York Public Library/Art Resource, NY)

Women generally parted their hair in the center and drew it over the ears smoothly or in waves and then into a bun or plaits at the back of the head. Pads, placed under the hair at the side, helped to give a wider appearance. For evening, curls were arranged at the back of the neck. In the 1860s, the quantity of hair massed at the back enlarged. False hair supplemented natural hair as required. In daytime, hair was usually confined in a net, called a **snood**. This was frequently made of colored silk or chenille.

Small, muslin day caps with long lappets, or ribbons, were still worn by some older or married ladies. Although bonnets continued to be worn, small hats were more fashionable by the 1860s, especially hats with low, flat crowns and wide brims. Other popular styles were hats with flexible brims; bergere straw hats, similar to those of the 18th century; sailor hats; and "pork pie" hats with low, round crowns and small brims turned up at one side. Beaded hairnets, lace kerchiefs, hair ornaments made of fresh or artificial flowers, artificial fruit, or jeweled hair ornaments were worn for evening. Unique styles were worn by African American women (see Global Connections).

Footwear

See Illustrated Table 13.3, page 373, for some examples of accessories of the period.

Stockings were made of cotton or silk. White was the preferred color, but colored and plaid stockings were also worn.

Most shoes worn for daytime had square toes and low heels. Some styles had rosette trimming over the toes. Shoes worn for evening were made of white kid or satin. In the 1860s, evening shoes were often colored to match the gown. Boots were cut to above the ankle and closed with lacing, buttons, or with elastic sides.

Accessories

Gloves tended to be short and fitted for daytime, except for sporty gauntlets with wide cuffs. White gloves, short in the 1850s and long and elbow length in the 1860s, were worn with evening dress. Fingerless mitts, often of lace, were worn for day or evening. Decorative accessories were sometimes made for

Illustrated Table 13.2

Typical Women's Hairstyles and Headdress: 1850–1870

Hairstyles

1851[1] 1859[1] 1864[1] 1866[1]

Head coverings

Bonnet, 1850[1] Bonnet, 1858[1] Bonnet, 1864[1]

Snood, 1864[1] Hat, 1865[2] Hat, 1867[1]

Indoor cap, 1866[1]

[1] Fashion magazines, 1850–1870

[2] Reprinted from *Fashions and Costumes from Godey's Lady's Book*, New York by S. Blum, ed., with permission by Dover Publications, Inc.

Global Connections

In West Africa married women wore a turbanlike headwrap outdoors. Custom dictated that a woman reveal her hair only to her husband within the house. Enslaved women in the American south brought the headwrap tradition with them.

At first, African American headwraps consisted of a simple cloth wrapped around the head and tied. Slaveowners viewed headwraps as a symbol of slavery. But enslaved women transformed the headwrap into a symbol of protest. They constructed elaborate headwear from large decorative textiles elaborately tied around the head as a symbolic statement of "resistance to loss of personal and communal identity" (Foster, 2010). *(Portrait of a Woman in a Blue Turban*, Eugène Delacroix c. 1827; oil on canvas; overall: 23¹/₂ x 19¹/₄ inches (59.69 x 48.895 cm); Dallas Museum of Art, The Eugene and Margaret McDermott Art Fund, Inc., in honor of Patricia McBride)

gowns so that the wearer could vary the appearance of the dress (Figure 13.13).

Popular hand-carried accessories included handkerchiefs, folding fans of moderate size, and small muffs. Parasols were small, dome shaped, often of silk, and lined inside. Carriage parasols had folding handles (see Illustrated Table 13.3).

A **Swiss belt**, cut wide with a triangular piece in front, was a popular accessory (see Figure 13.10).

Jewelry

The most commonly worn jewelry items were bracelets, earrings, brooches, and necklaces. Fashionable materials included coral, cameos, **cabochon stones** (i.e., cut in convex form but without facets), colored glass, and jet.

FIGURE 13.13 By 1868 the silhouette was changing. The waistline was higher and the skirt that fit smoothly at the hips gradually widened into a skirt with ornamentation at the back. A variety of decorative accessories could be placed over the dress to change its appearance. (Author's fashion plate)

Illustrated Table 13.3

Accessories: Crinoline Period, 1850–1870

Woman c. 1860 wearing necklace, bracelets, and rings

Decorative undersleeve, made for wearing under a wide dress sleeve, c. 1860s

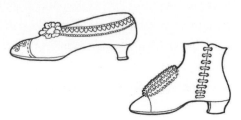

Women's footwear, c. 1860s

Men's footwear, c. 1860s

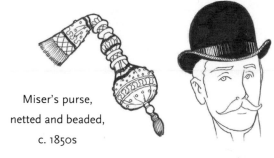

Miser's purse, netted and beaded, c. 1850s

Derby or bowler hat

Ladies muff, c. 1860s

Parasols
(a) and (b) Marquise parasol, that tips at the top, c. 1850s
(c) Carriage parasol that folds, c. 1860s

Cosmetics

The use of "paint" was considered to be in bad taste among "ladies of quality," but fashion magazines did offer regular advice about homemade cosmetic remedies, for example: "[A] tablespoon of gin thrown into lukewarm water will remove redness in the face produced by exertion" (*Godey's*, 1854, 91). *Godey's* also mentioned

> water to thicken hair and prevent its falling out: distil [sic] and cool as slowly as possible two pounds of honey, a handful of rosemary, and twelve handfuls of the curlings or tendrils of grapevines, infused in a gallon of new milk. (1864, 439)

Costume Components for Men

Garments

Men wore long or short cotton or linen underdrawers and an undervest of cotton or linen next to the skin in the warm months and, sometimes, wool in the winter (see Illustrated Table 13.1, page 365). Shirts showed no major changes in shape from earlier styles. Points of the collar extended to the jaw. With less of the shirt front exposed at the neck, shirts worn in the daytime lost their decorative tucking or ruffles. Evening shirts, however, had embroidered or ruffled fronts. Most shirts were white; some shirts for country or sportswear were colored. Ties and cravats were wrapped around the collar (Figure 13.14; see also 13.16).

As before, suits were made up of coats, waistcoats (vests), and trousers. Coats did not button shut but were worn open, leaving the waistcoat visible (see Figure 13.14). Dress coats (formerly called tailcoats) were cut with a short, square "cut-in" in front and tails at the back. Although they were worn for both day and evening for formal occasions in the 1850s, by the 1860s tailcoats were strictly evening dress. Evening coats were black, some with velvet-faced lapels.

Construction of the frock coat was the same as in the previous decade. It was fitted through the torso. The skirt was not overly full. In the 1860s the frock coat waistline dropped somewhat, and the waistline was less well defined. These coats lengthened after

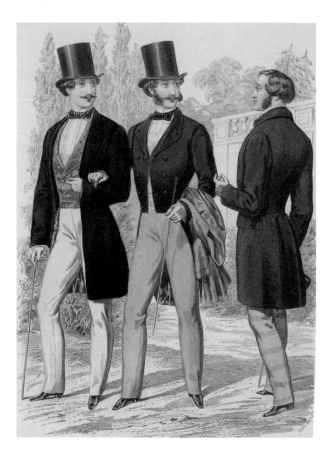

FIGURE 13.14 Men of the 1850s at left and right wear frock coats. The man at center wears a tailcoat. Generally, for daytime wear coats and trousers were not of the same color. Top hats were the most popular hat style for men. (The New York Public Library/Art Resource, NY)

1855, and remained longer for the rest of the period (Figure 13.15).

There were other popular coat styles as well. Morning coats (also called riding coats or Newmarket coats) curved back gradually from the waist, the curve becoming less pronounced in the 1860s. The **sack jacket** (or *lounging jacket* in England) was a loose, comfortable jacket with no waistline. Sack jackets had straight fronts, center vents in back, sleeves without cuffs, and small collars with short lapels (Figure 13.16). **Reefers** or **pea jackets** were loose, double-breasted jackets with side vents and small collars. These were also worn as overcoats.

Waistcoats for daytime ended above the natural waist (see Figure 13.14). Both single- and double-breasted

FIGURE 13.15 Adult men of 1868 wearing a variety of outdoor coats and jackets. By the late 1860s men's coats were less closely fitted and top hats were not so high. The young man third from left wears a pea jacket and the child second from left wears short breeches and a matching braid-trimmed jacket that looks to be of velvet. (The New York Public Library/ Art Resource, NY)

styles were worn; the latter had wider lapels. For evening, waistcoats were single breasted and longer.

Instep straps disappeared after 1850, but trousers fit close to the leg. Pegged-top styles, which were wider at the top and narrowed gradually to the ankle, were also seen. After 1860, legs widened somewhat. For daytime some were made of striped or checked fabrics. Bands made from colored strips of fabric covered side seams of some styles. Men commonly wore suspenders (or **braces** in England) to hold their trousers in place. As an alternative, some pants were constructed with a tab and buckle at the back of the waistband and did not require suspenders. An embroidered or needlepoint pair of suspenders was considered an appropriate gift from a lady to a gentleman.

A new sportswear garment called **knickerbockers** appeared after 1850. The name derives from the similarity of these pants to drawings of the dress of early Dutch settlers that were part of Washington Irving's book, *History of New York*. They were cut with loose legs and belted into a band that buckled just below the knee. The term was later shortened to **knickers**. Wearing knickerbockers for sports seems

FIGURE 13.16 Man c. 1850 wearing a sack jacket, a loosely fitted coat, introduced in the late 1840s for casual wear. (Fashion Plate, c. 1850)

to have originated from the practice of wearing fitted knee breeches for riding, shooting, and hunting.

Some garments were worn only in the privacy of one's home, such as dressing gowns, which were made in decorative fabrics and worn with nightcaps, and smoking jackets, which were loose jackets cut like a sack jacket and made in velvet, cashmere, or other decorative fabrics and worn with small, tasseled caps.

Outdoor Garments

The trend toward looser, more comfortable clothing was evident in overcoats. Some overcoats were fitted with a defined waist while others were loose, with no clear waistline definition. Combined coat-capes had a loose fit and capelike or full sleeves, or an over cape. (The term *paletot* continued to be used to refer to the general category of overcoats; see Figure 13.15). Other names for coat styles include:

- **Chesterfield**: either single- or double-breasted;
- **frock overcoat**: cut along the same lines as the frock coat, but longer;
- **Inverness cape**: a large, loose overcoat with full sleeves and a cape ending at wrist length; and
- **raglan cape**: in spite of the name, a full overcoat with an innovative sleeve construction. Instead of setting the sleeve into a round armscye, it was joined in a diagonal hole seam running from under the arm to the neckline.

In addition, there was a wide variety of capes or cloaks with sleeves. A man's cloak similar to the lady's talma-mantle was worn for evening. Waterproof coats, such as the mackintosh, continued in use. Men also wore large shawls over suits for outdoors. Some of the most famous photographs of President Abraham Lincoln show him wearing a dark shawl outdoors.

Hair and Headdress

Men wore their hair fairly short and either curly or waved. Long, full side whiskers were stylish. Mustaches became more popular in the 1850s; by the 1860s being clean shaven was no longer fashionable (see Figures 13.14–13.16).

The top hat was the predominant style of headcovering (see Figures 13.14 and 13.15). Other styles included the **wide awake**, with a low crown and wide brim and made of felt or straw; caps for casual wear; derbies (bowlers); and straw hats with flat crowns and narrow brims. The **Stetson hat** was born in 1865 when John B. Stetson, who was traveling in the western United States, made himself a broad-brimmed, high-crowned felt hat of beaver and rabbit skins. Cowboys adopted this practical, water-repellent, wide-brimmed, crushable hat, and Stetson began to manufacture these hats on his return to New Jersey (Watson, 1994).

Footwear

Important types of footwear included laced shoes, half or short boots with elastic sides or buttoned or laced closings, and long boots. Short or long gaiters or spatterdashers (spats) were added to shoes for sportswear.

Accessories

Men carried canes and umbrellas with decorative handles and wore gloves.

Jewelry

For men, jewelry was largely confined to watches and watch chains, tie pins, rings, and a variety of ornamental buttons and studs.

COSTUME FOR CHILDREN

Infants unable to walk were dressed in long gowns. From the time they began to walk until the age of 5 or 6, both boys and girls wore short skirts (Figure 13.17b). Infants wore caps indoors and out, which were intended to keep them from losing heat from their heads. Many infants' caps were quite decorative, made of cotton or linen and trimmed with elaborate embroidery and lace. Others were knitted or crocheted.

Costume Components for Boys and Girls

Girls wore shorter versions of the styles adopted by adult women (Figures 13.18 and 13.19). Skirts

FIGURE 13.17 Boy and girl (a) wear similarly cut Zouave jackets, the girl with a gathered skirt, the boy with a pair of trousers. Their leather boots reach to the ankle. A small boy (b), still dressed in skirts, wears a white shirt with belt and band trimmed in velvet, lace-trimmed drawers, knee-length stockings, and ankle-high boots. The man standing beside him wears a frock coat and light-colored trousers. (Photographs from the author's collection)

lengthened as girls grew. At age 4, girls and boys wore dresses ending just below the knee. Skirts for girls age 16 had gradually lengthened to 2 inches above the ankle. Older girls wore hoops to hold out their skirts. Pantalettes continued in use until the end of the period, after which they were no longer worn.

Footwear

Children were generally dressed in ankle-high boots or slippers (see Figure 13.17a and b) They wore striped or plain colored stockings.

Hair and Headdress

Boys generally had short hair; girls' hair was often dressed in tight ringlets around the face. Boys wore caps, straw sailor hats, small pillboxes, and smaller versions of men's hats. Girls' hats resembled those of adult women.

FIGURE 13.18 Plaid fabrics were popular for both adults and children, and dresses—like this one—had the full skirts typical of the period. (Image courtesy of National Gallery of Art)

FIGURE 13.19 Children in outdoor activities wear rather elaborate styles. The boys riding bicycles wear knickers or trousers with jackets and high boots. The girls' dresses, like those of adult women, have slightly elevated waistlines and skirts with more fullness at the back than in front. There are subtle differences in skirt lengths, with older girls having slightly longer skirts than younger girls. (*Children in the Park*, from *La Saison, Journal Illustre des Dames*, May 1869 (coloured engraving), Colin, H. (fl.1869)/Private Collection/Bridgeman Images)

Costume Components for Boys: After Age 5 or 6

After they were taken out of skirts, boys wore trousers or short pants cut similarly to adult men's clothing (see Figure 13.17a). Specific styles for boys included knickerbockers, which were cut full to the knee where they gathered into a band and buttoned or buckled to close (see Figure 13.19). Knickerbocker suits added a short, collarless jacket to these pants, and for older boys, a vest as well. Sailor suits were made up of trousers or knickers, a blouse with a flat, square collar and a V-shaped neck opening. The sailor blouse style was known as a "middy," derived from the word *midshipman*. Eton suits, tunic suits, and jackets plus trousers were all similar to those of the preceding period.

Outdoor garments were mostly smaller versions of adult men's coats, and they included inverness, Chesterfield, and ulster styles.

Knitted, wool jersey suits were worn at for swimming.

Summary

Themes

During the crinoline period we first encounter the theme of THE RELATIONSHIP BETWEEN FASHION AND THE WORK OF AN INDIVIDUAL DESIGNER. That designer was Charles Worth, father of the French couture, whose designs determined what was fashionable and what was not. He also played a significant role in changing the ACQUISITION OF APPAREL. With the

Visual Summary Table

Crinoline

Man: 1850–1870

Shirts with suits made up of coats
(tailcoats for dress, frock coats for
daytime) waistcoats, and trousers.
Sack jackets now used more.

Woman: 1850–late 1860s

Fitted bodices have sleeves set in at a
dropped shoulder. Waistline is close to
the anatomical waistline.

Woman: after 1857

Hoopskirts support full gathered or
pleated skirts. At first concentrated
all around, fullness gradually moves
toward the back.

Woman: late 1860s

Skirts are gored, have higher waistlines
and fullness concentrated at the back.

founding of the *Chambre Syndicale* in Paris by Worth's sons, the hegemony of Paris over fashion innovation was established.

Other changes in the PRODUCTION AND ACQUISITION OF APPAREL also have their beginnings in this period. During the crinoline period, fashion changes in women's clothing were concentrated more in variations of details than in major silhouette alterations. To be sure, the shape of the hoop-supported skirts did evolve from a domelike shape to one more pyramidal. The period might be considered a product of the Industrial Revolution and TECHNOLOGY. Surely it would have been difficult for so many women of all social classes to adopt the hoop so quickly without the factories that produced the steel from which the hoops were made and the sewing machines that permitted their assembly at relatively low prices and in great quantities.

The invention of the sewing machine radically altered the way clothing was made. POLITICAL CONFLICT gave impetus to this new technology in the United States when huge numbers of uniforms were required for Civil War soldiers.

The themes of POLITICAL CONFLICT and fashion came together when garibaldi blouses, Zouave jackets, and raglan sleeves became fashionable—named for an Italian general, a French military regiment, and an English Crimean War hero, respectively.

POLITICAL LEADERS and their families also appeared as influences on dress. Empress Eugénie of France was admired for her style of dressing. Queen Victoria, though not a fashion innovator, exemplified SOCIAL ATTITUDES that placed a high value on family life and reinforced GENDER DIFFERENCES in dress. While women were being confined inside the steel structure of the hoop, men were gaining greater comfort and freedom in their clothing. The sack suit, the closest 19th-century ancestor of the men's sport jacket of today, was a comfortable, nonconfining jacket that men accepted readily and have made a staple in their wardrobes ever since.

LEGACIES OF CRINOLINE PERIOD COSTUME STYLES

The term *crinoline* took on a new definition in the 1850s that it has retained to this day. Crinoline was a stiff fabric used in petticoats to hold out skirts. When hoopskirts were introduced, people took to calling them *cage crinolines* and then finally shortened the term to *crinoline*. Today the term *crinoline* is applied to any stiff petticoat, whether or not it includes a hoop of any kind. The crinoline experienced a revival with the introduction of the New Look in 1947 (see Illustrated Table 17.1, page 521) and again when mini-crinolines were shown in the late 1980s (Figure 19.33a, page 629). The crinoline appears in any period when wedding dresses have long, full skirts. See Modern Influences for an example of a theatrical use of a hoop.

Knickers, themselves a descendant of the knee breeches of the 18th century, have been fashionable for men, for boys, or for women ever since their

MODERN INFLUENCES

Contemporary entertainers, such as the Noisettes, sometimes return to the past to find inspiration for their costumes. Here the hoopskirt undergarment of the crinoline period serves as a theatrical addition to the outermost stage dress for a 2012 performance in Manchester, England. (Shirlaine Forrest/ WireImage)

introduction in the 1860s (see Illustrated Table 16.5, page 498). Levi's, a by-product of the 1849 Gold Rush, have had a long life as work clothing but also experienced fashion revival as sports clothing, children's play clothing, and finally as fashionable dress for almost any occasion.

REFERENCES

Cunnington, C. W., & Cunnington, P. (1970). *Handbook of English costume in the 19th Century*. London, UK: Faber and Faber.

Foster, H. B. (2010). Antebellum African Americans. In J. Eicher (Ed.), *Encyclopedia of world dress and fashion* (Vol. 3, pp. 514–516). New York, NY: Berg.

Foster, V. (1984). *A visual history of costume: The nineteenth century*. New York, NY: Drama.

Godey's Lady's Book. (1854). July.

Godey's Lady's Book. (1864). November.

Harper, I. H. (1898). The life and work of Susan B. Anthony. Vol. 1, ch. 7. Quote retrieved from http://quotes.dictionary.com/Women_are_in_bondage_their_clothes_are_a#XitcEiWmCTkHk6Hk.99

Hay, E. (1866). Dress under difficulties; or, passages from the blockade experiences of rebel women. *Godey's Lady's Book*, July.

Hegermann-Lindencrone, L. (1912). *In the courts of memory*. New York, NY: Harper.

Ratner, E. (1975). Levi's. *Dress, 1*(1), 1–6.

Sullivan, J. (2006). *Jeans: A cultural history of an icon*. New York, NY: Gotham.

Warner, P. C. (1993). The gym suit: Freedom at last. In P. A. Cunningham & S. V. Lab (Eds.), *Dress in American culture*. Bowling Green, OH: Bowling Green State University, Popular Press.

Watson, B. (1994). In the heyday of men's hats, fashion began at the top. *Smithsonian, 24*(3), 72.

	1870–1900	1870–1871	1872	1873	c. 1870–1910	1874
FASHION AND TEXTILES	Queen Victoria wears mourning dress for the rest of her reign after Prince Albert dies in 1861					
POLITICS AND CONFLICTS		War between France and Prussia. Napoleon III abdicates. Civil war in France				
DECORATIVE AND FINE ARTS				Mark Twain publishes his satiric novel *The Gilded Age*		
ECONOMICS AND TRADE					Arts and crafts movement	
TECHNOLOGY AND IDEAS			Steam-powered machine cuts multiple layers of cloth simultaneously			Impressionists show work at *Salon des Indépendants*
RELIGION AND SOCIETY	Women's participation in sports increases		Yellowstone Park becomes America's first national park			

The Bustle Period and the Nineties

1870–1900

1886	1880s AND 1890s	1890–1910	1892	1893	1896	1898	1899–1902

Art Nouveau styles develop and influence fashions

Vogue magazine begins publication

Labor protest erupts in riot when police shoot workers at Chicago's Haymarket Square

Spanish-American War; United States annexes Hawaii

British and South Africa fight Boer war

Gilbert and Sullivan operettas contribute to the aesthetic movement in the arts

Klondike Gold Rush

Sigmund Freud publishes papers leading to psychoanalysis

Census for 1890 reports 145 religious denominations in the United States

The bustle period derives its name from the device that provided the shape of a skirt silhouette with pronounced back fullness. In the 1890s skirts lost this extreme back fullness, and bodices developed "leg of mutton" sleeves. This last decade of the 19th century is often referred to as the Gay Nineties or, in France, *La Belle Époque*. Both names convey a sense of fun and good humor. The western world seemed to be emerging from the serious, moralistic tone of the Victorian era. Women were beginning to enter the work force and participate in sports, especially bicycling. The pre-Raphaelite, aesthetic, and Art Nouveau movements were each, in turn, reflected in dress.

HISTORICAL BACKGROUND: 1870–1890

By the time bustle skirts had become popular fashions, Queen Victoria had been ruler of Great Britain for just over 30 years and would remain Britain's ruler for 30 years more. During the earlier years of Victoria's reign, the British had come to share a common ideal with particular emphasis on the importance of morality and high standards of conduct.

The British empire had grown to include lands across the world. In 1870 industrial England was in the midst of a great economic boom. During the following 20 years, voting rights were extended and legislation mandated a cleanup of the slums and improved sanitary conditions. These years were not marked by any major internal or international upheavals for England.

In France, the period began with the shock of the Franco-Prussian War, when French armies were defeated and Napoleon III surrendered to the victorious Prussian armies. Peace returned after a revolution that ended the Second French Empire and replaced it with the Third Republic. The people of Paris endured a bloody civil war in the spring of 1871, a struggle between radicals and conservatives.

In the United States the Civil War had ended, the country was united from east to west by the railroads, and settlers were moving westward in ever-increasing numbers. Industrialization, urbanization, and immigration were continuing apace, and with them came the corresponding problems of labor strife arising from exploitation of laborers and poverty. But Americans remained optimistic (Mark Twain called this era the *Gilded Age*.) The long peace and economic expansion that followed the Civil War provided opportunity for many Americans to improve their economic status.

HISTORICAL BACKGROUND: 1890–1900

The American frontier was closing, and urban centers were expanding with new immigrants as the United States moved toward the new century. Labor strife and poverty continued to plague American cities (Figure 14.1).

In Europe, too, the social conventions of the Victorian era continued, but there were signs of changes in attitude. In England, the Prince of Wales, heir to the throne, was enormously popular, while the Queen was considered somewhat old-fashioned. The prince, a ladies' man, lived a lifestyle of which his mother disapproved. One of his favorite spots for escaping from parental constraints was Paris, then considered the pleasure capital of Europe. In popular dance halls like the Moulin Rouge, risqué dances and songs were performed. The Folies Bergère had opened and a new form of entertainment called the *striptease* became popular. Houses of prostitution flourished. They ranged from the lavish, beautifully furnished houses visited by the Prince of Wales to shabby rooms in the most degraded quarters of the city.

For those who came to Paris for more sedate pleasures, there were the fashion houses of Worth, Paquin, and others, as well as outdoor cafes, the theater, and tree-lined boulevards for strolling.

SOCIAL LIFE: 1870–1900

The first apartment house in New York City was built in 1870. This five-story walk-up was patterned after the apartment buildings of Paris. Urban centers grew

FIGURE 14.1 Haymarket Square in Chicago was a hive of activity on any given day. It was the site of labor strife in May 1886, when workers demonstrated to achieve an 8-hour workday. A bomb was thrown that killed and wounded both police and civilians. (Library of Congress Prints and Photographs Division Washington, D.C. 20540 USA)

as demand for housing increased. It was not long before this first luxurious building had inspired a host of imitations, including the notorious, crowded tenements that housed the poor.

Whether people lived in sprawling suburban Victorian houses, on farms, or in city apartments, western society in the 1870s was family oriented, and the father was the head of the household. Even so, increasing numbers of American women were entering the workforce. In 1890, 3,704,000 women were employed in a variety of jobs outside the home. By 1900 that figure had reached 5,319,000. Women were concentrated in occupations such as teaching, domestic and personal services (i.e., as nurses, laundresses, servants, and waitresses), bookkeeping and accounting, selling, and dressmaking. Many were employed in agriculture. More than 226,000 were farm owners or overseers, and 447,000 were listed as hired help on farms. There were even 60 female blacksmiths and more than 4,800 physicians and surgeons. Seven out of every 10 colleges had become coeducational by 1900.

The tendency for women to go out of the home to work was probably responsible for the development of less cumbersome clothing for women by the 1890s. Fashion magazines do not always accurately reflect this trend. However, photographs demonstrate that working women wore their skirts shorter and with relatively less decoration than those shown in magazines. Although clothing was becoming simplified, many of the items in historic costume collections reinforce the notion of excessive decoration and elaborate construction, because most women did not save their everyday clothing. Everyday clothing is more readily seen in mail-order catalogs and candid photographs of the period.

SPORTS FOR WOMEN

If sport is defined as recreational activity that requires somewhat vigorous physical exertion, women did not enter into real participation in active sports until well into the 19th century. True, women had ridden horses for recreation as well as for transportation for a number of centuries. They also ice-skated and played croquet, but it was after 1870 that women increasingly participated in tennis, golf, roller skating, hiking, and even mountain climbing. Women also "bathed" in lakes or the sea, but few did any real swimming. Bathing and riding required special dress. Other sports needed only slight modifications of daytime costume. Except for shortening skirts a little, tennis or croquet players and skaters or golfers tended to follow the fashions of the period. When cycling became the rage, however, a special costume was devised.

Calisthenics or gymnastics had been part of the curriculum in most women's seminaries and colleges since the 1860s. In the 1870s and 1880s, some colleges added team sports such as crew and baseball. The clothing worn for these sports was apparently made at home or by a dressmaker. After women began playing basketball in colleges in the 1890s, physical education uniforms appeared. By the early 20th century, the "gym suit" uniform had replaced the individually selected outfit. These were more practical than the Turkish trousers that had heretofore been worn in combination with either short, skirted dresses or bloused bodices. One author describes them as follows: "The bloomers shortened and widened to give the appearance of a short skirt and the separate blouse buttoned onto the bloomer waistband" (Warner, 1993, 23).

Bicycles first appeared in the early 19th century but had not really caught the public fancy. The English bicycle with a front wheel 5 feet high and a rear wheel of 8 inches intrigued a few manufacturers when it was shown in the Philadelphia Centennial Exhibition of 1876. By 1885 more than 50,000 Americans had taken up cycling, and by 1896 the number swelled to an estimated 10 million.

The first lady cyclists pedaled decorously in their long skirts, even while wearing bustles, but in the 1890s a bifurcated garment, a sort of full knicker, was devised as a practical costume for the sport (Figure 14.18, page 406). Although relatively few women actually adopted knickers (or **rationals** in England), the style did mark the first use of bifurcated garments for women that had achieved some modest success. Once these knickers had been accepted for a particular sport, they were also adopted for other activities such as mountain climbing. It was not until the late 1920s,

however, that large numbers of women began to wear anything approximating men's trousers.

Textile Technology

The technological advances in textile production, which had matured during the 19th century, resulted in better fabrics that were often less expensive. Power looms replaced handlooms, and the not always dependable natural dyestuffs gave way to more reliable synthetic dyes.

Various chemical processes were applied to textiles. To give silk fabric greater body, a process called **weighting** was used in which silk was treated with chemical salts. Unfortunately, excessive weighting made the fabric wear out much more quickly. Many weighted garments dating from the 1870s, when weighting first became common, to the late 1930s, at which point weighting was regulated and limited by law, show this damage in split or broken yarns. The performance of cotton fabrics could be improved by **mercerizing**, treating it with sodium hydroxide, which improved strength, receptivity to dyes, and luster.

Ready-to-Wear Clothing

By 1879 most men bought at least part of their clothing from stores. Corsets, crinolines, bonnets, and cloaks were about the only ready-made items that most ladies bought through the 1860s. The average housewife counted sewing among her many skills, and a dressmaker was easily employed for the more affluent. The entry of more women into the workforce after 1870 prompted changes in clothing production and consumption, as did the development of department stores. Underclothes and wrappers were the first women's garments to become available in stores. Advertisements for dresses, suits, and walking costumes followed. A vogue for shirtwaists and skirts in the 1890s gave a tremendous impetus to manufacturing and by 1910 "every article of female clothing could be purchased ready-made" (Kidwell and Christman, 1974, 137).

A number of technological developments made the move to mass production possible. The invention of the sewing machine was a major factor. In 1863 Ebenezer Butterick, a tailor, patented a special type of tissue-paper pattern that he sold successfully. The unique feature of these patterns was that they were made in different sizes. Prior to this, seamstresses had to enlarge small patterns printed in fashion magazines and adjust them to the correct size. Butterick's paper dress pattern helped standardize sizes, a necessity for ready-to-wear clothing.

Cutting out each garment by hand was a time-consuming process. Unless some way could be found to speed up this step, no great quantity of garments could be made efficiently. The first device for cutting large numbers of pattern pieces at the same time was a long knife that was worked up and down through slots in the table. This device could cut 18 layers of cloth at one time. A cutting machine powered by steam was introduced about 1872, but the device was stationary and the fabric had to be brought to it, making it awkward and cumbersome to use. After 1890, the use of electricity for manufacturing allowed the development of smaller, more efficient cutting machines. The first of these cut 24 layers of fabric; later models could handle up to 100.

The efficiency of the garment industry was also based on the piecework concept, in which each operator completed only one step in the manufacturing process. The division of labor among a number of different workers that was characteristic of less expensive clothing made it possible for even a novice to acquire sufficient skill to handle a single component of garment manufacturing.

Sociological factors also contributed to the development of the garment industry. The absorption of more women into the workforce on a full-time basis meant women had less time for dressmaking for themselves and their families, and at the same time it created a greater demand for clothing suitable for work. The dress industry developed over a period when great waves of immigrants—many of whom had excellent tailoring and dressmaking skills—were entering the United States and seeking work. Even the American ideal of a society in which "all men are created equal" helped foster acceptance of ready-made clothing that, as Kidwell and Christman (1974) put it, "served to obliterate ethnic origins and blur social distinctions." Nothing comparable evolved in western Europe; not only was the immigrant labor force lacking, but the more clearly defined social-class structure did not lend itself so readily to the acceptance of a mass-produced supply of clothing suitable for all but the wealthiest. Even in the United States, the rich continued to purchase their clothing in Paris or from custom dressmakers and tailors.

Merchandising of Ready-to-Wear

Department stores, which first appeared in the 1860s, stocked a wide variety of goods, including ready- and custom-made clothing. For customers who could not come to the city to shop, many stores published mail-order catalogs. In 1872 Aaron Montgomery Ward prepared and sent a catalog to farmers, offering them a variety of products available for purchase by mail. The success of the Montgomery Ward catalog inspired other companies to enter the mail-order business. Sears, Roebuck and Co. began operation in 1893.

THE VISUAL ARTS AND COSTUME

The entire Victorian period in the arts was markedly eclectic, featuring many styles that derived from earlier historical periods. In architecture, Gothic and Renaissance styles were among the more important examples of this tendency. Most of the important styles in furniture or interior design were also based on earlier furniture or architectural styles and included not only Gothic and Renaissance revivals, but also revivals of rococo, Louis XVI, and neo-Greek forms.

Revivals of historic styles were also evident in women's dress, particularly in the years between 1870 and 1890. Some dresses had hanging sleeves similar to those of the Middle Ages or the Renaissance, others had "Medici" collars, derived from the 16th and early 17th centuries, and many skirts were cut with polonaises inspired by the costumes of the 18th century. Shoes were made with "Louis" heels, modeled after those worn at the court of Louis XIV, and garments were given fashion names such as the "Marie Antoinette fichu" or the "Anne Boleyn paletot."

A reaction against the traditional and conservative nature of art was stirring, however. Artists such as Courbet and Manet had begun to challenge the traditional painting styles as early as the 1860s. The Impressionists, who received a hostile reaction not only from the traditional salon painters and critics but also from the public, followed them in the 1870s and 1880s. In 1874, their work was refused admission to the official French salon, a show of art works approved by the established art world. In response, they set up a separate show called the *Salon des Indépendants*, which became an annual event. By the 1890s the Impressionists had gained a substantial following among the public and had become the acknowledged leaders of the art world. The direct influence of Impressionist art on costume of the period was minimal. Their paintings, however, can provide

FIGURE 14.2 The first public exhibition of the work of Impressionist artists was in 1874. Their work transformed the work of Vincent van Gogh when he came to Paris in the 1880s. (Digital Image © The Museum of Modern Art/Licensed by SCALA/Art Resource, NY)

good illustrations of current fashion (Groom, 2012; Figure 14.2).

Aesthetic Dress

In the 1880s and 1890s, a dress reform movement directly related to attempts to reform the arts in England did have some impact on clothing styles. The dress reforms of the Bloomer movement proposed by the American women's rights proponents had been based chiefly on the need for more comfortable and convenient clothing for women. Aesthetic dress, of the latter part of the 19th century, had different philosophical origins.

Its origins lay in the **pre-Raphaelite movement**, a group of painters who opposed the direction of English art of the 1840s. They took their themes from medieval and Renaissance stories. Not only did they make costumes for their models to wear, but the women of the group also adopted these dresses for themselves. The costumes, though not wholly authentic, were based on drawings from books on costume history published in the 19th century. After the opening of Japan to the west in the 1850s, Japanese influences also appeared in pre-Raphaelite art. From the 1850s through the 1870s, pre-Raphaelite dress was limited to this group of artists and a few others. By the 1880s and 1890s, the costume had begun to catch on with those who espoused the **aesthetic movement** in the arts, a popularized form of pre-Raphaelite philosophy that attracted painters, designers, craftsman, poets, and writers. Japanese and Asian influences became more pronounced, especially in textiles and other decorative arts. The arts and crafts movement, with its rebellion against machine-made objects, grew out of the aesthetic movement (Figure 14.3). One of the major proponents of aestheticism was the poet and playwright Oscar Wilde. During his lectures on aestheticism, Wilde sometimes wore his own version of aesthetic costume: a velvet suit with knee breeches and a loosely fitted jacket, worn with flowing tie and a soft, wide collar.

Women's aesthetic costume generally had no stays. Sleeves were of the puffed, leg-of-mutton style.

FIGURE 14.3 British writer and artist William Morris led the arts and crafts movement. This wallpaper was among the household materials that he designed. (Image copyright © The Metropolitan Museum of Art. Image source: Art Resource, NY)

FIGURE 14.4 Couple in aesthetic dress, 1880s. Although the dress has some back fullness, it lacks the full bustle of the period and has sleeves that do not appear in mainstream fashions until the 1890s. The man's velvet jacket and shirt with a soft collar and tie are also part of aesthetic dress, as is his long hair. (Reprinted from *Great drawings and illustrations from Punch: 1841–1901* [p. 31] by S. Appelbaum & R. Kelly [Eds.] [1981] with permission by Dover Publications, Inc.)

Preferred fabrics were Asian silks and British Liberty prints, worn without petticoats. When the Liberty fabric shop opened in 1875, proprietor Arthur Lasenby Liberty's experience with Asian design made his products an immediate success.

The wearer had a languid, drooping appearance that contrasted with the stiffly constructed lines of fashionable, bustle-supported dresses. The satirists of the period had great fun mocking the aesthetes with their emphasis on "art for art's sake." Most of the illustrations of aesthetic dress come from the cartoons of George du Maurier, whose work appeared regularly in the British humor magazine *Punch* (Figure 14.4). The operetta *Patience*, written by Gilbert and Sullivan, also poked fun at the aesthetes (Figure 14.5). Indeed, its leading character was modeled on Oscar Wilde.

Art Nouveau

In the period between 1890 and 1910, yet another European reform movement in the arts had some influence on costume for women. **Art Nouveau** was an attempt by artists and artisans to develop a style with no roots in earlier artistic forms. Its proponents saw it as a revolt against the eclectic nature of art and design of the Victorian period.

Art Nouveau designs emphasized sinuous, curved lines, contorted and stylized forms from nature, and a

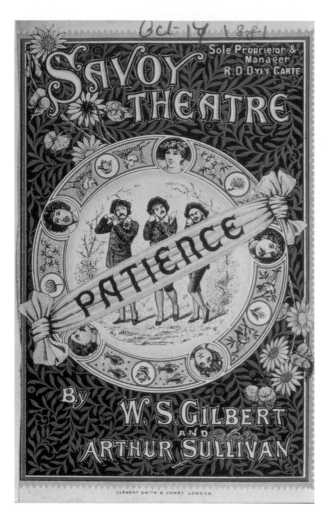

FIGURE 14.5 The operetta *Patience* by Gilbert and Sullivan both satirized and publicized participation in the aesthetic movement. (V&A Images, London/Art Resource, NY)

constant sense of movement. The silhouette of some women's dresses, especially in the first decade of the 20th century, echoed these lines. The stylized natural forms appeared in some dress fabrics, and embroidered patterns in Art Nouveau motifs were often applied to garments (see Figure 14.17, page 405). Jewelry, the metal clasps of handbags, hat pins, and parasol and umbrella handles often show Art Nouveau influences.

In a sense, the Art Nouveau movement formed a bridge between the artistic styles of the 19th century and those of the 20th century. Although Art Nouveau artists did not succeed in making a sharp break with traditional styles, this artistic philosophy that stressed the need for art to be divorced from the past led

eventually to the true revolution in art that arrived with modern, abstract art after World War I.

SOURCES OF EVIDENCE ABOUT COSTUME

Previously cited sources—clothing in museum collections, photographs, works of art, and magazines—continue to provide most of the information we have about costume at the end of the 19th century.

Portraits of men and women from these periods present more or less faithful renderings of clothing. Impressionist painters, active in these decades, did not all pay a great deal of attention to details of dress, although exhibitions have demonstrated how dress from museum collections can also match the dress depicted in Impressionist paintings (Groom, 2012). Depictions of dress in women's portraits of the late 19th century can present other problems, too. In the late 19th century, exhibits of 18th-century portraits of women held in New York and London inspired women of the upper classes to have themselves painted in garments modeled after the 18th-century dresses.

Hand-tinted fashion plates gradually disappeared as fashion magazines in the 1880s and 1890s adopted color printing. Fashion magazines began to use fewer drawings and more photographs, but color photographs of good quality were not available until the 1930s. When color was wanted, the magazines reproduced color drawings. In a study of proportions in fashion illustrations, Warner (1992) showed how fashion drawings often exaggerate proportions to provide a longer, leaner look and that even photographs can be shot from angles that provide a fashionable distortion.

COSTUME: THE BUSTLE PERIOD, 1870–1890

General Costume Components for Women
The confining nature of women's clothing, the heavy draperies and long trains, encumbering bustles, and the tight corseting necessary to achieve the fashionable silhouette prompted intense activity on the part of

Contemporary Comments 14.1

THE EFFECT OF FASHIONABLE GARMENTS ON WOMEN'S HEALTH

The Arena, *a periodical published in the late 19th and early 20th centuries, campaigned vigorously for women's dress reform. One of the often-voiced concerns was the effect of contemporary garments on the health of women. In the August 1891 issue, Abba B. Gould is quoted about her thoughts on what* The Arena *calls the "long, heavy, disease-producing skirts" of the bustle period.*

Do what we will with them, they still add enormously to the weight of clothing, prevent cleanliness of attire about the ankles, overheat by their tops the lower portion of the body, impede locomotion, and invite accidents. In short, they are uncomfortable, unhealthy, unsafe and invite accidents. (402)

In the same article, Mary A. Livermore observes:

The invalidism of young girls is usually attributed to every cause but the right one: to hard study— co-education—which it is said, compels overwork that the girl student may keep up with the young men of her class; too much exercise, or lack of rest and quiet at certain periods when nature demands it. All the while the physician is silent concerning the glove-fitting, steel-clasped corset, the heavy, dragging skirts, the bands engirdling the body, the pinching, deforming boot, and the ruinous social dissipation of fashionable society. (402–403)

Emily Bruce, a physician, participating in a symposium on dress reform in the February 1894 issue, notes:

The long, heavy skirt is scarcely less dangerous than the tight bodice. It impeded free and graceful movements by embarrassing and entangling the lower extremities, and picks up all sorts of evil things from the street and elsewhere, carrying them home to be distributed to all the family without their knowledge or consent. It aids the wicked bodice in compressing the waist, and drags upon spine, hips, and abdomen, producing a state of exhaustion very conducive to the development of disease. (318)

those promoting dress reform. See Contemporary Comments 14.1 for the views of some proponents of dress reform.

Back fullness was a feature of women's dress for most of the period. To support this fullness, a number of different structures, called *bustles*, were devised.

The Bustle

Initially the new back fullness was supported by the cage crinoline of the preceding period, which was worn with an added bustle. Some crinolines were shaped with greater fullness at the back. Subsequently, other bustle-support constructions developed. These ranged from padded, cushionlike devices to half hoops of steel. See Illustrated Table 14.1 (page 394) for examples of undergarments from the period 1870–1900.

The shaping of the back fullness, however, was not consistently the same for the entire period and three somewhat different subdivisions can be identified within the overall bustle period:

FIGURE 14.6 Dress on the left from c. 1867 shows the movement of fullness toward the back that began in the late crinoline period, while the 1873 dress on the right shows the style of the first phase of the bustle period, a sort of waterfall effect with much increased back fullness. (Putnam County Historical Society and Foundry School Museum)

1. 1870–1878: a full bustle created by manipulating the drapery at the back of the skirt (Figures 14.6 and 14.7);
2. 1878–1883: the sheath or cuirass bodice. During the period when the narrow, cuirass bodice (*kwi-ras'*) was fashionable, fullness dropped to below the hips, and a semicircular frame supported the trailing skirts (Figure 14.8); and
3. 1884–1890: large, rigid, shelflike bustles (Figure 14.9).

Garments

See Illustrated Table 14.1 (pages 394–395) for examples of undergarments from the period 1870–1900.

FIGURE 14.7 Daytime dress of 1874. Pleated and fringed trimmings were applied to the sleeves, to the bodice and its elongated basques, and to the skirt. (National Museum of American History, Smithsonian Institution)

Drawers changed very little from those of earlier periods. Chemises, made of cotton or linen, were generally short sleeved and round necked and extended to the knee. They became more decorative, with trimmings at the neck and sleeve and, often, ornamental tucks at either side of the front opening.

A garment combining the chemise and drawers into one was called a **combination**. At least one example of a combination was depicted in *Godey's Lady's Book* as early as 1858. The article stated, "This garment combining the chemise and drawers has very many advantages. We recommend it to ladies traveling, to those giving out their wash, and to ladies boarding. It is also decidedly cooler for summer." Some models were knitted; others, woven. Wool was preferred in winter. Widespread acceptance of combinations after 1870 was probably related to a desire for less bulky underclothing to wear beneath dresses that fit quite closely (see Illustrated Table 14.1, page 394).

Long, curved, and supported with strips of whalebone, steel, or cane, corsets were now shaped to achieve a full, curved bustline; narrow waist; and smooth, round hip curve. The fullness of petticoats increased and decreased as skirt widths changed.

In the early 1870s a new form of dress called a **tea gown** was introduced. Intended to provide some relief from the tight lacing, it was worn without a corset, loosely fitted, and softer in line than daytime or evening dresses. Ladies wore tea gowns at home with other women friends. Because supporters of dress reform also favored them, tea gowns were sometimes referred to as *rational* or *reform garments*.

FIGURE 14.8 The second phase of the bustle period is evident in this 1877 dress in which the skirt has narrowed through the torso and fullness is released at the bottom of the back allowing it to extend into a long train. (Putnam County Historical Society and Foundry School Museum)

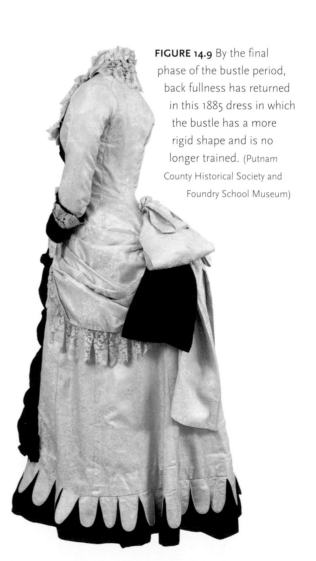

FIGURE 14.9 By the final phase of the bustle period, back fullness has returned in this 1885 dress in which the bustle has a more rigid shape and is no longer trained. (Putnam County Historical Society and Foundry School Museum)

Illustrated Table 14.1

Selected Undergarments for Women, Men, and Children: 1870–1900

A variety of bustle styles illustrated in fashion magazines of the 1870s and 1880, including:

Horsehair bustle

Bustle of hoops sewn into cambric

Horsehair ruffles attached to petticoat

BVD spiral bustle, "the only bustle that will not break down."

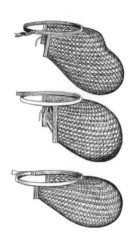

Three braided wire bustles of differing shapes

Taylor's star folding bustle, described as "light, cool, and comfortable."

Corset cover, 1880s[1]

Lady's muslin drawers, 1886[2]

[1] Reprinted from *Victorian Women's Fashion Cuts* by C. B. Grafton, 1993, with permission by Dover Publications, Inc.

[2] Reprinted from Bloomingdale Brothers, 1988. *Bloomingdale's Illustrated Catalog*, p. 26, New York, with permission by Dover Publications, Inc.

Illustrated Table 14.1

Selected Undergarments for Women, Men, and Children: 1870–1900 (continued)

Lace-trimmed muslin
chemise, 1886[2]

Lady's lace-trimmed
petticoat, 1890s[1]

Knitted combination underwear
of the type recommended by advocates
of dress reform, 1897[3]

Boy's drawers with attached
underwaist[5]

Men's drawers[4]

  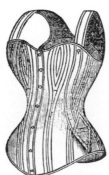 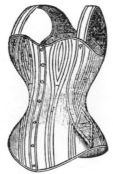

BABY'S. Age one year.

INFANTS'.
Ages 1 to 3 years.

CHILDREN'S.
For BOYS and GIRLS,
Ages 3 to 10 years.

YOUNG LADIES'.
Style 92.
For GROWING GIRLS.
Ages 12 to 16 years.

Corsets for children age 1 year up to adult, 1893[5]

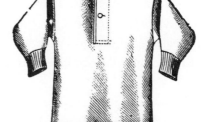

Child's vest[2]

---

[3] The New York Public Library/Art Resource, NY

[4] *The Delineator*, May 1893.

[5] Reprinted from *American Dress Pattern Catalogs, 1873–1909*, by N. V. Bryk, 1988, with permission by Dover Publications, Inc.

Other negligee items that were worn before the day's toilette was complete or before retiring included wrappers, dressing sacques, combing mantles, and breakfast jackets.

Throughout the period, two-piece dresses consisting of bodice and matching skirt predominated. The princess dress, cut in one piece from shoulder to hem, without a waistline seam, was an exception. To achieve a fit that followed body contours through the torso, princess dresses were cut with many vertical seams and vertical darts (long, shaped tucks).

Skirts and blouses, although seen less frequently than dresses, were also worn. Most were overblouses, cut loosely and belted at the waistline. Women wore Norfolk jackets (a men's coat style) with skirts. Princess-style overdresses were sometimes combined with a separate underskirt. When the outer fabric was looped up or draped over the hip the style was known as a **princess polonaise**.

Features of the Bustle Period

Daytime Dresses: 1870–1878

Bodices were generally of the fitted-jacket type with either shorter basques (i.e., extensions of the bodice below the waist) at front or back (or both) or longer basques forming a sort of overskirt at the back of the costume. Necklines were high and closed, square, or V-shaped. Open necklines were generally filled in with a decorative chemisette or lace frill. Even when the front of the bodice was cut low, the back neckline was high.

Closely fitted sleeves ended about three quarters of the way down the arm or at the wrist. Coat sleeves were fitted sleeves ending in a deep cuff. Sleeves were now set higher into the armhole, without a dropped shoulder.

Skirts generally matched bodices in color and fabric unless they were worn with a blouse rather than a bodice. Overskirts were often draped to produce an apronlike effect at the front. Both skirts and long basques were made with plenty of fabric, which was then looped or draped in various ways at the back of the skirt. The considerable fullness achieved in this way was supported by the bustle.

Evening Dresses: 1870–1878

Many women had two bodices made for each skirt; one for daytime, one for evening wear. Because evening dresses followed the same lines as daytime dresses, the chief differences between them were in the use of more decorative fabrics, greater ornamentation, and cut of sleeves and necklines. Many evening bodices either had off-the-shoulder sleeves, were sleeveless, were short sleeved, or had elbow-length sleeves finishing in ruffles. Necklines for evening were square, V-shaped, or round and low.

Daytime and Evening Dresses: 1878–1883

The silhouette (see Figure 14.8) was modified continually, with gradual year-by-year diminishing of bustle dimensions. The change began as early as 1875, with the **cuirass bodice**, a long jacket ending in a point at the front and fitting smoothly over the hips. This cut required less back fullness, and as a result bustle fullness decreased gradually. The decoration applied to dress became more asymmetrical.

Necklines, sleeves, and trimmings showed no radical changes. Long, heavily trained skirts fitted smoothly over the hips. Their decoration was concentrated low, at the back of the skirt. Skirts were held close to the knee in front by ties, restricting women's movements to small, mincing steps.

Daytime Dresses: 1883–1890

Bustles returned, but they differed from earlier styles in that the back fullness had more the appearance of a constructed, shelflike projection rather than the softer, draped construction of the 1870–1878 styles (Figure 14.9).

The bodices most frequently seen were fitted, jacket style with short basques, polonaise bodices, or belted over blouses (Figure 14.10; see also Global Connections).

Almost all daytime dresses of the 1880s had high, fitted, boned collars. The collars were either part of a

FIGURE 14.10 Women and men of the 1880s. Women's jacket-style bodices have basques extended below the waist and high collars typical of the period. Their hair is dressed on top of the head, off the neck. Most of the men wear frock coats. (Courtesy of Huntington Historical Society, Huntington, NY)

blouse worn under a jacket, part of the jacket, or part of the dress. Generally closely fitted, most sleeves ended above the wrist. As early as 1883 some sleeves developed a small puff at the sleeve cap. In 1889 this puff (called a **kick-up**) grew, becoming more pronounced, a forerunner of the extremely full sleeves that characterized the 1890s. Skirts usually ended several inches above the floor and only rarely had trains.

Evening Dresses: 1883–1890

Evening dresses had the same silhouette as daytime dresses but with increased trimming. Some were trained. Sleeves on ball gowns were short, covering just the shoulders. By the close of the 1880s, some evening dresses had broad or narrow shoulder straps in place of sleeves. Conservative ladies wore elbow-length sleeves.

Outdoor Garments

The variety of outdoor garments increased. Whereas crinoline-period styles relied heavily on cloaks

and capes, the bustle silhouette was more easily accommodated by coats or jackets. Jackets were closely fitted at the back and loose or fitted in front, where they generally extended below the waist. Some were knee length. They were cut to accommodate the bustle configuration of the particular year. Sleeves generally were coat style with turned-back cuffs (Figure 14.11).

Paletot, sacque (or sack), and *pelisse* are terms applied to a variety of coatlike garments, most of which were three-quarter length or reached to the floor. Another long coat was the **ulster**, a long, belted coat often made with a removable shoulder cape or hood. Full-length Chesterfield-style coats usually had velvet collars.

The **dolman** was a semifitted garment of hip-to-floor length that was shaped like a coat but had a wide-bottomed sleeve that was part of the body of the garment (a sort of coat or cape; see Figure 4.11). Fitted to the shoulder, cloaks and capes were cut in varying lengths; some were fitted in the back and loose in the front.

FIGURE 14.11 Outdoor garments for adult women and young girls. The garment at the far right is a dolman-mantle. (Italian fashion magazine, November 1874)

Global Connections

Sewing machines and clothing construction techniques that were needed to construct bustle dresses moved around the world along with Euro-American fashions. The ones depicted here are being made by court ladies in Japan. Japan had closed its ports to western trade until 1854 when U.S. Commodore Matthew Perry used naval might to persuade Japan to sign a treaty opening Japan to American contacts. After this date Euro-American dress appears in Japanese art, providing evidence that although traditional Japanese dress did not disappear, western dress became fashionable in certain situations. (Image copyright © The Metropolitan Museum of Art. Image source: Art Resource, NY)

FIGURE 14.12 Skaters of about 1890 wear street clothes for the active sport of ice skating, although women tended to favor skirts a bit shorter than those for street wear and kept their hands warm with muffs. (*Skating*, published by L. Prang and Co. [color litho], Sandham, Henry [1842–1912] [after]/Library of Congress, Washington DC, USA/Bridgeman Images)

Clothing for Active Sports

Although women were beginning to take more interest in active sports, the costumes worn for tennis, golf, yachting, or walking were made with bustles and elaborate draperies. The only concession to the activity of these pastimes was that dresses worn were cut slightly shorter (Figure 14.12).

A vogue for wearing wool knit fabric began when Lillie Langtry, an internationally famous stage personality, adopted a wool knit fabric as a tennis costume. Langtry was born on the British island of Jersey and was nicknamed "the Jersey Lily." As a result the fabric became known as **jersey**, the name by which it is still called today.

Bathing costumes consisted of bloomers or trousers with an overskirt and bodice. Gradually, the trousers were shortened to the knee and stockings covered the lower part of the leg. Bathing shoes or slippers and a cap completed the outfit. Sleeves decreased in size, and in 1885 some bathing costumes were sleeveless. Even with these modifications, ladies could do little real swimming; their activity in the water was

FIGURE 14.13 Group of women and children by the sea from *Der Bazar*, a German publication, of 1874. The three figures in the center are dressed in bathing costumes. (The New York Public Library/Art Resource, NY)

generally limited to a little splashing about in shallow areas (Figure 14.13).

Hair and Headdress

See Illustrated Table 14.2 (page 400) for some examples of hairstyles and headdress for the period from 1870 to 1900.

Usually hair was parted at the center, waved around the face, and pulled to the back of the head. Bangs or curled fringe covered the forehead. In the early 1870s, long hair was arranged in large braids, a chignon, or long curls cascading down the back of the head. False hair was used lavishly. As the costume silhouette grew more slender, hair was worn closer to the head and arranged in a confined bun or curls at the nape of the neck. High-boned collars were worn so widely after 1884 that most women dressed their hair off the neck and high on the top of the head in a bun or curls.

By the end of the 1880s only elderly women still wore day caps indoors. Hats and bonnets were exceedingly elaborate, with ribbons, feathers, lace, flowers, and flounces as trimming. When masses of large curls or chignons were concentrated at the back of the head, hats were worn either tilted up, perched on the front of the head, or set back, resting on the chignon. When hairstyles became simplified, hats and bonnets were built up higher, crowns were enlarged, and brimless toques were in style. For sportswear, a straw sailor hat with low flat crown and wide stiff brim was a popular fashion.

Footwear

See Illustrated Table 14.3, page 401, for some examples of footwear for the period from 1870 to 1900.

Usually stockings matched the color of the dress or shoes. Embroidered and striped patterns were popular. For evening in the 1870s, white silk stockings with colored **clocks** (a small design) were preferred, whereas black became more popular in the 1880s.

For both shoes and boots, pointed toes and medium-high heels predominated. Daytime shoes often matched dresses; evening slippers were of white kid or satin, often with floral or ribbon ornaments at the toe. Less fashionable than shoes, boots were

Illustrated Table 14.2

Selected Hats and Hairstyles for Women: 1870–1900

Hat, 1874, front view

Hat, 1874, side view

"Waterfall" hairstyle, 1876

Hat, 1885

Hat, 1885

Hairstyle, 1888

Hat and hairstyle, 1894

Contemporary fashion plates.

Illustrated Table 14.3

Selected Footwear for Women and Men: 1870–1900

Women's Footwear

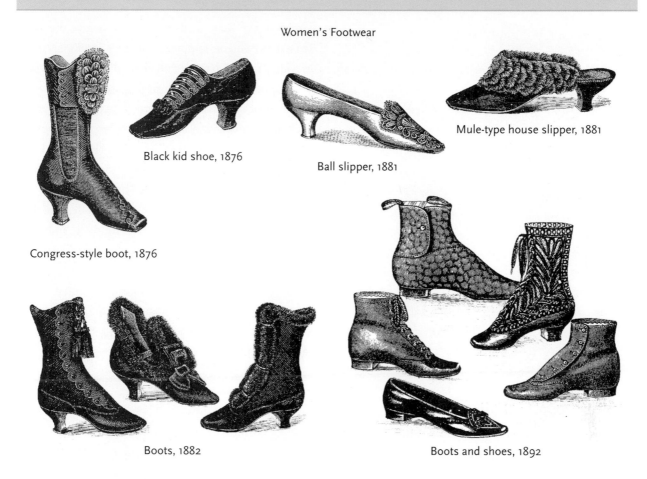

Black kid shoe, 1876

Ball slipper, 1881

Mule-type house slipper, 1881

Congress-style boot, 1876

Boots, 1882

Boots and shoes, 1892

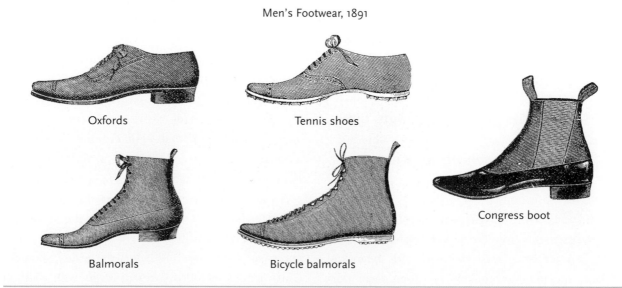

Men's Footwear, 1891

Oxfords

Tennis shoes

Congress boot

Balmorals

Bicycle balmorals

Women's Footwear: Reprinted from *Women's Footwear* by S. I. Blum, ed., 1974, with permission by Dover Publications, Inc.

Men's Footwear: *Jordan Marsh Illustrated Catalog of 1891*. Philadelphia: Athanaeum of Philadelphia.

usually cut to the lower calf, closed with laces, and shaped similarly to shoes. Rubber-soled shoes with canvas or buckskin tops were worn for sports such as tennis and boating; boots, for hiking and skating.

Accessories

See Illustrated Table 14.4 for examples of some popular accessories.

Glove lengths varied with sleeve lengths, longer gloves being worn with shorter sleeves. Evening dress required elbow, or longer, lengths. Although there were some large fur muffs, most were small.

Popular fan styles for evening included folding fans of gauze with painted decorations or large ostrich plumes mounted on tortoise shell or ivory sticks. Parasols were large in size, with ornate handles and long points, and they were trimmed with lace and ribbons.

Boas, which were long, narrow, tubular scarves of feathers or fur, were an important and decorative accessory.

Jewelry

Utilized for evening more than for day, popular items included bracelets, earrings (usually small balls or hoops), necklaces, and jeweled hair ornaments. With daytime dresses, women sometimes wore brooches.

Cosmetics and Grooming

Rouge and "paint" were unacceptable in polite, middle-class society, but face creams, beauty soaps, rice powder, and light scent were used.

COSTUME: THE NINETIES, 1890–1900

Costume Components for Women

Garments

See Illustrated Table 14.1 (pages 394–395) for examples of undergarments from the period 1870–1900.

Most underwear was trimmed with quantities of lace, tucking, embroidery, or other decoration. Drawers, chemises, or combinations comprised the layer of garments worn next to the body. They changed little from those worn during the bustle period.

Although the traditional style of corsets continued in use, a new corset shape was introduced that confined the waist and ended just below the bust. This removed the support that had previously been provided for the bosom and helped make a garment that supported the bust desirable. In an exploration of the history of the brassiere in America, Farrell-Beck and Gau (2002) showed that breast supporters had been patented as early as 1863. They noted that although the early designs were intended to provide a "more comfortable and healthful alternative" (1) to contemporary corsets, they apparently failed to produce the desired fashionable silhouette and none achieved commercial success. By the 1890s, however, women's magazines were carrying advertisements for garments known variously as short stays, bust girdle, bust corset, bust bodice, and strophium (a Latin name for the breast supporters of ancient Rome). These garments were forerunners of the brassiere.

Designed to fill out a deficient figure, "bust improvers" were made of flexible celluloid; others were made of fabric and stuffed with pads of cotton. Caroline Newell, one of the suppliers of bust supporters, used the phrase "All Deficiency of Development Supplied" (Farrell-Beck and Gau, 2002, 1) in advertisements. What had been called corset covers were now known as **camisoles**. It was usual to wear one or two petticoats.

Although vestiges of the bustle remained in pleats or gathers concentrated at the back of the skirt, the silhouette of the 1890s could be described as hourglass shaped. By mid-decade sleeve styles were large and wide at the top for both day and evening. Waists were as small as corsets could make them, and skirts flared out into a bell-like shape (Figures 14.14 and 14.15).

Two-piece dresses were constructed with lined and boned bodices that usually ended at the waist and had round or slightly pointed waistlines. A few had short basques, extending below the waist. Shoulder constructions included yokes or revers with width at the shoulder produced by ruffles or frills (Figure 14.16).

Illustrated Table 14.4

Bustle Period and Nineties Accessories: 1870–1900

New hat styles for men

(a) Homburg, c. 1870s

(b) Deerstalker, c. 1870s

(c) Fedora, c. 1880s

Men's neckwear

(a) Striped knotted necktie, c. 1880s

(b) Ascot, c. 1880s

Jewelry and watches, c. 1870–1890

(a) Brooch at neck and small, hanging earring

(b) Watch that pinned to the dress bodice

(c) Man's pocket watch

Lady's bags

(a) Handbag

(b) Travel bag

Parasol, c. 1876

Lady's embroidered lace fan, c. 1890

Feather boa, 1890

The expansion that had begun in the late 1880s with enlarged sleeve caps continued. Sleeves were still larger by 1893 and had become enormous by 1895. The leg-of-mutton sleeve had a full puff to the elbow, then a fitted sleeve from elbow to wrist or a wide top that narrowed gradually to the wrist. Other sleeves made of softer fabric were full for the length of the arm, ending in a cuff. After 1897 sleeve size generally decreased, and reminders of the larger sleeve styles could be seen in small puffs or epaulettes at the shoulder, the rest of the sleeve being fitted.

Most skirts were gored, fitting smoothly over the hips. They had some back pleating or fullness. The gores flared out to a wide bell shape. Skirts were lined with fabric. Some had bands of linen or buckram around the hem for stiffness. Fashion magazines and costume historians speak of skirts to the floor. However, candid photographs of working women show that for practical purposes, skirts of 3 or 4 inches from the floor were more often worn for work or sports.

The name for blouses, **shirtwaist**, was often shortened to **waists**. Styles ranged from blouses with

FIGURE 14.14 Couple from the 1890s dress for the photographer, she in leg-of-mutton–sleeved bodice and bell-shaped skirt; he in a sack jacket, waistcoat, and matching trousers. His handlebar moustache was a popular fashion in this decade. (Courtesy of Huntington Historical Society, Huntington, NY)

a　　　　　　　　　　b

FIGURE 14.15 Shirtwaists. Young woman of the 1890s (a) wears a decorative lace-trimmed shirtwaist blouse and skirt of brocade. (Courtesy of Huntington Historical Society, Huntington, NY) Simple shirtwaist (b) from 1894, cut like a man's shirt except for the leg-of-mutton sleeves. (Reprinted from *Victorian fashions and costumes from Harper's Bazaar: 1867–1898* by S. Blum [Ed.] with permission by Dover Publications, Inc.)

FIGURE 14.16 Tailor-made costume of 1895 has large, leg-of-mutton sleeves. The bell-shaped skirt would have had some fullness at the back, generally in the form of pleats or gathers. (Author's collection)

sketches of young men and women at the turn of the century—the Gibson girls and the Gibson men—did just that. Young people throughout the United States strove to imitate that look. Revivals of shirtwaists with leg-of-mutton sleeves in the late 1940s were called Gibson Girl blouses.

Tailor-mades (see Figure 14.16) were matching jackets and skirts, worn with a blouse. These were the predominant fashion for wear outside the home. Styles ranged from severely tailored costumes modeled after men's suits to elaborately decorated models with ruffles and lace trimmings. Even the most severely tailored, however, had the enlarged sleeves of the period. Tailors rather than dressmakers made these garments, hence the name.

Evening dresses had low necklines that were either square, round, or V-shaped. After 1893, off-the-shoulder lines were more common. These gowns had full sleeves, ending above or at the elbow, and were usually large and balloon shaped. When daytime sleeves grew smaller (c. 1897), evening dress sleeves also diminished to short, small puffs.

Evening dresses were frequently trained. The shape of skirts was like that of daytime dresses (Figure 14.17).

leg-of-mutton sleeves tailored to look like a man's shirt to styles covered with lace, embroidery, and frills (see Figure 14.15). Shirtwaists were among the first products of the growing American ready-to-wear industry.

Artists can sometimes capture the ideal look for a particular period. Charles Dana Gibson's pen-and-ink

FIGURE 14.17 Art Nouveau designs, such as this one made by the House of Worth in 1898, appeared in many evening gowns of the period between 1890 and 1910. (House of Worth (1858-1956) Evening dress. French. 1898-1900. White silk satin and black silk voided velvet, white silk net, black silk velvet. The Metropolian Museum of Art, Gift of Miss Eva Drexel Dahlgren, 1976 (1976.258.1a, b). Photograph by Sheldan Collins Image copyright © The Metropolitan Museum of Art. Image source: Art Resource, NY)

Outdoor Garments

Capes, many with high puffs at the shoulder to accommodate the large sleeves of dresses, were the most common outdoor garments. Styles included full capes of velvet or plush trimmed with fur or jet beading. Collars were high and standing, or the neck finished in a ruffle. Those coats that were worn could be fitted or full, had large sleeves, and ranged in length from short, hip length to three quarters or floor length. Chesterfield-style and ulster coats remained popular. The terms *sacque* and *dolman* gradually went out of use.

Clothing for Active Sports

Knickers (or *rationals* in England) worn with a fitted jacket were proposed as cycling costume in fashion magazines (Figure 14.18). Some of these knickers were constructed with considerable fullness so that when a lady dismounted from her bicycle they gave the appearance of a full skirt. Other cycling costumes included divided skirts or a skirt worn over knickers and blouses. Many women simply cycled in their shirtwaists and skirts or tailor-mades and maintained a dignified, if somewhat strained, upright position.

Bathing costumes of the nineties were not only no more practical for swimming than those of the bustle period but were perhaps even more cumbersome, because, by following the lines of the dresses, they contained more fabric. As a result, they often had large, puffed sleeves of elbow length, narrow waistlines, and full, bell-shaped skirts ending at about knee length. All this was worn over bloomers of the same length and with dark stockings that came to the knee. A few bathing costumes were cut with knickerbockers instead of skirts, but even these were very full.

Hair and Headdress

See Illustrated Table 14.2 (page 400) for some examples of hairstyles and headdress for the period from 1870 to 1900.

Many women wore their hair in a curled fringe at the front and twisted and arranged the rest of the hair in a coil or curl at the top. The Gibson Girl look favored an arrangement with deep, soft waves around the face. Hair was built up at the front in a pompadour. The ears were uncovered.

FIGURE 14.18 Velveteen bicycling costume of 1894. Sleeves are of leg-of-mutton type, fashionable for women's dress of the time. The fashion magazine caption used the term *turkish trousers*, not *bloomers*, in describing the garment. (S. Blum, ed., 1974. *Victorian Fashions and Costumes from Harper's Bazaar: 1867-1898.* New York: Dover.)

Now worn only outdoors, hats were small to medium in size; some had no brim. Trimming tended upward, with lace, feathers, and ribbons as the favored trims. For sportswear or work, women wore men's styles, including the fedora and the straw boater. Face veils were popular. For evening, hair decorations such as feathers, combs, and jeweled ornaments were worn.

Footwear

See Illustrated Table 14.3 (page 401) for some examples of footwear for the period from 1870 to 1900.

For daytime, stockings were made of cotton; for evening, black or colored silk. Shoes generally had slightly rounded toes, medium-high heels. Boots either laced or buttoned to close.

Accessories

Gloves were worn short during the day; long in the evening. Hand-carried accessories changed little from those of the bustle period. Boas remained popular.

Jewelry

The influence of Art Nouveau design was strong in many items of jewelry. Watches that pinned to the dress were a fashionable accessory item.

Cosmetics

Although only face powder and face creams were acceptable cosmetic items, a little tinting was sometimes added to these materials.

Costume Components for Men

Garments

See Illustrated Table 14.1 (pages 394–395) for examples of undergarments from the period 1870 to 1900.

Men's drawers were usually made of wool, although cotton knits were worn in the summer. They buttoned in front and had a drawstring at the back that could adjust the fit around the waist. When worn under trousers, drawers ended at the ankle, but those worn under knickers for sportswear were knee length.

Undervests, also called undershirts, were usually made of wool, although more expensive silk versions were also available. Hip length and with long sleeves, they buttoned in front.

Men also could purchase combinations or **union suits** that united drawers and undervests into one garment. See Figure 14.19 for examples of most of the garments worn by men of the 1890s.

Frock coats remained fashionable until the late 1890s when they were supplanted for formal daytime wear by morning coats. Morning coats curved back from well above the waist, thereby displaying the lower part of the waistcoat. Lounge coats or sack coats continued to gain in popularity (see Figure 14.14).

FIGURE 14.19 Men of 1899 in a wide variety of suits and coats. At upper left, men in business suits with sack jackets. At upper right, men dressed for evening in tailcoats and formal overcoats. At lower right, somewhat more formal business suits are cut with a waistline seam. Shorter outdoor jackets are worn with either top hat or a derby. Lower left, men wear (left to right) a Chesterfield coat, a double-breasted business suit, a frock-style overcoat, and a cutaway coat. (Library of Congress Prints and Photographs Division Washington, D.C. 20540 USA http://hdl.loc.gov/loc.pnp/pp.print)

These had no waist seam. They were cut straight or slightly curved in front and could be either single or double breasted. Reefers, similar in cut, were always square and the front double breasted, with slightly larger lapels and collar than the sack jacket. After 1890, reefers went out of use as suit jackets; they were chiefly worn as overcoats. Another popular style was the **Norfolk jacket**, a belted sport jacket.

At this period trousers were straight and fairly narrow, with daytime trousers cut slightly wider than those for evening. Knickerbockers were worn for golf, hiking, tennis, and shooting, together with knee-length stockings and sturdy shoes or high boots (gaiters).

Coats tended to button high in the 1870s and early 1880s; therefore, waistcoats became less important. Often they were made of the same fabric as suits. When patterned, waistcoats were made from plaids, checks, and woven figures. By the 1890s, coats were often worn open, and as waistcoats had now become more visible, some were made from quite decorative fabrics.

Shirts for formal daytime wear had stiff, starched shirt fronts, which after 1870 were plain rather than pleated. Just how much of the shirt front was visible through the coat front opening varied from year to year. Standing stiff collars gradually grew taller, the tallest being close to 3 inches high in the 1890s. Removable, starched collars and cuffs, common by the 1880s, came in a variety of shapes ranging from straight collars to those that folded over. Bow ties were popular. Longer neckties were knotted, the ends often held in place with a decorative tie stud. Colored shirts appeared in the 1890s, most of them striped. Some had plain white collars.

Evening dress for men consisted of tailcoats, which had tails about knee length that were slightly narrower at the bottom than at the top. In the 1880s the cut of the dress tailcoat altered somewhat, and a continuous, rolled collar faced in satin or some other silk fabric replaced the notched collar.

Evening waistcoats most often matched the rest of the suit and were usually double breasted. Formal shirts were white, generally plain, with two studs at the front. After 1889, some dress shirt fronts were pleated. Closely fitted collars and narrow bow ties were the fashionable evening wear. Fairly narrow trousers matched coats in color and generally had bands of braid covering the outer, side seams.

In the 1880s, a dress version of the sack suit jacket was introduced. It was called a *tuxedo* (after its origin in Tuxedo, New York) in the United States and a *dinner jacket* in England.

Outdoor Garments

To follow fashion in outdoor wear, men had to pay attention to the length of these garments. They were shorter in the 1870s, longer in the 1880s, and still longer in the 1890s. Major styles were Chesterfield or topcoats cut in frock coat styles (see Figure 14.19). The **Inverness cape** was a garment with full cape covering the shoulders and arms or a cape in front that fitted into the armscye in the back so that from the front the cape was visible but from the back the coat looked like a conventional overcoat with full sleeves. The **ulster**, a long, almost ankle-length coat, had a full or half belt and sometimes a detachable hood or cape.

Hair and Headdress

Generally men cut their hair short and used a side or, less often, center part. Mustaches were popular, worn with side whiskers or a beard, although during this time the trend moved toward clean-shaven faces with mustaches.

Most hat styles had been seen in earlier periods. Top hats were the favored dress hat and folding top hats were used for the opera or theater. Evening top hats were black, silk plush. Light gray, fawn, and white were all used in the daytime. Other styles included bowlers or derbies, **fedoras** (low, soft hats, with the crown creased front to back), **homburgs** (a variant of the fedora made popular by the Prince of Wales), and a variety of caps worn for sports.

Straw boaters, made of shellacked straw, were worn for sports. The **deerstalker cap** was made famous through the illustrations of Conan Doyle's Sherlock Holmes stories (see Illustrated Table 14.4, page 403).

Footwear

See Illustrated Table 14.3 (page 401) for some examples of footwear for the period from 1870 to 1900.

Patent leather shoes were used with both day and evening dress. They laced up the front. Elastic-sided shoes, sturdy high shoes for work or hunting, oxfords, and gymnastic shoes of canvas or calf with rubber soles were all popular styles.

Accessories

Accessories for men included such items as gloves and walking sticks.

Jewelry

It was not considered masculine for men to wear jewelry except for such things as tie pins, watches, shirt studs, and cuff links.

COSTUME FOR CHILDREN

The basic approach to dressing children remained constant throughout the 19th century. Infants and young children of both sexes were dressed alike.

Costume Components for Girls

Girls' dresses were like those of adult women in silhouette, but were shorter in length. As a result, early in the bustle period they had large bustle constructions. About 1880, when the adult cuirass style was worn, girls had dresses cut straight from shoulder to hem with a belt located just a few inches above the hemline, at the knee (Figure 14.20). When bustles enlarged again, young girls wore bustles. In the 1890s large leg-of-mutton sleeves also appeared in girls' dresses (Figure 14.21). Other style features included Russian blouses, scotch plaid costumes, smocked dresses, pinafores, and sailor dresses (Figure 14.22).

Costume Components for Boys

After age 5 or so, boys no longer wore skirts but changed to trousers or knickers. By 1890, the age of breeching had dropped to about age 3 (Paoletti, 1983).

FIGURE 14.20 Marthe Bernard, 1879, in a portrait painted by Impressionist painter Auguste Renoir, wears a black velvet dress with lace color and cuffs and the low-set waistline typical of girls' dresses of this period. A large bow at the back echoes the back fullness commonly found in adult women's dresses. (Erich Lessing/Art Resource, NY)

Boys' knickers of the 1870s became more fitted, resembling 18th-century knee breeches. In the 1880s they were like short trousers ending at the knee (Figure 14.23).

Suit styles for boys included Eton suits, like those of the crinoline period, sailor suits (see Figure 15.6, page 430), and tunic suits with a narrower skirt and slightly lower waistline than earlier styles.

Boys wore reefers, cut like those for men; blazers, made of striped or plain-colored flannel, loosely fitted, with patch pockets, and generally worn for sports; and Norfolk jackets, especially with knickers. Shirts usually had stiff, high collars. Boys wore smaller versions of adult men's outerwear.

FIGURE 14.21 Nez Perce Native American girls, c. 1900, wear dresses with sleeves that resemble women's leg-of-mutton sleeves. (Courtesy of Idaho State Historical Society. Photo 63.221.317 by E. Jane Gay)

FIGURE 14.22 Village children, painted in 1890 by John Singer Sargent, wear pinafores over their dresses, a typical way to assure that their clothing is not soiled. (Yale University Art Gallery/Art Resource, NY)

Costume for Boys and Girls

Table 14.1 summarizes typical stages in the acquisition of adult clothing by children in the late 19th century.

Influences from Aesthetic Dress

The aesthetic movement influenced children's clothing. **Kate Greenaway styles** (based on illustrations by Kate Greenaway, an aesthetic movement illustrator of children's books who showed little girls in dresses derived from Empire styles) became popular and were imitated in girls' dresses for the 1880s and 1890s. Kate Greenaway styles have been revived periodically ever since for children and have influenced women's styles as well. **Little Lord Fauntleroy suits** consisted of a velvet tunic, ending slightly below the waist; tight knickerbockers; a wide sash; and a wide, white lace collar. This outfit was based on clothing worn by the hero of the children's book of the same name (see Figure 14.23). The similarity of this costume to that worn by Oscar Wilde was no coincidence. According to Cunnington and Beard (1972), the author of *Little Lord Fauntleroy* was influenced by the comments of Wilde on his trip to the United States in 1882, when he declared that the Cavalier dress on which he based his "aesthetic" costume was the most artistic male dress ever known. With this costume some boys wore long, curling locks. Many children's books of the time characterized the wearers of the Fauntleroy costume as "mama's boys," while boys forced to wear the costume were depicted as hating every moment and longing for the day when the barber would relieve them of these obnoxious curls. The truth is that relatively few boys actually wore Little Lord Fauntleroy suits.

Hair and Headdress

Boys wore their hair slightly longer until they were out of skirts; afterwards their hair was cut short like adult men's. Girls' hair was long and natural waves were encouraged. Large bows were a popular hair ornament. Boys wore caps. Both boys and girls wore sailor hats and other styles modeled on adults' hats.

TABLE 14.1 Typical Stages in the Acquisition of Adult Clothing in the Late 19th Century

STAGE	BOYS	GIRLS
infant	long white dresses	long white dresses
toddler	short dresses	short dresses
small child	dresses or tunic suits	short dresses
school-age child	suit with short trousers	somewhat longer dresses
adolescent	suit with long trousers; no adult formal wear	somewhat longer dresses; no revealing formal evening dresses
adult	formal wear permitted	hair worn up; dresses to ankle; décolletage for formal evening dress

Note: A survey of child-care manuals, etiquette books, and advice. Reprinted from Paoletti, J. (1983). Clothes make the boy. *Dress, 9*(1), 19.

FIGURE 14.23 Boy dressed in Little Lord Fauntleroy suit. Although the suit is made from wool rather than velvet, the wide lace collar and cuffs, knickers, bow at the neck, and long hair are typical of the style. (Author's collection)

MOURNING COSTUME: 1850–1900

Wearing special dress that signifies bereavement is not unique to any period. However, social custom in the second half of the 19th century seemed to place far greater emphasis on conforming to a rigid and far-reaching code of etiquette for mourning than in most previous or subsequent periods. Taylor (1983), in an extended study of mourning costume and customs, indicated that several factors were influential in the increased emphasis on appropriate mourning costume in the 19th century.

One factor was the more widespread imitation of royal and upper class behavior and dress by the middle class. When Prince Albert, husband of Queen Victoria, died in 1861, the queen put on mourning not only for the requisite period but for the rest of her life. In so doing, she set a highly visible example for others to follow. Another important influence was the widespread availability of fashion magazines, which frequently published articles about proper mourning etiquette and reported on the mourning dress of famous people.

Custom not only prescribed colors and fabrics for mourning but established stages and gradations of mourning. Although men were not required to do much more than wear a black armband, widows had to wear deep mourning for a year and a day. Deepest or first mourning consisted of black crape-covered dresses, black accessories, and even, in some cases, black underwear. **Mourning crape** was a black, silk fabric with a crinkled or uneven surface texture. The preferred modern spelling for similar fabrics in various colors is *crepe*; however, when used for

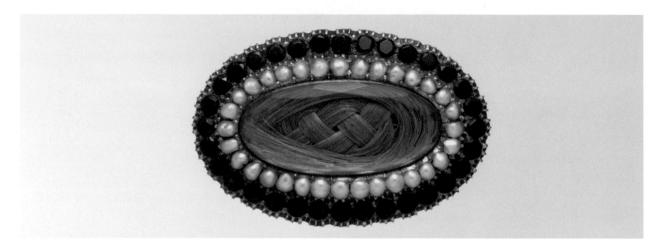

FIGURE 14.24 The bereaved Victorian might wear special jewelry that included the hair of the loved one. Victorian mourning dress was rigidly prescribed. (Detail: Image copyright © The Metropolitan Museum of Art. Image source: Art Resource, NY)

mourning in the 19th century, it was spelled *crape*. Widows wore second mourning for 21 months (black with crape trimming) and ordinary mourning (in which crape could be omitted altogether and black clothing trimmed in black was worn) for at least 3 months (Figure 14.24). Even children wore black or white trimmed in black.

After the first decade of the 20th century, the rigid etiquette surrounding mourning diminished. Taylor (1983, 266–267) explained:

It was the terrible slaughter of the First World War that undoubtedly caused the major breakdown in funeral and mourning etiquette. . . . As the war continued the survivors had somehow to face up to the loss of almost a whole generation of young men and the creation of a new army—this one of widows and fatherless children. . . . The sight of millions of women of all ages shrouded in crape would have been too much to bear.

Summary

Themes

Important themes of the late 19th century include PRODUCTION AND ACQUISITION OF TEXTILES AND APPAREL AND TECHNOLOGY. The budding American women's ready-to-wear industry, born in the last decades of the 19th century as a result of socioeconomic changes and technological advances in the United States, was beginning to be a factor in women's fashion. It made possible the mass production and distribution of fashionable items such as the shirtwaist.

The more rapid movement of fashion changes for women, the more static nature of styles for men, and the transformation of certain segments of the ready-to-wear industry into a fashion industry foreshadowed important trends that would continue in the 20th century.

FASHION, a constant theme since the Middle Ages, stands out as styles for women in the years between 1870 and 1900 went through a more rapid series of changes than did styles of any preceding period of comparable length. None of the distinct phases of costume can be said to have lasted even ten years. These changes were gradual, progressing year by year as the silhouette changed from emphasizing the draped bustle, narrowing to the slim cuirass bodice with both decorative detailing and training at the

Visual Summary Table

Bustle and Nineties

Man: 1870–1900
Shirts and neckties, vests, coats, and trousers. Coat alternatives were frock coats, morning coats, sack coats, and Norfolk jackets.

Man: 1870–1900
The tuxedo, an evening suit with a sack jacket, appeared in the 1880s.

Woman: 1870–1878
Mostly two-piece dresses, closely fitted bodices, sleeves set in at the shoulder. Fullness concentrated at the back of the skirt falls in ruffles and draperies supported by a bustle.

Woman: 1878–1883
The bustle diminishes and skirt fullness drops toward the floor. Bodices lengthen, fitting smoothly over the hip, then becoming wider below the knee.

Woman: 1883–1890
The bustle returns as a shelflike, rigid form at the back. Skirts are rarely trained. Details include high, standing collars and long, fitted sleeves for daytime.

Woman: 1890–1900
A few pleats at the back of the skirt replace bustles. Dresses are hourglass shaped, with very large sleeves, small waistlines, and skirts shaped like an inverted cone.

back, and returning to back fullness again in the rigid structure of yet another sort of bustle. When the bustle finally subsided, it was superseded by the hourglass silhouette of the 1890s.

Men's costume, contrariwise, showed little change in silhouette. The items of a man's wardrobe remained constant and varied little from year to year, except in details such as the length of coats or the width of trousers or lapels.

The theme of CHANGES IN SOCIAL BEHAVIOR is also reflected in women's apparel. The movement of more women into the workplace was evident in such practical styles as tailor-mades and shirtwaists. Bicycling bloomers, bathing costumes, and gymnastic clothing demonstrated that women were beginning to feel free to participate in active sports.

As has been true so often before, RELATIONSHIPS BETWEEN COSTUME AND DEVELOPMENTS IN THE FINE AND APPLIED ARTS are evident. Not only do the enormously elaborate bustle-period dresses find a parallel in the Victorian parlors with their wealth of pattern and knickknacks, but costume also shares the tendency of furniture and architecture to revive styles of the past. As new artistic movements emerged, clothing styles reflected these as well. Those who shared this artistic philosophy adopted aesthetic dress. And as the century ended, Art Nouveau motifs could be seen not only in fabrics, jewelry, and accessories but also in a sinuous, S-shaped silhouette that was developing in women's dress.

LEGACIES OF BUSTLE AND NINETIES COSTUME STYLES

Although the bustle in its fullest form has not truly returned since 1890, the focus of fullness at the back of women's skirts is an idea that comes and goes (see Modern Influences). It most frequently appears in evening or wedding gowns. The figure-revealing styles of the 1990s even produced their own version of the bustle, a padded girdle called the *wonderbutt* (see Illustrated Table 19.1, page 627).

Norfolk jackets, with their distinctive cut, are revived from time to time. Their most recent revival in men's dress was in the late 1960s and 1970s.

Although the leg-of-mutton sleeves of the nineties show remarkable similarities to sleeve styles of the 1830s, their incorporation into shirtwaist blouses was something new. Styles derived from shirtwaist blouses, often called the *Gibson Girl* look, have experienced revivals. Around 1947 they became a fad for adolescents and returned again, with less sleeve fullness, in blouses of the latter part of the 1980s.

MODERN INFLUENCES

Past styles constantly undergo revivals. The bustle dress is one that reappears, often for evening or special occasions. The red-carpet entrance to film award ceremonies is one of the places where dramatic designs are often seen. This dress was photographed at the Venice Film Festival in 2011. The actress is Fumi Nicado, and her dress with its pronounced bustle was made by **Film Magic.** (Danny Martindale/FilmMagic)

REFERENCES

Cunnington, C. W., & Beard, C. (1972). *A dictionary of English costume 900–1900*. London, UK: Adam and Charles Black.

Farrell-Beck, J., & Gau, C. (2002). *Uplift. The bra in America*. Philadelphia, PA: University of Pennsylvania Press.

Groom, G. (2012). *Impressionism, fashion, & modernity*. Chicago, IL: The Art Institute of Chicago.

Kidwell, C. B., & Christman, M. C. (1974). *Suiting everyone*. Washington, DC: The Smithsonian Institution Press.

Paoletti, J. (1983). Clothes make the boy, 1860–1910. *Dress*, 9(1), 16–20.

Taylor, L. (1983). *Mourning dress: A costume and social history*. London, UK: George Allen and Unwin.

Warner, P. C. (1992, November). The thin ideal: A matter of proportion and history. *ITAA Proceedings*. Annual conference conducted at the meeting of International Textile and Apparel Association, Monument, CO.

Warner, P. C. (1993). The gym suit: Freedom at last. In P. A. Cunningham & S. V. Lab (Eds.), *Dress in American popular culture*. Bowling Green, OH: Bowling Green State University, Popular Press.

PART SIX

From the Twentieth to the Twenty-first Century

The beginning of the 20th century was, for many, almost a magical period. It seemed to mark a turning point—a new era—and it was punctuated by special celebrations, expositions, pronouncements by public officials, and a rash of predictions about what the world would be like by the turn of the next century. And yet, had people been able to look into the future to see the events of the next 100 years, it is likely they would have chosen 1914 rather than 1900 as the beginning of a new era since World War I so radically changed life.

In 1914 World War I began, and nothing ever seemed the same again. For Americans especially, World War I marked the beginning of an expanded role in international politics and economics from which the country, try as it might, could never pull back.

In the 1920s, general prosperity was the norm for most Americans, the single largest exception being farmers. The country entered a period of reaction to the war that brought with it a revolution on the part of the young against traditional mores and values. Technology expanded, the buying power of individuals increased, and life for most people, though more frenetic, was marked by a higher standard of material comfort than ever before.

When the 1929 stock market crash ushered in the Great Depression of the 1930s, all this changed. Not only the farmers but also large numbers of middle-class Americans experienced varying degrees of poverty. The impact of the Depression was worldwide. The stage was slowly set for another international conflict when fascist dictator Benito Mussolini rose to power in Italy in the 1920s, and Adolf Hitler, in Germany, in the 1930s. War began in 1939 when Germany invaded Poland. The United States stayed out of World War II until the Japanese bombed Pearl Harbor in 1941.

The end of the war in 1945 was marked by yet another 20th-century milestone, the development of atomic power. The United States emerged from the war as a "super power," along with the Soviet Union. The older European powers that had exercised western world leadership for so many centuries had been devastated by the war and had to begin to rebuild. At the Yalta Conference in February 1945, the leaders of Britain, Russia, and the United States outlined preliminary proposals for an international association to replace the League of Nations. The United Nations came into being on October 24, 1945.

The postwar period was marked politically by the Cold War between the Soviet Union and the United States and economically by a period of prosperity. In the United States, World War II veterans flooded college and university campuses, married or returned to married life, produced a bumper crop of babies, and moved to the suburbs in large numbers. The Korean War (1950–1953) disturbed the return to peacetime life for some Americans.

The Space Age began in 1957 when the Russians announced that they had launched the first Earth-orbiting satellite. Americans made intense efforts to catch up. When John F. Kennedy was elected president in 1960, he vowed that Americans would reach the moon by 1970, and indeed the first manned moon landing took place on July 20, 1969.

The 1960s in the United States was a decade of protest and demonstrations. The civil rights movement pressed its demands for racial equality through passive resistance and mass demonstrations in the early 1960s. When students of the late 1960s first opposed the escalating war in Vietnam, they borrowed these same tactics.

In the 1970s the U.S. government resumed diplomatic relations with China, and an American president resigned from office. By the 1980s a new wave of immigration and the computer revolution changed American life.

The European Economic Community continued to grow and prosper in the 1970s and into the 1980s. In an effort to integrate Europe after World War II, a number of European countries formed the European Union by treaty in 1992. It was part of an effort to integrate Europe.

The Soviet Union maintained its control over eastern Europe until the strain of the Cold War undermined the Soviet economy and forced the Soviet system to collapse. While the Soviet economy was deteriorating, the economies of Asian countries that followed the Japanese model were booming. That boom ended when the Japanese economy went into a severe decline in the last decade of the 20th century.

As the 21st century approached, many feared that computers, which had taken on a great many routine functions, would suddenly fail, causing malfunctions in a host of essential services. The problems predicted by the Y2k scare, as it was called, never happened, and the world passed easily into a new millennium.

The years after 2000 brought terrorist attacks to the United States and American-led wars in Afghanistan and Iraq. The Great Recession and enhanced communications via the Internet brought changes to production and consumption practices. Visible differences between 1900 and 2014 were many, but changes in attitudes and values were even more dramatic.

ART AND COSTUME

With the advent of photography, contemporary clothing was no longer depicted only by drawings, paintings, and sculpture. Indeed, in the century following advances in photography, artists themselves moved away from representing photographic-like reality and moved gradually from impressionist representations of the world toward greater abstraction. In earlier centuries the work of artists showed how clothing was worn, and at the same time the lines, proportions, and decoration of clothing embodied the artistic spirit or zeitgeist of the times. In the 20th century, much of the art does not inform us about clothing, but we can still see many connections between the visual arts and dress in areas such as line and proportion and in the design of textiles. These parallels are sometimes quite obvious, as in the Art Nouveau and Art Deco periods (Figure VI.1), and at other times more subtle, tenuous, or even superficial.

Whether clothing can be considered an art has been hotly debated. In earlier centuries this question was not even considered. It arose only after the establishment of the haute couture and the elevation of the fashion designer to the role of a creative genius shaping new and original styles. If we accept the idea of the designer as an artist working in the medium of clothing, then it is not surprising to find that, like other artists of any period, the designer will be sensitive to the zeitgeist—the spirit of the age—and that the creations of the designer will reflect that period. The designer however, must work within the constraints of what is wearable. Designers often turn to current art, events, and media for design ideas, and reflections of all frequently appear in their creations.

GLOBALIZATION OF FASHION

By 1900 mass production of some kinds of clothing had begun, especially in the United States. The haute couture provided original styles that were often copied by home sewers, dressmakers, and, gradually, as mass production increased, by manufacturers of women's dress. Though American designers gained some recognition in the years before and after World War I, they did not become very widely known or publicized by the fashion and

FIGURE VI.1 Art Nouveau influenced art, architecture, interior design, architecture, textiles, and jewelry. The maker of this woman's pin, René Lalique, was one of the best known French Art Nouveau artists. (© The Calouste Gulbenkian Foundation/Scala/ Art Resource, NY.)

popular press until World War II. At this point, the German occupation of Paris closed off the haute couture to the countries fighting Germany and its allies.

A number of design centers emerged in countries around the world after the war. The couture had to share the spotlight with emerging, upscale, ready-to-wear designers and customers. Beginning in the 1970s and accelerating in the 1980s and after, the production of clothing tended to move from more affluent countries to low-wage countries. Western fashion sometimes gained a foothold in areas where local ethnic dress had formerly predominated. Sometimes ethnic styles and western fashions merged or controversy grew out of a desire of immigrants to maintain dress practices of their ethnic or religious backgrounds.

NEW MEDIA DEPICTIONS OF DRESS

Three additional media sources emerged in the 20th century: motion pictures, television, and the Internet. By the 1920s motion pictures were playing in both urban and rural areas. When leading actors and actresses wore contemporary clothing, they were seen by millions of individuals. Although some trends began after they were seen "in the movies," it is not entirely clear whether, as a general rule, the styles shown in films followed current trends or initiated them (Figure VI.2). If the costume designer for a film was using costume to delineate a character, the clothing did not necessarily simply reproduce a current style.

Styles shown in films set in earlier historic periods may not be trustworthy. Even when garments are reasonably authentic, makeup and hairstyles often bear little resemblance to the styles of the historic period depicted but rather reflect the period in which

the film was actually made. When a famous actress appears in a period film, she may have her own designer whose task it is to set off the star's physical charms rather than to produce authentic costumes.

As a record of contemporary costume, TV dramas have some of the same problems as motion pictures. However, costume designers for shows such as soap operas generally selected costumes from styles available in stores or from manufacturers. Any source of information about costume taken from TV dramas or motion pictures should be evaluated carefully. Insofar as possible, one should ascertain whether the clothing was designed and intended to serve a specific dramatic purpose or purchased from ready-to-wear sources.

On the other hand, once the motion picture camera was available to the press, many actual events were filmed, and these accurately depict the clothing being worn by real people. Such footage was seen in newsreel films, and a great deal of early film material has been utilized in documentary motion pictures. With the advent of television after World War II, the amount of film and video material increased dramatically.

Because of the prevalence of the Internet, future generations studying dress history should have no difficulty determining what was worn in public in the 20th century and beyond. Designer websites, fashion blogs, and social media offer countless research potential. However, these sites may also spread myths, as information and images are often reused without accuracy and attribution. Future dress history scholars would be wise to continue to draw from a wide range of primary and secondary sources in researching the past.

FIGURE VI.2 Stage and screen star Fred Astaire preferred tailored looks and was often on best-dressed lists. (John Meek/The Art Archive at Art Resource, NY)

	1900	1901	1903	1905	1909
FASHION AND TEXTILES	International Ladies Garment Workers Union founded				
POLITICS AND CONFLICTS		Queen Victoria dies; Edward VII assumes the throne			
DECORATIVE AND FINE ARTS	*Exposition Universelle* held in Paris; couturiers display their designs	First Paris exhibit by Pablo Picasso	*The Great Train Robbery*, first feature film, released		The Russian ballet company Ballet Russes appears in Paris
ECONOMICS AND TRADE				Henry Ford makes first Model T automobile	
TECHNOLOGY AND IDEAS			First successful flight by Orville and Wilbur Wright at Kitty Hawk, NC	Einstein formulates the theory of relativity	
RELIGION AND SOCIETY	Americans depend more and more on manufactured goods, such as clothing bought from department stores				

CHAPTER FIFTEEN

The Edwardian Period and World War I

1900–1920

1910	1911	1912	1913	1914	1917	1919
Women's Wear Daily begins publication	Fire in Triangle Shirtwaist Co., New York	Poiret, designer of the "lampshade effect," uses hobble skirts in costumes				
	Woodrow Wilson elected U.S. president			Outbreak of WWI; the United States enters the war in 1917; war ends in 1918	Russian revolution overthrows czarist government	
Vernon and Irene Castle's success as a dance team helps launch a dance craze in the United States	Cubists exhibit in *Salon des Indépendants* in Paris					The Bauhaus is established as a center for contemporary design in Germany
				World War I impacts the availability of colors and certain fabrics for clothing		
			G. Sundbäck invents the slide fastener— later called the *zipper*			
				The use of mourning dress lessened due to the number of casualties from WWI		

Innovative designers such as Paul Poiret and Mariano Fortuny established themselves as fashion leaders in the haute couture. Women, now much more fully engaged in the work world and outside the home, fought for the right to vote; their efforts were crowned with success in the United States at the end of the second decade. Technological advances had made mass production of clothing possible, and ready-to-wear could be bought in large department stores or by mail order. The automobile industry boomed. Peace was shattered when World War I erupted in Europe in 1914. The United States entered in 1917, and the fighting continued until near the end of 1918.

HISTORICAL BACKGROUND

From 1900 to 1920, many societal, political, and technological changes occurred that dramatically altered life for many people. Innovations such as the telephone and cable cars and trolleys made communication and travel easier. With enhanced interest and access to college and university education, and increased variety and complexity of jobs, more people needed simpler, easier to acquire clothing. By the beginning of the 20th century, ready-to-wear clothing, offered in a variety of styles, quantities, and prices, was available in almost all markets. Ready-to-wear clothing mass produced by garment manufacturers transformed clothing "made for somebody" to clothing "made for anybody" to clothing "made for everybody" (Kidwell & Christman, 1974, 75–77). The proliferation of fashion magazines and the flourishing of steam and cruise lines would spread fashion ideas more quickly than ever before (Leach, 1993). Marketing and advertising of fashion, along with increased numbers of both small and large companies to produce garments, would also intensify the pace of fashion change (Leach, 1993). World War I, known then as the Great War, would have lasting impact even on our lives today. Related to dress and clothing, these influences include innovations in plastic surgery, mass-produced prosthetics, and the sweater, trench coat, and wristwatch.

The United States

Writers have called the years preceding World War I in America "the good years," "the confident years," "the age of optimism," "the innocent years," and even "the cocksure era." These terms reflect a sense of well-being that seemed to pervade the country.

The total population of the United States in 1900 was something over 76 million, 40 percent of whom lived in urban areas. Only 41 million of these Americans were native born, and almost half a million new immigrants entered the country each year. There were 45 states: New York had the largest in population; Nevada, the smallest.

The country was coming to depend more and more on a host of useful devices. The telephone, the typewriter, the self-binding harvester, and the sewing machine were commonplace. Electricity was installed in many American homes. By 1900, 8,000 automobiles were registered in the United States.

At the drugstore soda fountain, ice cream sodas were a dime, and orangeade was a nickel. Beef was $0.10 a pound, and spring chicken, $0.07 a pound. Ladies could buy a tailor-made suit at the department store for $10.00 and a pair of shoes for $1.50. At the same time, the average wage was $12.00 a week, or $0.22 an hour. Five percent of the population was unemployed; almost 11 percent were illiterate.

The Wright brothers made the first successful flight in 1903 (Figure 15.1). In the same year, a 12-minute movie, *The Great Train Robbery*, was released. Movies as well as movie stars helped promote clothing. Actresses such as Mary Pickford and Annette Kellermann and dancers Vernon and Irene Castle helped spread fashion information and even create style trends (Figure 15.2). The influence of the stars paved the way for fan magazines.

Great Britain and France at the Turn of the Century

The accession of Edward VII to the throne of the British Empire in 1901, after the almost 70-year reign of his mother, Queen Victoria, raised in some British the hope for a fresh approach in politics. When Edward

FIGURE 15.1 A 1908 illustration from *Le Petit Journal*, Paris, August 30, 1908, depicting Wilbur Wright's first flight in Europe. The invention of flight opened the doors to the commercial and military potential of aviation, commercial travel, and artistic expression, with flight motifs appearing on jewelry, games, postcards, and in cartoons. (HIP/Art Resource, NY)

FIGURE 15.2 For dancing with her partner Vernon, Irene Castle adapted her clothes by shortening them and using soft, flowing fabrics. She epitomized the vogue for short hair and clothes that did not restrict movement well before these looks were popular. (© CORBIS)

became king, Britain was involved in the Boer War in South Africa, and the war dragged on another year.

Edward was a genial and worldly man with a wide range of interests. While Prince of Wales, he displayed an especially keen interest in women and led such an active social life that his lifestyle earned the disapproval of the queen. One of the most popular cartoons of the era showed a rotund Prince of Wales standing in the corner while the queen scolded him.

Edward's name is generally applied to the first decade of the century—the Edwardian period. He brought to the English throne an emphasis on social life and fashion that had been absent during the long years of Victoria's widowhood.

In France, in the period from 1900 to just before World War I, a political system emerged that permitted a high degree of individual freedom. A remarkable number of creative artists and scientists were active

at the time. Important authors include Zola, de Maupassant, Anatole France, Verlaine, and Mallarmé. Monet, Manet, Renoir, Degas, Cezanne, and Gauguin are among the important painters of the era. The 1911 exhibition of Cubism in the *Salon des Indépendants* in Paris caused a scandal and brought the art form to the attention of the general public (Figure 15.3). Notable musical composers include Massenet, Saint-Saëns, Bizet, Debussy, and Ravel. In science, the names of Pierre and Marie Curie and Louis Pasteur stand out.

WORLD WAR I

Events that led to the beginning of World War I developed rapidly and unexpectedly. The major European powers confronted each other in two heavily armed alliance systems. Germany feared encirclement

FIGURE 15.3 Cubist artists, such as Pablo Picasso, worked with and from differing perspectives to transform otherwise complex forms into simpler geometric shapes and abstractions. Artists such as Sonia Delaunay created bold geometric Cubist shapes and patterns in textile designs. (© Harvard Art Museum/Art Resource, NY. © 2014 Estate of Pablo Picasso/ Artists Rights Society (ARS), New York)

by hostile powers. However, because of Germany's rise to power, other nations feared German domination of Europe. Indeed, some German leaders dreamed of such a goal.

The assassination of Archduke Franz Ferdinand, heir apparent to the Austro-Hungarian throne, provided the spark for war. The Austro-Hungarian government, convinced of Serbian responsibility for the assassination, used the assassination as an excuse to declare war on Serbia. After Russia refused to stop mobilizing in defense of Serbia, Germany declared war on Russia and 2 days later Germany declared war on France, Russia's ally. Germany took these actions because the war plan required attacking first France and then Russia. To attack France, German armies marched through Belgium, whose neutrality had been guaranteed by the European powers. Consequently, Britain entered the war as an ally of France and Russia in defense of Belgium.

To Americans, the war was far away. The average man and woman on the street, though likely to sympathize with the French and British and aghast at "the rape of Belgium," or the invasion and occupation of neutral Belgium by the Germans, thought the United States was well out of it. But as the war dragged on, American sentiment changed, and on April 2, 1917, President Woodrow Wilson called for a declaration of war against Germany.

When the fighting stopped on November 11, 1918, more than 10 million soldiers had been killed, and more than 20 million wounded. Three great empires had collapsed. Western civilization had been forever changed.

The Effect of the War on Fashions

The war influenced styles of the period in Europe and America from 1914 to 1918 in a number of ways. The most obvious of these was in a move by women into more comfortable, practical clothes required for their more active participation in the variety of jobs that they had taken over for men away at war. The prevailing dress during World War I had a relatively short skirt, several inches above the ankles. The skirt was fairly wide around the hem, a distinct change from the hobble skirt that had been the rage about 1912. The fit through the body was comfortable. Military influences were evident in the cut of some jackets and coats that followed the lines of officers' tunics (see Figure 15.19).

The war also affected colors and fabrics. Wool was in short supply, because it was diverted to the manufacture of uniforms for fighting men. The scarcity of chemicals used for certain dyestuffs restricted somewhat the use of dark colors. Contemporary Comments 15.1 describes the impact of fabric shortages.

After the war, some of the clothing worn by soldiers passed into use by the general public. Sweaters were issued to soldiers, and the men who had become used to wearing these comfortable garments adopted them for general sportswear. For warmth, the army issued a sleeveless vestlike garment to wear under the uniform. After the war, these were sold as army surplus. The success the surplus stores had in selling these garments led manufacturers to add sleeves and make jackets over the same general pattern, and the buttoned and, later, zippered jacket for outdoor wear

Contemporary Comments 15.1

IMPACT OF WORLD WAR I ON TEXTILE SUPPLIES

World War I disrupted fiber supplies. In the Journal of Home Economics *for March 1918, Amy L. Rolfe of the Department of Home Economics, University of Missouri, analyzes the impact of the war in "What We Shall Wear This Year and Next" (125–129).*

Few persons realize the very small amount of textile fibers, which can be purchased by our clothing manufacturers or the causes which have brought about such conditions. . . . There is so little raw wool on the market, and so much of that is being commandeered by the government for soldier's uniforms and blankets. . . .

Before the war the United States grew only two-thirds of the wool used in our mills and the remaining third came from abroad. Now none is imported except from South America for the Allies have use for all they can get. Besides that used for uniforms and blankets, millions of yards of worsted cloth, costing $3 a yard and known as shalloon and shell cloth are being used in bagging or covering both the propelling and explosive charges for the big guns. Every bit of wool used in this way is entirely destroyed. . . .

The draft has taken spinners from the mills in great numbers and new workers must be trained before they can use their hands skillfully. . . .

For these and various other reasons it seems very improbable that there will be much wool to be worn by the civilian population next year. . . .

The cotton situation is almost as bad as the wool situation, although the United States has the advantage as it grows more than half the cotton in the world. . . . [T]he price of raw cotton has risen to alarming heights. . . . [A] bale of cotton is needed to fire one of the large guns, vast quantities are used for the unbleached muslin and gauze used in Red Cross work, and a still greater amount is commandeered by the government for khaki uniforms and tents. . . .

The use of linen as a substitute is more impossible still. Millions of yards of linen are needed for aëroplane wings. . . . The reason for the shortage of linen is that much of the flax of the world has been grown near the German border and has been trampled down and broken by the warfare that has been going on there. . . .

Most of our silk comes to us from China and Japan and so the supply of that material should be little influenced by the war. . . . [A] series of experiments being conducted at the front . . . may result in the use of all of the silk which it is possible to procure. As the boys "Somewhere in France" are sent into the trenches they are provided with silk underwear. It is thought that silk will prove to be gas resisting and also will be less irritating to the wounds than cotton. . . .

As wool, cotton, linen, and silk comprise the list of fibres which are commonly used for clothing, . . . we in the United States . . . must do our bit by conserving the supply of textiles. The manufacturers will help us to do this by using as little material as possible in their ready to wear garments. Skirts will be comfortably narrow, suit coats will be short, single breasted with small lapels and collars. Ornamental revers, patch pockets, and belts will be eliminated. Conservative styles will be in vogue because people will know that whatever they buy this year they must expect to wear much longer than usual.

was born. Another postwar style that originated during the war was the trench coat. Originally designed as a British military officer's coat, this water-repellent coat of closely woven cotton twill was belted at the waist. It became a standard item of rainwear for men, and after several decades it was also adopted by women. Prior to World War I, most men carried pocket watches with chains draped across their vest fronts. During the war many military men wore wristwatches for the ease they provided, and thus wristwatches became the preferred timepiece.

INFLUENCES ON FASHION

In addition to World War I, other notable fashion influences included French haute couture, Asian art, and important societal changes such as women's roles.

The French Couture and Paul Poiret

The turn of the century was marked by a major exposition in Paris, the *Exposition Universelle*. In one of the exhibit halls members of the Parisian haute couture—the leading fashion houses of the era—showed their designs. The most important design houses of the time were Doucet, Paquin, Rouf, Cheruit, Callot Soeurs, Redfern, and Worth.

Charles Worth had died in 1895 and had been succeeded by his two sons, Gaston and Jean Philippe. In the early part of the century Gaston engaged a young designer named **Paul Poiret** (*pwar-ay'*). Gaston saw in Poiret's work the kind of change he felt was needed for styles, but Jean Philippe disagreed. Poiret left the House of Worth and in a few years opened his own establishment. In any fashion period there may be designers whose influence is so great or whose work

so captures the spirit of the age that they seem to serve as a focal point for style in that time. Poiret was such a figure. He was not only an outstanding designer but also a colorful character whose personal idiosyncrasies help perpetuate his legend.

Between 1903 and World War I, Poiret reigned supreme in the Parisian couture. His customers submitted to his every wish, and he altered their way of dressing. The first radical step he took was to do away with corsets. Although he made gowns that were loose and free through the body, he put women into **hobble** skirts with hems so narrow they could hardly move. He once said, "I freed the bosom, shackled the legs, but gave liberty to the body" (Lyman, 1972, 63).

One of Poiret's major talents was for the use of vivid colors. Many writers have credited the color and Asian-influenced styles he devised to the popularity of the Ballet Russes (the Russian ballet company that took Paris by storm in 1909) as well as the costumes designed for the dancers by artist Léon Bakst. Poiret disclaimed the influence of Bakst, saying he had already begun to use vivid colors and a new style with strong Asian overtones before the arrival of the ballet. No matter which version of the development of these styles is accurate, the two complemented each other and helped reinforce the popular lines and colors of the time (Figure 15.4).

FIGURE 15.4 Among the designs for which Poiret was known were dresses with an overskirt wired to give a "lampshade effect." The first version was made for his wife for a ball called "The Thousand and One Nights." The dress was worn over harem pants. The version shown here, worn over a skirt, was called *sorbet* and dates from 1911. (V&A Images, London/Art Resource, NY.)

In 1912 Poiret designed costumes for a show called *Le Minaret*. He put the women into hobble skirts over which he placed wide tunics. The tunic and hobble skirt became the rage. One of his designers—who called himself Erté—was an artist who, in turn, became a prominent fashion illustrator and designer for the stage as well as for women's clothing. Erté designed hundreds of covers for *Harper's Bazar* (spelled *Harper's Bazaar* from 1929 on) with illustrations appearing in other fashion magazines such as *Vogue*.

In addition to the styles he created, Poiret was an innovator in other ways. He traveled abroad with a group of fashion models on which he showed his designs. He was also the first couturier to market a perfume, which he named after his daughter.

During and after World War I, the theatrical, colorful styles so characteristic of Poiret's work became outmoded. He never adjusted to the newer lines and look, and although his business continued into the 1920s, he grew less and less successful. Eventually he dropped from public sight and died in 1943.

Fortuny

While Poiret was a designer whose work seems to be uniquely suited to his times, the Spanish-born Mariano Fortuny y Madrazo (generally called Fortuny) was one of those rare designers whose work seems timeless. An artist who began exhibiting in the 1890s and continued to paint all of his life, Fortuny designed clothing and textiles from 1906 to 1949. In the catalogue of a 1981 exhibition of his work, Fortuny's biographer, Guillermo de Osma wrote:

> Fortuny's clothes, like the rest of his work, were quite outside accepted convention. He was not a couturier but rather a creative artist of dress. . . . His fabrics were conceived like paintings; he built up colors in layers, playing with the effects of light and transparency, printing and retouching to create textures and harmonies of color that were impossible to repeat. (Fortuny, 1981, 8)

Fortuny drew upon the past and non-European cultures as inspiration for his designs. Among the most notable were ancient Greek styles that inspired

FIGURE 15.5 The pleated gowns of Fortuny (1915–1935) were usually made in bright solid colors, while his patterned fabrics were in rich, often dark shades influenced by Renaissance and Asian designs. (Artist: Mariano Fortuny y Madrazo [Spanish, b.1871, d.1949], evening jacket, 1934, silk velvet; Cincinnati Art Museum, Gift of Mr. and Mrs. Charles Fleischmann in memory of Julius Fleischmann, 1987.67)

his **Delphos gown**, probably his most famous design, and Renaissance and Asian motifs that appear in many of his textile designs (Figure 15.5). Just how he achieved the pleating for his Greek-inspired gowns is not known. The pleats were removed by dry cleaning, so his clients returned garments to his atelier for cleaning and repleating.

Fortuny's clients were dancers, actresses, and well-to-do women. He was never part of the popular fashion market (in fact Fortuny was largely ignored by the influential fashion press), but Poiret knew and admired his work, as did other designers. Museums continue to collect his work, and many designers, such as Mary McFadden, cite Fortuny as an influence.

TABLE 15.1 Haute Couture Designers: 1900–1920

DESIGNER OR FOUNDER	COUTURE HOUSE AND DATE OF OPENING	NOTABLE CHARACTERISTICS
Marie Gerber, Marthe Bertrand, Régine Tennyson-Chantrelle, and Joséphine Crimont	Callot Soeurs, 1895	French couture house founded by four sisters. From 1916 to 1927, it became one of the great dressmaking houses famous for 18th-century inspired designs. Closed in 1937.
Jacques Doucet (c. 1860–1932)	The House of Doucet, 1895	A competitor of Worth, Doucet favored 18th-century styles and lace.
Christoff von Drécoll (1851–1933)	Drécoll, 1896	One of the most prestigious couture houses in Paris from 1900 to 1925. Architectural designs with elegant lines. Closed in 1963.
Fortuny (1871–1949)	Fortuny, 1906	Designed fabrics, originated a singular style of pleating. Timeless clothing styles worn by women who valued their uniqueness.
Jeanne Paquin (1891–1956)	House of Paquin, 1891	Fur-trimmed tailored suits, furs, evening dress, and fine workmanship. Closed in 1956.
John Redfern (1853–1929)	House of Redfern, 1881	London-based dressmaker for Queen Victoria, maker of jersey suit for actress Lillie Langtry in 1879, designer of first woman's uniform for the International Red Cross in 1916. Closed in the 1920s.

From Tortora, P. G., & Keiser, S. J. (2013). *The Fairchild books dictionary of fashion* (4th ed.). New York, NY: Bloomsbury.

Other influential designers of the period 1900 to 1920 are listed in Table 15.1.

ASIAN ART STYLES

Art movements and fashion trends are often connected. Influences from Japanese art on Impressionist painters and other European artists of the latter part of the 19th century probably had their roots in the opening of Japan for trade in the 1850s. It is likely that the Japanese and Chinese influences that can be observed in women's clothing, especially in the years after 1907, derive from late–19th-century trends in the fine and decorative arts (see Figures 15.13 and 15.17).

The style connections to east Asia were plentiful. Kimonos became popular for leisurely at-home wear for both men and women (see Global Connections). The cut of women's clothing grew less structured. Fabric designs and colors showed Asian influences, as did the design of haute couture. Reporting on an analysis of women's fashions of the 1910s and 1920s, Kim and DeLong (1992) noted that "virtually every category of garment type eventually was influenced, from morning jackets to afternoon frocks and evening gowns" (24).

The Changing Social Roles of American Women

Although larger numbers of women entered the workforce (more than five million in 1900), many men and women considered the woman's place to be in the home. Concessions to the more active life that women were leading are evident in the styles, as skirts grew somewhat shorter and the shirtwaist blouse and skirt were widely adopted. Business was employing increasing numbers of women, especially as typists.

However, even the more affluent married woman who saw her role as wife and mother was getting out of the house more often. Women's clubs increased in membership to more than one million by 1910. These groups focused on self-improvement or charitable works.

The woman's suffrage movement stepped up its campaigning for women's rights, but President Grover Cleveland spoke for many men, and women

Global Connections

This kimono from London's Victoria and Albert Museum was the type often exported to the west in the craze for all things Japanese. Dated to 1870–1900, the kimono is made of crepe silk, with embroidery and freehand paste-resist (*yuzen*) and stenciled (*kata kanoko*) designs. The kimono is an enduring symbol of Japanese culture. A kimono is constructed from rectangular lengths of cloth that are sewn together with minimal cutting in order to avoid wasting material. The full kimono ensemble includes many accessories selected to coordinate with the designs and colors of the kimono. These elements often demonstrate social status and personal identity. (V&A Images, London/Art Resource, NY)

as well, when he declared, "Sensible and responsible women do not want to vote. The relative positions to be assumed by man and woman in the working out of our civilization were assigned long ago by a higher intelligence than ours" (Bingham, 1969, 95).

By the second decade of the century women were becoming even more adventurous. They drove cars, went to work in increasing numbers (more than seven million in 1910 and a million more by 1920), and engaged in a variety of active sports, from bicycling to swimming to bobsledding. The clothes required for these active, competitive sports helped modify the prevailing norms regarding women's acceptable roles in society.

As women became more emancipated, support for the vote for women grew. After 1910, a series of public marches and rallies were held, each one larger than the last. The war caused a decrease in the activism of the suffragists and, at the same time, dramatized the place of women in American society as women filled jobs left behind by departing soldiers. Women worked in traditional occupations such as teaching, as well as in positions previously barred to them, such as factory workers, police officers, railroad workers, and traffic conductors. Women became auto mechanics and operated elevators. On June 4, 1919, after the war had ended, Congress passed the 19th Amendment, which guaranteed that the right to vote could not be restricted because of sex.

The Automobile

The role of the automobile in American society is so thoroughly established that it is difficult to imagine what life must have been like before it came on the scene. In 1900, the auto was a toy of the rich. Automobiles, or *bubbles* as they were sometimes called, cost upwards of $3,000 at a time when the average weekly wage was $12.

At first they were used for sport. Auto racing became a social event. In 1905, when the second Vanderbilt Cup Race was held, Manhattan society turned out in force. The newspapers reported descriptions of the crowds and their clothing. For example, one woman wore tweed, a fairly sensible choice, while another dowager (or dignified widow) "dripped pearls" and yet another woman wore a large Gainsborough picture hat (Lord, 1965, 108).

Automobile drivers had no problems about what to wear. A long cotton or linen **duster**, a cap with a visor (worn backwards at high speeds to prevent its being blown off), and goggles became customary automobiling costume for men. Ladies wore face veils (green was preferred as it cut down on glare); their coats sometimes had a more stylish cut, but like men's coats they covered the costume beneath completely. Cars were open and roads were unpaved, so the term *duster* was appropriate (Figure 15.6).

In 1908 Henry Ford made the first Model T, which sold for $850. The car was no longer a toy for the rich. By the end of the next decade Americans had purchased more than four million Model T Fords, and the age of the automobile had arrived (Figure 15.7).

American High Society

Although the average woman in small-town America had no direct contact with the wealthy and socially prominent, she easily kept abreast of their doings through the press, particularly through the many magazines sold across the nation. Around the turn of the century, mass-circulation magazines in the United States were available at low prices and in great variety. Their cost was kept low by the increasingly large quantities of advertising they carried.

Fashion magazines such as *Vogue* and *Harper's Bazar* and women's magazines including *The Delineator, Ladies' Home Journal,* and *McCalls,* which carried a good deal of fashion information, frequently printed photographs and drawings of the wealthy and stories of their latest escapades. The balls and weddings of the socially prominent were described in minute detail in *Vogue,* and a drawing of a bride's wedding dress often accompanied the article. From these photographs, articles, and drawings, fashion-conscious women across the country kept up with the

FIGURE 15.6 The duster, in tan, showed the effects of dirt kicked up by open automobiles less than if it were made in a darker or lighter shade (c. 1905). The small boy wears a sailor suit. (Photographed at Fashion Institute of Technology Galleries, "All-American: A Sportswear Tradition")

latest fashions in "society." By selecting similar styles from the growing number of pattern catalogues and ready-to-wear items, women of more limited means were able to obtain less-expensive versions of the most popular garments.

THE PRODUCTION AND ACQUISITION OF CLOTHING

The ready-to-wear industry in America expanded and became a mature industry by 1920. Although some women continued sewing their own dresses and other women and men patronized custom dressmakers and

FIGURE 15.7 Henry Ford's Model T transformed American life, making travel possible and supporting a number of related industries such as metal, glass, rubber, leather, and textiles. Open cars with unpaved roads necessitated specialized clothing, which was made obsolete as cars became enclosed and roads paved. (© Bettmann/CORBIS)

tailors, almost all Americans purchased at least some elements of their wardrobes ready-made. The patterns of mass production and the sale of ready-to-wear clothing in the United States established in the first two decades of the 20th century dominated middle-class American clothing consumption practices throughout the century (Figure 15.8).

FIGURE 15.8 Marshall Field & Company was an upscale department store in Chicago, Illinois. During the era of this image, c. 1907–1910, the department store occupied the entire block bounded by State, Washington, and Randolph streets and Wabash Avenue in Chicago's Loop. (F&A Archive/ The Art Archive at Art Resource, NY)

SOURCES OF INFORMATION ABOUT COSTUME

Clothing, photographs, magazines, and an enormous variety of mail-order and store catalogues dating from the period are readily available for study. To all these, was added a new medium of communication: motion pictures. Fashion shows and exhibitions were filmed and shown as part of newsreels. Fashionable clothing was worn by heroines in popular serial films (Leese, 1991). While filmed fashion shows and feature films showed high fashion worn by actresses and actors, newsreels of current events provided views of ordinary individuals.

COSTUME: 1900–1920

Between 1900 and 1920, women's fashions in Europe and America changed with remarkable rapidity. Examination of daytime and evening styles from this period is, therefore, simplified by subdividing the examination of women's dress into the following phases:

- Edwardian styles or styles with emphasis on an S-shaped silhouette, c. 1900–1909;
- Empire revival and the hobble skirt, c. 1909–1914;
- 1914–1918: World War I; and
- 1918–1919: postwar styles.

Costume Components for Women: 1900–1908

Garments

Frilly, decorative petticoats and drawers continued to be popular. Eyelet insertion with ivory, pink, or blue ribbon threaded through was a popular trim for all kinds of underclothing, as were ruffles and lace edging.

The bust supporter of the 1890s was modified to make it more suitable for supporting the fashionable silhouette of the new century. The name **brassiere** seems to have appeared first in 1904 when the Charles R. DeBevoise Company used the name in promoting its product. The following year, Gabrielle Poix filed a patent in which she called her design a *brassiere* (Farrell-Beck and Gau, 2002). The brassiere gradually became a basic item of underwear for adult women. See Illustrated Table 15.1 for examples of undergarments from the period 1900–1920.

Dresses were generally one piece, with bodices and skirts sewn together at the waistline, although some dresses were princess line as well (cut from shoulder to hem without a waistline seam). The shape of dresses seemed based on an S-shaped curve (Figure 15.9). Typical dresses had high-boned collars, full, pouched bodices, also called a *pouter-pigeon silhouette* (Figure 15.10), and skirts that were flat in front and emphasized a rounded hipline in the back. After hugging the hips, skirts flared out to a trumpet shape at the bottom (Figure 15.11).

Except for tailor-mades and shirtwaist styles made in imitation of men's shirts, the emphasis on frilly and much-decorated clothing required soft fabrics. Decorations included tucking, pleating, lace insertions, bands of applied fabric, lace, and embroidery. The popular white, frilly cotton or linen dresses with this decoration were referred to as **lingerie dresses**, probably because the fabric and decoration so much resembled women's undergarments or lingerie of the period (see Figure 15.10).

It is in this decade that the first advertisements for ready-to-wear maternity dresses appeared. In earlier periods women or their dressmakers adapted current

FIGURE 15.9 The predominant silhouette for women after the turn of the century was described as S-shaped with a full, pouched bosom and a rounded hipline. High, standing collars were almost universally seen on dresses. (Author's fashion plate)

styles to accommodate expanding figures. Stand-alone retail establishments, such as Lane Bryant, emerged for the plus-sized women during this period (Keist, 2012).

Bodices were often quite complicated in construction. The full-bosomed cut was almost universal. Most bodices closed with hooks and eyes or hooks and bars. High-boned collars predominated. Other styles were square cut, V-shaped (with or without collars), or sailor collars. Frilly ruffles, called **jabots**, were often placed at the front of the neck. In the first half of the decade, sleeves were generally long and made in either closely fitted or bishop style. The **bishop sleeve** was gathered into the armscye (or armhole) and full below the elbow with fabric puffed or pouched at the wrist. In the last half of the decade, sleeves were shorter (often

Illustrated Table 15.1

Selected Undergarments for Women, Men, and Children: 1900–1920

Lady's corset cover
and drawers, 1907[1]

Lady's petticoat, 1905[2]

Lady's corset, 1907[1]

Ladies' corsets, 1917[3]

Children's corsets, 1917[3]

Cambric brassiere, 1917[4]

Man's union suit and drawers, 1914[5]

Lady's corset cover
and drawers, 1914[5]

Petticoat
combination, 1917[3]

[1] McCall's® Image Courtesy of the McCall Pattern Company copyright © 2014

[2] Courtesy, *The Delineator,* April 1905.

[3] Courtesy, Fairchild Publications.

[4] Reprinted from *Women's and Children's Fashions of 1917; The Complete Perry, Dame & Co. Catalog.* 1992. Mineola, NY: Dover, pp. 68, 142, with permission of Dover Publications

[5] Courtesy, Reprinted from *In Home Pattern Company 1914, Fashions Catalogue.* 1995, pp. 63, 73, with permission by Dover Publications.

FIGURE 15.10 This high-school graduate of 1904 wears a lace-trimmed, ruffled white lingerie dress with a high, boned collar. (Courtesy of Melissa Clark)

FIGURE 15.11 Gored skirt pattern of 1907 shows that skirt patterns were generally made in varying lengths, ranging from those short enough to show the shoes to those that reached to the floor. (McCall's® Image Courtesy of the McCall Pattern Company copyright © 2014)

three quarter length). Some sleeves were wide at the end and finished with either ruffles or attached under sleeves. Japanese influences were evident in kimono-style sleeves.

The shape of skirts was achieved by goring. In **goring**, the shape of a skirt is created by using a number of panels shaped so that when joined they fit the body in some areas, usually over the hips, and flare out in others, usually toward the bottom. From waist to knee, skirts fit closely, and from that point on were full and flared to the hem. Some skirts had pleats at center back. Lengths varied with some skirts, ending several inches off the ground, while others had trains (see Figure 15.11).

The garment called a **tailor-made**, which today would be called a woman's suit, was an important item of clothing for women. Jackets varied in length, ending anywhere from the waist to below the hip. Shorter jackets were generally fitted; long jackets were sometimes loose and sacklike. Many tailor-mades imitated the cut of men's jackets.

Separate blouses (shirtwaists) came in great variety and displayed features much like the bodices of daytime dresses (Figure 15.12). Mail-order catalogues advertised a wide range of skirt styles with which these blouses were worn; they pictured skirts that incorporated pleating, decorative stitching, applied braid trim, and ruffled hems.

More affluent women wore soft, less-fitted **tea gowns** in the late afternoon. The gowns created by Fortuny were often worn as tea gowns. Women of lesser means wore **wrappers**, loose fitting, one-piece garments for relaxing at home.

Evening dresses followed the same silhouette as daytime dresses. For evening, necklines were generally low and square, round, or V-shaped. Some had lace or sheer fabric scarves at the neck. Ruffled,

Arranged full and loose around the face, hair was pulled into a chignon, or bun, at the back of the neck. An important style, the **pompadour**, had hair built high in front and at the sides around the face (see Figure 15.12). The first permanent wave was given in London in 1904.

Large in scale, popular hat styles included brimless toques and large-brimmed **picture hats**. Decoration was lavish with artificial flowers, lace, buckles, feathers, and birds' wings. In 1905, a single page of the Sears, Roebuck catalogue showed 75 different styles of ostrich-feather decorations. The slaughter of birds for feathers to decorate hats resulted in the near extinction

FIGURE 15.12 At a church outing, c. 1901, young ladies wear cotton dresses or shirtwaists and skirts; young men wear white shirts and bow ties. Almost all of the women have arranged their hair in a pompadour. (Courtesy of Almeda Brackbill Scheid)

decorative sleeves covered the upper part of the arm. There were also sleeveless styles with shoulder straps. Skirts were full, extending to the floor. Gowns often had trains made from soft fabrics that were longer at the back and trailed along the floor.

Outdoor Garments

Outdoor garments consisted chiefly of cloaks and capes with high-standing (Medici) collars and wide revers, and coats that were fitted or unfitted and made in many different lengths. Some coats were fitted at the back, loose in the front. Capes were especially popular for evening wear. Asian influences were evident in kimono-style coats (Figure 15.13).

Hair and Headdress

See Illustrated Table 15.2 for some examples of hairstyles and hats from 1900 to 1920.

FIGURE 15.13 Both the cut of this theater coat, c. 1900, and the embroidered bamboo motifs are inspired by the Asian influences that entered fashion from the late 1800s into the early 20th century. (Image copyright © The Metropolitan Museum of Art. Image source: Art Resource, NY)

Illustrated Table 15.2

Selected Hairstyles and Hats for Women: 1900–1920

Hats, 1905   Hair, 1907   Hat, 1907

Hats, 1909   Hats, 1912

Hair, 1912   Hair, 1919   Hats, 1919

Reproduced from contemporary fashion and pattern magazines.

of many birds. In 1906, Queen Alexandra of England tried to set a good example by refusing to wear any hats decorated with wild-bird feathers. By the second decade of the century, some countries were banning the importation of most kinds of feathers. Fortunately for the birds, the fashion for large hats subsided after about 1914.

Hair ornaments worn for evening included feathers, jeweled combs, and small skullcaps of pearls called *Juliet caps*, after the heroine of *Romeo and Juliet*.

Footwear

See Illustrated Table 15.3 for some examples of footwear from 1900 to 1920.

Generally, stockings of dark or neutral cotton lisle were worn for daytime, and silk, for formal wear. Some were decorated with colored clocks (designs knitted into the stocking) or lace insertion.

Shoes had pointed toes, long, slender lines, and heels about 2 to 2$^1/_2$ inches high that were curved in the so-called Louis style. Boots were less fashionable

Illustrated Table 15.3

Selected Examples of Footwear for Women: 1900–1920

Women's dress shoe, 1904[1]

Women's boot, 1904[1]

Women's dress shoes, 1911[2]

Women's boots, 1917[3]

[1] *Chicago Mail Order and Millinery Company Catalogue, 1904–1905.*

[2] *The Ladies' Field*, October 7, 1911.

[3] Reprinted from *Women's and Children's Fashions of 1917: The Complete Perry, Dame & Co. Catalogue.* 1992. Mineola, NY: Dover, pp. 68, 142, with permission of Dover Publications.

than shoes, but when worn, they were high and closed by buttons or laces.

Accessories

See Illustrated Table 15.4 for some examples of popular accessories.

Among the important accessories were large, flat muffs and suede or leather daytime handbags or beaded evening bags. Decorative lace or silk parasols were trimmed with fringe or lace. The less decorative and more serviceable umbrellas were made of oiled silk. For evening, women carried long folding fabric fans or ostrich fans. The most popular belts were triangular shaped. Swiss belts were revived from the 1860s. Ruffles, boas, ribbons, or cravats were worn around the neck.

Jewelry

The most worn types of jewelry included clasps, brooches, pendants, necklaces, chains, dog collars and long necklaces, and pendant or single-stone earrings. Jewelry was often made in the Art Nouveau style (see Figure VI.1, page 419). Such items were available in all qualities and price ranges.

Costume Components for Women: 1909–1914

Garments

The quantity of underclothing worn by women decreased. Most women continued to wear corsets, even though Paul Poiret claimed that his designs liberated women from these garments. The new brassiere was especially suitable, when combined with a straight corset, for the revival of the Empire line in dresses. Many women wore combination underwear, ornamented with lace and embroidery, rather than drawers (frequently referred to as **knickers**) and a chemise. A narrower silhouette after 1909 required narrower petticoats. The princess petticoat, which combined a camisole-type top with a petticoat into a single princess-line garment, became popular. See Illustrated Table 15.1, page 433, for examples of undergarments from the period 1900–1920.

Dresses were likely to be one piece, although skirts, blouses, and tailor-mades had also become a permanent part of women's daytime wardrobes. By 1909 the S-shaped curve of the Edwardian period was being replaced by a straighter line. The size of the full, pouched bodice decreased, and the location of the waistline moved upward. Skirts narrowed and grew shorter. The high-boned collar gradually went out of fashion. This collar had been part of women's costumes for such a long time that the clergy were outraged that women showed their necks, while health experts expressed fear for women's health and predicted an increase in pneumonia and tuberculosis.

An Empire revival led to use of a silhouette with an elevated waistline as well as a number of details that were considered to have originated during France's First Empire (Figure 15.14). These included military

FIGURE 15.14 A revival of the Empire waistline around 1912 was accompanied by a straighter, narrower skirt. (*The Delineator*, August 1912)

Illustrated Table 15.4

Accessories: 1900–1920

Ostrich feather fan

c. 1900–1910

Women's neckwear

(a) Jabot, c. 1900–1910 (b) Small silk ruffle, 1902

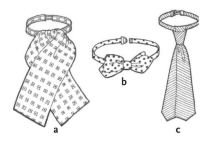

Men's pre-tied neckwear

(a) Ascot (b) Bow tie (c) Necktie

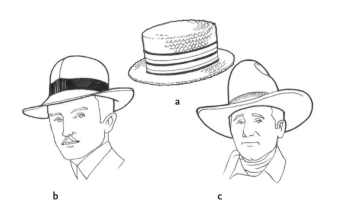

Men's hats popular c. 1900

(a) Straw boater (b) Panama hat (c) Stetson hat

Women's handbags

(a) Alligator handbag, 1913

(b) Beaded evening handbag, 1915

Art Nouveau ornamentation

(a) Belt buckle (b) Bracelet (c) Parasol (d) Man's suspenders collars, ruffled jabots, and wide revers, or lapels. As is true with most costume revivals, these latter details were only very loosely based on men's costume of the early 1800s. Asian influences were evident in the cut and draping of some styles.

Although some vestiges of the frilliness of the Edwardian period remained, bodice styles gradually simplified. Front-buttoned closings were used for many garments. Sleeves tended to be tight fitting, ending below the elbow or at the wrist, with cuffs of contrasting colors. Shorter, kimono-style sleeves reflected the impact of Japanese styles.

From 1909 to 1911, a narrow, straight skirt predominated, but by about 1912 a number of different skirt styles of more elaborate construction had become popular (Figure 15.15). Whether the skirt was single or multilayered, however, it maintained an exceptionally narrow circumference around the ankles. Women could barely take a full step in the most extreme of these skirts, which were called **hobble skirts**. Some were so tight that a slit had to be made at the bottom to enable women to walk. **Peg-top skirts**, with fullness concentrated at the hip then narrowing gradually to the ankles, were also popular. Tunics were worn over underskirts. Tunics varied in shape from narrow tubes, to wide, full-bottomed styles to multiple layers of tunic

skirts. Paul Poiret designed a number of very exotic styles including the **minaret tunic**, a wide tunic, boned to hold out the skirt in a full circle and worn over the narrowest of hobble skirts. He also introduced the harem skirt, a full Turkish-style trouser that did not attract significant following.

Jackets of tailored suits were cut to below the hips, with an overall line that was long and slender (Figure 15.16). Narrow skirts were slit at the side or front.

Man-tailored shirtwaist blouses complete with neckties and high, tight collars were worn with separate skirts or tailored suits (see Figure 15.15).

For evening, both Empire revival and Asian influences were evident. Most evening dresses had tunics or layers of sheer fabric placed over heavier fabric. Trains were popular. Sleeves were short, often kimono style and of sheerer fabric than the body of the dress. Decorative touches included wide cloth belts or sashes; gold and silver embroidery; and lace, beading, and fringe (Figure 15.17).

Outdoor Garments

For daytime, coats were long or three quarter length. Some closed at far left in a sort of wraparound style. Evening coats were looser, cut full across the back and

FIGURE 15.15 Almost all of the fashionable variations of skirt styles can be seen on the members of the Gamma Phi Beta sorority at Michigan State University in 1914. These include tight hobble skirts, some plain and others with single and multilayered tunics, and peg-topped skirts. (Courtesy of Marilyn Guenther)

FIGURE 15.16 Suits and a coat advertised in the October 1909 *Ladies' Home Journal* reflect the new, more slender line and the longer suit jackets that became fashionable. (Printz-Biederman Co., 1909)

FIGURE 15.17 Evening gown, c. 1912, has a somewhat kimono-like sleeve treatment that reflects the pervasive Asian influences in women's dress and in the yellow chiffon with bead and braid trim typical of the materials used in evening gowns at this time. (ICHi-59706, CHM staff, Chicago History Museum)

often with capelike sleeves. Some elaborately ruffled capes were also worn for evening.

Hair and Headdress

See Illustrated Table 15.2, page 436, for some examples of hairstyles and hats from 1900 to 1920.

Hair was less bouffant now. The hair was waved softly around the face and pulled into a soft roll at the back or toward the top of the head.

Large hats included those emphasizing height, the brimless toque style, or hats with turned-up brims. Face veils were popular. Hats were decorated with artificial flowers, feathers, and ribbons. The fashion press noted the revival of tricorne hats, which they identified as part of the Directoire styles. (In actuality,

tricornes were worn not in the Directoire or empire periods, but earlier.)

Footwear

No radical changes occurred.

Costume Components for Women: 1914–1918

Garments

Brassieres, which were worn with a corset that ended below the bust, were now widely available. A combination garment that put together a camisole with a skirt that buttoned under the crotch to form drawers was called **cami-knickers**. This garment was especially popular when skirts grew shorter. Wider skirts required fuller petticoats. See Illustrated Table 15.1 (page 433) for examples of undergarments from the period 1900–1920.

One-piece dresses were still preferred over two-piece styles. Coat dresses, either single or double breasted and belted or sashed at the waist, were stylish. During the wartime years the silhouette of women's clothes grew wider, and skirts, shorter. Hems rose to 6 inches from the ground in 1916 and as much as 8 or more inches from the floor in 1917. Throughout the period the waistline was at normal placement or slightly above (Figure 15.18).

The fit of bodices was easy, and waistlines were defined, often with loose-fitting belts. Necklines tended to be V-shaped or squared. Some necklines were edged with sailor collars. Sleeves were generally straight and fitted. Skirts were full, the fullness achieved through pleating, gathering, or with gores.

Tailored suits became even more popular during the wartime years, and some had a distinctively military look. Jackets were long and belted at or slightly above the natural waistline (Figure 15.19).

Special features of the blouses worn with skirts or suits included sleeves and yokes cut in one; leg-of-mutton sleeves; and Medici or standing collars with necks that were either open, round, or square at the front. Knitted sweaters that pulled on over the head (**pullovers**) became popular after 1915. Pullovers had no discernible waist, were belted at the hip, and had long sleeves. Gabrielle Chanel, the designer who became very influential during the 1920s, is often given credit

FIGURE 15.18 McCall patterns of 1915 shows the shorter hemlines with easier cut and fit in both dresses and women's suits that appeared by mid-decade. (The New York Public Library/Art Resource, NY)

FIGURE 15.19 Suits of the World War I period were softer, shorter, and more practical and frequently, as in this example, showed a military influence in color and styling. (The New York Public Library/Art Resource, NY)

for being the first person to interest women in knitted pullover sweaters about the time of World War I.

The lines of daytime and evening dresses were similar, although waistline placement for evening tended to be slightly higher than the natural waistline. Skirts were full, many having tiers of ruffles, floating panels of fabric, or layers of varying lengths. At the neck, the décolletage might be filled in with flesh-colored or transparent fabric. Sleeves were short or to the elbow. Sleeveless dresses had only narrow straps over the shoulder. Fashionable trimmings were made with beading, gold, and silver embroidery (Figure 15.20).

Outdoor Garments

Coats grew wider to accommodate wider skirts. One popular style had a full back; others were full but loosely belted. Three-quarter–length coats were popular in 1916 and after. Military influence was evident in some coats.

Hair and Headdress

See Illustrated Table 15.2 (page 436) for some examples of hairstyles and hats from 1900 to 1920.

During the wartime period, hair was worn closer to the face and shorter. More women tried permanent waves. Hats were high rather than wide, and were smaller than before the war. They were made with and without brims and were often worn with face veils.

Footwear

See Illustrated Table 15.3 (page 437) for some examples of footwear from 1900 to 1920.

Stockings were dark for daytime, but pale for evening. Rayon (called artificial silk) stockings were introduced as an alternative to silk (see page 465 for a more complete discussion of rayon).

Shoes styles did not change radically, but shoes were more visible as hemlines rose. High-buttoned shoes or shoes with spats kept feet warm in cold weather.

Cosmetics

Tonics, creams, and makeup including foundation, rouge, and eye liner were used. Beauty entrepreneurs Elizabeth Arden and Helena Rubinstein provided

FIGURE 15.20 Evening dress, c. 1916. Evening dresses of mid-decade, like daytime dresses, were shorter and fuller than those of previous years. Lace and sheer fabrics often appeared in evening wear. (Kharbine-Tapabor/The Art Archive at Art Resource, NY)

cosmetics in their New York salons. Annie Turnbo Malone and Madame C. J. Walker provided complexion and hair care products specifically designed for African American women.

Costume Components for Women: 1918–1920

The postwar period is really a transitional period from wartime styles to the styles of the 1920s. By 1918, the war had the effect of curtailing the supply of fabrics, and the silhouette grew narrower again. In 1918 and 1919, dresses with narrow hems had waistlines that were rather wide, which produced a silhouette described as "barrel shaped." In 1919 after the end of

FIGURE 15.21 By the end of the decade, c. 1919, skirt lengths for adult women dropped once again, and fashionable dresses began to show the loosely fitted silhouettes that would become characteristic of the 1920s. Young girls wore shorter skirts. (Advertisement for Grand Bazar de l'Hotel de Ville, winter 1919 (colour litho), French School, (20th century)/Bibliotheque des Arts Decoratifs, Paris, France/Archives Charmet/Bridgeman Images)

the war, fashion designers turned back to narrower skirts, and hemlines gradually dipped to the ankle again. The silhouette remained loosely fitted through the waist. Jeanne Lanvin, a fashion designer of the period, is credited with creating the chemise dress, a straight tube of the type that was to become so fashionable in the 1920s (Figure 15.21).

COSTUME COMPONENTS FOR MEN

Garments

Wool was the primary fabric for men's underwear, although cotton was coming into use as well. Heavier knits were used for winter, lighter for summer. Union suits, with drawers and underwear in one, were popular. In summer, drawers had short legs; in winter, long. See Illustrated Table 15.1 (page 433) for examples of undergarments from the period 1900–1920.

Suits, consisting of jacket, vest, and trousers and worn with a shirt and necktie, were appropriate dress for professional and business employees during the workweek. Laboring men wore sturdy work clothes. All men wore suits for important social occasions. For informal social occasions or during their leisure time, men wore sport jackets, trousers, and shirts of various kinds. Some active sports required special clothing, as did formal evening or daytime events.

Except for summer when lighter weight flannel and linen fabrics were worn, suit jackets and trousers were generally dark in color, and dark blue wool serge was the most popular fabric. Jackets, whether they were part of a suit or a separate garment, showed some variations in cut. Both single- and double-breasted suits were made, the popularity of each varying from year to year. In the early years of the century, jackets and coats were cut long, buttoned high, and had small lapels. Their full cut through the torso gave men an almost barrel-chested appearance (Figure 15.22). During World War I, jackets and coats gradually shortened. Silhouettes narrowed; shoulder lines became less padded and more natural.

Types of jackets included frock coats, which were worn only by dignitaries on formal occasions or by elderly men, and morning coats, still seen for formal occasions during the day. Before the war, morning coats were worn as suits with matching coat and trousers or with contrasting waistcoat and striped trousers. After the war, the use of morning coats was limited to the upper classes or political leaders who donned them as formal dress for weddings, diplomatic receptions, or inaugurations. Men continued to wear three-piece suits, which narrowed in the second decade of the century (Figure 15.23). Formal occasions required a top hat; for less formal events a man might wear a derby or homburg.

Sack jackets became the standard suit jacket for men during the 20th century. They were worn for all occasions and even appeared for leisure time wear as

FIGURE 15.22 Golf clothing, 1912. On the left, knickers and a Norfolk jacket; on the right, a plaid suit with a half belt at the back. (*Sartorial Arts Journal*, 1912)

FIGURE 15.23 Men, 1912. Men's three-piece suits, at left, narrowed in the second decade of the century. The Chesterfield coat, at right, continued to be popular, and an athlete, at center, competed in knickers and knee socks worn with an early type of athletic shoe. A knitted sweater was often paired with a colorful shirt. (The New York Public Library/ Art Resource, NY)

sport jackets. American tailors called these coats *sack jackets*, and the British preferred the term **lounge coat**.

Vests were routinely worn as part of men's suits. Just after the turn of the century, vests were light or colored, but by the 1910s vests generally matched the suit with which they were worn.

When worn under coats and vests, shirts were visible only at the collar, above the vest, and at the end of the sleeves. Some shirts, particularly those for more formal dress, had stiffened fronts. Both white and colored shirts were worn, as well as patterns such as polka dots or stripes (Figure 15.24). In the first years of the century, collars were high and stiff. The height of collars gradually decreased, and both soft and stiff collars were worn. Shirts worn by soldiers had softer collars. After the war men, continued to prefer these

less rigidly starched shirt collars, which were either part of the shirt or detachable. Changing the collar and cuffs made it possible to wear the same shirt for several days, giving the appearance of having on a fresh shirt.

Necktie varieties included bow ties, which could be purchased already tied to clip into place. Other styles were **four-in-hand** ties, today's standard necktie, and **ascots**, which were ties with wide ends worn with one end looped over the other and held in place with a tie pin (see Illustrated Table 15.4, page 439).

Trousers were generally cut loosely around the hips and narrower toward the bottom. Some had turned-up cuffs; others had no cuffs. Trousers were worn with and without sharply pressed creases. Applied waistbands were becoming more popular.

FIGURE 15.24 Menswear was rarely colored in the 20th century. Dark blue pinstriped suits were worn for business before World War I. For leisure and sports, however, more colorful shirts could be worn. (The New York Public Library/Art Resource, NY)

Men's evening dress consisted of tailcoats or tuxedo jackets with matching trousers and a dark or white waistcoat. Dinner jackets were tuxedo style, sack cut, and generally single breasted. Tailcoats were double breasted, but worn unbuttoned, and had rolled lapels or notched collars and lapels. Most evening jackets had lapels faced in silk (Figure 15.25). Trousers for evening matched the jacket, had no cuffs, and sported a row or two of braid placed along the outer seams.

Generally dress shirts had stand-up collars and were worn with white bow ties. Shirts closed with studs. After about 1910 shirt fronts were pleated and had wing collars. After 1915, black bow ties for evening were gaining acceptance.

Outdoor Garments

Sweaters were generally worn by working class men: collarless cardigans that opened down the front, V-necked pullovers, and high-collared styles similar to the modern turtleneck (Figure 15.26).

Overcoats were full to accommodate the wide cut of men's suits in the first decade, then became more fitted in the second decade. Lengths varied, some almost ankle length, others below the knee at midcalf, and others short. **Top coats** ended at the hip. The top

FIGURE 15.25 Men, 1909. The tailcoat and white tie continued to be worn as formal wear (see man at left), but the tuxedo worn by the two men on the right was fast becoming an important style for evening dress. (Courtesy of The Advertising Archives)

FIGURE 15.26 Young man of the turn of the century dressed (probably to play baseball or football) in a turtleneck sweater and padded knickers. (Courtesy of Huntington Historical Society, Huntington, NY)

coat was worn by affluent men who could afford more than one overcoat. Basic overcoat styles included:

- Chesterfields and raglan-sleeve coats, with versions for evening having velvet collars;
- ulsters, made with whole or half belts and detachable hoods or capes;
- Inverness coats, with single or double capes;
- the mackintosh, the name given to almost any kind of rainwear (the process patented by Charles Mackintosh for placing a layer of rubber between two layers of cloth was still a popular means of applying a waterproof finish to fabric. Other waterproof finishes were made by oiling fabric to make "slickers"); and
- the trench coat (credited to Thomas Burberry during World War I), a belted twill cotton gabardine

of very close weave with a chemical finish that made the coat water repellent. Trench coats became fashionable for civilian wear after the war.

After the war, military influences were especially evident in outdoor wear. Collars took on a military shape, high and fitted, and coats became shorter. Other postwar styles included fur coats. Raccoon was especially popular for motoring. Many coats had fur collars and fur linings.

In the early years of the period, jackets and casual coats were limited to working class men who wore heavy corduroy, leather, wool, and other utilitarian fabrics. Some jackets were associated with particular occupations, such as lumber jackets. After the war, interest in outdoor sports increased and, as a result, jackets for recreation were adopted by the public at large.

Clothing for Active Sports

Antecedents of the modern sport jacket, worn with unmatched trousers can be seen in the **blazer**, which was worn for tennis, yachting, or other sports. One account of the origin of the blazer reports that in 1837 when Queen Victoria reviewed the crew of HMS *Blazer*, the captain had no uniforms for his men, so he had them dress in dark blue jackets with shiny brass buttons in a parade honoring the queen. The queen is said to have decreed that henceforth jackets of this style would be called *blazers* (Attaway, 1991). Other sources claim the name came from the "blazing" red color of these jackets worn for sports. The Norfolk jacket was an English style of belted jacket for golf, bicycling, and hiking. Knickers, long stockings, sturdy shoes, and a soft cap with a visor were often combined with these jackets.

Outfits for riding differed from the traditional 19th-century morning coat, breeches, and boots. Instead, a jacket with a flared skirt was worn with **jodhpurs**, a pair of trousers fitted closely around the lower leg and flaring out above the knee. Jodhpurs are another example of cross-cultural influences on western dress, originated in India where they were adopted by British colonials and subsequently spread throughout the west.

In England, swimming suits consisted of a pair of drawers, but men in the United States were more likely to wear either a knitted wool suit made up of fitted knee-length breeches and a shirt with short or no sleeves or a one-piece, short-legged, round-necked, sleeveless tank suit. Kidwell (1968) believed that bathing dress in the United States developed a more conservative character because men and women bathed together rather than separately, as was the custom in England until about 1900.

Some men wore sport coats and flannel trousers for driving; however, placing long linen dusters or leather motoring coats over clothing was more practical. Men wore goggles and peaked caps, which were worn with the peak at the back to keep them from blowing off.

Loungewear and Sleepwear

Menswear at home consisted of dressing gowns and smoking jackets, some of which had quilted lapels and were made in decorative fabrics. Nightshirts were still worn by many men, but others wore pajamas.

Hair and Headdress

Generally hair was short. The war helped diminish the popularity of beards and mustaches, as they were more difficult to keep clean in combat zones and interfered with gas masks.

Hat styles remained much the same as those in the latter part of the 19th century and included top hats, now only for formal occasions; soft felt hats with the names *homburg* or *trilby*; derbies; and caps for leisure. Western-style Stetson felt hats were worn in some parts of the United States. For summer, men used panama straw hats, straw boaters, and linen hats made in derby or fedoralike shapes (see Illustrated Table 15.4, page 439).

Footwear

Stockings were usually neutral colors. Some were made with a few stripes or in multicolored styles. Stockings had ribbed tops and were held up with elastic garters.

In the early part of the century shoes had long, pointed toes, and they laced or buttoned to close. Many were cut high, above the ankle. For evening, black patent leather slippers were popular. After 1910, oxfords (low, laced shoes) increased in use. Some had perforated designs on the toes. Others were two-toned. White buckskin oxfords were popular for summer. Sturdy, laced high shoes were still favored by many for everyday. By the end of the decade, rounded, more blunt toes were more popular.

Accessories

Walking sticks were popular until automobiles came into widespread use. Other accessories for men were gloves, handkerchiefs, and scarves.

Jewelry

Jewelry was mostly limited to tie pins, shirt studs, rings, and cuff links. Wristwatches gained popularity as a result of their wartime use and because of the increased use of automobiles. The inconvenience of pocket watches to soldiers and drivers proved the value of wristwatches.

COSTUME COMPONENTS FOR CHILDREN

Throughout history, children's clothing shows clear similarities to that of adults. At times, particularly in the 20th century, the special needs of children for practical clothing have been recognized. Moore (1953) called the Edwardian period a time of transition in children's clothing as styles moved from impractical to more practical dress.

Costume Components for Girls

Garments

Many girls of all ages wore white, light-, or cream-colored lingerie dresses (one of the less practical styles), cut with waistlines low on the hip. Decoration consisted of embroidery, smocking, and lace. Other styles had more natural waistline placement and full-bloused bodices similar to those of adult women.

For school, navy blue serge was popular, as were sailor dresses and sailor hats and pinafores, which were placed on top of other dresses to protect them (Figure 15.27).

A style favored about 1910 had a large, cape collar; low waist; and sleeves full to the elbow, then tight to the wrist. After 1910 there was less white and more color in "best" dresses.

From 1914 to 1917 belts dropped low, to the thighs, foreshadowing the flapper styles that would take hold during the 1920s (Figure 15.28). Throughout the period skirts for young girls were about knee length. For older girls they were longer but still a practical length.

Physical Education Uniforms

Gym tunics, which were worn over blouses, had sleeveless yokes, square necks, and belted, full pleated bodices. This style remained popular in subsequent periods as well.

FIGURE 15.27 Children of 1912 were provided with more practical clothing. Young boys wore short pants. Girls also tended to wear pinafores over their dresses. As young women reached their teens (figure at right in lower row), they wore dresses like those of adult women. (McCall's® Image Courtesy of the McCall Pattern Company copyright © 2014)

FIGURE 15.28 By 1917 young girls were wearing colorful dresses with a silhouette similar to those of adult women, though shorter in length. Waistline placement was somewhat variable, ranging from slightly above the anatomical waist to lower at the hip. (Reprinted from *Women's and Children's Fashions of 1917: The Complete Perry, Dame, & Co. Catalog*, inside of back cover, with permission by Dover Publications, Inc.)

Costume Components for Boys

From 1900 to 1910, most small boys were still dressed in skirts until the age of 3 or 4. These dresses followed the same lines as those for girls. From 1910 to 1920, little boys were more likely to be dressed in rompers and, when a little older, in knickers.

Garments

Boys could choose from sailor suits (see Figure 15.6), Eton suits, Norfolk jackets, and sack suit jackets, all with or without belts. Younger boys wore jackets with shorts or knickers, and older boys wore them with long trousers.

Outdoor Wear

Outside, boys wore mackinaw coats in plaid or plain colors, Norfolk jackets, long cardigan sweaters, or turtleneck sweaters.

Costume Components for Boys and Girls

Innovative styles pictured in mail-order catalogues of 1914 included knitted tops and leggings for small boys and girls and sleeping garments with feet.

Footwear

High-laced shoes were worn by either boys or girls. For dress wear, girls wore flat slippers with one or more straps across the instep or a flat shoe with an ankle strap. Stockings from 1900 to 1910 tended to be knee length. During the war these shortened for girls. Boys wore knee-length socks with knickers.

Summary

Themes

Many themes can be identified in the styles of the first two decades of the 20th century. Rapid FASHION CHANGE is seen in women's clothing and relative stability in styles of men's clothing. TECHNOLOGY in everyday life, as seen in the increasing use of automobiles, and SOCIAL CHANGES, such as the entry into the workforce by more women both before and during World War I, probably helped establish styles for women that were shorter, less confining, and more practical. The theme of PRODUCTION AND ACQUISITION OF TEXTILES AND APPAREL was evident in the growing availability of ready-to-wear clothing of all kinds. Mail-order catalogue retailing helped make fashionable clothing available in rural as well as urban regions.

The specific styles of this period can be related to themes such as THE RELATIONSHIPS BETWEEN COSTUME AND THE WORK OF INDIVIDUAL DESIGNERS, such as Paul Poiret and Fortuny, and also to CROSS-CULTURAL INFLUENCES from Asia. Furthermore, a NEW MEDIUM OF COMMUNICATION, motion pictures, not only served to spread styles but also added to SOURCES OF INFORMATION ABOUT COSTUME for future costume historians.

POLITICAL CONFLICT was once again an important theme. World War I had an impact not only on the styles of the wartime period, when military influences were evident in the cut and colors of both men's and women's clothing, but also on styles after the war. Garments that had been part of military clothing,

Visual Summary Table

Edwardian Period and World War I

Man: 1900–1920
Suits of jackets, vests, and trousers worn with white, colored, or figured shirts. Sack jackets predominate; morning coats for formal occasions.

Man: 1900–1920
Until World War I, suits are cut full through the torso. During and after the war, silhouette narrows. Norfolk jackets are worn for daytime, frock coats have limited use.

Woman: 1900–1908
S-shaped silhouette with full bosom and morning-glory–shaped skirt. Much use of frilly, lacy fabrics. Many women wear two-piece, tailor-made suits.

Woman: 1909–1914
Waistline moves higher with Empire-style revival. Skirt lines become straighter. Hobble skirts, very tight around the ankles, are fashionable.

Woman: 1914–1918
Skirts shorten and grow wider. Waistline is still slightly elevated. Military influences are evident.

Woman: 1918–1920
Silhouette narrows, skirts lengthen. Some dresses are barrel shaped, wider at the waist, more closely fitted at the hem. An unfitted line begins to appear.

such as trench coats, sweaters, and wristwatches, were carried over into civilian use after the war.

LEGACIES OF EDWARDIAN AND WORLD WAR I STYLES

Many of the revivals of Edwardian style have been in menswear. King Edward VII of Britain had popularized the homburg hat. President Dwight Eisenhower brought the style to public notice again when he wore a homburg to his inauguration in 1952. The Teddy Boys, British adolescents of the 1950s, adopted suits with styling similar to that of Edwardian men, and this narrower cut was adopted for mainsteam menswear as well.

In the 1960s mod styles again drew on Edwardian fashion for inspiration and in the 1990s the mod styles were themselves revived. Another repetition of early–20th-century styles can be seen in the striped shirts with white collars that returned to menswear in the early 1980s.

The Edwardian lingerie dress and the frilly undergarments with embroidered and lace trimming worn under them also inspired fashions in outerwear and underwear in the 1980s. And in one of the most unusual revivals seen to date, women who had collected original Delphos gowns made by Fortuny about the time of World War I began wearing them. Designer Mary McFadden became known for her pleated gowns of the 1980s and 1990s that derived from the Fortuny styles. Twenty-first–century designers continue to use frilly, softer feminine looks popular during periods of the Edwardian time (see Modern Influences).

REFERENCES

Attaway, R. (1991). The enduring blazer. *Yachting, 170*(4), 60–65.

Bingham, C. (1969). *The affairs of women: A modern miscellany.* Sydney, Australia: Currawong Publishing Co.

Farrell-Beck, J., & Gau, C. (2002). *Uplift: The bra in America.* Philadelphia, PA: University of Pennsylvania Press.

Fortuny. (1981). [Catalog of an exhibition at the Galleries at the Fashion Institute of Technology]. April 14 through July 11. New York, NY.

Keist, C. (2012). *The new costumes of odd sizes: Plus sized women's fashions, 1910-1929* (Doctoral dissertation). Iowa State University, Ames, IA.

MODERN INFLUENCES

The pleating used by Fortuny has served as inspiration for countless designers throughout the 20th and 21st centuries, including Madame Gres, Mary McFadden, Issey Miyake, and Stella McCartney. In the spring 2014 collection by Belgian designer Dries Van Noten, Fortuny influence can be seen in the small rosette of pleats. This example shows how a designer will take an idea and modify it, transforming the past to live again in the present. (Giannoni/ WWD/© Conde Nast)

Kidwell, C. (1968). *Women's bathing and swimming costume in the United States.* Washington, DC: Smithsonian Institution Press.

Kidwell, C. & Christman, M. (1974). *Suiting everyone: The democratization of clothing in America.* Washington: The Smithsonian Institution Press.

Kim, H. J., & DeLong, M. (1992). Sino-Japanism in western women's fashionable dress in *Harper's Bazaar, 1890–1927. Clothing and Textiles Research Journal, 11*(1), 24–30.

Leach, W. (1993). *Land of desire: Merchants, power, and the rise of a new American culture.* New York: Vintage Books.

Leese, E. (1991). *Costume design in the movies.* New York, NY: Dover.

Lord, W. (1965). *The good years.* New York, NY: Bantam Books.

Lyman, M. (1972). *Couture.* Garden City, NY: Doubleday.

Moore, D. L. (1953). *The child in fashion.* London: B. T. Batsford.

	1920	1922	1924	1925	1927	1929
FASHION AND TEXTILES			U.S. Department of Commerce establishes name *rayon*			
POLITICS AND CONFLICTS	Warren G. Harding elected U.S. president					
DECORATIVE AND FINE ARTS			Founding of the surrealist movement with Breton's *Manifeste du Surréalisme*	Publication of *The Great Gatsby* by F. Scott Fitzgerald	Sound comes to motion pictures in *The Jazz Singer*	
ECONOMICS AND TRADE		Commercial radio broadcasting to the public begins				Stock market crash
TECHNOLOGY AND IDEAS				B. F. Goodrich registers the trademark *zipper*	Charles Lindbergh makes first flight across the Atlantic Ocean	
RELIGION AND SOCIETY	United States ratifies the 19th Amendment, giving women the right to vote; 18th Amendment (Prohibition) is passed					

The Twenties, Thirties, and World War II

1920–1947

1932	1933	1934	1938	1941	1945	1947

The film *It Happened One Night* shows Clark Gable without an undershirt, and men's undershirt sales drop sharply

U.S. regulations restrict clothing manufacture and ration leather goods

Christian Dior introduces the New Look

Franklin D. Roosevelt elected U.S. president; the New Deal begins

Hitler comes to power in Germany; repeal of Prohibition

Japan bombs Pearl Harbor and the United States enters WWII

Roosevelt dies and Harry S Truman becomes U.S. president; atomic bombs are dropped on Hiroshima and Nagasaki; Japan surrenders

First use of Technicolor process in motion pictures

Nylon fiber first marketed by E. I. du Pont de Nemours Company

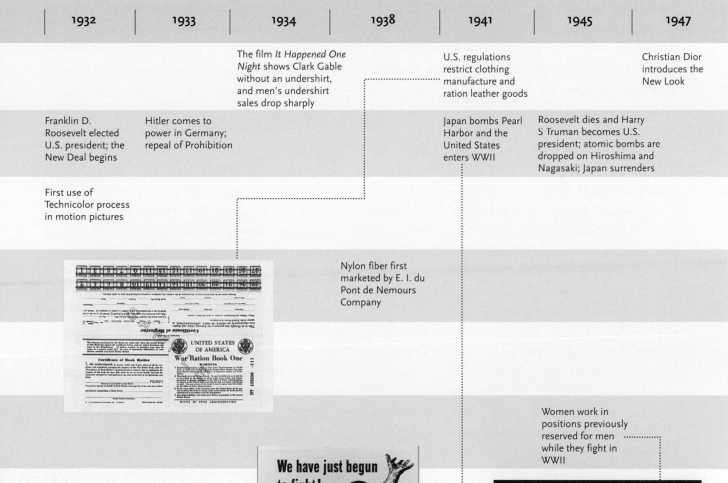

Women work in positions previously reserved for men while they fight in WWII

The twenties were characterized by prosperity and radical changes in clothing for women; the thirties, a worldwide Great Depression; and the forties, World War II. In these 27 years the American ready-to-wear industry thrived. Before the war the French *haute couture* created styles that were copied around the world. When access to French designers was cut off by the war, American designers were featured by the fashion press. The artistic developments of Art Deco, Cubism, fauvism, expressionism, and surrealism were reflected in fashion. Automobiles made shorter skirts practical, and the fashions shown in motion pictures were seen by millions of people.

HISTORICAL BACKGROUND

With the end of World War I, Europe and the United States hoped for a return to normalcy. U.S. President Woodrow Wilson, a strong proponent of the League of Nations, campaigned arduously for ratification of the Treaty of Versailles and membership for the United States in the League. These efforts cost him his health—he suffered a breakdown in 1919—and he was an invalid for the remainder of his 17 months in office. In the end, the Senate defeated the treaty, and the United States never joined the League of Nations.

Warren G. Harding was elected president of the United States in 1920. During his administration a separate peace resolution was approved, and the "official business" of World War I finally was concluded.

The Twenties

In the wake of World War I, imperial monarchies in Austria-Hungary and Russia collapsed. Germany, reduced in size, became a republic; Austria-Hungary split into small, weak states. In Russia, following the fall of the czar and the demise of a weak democratic government, the communists, led by Vladimir Lenin, seized power in 1917 and established a centralized government with the Communist Party as the only legal party. To enforce its will, the communist government established a secret police to persecute political opponents and maintain the tyranny of the party.

Josef Stalin emerged victorious in the power struggle after Lenin's death. Stalin decreed forced industrialization and collectivization of agriculture. He then launched a purge of the people to break resistance to his policies and to eliminate all possible opposition. Millions of Russian men and women were killed or imprisoned, and millions more were shipped to slave-labor camps in Siberia.

Italian parliamentary government succumbed in 1922 when the fascist party, led by Benito Mussolini, came into power.

In the meantime in the early 1920s the United States settled down to a period of unequaled prosperity. From 1923 to 1927 business was booming. A survey of the consumer goods that sold most actively provides a key to the interests and lifestyle that developed over the period. Leading the sales charts were automobiles. Radios (commercial broadcasting to the public began in 1922), rayon, cigarettes, refrigerators, telephones, cosmetics, and electrical devices of all kinds were sold in huge quantities (Figure 16.1). The purchasing power of the dollar increased twofold for most Americans. There was a boom in higher education, self-improvement books sold briskly, and travel abroad increased. In 1928, 437,000 people left the United States by ship to visit some distant place.

Life changed significantly, particularly for women. More women matriculated from high school and college than ever before, entered the workforce, and in 1920—with the ratification of the 19th Amendment—gained the right to vote.

This prosperity, however, had a dark side. Although business was thriving and most people were increasingly affluent, the American farmer was experiencing hard times. The demand for agricultural products was fairly stable and the export market dropped off, creating surpluses. Cotton went into decline as rayon, a manufactured fiber, became more popular.

Another cloud on the horizon was Prohibition. The 18th Amendment was passed and the distilling,

FIGURE 16.1 Radios broadcasted news and entertainment, including comedies, drama, and sports. Families and friends gathered nightly around the radio at home to listen to programming together. (The Advertising Archives)

flying records and short-lived line of medium-priced women's sportswear replete with notions from aviation—a parachute cord for ties or belts, ball-bearing belt buckles, and propeller wings for buttons—brought added attention to flying. Passenger service was beginning by the end of the decade. A cross-continental flight combined with rail transportation (it was too dangerous to fly at night, so by night passengers took the train) took 2 days. And the first airmail service was initiated.

Changes in the Social Life of the Twenties

After World War I had ended, the social climate in Europe and in the United States changed. This change was especially pronounced in the United States. Not only had the war left people wondering whether their efforts were justified, other disturbing

FIGURE 16.2 Charles Lindbergh's nonstop flight from New York to Paris galvanized public acceptance of the airplane and commercial aviation. (National Portrait Gallery, Smithsonian Institution/Art Resource, NY)

brewing, and sale of alcoholic beverages became illegal in 1920. In the long run, the amendment was ignored by many. In the process of violating the law, a new institution, the speakeasy—a clandestine drinking club for drinking, dining, and dancing—replaced the saloon. When Prohibition was repealed in 1933, the speakeasy made a rapid transition into the nightclub.

Several other American institutions planted their roots firmly during the 1920s. One was the chain store. National or regional chains of stores served to bring prices of consumer goods down and increase purchasing power. Installment buying took a firm hold, too.

With the spectacular success of Charles A. Lindbergh's transatlantic flight in 1927, flying took on new importance (Figure 16.2). Amelia Earhart's

FIGURE 16.3 The "flapper" and "sheik" as drawn by John Held Jr. became the personification of "flaming youth" and 1920s styles: He is in his colorful argyle pullover, and she has her stockings rolled and her lips and cheeks rouged. (John Held Jr., "The Petting Green," *Life*, March 3, 1927)

notions, such as the sexual theories of Sigmund Freud and the changing social roles of women, resulted in a revolution in mores and values, especially among the young. Reactions varied. There were the romantic cynics such as novelist F. Scott Fitzgerald and his heroes and heroines: escapists who followed a ceaseless round of parties and pleasure. There was an increasing number of isolationists who saw America as having no important ties to Europe or the rest of the world. And of course, there were the average citizens who were increasingly bewildered by the antics of the pleasure seekers.

Writers of the period spoke of a revolution in morality, evident in the behavior of the young, particularly women. Until World War I, there were certain standards of behavior expected of "ladies." They were not supposed to smoke, to drink, or to see young men unchaperoned; certainly a lady was expected to kiss only the boy she intended to marry. By the 1920s, all this had changed. The **flapper**, as she was nicknamed, seemed free from all of the restraints of the past. She smoked and drank, she necked in parked cars, she danced the Charleston until all hours of the night, and she dressed totally different from her predecessors. She was caricatured perfectly by John Held Jr., whose drawings of flappers appeared often on the covers of *Life* magazine (Figure 16.3). According to writer Marilyn Horn,

> the sensitivity of fashion to social problems provides a visible index of agitation and unrest. Drastic changes in clothing patterns are evidence of changes elsewhere. (1975, 107)

Women's costume of the 1920s provides visible evidence of the agitation and unrest of which Horn spoke. Never before in the history of costume in the civilized west had women worn skirts that revealed their legs. Except for a brief period after the French Revolution, women's hair had never been cut so short nor had flesh-colored stockings been worn. Trousers had heretofore been strictly a man's garment. (Earlier attempts to introduce bifurcated garments for women had utilized bloomers, which were cut differently from a man's trousers). Rouge and lip color had not been used by "nice" girls. But during the 1920s all of these things became commonplace. These were visible changes in acceptable dress for women that paralleled changes in the social roles of women.

The Thirties

Toward the end of the decade, the 1920s prosperity bubble burst. Business had been faltering after about 1927, but the stock market continued to rise to what astute financial observers felt were dangerous heights. On October 29, 1929, the stock market collapsed, the last of several drops that had each been followed by recovery. This time the recovery never came. The United States and Europe sank into the period now known as the Great Depression.

Unemployment was widespread. American farmers who had never participated in the prosperity of the 1920s were affected even more sharply during the Depression. Those of the midwest were further devastated by natural disasters that included floods and the decade-long Dust Bowl, a series of storms that lifted huge clouds of dust into rural areas and cities alike.

The labor movement, which had made gains in the United States during World War I and shortly after, had no great successes in the 1920s, but during the 1930s unionization advanced. These advances were accompanied by violence and strikes, as industrialists did not capitulate to labor without resistance.

At the same time, not everyone was poor. Many individuals and families retained their wealth. Women turned to *Vogue* and *Harper's Bazaar*, and men, to *Esquire*, for fashion news. They vacationed on the Riviera, in Palm Springs, or at Newport, Rhode Island. They made headlines in the gossip columns and socialized with movie stars (see Contemporary Comments 16.1 about the effect of the Depression on styles even for the wealthy).

International Political Developments

In Germany, democracy fell victim to the Depression when a government headed by Austrian-born Adolf Hitler, leader of the Nazi party, came into power in 1933 and established a one-party dictatorship. Soon Hitler began to rearm Germany, evading the restrictions of the Treaty of Versailles.

In 1935, fascist Italy invaded Ethiopia, and in 1936, Italy and Germany formed the Rome–Berlin Axis. In 1938, Germany annexed Austria and part of Czechoslovakia. World War II began on September 1, 1939, with the German invasion of Poland. German forces overran Norway, Denmark, France, and the Low Countries in 1940, but the invasion of Russia in 1941 proved a disaster for Hitler's armies. The United States remained outside of the war but was clearly sympathetic to the British and French.

In east Asia the Japanese parliamentary government moved toward military dictatorship when Army officers precipitated a clash in an outlying province of China in 1931 and moved swiftly to occupy that province. China, lacking an effective central government, failed to stem Japanese aggression. In 1937, a clash between Japanese and Chinese forces turned into a full-fledged war.

Meanwhile, Japanese leaders, convinced that the United States blocked their path to an empire in Asia, ordered the December 7, 1941, attack on Pearl Harbor (Figure 16.4). The U.S. Congress then passed a resolution on December 8, 1941, to declare war against Japan. Three days later, Germany and Italy declared war on the United States, which became fully involved in the war effort.

FIGURE 16.4 World War II (1939–1945) was the deadliest and most destructive war in history. More than 50 nations in the world were fighting, with more than 100 million soldiers deployed. (Eileen Tweedy/The Art Archive at Art Resource, NY)

Contemporary Comments 16.1

IMPACT OF THE DEPRESSION ON PARIS FASHIONS

The impact of the Depression on Parisian fashions is noted on July 28, 1932, in the New York Times *(page 2, column 6).*

HARD TIMES HIT PARIS SOCIETY MANY WEAR LAST YEAR'S GOWNS

By the Associated Press
Paris. July 20 (by mail)

Europe's smart set is feeling the pinch of hard times.

Summer soirees held in Parisian embassies, long famous for the brilliance of the women's costumes, this year reveal many gowns of last year's vintage worn with jewels worth hundreds of thousands of dollars. The jewels remain as souvenirs of more prosperous days, while the price of a new frock is often lacking.

Many of the wealthiest women who have not yet felt the pinch are dressing more simply than last year, since they feel ostentatious costume is bad taste these days.

White satin gowns are favorites with many smart women for formal embassy functions, since they can be worn with different jewels and varicolored wraps and slippers. They follow somewhat classic lines, which have not varied markedly within the last two years and may be worn without appearing hopelessly out of date.

Courtesy of the Associated Press.

Wartime industrial production brought the United States out of the Depression. In the late 1930s, recovery had begun, but this recovery was not complete when the war began.

World War II

Because they were outside of the fighting zones, Americans did not experience devastation of homes and communities during World War II. The war was brought home more directly by the draft and military casualties. Scarce goods, largely foodstuffs and gasoline, were rationed. Few clothing items were actually rationed, except for shoes made of leather, which was in short supply. Guidelines called the **L-85 Regulations** restricted the quantity of cloth that could be used in clothing (Figure 16.5). Savings in fabric were made by eliminating trouser cuffs, extra pockets,

and vests with double-breasted suits, and by regulating the width of skirt hems and the length of men's trousers and suit jackets. Some garments, such as wedding dresses and burial gowns, were exempt from restrictions. Women also "made-do and mended," recycling out-of-fashion clothing and textile scraps into new clothing for themselves and their families (Mower and Pedersen, 2013). (Contemporary Comments 16.2 summarizes these restrictions on women's styles).

Many fabrics available before the war were in short supply. Nylon, introduced at the New York World's Fair in 1939, was diverted to military use. Wool was scarce. Silk supplies were disrupted because of the war in the Pacific. Natural rubber was unavailable for civilian use.

Because most able-bodied men enlisted or were drafted into the armed services, women entered

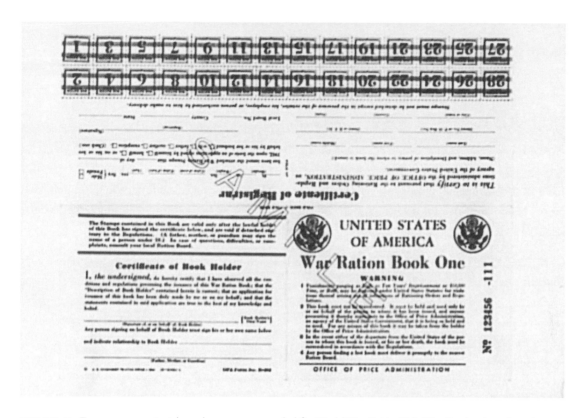

FIGURE 16.5 To preserve materials and manpower needed for World War II, the U.S. War Productions Board issued regulations governing the styles of outerwear (L-85) and underwear (L-90). Capitalizing on the press regarding the orders, some fashion designers used even less fabric than required. (Library of Congress Prints & Photographs Division Washington, DC 20540, http://hdl.loc.gov/loc.pnp/pp.print)

factories and took on jobs that were formerly held by men (Figure 16.6). In factories, women required specialized kinds of clothing, and coveralls, slacks, and turbans were generally adopted for jobs involving active physical labor.

The war in Europe ended in May 1945 but continued in the Pacific until September. With the cessation of hostilities the countries involved turned to rebuilding their devastated lands. The United States emerged from the fighting with its land unscathed and its economy intact, but millions of families had experienced the loss of one or more men in battle.

FIGURE 16.6 While the most lasting image of women's patriotism during World War II is Rosie the Riveter, women also volunteered with the Red Cross and served in the military. When men returned home from the war, many women were laid off from their positions. (Art Resource/Art Resource, NY)

GENERAL LIMITATION ORDER L-85

On April 8, 1942, Women's Wear Daily *published the "General Limitation Order L-85, Restrictions on Feminine Apparel for Outerwear and Certain Other Garments." Reproduced here are some of the major items in the order.*

The fulfillment of requirements for the defense of the United States has created a shortage in the supply of wool, silk, rayon, cotton and linen for defense, for private account and for export; and the following Order is deemed necessary and appropriate in the public interest and to promote the National Defense.

(d) GENERAL EXCEPTIONS: The prohibitions and restrictions of this Order shall not apply to feminine apparel manufactured or sold for use as:

1. Infants and Toddler's Apparel, size range from 1 to 4;
2. Bridal Gowns;
3. Maternity Dresses;
4. Clothing for persons who, because of abnormal height, size or physical deformities, require additional material for proportionate length of skirt or jacket or sweep of skirt or width of sleeve;
5. Burial Gowns;
6. Robes or Vestments as required by the rules of Religious Orders or Sects

or when manufactured for or sold to the [armed forces.]

(e) GENERAL RESTRICTIONS

1. more than two articles of apparel at one unit price.
2. any garment of multiple units, any of which contains wool cloth to be sold at a unit price.
3. French cuffs on sleeves.
4. double material yokes.
5. balloon, dolman, or leg-of-mutton sleeves.
6. fabrics which have been reduced from normal width or length by overall tucking, shirring, or pleating, except for minor trimmings.
7. inside pockets of wool cloth.
8. patch pockets of wool cloth on a lined wool cloth garment.
9. interlinings containing any virgin or reprocessed wool.

The order went on to identify specific restrictions for women's misses and junior misses coats, daytime and evening dresses, suits, jackets, separate skirts and culottes, slacks and playclothes, and blouses and also for teenage girls and children's apparel in the categories of dresses, coats, rainwear, slacks and playclothes, snow and ski suits, and nurses' and maids' uniforms. Specific limitations, identified in tables appended to the order, were placed on the length and circumference of skirts and the width of jackets. Some notable restrictions included:

- no coats with "separate or attached cape, hood, muff, scarf, bag or hat";
- no daytime or evening dresses "with a separate or attached belt exceeding 2 inches in width";
- no evening dresses or suits or skirts and culottes "with a hem exceeding 2 inches in width";
- no jackets "with sleeves cut on the bias or with cuffs on long sleeves"; and
- no slacks "with a cuff."

INFLUENCES ON FASHIONS

Influences on fashion included movies, royalty and café society, sports, and the automobile.

The Movies

Silent films had, by the 1920s, become a part of everyday life. In addition to providing a diversion, movies brought visions of glamorous actors and actresses into every small town across America. Life depicted in films helped reinforce the hedonistic attitudes and helped spread urban tastes, urban dress, and an urban way of living.

Film stars became fashion setters. Rudolph Valentino was the idol of millions of American women, and men copied his pomaded, patent-leather–look hair. In her first major film role, actress Joan Crawford personified the fast-living flapper of the 1920s, and women across the country imitated her makeup, hairstyle, and clothes.

With the beginning of talking pictures in 1927, films became more popular than ever. In the early 1930s reaction in the United States against some films that were thought to have too much nudity and sex led to a strict code of propriety as to what could or could not be shown on the screen. Many films of the 1930s did not at all reflect the bleak economic picture of the Depression. Women were lavishly gowned and houses magnificently furnished. In the film *Letty Lynton*, Joan Crawford wore a dress with dramatic, large ruffled sleeves. This dress inspired a host of imitations at all price levels (Figure 16.7). Off screen, the movie star was a fashion influence. Greta Garbo's broad-shouldered, natural beauty was one ideal of feminine beauty of the era. Women bleached their hair blonde in imitation of Jean Harlow. Thousands of mothers

a

b

FIGURE 16.7 This large-sleeved dress (a) was worn by Joan Crawford in the 1932 film *Letty Lynton* (Hulton Archives/Getty Images). It became popular with the public and inspired many imitations, such as this version (b) from the spring 1933 Sears, Roebuck catalogue. (Detail: The Art Archive at Art Resource, NY) curled their daughters' hair into ringlets like those of Shirley Temple, the famous child star.

During the war movies stressed patriotic themes. Among the screen heroes of the day were the clean-cut American boy Van Johnson and the rugged individualist Spencer Tracy. Teenage girls wore pageboy hair like June Allyson or draped a wave over one eye in the peekaboo style of Veronica Lake. Movie studio publicity offices printed pin-up pictures of actress Betty Grable in a backless bathing suit and high heels. Films were made in Technicolor, and Americans flocked to the movies throughout the war.

Royalty and Cafe Society

European royalty and ex-royalty, as well as cafe society, influenced fashion. During the 1920s and 1930s one important style setter was the British Prince of Wales (later known as the Duke of Windsor). He ascended to the throne as King Edward VIII in 1936, but abdicated after less than a year to marry American divorcée Wallis Simpson. During the 1930s wealthy Americans and Europeans were photographed at fashionable resorts in the United States and abroad. The rich wore much of the sportswear that became popular for tennis, riding, and skiing. Few others had the leisure and money to engage in these activities in the 1930s. Some of the debutantes of the late 1930s caught the imagination of the public, and gossip columns were full of news about coming-out parties, cotillions, and charity balls. Brenda Frazier, a famous debutante, helped publicize a new style, the strapless evening gown.

Sports

The numbers of participants in both spectator sports and active sports increased. Attendance at sporting events in the 1920s broke all previous records. Baseball, college football, boxing, tennis, and golf were widely followed. Seeing women as leading sports figures was a new phenomenon. The interest in watching sports had the logical side effect of increasing participation in sports, and widespread prosperity made this participation easy for many. Sports stars appeared in films, so that a national audience that would otherwise

have seen them only in photographs knew them through these films.

As active sports for everyone became more widespread, sports clothing became more important. Special dress was required for sports such as skiing and tennis. The move to expanded outdoor recreation reinforced the need for practical, casual dress and established **sportswear** as a separate category of clothing. This new type of clothing, worn for leisure time but not dedicated to one particular sport, entered the vocabulary of fashion and also became a merchandising term. California, which had created clothing for the film stars of Hollywood, became particularly adept at creating sportswear.

Throughout this text, *sportswear* refers to clothing for men and women that is worn for leisure or informal situations, while clothing for sports is discussed under the heading of the clothing for active sports.

The Automobile

Once the automobile became practical transportation rather than a sport, special costume for motoring disappeared. As women began to drive routinely, the need for shorter and less cumbersome skirts was evident. Although daytime skirts dropped fairly low to just above the ankle in the early 1930s and again in the 1950s, skirts have not reached all the way to the floor for everyday wear since 1910, and it is possible that the automobile has been, in part, responsible for this.

The automobile also may have been responsible for the abandonment of the parasol, or sun shade. Women walked less, and parasols were both impractical in open cars and unnecessary in closed vehicles. Cars encouraged the use of wristwatches (which were easier to look at while driving than pocket watches) and probably made smaller hats preferable. Canes and walking sticks went out of style.

Cars allowed workers to live in suburban areas and commute to the city and made new recreational opportunities possible by carrying individuals and families out of the city and into the countryside. These recreational aspects of car use contributed to the growing use of casual sport clothes.

Technological Developments Affecting Fashion

For centuries, fabrics available for clothing had been limited to those found in nature. Although people in a few parts of the world used unusual local materials for garments, western societies tended to utilize four natural fibers: cotton, linen, silk, and wool. As early as the 1880s, Count Hilaire de Chardonnet of France had manufactured a new fiber from cellulose. Called **artificial silk**, the fiber did not gain rapid acceptance, as it was too lustrous and did not wash well. Gradually it was improved, and by 1924 the National Retail Dry Goods Association coined the fiber **rayon**, which was used fairly widely. A second and quite different manufactured fiber came into commercial use after World War I. It, too, was called *rayon* until the 1950s when it was given a separate name, **acetate**, to distinguish it from rayon. Throughout the 1920s and increasingly in the 1930s, rayon fabrics (including acetate) were used, mostly in women's clothing.

The first **nylon** fibers were marketed by E. I. du Pont de Nemours Company in 1938. Shown at the 1939 World's Fair, nylon quickly gained favor for use in women's underwear and stockings. This strong, durable fiber was put to military use during World War II. No longer accessible to the general public at that time, nylon was not readily available again until after the war.

Unless individuals were to wear only loose, unfitted clothing that could be put on over the head, some means of closure had to be used. Lacing and buttons were the chief means of fastening garments shut until the 19th century when a wide variety of metal hooks and eyes were developed.

Whitcomb L. Judson from Chicago had invented the zipper in 1891. He called this first version a *clasp locker*. An imperfect device (it kept falling apart), the design was improved by Gideon Sundbäck, who went on to manufacture **hookless fasteners** that were sold for use in corsets, gloves, sleeping bags, money belts, and tobacco pouches. In the 1920s, B. F. Goodrich bought hookless fasteners for closures on rubber boots. It was Goodrich who first used the term **zipper**, calling the boots *zipper boots*. Goodrich registered the word *zipper* as a trademark in 1925, but zippers were so widely used in the 1930s and afterwards that *zipper* became a generic term applied to any toothed, slide fastener (Berendt, 1989).

By the mid-30s, the zipper was a well-known device, but was not universally used. Zipper manufacturers mounted a campaign to get men's trouser and suit manufacturers to use zippers in trouser fly closings. This objective, which took considerable effort to accomplish, was helped when the Prince of Wales, his brother the Duke of York, and his second cousin started to wear zippered trousers.

Use of zippers in women's high-fashion clothing grew after couturiers incorporated them into their collections. Charles James was the first major designer to use the zipper as a decorative element when in 1933 he spiraled a long zipper all around one of his dresses (Friedel, 1994). Schiaparelli put colored plastic zippers into her designs as decorative elements in 1935. Paquin, Molyneux, and Piguet used zipper closures in their 1937 collections (Friedel, 1994). As one *Life* reporter commented in the 1937 article "Now Everything's Zippers," seemingly, "Overnight . . . the zipper which had been an accepted functional gadget for smooth, secure closings, became an important as a style element" (Friedel, 1994, 192).

By the early 1940s the zipper was well established as a closure and appeared in clothing in all price ranges. After the beginning of World War II, the supply of zippers was curtailed because of metal shortages.

The French Couture

The French couture maintained its position as the arbiter of style in clothing for women from 1920 until the German occupation during World War II cut Paris off from contact with England and America. Although the couture in general was influential, in each period certain designers stood out from the rest. Just as Poiret had occupied a special place among the designers of the late Edwardian period and before World War I, so did the designs of Chanel typify the style of the 1920s, Vionnet the early 1930s, and Schiaparelli the later 1930s.

FIGURE 16.8 Gabrielle "Coco" Chanel, wearing one of her signature cardigan suits in 1929, was one of the best models for her own designs. (Sasha/Getty Images)

Gabrielle "Coco" Chanel began to work as a designer before World War I. During the war she had a small shop at Deauville, a seaside resort, where she had great success in making casual knit jackets and pullover sweaters. She designed comfortable, practical clothes, buying sailor's jackets and men's pullover sweaters that she combined with pleated skirts. Soon she was having these garments made especially for her own clients.

After the war she returned to Paris and set up a salon that became one of the most influential in Paris. She is credited with making the suntanned look and costume jewelry popular, but her real genius lay in designing simple, classic wool jersey styles (Figure 16.8).

In the late 1920s Chanel went to Hollywood briefly to design for films. It had been the practice to dress film stars in the most elaborate costumes possible, even when these were not appropriate for the time of day. Chanel insisted that the costumes be appropriate for the action of the drama, and in this way she was responsible for a new authenticity in film clothes. She continued to be a leading fashion designer throughout the 1930s. Chanel closed her shop during World War II, and she did not reopen after the war. In 1954 she came out of retirement and surprised the fashion world by reentering the couture. She went on to have a highly successful second career as a leading couturier.

Madeleine Vionnet began to work as an apprentice in a dressmaker's shop at the age of 13. She worked at the important fashion house of Callot Soeurs and later for Doucet. Her plain, unadorned, but well-cut designs were not acceptable to Doucet where elaborate and lavish clothes were the mode, so she left in the years before World War I to set up her own shop. She was not especially successful until after the war in the early 1920s, at which time the house of Vionnet became part of the haute couture.

Her distinctive talent was in cutting dresses. She originated the **bias cut**, a technique for cutting clothing to utilize the diagonal direction of the cloth, which has greater stretch and drapes in such a way that the body lines and curves are accentuated. During the 1930s, when this cut was especially fashionable, she was one of the most sought-after French designers. She has been compared to an architect or sculptor (Figure 16.9). She completely understood the medium of fabric and, through cutting and draping, created styles of such simplicity and elegance that they are still admired. She retired in 1939, and although she lived until 1975, she never returned to the couture.

Elsa Schiaparelli, an Italian designer, worked in Paris in the 1930s where she began by creating sweaters in bizarre designs. She had a flair for the theatrical. By the end of the 1930s she was an exceedingly popular designer whose emphasis on color and unusual decorative effects was widely praised. She is credited with being among the first in the couture to use

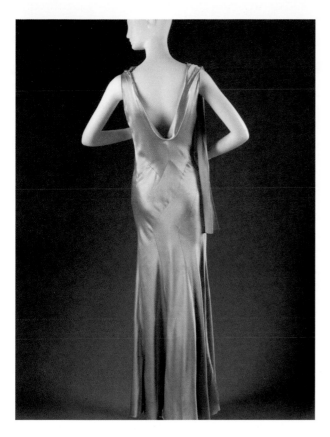

FIGURE 16.9 Madeleine Vionnet was renowned for superb workmanship and her ability to structure garments using a special design technique called *bias cut* that made use of the way fabrics draped on the body. This backless evening dress with its bias-cut panels from 1932 is typical of high-fashion formal gowns. (Image copyright © The Metropolitan Museum of Art. Image source: Art Resource, NY)

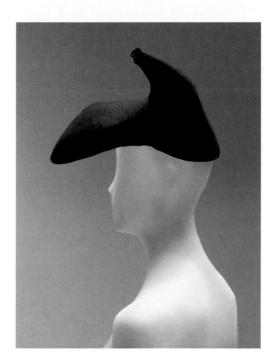

FIGURE 16.10 Schiaparelli was influenced by surrealist art, evident in this hat that resembles a high-heeled shoe, 1937–1938. The hat was made to be worn with a black dress and jacket embroidered with red lips suggestive of those belonging to the voluptuous actress Mae West. (Image copyright © The Metropolitan Museum of Art. Image source: Art Resource, NY)

zippers as colorful ornaments on pockets and dresses. Her other innovations included the first evening dress with a matching jacket and skirts to match sweaters. She worked with artists such as Salvador Dali (Figure 16.10; see also surrealism, page 472) who designed fabrics for her. She had a talent for gaining publicity for her work. In the mid-1930s Schiaparelli labeled a vivid pink color that she used *shocking pink*. When the war broke out, she came to the United States where she continued to work during and after the war.

Although some couturiers left France or closed their businesses during the war, many continued to operate in isolation during the Nazi occupation of Paris (1940–1944). As a result, the international influence of the couture was curtailed during this period. In an

in-depth study, *Fashion under the Occupation*, Veillon (2002) described dress of the period as reflecting two trends, one in which the majority of the population managed to get along and create their own style of dress and the other, the rich minority, which was almost unchanged. By maintaining its creation of high-fashion designs, the couture managed to preserve its techniques and its workforce so it could continue in the postwar period.

Chanel, Vionnet, and Schiaparelli were only three of the influential Paris-based designers of the 1920s and 1930s. Other important couturiers of the 1920–1947 period are listed in Table 16.1.

American Designers

Because international press coverage could not be given to the designs created in Paris during the war, a number of talented American designers were featured in magazines like *Vogue* and *Harper's Bazaar*

TABLE 16.1 Designers of the French Couture: 1920–1947

DESIGNER OR FOUNDER	COUTURE HOUSE AND DATE OF OPENING	NOTABLE CHARACTERISTICS
Gabrielle "Coco" Chanel (1883–1971)	Chanel, 1914	Simple and classic designs.
Alix Grès (1903–1993)	Alix, 1934	High level of craftsmanship, soft draping designs.
Jacques Heim (1899–1967)	Heim, 1923	Well-made clothes that reflected current trends.
Jeanne Lanvin (1867–1946)	Lanvin, began as milliner in 1890	Emphasized more ornate designs; originated robe de style, popular gown of the 1920s.
Lucien Lelong (1889–1958)	Lucien Lelong, 1919	Not himself a designer, his house was "famed for elegant, feminine clothes of refined taste and lasting wearability." Among the designers who worked for him were Dior, Balmain, Givenchy.
Main Rousseau Bocher (1890–1976)	Mainbocher, 1929	American, opened Paris salon in 1929, moved to New York during World War II; designed wedding dress for Duchess of Windsor.
Edward Molyneux (1891–1974)	Molyneux, 1919	"Well-bred, elegant, fluid" lines.
Jean Patou (1887–1936)	Patou, 1914	"[S]pecialized in lady-like, elegant, uncluttered country-club clothes." In 1929 he led the way to longer skirt lengths, natural waistlines.
Robert Piguet (1901–1953)	Piguet, 1933	Used freelance designers, including Givenchy and Dior, who said that he "taught the virtues of simplicity."
Nina Ricci (1883–1970)	Nina Ricci, 1932; ceased designing in 1945 but the house continued with other designers	"Graceful, with superb, detailed workmanship."
Marcel Rochas (1902–1955)	Rochas, c. 1924	Color, lots of decoration, and "fantastic" ideas in fabrics and designs.
Maggie Rouff (1897–1971)	Rouff, 1929	"Standing for refined, feminine elegance."
Elsa Schiaparelli (1890–1973)	Pour le Sport, 1929; Schiaparelli, 1935	Original, with flair for the unusual and for garnering publicity.
Madeleine Vionnet (1876–1975)	Vionnet, 1912	Noted for bias cut, exceptional technical skills. (See page 467.)

All quotes from Calasibetta, C. M. (1988). *The Fairchild dictionary of fashion* (2nd ed.). New York, NY: Fairchild Publications; and Stegemeyer, A. (1996). *Who's who in fashion* (3rd ed.). New York, NY: Fairchild Publications.

to an extent that might not have been possible had they been competing with the French couture. Once established, these designers continued to have a substantial following—although the operation of the fashion industry in America was quite different from that of the French couture.

A trade association called the *Chambre Syndicale de la Couture Parisienne* represents the French haute couture. This group defines **haute couture** as firms that create garments that may be sold to private customers or to other segments of the fashion industry who also acquire the right to reproduce the designs. In the period between the wars, the designs of the French haute couturiers were sold to private customers and to retail stores where they were resold or copied and sold to customers of the store. Through this system the designs originated by the couturiers influenced international fashions (Latour, 1956).

In the United States, by contrast, fashion designers generally worked for ready-to-wear manufacturers. Although many of the fine department stores in large cities maintained custom dressmaking or tailoring departments and smaller towns and cities had a number of local dressmakers, most American women purchased their clothing ready-to-wear in local stores.

The American fashion designer, therefore, usually worked for the dress manufacturer. He or she prepared a line of designs for a given season. Most dress firms produced clothing for four seasons: spring, summer, fall, and holiday. Some also had a resort line. These clothes were shown in New York to buyers for stores across the country. In lower-priced dresses, salespeople took samples directly to the stores. Buyers placed orders for items from the line. Those designs that did not receive an adequate number of orders were not put into production.

American designers for the most part worked in this system. Even the highest priced fashions of the 1930s and 1940s were produced in this way. One exception to this rule was **Mainbocher**, an American-born designer who went to Paris in the 1920s to work as a fashion editor. He opened his own couture house in Paris in 1929. He designed Wallis Simpson's wedding dress (she married the Duke of Windsor in June 1937). When the war came, he left Paris and returned to New York where he continued to work as he had in Paris, following the practices of the French couture.

Among the American fashion designers of the period between 1920 and the end of World War II, certain figures stand out. **Claire McCardell** is one such figure. Sally Kirkland (1975), writing about McCardell in *American Fashion*, said, "Many think Claire McCardell was the greatest fashion designer this country has yet produced. Certainly she was the most innovative, independent, and indigenous of American designers" (211).

Claire McCardell was born in Frederick, Maryland, in 1905. She studied at the Parsons School of Design and in Paris. Her first individual collection was done

for Townley Frocks in 1931 when the head designer with whom she worked was killed accidentally. She remained with this firm until 1938, when it closed. She designed chiefly sportswear and casual clothes for Townley. After 1940, she designed under her own name. She had her greatest success in the 1940s and 1950s. Her clothing was considered radical at first and was difficult to sell, but when women found her designs comfortable and flattering, they looked for more of the same.

Some of the important styles and design features that she is credited as originating or making popular include matching separates, a new idea at the time; dirndl skirts; the **monastic**, a bias-cut, full tent dress that when belted followed the body contours gracefully; hardware closings; spaghetti or shoestring ties; the diaper bathing suit; ballet slippers; and the poncho (Figure 16.11). She died in 1958.

Another prominent American designer, **Adrian**, gained his earliest recognition as a designer for films. Throughout the 1920s and 1930s he designed for both contemporary and period films, and the name Adrian became synonymous with high fashion and glamour (Figure 16.12). In 1941 he opened his own business. With Paris designs inaccessible as a result of the war, he saw that American design would become more important. Known for subtle details, he designed "in the round," thinking about how a woman would look from all angles, a result of his work in films (Horyn, 2002).

The firm of Adrian Ltd. continued in business throughout the 1940s but had to be closed in 1952 when the designer had a severe heart attack. His recovery was long and slow. When he felt ready to return to active work it was to design costumes for the musical comedy *Camelot*; however, he died in 1959 before he was able to complete the project.

Two other American designers who came to prominence during the wartime period were **Norman Norell** and **Pauline Trigère**. Norell was a native of the United States; Trigère was French and came to America in 1937. Although both Norell and Trigère were more influential in the period discussed in the

a

b

c

d

FIGURE 16.11 Some of the styles originated by Claire McCardell during her career: (a) the popover, c. 1942; (b) the draped bathing suit, c. 1944; (c) railroad stitched denim with a bib front and low back, c. 1944; and (d) string-tied Empire-line dress, c. 1944. (*Women's Wear Daily*, March 24, 1958. Courtesy of Fairchild Publications, Inc.)

Color Forecast
by Adrian of Hollywood

Guatemalan pink linen jacket...
mauve sheer wool skirt...
eloquent colors punctuated
with vivid plaid

Exclusively at **NAN DUSKIN**
in Philadelphia

next chapter, they were active in the 1940s as well (Figure 16.13). Both worked for Hattie Carnegie for a time before forming other businesses (see Table 17.2, page 517).

After the end of World War II, the French couture resumed its operation and its primacy as the center of international fashion design. American designers had, however, shown that they could create innovative and original styles and had earned an important place in the world of fashion design. In recognition of the importance of American design in the postwar period, fashion magazines continued to give extensive coverage to American designers as well as featuring Paris design.

Théâtre de la Mode

Paris was liberated from foreign occupation in the autumn of 1944. To convince the world that the

FIGURE 16.12 Tailored suit with large, square shoulder pads created by American designer Adrian in 1945 and typical of the sophisticated designs for which he was famous. (Courtesy of Nan Duskin)

FIGURE 16.13 Although Schiaparelli was most closely associated with the color called *shocking pink*, American designer Norman Norell also used this color for a dramatic effect in a 1941 design. (Illustration by Eric. Courtesy of Vogue Copyright 1941 [renewed 1961] by Condé Nast Publications, Inc.)

FIGURE 16.14 The *Théâtre de la Mode* of 1944 displayed 27-inch mannequins (right) on a miniature set (below). This traveling exhibit of the latest fashions from the haute couture not only featured the work of more than 40 French couturiers but also raised funds for war relief. (Collection of Maryhill Museum of Art)

couture was once again ready to provide leadership in fashion design and to raise money for war relief, the *Chambre Syndicale* organized an exhibit of miniature mannequins, 27 inches tall, dressed in clothes designed by more than 40 of the leading French couturiers. Included not only were dresses, suits, and coats but also shoes, hats, gloves, belts, and real jewelry. Shown in nine miniature stage sets, the almost 200 small-scale figures traveled throughout Europe and the United States until 1946 (Figure 16.14). Acquired by the Maryhill Museum in Goldendale, Washington, in 1952, they went on a second world tour in the 1990s visiting Paris, New York, Baltimore, Portland, and Tokyo.

ART MOVEMENTS AND THEIR INFLUENCE ON FASHION

The term **Art Deco** derives from the Exposition Internationale des Arts Décoratifs et Industriel Modernes, the name of an exposition held in Paris in 1925. The term has been applied to art typical of that produced in the 1920s and 1930s. Geometric forms that could be derived from artistic expressions of the past or present characterized Art Deco styles. Egyptian and Mayan motifs can be seen in Art Deco, as well as designs related to modern art movements such as Cubism, fauvism, and expressionism.

Art Deco influences are especially notable in the fashions of the 1920s, when the geometric lines of many garments can be seen to echo Art Deco style lines. Art Deco style can be observed in many fabric prints, embroideries, beaded decorations, and jewelry (see Illustrated Table 16.4, page 489). Art Deco styles underwent a revival in the 1970s.

Surrealism, literally "beyond the real," was a literary and art movement that began in the 1920s, influenced by Freudianism (Figure 16.15). Artists such as the Italian Giorgio de Chirico, the Spanish Salvador Dali, and the French René Magritte painted nonconventional scenes and objects, drawing on the subconscious imagination. By the 1930s surrealism could be seen as an influence on fashion (Martin, 1987).

Elsa Schiaparelli was a friend of many surrealist artists, and surrealist influences are especially pronounced in her work of the 1930s. Among the surreal aspects of her work were the use of body parts such as eyes, mouths, and hands in unexpected places on garments or in prints. One organza dress had a painted lobster on the skirt. Suits had butterflies or cicadas as buttons. A hat was shaped like a shoe (see Figure 16.10). Not only Dali but also surrealist writer, film director, and artist Jean Cocteau created fabrics and embroideries for Schiaparelli.

Fashion photographers of the 1930s frequently used surrealistic settings for their photographs of fashions. During and after the war, interest in surrealism in fashion waned, but in the 1980s fashion designers

FIGURE 16.15 Artist Jean (Hans) Arp created works such as *Clock*, 1924, derived from nature (two birds in the image) and the everyday environment; his works were marked by irregular but supple contours reflecting a world constantly in flux. Arp was connected to the surrealist and constructivist art movements. (© CNAC/MNAM/Dist. RMN-Grand Palais/Art Resource, NY.)

such as Lacroix and Lagerfeld incorporated surrealist motifs in their collections.

SOURCES OF INFORMATION ABOUT COSTUME

Photographs of fashions had been appearing in fashion magazines since the late 19th century. By the 1920s some fashion photographers were trying to create increasingly artistic effects. As a result some fashion photographs might be called fashion *art* photography and others fashion *information* photography. Fashion art photographs sometimes prevent the viewer from getting the maximum information about the details of clothing being shown. Fashion information photographs present a clear, undistorted view of items of dress.

During the 1920s and early 1930s, color illustrations used in fashion magazines had to be drawings. The technology for reproducing color photographs improved by the late 1930s making use of color photographs possible.

COSTUME: 1920–1947

Costume Components for Women: 1920–1930

Garments

As depicted in mail-order catalogues, undergarments came in a wide variety of styles. Items included brassieres, which had to first flatten and then, toward the end of the decade, uplift the bosom in order to provide the current fashionable shape. Drawers or knickers became **panties** in the 1920s. These were short, buttoned or elasticized at the waistline, and often very decorative.

An evolution of the combination was a garment alternately known as **cami-knickers**, **step-ins**, or **teddies**, a combination of the camisole and panties. A straight-cut chemise or petticoat was renamed the **slip**, and was comparable to the garment called by that name today. Larger women wore corsets. These were boned or made with elastic panels, or both. Garters suspended from the corset held up the stockings; women who did not wear corsets wore garter belts or garters to hold up their stockings. See Illustrated Table 16.1 for examples of undergarments during the years between 1920 and 1947.

A figure with a flat bosom and narrow hips was the ideal. The fashionable silhouette was straight, without indentation at the waistline. When a dress had a belt, the belt was placed at the hipline. Most dresses were one piece (Figure 16.16).

At the beginning of the period, skirts were long and reached almost to the ankle, tending downward in 1922 but gradually moving upward in 1924 and after. By 1925 they were about 8 inches from the floor, by 1926–1927, 14 to 16 inches, some even as short as 18 inches from the ground. Once skirts reached this elevation, they remained relatively stable in 1928–1929, then began to lengthen again (Richards, 1983). The first move toward longer lengths was observable in a tendency to cut skirt hems unevenly with panelled, flared, scalloped, or pointed segments of the skirt. By the end of the decade, skirt lengths had dropped

FIGURE 16.16 Styles of 1922 reflect the introduction of a new silhouette: narrow, with a dropped waistline. In the postwar period, hemlines had lengthened. (The New York Public Library/Art Resource, NY)

(Figure 16.17 gives a diagrammatic representation of skirt lengths throughout the 1920s).

For daytime one-piece styles predominated. Some coat dresses had crossover, right to left, closings. Necklines usually ended at the base of the throat or lower, with round, V-shaped, bateau, or cowl styles. Round, high, and V-necklines often were finished with collars or bias ruffles. When dresses had sleeves, they were often long. Many dresses were sleeveless. Most bodices were plain and cut straight to the hip. Some had embroidered decorations or pleating. Skirts were more complex in cut than bodices, often utilizing bias cutting to produce interesting effects. Skirts had pleats and gathers placed off center, scalloped hems, godet insets, and paneled effects that achieved **handkerchief skirt** styles.

Illustrated Table 16.1

Selected Undergarments for Women, Men, and Boys: 1920–1947

Woman's brassiere, 1923[1]

Woman's corset, 1923[1]

Woman's step-in chemise, 1923[1]

Brassiere and girdle, 1930s[2]

Slip and panties, 1934[3]

Brassiere, World War II period; due to shortage of broadcloth, these brassieres were made of printed calico[2]

[1] Reprinted from Franklin Simon & Co. 1993. *Franklin Simon Fashion Catalog for 1923*, Mineola, NY, pp. 83, 88, with permission by Dover Publications, Inc.

[2] Based on illustration from The Maidenform Museum, New York, NY.

[3] Fairchild Publications, Inc.

Illustrated Table 16.1

Selected Undergarments for Women, Men, and Boys: 1920–1947 (continued)

Men's undershirts and undershorts, 1922[4]

Boy's boxer shorts and undershirt, 1930s[5]

Men's jockey-type under shorts, undershirt, long underdrawers, and T-shirt, 1938–1939[3]

[4] Reprinted from *Everyday fashions of the twenties* by S. Blum, 1981, p. 190, Mineola, NY, with permission by Dover Publications, Inc.

[5] Reprinted from *Everyday fashions of the thirties* by C. B. Grafton, 1993, p. 55, Mineola, NY, with permission by Dover Publications, Inc.

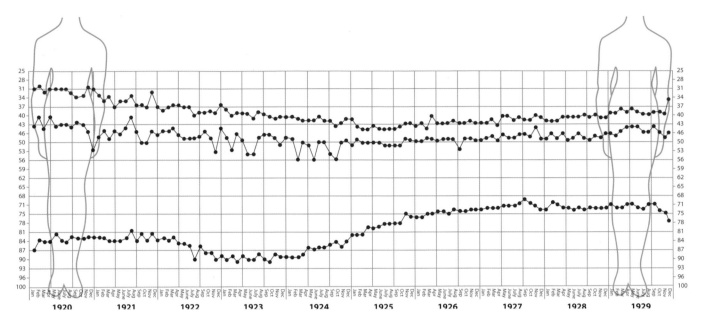

FIGURE 16.17 Location of the average waistline, hipline, and hemline during the 1920s as calculated according to percentage of total figure height. (From Richards, L. [1983]. The rise and fall of it all: The hemlines and hiplines of the 1920s. *Clothing and Textiles Research Journal*, 2[1], 47)

Separate blouses and sweaters were popular. Most were elongated, low-hipped, and straight, and worn over, not tucked into, the skirt (Figure 16.18). Middy blouses were fashionable.

Tailored suits had matching jackets and skirts, with jackets ending at the hip or below. The Chanel suit, a cardigan-style jacket and skirt made from wool jersey (see Figure 16.8), was very popular. When suits were belted, the belt was placed well below normal waist placement. Some opened at the center front, closed on the left. Long lapels that rolled to a low closing were fashionable. **Ensembles** were matching dresses and coats or matching skirts, overblouses, and coats.

Made in the same lengths as daytime dresses, evening dresses grew shorter as daytime dresses grew shorter. Generally sleeveless, with deep V- or U-shaped necklines, some evening bodices were supported over

FIGURE 16.18 Skirt lengths of mid-decade had grown shorter, reaching just to the knee. Belts were placed at the hip for day wear and for active sports. Hip-length cardigan-style jackets were especially popular for jacket and skirt ensembles or suits. Cloche-style hats were worn over short, bobbed hair. (© Amoret Tanner/Alamy)

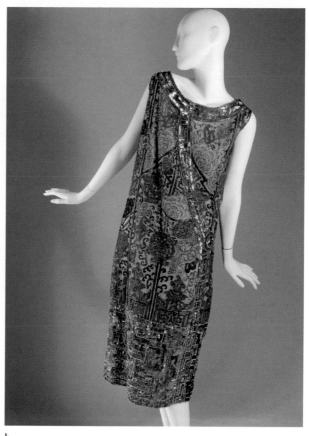

a

b

FIGURE 16.19 (a) This dress was designed by Jeanne Lanvin and has the wide skirt she created in the *robe de style*, an alternative silhouette for some dresses of the 1920s. (Evening dress, metallic sequin and beading, c. 1925, USA. The Museum at FIT, 81.12.23. Photo © The Museum at FIT) (b) Although this beaded, unfitted evening dress, c. 1925, is cut in the typical tubular, chemise style characteristic of the period, it also utilizes Chinese ornamental motifs, which appeared in some 1920s dresses (Image copyright © The Metropolitan Museum of Art. Image source: Art Resource, NY).

the shoulder by small straps. Skirts of evening dresses were often more complex in cut than daytime dresses and used such effects as floating panels, draped areas, or layered skirts. In 1919 Jeanne Lanvin introduced a bouffant skirt, reminiscent of the crinoline period. An evening dress of this type with a dropped waistline and full skirt, called the **robe de style**, was a popular alternative to the tubular silhouette (Figure 16.19a). As the decade progressed, the tendency to cut skirts unevenly also appeared in evening styles.

Beading was a popular means of ornamenting evening dresses and sometimes covered the entire dress (Figure 16.19b). Fashionable fabrics included chiffon, soft satins, and velvets (and for the *robe de style* garments, silk taffeta). Geometric Art Deco designs were frequently used as fabric patterns. Cross-cultural decorative motifs, such as those from China, also appeared (see Global Connections).

Plus-sized women's garments followed the general silhouette but often included additional design details or fabric panels to flatter the figure (Keist and Marcketti, 2013).

Outdoor Garments

The most characteristic coats closed over the left hip, often with one large decorative button or several small ones. Some coats, known as **clutch coats**, had to be held shut because they had no fastening.

Young women (and young men) wore raccoon coats for motoring or to football games. Fur and

Global Connections

In the 1920s, garments, particularly those influenced by Art Deco, included medallions of Chinese embroidery, Chinese-style frog closures, and Chinese characters (Steele and Major, 1999). This traditional Chinese silk brocade jacket in the Manchu style belonged to a young boy in the early 20th century. The jacket's design incorporates many symbols that represent species or objects thought to have protective qualities: the bat or *fu*, for happiness, the dancing lion or *nen*, often used for

celebrations, and the swastika or *wan* for good fortune. As Martin and Koda (1994) stated, "Eastern ideas of textile, design, construction, and utility have been realized again and again as a positive contribution to the culture of the West" (11). (In the permanent collection of the Textiles and Clothing Museum, College of Human Sciences, Iowa State University, Ames, IA. 1042)

fur-trimmed capes and wraps were popular among the more well-to-do. Sweaters, long and belted low, were popular as sportswear.

Sleepwear

Night clothing consisted of either nightgowns or pajamas, both of which had long, straight lines.

Hair and Headdress

See Illustrated Table 16.2 for some examples of hairstyles and hats from the period of 1920 to 1947.

Women's hairstyles of the 1920s constituted one of the more revolutionary developments in fashion. Except for the empire period, in which short hair was fashionable, no other earlier costume periods can be cited in which women cut their hair short. Viewed at first as a radical style, by 1923 it had become accepted fashion, and college girls across the country were singing (to the tune of *Jingle Bells*), "Shingle bob,

shingle bob, cut it all away." To have one's hair **bobbed** was to have it cut. The **shingle** was an exceptionally short cut in which the back hair was cut and tapered like that of a man. Although the most fashionable cut was short with the hair tapering off to the nape of the neck, many variations were seen. Some women cut their hair short, with bangs at the front and the hair turned under at the ends on the sides and in the back. Others followed the extreme **Eton crop**, a style in which hair was exceptionally closely cropped and dressed like that of the men. Frederick Lewis Allen (1931) pointed out the widespread nature of the style for short hair in the United States: "In the latter years of the 1920s bobbed hair became almost universal among girls in their 20s, very common among women in their 30s and 40s, and by no means rare among women of sixty" (87–88).

Some women wore their bobbed hair straight, others with a **marcel wave**, a style made up of a series

Illustrated Table 16.2

Selected Hairstyles and Hats for Women: 1920–1947

Woman's hairstyle, 1921

Bobbed hair, 1922

Woman's cloche-style
hat, 1921

Woman's hat, 1926

Woman's hat, 1928

Women's hats, 1933

Woman's hat, 1937

Woman's "upsweep"
hairstyle, 1941

Stocking cap, 1943

Flowered hat with
face veil, 1943

Hat with a one-sided
look, 1944

of deep waves all over the head. The old-fashioned, open hairpin was replaced by the **bobby pin**, with its tight spring clip. By the end of the decade, however, women started to let their hair grow again, and small curls began to appear at the back of the head. Of course, some women never did cut their hair, but even those with longer hair usually wore it dressed straight or waved close to the face with a tight bun at the back of the neck.

Because they were worn with short hair, hats could be fitted close to the head. Just as the bob was the prevailing hair style, a small, closely fitted hat called the **cloche** became the predominant hat form. In general, cloches had small or larger brims that turned down around the face. Some larger summer hats with wide, down-turned brims hid the face almost entirely. Berets were popular for sports. Headbands were colloquially known as **headache bands**. Some that were jeweled and others with tall feathers attached were popular for evening, as were turbans.

Footwear

See Illustrated Table 16.3 for some examples of footwear from the period of 1920 to 1947.

Short skirts caused women to focus greater attention on hosiery. In the early years of the decade, dark stockings or white stockings continued in use, but as skirts grew shorter, tan- or flesh-colored stockings replaced them. More luxurious stockings were silk, but rayon was coming into widespread use for less-expensive stockings. Cartoons by John Held Jr. depicted the flapper of the period in stockings rolled below the knee, a skirt above the knee, and rouge on the knees.

Heels were 2 to $2^1/_2$ inches high; toes were pointed or rounded. Commonly seen styles included pumps with a strap across the instep or T-shaped straps that crossed the instep and ran down the center of the foot. Oxfords were worn, especially for sports. Dressy evening slippers were made of fabric or gold or silver leather.

Women wore Russian-style, wide-topped boots. (One photo of the period shows how neatly a flask of bootleg whiskey fit into the top of this boot.) Young women affected the style of wearing their overshoes for bad weather, or galoshes, open and flapping. Some have attributed the origin of the term *flappers* to this practice, although a variety of sources are claimed for the word. Another suggested origin is the large hair bows worn by young girls in the post–World War I period, which flapped on the backs of their heads. Most dictionaries of word origin indicate the word comes from the flapping wings of young birds, making an analogy to the young human "fledgling" of 15 or 16 who is "trying her wings." The term had been applied to young girls before the 1920s, and the use of the word probably received reinforcement from the flapping of galoshes on the young girls of the 1920s. In the 1920s it was applied quite specifically to fashionable and modern young women in their late teens and 20s.

Costume Components for Women: 1930–1947

Garments

In a change from the straight lines of the 1920s, undergarments of the 1930s and 1940s emphasized the curves of the figure. Brassieres of the 1930s were cut to lift and emphasize the breasts. Corsets extended to slightly above the waist. Rigidly boned corsets were still worn by large women, but smaller women wore corsets in which the shaping was achieved by elasticized fabric panels. Terminology changed: Panties became **panty briefs** and then **briefs** as they grew shorter in order to fit under active sportswear. Older women continued to wear fuller, looser drawers or bloomers. Slips fitted the torso and were fuller in the cut of the skirt. Lower priced underwear was made of cotton, rayon, or acetate; more expensive garments were silk. See Illustrated Table 16.1 (page 474) for examples of undergarments during the years between 1920 and 1947.

One-piece dresses, skirts and blouses, and tailored suits remained the staples of women's wardrobes for daytime wear. The beginning of a change in

Illustrated Table 16.3

Selected Examples of Footwear for Women: 1920–1947

Dress shoes, 1927

Dress shoes, 1933

1941–1947
Wartime shoes made without leather (a) Jungle cloth, fleece lining, sisal soles
(b) Gabardine wedge-soled oxford with composition soles
(c) Gabardine open-toed pump with plastic soles

Platform-soled shoes, 1947

silhouette came in the late 1920s when hemlines began to lengthen and belts moved gradually closer to the natural waistline. The silhouette of the 1930s emphasized the natural form of the woman's body. Bosom, waistline, and hips were clearly defined by the shape of clothing (Figure 16.20).

Hemlines fell early in the decade. They were about 12 inches from the ground for the first several years, and by 1932 went as low as 10 inches. Indeed, some illustrations of high-fashion garments show a hemline that comes almost to the ankle. By mid-decade, skirt lengths started upward again, 13 or 14 inches off the ground, and by the end of the period skirt lengths had reached 16 or 17 inches from the floor.

The wartime period, with its restrictions, essentially froze styles of the late 1930s and 1940–1941. By the beginning of the war, skirts had become shorter, ending just below the knee, and had grown fuller.

FIGURE 16.20 Daytime dresses of 1933 show the fitted line, bias cut, and interesting sleeve variations of the early 1930s. (*Women's Wear Daily*, spring 1933. Courtesy of Fairchild Publications, Inc.)

Shoulders had broadened, and shoulder pads were inserted into all garments to provide greater width. Bias cut was rarely used.

Necklines for daytime were generally high. In the first half of the decade, cowl necklines, cape collars, and soft finishes such as bows and jabots predominated (see Figure 16.20). Later, V-necklines (Figure 16.21) and collared dresses were more important. Yoke constructions were common. Sleeve styles included those that were long and full and gathered to a wristband at the end. Others styles were short, many with a capelike construction. Full sleeves were cut in raglan style or as **magyar** or **batwing** sleeves. At the end of the decade, short, puffed sleeves came back into fashion.

Most skirts were cut with several gores. Some had bias-cut pieces set into a yoke that covered the hips to create a skirt that was narrow but

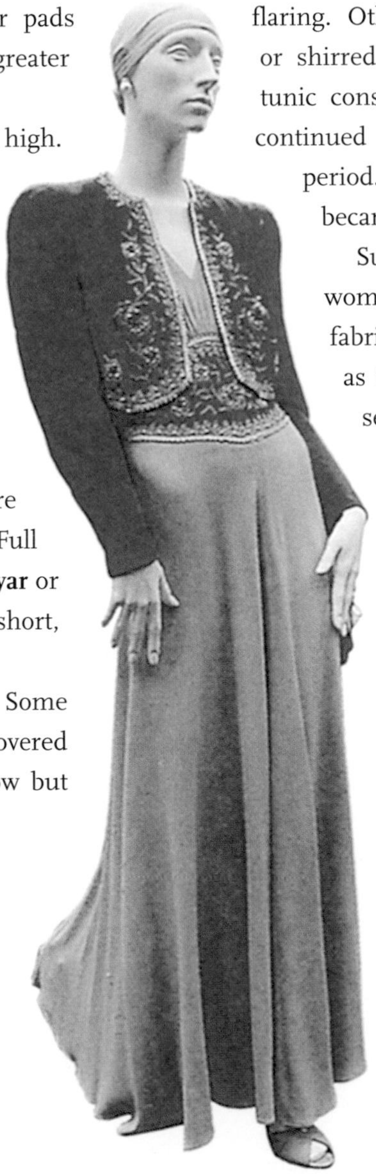

FIGURE 16.21 Dinner dress and jacket, mid- to late 1930s, made in bias cut of silk crepe. The metal zipper used to close the jacket was an innovation not previously seen in high fashion. (Courtesy of Texas Fashion Collection, University of North Texas, Gift of Lou Ann Zellers)

flaring. Others were made with box pleats or shirred sections, and a few had layered tunic constructions. All these constructions continued to be used until the end of the period. Toward the end of the 1930s, skirts became wider.

Suits remained a basic item of women's wardrobes. Made in firmer fabrics, their lines were not as supple as that of most dresses (Figure 16.22; see also Figure 16.12). Some styles were clearly modeled after men's suits. Except for some square, boxy jackets of the early 1930s, suits curved in to fit closely at the waist. Styles were both single and double breasted; some were belted. Jacket lengths were shorter in the early 1930s, longer toward the end. Lapels were wide in the early years, narrower and longer later.

Wartime suit styles included bolero suits with short, curving jackets that ended above the waist or **Eisenhower jackets**, based on military jackets that were slightly bloused above the waist and gathered to a fitted belt

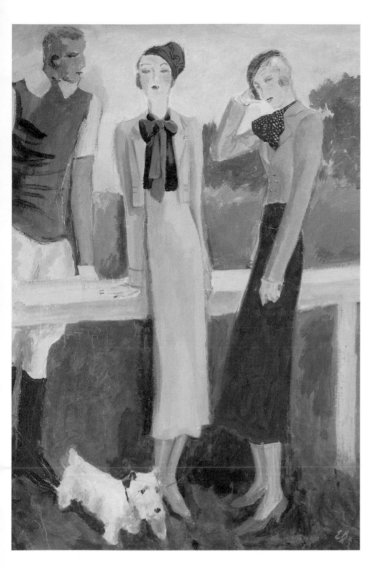

FIGURE 16.22 Suits of the early 1930s had longer skirts and softer lines than those of the later 1930s. (Eduardo Garcia Benito © 1932 Condé Nast Publications)

FIGURE 16.23 Although it began as a military style worn by General Dwight Eisenhower, after whom it was named, the short, belted Eisenhower jacket was made for women as well. (V&A Images, London/Art Resource, NY)

at the waist, and named after the Supreme Allied Commander Dwight Eisenhower, who wore this type of jacket (Figure 16.23).

Both casual and dressy versions of blouses, sweaters, and skirts were available. Retailers classified the more casual versions into a new category of clothing called sportswear. Blouses were constructed in much the same way as dress bodices. Pullover wool sweaters were made in decorative patterns or plain colors with short or long sleeves. Sometimes belts were worn over sweaters. Matching short-sleeved sweaters and long-sleeved cardigans were popular in the early forties. In

the mid-1940s adolescents wore large, loose pullovers called **sloppy joes**. Sweaters were especially popular during the war. Movie stars who were photographed in tightly fitting sweaters for pin-up pictures were called *sweater girls*.

In the 1930s skirts were generally cut without much fullness. Construction details included gores, pleats that released fullness low and below the hip, topstitching, and panel insets. In the 1940s, and during the war, skirts were fuller and shorter (Figure 16.24;

FIGURE 16.24 Suit of 1940, the year before the United States entered World War II, has the shoulder line, waistline placement, skirt shape, and length that became virtually frozen during the wartime period. The coat loosely fitted and with raglan sleeves, is one of a number of different coat types worn c. 1940. (Courtesy of *Vogue*, August 1, 1940, p. 41 © Condé Nast Publications)

see also Figure 16.23). About 1945, **dirndl** (*dirn'del*) **skirts** (*full, gathered skirts*) became fashionable.

Evening and daytime dress lengths were markedly different. Evening gowns always reached to the floor. Bias-cut styles were utilized until the late 1930s. Such dresses followed the body to the hips, where they flared out. Other common characteristics of evening dresses included bare-backed gowns cut low to the waist at the back, halter-type sleeveless bodices, and full, capelike or puffed sleeved styles (see Figures 16.7 and 16.9).

Toward the end of the 1930s, less ornamentation, less detail in construction, and more severe lines were more common. Evening styles included blouses and skirts and evening suits with long skirts and matching jackets of plain, uncluttered lines. Under these, soft, frilly, and often backless or sleeveless blouses or bodices were worn (see Figure 16.21).

Strapless gowns appeared in Hollywood films of the late 1930s. The tops of these dresses fitted tightly and were held in place by boning sewn along the inside seams.

Outdoor Garments

In the early 1930s many coats were cut with decorative detailing around the necklines and shoulderlines. Large collars were often made of fur. Some coats had leg-of-mutton sleeves. Closings tended to be at the left, often with only one button. Overall, the line was slender until the latter part of the decade when more boxy, fuller coats, some in three quarter length, some ending at the hip, and some in full length were popular.

Many coats of the 1940s had features such as large collars and revers, heavily padded shoulders, and raglan and dolman sleeve constructions. Some had plain, straight boxy shapes. Fur coats were popular and the increased affluence of Americans who worked in highly paid wartime industry brought these coats within the means of many more women. Military influence was evident in the war years, when the military trench coat was often seen.

Sleepwear

Women wore nightgowns or pajamas.

Hair and Headdress

See Illustrated Table 16.2 (page 479) for some examples of hairstyles and hats from the period 1920–1947.

In the early years of the 1930s, hair was relatively short, softly waved, and with short, turned-up curls around the nape of the neck. As the decade progressed, fashionable hairstyles grew longer. Toward the end of the decade, the **pageboy bob** (straight hair turned under at the ends) and hair dressed on top of the head in curls or braids (the **upsweep**) were more fashionable. During the war some women arranged the hair in a high pompadour at the front and sides of the face while making a long, U-shaped roll at the back. Others wore a short, curly hairstyle called a **feather cut**.

In the early 1930s, hats were small in scale, of many different shapes, and usually tipped either to one side, front, or back at an angle. In the later 1930s, berets, sailor hats, and wider brimmed styles were seen. When upswept hairstyles were worn, higher hats and small hats with face veils were fashionable. Milliners found inspiration in many sources, including the Middle Ages, and some hats were shown with wimplelike scarves draped under the chin and attached to the hat at or above the ear. Hats and hair ornaments became fashionable for evening, especially turbans, decorative veils, artificial flowers, and ribbons. Snoods returned to fashion for the first time since the Civil War era, possibly as a result of the popularity of motion pictures such as *Gone With the Wind* and *Little Women*.

In the 1940s, hats tended to be small, among them pillboxes and small bonnets. Many women went hatless, but to be considered well dressed, a lady had to wear a hat. Women working in wartime factories covered their hair with turbans or wore snoods to protect hair from getting caught in the machinery.

Footwear

See Illustrated Table 16.3 for some examples of footwear from the period 1920–1947.

Stockings were made in flesh tones of silk or rayon and seamed up the back. Cotton and wool stockings were for sportswear. Ankle socks were worn by young girls and for sports. In the 1940s teenaged girls wore ankle socks so constantly that adolescent girls came to be known as **bobby-soxers**. Shortages of fabrics for stockings during the war led women to paint their legs with **leg makeup** to simulate the color of stockings. Some even went so far as to paint a dark line down the back of the leg in imitation of the seams (Figure 16.25).

During the war, leather shoes were rationed. Each adult was entitled to two new pairs per year. Shoes

FIGURE 16.25 When World War II caused silk supplies to dry up, many women preferred to paint their legs with makeup rather than wear ill-fitting rayon stockings. (Courtesy of The Advertising Archives)

made of cloth were exempt from restriction, so cloth shoes with synthetic soles were readily available.

Costume Components for Women: 1920–1947

Sportswear

Throughout the period from 1920 to 1947, women were becoming more active participants in sports. As a result, women adopted both specific costumes for individual sports such as tennis, swimming, and skiing, and general informal dress for spectator sports and outdoor activities (Figure 16.26; see also

A man's silk shirt, beautifully tailored, worn with the briefest of jersey trunks

Three handkerchiefs, in three contrasting colours, all knotted together

An Oriental sarong tied on over a thin lisle sweater, lisle trunks; plus a bandanna and bracelet

Riviera

Like a French porter's – this blouse, cinched with a wide webbing polo-belt, over a pair of tailored linen slacks

A jacket made of shirting, exactly like a man's pyjama-coat, and flannel shorts – new for tennis, boating, or the beach

All models on this page from Best

FIGURE 16.26 Women's sportswear had become an important part of their wardrobes by the 1930s. In this feature from *Vogue*, November 15, 1937, sportswear includes a range of items for active sports and leisure. (*Vogue* © 1937 Condé Nast Publications, Inc.)

Figure 16.8). By 1928 such clothing was referred to as "spectator sports styles" by fashion magazines. By the 1930s, the clothing industry identified this new category of clothing as *sportswear*.

Except for basically unsuccessful attempts by dress reformers of the 1860s to introduce bloomers and the knickers worn by women for cycling, trousers for daytime wear had remained essentially a man's garment until the 1920s. Harem skirts had been introduced by Poiret in the preceding period. These exotic bifurcated garments were unlike men's trousers and were not widely worn. In the late 1920s, women began to appear in garments made like men's trousers for casual wear. The general term **slacks** was used to designate these garments. By the 1930s the style was well established, but slacks (and one-piece playsuits) remained largely a sportswear item (Figure 16.27). During the war many women found slacks a useful garment for working in factories.

In the 1930s jeans had a short run as a fashion item when *Vogue* magazine ran an advertisement depicting two society women in tight-fitting jeans, a look it called *western chic*. Adolescent girls began to wear men's work jeans in blue denim for casual dress (Ratner, 1975).

In the 1920s and on into the early 1930s, women wore beach pajamas. These were long, full trousers with matching tops, either separate or seamed together, worn for leisure activities (Figure 16.28). Some even had large, matching hats.

a
b

FIGURE 16.27 Sportswear of the 1940s: (a) slacks and a crepe blouse; (b) a one-piece playsuit. (Division of Home and Community Life, National Museum of American History, Smithsonian Institution)

FIGURE 16.28 Colorful lounging pajamas and beach pajamas were two of several ways in which women were able to wear the trousers that had heretofore been worn exclusively by men (c. 1929). (Courtesy of Belding Hemingway Company, Inc.)

Clothing for Active Sports

White clothing was traditional for tennis. Like dress skirts in the 1920s, tennis dresses grew shorter and remained shorter even when daytime dresses lengthened again. In the 1930s, bodices of tennis dresses were sleeveless and collarless; skirts were either short or divided culotte-style; and shorts were also commonly worn for tennis. No special costume was required for golf, but tweed skirts with pullover sweaters worn over a blouse seemed to be favored.

Costume for swimming altered radically (Figure 16.29). In the early 1920s, a fairly voluminous two-piece tunic and knickers was a carryover from the 1910s. Gradually the knickers grew shorter, armholes grew deeper, necklines plunged lower, and one-piece tank suits were adopted by women. Knee-length stockings were worn only in the first years of the 1920s. By the end of the 1920s, the modern concept of costumes in which women could really "swim" rather

than "bathe" had been established. The first women to wear the more revealing tank suits, however, were often arrested for indecent exposure.

In the 1930s, bathing suits with halter tops or low-cut backs became popular. These lines were similar to those seen in some evening gowns. Bathing suits were made from knitted wool, rayon, acetate, and cotton. In the early 1930s, **Lastex**®, a fabric made from yarns with a rubber core covered by another fiber, was used to make bathing suits that had stretch and were more form fitting and wrinkle-free than other fabrics. It was also in the 1930s that two-piece bathing suits with either a brassierelike or halter top and shorts made their first appearance. Women could choose from an assortment of bathing suit styles including one-piece or two-piece styles with either shorts or skirtlike constructions.

Ski clothes consisted of full trousers and a sweater or, especially in the 1930s and after, matching jackets. Closely fitted ski clothing was not introduced until after World War II. Women wore jodhpurs with high riding boots, shirts, and tweed jackets for riding horses.

Accessories

See Illustrated Table 16.4 for examples of some popular accessories.

Umbrellas were practical, rather than fashionable, with either long or short handles and made in conservative colors. Parasols were hardly ever used. Fans made of ostrich feathers were carried in the evening during the 1920s, but fans were not much used after this decade.

Handbags ranged in size from large leather bags to dainty, beaded evening bags barely big enough to hold a handkerchief and a lipstick. From a vast variety a few especially fashionable items stand out in each decade. In the 1920s, some fashionable evening bags were made from brocade, embroidered silk, glass or metal beads, or wire mesh in gold and silver. Daytime leather bags were often flat envelope types held by small straps. In the 1930s, some bags were mounted on frames and had straps and others were pouch shaped. In the 1940s, shoulder strap bags became especially popular.

a

b

c

d

FIGURE 16.29 Bathing suits show marked evolution in the period from 1920 to 1947. (a) A black wool knit bathing suit from 1925–1927, made in one piece, with trunks attached at the waist. This suit was made by Gantner and Mattern Company and worn in California (Division of Home and Community Life, National Museum of American History, Smithsonian Institution). (b) "Trio of Striplings," January 1, 1934 (Pierre Mourgue © 1934 Condé Nast Publications). (c) "Swoon Suit" from Cole of California, May 1, 1939 (Courtesy of *Vogue* magazine, Condé Nast Publications). (d) "Perfect Form" bathing suit from June 1944 (Courtesy of *Vogue* magazine, Condé Nast Publications).

Illustrated Table 16.4

Accessories: 1920–1947

Fur neckpiece, 1930s

Popular jewelry in the 1920s: Drop earrings, long pearl or bead necklace, and bracelet

Men's neckties, 1920–1947, shapes varied, as did widths

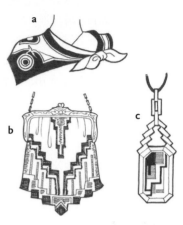

Accessories showing Art Deco influence (a) Woman's neck scarf, 1930 (b) Mesh handbag, c. 1920s, with geometric pattern (c) Art Deco pendant

Umbrellas, 1937 (a) See-through plastic umbrella (b) Oiled silk umbrella with decorative handle

Stocking styles for women, 1930 (a) Figured knitted stocking for casual wear (b) Long flesh-colored silk dress stocking, seamed up the back

Men's socks (a) Man's black silk socks with embroidered clocks, 1923 (b) Man's patterned golfing socks

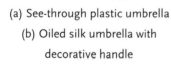

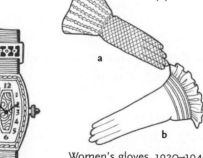

Handbags (a) Envelope style handbag, 1923 (b) Wood-bead handbag, 1938 (c) Cordé handbag, 1940s

Wrist watch, 1923

Women's gloves, 1920–1940 (a) Gauntlet-styled glove (b) Glove trimmed with ruffle

Sunglasses, 1939

Throughout the period women were expected to wear gloves outdoors in the daytime. In the 1930s, long evening gloves appeared. During the war, cotton gloves replaced leather because of shortages. Gloves often matched dresses or hats or handbags in color or fabric.

An important accessory in the mid-1940s, scarves were made of fabrics that contrasted with dresses. Throughout the period fur scarves, stoles, and skins were worn around the neck; often the head and paws of the animal were retained for decoration.

Jewelry

In the 1920s jewelry was plentiful, especially long, dangling earrings that looked good against short haircuts and long necks. Many brooches, bracelets, and shorter necklaces were made with Art Deco designs. Long strands of pearls or beads were popular accessories.

By the 1930s jewelry was more subdued, in keeping with the depressed economy, and included short pearl necklaces and jeweled clips in pairs placed at the neckline or on collars. Although earrings were generally worn in the evening, many fashion magazines showed women modeling daytime dresses without earrings.

Upswept hairstyles of the 1940s contributed to greater interest in earrings, many of which were large in scale. Rhinestones were popular for evening. Other jewelry included brooches for collars and lapels, short necklaces, and bracelets.

Cosmetics and Grooming

During the 1920s, cosmetics (popularly called **makeup**) became an accepted part of women's fashion. Prior to this time most women who used cosmetics did so in secret. In the 1920s, cosmetics became essential to achieving a fashionable look. This notation from *Only Yesterday* serves to dramatize the magnitude of the change that took place. In 1917, according to Frances Fisher Dubuc, only 2 people in the beauty culture business had paid an income tax; by 1927, 18,000 firms and individuals in this field reported income (Allen, 1931).

Fashionable ladies plucked their eyebrows into a narrow line, which was then emphasized with eyebrow pencil. Bright shades of rouge and lipstick were preferred. Lipstick in a round metal tube had been invented in 1915. Some flappers even went so far as to rouge their knees. Powder completed an almost masklike appearance that the most fashionable women attempted to achieve.

COSTUME COMPONENTS FOR MEN

Less dramatic changes took place from the 1920s through the end of World War II in men's wear. Among the well-to-do, the English tailor retained his reputation as the best in the world. The English tailor was to men's clothing what the French couturier was to women's.

Fashion influences in England were also given a boost by the popularity of the youthful Prince of Wales. The prince, who after his abdication from the throne was known as the Duke of Windsor, was always very much interested in clothing, and his adoption of a style was sure to give it importance throughout the menswear industry.

Hollywood's leading men also influenced styles. The appearance of leading men on the screen in unusual clothing was likely to start a new trend. Matinee idols known for their taste and style often ordered their clothing from British tailors.

Sack suits remained the basis of suits for almost every occasion. Vests, trousers, and jackets matched in color and fabric. Only wealthy and prominent individuals still wore morning coats, and then only for very formal occasions. Those who could afford variety in their wardrobes wore white suits for summer. F. Scott Fitzgerald's character Jay Gatsby was portrayed in a white suit at his fabulous summer parties on Long Island, and the white linen or flannel suit became symbolic of an upper class lifestyle.

Garments

As underwear for more conservative men, one-piece knitted union suits were available with short or long sleeves or legs. Other underwear had no sleeves and ended at the knee or above. **Boxer shorts** were introduced in the 1930s. The shorts worn by professional boxers inspired this style. Other new styles of the 1930s included **athletic shirts** of knitted cotton that were adapted from the top of tank swimsuits and fitted brief knit shorts, patented in 1935. The trademark name for these knitted briefs, **Jockey shorts**, has since become an almost generic designation for this style of men's underwear. Made initially without a front opening, these shorts added a Y-shaped front opening in 1942. During World War II servicemen wore knit undershirts with short sleeves called **T-shirts**. After the war civilian men continued to wear these undershirts, and they eventually found their way into general sportswear as well. See Illustrated Table 16.1 (page 474) for examples of undergarments during the years between 1920 and 1947.

In the 1934 film *It Happened One Night*, actor Clark Gable appeared bare chested and without an undershirt. *Esquire's Encyclopedia of 20th Century Men's Fashion* credits this film with beginning a fashion for going without undershirts, which severely affected the underwear industry. As another example of the influence of motion picture on clothing, the **Wallace Beery shirt** was a ribbed-knit undershirt with a buttoned vent at the front of the neck worn by the character actor of that name (Schoeffler and Gale, 1973). This shirt is more likely to be called a **henley shirt** today.

Business suits of the 1920s featured jackets with fairly natural shoulderlines, fairly wide lapels, and pronounced waists. Single- and double-breasted styles were worn, and sleeves were short enough to show at least 1/2 inch of shirt cuff (Figure 16.30). During the 1920s, trouser legs widened. The impetus for wider trouser legs may have come from a fad that developed at Oxford College in England. Students were forbidden

FIGURE 16.30 Menswear fashions from the 1920s. (*Men's Wear Review*)

by dress regulations from wearing knickers to classes. To be able to change quickly from the acceptable long trousers to knickers, students took to wearing trousers with excessively wide legs that could be slipped on over the knickers. After classes, off came the **Oxford bags** (Schoeffler and Gale, 1973). The style spread to other young people, and Oxford bags with legs as wide as 32 inches in diameter were soon seen in America, too. Although most men never wore Oxford bags, trousers grew generally wider and remained fuller in cut.

Manufactured in white and in colors, shirts had narrow collars. Some had button-down collars (a new form), other collars were designed to be pinned together under the tie with a tie pin, and some had a tab to fasten the points of the collar together under the tie. The **Barrymore collar** (named after actor John Barrymore) had long points. Four-in-hand neckties, bow ties, and ascots made up the repertory of neckwear.

Turtleneck jerseys, around for about 30 years as sportswear, gained popularity for a time as a substitute for shirts and ties when, in 1924, actor Noel Coward initiated the style.

In the 1930s, suits were made from such popular fabrics as lightweight worsted wools, gabardine, and linen (see Figure 16.33). Rayon was the first manufactured fiber to gain widespread use. It was made into suits, as well as other garments. After the Prince of Wales wore a plaid suit while on a visit to the United States, plaid suits became more popular, along with pinstripes and summer suits in light colors.

Jackets grew wider at the shoulders, more fitted at the hips. In the latter part of the decade a style known as the **English drape suit** was introduced and became the predominant cut for suits. This style, which was cut for comfort, fell softly with a slight drape or wrinkle through the chest and shoulders because it had more fabric there.

The width of trousers decreased in the 1930s. Manufacturers began to use zippers rather than the customary buttons for fly closings—a major change.

White was considered more traditional for shirts, but they were also made in colors and with stripes or checks. Collar styles included tab and button-down styles. **California collars**, seen on film actors such as Clark Gable, had shorter, wider points than the Barrymore collar of the 1920s. **Windsor**, or spread, collars were worn with the larger Windsor tie knot. Some collars also had short, rounded shapes.

Wartime restrictions in the 1940s modified the English drape cut somewhat. To conserve wool fabric, which was in short supply, restrictions were imposed on the quantity of fabric that could be used in suits. The American War Production Board decreed maximum lengths for jackets and trouser inseams in each size, ruled out making suits with two pairs of trousers, and eliminated waistcoats with double-breasted suits, cuffs, pleats in trousers, and overlapping waistbands (Figure 16.31).

The **zoot suit** was thereby officially eliminated, although bootleg tailors continued to provide the garment to individuals who could pay for it. The origins of the zoot suit are debated. This unusual fashion is said by some to have originated with Mexican-American immigrant workers (called *pachucos*) in southern California; others claim it was first worn by an African-American bus driver in Gainesville, Georgia. Eventually, its association with an

FIGURE 16.31

Drawing from June 1942 of a suit that conforms to the War Production Board regulations for men's suits. Specifications included shorter jackets with no patch pockets, belts, vents, pleats, tucks, or yokes; no vests with double-breasted suits; and no pleats, tucks overlapping waistbands, or cuffs on trousers. (Courtesy of Fairchild Publications, Inc.)

FIGURE 16.32 Three young men wearing the pegged trousers of the zoot suits, with the men in the middle and at right of the photograph also wearing the oversized, wide-shouldered, long jackets characteristic of the zoot suit. (Douglas Miller/Getty Images)

especially athletic type of dance, called jitterbug, and with popular African-American musicians led teenage boys of many ethnic groups to adopt the styles in the early 1940s. The suit was an extreme form of the sack suit of this period. The jacket was long, with wide shoulders and long, wide lapels. The trousers were markedly pegged (Figure 16.32). Even girls' jackets showed some influences.

Some minority youth became alienated and disaffected as a result of social upheavals related to World War II. In 1943 conflict broke out between Latino Americans and predominantly white servicemen. During fights between the two groups, servicemen removed zoot suits from their Latino adversaries by force. As a result, the subsequent riots that broke out were known as the "zoot suit riots." The violence spread to other cities, such as Detroit, New York, and Philadelphia and was followed by the worst race riots in American history up to that time (Cosgrove, 1984).

Evening dress from 1920 to the 1940s underwent changes. Tailcoats were reserved for the most formal occasions. For evening, jackets generally were of the tuxedo type, made in black or midnight blue (see Figure 16.30). Tuxedos had either rolled collars faced in silk or notched collars. Lines of jackets followed the lines of daytime business suits. In the 1920s, single-breasted styles were preferred; in the 1930s, double-breasted styles were more popular. From the late 1920s on, some men substituted a **cummerbund**, a wide, pleated fabric waistband, for the waistcoat. Waistcoats after the 1930s often had a sort of halter-type construction and no back. In the 1930s and after, white dinner jackets, especially for summer, were worn. Wartime restrictions required that all dinner jackets be single breasted. Evening trousers followed the lines of daytime trousers (but with no cuffs) and added a line of braid following the outer seam line. White shirts with starched fronts that closed with two shirt studs were worn with tailcoats throughout the period. With dinner jackets and tuxedos, soft-fronted shirts were acceptable after the late 1920s. Dark bow ties were worn with dinner jackets; white bow ties, with tails. Except for more affluent men, most did not own evening clothes but instead rented them for special events.

Outdoor Garments

Generally outdoor garments followed the predominant jacket silhouette. Coat styles included Chesterfields and raglan-sleeved coats, with either buttoned front closings or fly-front closing in which a fabric placket obscured the buttons.

In the 1920s, raccoon coats were popular among the young college crowd and served as a hallmark of the successful collegian or "sheik." Men who could not afford these coats might pool their resources to buy one coat that they could then share (Berendt, 1988). Women also adopted the look. Tweed and herringbone-patterned fabrics were used for casual coats.

Polo coats made of tan camel's hair were worn by a British polo team playing exhibition matches in the United States and the style swept the United States and continued on into the 1930s (see Figure 16.30). The classic cut of this coat was double breasted, with a six-button closing, and a half belt at the back. Camel's hair coats included single-breasted box coats, belted raglan-sleeved coats, and wraparound coats without buttons that tied with belts. Trench coats, slickers, and waterproof coats modeled after fishermen's foul-weather gear were worn as rain coats.

In the 1930s many of the styles seen in the 1920s continued, and some new styles were added, such as the **English guards' coat**, a dark blue coat with wide lapels, an inverted pleat in the back, and a half belt. **Zip-in linings**, a new feature, made cold-weather coats convertible to use in warmer temperatures.

Informal coat styles included short jackets with knitted waistbands and cuffs, **parka jackets** with hoods (copied from Eskimo cold-weather wear), and **lumber jackets** or **mackinaws** (sturdy jackets made of heavily fulled wool). The affluent wore leather jackets.

In the 1940s, styles showed marked military influences and included **pea jackets**, which were the double-breasted dark box jackets of American sailors, and Eisenhower or **battle jackets**, which were short, waist length, bloused jackets the lower edge of which was attached to a belt of the same fabric (see Figure 16.23).

Informal Daytime Clothing, or Sportswear

From 1920 to 1947, a whole new category of clothing developed. It is generally classified as sportswear but would perhaps be more accurately termed *leisure* or *casual* clothing. It was worn not only for active sports but also during a man's leisure time.

Jackets without matching trousers, cut along the lines of business suit jackets and worn with contrasting fabric trousers were known as **sport** or **casual jackets** (Figure 16.33). Sport jackets were made in more colors and fabrics than regular suit jackets and were worn with vests in matching or contrasting colors, pullover

FIGURE 16.33 Men's business suits of various colors could be single or double breasted; consisted of trousers, vest, and jacket; and were generally worn with a fedora-style hat. Sports jackets were contrasted in color with trousers and might be worn with straw or panama hats. (Town and Country Outfits, from *Vanity Fair*, April 1931 [colour litho], American School [20th century]/Bibliotheque des Arts Decoratifs, Paris, France/Archives Charmet/Bridgeman Images)

sweaters, or shirts. Some were cut with half belts or were belted all the way around. Golfers adopted Norfolk jackets with a pleat in the back. The Prince of Wales made tweed jackets popular. **Bush jackets**, short-sleeved tan cotton jackets with four large flapped pockets made to imitate styles worn by hunters and explorers in Africa, were popular for casual wear in the 1930s.

During the 1920s sport jackets were often combined with knickers or **plus fours** (a fuller version of knickers) and argyle socks. In the 1930s, trousers or shorts replaced knickers to some extent. **Walking shorts**, based on military costume of British Colonial soldiers, had been adopted by the well-to-do for vacation wear. They were worn with knee-length stockings and often had matching shirts. Trousers for sportswear were made in a variety of colors and patterns including plaid, checked, and striped designs.

Shirts for leisure, as opposed to those for wearing with suits, were a new development in menswear. Styles included **polo shirts**, which were knitted shirts with attached collars and short, buttoned, neck vents. They usually had short sleeves. This style originated as costume for polo players, but was adopted generally for informal wear in the 1920s and after.

In the 1930s and after, men wore **dishrag shirts** of net fabric that were first seen on the Riviera; **basque shirts**, striped, wide, crew-necked shirts; and dark blue linen sport shirts patterned after one worn by the Prince of Wales. In the late 1930s, men bought **cowboy shirts** in bright colors and fabrics with button-down pockets on the chest and pointed collars, and **western shirts** in solid or plaid wool or gabardine with crescent-shaped pockets in front. About 1938, **Hawaiian shirts** printed in vivid colors entered mainstream fashion (Figure 16.34).

Sweaters were popular for golfing and other sports. Multicolored sweater patterns were worn in imitation of a sweater worn by the Prince of Wales in the 1920s. Turtleneck sweaters were popular in the 1920s and the 1930s.

Clothing for Active Sports

For tennis, knitted white shirts worn with white flannel trousers were popular until the 1930s when some men substituted white shorts for the trousers. White was mandatory as a color on tennis courts. Many clubs forbade play to those wearing colors.

The **Lacoste® knit tennis shirt**, made along the lines of a polo shirt, was introduced in the 1920s. René Lacoste, a well-known player who had been nicknamed "the Crocodile," designed a short-sleeved cotton knit shirt with a longer tail in back so it would not pull out when he was playing tennis. He marketed this shirt,

FIGURE 16.34 Hawaiian shirts made a strong impact in the menswear market in the late 1940s. (Matthew Cole/ Shutterstock)

FIGURE 16.35 Golf outfit; jacket from 1930, knickers from 1928 (left). (Division of Home and Community Life, National Museum of American History, Smithsonian Institution)

FIGURE 16.36 Ski outfit. The pants are from 1940 and the jacket is from 1937. The skis, goggles, gloves, boots, and ski poles all date from the same period (right). (Division of Home and Community Life, National Museum of American History, Smithsonian Institution)

using a crocodile as the logo. The shirt became very popular and was worn not only for tennis but also as general sportswear.

Clothes for golf consisted mainly of shirts, sweaters, or jackets combined with knickers in the 1920s and slacks or shorts in the 1930s and after (Figure 16.35).

In the 1920s, one-piece swimsuits were held on over the shoulders with shoulder straps. As an alternative, knit pullover shirts with or without sleeves were worn with short trunks. The pullover was worn either out, over the trunks, or tucked into trunks that were belted at the waist. Upper sections of bathing suits often had deep armholes and straps across the armhole to maintain a snug fit. In the 1930s, tops decreased in size until eventually men stopped wearing any covering for the upper part of the body, and by the 1940s only bathing trunks were worn.

Skiing was taken up by large numbers of people only after World War I. In the 1920s, skiers wore wool

sweaters and plus fours. In the 1930s, wind-resistant jackets were adopted and worn with long trousers cut full and gathered into an elasticized cuff at the ankle (Figure 16.36).

Sleepwear

Pajamas had largely replaced nightshirts. The cut varied: in the 1920s, the jacket was long, below the hip, and often belted. Russian influence was evident in the late 1920s and 1930s in styles that had standing collars and closed far to the left. Some pajamas buttoned down the front; others slipped pm over the head. Robes ranged from kimono-style silk to ornately patterned flannels that buttoned down the front and tied shut with a corded belt.

Hair and Headdress

Throughout the period hair was short. In the 1920s, many men controlled their hair with glistening hair dressings and pomades in imitation of the film star Rudolph Valentino, whose hair looked as if it were plastered to his head. Faces were generally clean shaven. Some men wore pencil-thin mustaches. In the 1930s, hair was worn waved and parted on the side. Mustaches were more likely to be worn by older men. Mustaches went out of fashion in the 1940s. Some authors attribute the decrease in popularity of mustaches in the 1940s to the fact that the German dictator Adolf Hitler wore a mustache.

Hat styles altered very little. Major forms continued to be fedoras (becoming more popular), derbies (becoming less popular), homburgs, straw boaters and panama hats, and sports caps. During the 1930s, the pork pie—a low-crowned, soft felt hat that could be rolled up—was used for sportswear.

Footwear

Stockings became more colorful as a result of the availability of machinery for making fancy, patterned hosiery. In the 1930s, argyle, chevron, and diamond-patterned socks were popular. Elastic-topped socks were introduced and did away with the need for garters.

High shoes went out of style in the 1920s, and oxfords became the predominant style. White and two-toned shoes were worn in summer. Moccasin-type shoes were introduced in the 1930s, adapted from shoes worn by Norwegian fishermen and nicknamed **weejuns**. Other 1930s styles included sandals; cloth shoes for summer; crepe-soled shoes; and higher shoes that ended at the ankle, closing either with laces (**chukka boots**) or a strap and buckle across the ankle (**monk's front**).

Wartime rationing made leather shoes and tennis shoes with rubber soles scarce. Composition soles were used to conserve leather.

Galoshes or overshoes and rubbers changed little over this period. Galoshes closed at the front with snaps or zippers. Synthetic rubber material was used during the war.

Accessories

Men used relatively few accessories, mainly gloves, handkerchiefs, scarves, umbrellas, and canes. Sunglasses were first manufactured at the request of Army Air Corps flyer Lieutenant John Macready, who wanted lenses for goggles that would deflect the sun's rays. The manufacturer, Bausch and Lomb, went on to market them to the general public.

Jewelry

As before, jewelry was largely functional: watches, tie pins, shirt studs, cuff links, and rings.

COSTUME COMPONENTS FOR CHILDREN

See Illustrated Table 16.5 for some examples of children's clothing from the period 1920–1947.

Costume Components for Girls

Garments

Toddlers wore loose, smocklike dresses that often had a yoke at the neck. Many had matching bloomers that could be seen beneath the short skirts. Smocking and embroidery were favored decorations.

In the 1920s young girls' dresses, like those of adults, were unfitted. In the 1930s waistlines of dresses returned to anatomical placement. Older girls' dresses often had fitted bodices with skirts attached and a sash tied in the back. Skirt fullness varied according to whether adult skirt styles were wider or narrower. Puffed sleeves were commonly seen.

For school, skirts and blouses were common in the 1930s and 1940s. Some skirts had straps or suspenders. Once pants had been accepted for women, young girls wore pullover and cardigan sweaters and slacks for sportswear. The popularity of child actress Shirley Temple influenced clothing styles for little girls in the 1930s.

Outdoor Garments

In the 1920s, girls wore straight, narrow coats. Princess-line coats, often with fur-trimmed collars, were popular in the 1930s, and in 1944 the Sears, Roebuck catalogue showed a cross section of coats for young girls including princess line, single-breasted Chesterfields with velvet collars, **boy coats** that were cut straight with patch pockets, and wrap coats that had tie belts. Leggings were available to match dress coats for cold weather.

Costume Components for Boys

Garments

The custom of dressing small boys in skirts had ended. They wore romper suits or short pants instead. The custom of dressing small boys in blue and small girls in pink seems to have begun around the 1920s in the United States. Prior to this time, shades of red had been considered "masculine" colors, and were more likely to be worn by boys than girls. Indeed,

Illustrated Table 16.5

Children's Clothing Styles: 1920–1938

Girl's dress, 1926

Boys' clothing, 1926

Girls' clothing, 1933

Girls' dresses, 1938

this gender-related color assignment was not firmly established until around 1940 (Kidwell and Steele, 1980). Although boys' styles showed some minor differences from decade to decade, a boy could expect to spend the first few years of his life in short pants, then graduate to knickers, and finally into long trousers (see Illustrated Table 16.5).

For dress occasions in the 1920s, boys wore long belted jackets or Norfolk jackets. By the 1930s and 1940s, jackets were less likely to be belted, shorter, and cut like those of adult men. Some had matching vests.

In the 1930s, polo shirts were common for everyday dress. Cotton knit pullovers with napped under surfaces appeared in the early 1930s, and by the 1940s this garment was being called a **sweatshirt**. Throughout the period boys wore sweaters of all types: cardigans, pullovers, and sleeveless pullovers. Turtleneck sweaters went out of fashion after the 1920s.

Outdoor Garments

Dress coats followed the lines of men's dress coats in each decade. For everyday wear in the 1920s, mackinaws remained popular, and a lumberjack jacket with knitted waistband ending just below the waist was worn. In the 1930s, fingertip-length, boxy jackets were added, and in the late 1930s and early 1940s, poplin jackets and waterproof parkas appeared. During the war years boys wore Eisenhower jackets.

Costume Components for Boys and Girls

Garments

As athletic shorts and sleeveless undershirts became available for men and brief panties for women, they also were made for children.

Beginning in the 1930s and in subsequent decades, children wore jeans as play and everyday clothing. Teachers complained that the rivets on the back pockets made holes in wooden school seats, so this feature was discontinued (Ratner, 1975). Overalls made of blue denim and pants of the same fabric appeared in the boys' section of the 1923 Sears, Roebuck catalogue with the caption "for work or play" and henceforth

were a consistent feature of work or playclothes for boys, especially in rural areas. In the 1940s they also appeared as playclothes for girls.

Preschool boys and girls continued to wear sailor suits and dresses, respectively. Other items also appeared. In the 1920s, Tom Mix (a popular cowboy movie star) outfits were advertised. The same page of the Sears, Roebuck catalogue advertised Indian suits (Native Americans were referred to as *Indians* at that time), policeman suits, and other cowboy outfits. In the 1930s, cowboy and Indian suits remained popular, and baseball players' suits and flyers' uniforms were added. The availability of space suits reflected the popularity of cartoons and films such as those about Buck Rogers (Figure 16.37). Girls could wear nurses' uniforms and, sometimes, cowgirl or Indian dresses. In the 1940s, during the war, boys could choose from officers' suits from the army, navy, or marines and from admirals' suits, aviators' suits, or sailors' suits; girls chose from dresslike uniforms worn by women's auxiliary (WAAC) or volunteer military units (WAVE).

Outdoor Garments

There was little difference between snowsuits for preschool boys and girls other than color, pink being reserved for girls. For small children, there were one-piece snow suits; for older children, two-piece jackets

FIGURE 16.37 Page from a 1935 Sears, Roebuck catalogue. The interests of small boys of this period are reflected in the Indian and aviator costumes and Buck Rogers's space suit that could be purchased. (Courtesy of Sears, Roebuck & Co.)

and leggings. In the 1930s, water-repellent fabrics were used. In the 1940s, hooded jackets were popular.

In the 1920s and 1930s rubberized cloth or oiled slicker material was used for rainwear. By the late 1930s, water-repellent fabric replaced oiled slicker fabric. For true waterproofing, rubberized fabrics were required. During the war when rubber was scarce, rainwear was made of synthetic rubber.

Clothing for Active Sports

Swimsuits followed adult styles.

Sleepwear

From the 1920s on, much of the sleepwear for young children was in the form of footed pajamas, sometimes called **sleepers**. Older boys wore pajamas almost exclusively, whereas girls wore either pajamas or nightgowns.

Costume Components for the Teenage Market

The concept of a stage of development called *adolescence*, defined as the years between ages 13 and 18, first appeared in the work of psychologist G. Stanley Hall in 1904. In exploring the emergence of teenage girls' culture, Schrum (2004) saw that serious marketing to teens began in the 1920s and was well established by the 1940s. As evidence she pointed to teen-centered marketing in stores, new sizes and styles, and the use of advertising terminology such as *junior miss*, *high school shop*, and *sub-debs*.

One of the major concerns for adolescent girls was the point at which to start wearing a bra. Special bras were marketed to developing girls, and peer pressure was a major force when it came to making this choice. Although the garment industry also tried to market girdles to teenage girls, these efforts were less successful.

Preferences in school clothing gradually changed. In the 1920s dresses with stockings, pumps, oxfords, or sandals were preferred. In the 1930s the preference was for blouses and skirts, though dresses were also worn. Ankle socks became more important, and the term *bobby sox* used for ankle socks had come into use by 1936. By the 1940s adolescent and college-age girls made skirts and sweaters into veritable uniforms. To skirts and sweaters they added white ankle socks and either loafers or saddle shoes. The favorite hairstyle was a long pageboy cut.

In the mid-1940s adolescent girls wore large, loose sweaters known as *sloppy joes* or put on cardigan sweaters backward.

High school proms required formal, floor-length dresses.

Summary

Themes

A theme evident in any consideration of styles between the first and second World Wars is that of CHANGES IN SOCIAL BEHAVIOR, especially for women. Clothing styles for men continued the trends begun before the 1914 war. Wardrobes for men who were white-collar office workers and for blue-collar laborers offered relatively little choice. The former was confined to a suit with vest, white shirt, and necktie for business, and the latter, to sturdy, washable work clothes. In clothing for leisure, however, men were able to exercise a wider degree of selection from a broader range of styles.

Women's clothing in the 1920s incorporated elements that had rarely appeared in earlier historical periods and that provided visible evidence of CHANGES IN THE ROLES OF WOMEN. The radically shorter skirts, cropped hair, acceptability of cosmetic use, and adoption by women of traditionally masculine garments such as trousers showed that women had rejected patterns in feminine dress that had been

Visual Summary Table

1920–1947

Man: Business Suit, 1927/1928
Chief elements continue to be shirt, vest, jacket, and trousers. Trousers slightly wider in the 1920s than in previous decade.

Man: English Drape Suit, 1938
English drape style jackets have wider shoulders. Men wore sports jackets for casual dress.

Woman: Dress, 1926
Typical style: flat bosom, unfitted waist, and belt placed at the hip. Skirts shortest c. 1926–27, longer again by 1930. Pants seen for sports and outdoors.

Woman: Dress, 1933
Garments now follow body curves. Waist is again at anatomical position. Bias cut often used. Skirts, long at the beginning of the decade, gradually shorten.

Woman: Dress and Jacket, 1941
The lines of dresses just before the war are "frozen" by the war at shorter lengths, somewhat fuller skirts, and broad, padded shoulders.

established for hundreds of years, just as they were rejecting patterns of behavior for women that had confined them to more limited roles in society.

The importance of the RELATIONSHIP BETWEEN COSTUME AND THE WORK OF INDIVIDUAL DESIGNERS continued to grow, as designers such as Chanel, Vionnet, and Schiaparelli had a great impact on styles that were copied by the American fashion industry at all levels. THE RELATIONSHIPS BETWEEN COSTUME AND DEVELOPMENTS IN THE FINE AND APPLIED ARTS can be seen in Art Deco design motifs on textiles of the 1920s and in Schiaparelli's incorporation of surrealistic elements in her designs.

ECONOMIC EVENTS can be identified as another important theme, which was evident in the extremes of prosperity in the 1920s and depression in the 1930s. Clothing styles of the two decades contrast almost as sharply as economic trends, with the lavish, beaded gowns of the 1920s giving way to the simpler, more subdued lines of the 1930s.

TECHNOLOGY made new fibers available. Rayon was used throughout these periods, and nylon was introduced just before World War II. As always, the POLITICAL CONFLICT of World War II affected apparel, removing nylon from the consumer market, cutting off supplies of silk from east Asia, and leading to restrictions on the cut of clothing. The war also served to bring American fashion designers to the forefront of fashion design, as Paris was occupied by the Germans.

LEGACIES OF STYLES OF THE 1920S AND 1930S

Fashion designers of the post–World War II period often turned to the past for design inspiration. In those periods when unfitted styles have been popular, the 1920s have often served as the source (see Modern Influences). The 1960s was such a period. Other 1920s revivals could be seen in the 1980s and 1990s. Art Deco design motifs came to prominence again in the

1970s after several art exhibitions focused attention on these styles of the 1920s and 1930s.

When Chanel reopened her couture house in the 1950s, she also revived her signature cardigan suit. This suit continues to be reworked by subsequent designers at the house of Chanel and has maintained its popularity.

Both the platform-soled shoes and the big shoulder pads of the 1930s have been seen again. Platform soles grew to extreme heights in the 1970s, then returned again in the 1990s. Big shoulder pads reentered the fashion scene in the early 1980s, and some form of these pads continued into 2008.

In their constant mining of the past, fashion designers have not overlooked the 1930s. Often these revivals followed the release of films set in the 1930s. The first was in 1967 with 1930s-style sweaters and berets from the film *Bonnie and Clyde*. Some designs

MODERN INFLUENCES

When unfitted evening dresses are in style, the cut and styles of dresses of the 1920s are often revived, as in this example from 2009. (Giannoni/WWD/© Condé Nast)

of the 1980s and the 1990s clearly came from bias cut styles of the 1930s, as did some printed textile designs.

REFERENCES

Allen, F. L. (1931). *Only yesterday*. New York, NY: Harper and Row.

Berendt, J. (1988). The raccoon coat. *Esquire, 109*(1), 22.

Berendt, J. (1989). The zipper. *Esquire, 111*(5), 42.

Cosgrove, S. (1984). The zoot suit and style warfare. *History Workshop Journal, 18*, 77–91.

Friedel, R. (1994). *Zipper*. New York, NY: Norton.

Horn, M. (1975). *The second skin*. New York, NY: Houghton-Mifflin.

Horyn, C. (2002, April 30). Silver screen or mezzanine: His designs were for all. *New York Times*, B8.

Keist, C. N., & Marcketti, S. B. (2013). The new costumes of odd sizes: Plus-sized women's fashions, 1920–1929. *Clothing and Textiles Research Journal, 31*(4), 259–274.

Kidwell, C. K., & Steele, V. (1980). *Men and women: Dressing the part*. Washington, DC: Smithsonian Institution Press.

Kirkland, S. (1975). *American fashion*. New York, NY: Quadrangle/New York Times Book Co.

Latour, A. (1956). *Kings of fashion*. London, UK: Weidenfeld and Nicolson.

Martin, R. (1987). *Surrealism and fashion*. New York, NY: Rizzoli.

Martin, R., & Koda, H. (1994). *Orientalism: Visions of the east in western dress*. New York, NY: Metropolitan Museum of Art.

Mower, J. M., & Pedersen, E. L. (2013). Pretty and patriotic: Women's consumption of apparel during World War II. *Dress, 39*(1), 37–54.

Ratner, E. (1975). Levi's. *Dress, 1*, 3.

Richards, L. (1983). The rise and fall of it all: The hemlines and hiplines of the 1920's. *Clothing and Textiles Research Journal, 2*(1), 42–48.

Schoeffler, O. E., & Gale, W. (1973). *Esquire's encyclopedia of 20th century men's fashion*. New York, NY: McGraw-Hill.

Schrum, K. (2004). *Some wore bobby sox: The emergence of teenage girls' culture 1920–1945*. New York, NY: Palgrave Macmillan.

Steele, V., & Major, J. S. (1999). *China chic: East meets west*. New Haven, CT: Yale University Press.

Veillon, D. (2002). *Fashion under the occupation*. New York, NY: Berg.

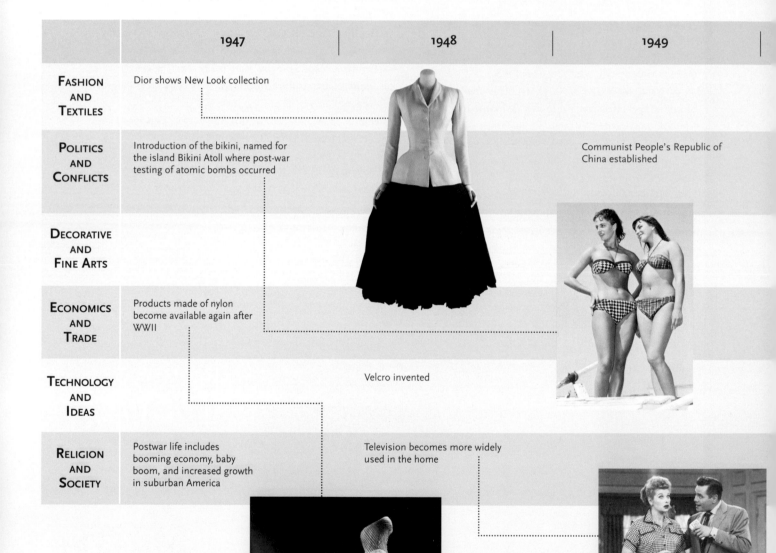

	1947	1948	1949
FASHION AND TEXTILES	Dior shows New Look collection		
POLITICS AND CONFLICTS	Introduction of the bikini, named for the island Bikini Atoll where post-war testing of atomic bombs occurred		Communist People's Republic of China established
DECORATIVE AND FINE ARTS			
ECONOMICS AND TRADE	Products made of nylon become available again after WWII		
TECHNOLOGY AND IDEAS		Velcro invented	
RELIGION AND SOCIETY	Postwar life includes booming economy, baby boom, and increased growth in suburban America	Television becomes more widely used in the home	

The New Look: Fashion Conformity Prevails

1947–1960

1950	1952	1953	1954	1955	1957	1959

Acrylic fibers mass-produced

Chanel reopens her couture house

Dior introduces the A-line

Yves Saint Laurent becomes designer for House of Dior

Korean War begins

Dwight Eisenhower elected U.S. president

Korean War ends

U.S. Supreme Court declares school segregation unconstitutional

Civil Rights movement begins with bus boycott in Montgomery, AL

Alaska becomes the 49th state; Hawaii becomes the 50th state. Castro comes to power in Cuba

Jack Kerouac publishes *On the Road*, a novel considered the testament of the "beat" generation

Rapid development of air travel in post-WWII era

Polyester fibers become available commercially

Russians launch Sputnik, the first space satellite

The Cold War affects politics and daily life

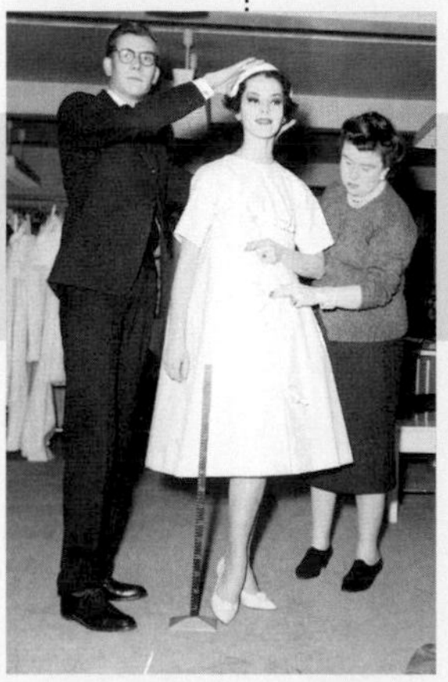

In 1947, after World War II, Parisian fashion turned in dramatic new directions that the press labeled the *New Look*. These styles dominated fashion design until the mid-1950s when some silhouette changes began to appear. Although Paris remained the preeminent fashion center, there was an internationalization of dress as other design centers emerged. Many clothes were made from new and popular easy-care synthetic fabrics such as nylon, polyester, and acrylic. The medium of television provided another platform for viewing current fashions. Teddy Boys in Britain and beatniks in the United States were among the first subcultural groups to develop unique fashion statements.

HISTORICAL BACKGROUND

During the 1950s the world became a much smaller place. The rapid development of air travel, the almost instant transmission of news from one part of the world to another, and the transition from national to globally interdependent economies spread fashion and other information faster than ever before (Figure 17.1). It was no longer possible to understand the historical background of a period by examining developments only in western Europe and North America.

Europe was devastated at the end of World War II and divided into capitalist and communist economies. In the Middle East and in Asia, World War II ended European imperialism. The Soviet Union's successful launch of the world's first artificial satellite, Sputnik I, ushered in new political, military, technological, and scientific developments. It marked the start of the space age and the "race to space" between the United States and the Soviet Union. Americans fought the Cold War abroad and racism at home.

Eastern and Western Europe

World War II left millions of Europeans homeless who faced food shortages, inadequate transportation, and cities in shambles. The political vacuum left in central Europe following the defeat of Nazi Germany and its allies was filled by the victorious Allied armies who,

FIGURE 17.1 During the 1950s, flight attendant uniforms tended to be mannish and military inspired in style and color. During the 1960s through 1980s fashion designers, including Emilio Pucci and Oleg Cassini, designed more fashion-forward uniforms. (NGS Image Collection/The Art Archive at Art Resource, NY)

in effect, partitioned Europe into pro-western and pro-Soviet spheres of influence. In western Europe, parliamentary governments and capitalist economies revived. For example, by 1949 the western zone of a divided Germany had a new democratic constitution. With a new economic policy West Germany soon began a period of sustained economic growth that made it an industrial power by the end of the 1950s.

In eastern Europe, the states under Soviet occupation were compelled to follow the Soviet political and economic model and to support Moscow's foreign policies. The German Democratic Republic, commonly referred to as East Germany, became a state within the eastern Soviet bloc. Divided Europe now became the center of the power struggle known as the Cold War. During the Cold War, the United States under presidents Truman and Eisenhower tried to contain communism in general and the Soviet Union in particular.

European countries were vulnerable to Soviet domination because of their need to repair their war-damaged economies. To aid in repairing their economies the U.S. government instituted the Marshall Plan in 1948. Although the Soviet Union and its satellite states rejected the Marshall Plan, this aid restored the economic well-being of western Europe and provided a market for American products. By 1952, as a result of Marshall Plan aid, industrial production in western Europe surpassed prewar levels.

In 1949 the United States and Canada joined the western European nations to form the North Atlantic Treaty Organization. In this agreement the members pledged to assist each other should there be an attack. In addition, in 1951 France and Germany joined the European Coal and Steel Community in which their coal and steel production was combined and supervised by an international authority. This agreement led to the creation in 1957 of the European Economic Community in which six European states, including France and Germany, pledged to gradually eliminate all restrictions on trade movements, capital, and labor.

In the postwar years, Europe underwent major social changes, including a spurt in population growth. Europe also experienced an exodus of people from the rural areas to the cities. As a result, the new society of Europe came to be dominated by the cities, and the new urban culture came to resemble that of the United States—white collar, middle class, and oriented toward a consumption economy. There was almost a class revolution in transportation. Before World War II only wealthy Europeans could afford automobiles. Most people traveled by streetcar or bicycle. In the 1950s, however, the number of automobiles more than doubled, and there was an increase in motor scooters. Highway systems were

limited, and as a result the narrow, medieval streets were soon clogged with traffic.

The Middle East and Asia

At the end of World War I, Britain and France dominated the states that were once part of the Ottoman Empire. But World War II undermined the Anglo-French influence in the Middle East. Major changes came as a new generation, often led by young, radical army officers, seized power.

A United Nations 1947 resolution intended to divide Palestine between Arabs and Jewish refugees from European persecution. The Arabs rejected the partition plan, and war ensued. The Jews held off their attackers, established the state of Israel in 1948, and received both United Nations and U.S. recognition. A truce came in 1949.

Imperialism was undermined in some parts of the east, while communism ruled in other nations. Britain granted independence to India in 1947. Ultimately three separate states were created: India, Pakistan, and Bangladesh. The Netherlands gave Indonesia freedom in 1949. Only France attempted unsuccessfully to retain power in Indochina. China came under the communist rule of Mao Zedong in 1949 after the government of Chiang Kai-shek was forced to flee to the island of Taiwan.

The Soviet Union

In 1953, the death of Soviet dictator Josef Stalin brought changes to the Soviet Union. Nikita S. Khrushchev, secretary general of the Communist Party, denounced Stalin's crimes in a speech in February 1956 to the 20th Congress of the Communist Party of the Soviet Union. Communists outside the Soviet bloc in western Europe hoped that Khrushchev's speech meant a lessening of Soviet control over eastern bloc states. But in 1956 the new Soviet leadership would not allow Hungary to embark on a policy of neutrality in the Cold War or to hold free elections. Soviet troops put down the Hungarian rebellion and installed a puppet who would follow Moscow's desires. The Soviet Union still controlled its new empire.

The United States

The post-war years were a time of technological innovations, particularly in efforts to win the "space race." Great strides were also made in the civil rights movement.

The Cold War Heats Up

Following the death of Franklin D. Roosevelt, Harry Truman became president in 1945. One of Truman's first decisions was to drop the atomic bomb on Japan. In 1949 Americans were shocked to learn that the Soviet Union had developed the capacity to produce atomic weapons. Frightened by Soviet progress, Truman ordered the development of a thermonuclear weapon—the hydrogen bomb. The first American H-bomb was exploded in 1952. Soviet authorities exploded their first H-bomb in 1955. The arms race to develop and control weapons was under way.

The Cold War appeared to be heating up in June 1950 when communist North Korean troops crossed the 38th parallel, the dividing line between North and South Korea. President Truman ordered American forces under the command of General Douglas MacArthur to defend South Korea. The Korean War worsened when Chinese troops entered the war in support of their North Korean allies. Eventually the fighting came to a stalemate, and after protracted negotiations a truce was signed in 1953.

Anticommunism and McCarthyism

As the Cold War intensified, many Americans wondered why the United States now seemed to be a nation in peril. Some Americans blamed a communist conspiracy for the nation's troubles. The Truman administration decided to set up the Federal Employee Loyalty Program to determine whether foreign agents—communists—were undermining the nation's strength. No communist plot was uncovered. Another government anticommunist group was the House Un-American Activities Committee within the House of Representatives. Members investigated alleged disloyalty and subversive activities on the part of citizens, public employees, and even members of the Hollywood film industry. More than 300 artists, including actors and screenwriters, were blacklisted, or denied the opportunity to work.

One of the most vocal anticommunists was an unscrupulous politician, Senator Joseph McCarthy from Wisconsin who, exploiting fears of a communist plot, issued charges that numbers of communist agents were in the Department of State. A clever demagogue, McCarthy never attempted to prove his charges.

McCarthy was riding high as his pursuit of alleged communists turned into a witch-hunt. Even Dwight Eisenhower, elected in 1952, could do nothing. McCarthy went unchallenged until 1954 when he took aim at the army in a search for communist spies at Fort Monmouth, New Jersey. In a series of televised hearings, a new spectacle for the American viewing public, McCarthy's arrogance and lies, revealed on television, undermined his power. In December 1954 the Senate summoned enough courage to censure McCarthy. He was no longer a force in American politics.

Postwar Life

The 1944 GI Bill provided benefits to veterans of World War II and the Korean War, including educational subsidies, and many of them took advantage of these benefits by returning to college. The college students of the immediate postwar period and the generation of students who followed have been described as

> studious, earnest, rather humorless, bent on getting an education not for its own sake but because it clearly would, under the emerging national system, lead surely and inevitably to a good job and the solution to the youth problem of not so long before—economic security. (Brooks, 1966, 162)

Building on college campuses increased, as both men and women attended college.

The Beginning of Social Protest

In the decade of the 1960s, the **silent generation**, those born between the Great Depression and World War II, gave way to more vocal youth. The predecessors of the youthful protests movements of the 1960s were the **beatniks**, who appeared in the latter part of the 1950s. Beginning as a literary movement that included writer Jack Kerouac and poets Allen Ginsberg and Gregory Corso, the "beats" adopted eccentric habits of dress and grooming—"beards, pony tails, dirty sneakers, peasant blouses" (Brooks, 1966, 232). They experimented with drugs, turned to eastern mysticism, especially Zen Buddhism, and rejected the "square" world. Contacts with French existentialists led to the adoption of black clothes, especially turtlenecks and berets for men and leotards, tights, and ballet slippers for women

FIGURE 17.2 French existentialist-influenced dress for male beatniks included dark clothes, turtleneck tops, berets, sandals, small pointed beards and moustaches. (Courtesy of Fairchild Publications, Inc.)

(Figure 17.2). The end of the beatnik culture did not end rejection of contemporary culture for the creation of subcultures that influenced fashion and society.

Civil Rights Movement

During the Eisenhower administration, civil rights came to dominate much of American life. During the Truman years, Congress had rejected civil rights legislation proposed by the president. A breakthrough came in the unanimous Supreme Court decision in the case of *Brown v. the Board of Education of Topeka*. On May 17, 1954, the court overturned the doctrine of separate but equal in public education and held that separate educational facilities were inherently unequal. A year later the Supreme Court directed that school authorities draft plans for desegregation of public schools and ordered action "with all deliberate speed" (Daugherity and Bolton, 2008).

The states of the deep south took steps to avoid compliance with the orders of the Supreme Court. Resistance to the court's decision erupted in 1957 when a mob in Little Rock, Arkansas, threatened African-American students who were attempting to enter Central High School. A reluctant President Eisenhower ordered federal troops to restore order and to protect the African-American students.

Congress took limited action by passing the first Civil Rights Act in 82 years, designed to help African Americans to vote. In a series of decisions over the next few years, the Supreme Court struck down segregation in interstate commerce, buildings, interstate bus terminals, and airports. African Americans themselves undertook personal campaigns aimed at ending segregation. In Atlanta, Georgia, a year-long bus boycott led by Dr. Martin Luther King Jr. helped end segregation on buses. In 1960 four young African-American men remained seated at a lunch counter in Greensboro, North Carolina, when a waitress refused to serve them. Thus began the first of a number of "sit-in" demonstrations against segregation. By 1960, however, only limited progress had been made in ending segregation in the United States.

INFLUENCES ON FASHION

The changing patterns of life in the United States and western Europe had a major impact on what people wore.

The Silent Generation's Move to the Suburbs

By 1947 many American women had returned to full-time homemaking after working for pay during World War II. By producing a bumper crop of babies, families created a **baby boom**. A family-oriented lifestyle was emphasized as women's magazines stressed togetherness even as women contributed to the family income by working outside of the home.

As the American highway systems expanded during the Eisenhower administration, many urban families moved to the rapidly growing suburbs. The interstate allowed for family travel, and fast-food restaurants proliferated for quick and easy meals. Camping became a popular form of recreation. All these changes were accompanied by the development of sportswear departments for men, women, and teens. The proportion of leisure clothing in the suburban American's wardrobe signaled a tendency that accelerated as the period progressed.

The newly created suburbs produced a changed lifestyle for large numbers of Americans. Part of that lifestyle was the suburban shopping mall. Shopping malls supplemented, and later replaced, downtown department stores; shopping had become almost a form of recreation. American adolescents found the shopping mall an especially appealing place to congregate.

The Young

Changes in the socioeconomic status of adolescents had begun during World War II. Before the war, many young people became wage earners and members of the workforce soon after they entered their teens. But the postwar socioeconomic changes kept many young people dependent on their families for a longer period of time—through high school and even beyond—and this accentuated the period of adolescence as a

separate stage of development. The teen market grew rapidly, and teenage fashions and fads played an important role in the garment industry. Magazines such as *Seventeen* (first issued in 1944) and *Young Miss* (in 1955) targeted the teen market.

But it was in Britain in the late 1940s and 1950s that the **Teddy Boys** created the first truly independent fashions for young people. Teddy Boys were working-class British adolescents who adopted styles in menswear that had a somewhat Edwardian flavor (named after King Edward VII, 1901–1910): longer jackets with more shaping, high turned-back lapels, cuffed sleeves, waistcoats, and well-cut, narrow trousers. Teddy Boys adopted an exaggerated version of these styles, somewhat akin to the prewar zoot suit, an earlier example of a style popular with less affluent youth (see pages 492–493). They wore elongated, loose jackets with wide, padded shoulders and, often, a velvet collar. Trousers were very narrow, tight, and short enough to allow garishly colored socks to show. They added narrow neckties. In the 1950s, flat, broad shoes were replaced by **winkle pickers**, shoes with exaggeratedly pointed toes. Hair was somewhat longer, with sideburns and a duck-tailed shape cut at the back, known as a **DA** (short for *duck's ass*; Ewing, 1977; Figure 17.3).

The female companions of Teddy Boys, Teddy Girls, wore long gray jackets over tight, high-necked black sweaters and black skirts. They combined dark stockings with a feminized version of the winkle pickers that had very high heels and pointed toes.

Ewing (1977) noted that the Teddy Boy phenomenon had a threefold significance: It was the first outfit to be promoted by the young, for the young; it was the first fashion to begin among the lower classes; and it was the first fashion to be the outward evidence of a lifestyle cult.

Unlike the zoot suit, some elements of Teddy Boy styles, such as the narrow-toed shoes and the hairstyles, penetrated mainstream fashion. Teddy Boy styles were only the beginning of a new phenomenon that was to characterize subsequent fashion periods, that of the origination and adoption of style changes by a young, less affluent subgroup within the larger society.

FIGURE 17.3 Three British adolescent boys dressed in the Teddy Boy styles of the post–World War II period. (© Bettmann/CORBIS)

FIGURE 17.4 The television series *I Love Lucy* aired from 1951 to 1957. Several episodes prominently featured fashion, particularly in Season 4 in which Lucy is a model in a Don Draper fashion show and in Season 5 when Lucy desires a Parisian gown. (The Kobal Collection at Art Resource)

Television

Television became commercially available to the American public about 1948, but in that year only 20 stations were on the air and only 172,000 families had sets. According to the 1950 census, five million families reported having a TV set in the house (Brooks, 1966; Figure 17.4). As a medium for the spread of fashion information, influences from television were more evident among the young. Styles directly attributable to television included white buckskin shoes (called **white bucks**) after singer Pat Boone wore these shoe styles; Elvis Presley look-alike pompadours; a slick, combed-back hairstyle copied from a character named "Kookie" on a show called *77 Sunset Strip*; and a fad for Davy Crockett coonskin caps.

When Lucille Ball allowed the story line of *I Love Lucy* to incorporate her pregnancy into the TV show, more attention was paid to maternity clothing (Figure 17.5). But as Milbank (1989) pointed out,

> For the most part, early television depicted a sanitized view of family life, with exaggeratedly middle-class housewives as the most prevalent female characters. Women wanting to emulate television fashions would have concentrated on the ball gowns and cocktail dresses worn by singers [and actresses]. (179)

Other notable TV families included those on *The Donna Reed Show* and *Father Knows Best*.

Internationalism

Air travel made it possible for people of the postwar period to move easily from one place to another. The

FIGURE 17.5 During the baby boom, even international couturiers designed lines of maternity clothing. Left to right, designs created in 1956 by Miguel Dorian of Spain, Givenchy of France, and Norman Hartnell of England. (Courtesy of Fairchild Publications, Inc.)

relatively low cost of this transportation and its speed (compared with ship travel), coupled with an increased affluence for many Americans, encouraged more of them to travel abroad. In 1929, 500,000 Americans traveled abroad. In 1958 the number of Americans who went abroad reached 1,398,000, and they spent an estimated $2 billion in their travels (*New York Times*, as cited in Brooks, 1966). Travelers returned with fashion goods from the countries they visited. They also became more receptive to imported goods sold in the United States.

Steady increases in imports were seen as a serious threat by labor and management in the American garment industry. These imports were at first chiefly from western Europe and tended to be

high fashion with fairly high prices. Advertisements and promotions by sophisticated western European countries created a demand for fashionable Italian, French, and British goods. In the 1960s, developing countries in Asia, Africa, and South America began to export goods, which cost much less than European goods. Because of their low prices, these gradually came to dominate the low- and mid-price markets. Retailers liked the imported goods because they often took a higher markup on these items than on domestic goods.

High-fashion design took on a more international flavor. The French position as the sole arbiter of fashion for women was challenged not only by American designers who rose to prominence during

World War II but also by English, Italian, and even a few Irish and Spanish designers.

The Fabric Revolution

Before World War II clothing was made from a limited number of fibers: natural fibers (silk, wool, cotton, and linen) and manufactured fibers (rayon and acetate). The successful marketing of nylon, invented before the war but not given wide distribution to the civilian population until after the war, ignited the production of other synthetic fibers (Handley, 1999). The major apparel fibers that came onto the market in the 1950s included modacrylics (1949), acrylics (1950), polyesters (1953), triacetate (1954), and spandex (1959; Figure 17.6). Other fibers were also developed, but these either had limited use or were found mostly in household textiles or industrial applications. Many companies that had formerly been chemical companies began to manufacture fibers, which were chiefly derived from chemical substances.

One of the characteristics of most of the postwar fabrics was that they were easy to care for. With the more casual lifestyle that had evolved, and with the virtual disappearance of servants from the middle-class household, these fabrics were easier to maintain and rapidly gained consumer acceptance. The expansion of travel helped to promote **drip-dry** fabrics. In the late 1950s, there were **wash-and-wear** fabrics. In the 1960s, wash and wear was replaced by **permanent press**, which were chiefly cotton and cotton blended with polyester. Some wool fabrics were given special treatments to render them more readily washable. These new synthetic fibers may also have contributed to the popularity of the full skirts of the period which were held out by lightweight, permanently stiffened nylon petticoats (Figure 17.7).

With manufactured fibers, and especially with blends, American consumers found it hard to identify fibers and know how to care for them. To help consumers, Congress passed the Textile Fiber Products Identification Act in 1960; this legislation required textile products to be sold with labels identifying the fiber content.

The Changing Couture

Since the establishment of the French haute couture in the 19th century, member designers have been considered the primary source of major fashion trends. The *Chambre Syndicale de la Couture Parisienne* is a business association that serves to promote the products of its designers. Membership in the *Chambre Syndicale* requires that new style ideas are developed and shown several times each year. In the postwar period potential customers and the fashion press attended fashion shows presented by each couturier (designer).

Garments shown and sold by couture houses are called **originals**. The term *original* does not mean the garment is the only one of its kind but that it was

FIGURE 17.6 Du Pont trademarked their acrylic fibers as Orlon. This 1955 advertisement for a sweater twin set proclaims the perfect combination of the fiber's "luxury and practicality." (© Jeff Morgan 11 / Alamy)

FIGURE 17.7 During World War II, the production of nylon was channeled to support the war effort. Following the war, nylon moved from a fiber used mainly for hosiery to a staple of sleepwear and outerwear, including its use in this Charles James evening gown with silk chiffon, silk satin, and nylon chiffon from 1951. (Digital Image © 1951 Museum Associates/LACMA. Licensed by Art Resource, NY)

made in the establishment of the designer. More than one original can be made of any style. Prices for originals are very high, but so are expenses. Most French couture houses at the time did not make profits on their haute couture operations. Instead, they established auxiliary enterprises such as perfume sales and "signed" accessory items, the manufacture of which had much lower overhead costs. These more affordable items became the profitable part of their businesses and supported the costly couture.

Prominent Designers of the Postwar Couture

Some individual members of the French couture continued designing in Paris throughout World War II, but most left Paris or closed their ateliers. Mainbocher and Schiaparelli went to New York; Balenciaga went to neutral Portugal. Chanel gave her last show in 1940. Once the war ended, the couturiers planned for a revival of their businesses. This revival was given an enormous push forward by the collections of 1947 and the New Look, the name given by the fashion press to the collection mounted by **Christian Dior** (Figure 17.8).

FIGURE 17.8 The designs Christian Dior created in the late 1940s and 1950s have been described as romantic and were seen, at the time, as a return to luxurious fashion like that of the past. (Image copyright © The Metropolitan Museum of Art. Image source: Art Resource, NY)

Dior had worked before the war for Piquet and after, briefly, for the House of Lucien Lelong (Lelong was not a designer but ran an establishment carrying his name). In 1945 Dior was offered financial backing to open his own establishment, and in 1947 the House of Dior made fashion history. The new styles were successful overnight, and the House of Dior became one of the most influential of the houses in the haute couture. Dior remained a celebrated designer until his death in 1957 (Palmer, 2009).

Another major designer of the postwar period was **Cristobal Balenciaga**. The Spanish-born Balenciaga opened his first Paris establishment in 1937. When he returned to Paris after the war, he became a favorite of Carmel Snow, editor of *Harper's Bazaar* who often featured his work in the magazine. His work showed a mastery of almost sculptural forms and shapes, and his styles were frequently well ahead of their time (Figure 17.9). A major force in the haute couture for the 1950s and on into the 1960s, he suddenly and unexpectedly closed his establishment in 1968. Balenciaga died in 1972.

Chanel did not reopen her atelier until 1954. Once again she became a major force in the couture, continuing to influence styles until she died in 1971.

The couture remained a vital, active force in fashion throughout the 1950s and early 1960s. Interest in the couture remained exceptionally high and many other Parisian couturiers were active in the postwar period. Table 17.1 lists major French designers of the period between 1947 and 1960.

The American Mass Market

In the American sportswear market, U.S. designers were originating most of the designs in the 1930s and 1940s. The potential elimination of Paris as a design center during World War II had allowed American designers to flourish. Some created custom-made clothing for an exclusive clientele, such as Mainbocher and Charles James, while others worked in the higher priced ready-to-wear market, such as Claire McCardell, Norman Norell, Pauline Trigère, Arnold Scaasi, and James Galanos. These designers developed a strong

FIGURE 17.9 Balenciaga was known for his skill in cutting and structuring the clothes he designed. This quality is visible in this red linen suit from 1952. (Horst P. Horst © 1952 Condé Nast Publications)

following and influenced styles, making New York a postwar center of design. Other designers, many of whose names have been lost to history, worked anonymously under company labels. Table 17.2 lists major American designers of the postwar period.

The American mass market was organized to originate, manufacture, and distribute clothing to retailers throughout the United States. The pre–World War II mass-market designers generally seemed to draw their inspiration from styles presented by fashion designers in Paris. Initially this clothing was purchased by a fashionable, moneyed elite, a situation that continued for moderate and lower priced ready-to-wear throughout the 1950s. However, especially in higher priced lines, innovative and creative American designers also created new styles, and their work was regularly reported by the fashion press.

TABLE 17.1 Influential Paris-Based Designers, 1947–1960

DESIGNER	COUTURE HOUSE AND DATE OF OPENING	NOTABLE CHARACTERISTICS
Cristobal Balenciaga (1895–1972)	Balenciaga, 1937	Innovative designer, major influence after WWII, considered a master craftsman (see page 515).
Pierre Balmain (1914–1982)	Balmain, 1945	"Known for wearable, elegant clothes . . . daytime classics, extravagant evening gowns."
Marc Bohan (1926–)	Chief designer and artistic director of Christian Dior, 1958–1989, after which he became head designer at Jean Patou.	High-quality workmanship and "refined and romantic clothes."
Pierre Cardin (1922–)	Cardin, 1950	Created many innovative and exciting designs in the 1950s and 1960s for women; began designing for men in 1958.
Gabrielle "Coco" Chanel (1883–1971)	Chanel, 1914; closed house during both world wars; first postwar collection, 1954. House of Chanel continued under various designers, most notably Karl Lagerfeld (see Table 19.2).	"Trademark looks included the little boy look, wool jersey dresses with white collars and cuffs, pea jackets, bell-bottom trousers, bobbed hair, and magnificent jewelry worn with sportswear. Other widely copied signatures were quilted handbags with chain handles, collarless jackets trimmed with braid, beige sling-back pumps with black tips."
Christian Dior (1905–1957)	Dior, 1947. After his death the house continued with other designers: Yves Saint Laurent until 1960, Marc Bohan until 1989, Gianfranco Ferré until 1996, John Galliano in 1997.	Originated the New Look, spring 1947 (see page 514), with the sensuous line, loosened the waist, 1952; H-line, 1954; and Y-line, 1955.
Jacques Fath (1912–1954)	Jacques Fath, 1937. Closed in 1957; the company was reopened in 1992; and in March 1997 was bought by the group EK Finances and now produces a prêt-a-porter line.	"Designed elegant, flattering, feminine, sexy clothes."
Hubert de Givenchy (1927–)	Givenchy, 1952; sold to LVMH, 1988; announced his retirement, 1995, following presentation of his final haute couture collection; British designer, John Galliano, was named to succeed him; then Alexander McQueen, 1996; in 2001, Julien MacDonald.	"Noted for clothing of exceptional workmanship, masterly cut, beautiful fabrics."

All quotes from Calasibetta, C. M. (1988). *The Fairchild dictionary of fashion* (2nd ed.). New York, NY: Fairchild Publications; Calasibetta, C. M. (2003). *The Fairchild dictionary of fashion* (3rd ed). New York, NY: Fairchild Publications; Stegemeyer, A. (1996). *Who's who in fashion* (3rd ed.). New York, NY: Fairchild Publications; and Stegemeyer, A. (2004). *Who's who in fashion* (4th ed.). New York, NY: Fairchild Publications.

Popular designs originated by couture and American ready-to-wear designers working in higher priced lines were quickly copied by designers for lower priced lines. These pirated copies are known in the garment industry as **knock-offs**.

American Retailers and the Couture

Some exclusive American retail stores purchased designer originals that they sold to their customers. These garments were very costly because of import duties. The price of an original Chanel suit in 1958 at one specialty shop in Philadelphia was $3,500, the cost of a mid-priced automobile at the time.

In order to make high-fashion design available to American women, department stores such as Ohrbach's, Macy's, and Alexander's in New York bought original designer garments and, by arrangement with the designer, made relatively faithful **line-for-line copies** sold at much lower prices than the originals commanded. American designers and manufacturers

TABLE 17.2 Major American Fashion Designers of the 1950s

DESIGNER	AFFILIATION	NOTABLE CHARACTERISTICS
Gilbert Adrian (1903–1959)	Known first as designer for motion pictures; entered retail business, 1941; switched to wholesale, 1953.	Known for big-shouldered suits, dolman sleeves (see page 469).
Hattie Carnegie (1889–1956)	Hattie Carnegie Inc., established 1918.	Designed custom-made and ready-to-wear for well-to-do and celebrities for a long time. Influenced many American designers who worked for her.
Lilly Daché (1904–1989)	Leading milliner, as well as dress designer; added perfume and cosmetics in 1954. Closed business in 1969.	Draped turbans, half-hats, colored snoods.
Anne Fogarty (1919–1981)	Designed for Youth Guild, 1948–1057 and Margot Inc. 1957–1962. Established Anne Fogarty Inc., 1962 until her death.	Originated "paper doll" silhouette, 1951, with full skirt, small waist; known for Empire dress revival.
James Galanos (1929–)	Opened own business in Los Angeles, 1951. He closed his business and retired in 1998.	"Known for luxurious day and evening ensembles" as well as other types of clothing. Designed both inaugural gowns for Nancy Reagan.
Elizabeth Hawes (1903–1971)	Opened own shop in New York in 1928.	Known for simple and soft designs that followed natural proportions. Her first book *Fashion Is Spinach* (1938) was on fashion and the fashion business.
Charles James (1906–1978)	Had salons in London and Paris in the 1930s, and a custom-made business in New York in the 1940s and 1950s.	Considered to be among the most original of American designers. Known for lavish ball gowns, architectural shapes.
Tina Leser (1910–1986)	Designed for Edwin H. Foreman, Inc., 1943–1952. Opened own company, Tina Leser Inc., 1952.	Especially known for sportswear with influences from Mexico, Haiti, Japan, and India. Used cashmere in dresses.
Claire McCardell (1906–1958)	Except for 2 years at Hattie Carnegie, did most of her designing for Townley Frocks, Inc.	"Specialized in practical clothes for the working girl." Considered one of most innovative and creative of all American designers (see page 534).
Sally Milgrim (1891–1994)	Custom designer, with husband owned The Milgrim stores; last store closed 1990.	Known for evening wear. Designer of Eleanor Roosevelt's inaugural ball gown in 1933.
Norman Norell (1900–1972)	Worked for Hattie Carnegie from 1928–1940; a partner in Traina–Norell until 1960; then established Norman Norell Inc.	"Known for precision tailoring, . . . purity of line, conservative elegance." First designer elected to Coty Hall of Fame in 1958. A major figure in the American fashion industry until his death in 1972 (see page 469).
Mollie Parnis (1905–1992)	Active since 1939 when she and her husband founded Parnis-Livingston; then Mollie Parnis Inc., until 1984.	"[S]pecialized in flattering, feminine dresses and ensembles for the well-to-do woman over 30."
Claire Potter (1903–1999)	Worked under name "Clarepotter" in 1940s and 1950s, as Potter Designs Inc. in 1960s.	Known for sportswear designs, informal and more formal evening clothes.
Adele Simpson (1903–1995)	Adele Simpson, 1949–1991.	"Known for pretty, feminine clothes in delicate prints and colors."
Gustave Tassell (1926–)	Opened own firm in Los Angeles, 1956; designed for Norell, Inc., after Norell's death, from 1972 to 1976; then opened his own firm.	"Known for refined, no-gimmick clothes with stark, clean lines."
Pauline Trigère (1912–2002)	Worked for Hattie Carnegie, then opened own business in 1942, which she closed in 1993.	Highly regarded designer, with extensive licensing operation. Used unusual fabrics and prints, and "intricate" cuts (see page 469).
John Weitz (1923–2002)	Began with sportswear for Lord & Taylor, licensed designs in 1954, and opened his men's wear business in 1964.	One of the earliest to design both men's and women's apparel, and to begin licensing. Known for designs of practical sportswear.

All quotes from Calasibetta, C. M. (1988). *The Fairchild dictionary of fashion* (2nd ed.). New York, NY: Fairchild Publications; and Stegemeyer, A. (1996). *Who's who in fashion* (3rd ed.). New York, NY: Fairchild Publications.

also pirated French and American designs, sometimes selling copies of Monsieur X, Monsieur Y, or Monsieur Z. Knowledgeable customers were aware that Monsieur X was Dior, Monsieur Y was Jacques Fath, and Monsieur Z was Givenchy.

New Centers of Fashion Design

In the postwar era, a number of fashion design centers other than Paris also became important. When travel had been by ship or required lengthy and slow airplane trips, there was a certain practical aspect to having a single important center for fashion design. In the postwar period jet travel made reaching any of the major cities of the world faster and easier. The fashion press could cover shows in diverse parts of the globe with ease. By the 1950s Florence, Rome, and London had joined Paris and New York as important centers of fashion design (see Table 18.2, pages 560–561, for important fashion designers of the 1950s from international fashion centers other than Paris).

Design for men's clothing had no fashion center comparable to Paris and no organization comparable to the couture. As early as the 18th century, England had a reputation for fine tailoring, but a high level of interest in fashion was not considered manly. In the period from after World War II to the early 1960s this began to change, and centers for design for men as well as for women expanded.

COSTUME FOR WOMEN: 1947–1960

The discussion of fashion in this chapter is divided between consideration of the New Look (1947 to about 1954) and the gradual emergence of a softer, easier style (1954–1960). In the period after World War II definitive style changes entered onto the fashion stage at various points in each decade; therefore, some of the major trends in fashion persisted from one decade to another.

Seldom does fashion change almost overnight, but in 1947 an exceptionally rapid shift in styles took place. After the war, western nations began to recover from the wartime devastation. World War II ended in August 1945. After a little more than a year in which there were no major fashion upheavals, French designer Christian Dior caused a sensation by introducing a line of clothing at his spring 1947 show that deviated sharply from the styles of the wartime period and came to be known as the New Look (Figure 17.10). It was accepted rapidly and became the basis of style lines for the next ten or more years. Contemporary Comments 17.1 (page 519) reprints the description of the New Look collection from *Vogue*.

FIGURE 17.10 Suit from the Dior New Look collection of March 1947. (Art Resource/Metropolitan Museum of Art)

Contemporary Comments 17.1

THE NEW LOOK COLLECTION

Vogue *reports on the New Look collection in 1947.*

If there could be a composite, mythical woman dressed by a mythical, composite couturier, she would probably wear her skirt about fourteen inches from the floor; it might have, for its working model, a flower: petals of padding and stiffening sewn beneath the cup of the skirt; or it might be a long, straight tube beneath a belled and padded jacket. Her waist could be as small and nipped-in in cut as tight bodice and padded hips could make it. Her shoulders would be her own (or it would seem so); her arms traced closely in cloth. Her hat engaging but not silly—a gendarme hat; a hat with a broken brim; a mushroom hat which at eye level would have an almost flat surface with crown slipping into brim; or a thicket of straw and flowers. She might wear a high-necked, boned-collar blouse, or she might wear a suit with a low-necked collar; there would probably be a fan of pleating somewhere about her; and she would, without question, wear opera pumps—pointed, high-heeled.

Reprinted courtesy of *Vogue* magazine, April 1947, p. 137.

Style Features of the New Look for Women

The major style elements of the New Look and the changes that it brought were the following:

- Skirt lengths dropped sharply. Examination of fashion magazines of the preceding months shows that there was already a tendency toward somewhat longer skirts. Many other designers in the spring of 1947 also showed longer skirts, but to the woman on the street who had worn her skirts just below her knees for the preceding 4 or 5 years, the change was radical. Although there were pockets of resistance to the longer skirts (in the United States groups of women banded together to form Little Below the Knee Clubs and declared they would not lengthen their skirts), the change seemed irresistible and within a year the longer skirt lengths were widely adopted.
- The square, padded shoulder that had been worn since the late 1930s was replaced by a shoulder line with a round, soft curve (achieved by a shaped shoulder pad).
- Many designs had enormously full skirts. One of Dior's models had 25 yards of fan-pleated silk in the skirt.
- Other designs had pencil-slim skirts.
- Whether the skirt was full or narrow, the waistline was nipped in and small. The rounded curves of the body were emphasized. Many daytime and evening dresses were cut quite low. The curve of the hip was stressed. In jackets with basques—sections that extended below the waist—the basque was padded and stiffened into a full, round curve.

Once established, the New Look influence permeated women's clothes throughout the greater part of the 1950s.

Costume Components for Women: 1947–1954

Garments

To achieve the fashionable look, women returned to more confining underclothing than had been seen since before 1920. Fortunately for the comfort of women, many of the undergarments required to maintain the soft curves of the New Look were made of newer synthetic fabrics that pulled the body into the requisite shape without the rigid, painful bones and lacing of the early 20th century (see Illustrated Table 17.1 for examples of undergarments from the period between 1947 and 1960). The necessary underwear included brassieres. Nicknamed *bras*, these emphasized an uplift. For wearing under some of the strapless evening gowns, strapless brassieres were available both in short lengths or constructed to extend to the waist. The longer version was known as a *merry widow*. These were boned with synthetic materials. By the 1950s whalebone was no longer in use. However, the term *boning* had come to be applied to any kind of material shaped like whalebone and used to provide stiffening in undergarments, strapless evening gown bodices, or hoops, all of which were popular in this period. Although the sections between the bones were generally made of elasticized fabrics or synthetic power net, wearing these confining garments did occasion some degree of discomfort.

Many women wore waist cinchers, boned or elasticized fabric worn to narrow the waistline to the desired size. Garments that had been called *corsets* in earlier periods were now generally referred to as **girdles** or **foundation garments**. They usually extended well above the waistline in order to narrow the waist and were made of elasticized panels with some stretch combined with panels of firmer, nonstretching fabrics. Some closed with zippers; others had enough stretch to simply pull on over the hips.

In order to hold out the skirts of the New Look dresses, full petticoats were required. Starched crinoline half-slips (at this time crinoline was any open-weave, heavily sized fabric) were used, but permanently stiffened nylon plain-weave fabrics or nets were generally preferred for these garments, because they required less maintenance and were lighter in weight. Beneath the full skirts, slips with full skirts, often with a ruffle around the hem, were worn while the narrower skirts required a straight slip.

Under evening and wedding dresses, a hoop petticoat might also be used.

This period was marked by what might be called a dual silhouette for daytime garments, because both exceptionally full and narrow skirts coexisted. The long, narrow skirts required the bottom of the skirt be slit or have a pleat of some type to allow a full stride. Fullness was achieved by goring, pleating, gathering, or cutting garments in the princess style, without waistline seams (Figure 17.11).

Necklines were plain, round, or square and ended either close to the neck or lower. Many dresses had small (square or round) Peter Pan collars, larger (square or round) collars, and Chinese-style, or mandarin, standing collars.

Most sleeves were close fitting, the most popular styles being short cap sleeves just covering the shoulder; short, medium, and longer set-in sleeves that fit the arm closely; and "shirt sleeves" similar to those on men's shirts, but fuller.

Some notable dress styles included summer jacket dresses, usually sleeveless with small straps or halter tops and a short jacket or bolero; shirtwaist dresses with full skirts; and coat dresses with full skirts, some in the princess style, buttoning down the front. Some dresses of the early 1950s had dropped waistlines.

Although some full-skirted suits were worn, most tended to be made with narrow skirts. Jackets fit close at the waistline, extending below the waist where they either flared out into a stiffened peplum (a short extension below the waist) or had a rounded, stiffened, and padded hip section ending several inches below the waist (Figure 17.12). Suit necklines varied in placement, but tended to stand away from the neck somewhat. Collar styles included Peter Pan, rolled, notched, and shawl types.

Maternity Dresses

Most maternity dresses were two-piece, with loosely fitted tops over narrow skirts that had a stretch panel or open area to accommodate the expanding figure (see Figure 17.5). The baby boom of the 1940s and 1950s, together with Lucille Ball's very public pregnancy on

Illustrated Table 17.1

Selected Undergarments for Women, Men, and Boys: 1947–1960

Waist cincher, c. 1946[1]

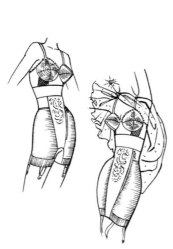

Girdles of the late 1940s and the 1950s with elasticized extensions above the waist for achieving the small-waisted silhouette of the period[2]

Full-skirted, permanently stiffened petticoat, late 1940s and 1950s[2]

Advertisement for a Maidenform brassiere; this "I dreamed I went walking . . ." series of advertisements was exceptionally popular In the 1950s.[3]

Maternity slip and panties, 1953

Slip, c. 1950–1953

Boy's knit athletic shirt and cotton knit briefs, 1950[4]

Men's T-shirt and boxer shorts

---

[1] Fairchild Publications.

[2] Stern's Department Store.

[3] Courtesy of Advertising Archives

[4] *Boys' Outfitter*, 1950, Fairchild Publications.

9. Playing tennis? A dress short as shorts, in tucked white piqué. $30; Abercrombie & Fitch.
10. Bathing suit. (Make it two, one for morning, one for afternoon.) This halter-neckline suit, in gingham, $30. From Lord & Taylor.
11. A dressing gown, discreetly cut, that can be worn down to breakfast. Here, full-skirted, in sheer eyelet nylon. $85; Bonwit Teller.

12. For lunch or cocktails, in or out, a dress not too bare without a cardigan. In rayon-and-cotton pinwale cord, $45; Lord & Taylor.
13. An evening dress, short. Here, a strapless dress, sleeveless jacket, of embroidered Swiss organdie. $125; Bergdorf Goodman.
14. What to arrive and leave in. Could be this city-country silk Shantung, line-stitched, the sleeves coolly deep. $80; Bergdorf Goodman.
15. Beach pieces: dotted Swiss blouse and brassière; piqué shorts. $30; Lord & Taylor.
16. Bathing suit (see 10). This, all one piece, in cotton broadcloth. $11; Arnold Constable.

FIGURE 17.11 *Vogue*, May 15, 1951, suggested these items be included in packing for a weekend in the country. Note especially the examples of both full-skirted dresses for day (Number 12) and evening (Number 13) contrasted with the slim skirt of Number 14.

(Courtesy of Vogue Magazine/Condé Nast Publications)

FIGURE 17.12 A typical example of a suit from the 1950s with a nipped-in waistline and shaped peplums. Skirts of suits and dresses were either very full with wide hemlines, or narrow and so closely fitted that a pleat or slit was needed at the center of the back to allow the wearer to take a full stride. (Serge Balkin © 1951 Condé Nast Publications)

the *I Love Lucy* show, brought a focused attention on maternity clothes. Even so, maternity clothes for advertisements were photographed on nonexpectant women.

Dresses for day and evening were usually the same length. Evening dresses that were the same length as daytime dresses were referred to as **ballerina length**, and these predominated. They were especially popular with high school and college students and were worn over stiff crinolines. Paris designers continued to show some long gowns, and pattern catalogues included patterns in both lengths (Figure 17.13; see also Figure 17.8). Bridal gowns were generally floor length. Wide skirts were preferred for evening, but some narrow-skirted styles had elaborate puffs of fabric at the hips, called **fish tails** (i.e., wide areas around or at

the back of the hem). Strapless bodices predominated, and they were often boned.

Outdoor Garments

Coats either followed the silhouette, having fitted bodice areas and full skirts, or were cut full from the shoulders. Most fitted coats were cut in the princess line and belted; full coats had a good deal of flare in the skirt. Sleeve styles included kimono and raglan types. Some had turned back cuffs ending well above the wrist; long gloves were worn with these (Figure 17.14). Fur coats were popular with affluent women. Princess-line coats were generally made of less bulky furs.

FIGURE 17.13 Both full-length (see Figure 17.8) and short, ballerina-length evening gowns were popular during the period when New Look styles predominated. (Henry Clarke © 1953 Condé Nast Publications)

FIGURE 17.14 A variety of coat styles were worn over the New Look styles. These coats were either short enough or had wide enough skirts to accommodate the wider skirts of the period. (© Vogue Magazine/Condé Nast Publications)

Jackets ending above the waist, called **shorties** or **toppers**, were a convenient way to accommodate wide skirts. Longer jackets, full and flaring from shoulder to hem, were also worn.

Sportswear

Casual garments worn during leisure time and in informal situations became an increasingly large part of the wardrobe. Retailers called such clothing *sportswear*. Skirts were either very full or narrow. Lines of blouses were shaped to follow body contours with darts or seams so that they fit smoothly through the bust and rib cage. They were similar in cut to dress bodices.

Sweaters, worn either tucked into the skirt or outside with a belt, fit close to the body. Many sweaters had smooth shoulder lines achieved by knitting sleeve and body in one. Variations included matching cardigans and pullovers or **sweater twin sets** (see Figure 17.6),

evening sweaters with beaded or sequin decorations (or both), and in the 1950s bolerolike cardigans called **shrugs**.

In the early part of the period, shorts were upper thigh length and fairly straight (see Figure 17.11). Knee-length Bermuda shorts were adopted about 1954 and until the late 1950s virtually replaced shorter styles (Figure 17.15). Narrow pants fit the leg so closely that shoes had to be taken off in order to pull on the pants (see Figure 17.15). Pant lengths included those ending at the ankle; **houseboy pants** ending at the calf; and shorter, midcalf-length pants that were given the fashion name **pedal pushers**. Other styles had names that changed from season to season, according to advertising copywriters' whims.

Clothing Worn for Active Sports

Designer Jacques Heim is credited with introducing in Europe a scanty, two-piece bathing suit—smaller

FIGURE 17.15 Bermuda shorts and narrow slacks were important sportswear styles of the early 1950s. (Butterick® Image Courtesy of the McCall Pattern Company copyright © 2014)

than any that had ever been seen before—that he called the *atom*. Soon a new version was advertised as smaller than the atom. French engineer Lous Réard named his design a **bikini** after the Pacific atoll where atomic tests were then being conducted. He hoped his bikini would be just as explosive as these nuclear tests. Although bikinis were worn on the beaches of Europe, American women did not adopt them but continued to wear one- or two-piece suits that covered more of the body. Many bathing suits were cut with bottoms like shorts, while others had skirtlike constructions, and a few had full bloomers. Cotton, nylon, and Lastex were the most popular fabrics (Figure 17.16).

Shorts, trousers, or skirts and sweaters were worn on golf courses. Cotton golf dresses were constructed with extra pleats of fabric at the shoulders to accommodate the golf swing.

As slacks narrowed, so did ski pants. Stretch yarns, used since 1956, made it possible to make ski pants fit the leg tightly. Closely woven nylon windbreakers were worn as jackets, and skiwear was made in bright colors. The rapid increase in the number of skiing enthusiasts in the United States made for greater variety in skiwear styles.

Tennis clubs required players to wear white. Women's tennis outfits had short skirts (see Figure 17.11); however, players on public courts were likely to wear ordinary sportswear consisting of colored shorts with knitted tops.

Sleepwear

Nightwear followed the trend toward fuller skirts and figure-hugging bodices, although tailored pajamas were also available. Advertising in fashion magazines

a   b

FIGURE 17.16 (a) American women of the 1950s chose to wear one- or two-piece bathing suits of modest cut. (Henry Clarke © 1955 Condé Nast Publications) (b) European women, in contrast, adopted the bikini, a two-piece bathing suit smaller than any ever worn before. (© Bettmann/CORBIS) and mail-order catalogues emphasized nightgowns, and a wide variety of sheer and full-skirted models were available. Toward the end of the 1950s pastel sleepwear was superseded by more colorful prints in floral and abstract patterns.

Hair and Headdress

See Illustrated Table 17.2 for some examples of hairstyles and hats for the period from 1947 to 1960.

Short hair had become fashionable with the New Look. In the mid-1950s, longer hair was again in fashion.

Worn for all but the most casual occasions and especially when attending religious services, hats ranged from those that were small in scale, to large, wide-brimmed picture hats. In the later 1950s, hats were consistently small and fit the head closely. Also seen were some turban styles in brightly colored prints or plain colors.

Footwear

See Illustrated Table 17.3 for some examples of footwear for the period from 1947 to 1960.

The terminology applied to stockings was somewhat confusing. *Stockings* and *hosiery* were generic terms that referred to items ranging from long, sheer stockings (also called *hose*) to ankle-length, cotton stockings (often called *socks* or *anklets*). Women called their long, sheer stockings **nylons**, as these were inevitably made of nylon. Some were seamed (more popular), others seamless. Seams were often stitched in dark thread with reinforced heels made in dark yarn and extending several inches up the back of the ankle.

Through the 1940s and mid-1950s, rounded toes and very high heels and open-toed, ankle-strap, sling-back, or sandal styles were worn for dress. Lower heeled and flat shoes were also available. With more people living in the suburbs, there was an increase in casual styles, which included moccasins, loafers, ballet slippers, and canvas tennis shoes, called **sneakers**.

In the mid-1950s, toes of shoes grew more pointed and heels narrowed. High-heeled shoes had "stiletto heels" made with a steel spike up the center of the heel to prevent the narrow heel from breaking.

Accessories

See Illustrated Table 17.4 for examples of popular accessories for the period from 1947 to 1960.

Gloves were worn as an accessory for many occasions, made from cotton and nylon, knitted in a variety of weights and textures and colors, as well as leather. They ranged from very short to elbow-length styles worn with strapless evening gowns.

Handbags tended to be moderate in size, usually with small handles.

Jewelry

Popular jewelry items included necklaces (usually fitting close to the neck), bracelets, and earrings. Costume jewelry included rhinestones, colored stones, and imitation pearls in a variety of colors.

Cosmetics

Women favored bright red lipstick and used face makeup in natural skin tones, mascara on eyelashes, and pencil on eyebrows. After 1952, eye makeup became more pronounced, and some women drew a dark line around the eyes. About 1956 colored eye shadow began to appear in fashion magazines. Nail polish was available in many shades of pink and red.

Silhouette Changes: 1954–1960

The precise point at which the general public gave up the styles influenced by the New Look in favor of the unfitted look that became the predominant style of the better part of the 1960s is difficult to identify. Balenciaga had introduced the unfitted dress style as early as 1954 (his suits were unfitted from 1951 on), and Dior presented the **A-line** in his collection of 1955, but the unfitted look or **chemise styles** in dresses did not catch the public fancy immediately (Figure 17.17). By 1957 most suits had shorter jackets, loosely fitted and ending shortly below the waist. Some blouson (full-backed) styles were shown, and skirts had been growing gradually shorter and narrower. Coats were straighter, and hair was longer and showed a tendency to be arranged in styles that were higher and wider around the face.

Illustrated Table 17.2

Typical Hats for Women: 1947–1960

Hats, 1948[1]

Small hat, 1953[2]

Wide-brimmed
hat, 1954[3]

Small-brimmed
hat, 1955[4]

---

[1] *Charm,* April 1948.

[2] *Women's Wear Daily*, December 9, 1955, Fairchild Publications.

[3] *Women's Wear Daily*, December 9, 1954, Fairchild Publications.

[4] *Women's Wear Daily*, December 9, 1955, Fairchild Publications.

FIGURE 17.17 Both Dior
and Balenciaga showed
unfitted silhouettes in their
1955 collections. Balenciaga
(a) shows an unfitted, tunic
dress. Dior (b) introduces a
so-called A-line silhouette.
(Courtesy of Vogue Magazine/
Condé Nast Publications)

a

b

Illustrated Table 17.3

Selected Examples of Popular Footwear: 1947–1960

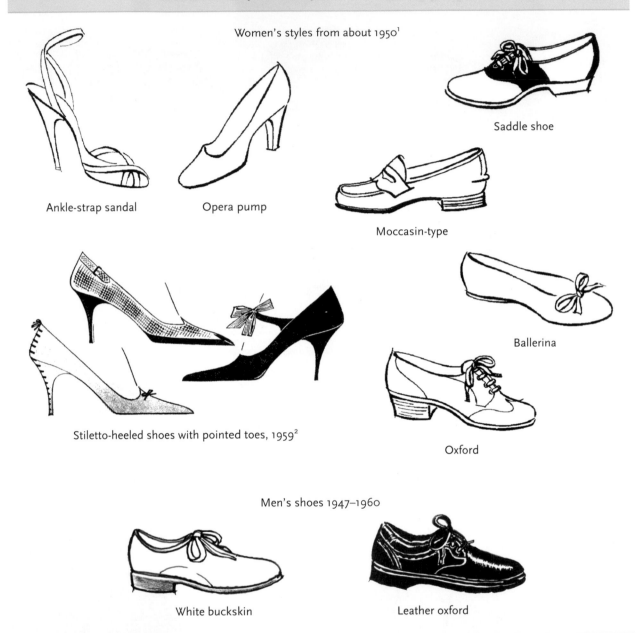

Women's styles from about 1950[1]

Saddle shoe

Ankle-strap sandal   Opera pump

Moccasin-type

Ballerina

Stiletto-heeled shoes with pointed toes, 1959[2]

Oxford

Men's shoes 1947–1960

White buckskin   Leather oxford

[1] *Department Store Economist*, October 1950.

[2] *Women's Wear Daily*, July 24, 1959.

By 1958, some women had bought unfitted dresses like the chemise type (Figure 17.18) or the A-line **trapeze** (Figure 17.19), but many others continued to resist the style. Even as late as the early 1960s, fashion magazines continued to show both new styles in the unfitted cut and dresses that followed the narrow-waisted, full-skirted silhouette associated with the New Look. By the mid-1960s, however, the unfitted style was almost universally worn, and this style had become the dominant silhouette.

Illustrated Table 17.4

Accessories: 1947–1960

Men's hats and hairstyles

(a) Driving cap for suburban wear, (b) Porkpie hat, c. 1950, (c) Fedora, c. 1956,

(d) Alpine hat, c. 1950, (e) DA or duck-tail hairstyle, 1950s

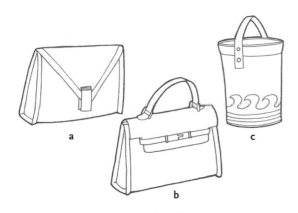

Women's handbags

(a) Clutch bag, (b) Kelly bag, (c) Bucket bag, c. 1955

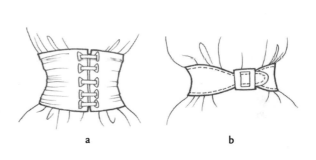

Women's belts

(a) Cinch belt, 1940s and 1950s, (b) Contour belt

Man's cummerbund

Women's jewelry

(a) Pearl choker and earrings, (b) Bracelet watch,

(c) Long chains and bead necklaces

FIGURE 17.18 A variety of unfitted chemise styles featured in *Women's Wear Daily* in late 1957. (Courtesy of Fairchild Publications, Inc.)

FIGURE 17.19 An example of the A-line dress called the *trapeze*, which was designed by Yves St. Laurent for Christian Dior in 1958. (AP Images)

COSTUME COMPONENTS FOR MEN

The major elements of men's costumes immediately after the war showed no significant changes, and styles made no radical departures from those of the wartime period and before. In time, however, the wide-shouldered silhouette altered, and styles for men became more diverse in the 1950s.

Garments

Boxer shorts, jockey-type shorts, athletic shirts, and T-shirts remained much the same, but the variety of fabrics and colors in which these items were manufactured increased. See Illustrated Table 17.1 (page 521) for examples of undergarments from the period between 1947 and 1960.

No postwar change in men's fashions occurred that equaled the radical New Look change in women's styles of 1947, although the menswear industry tried to promote a different look for men. *Esquire*, a men's magazine with a heavy emphasis on fashion, introduced the term **Bold Look** for men in October 1948 (a year after the New Look made its appearance). This was not a radical change in fashion but rather a continuation of the English drape cut with greater emphasis on a coordination between shirt and accessories and the suit.

Broad-shouldered jackets had lapels with a long roll. Double-breasted suits predominated (Figure 17.20). Jackets were somewhat longer than during the wartime years. After wartime restrictions were lifted in the United States in 1945, most pant legs were cuffed.

Shirts tended to have wide collars. Cotton fabric had long been favored for shirts, but as nylon again became available to the civilian population, some shirts were made of nylon.

In the 1950s, the Edwardian influences, evident in the Teddy Boy styles, moved mainstream menswear away from the English drape cut. The outcome was a suit with less padding in the shoulders, and a narrower silhouette. Single-breasted styles prevailed (Figure 17.21). Dark gray (called *charcoal*) was the most popular shade. The title of a popular novel, *The Man in the Gray Flannel Suit*, and a film based on the book starring Gregory Peck were indicative of the wide use of this suit for career-minded businessmen. The 1950s are sometimes nicknamed the **era of the gray flannel suit**.

FIGURE 17.20 A post–World War II double-breasted, wide-shouldered suit from 1950. (The New York Public Library/Art Resource, NY)

FIGURE 17.21 Narrower lapels and single-breasted cut characteristic of the early 1950s. (Courtesy of Fairchild Publications, Inc.)

It was the shirts worn with the gray flannel suits that provided touches of color—sometimes pink or light blue. Shirts most often had small collars either in the buttoned-down style, or they were fastened together under the tie with tie pins. Television helped bring color to men's shirts. The early black-and-white TV cameras caused white shirts, which were traditionally worn with business suits, to appear somewhat dingy. Men on television wore blue shirts, which appeared much more "white" to the camera. Shirt manufacturers started to produce colored shirts to wear with suits. This change met with resistance when some employers banned colored shirts with business suits. As polyester fibers came into widespread use, they were blended with cotton to make "wash and wear" shirts that wrinkled less than all-cotton shirts.

Vests were also produced in bright colors for informal occasions.

Suits altered somewhat in cut in the late 1950s, as men abandoned the gray flannel suit. Fashion writers called the new suits—with shorter jackets, a closer fit through the torso, and rounded, cutaway jacket fronts—**continental suits** (Figure 17.22). These new styles continued into the 1960s.

FIGURE 17.22 Three popular suit jacket styles of 1958: Left to right, the ambassador, the continental, and the Ivy League styles. Illustration appeared in the *Daily News Record*, November 4, 1958. (Courtesy of Fairchild Publications, Inc.)

Evening wear consisted of tuxedos or dinner jackets. Tailcoats were rare, worn only for very formal occasions. The cut of jackets for evening followed the prevailing cut of jackets for daytime. White dinner jackets were worn in summer. About 1950 a light blue dinner jacket in a color called *French blue* was noted by *Esquire*, but otherwise evening styles remained quite conservative.

Outdoor Garments

In the 1950s designers of outdoor garments turned away from the large-scale, broad-shouldered styles of the late 1940s and made coats with trimmer, narrower lines. The predominant line of overcoats in the 1950s had natural shoulders and more slender cuts. Some specific styles included tan polo coats; tweed, checked, and small-patterned fabric coats; and raglan-sleeved coats. In the late 1950s the wraparound, belted coat was revived.

Coats for casual wear were generally either hip or waist length, made in light or sturdy fabrics, lined or unlined, had set-in or raglan sleeves, and either buttoned or zippered closures. The great variety of casual coats reflected an increased emphasis on leisure activities.

Sportswear

The clothing favored by college students, called the *Ivy League Look* by fashion promoters, influenced some of the sportswear styles. Sports jackets reflected the cut of business suits. During the gray flannel era, sports jackets of tartan plaids were popular. In the mid-1950s, sports jackets cut along the lines seen in continental suits (see Figure 17.22) had interesting textures achieved by using raised cord or slub yarns with thick and thin areas. Leather-buttoned corduroy jackets, in checked and plaid and Indian madras plaids, were also fashionable (Figure 17.23; see also Global Connections).

In the 1950s, casual trousers were slim and straight. Among the important Ivy League styles were **chinos** (khaki-colored, twill-weave, cotton trousers) with a small belt and buckle at the back. These were

FIGURE 17.23 Popular sportswear items ranged from sport and knit shirts to sport jackets, including many items made from manufactured fibers or blends (or both). (Courtesy of Fairchild Publications, Inc.)

In the immediate postwar period, sports shirts reflected the wide-collared styling of more formal shirts. They were made in bright colors; plaids were especially popular. In the 1950s, small-patterned fabrics in shirts with buttoned-down collars were preferred. Knitted shirts and sweaters of all kinds were worn throughout the period, including T-shirts and polo shirts.

Clothing for Active Sports

In the early 1950s, tailored trunks were preferred for swimming, especially medium-length boxer shorts. Men sometimes wore sets of matching sports shirts and trunks. By the end of the 1950s, varieties of trunks similar to Bermuda shorts, even-longer Jamaica shorts, and tailored trunks were all worn.

Sleepwear

In the postwar period, men preferred pajamas to nightshirts.

Hair and Headdress

After World War II, some men continued to wear short crew cuts like those given to soldiers. When the hair was cut flat on top, it was called a **flat top**. In the 1950s, a contrasting longer hairstyle, inspired by the Teddy Boys in England and singer Elvis Presley in the United States, had a curly pompadour in front and hair at the back brushed into a "DA," a point that resembled a duck's tail. While crew cuts and DAs were worn by younger men, older men tended to compromise somewhere between the two, with hair long enough to be combed back from the forehead.

generally combined with button-down shirts and crew-neck sweaters.

In the late 1950s, self-belts and beltless trousers were worn. Slacks tapered to the ankles and were cuffless. About 1954 Bermuda or walking shorts, a style of the 1930s, were revived for general sportswear. These were combined with knee-length stockings. Some attempts were made to incorporate Bermuda shorts into walking suits, which were business suits with Bermuda shorts instead of trousers, but these styles never captured any significant segment of the market.

Global Connections

The madras used in men's and women's clothing derived from a cloth made in south India. It is recognized as a yarn-dyed fabric featuring plaid, striped, or checked patterns (Evenson, 2012). A truly global cloth, madras (or *injiri* to the Kalabari people of southern Nigeria) textiles are used as wrappers. Women artisans pull or cut threads of the cloth to create open-work, geometric patterns (Erekosima and Eicher, 1982). American sportswear designer Claire McCardell was known for her innovative use of fabrics, including this 1950s madras cotton halter-style sundress. Within the United States, retailers such as Brooks Brothers, L.L. Bean, and Ralph Lauren, routinely offer madras in light-weight, summer garments (Evenson, 2012). (Image copyright © The Metropolitan Museum of Art. Image source: Art Resource, NY)

During the 1950s, hats continued to be much the same as in the prewar period, with the fedora the staple of men's head wear. In 1952 President Dwight Eisenhower helped reestablish the homburg when he wore one to his inauguration rather than the customary top hat. Straw hats for summer followed the lines of the fedora, and hat brims decreased in size. For winter a narrow, Russian-style hat made of curled Astrakhan fur or its imitation in synthetic fiber fabrics gained popularity among businessmen. Some of these hats were made with ear flaps that could be tucked inside the hat or folded out on especially cold days.

Sporty hats for suburban and leisure wear appeared. These included the Tyrolean hat with a sharply creased crown, a narrow brim turned up in back and down in front, and a cord band with a feather or brush decoration. Sports car drivers wore flat-crowned caps with visors, and some men wore flat, crowned, small-brimmed, round porkpie hats (see Illustrated Table 17.4, page 529).

Footwear

Synthetic fibers made possible one-size, stretch stockings. These were available in a variety of patterns and styles. Antistatic finishes were added to stockings to combat the tendency of synthetic-fabric trousers to cling to synthetic-fiber stockings.

By varying the type of leather used, the color, and style detailing, manufacturers could use the same type of shoes for either dress or casual wear. Among the more popular styles were oxfords, brogues (a type of oxford with perforations at the tip and side seams), and moccasins. White bucks were part of the uniform of casual clothing for college students. Imported Italian shoes were fashionable, especially for dress, in the mid-1950s.

Accessories

For men accessories were limited to functional items: wristwatches; handkerchiefs; umbrellas; and jewelry such as rings, identification bracelets, cuff links, and tie pins.

COSTUME COMPONENTS FOR CHILDREN

As in all previous periods, styles for children displayed many elements of adult styles. The sociocultural events and technological changes that influenced adult clothing were also reflected in developments in children's clothing. For example, the synthetic and synthetic-blend wash-and-wear fabrics of the 1950s and, later, permanent press found a ready market in children's clothing.

In the 1950s, plaid vests and miniature gray flannel suits just like those for their fathers were made for boys, while most pattern companies of the period included several patterns for mother–daughter look-alike outfits. One is tempted to see in these styles a reflection of the emphasis on family togetherness that was characteristic of the United States in the 1950s (see Illustrated Table 17.5 for some examples of children's styles from 1947 to 1960).

Costume Components for Infants and Preschool Children

After the late 1950s, long pants up to about size 3 were made with gripper-snap fasteners up the inseam and around the crotch area to facilitate changing diapers without having to take off the entire garment. For children at the crawling stage, knees were reinforced.

Small girls, age 1 to 4, were dressed in loose, yoked dresses. Boys wore romper suits or short pants. Both boys and girls wore long corduroy pants or overalls.

Illustrated Table 17.5

Children's Clothing Styles: 1947–1960

Toddlers' styles, 1955[1]

Princess-style coats, 1955[2]

Full-skirted dress, 1960[3]

[1] *Infants and Children's Review,* August 1955.

[2] *Vogue,* March 1, 1955.

[3] Butterick Patterns, courtesy, Vogue/Butterick Pattern Company Archives/Library.

Costume Components for Girls

Garments

Echoing the silhouette of adult women's styles of the 1940s and 1950s, girl's dresses had full skirts and fitted bodices. Princess-line styles, full circular skirts, and jumpers all conformed to the predominant shape.

The most frequently seen styles for blouses and tops were tailored shirts, which often had rounded Peter Pan collars, knit polos, T-shirts, and other knit tops.

Girls' pants followed the cut of adult styles. For play or active sports, girls wore shorts or pants, including Bermuda or walking shorts, pedal pushers, and other lengths that carried the same fashion names as those for women.

Hair

Hair tended to be short.

Costume Components for Boys

Garments

The practice of dressing young boys in jackets and knickers in the years prior to adolescence was abandoned after the war. Although suits with short pants were available for very young boys, most boys' suits had long pants and were like those of adult men. Younger boys wore Eton jackets; boys of all ages wore blazers.

Dress shirts were worn with suits and jackets. The most common casual shirt styles were knitted T-shirts that were pulled over the head and polos with collars and buttoned vents at the front; in cold weather woven sports shirts and plaid flannel shirts were worn. In the late 1940s, there were western-style shirts with yoke and cuffs in contrasting colors to the body of the shirt.

Hair

Usually hair was cropped short or cut in a crew cut.

Costume Components for Boys and Girls

Outdoor Garments

Dress coats were made in miniature versions of classic styles for men and women. The enormous variety of jackets available included buttoned and zippered jackets with knit waistbands and cuffs in fabrics ranging from lightweight poplin to leather. Hooded parkas, boxy jackets, pea jackets, and melton (a dense, wool fabric) toggle coats with wood or plastic "toggle" closings were also popular.

Notable Youthful Fads

Fads are styles of intense popularity worn by a large number of people for a very short time. Adolescents, especially girls, seemed to be prone to the adoption of fad styles. Fads notable in the late 1940s included long, full black skirts, worn with leg-of-mutton-sleeved plaid blouses and flat ballet slippers, and denim jeans, worn with saddle shoes and a large shirt with a loose tail. In the 1950s, fluffy bedroom slippers were a fad, as were **poodle skirts**, full-circle felt skirts with a poodle (or other design) appliquéd in a contrasting color of felt. Rhinestones were used for the dog's eyes and collar. Such skirts were generally worn with ankle socks, two-tone saddle shoes, a white shirt, and a small scarf tied around the neck.

Summary

Themes

The importance of the theme of RELATIONSHIPS BETWEEN COSTUME AND THE WORK OF INDIVIDUAL DESIGNERS is evident: the New Look styles, introduced by Christian Dior in 1947, signaled a sharp change in women's fashion and marked the beginning of the postwar styles. For another decade the silhouette of women's clothing continued to follow the pattern

Visual Summary Table

The New Look: Fashion Conformity Prevails

Man: 1947–1950

The prewar, full shoulder line, double-breasted suits, with somewhat longer jackets and cuffed pants return.

Man: 1950–1960

Lines slimmer, based on Edwardian styles of the Teddy Boys. Suits are often made in gray wool flannel. Some colored shirts begin to appear.

Woman: 1947–1960

As war restrictions end, the New Look appears with rounded shoulders, narrow waist, and longer skirts, either very full or very narrow and straight.

Woman: 1955–1960

First move toward different silhouettes as less-fitted garments, chemise, trapeze, and A-line garments appear in Paris.

established by Dior in 1947. Throughout this period the PRODUCTION AND ACQUISITION OF TEXTILES AND APPAREL were much influenced by designers, as the French couture was followed closely by well-to-do women and celebrities who patronized the couturiers and by slightly less affluent women who bought line-for-line copies of Paris designs from American retail stores. At the same time a growing internationalism in fashion was reflected in the establishment of fashion design centers in other major European cities.

Themes related to SOCIAL GROUP MEMBERSHIP can also be identified in the dress that both the Teddy Boys and the beatniks used to set themselves apart and, at the same time, to express dissatisfaction with the broader society.

CHANGES IN PATTERNS OF SOCIAL BEHAVIOR were evident as more Americans moved to the suburbs, where their clothing needs changed, along with their lifestyles. The emergence of adolescence as an identified stage of development between childhood and adulthood was also reflective of changes in social behavior. Moreover, these changes were related to the theme of ECONOMICS, as adolescent purchasing power grew, allowing them to acquire popular fad items.

The new medium of COMMUNICATION, television, served to spread fashion information rapidly, while TECHNOLOGY made a host of new fibers available for use in clothing.

FASHION was an omnipresent theme of the 1950s. The first stirring of change from the New Look silhouette had begun as early as the mid-50s when designers such as Balenciaga and Dior showed some unfitted dress styles as part of their collections. By the end of the 1950s straight, shorter dresses were beginning to appear in retail stores. They met with little success, possibly because they were too radical a departure from the established, figure-hugging shapes.

But these styles, like some of the social changes that were just beginning to simmer beneath the smooth-appearing surface of the postwar society, were a harbinger of things that would come to occupy the attention of the world by the middle of the next decade.

LEGACIES OF NEW LOOK STYLES

Of the New Look styles that were utilized by fashion designers of the late 1980s and 1990s, probably the most notable were corsets. Although transformed with beading and other ornamentation and given the name *bustier*, the shape and structure of these garments are very like the merry widow of the New Look (see Modern Influences). These styles continue to resurface in haute couture designs of the 21st century.

Short, wide-skirted "mini-crinolines" had antecedents not only in the 19th-century crinoline period, but also in the New Look. Frequently they were strapless, an important feature of the longer but similarly shaped evening dresses of the New Look.

MODERN INFLUENCES

In the late 20th century and the 21st century, the corset of the 1950s was revived as the bustier. Pairing celebrity and fashion, Jean Paul Gaultier designed the corset-style body suit worn by Madonna in her 1990 Blonde Ambition World Tour. In this spring/summer 2014 haute couture show, Gaultier designed an ornately decorated bustier, worn as outerwear, paying homage to burlesque showgirls and butterflies. (Giannoni/WWD/ © Condé Nast Publications)

REFERENCES

Brooks, J. (1966). *The great leap: The past twenty-five years in America*. New York, NY: Harper and Row.

Daugherity, B. J., & Bolton, C. C. (2008). *With all deliberate speed: Implementing Brown v. Board of Education*. Fayetteville, Arkansas: University of Arkansas Press.

Erekosima, T. V., & Eicher, J. B. (1982). Kalabari cut-thread and pulled-thread cloth. *African Arts, 14*(2), 48-51, 87.

Evenson, S. L. (2012). Indian madras: From currency to identity. *Berg encyclopedia of world dress and fashion. Online exclusive* (Vol. 10).

Ewing, E. (1977). *History of children's costume*. New York, NY: Scribners.

Handley, S. (1999). *Nylon: The story of a fashion revolution*. Baltimore, MD: Johns Hopkins University Press.

Milbank, C. (1989). *New York fashion: The evolution of American style*. New York, NY: Abrams.

Palmer, A. (2009). *Dior*. London, UK: V&A Publishing.

	1960	1961	1962	1963	1964	1965	1966
FASHION AND TEXTILES						American sportswear manufacturer introduces "mod" clothes to U.S. market	
POLITICS AND CONFLICTS	John F. Kennedy elected U.S. president	Berlin Wall erected		Assassination of President Kennedy	Congress passes Civil Rights Bill		
DECORATIVE AND FINE ARTS			Pop art symposium at Museum of Modern Art	The Beatles have their first successful record			
ECONOMICS AND TRADE							
TECHNOLOGY AND IDEAS		Russians put first man in space	Rachel Carson's *The Silent Spring* published				
RELIGION AND SOCIETY	Food and Drug Administration approves oral contraceptive, "the pill"			Betty Friedan's *The Feminine Mystique* published			National Organization for Women founded

The Sixties and Seventies: Style Tribes Emerge

1960–1980

1968	1969	1970	1973	1974	1976	1977

Rise of punk fashions

Assassinations of Robert Kennedy and Martin Luther King Jr.

Four students killed in antiwar demonstration at Kent State University

Nixon resigns amid Watergate scandal; Gerald Ford becomes president

Jimmy Carter elected president

Woodstock music festival celebrates hippie counterculture

Japanese designers gain international notice

Yom Kippur Arab–Israeli War and oil embargo

Apollo II lands on moon

Parisian haute couture designers began to expand by adding lines for men and ready-to-wear (prêt-a-porter). Fashion originating outside Paris continued to garner attention, with international locations such as Africa and India influencing western fashion. Social unrest from the civil rights movement, feminism, and anti–Vietnam War protestors contributed to mainstream fashion. Trousers were added as a garment option for both day and evening wear for women, and youthful protestors initiated the widespread adoption of blue jeans. The concept of "style tribes" emerged, groups whose styles diverged from mainstream fashion. Hippies, mods, and punks were among the earliest of these groups. The fashion industry looked for countries where manufacturing was cheaper. Concerns over energy sources and environment permeated society and affected fashion.

HISTORICAL BACKGROUND

The years that encompassed the Vietnam conflict were marked by social upheaval and turmoil in the United States. Opposition to the war among the young, continuing efforts to right the wrongs of segregation and racial discrimination, the rise of feminism, and the budding environmental movement all contributed to a period of tumult that was clearly reflected in the fashions of the period.

Europe and the Soviet Union

The space age began in 1957 when the Soviet Union launched the first satellite to orbit the earth. This feat shocked Americans, as it demonstrated the gap in technology between the United States and Russia. In 1960 President John F. Kennedy vowed that the United States would reach the moon by 1970. The first manned moon landing occurred in 1969.

By the mid-1960s, the European Economic Community had created a single market for its economic resources. The 12 member nations abolished all tariffs affecting trade among them and set up a common tariff on goods imported from other countries.

In contrast, the Soviet Union continued to keep a tight control over its satellite states in eastern Europe. In 1968, when the Czechoslovak Communist Party sought to grant freedom of the press to make the party more popular, troops from the Soviet Union and other communist states invaded Czechoslovakia and restored repressive communist rule. Dissent continued within the Soviet Union during the 1970s. Even the renowned Soviet writer and Nobel Prize–winner Alexander Solzhenitsyn was exiled because of his writings.

The Soviet people had been promised more consumer goods and greater investment in agriculture in the 1970s. These promises were never fulfilled because of crop failures and spending on heavy industry and defense. Dissatisfaction grew as a ten-year war in Afghanistan proved costly in Soviet lives and money.

The Middle East

On Yom Kippur, October 6, 1973, the holiest day of the Jewish calendar, Egyptian and Syrian troops attacked Israel. After some months of fighting in which Israel prevailed, Egypt accepted a cease-fire in November 1973; Syria accepted in May 1974. Meanwhile, the Organization of Petroleum Exporting Countries (OPEC) imposed a brief oil embargo on the United States and other nations supportive of Israel.

Tensions in the Middle East eased after a summit conference between President Anwar Sadat of Egypt, Prime Minister Menachem Begin of Israel, and President Jimmy Carter at the presidential retreat Camp David in September 1978. The resulting Camp David Accords ultimately led to a 1979 Israeli–Egyptian peace treaty, the withdrawal of Israeli troops from the Sinai Peninsula, and the establishment of diplomatic relations between Egypt and Israel.

Earlier that year the government of Shah Mohammed Reza Pahlavi of Iran, whose autocratic policies antagonized religious leaders, was overthrown. After the Shiite Ayatollah Ruhollah Khomeini established an Islamic fundamentalist republic in which all institutions, laws, and economic and social policies were based on Islam, Khomeini's followers seized the American embassy and took the personnel hostage; they were not released until January 1981, minutes after Ronald Reagan was inaugurated as president.

Africa and the End of Colonialism

In 1957 the Gold Coast, now known as Ghana, became the first African state to be granted independence by Britain. By the mid-1960s Britain, Belgium, and France had freed most of their African colonies. The French government, however, supported by French men and women living in Algeria, opposed independence for Algeria; a bitter war followed until Algeria became independent in 1962. Freedom, however, did not solve the problems of the African people. Coups, civil wars, and famines continue today.

The Emergence of Japan as an Economic Power

For many of the people of Asia, political freedom meant economic freedom as well. Led by Japan, many Asian countries experienced an industrial expansion. Much of Japanese industry, destroyed by bombings, was replaced by new plants often more modern than those to be found within the United States. The United States helped the recovery of Japan by providing technological information. Japan made significant increases in output thanks to weak trade unions, low wages, high savings rates, demanding schools, and lifetime employment. Soon South Korea, Hong Kong, Singapore, and Taiwan followed Japan's example.

Japan created the economic model that set the pace for other industrialized nations and those that aspired to compete in the now worldwide market. The Japanese invested in new technologies to make their production cheaper and more efficient. As a result, their products became noted for high quality and high standards of performance. No longer was the pre–World War II phrase *cheap Japanese import* valid. Japan's quality products—computers, cameras, binoculars, radios, tape recorders, television sets, and automobiles—were sold throughout the world. By the 1990s Japanese automobile manufacturers even built their own plants within the United States.

In textiles the Japanese pioneered new technologies in the synthesis of manufactured fibers. In the 1960s and 1970s, before higher costs of wages and production in Japan drove the Japanese to move the manufacture of textiles to lower wage southeastern Asian countries, the Japanese produced high-quality natural and manufactured textiles that were utilized by American and European clothing firms.

It was also in this decade that some Japanese fashion designers gained international notice (Figure 18.1). Most worked in Japan, but Kenzo, who had come to Paris in 1965, opened his own ready-to-wear boutique in 1970 (Kawamura, 2004).

FIGURE 18.1 In 1971, Japanese fashion designer Kenzo Takada examines sketches for his upcoming line. (Christian/WWD/© Condé Nast)

The United States

The 1960s and 1970s were a time of dramatic political and societal change. Great strides were made in the civil rights and women's movements, and environmental activism. Yet, protests, revolts, and violence led to disenchantment for some.

The Kennedy Administration

The election of President John F. Kennedy in 1960 began a decade that contrasted markedly with the Eisenhower years (Figure 18.2). In 1962, after American spy planes discovered that the Russians were installing nuclear missiles in Cuba, the United States and the Soviet Union went to the brink of war. In this Cuban missile crisis President Kennedy ordered a naval blockade of Cuba, and eventually Soviet Premier Nikita S. Khrushchev agreed to withdraw the missiles, which avoided a nuclear conflict.

The assassination of President Kennedy in 1963 stunned the American public. Lyndon B. Johnson succeeded Kennedy.

The Civil Rights Movement

The issue of civil rights became more pressing. As early as 1962, federal troops were used to enroll an African-American student at the University of Mississippi. Similar action was taken in 1963 at the University of Alabama. To show their concern about civil rights, over 250,000 demonstrators gathered on the National Mall in Washington, D.C., in August 1963 to hear Dr. Martin Luther King Jr. proclaim, "I have a dream that one day this nation will rise up, live out the true meaning of its creed: We hold these truths to be self-evident, that all men are created equal" (King, 1963).

The assassination of President Kennedy in 1963 shocked the nation, but it did not halt the civil rights movement. In the administration of Lyndon B. Johnson, the cause of civil rights became a major force in American life. After a Senate filibuster had been broken, Johnson was able to sign the Civil Rights Act of 1964, the most far-reaching civil rights law ever enacted by Congress. Another important law, the Voting Rights Act of 1965, ensured every American

FIGURE 18.2 John F. Kennedy was the youngest man elected U.S. president; he was also the youngest president to die. From 1960 to 1963, First Lady Jacqueline's styles were widely copied, from her bouffant hairstyle and crisp coats and suits to her trim pumps and gilt-chain handbags. (© Bettmann/CORBIS)

the right to vote and authorized the attorney general to dispatch examiners to register voters.

Despite the passage of these laws, riots broke out in American cities during the summers of 1965 (in Los Angeles), 1966 (in Chicago, Cleveland, and 40 other cities), and 1967 (in Newark and Detroit). These riots erupted because civil rights legislation alone could not change residential segregation in urban centers.

By the mid-1960s, among African Americans dissatisfied with the nonviolent tactics of Martin Luther King Jr., the new rallying cry became "Black Power." The most articulate spokesperson for Black Power was Malcolm X, born Malcolm Little. The "X" represented his lost African surname. He rose from a disadvantaged childhood to a leadership position in the Black Muslim movement. Later, Malcolm X broke with the Nation of Islam and established his own organization committed to establishing an alliance between African Americans and the nonwhite people of the world. In 1965, black Muslim assassins shot and killed Malcolm X.

When Martin Luther King Jr. was assassinated on April 4, 1968, in Memphis, Tennessee, the civil rights movement lost its most charismatic leader and his death was mourned worldwide. Rioting followed in over 60 American cities, including Chicago and Washington, D.C.

In the same year Richard M. Nixon was elected president. He tried unsuccessfully to undo the civil rights legislation enacted during the Johnson administration. The Supreme Court, however, ordered a quick end to segregation in schools. As a result, more schools were desegregated in Nixon's first term than during the Kennedy–Johnson administrations.

The revelation that President Nixon attempted to cover up White House involvement in the Watergate scandal led to Nixon's resignation under threat of impeachment on August 9, 1974. His successor, Gerald R. Ford, grappled with a domestic economy that was hit by a quadrupling of oil prices as a result of the Arab oil embargo that followed the Yom Kippur War.

Jimmy Carter, a former governor of Georgia, defeated Ford in the presidential election of 1976. Important events during Carter's single term included a treaty turning the Panama Canal over to the government of Panama by 1999 and the 1979 peace treaty between Israel and Egypt. Unemployment remained high, and inflation soared ten percent in 1978. Another fuel shortage in 1979 forced motorists to wait in long lines at gasoline pumps.

War in Vietnam

Fearing the repercussions if another country came under communist rule, President Kennedy had authorized more aid to the South Vietnamese government that was struggling against Vietnamese communists, the Vietcong. When President Johnson assumed office following Kennedy's death, he authorized the dispatch of American ground combat troops to Vietnam to repel any attack on American military personnel. By 1965 the United States was effectively at war in Vietnam (though Congress never declared war). This bitter struggle soon aroused widespread opposition across the nation and provoked violent antiwar demonstrations on many American college campuses. Students publicly burned their draft cards, and antiwar demonstrators blocked the entrance to army installations and draft headquarters.

The Thaw in Relations with China

A major change in foreign policy occurred in the 1970s. Since 1949, Chinese–American relations had been in a deep freeze. The thaw began with a visit to Beijing by President Nixon in February 1972, where he engaged in discussions with Chinese leaders over questions related to Korea, Japan, and Taiwan. Nixon also offered trade concessions, credits, and technical assistance.

Nixon hoped there would be a trade-off: Chinese pressure on the North Vietnamese to be more conciliatory in discussing armistice terms. However, Chinese influence on North Vietnam had been overestimated, and it was not until January of 1973 that the United States finally signed an armistice, agreeing to withdraw its troops from Vietnam by April of that year. Nixon's opening to China led to increased trade with the United States, ranging from clothes to toys and beer.

Energy

Following the Yom Kippur War (1973–1974), OPEC instituted an embargo on oil shipments to the United States. Imports of oil dropped and prices quadrupled—a signal that OPEC had taken control of oil output and pricing. Although this first fuel crisis had a relatively brief impact, it served to awaken Americans to the need to conserve energy. Higher oil prices also led to higher costs for synthetic fibers, such as polyester, made from petroleum-derived chemicals.

A calm and stable oil market from 1974 to 1978 was followed by a crisis in 1979, when the fall of the shah of Iran's government led to another oil shortage. Gas stations began to close early and on weekends.

Gas lines often stretched for blocks. President Carter went on television, dressed casually in a sweater, and devoted one of his trademark fireside chats to energy in an effort to arouse public support for his new energy program, which he styled "the moral equivalent of war" (Carter, 1977). Although his energy program fared poorly in Congress, Carter issued a presidential proclamation prohibiting commercial, government, and public buildings from using air conditioning to lower temperatures below 78 degrees or using heating systems to raise temperatures above 65 degrees. Americans were urged to reduce heat and air-conditioning levels in their homes and offices. During the daytime those who lived or worked at lower temperatures wore more layers of clothing, including sweaters and jackets that could be added or subtracted. Mail-order catalogues of the period showed more warm nightgowns, pajamas, and robes.

The oil shortage gradually ended as the demand for oil decreased because of world recession, energy-saving measures, and the installation of energy-saving equipment. President Reagan removed controls on oil prices in January 1981. During the subsequent years, as oil prices stabilized, the goal of energy independence was abandoned as the memories of the oil crises of the 1970s faded.

Environment

By the 1970s, public concern over environmental problems increased substantially. The National Environmental Policy Act of 1970 established the Environmental Protection Agency and subsequent legislation addressed concerns about drinking water, nuclear waste, toxic-waste cleanup, and ocean dumping of sewage sludge.

Changes in Family Life and the Role of Women

The 1970s saw changes in the American family. The divorce rate doubled and the marriage rate dropped to a low of 10 marriages per 1,000 people in 1976. Those who did marry waited until they were older. Consequently, the birth rate slipped below the rate required to replace the population. Nevertheless, four fifths of those who were divorced remarried within 3 years. Frequent divorces combined with remarriage produced so-called blended families. The change in traditional marriages encouraged a proliferation of couples who lived together without legal or ecclesiastical sanction. It was estimated that the number of unmarried couples who established households tripled to 1.6 million, and it signaled a change in public opinion regarding cohabitation.

The number of households headed by women increased, which forced more women into the work force. By 1976 only 40 percent of American jobs provided enough income to support a nuclear family, which led more married women to seek paid employment. It was estimated that by 1976 one half of American mothers worked outside the home. Despite these gains, women suffered discrimination in wage rates compared to equivalent positions occupied by men, and opportunities for advancement were limited.

The gradual addition of millions of women to the work force changed fashion. Merchandisers noticed the change in shopping patterns, as working women shopped in the evenings and on weekends. They bought clothing for work and for play. As more women entered managerial positions in the corporate world in the 1970s, they wore a feminized version of the man's business suit: a tailored jacket, a moderate-length skirt, and a tailored blouse. This style was recommended for women who wanted to "dress for success."

Social Protest Movements

To the consternation of their elders, and unlike the silent generation, young people of the 1960s demanded to be heard. The beatnik phenomenon of the 1950s faded, but 1960s youths became increasingly involved in political movements. During the late 1960s and early 1970s the civil rights proponents, hippies, feminists, and environmentalists made their dissatisfactions known.

College Student Protests   By the mid-1960s student unrest on college campuses drew increasing media coverage, particularly on television. Antiwar protests, demonstrations, and student strikes spread from campus to campus. The *New York Times* spoke of a student "revolt against conformity, boredom, and tediousness of middle-class life," and students began calling for a greater voice in college governance (Spiegel, 1965, 17).

The Hippies Another expression of youthful revolt against the values of the adult society, the hippie movement, surfaced in 1966. Young people, most of them from middle-class families, responded to the call from Timothy Leary, a proponent of the use of the psychedelic drug LSD, to "turn on to the scene; tune into what's happening; and drop out of high school, college, grad school" (Burns and Siracusa, 2007, 200). Beginning in California in the Haight-Ashbury district of San Francisco, the movement, which became a drug-using subculture, spread across the country. The hippie philosophy stressed love and freedom from the constraints of "straight" society. On Easter Sunday 1967, in New York's Central Park, 10,000 young people—not all of them hippies—gathered to honor love. In Philadelphia on May 15 of the same year, 2,500 hippies held a "be in," a gathering honoring the notion that everyone had the right to "be" (see Figure 18.4).

The Feminist Movement The 1960s saw the second wave of the feminist movement as many American women began to question traditional values. A call to action came with the publication of *The Feminine Mystique* by Betty Friedan in 1963. The author described the frustration of college-educated women who felt trapped in the routine of housework and child care. Her book was a call for women to rethink their role in American life. The National Organization for Women, formed in 1966, announced a program calling for equal rights, equal opportunity, and an end to discrimination on the basis of gender. In 1973 many women applauded the Supreme Court's decision in *Roe v. Wade* legalizing abortion on the basis of the right to privacy. Earlier, a sexual revolution had occurred after the Food and Drug Administration in

1960 approved an oral contraceptive popularly known as "the pill."

The Environmental Movement With the publication of Rachel Carson's book *The Silent Spring* in 1962, Americans became aware of the dangerous effects of the powerful pesticide DDT, which killed birds and wildlife as well as insects. Her book jolted American complacency about the environment and helped ignite the environmental movement, which celebrated the first Earth Day in April 1970.

Environmentalists also recognized that hunting and loss of habitat through development posed a threat to a number of animal species. These animals were considered endangered and threatened with extinction. Among these threatened animals were American crocodiles, cheetahs, tigers, snow leopards, and Asiatic lions, the pelts of which were used for fashionable clothing and accessories. The United States passed the Endangered Species Act in 1973 to afford protection to such animals. International agreements were initiated in 1975. Taking advantage of the public awareness of the danger to wild animals posed by using their pelts for clothing, manufacturers of high-pile synthetic fabrics created **fake furs**, which were promoted as an environmentally sound alternative to real fur.

THE IMPACT OF SOCIAL CHANGE ON FASHION

The notion of using dress to proclaim ideology or membership in a specific group did not originate in the 1960s. Throughout the history of dress some individuals have chosen to wear clothing that identifies them as members of a particular group. Others have deliberately avoided fashionable dress in order to show that they differed from the rest of society in religious or ideological beliefs (e.g., the Amish, the Quakers, and the Puritans), in artistic preferences (the aesthetes), or in politics (the *sans culottes* of the French Revolution).

In the mid-20th century, subcultural dress was especially notable in the zoot suit in the 1930s and

1940s (see page 492), the Teddy Boys in Britain in the late 1940s and 1950s (page 510), and with the beatniks of the 1950s and early 1960s in the United States (page 509). Most of these styles originated among the young who often congregated in groups on the street. As a result such fashions became known as **street styles**.

Writer Ted Polhemus (1994), in his book *Street Style*, labeled these subcultural groups **style tribes**. He said,

> *Style isn't just a superficial phenomenon . . . and encoded within its iconography are all those ideas and ideals which together constitute a (sub)culture. Like-looking is like-thinking and in this sense the members of a style tribe have a great deal in common. (26)*

This tendency for young people, especially adolescents, to identify with a particular group and to try to set themselves apart from the mainstream culture through their dress accelerated in the 1960s and 1970s. Although street styles were intended to make a statement about being different from the mainstream, these countercultural fashions also provided nourishment for the fashion industry, ever hungry for new ideas. Descriptions of the most influential tribes of 1960–1980 follow.

The Mods

The **mods** and the **rockers** were groups of young people in Britain in the mid-1960s. Rockers were rough and tough, rode motorcycles, and wore black leather jackets. They vied with the mods, who were "up for love, self-expression, poetry, and getting stoned." The mod fashion statement was "elegance, long hair, granny glasses, and Edwardian finery" (McCloskey, 1970, 109). In the contest for dominance over the allegiance of young Britons, the mods won, and the importance of the rockers gradually faded away.

The center of mod activities was on Carnaby Street and on Portobello Road in London. The Beatles, then rising to fame in the popular music field, adopted mod-influenced clothing and, in turn, helped spread the popularity of the style. One of the ideas described as central to the mod fashion concept was the notion that men as well as women were entitled to wear handsome and dashing clothing (Figure 18.3). In 1965 American sportswear manufacturer McGregor

FIGURE 18.3 Mary Quant (at the far right) is closely associated with merchandising and popularizing the mod styles of the 1960s. The range of types of clothing associated with the mods is shown here, including miniskirts and maxi, full-length "granny dresses." (AP Images)

FIGURE 18.4 (a) Hippie couple of 1969 is dressed in clothing that was popular among this group: tie-dyed shirts and blouses, necklaces for both men and women, long hair and beards for men, headbands, and bright colors (© Henry Diltz/Corbis). (b) Fashionable dress designed by Giorgio di Sant'Angelo inspired by clothing worn by hippies. Such designs were often called "hippie-gypsy" styles. (Image copyright © The Metropolitan Museum of Art. Image source: Art Resource, NY)

produced and distributed mod styles in the United States.

The Hippies

In the meantime, the appearance of the hippies in the United States caused ripples in the fashion industry. Following the 1967 hippie gatherings, media coverage made the colorful hippie costume familiar: long hair for men and women; beards, headbands, and love beads for men; and long skirts and gypsylike dresses for women. Hippies assembled imaginative costumes from used clothing purchased in thrift shops. By 1968 Ken Scott, an American designer, had already designed a collection that included what he had called a "hippie-gypsy look" (Figure 18.4).

Young people gathered together at popular music concerts, such as the Woodstock Music and Art Fair attended by 200,000 in August of 1969. The beads, feathers, and bandannas that some of them wore were copied by others. *Newsweek* described Woodstock as

> *different from the usual pop festival, not just a concert but a tribal gathering, expressing all the ideas of the new generation: communal living away from the cities, getting high, digging arts, clothes, and crafts exhibits, and listening to the songs of revolution. ("Age of Aquarius," 1969, 88)*

Some joined communes or became involved in mystical religions led by gurus, religious teachers from India. Interest in Indian religions may have been a factor in the widespread popularity of styles inspired or influenced by clothing from India.

Both mod and hippie styles stressed long hair for men and women and greater color and imagination for men's clothing. Both were adopted, first by young people and slightly later for mainstream fashion. *Esquire* magazine proclaimed a **Peacock Revolution** for men, and fancifully colored and styled garments ranging from underwear to evening wear appeared in stores.

Antiwar Protesters and the Adoption of Jeans

In the 1960s young people protesting against the establishment adopted blue jeans as a symbol of solidarity with working people. In tracing the history of jeans as a symbol, Richard Martin and

FIGURE 18.5 Spiked, pink hair and black leather jacket with metal trim that were characteristics of punk styles of the early 1980s provide a marked contrast with more conservative men's dress of the period. (Chris Steele-Perkins/Magnum Photos)

Harold Koda (1989, 47) pointed out that as early as 1950 jeans were "associated with the American West and disestablishment behavior." In the play and subsequent 1955 movie *Blue Denim*, jeans were associated with youth and rebellion. The association with the counterculture was dramatized for the American public in the 1960s when jeans became a kind of uniform for the young antiwar protesters. Young people began to use jeans as a medium of self-expression. They embroidered designs on them, added patches, and painted messages.

It was not long before the fashion industry marketed these work-pants-as-protest-uniform as a hot fashion item. By 1970 jeans were an international success. Young Americans traveling in the Soviet Union and its satellite states, an area often referred to as the Iron Curtain, reported trading their blue jeans for enormous quantities of local goods.

Punk Styles

Striving to dramatize their alienation through their garb, devotees of punk rock music in 1977 began wearing messy, baggy, and ripped up clothes. Boys generally wore black leather. Girls wore micro-miniskirts with black fishnet stockings. Fabrics were purposely made with holes, tears, and stains. Accessories included safety pins, worn as earrings or through the skin, and razor blades. Punks wore black eye makeup; two-toned purple lips; and hair painted green, yellow, and red (Figure 18.5).

British fashion designer Zandra Rhodes quickly incorporated punk ideas into her 1977 collection, bringing punk style to a wider audience. **Punk styles** never dominated mainstream fashion but remained a viable alternative among some young people even after the millennium.

The Women's Movement

Feminists in the 19th century supported dress reform because they viewed women's clothing as a limit on their freedom. Some feminists in the 1960s also saw clothing as symbolizing oppression. To dramatize their liberation from social as well as physical constraints and to protest against the Miss America contest, which they saw as glorifying women for their beauty alone, a few feminists demonstrated and burned brassieres outside of the pageant in Atlantic City in the fall of 1968.

Although the majority of women did not abandon bras or burn them, many women no longer wore corsets, and underclothing became much less confining. Many bra styles were less rigid, molded from knitted synthetic fibers rather than cut and sewn to produce maximum uplift, as in the 1950s.

Some of the fashion developments in the late 1960s and the 1970s have been viewed as symbolic of changes in women's roles: the acceptance, especially by young people, of similar garments for men and women such as blue jeans, T-shirts, and pantsuits—which became an important component of women's wardrobes in the 1970s (Figure 18.6)—and the aforementioned changes in undergarments.

The Civil Rights Movement

Along with the accomplishments of the civil rights movement of the 1960s came a new consciousness of African culture, traditions, and art that was expressed in the phrases *black pride* and *black is beautiful*. Many African Americans adopted styles in dress that reflected interest in their African heritage, wearing traditional African garments such as **dashikis** (collarless, wide shirts with kimono-type sleeves) and caftans (similar garments in longer lengths). These and other garments were fabricated from textiles made in traditional designs, such as **kente cloth** (see Global Connections), mud cloth (in which fermented mud is used to produce designs), tie-dyed fabrics, and handsome embroideries.

The **afro** hairstyle, full and fluffy and taking advantage of the curl natural to the hair of many African Americans, was widely adopted by both men and women in the late 1960s and early 1970s. Styles in afros have changed periodically. By 1976 afros were cut shorter, closer to the head. **Cornrow braids**, a traditional African way of arranging the hair in myriad small braids, were worn by women in the 1970s and after (see Illustrated Table 18.2, page 572).

FIGURE 18.6 Example of unisex styles, 1968. (© Bettmann/CORBIS)

Jewelry was constructed in traditional designs, much of it imported from Africa, and utilized materials native to Africa: amber, ivory, and ebony.

Initially those African Americans who wanted to make a statement of black pride wore African-inspired clothing both at home and on the job. By the mid-1970s, these clothes were more likely to be worn at home as leisure wear or for social occasions.

African-inspired fashions penetrated the mass market. In the film *10*, actress Bo Derek wore her blond hair in cornrow braids (see Illustrated Table 18.2, page 572). When black women had adopted the style in the 1970s, it took from 2 to 6 hours to arrange the cornrows and cost $50. Later, when this style was promoted as a part of mainstream fashion about 1980, it took up to 10 hours to arrange and cost $300.

Global Connections

Kente cloth is a complex, elaborate, multicolored, woven design made on narrow-strip looms. Made by the Ashanti of Ghana and the Ewe of Ghana and Togo, it is one of the best known and highly prized textiles of West Africa (Plumer, 1971). Traditionally, the narrow woven cloth was worn by men in a toga-style (as seen in this image of a Ghanaian official holding a staff and wearing locally woven kente cloth in 1964) and by women as an upper and lower wrapper. Kente is composed of 3- to 4-inch strips woven on a horizontal treadle loom and then sewn together to make a larger cloth. The intricate warp and weft designs are distinguished by their names, each expressing different proverbs or ideas. The symbolism of colors, motifs, and designs has led to the

use of kente cloth as a powerful emblem of heritage and achievement. Since the 1960s adoption of kente by African Americans, it has spread into general fashion (Ross, 1998). (Werner Forman/Art Resource, NY)

FIGURE 18.7 Paris-based American designer Patrick Kelly poses with his models. The models wear his women's fashions, including colorful dresses and skirts in a variety of fabrics. (© Julio Donoso/Sygma/Corbis)

African Americans continue to have a strong impact on contemporary fashion. *Ebony* (first issued in 1945) and *Jet* (1951) chronicled fashion and society. The Ebony Fashion Fair (launched by Johnson Publishing Company) traveled throughout the United States from 1958 through 2009 bringing American fashion to mainly black female audiences (Bivins & Adams, 2013). Black fashion models began to appear in high-fashion magazines in the 1960s, and gradually newspapers and magazines came to include greater racial and ethnic diversity in the presentation of fashion illustrations. In the same period a number of African-American fashion designers rose to the top levels of American fashion design (Figure 18.7).

OTHER INFLUENCES IN FASHION

See Table 18.1 for a summary of media influences on fashion: 1960–1980.

TABLE 18.1 Media Influences on Fashion: 1960–1980

MEDIA	DATES	STYLE INFLUENCES
motion pictures	1960s	French actress Brigitte Bardot: long hair, knee length boots
	1970s	*The Last Picture Show, Grease, American Graffiti:* revival of 1950s styles
television	1960s	television news shows pictures of hippies, anti-war protesters, and their (initially) unique clothing
popular music performers	1960s	the Beatles: long hair, mod-style outfits worn for performances
popular music concerts and festivals such as Woodstock	1969	opportunities to exchange fashion information

The White House

Political leaders often become style leaders. This has been true of royalty for centuries and is often true today for political leaders, especially if they are considered attractive. When President Kennedy went bare-headed to his inauguration in 1961, hat use among men declined. Jacqueline Kennedy became a major influence on styles. The press paid close attention to her inaugural ball gown (Figure 18.8). Bouffant hairstyles, pillbox hats, A-line skirts,

FIGURE 18.8 Drawings from the Associated Press show three items of evening wear worn by Jacqueline Kennedy for the inaugural festivities in 1961. They are from left to right: a white silk ottoman gown designed by Oleg Cassini for the inaugural gala; a slim sheath for the inaugural ball of *peau d'ange* silk under chiffon, the silver-embroidered bodice visible under a transparent overblouse of white chiffon, designed by Bergdorf Goodman; and an evening wrap designed by Bergdorf Goodman to be worn with the inaugural ball gown. This sweeping cape is made of *peau d'ange* completely covered with three layers of white chiffon, and the simple stand-up collar fastens with two buttons. (Courtesy of Fairchild Publications, Inc.)

low-slung pumps, Empire-style evening dresses, and wraparound sunglasses were some styles associated with her. She remained a fashion leader in the years after she was no longer the First Lady. The Ford, Nixon, and Carter families were not viewed as major influences on fashion.

Political Events

Political events, as well as political figures, can influence fashion. Among the influences from the Vietnam War were the adoption of jeans by youthful antiwar activists and military-inspired clothing. Other examples include *Newsweek*, which published an article on July 12, 1971, that described a "Vietnam vogue" seen in St. Tropez, France, which consisted of army-style clothing. The *New York Times* reported interest in army fatigues in 1975 and *Gentlemen's Quarterly*, a men's fashion magazine, featured U.S. Navy–style pea jackets in the same year.

When President Nixon announced his intention to go to China in 1972, Chinese-influenced styles began

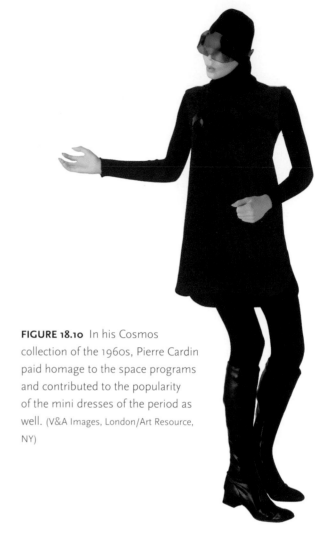

FIGURE 18.10 In his Cosmos collection of the 1960s, Pierre Cardin paid homage to the space programs and contributed to the popularity of the mini dresses of the period as well. (V&A Images, London/Art Resource, NY)

FIGURE 18.9 Yves St. Laurent dress with Chinese motifs and diagonal bodice closing in 1977–1978 at a time when western styles were influenced by Chinese textiles and cuts. (Yves Saint Laurent, evening ensemble, Black silk crepe and turquoise damask, 1977–1978, France. The Museum at FIT, 88.73.1. Photo © Museum at FIT)

appearing at once. These ranged from actual Chinese clothing to textiles, accessories, design motifs, and adaptations of Chinese styles (Figure 18.9).

The Space Age

Some fashions of the 1960s reflected interest in the growing aerospace developments. Fashion design in the mid-1960s reflected the space race both directly and indirectly. Couturier André Courrèges showed what he called a "Space Age collection" in 1964. Fashion models wore helmets; the lines were "precise and unadorned" and the shapes geometrical (Figure 18.10).

Designers used materials similar to those required for the technological advances that accompanied space exploration. Although invented in 1948, Velcro, a synthetic fiber staple tape used for closures, became more popular when Apollo astronauts used it to secure pens, food packets, and equipment they didn't want floating away. Paco Rabanne made dresses of square pieces of plastic held together with metal rings; vinyl was used for rainwear and outerwear. The most extreme of these styles were not widely adopted, but the clean, geometric lines and plastic jewelry and accessories in geometric shapes were often seen.

The Fine Arts

Op art (short for *optical art*) and **pop art** (short for *popular art*) entered the art world during the 1960s. Pop art featured glorified representations of ordinary objects such as soda cans and cartoon figures (Figure 18.11). Op art created visual illusions through largely geometric patterns. The op art designs translated readily into fabric and soon appeared in fabrics for clothing (Figure 18.12). Saint Laurent placed large op art designs on garments.

Geometric lines were also evident in fashions inspired by the paintings of the early–20th-century Dutch painter Piet Mondrian as inspiration. The most famous of these was Saint Laurent's 1965 **Mondrian dress**, which was widely copied (Figure 18.13). Both Art Deco and Art Nouveau designs were also revived.

In the 1970s, museum blockbuster exhibitions excited designers and the public. The discovery of the tomb of the Egyptian King Tutankhamen (Tut) in the 1920s had served as a catalyst for Egyptian-inspired designs. In the mid-1970s a major show of the treasures from the King Tut's tomb opened in London, then traveled around the world; in its wake jewelry, makeup, and some clothing items of Egyptian derivation appeared (see Illustrated Table 18.4, page 575).

FIGURE 18.11 Andy Warhol, who began his career as a fashion illustrator, created this paper "Souper Dress," 1966–67, with images from Campbell's soup cans. Art critic Lawrence Alloway (1926–1990) first used the term *pop art* in 1958, defining it as "popular (designed for a mass audience); transient (short term solution); expendable (easily forgotten); low cost; mass produced; young (aimed at youth); witty; sexy; gimmicky; glamorous; and big business" (Livingston, 2009). (Image copyright © The Metropolitan Museum of Art. Image source: Art Resource, NY)

FIGURE 18.12 Many of the fabrics inspired by op art (short for *optical art*) included dramatic designs in black and white. (Henry Clarke © 1965 Condé Nast Publications)

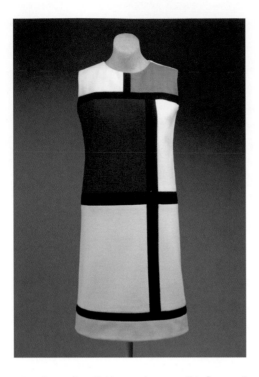

FIGURE 18.13 Surrealist, Cubist, and op art all influenced fashion in the 1960s. This Yves Saint Laurent garment draws on the style of Dutch abstract painter Piet Mondrian. (Image copyright © The Metropolitan Museum of Art. Image source: Art Resource, NY)

The 1970s also saw the origin of **wearable art**, the combination of clothing and fiber art, which probably had its antecedents in the decoration of clothing used by hippies. Artists who created wearable art often combined a variety of techniques such as crocheting, knitting, embroidery, piecing, special dyeing techniques, and painting on cloth. They used feathers, beads, layers, and slashing. Each garment created was a unique work of art (Figure 18.14; see also Figure 18.4b).

Ethnic Looks

The variety of sources that inspired design included Native-American dress, styles from countries such as India, traditional eastern European folk costume, and the aforementioned African-inspired styles.

THE CHANGING FASHION INDUSTRY

How and why fashions change has been a matter of debate among scholars. One of the most widely accepted theories about fashion change is the so-called **trickle-down theory** in which upper class individuals initiate styles. These styles are then imitated by the next, lower class within the society. Their clothing, in turn, is imitated by a still lower class. As the highest class individuals see the styles they originated copied by those lower in social status, they change these styles, and the cycle of imitation begins again.

From the medieval period, when fashion seems to have first become an important factor in the development of clothing styles in western Europe, until the 1960s, this explanation worked reasonably well. By the 20th century, a vast fashion industry had developed that expedited the design, manufacture, and distribution of clothing to all social classes, except the abject poor or cultural subgroups that rejected modern, fashionable dress.

FIGURE 18.14 Wearable art, consisting of original pieces by innovative designers, first became important in the 1965–1975 period and has continued to be a distinctive part of modern fashion. Shown here is *Celebration Cape #1*, an original design by Robert Hillestad. (Photo by John Nollendorfs)

Increasing Variety in Fashion Segments

In the 1960s, some popular styles seemed to originate not with the well-to-do but with less affluent individuals and with style tribes or subcultures such as the hippies in the United States and the mods in Britain. Some have called this phenomenon the **bottom-up theory**, in contrast with "trickle down."

The causes of fashion change are undoubtedly more complex than either the trickle-down or bottom-up theories suggest. Even as early as the 1920s, clothing for men and women became more diversified. In previous centuries, fashionable dress could fairly easily be divided between everyday dress and dress for special social occasions. By the 20th century, men and women had added to their wardrobes clothing for active sports. As more women entered the work force in larger numbers, they bought clothing suitable for work. Shortly before World War II, psychologists defined a stage of development they called *adolescence*, and clothing with certain unique features was manufactured for this age group. Adolescents were prone to fad behavior in which an element or item of clothing had a short, very intense burst of popularity. *Seventeen* magazine reported in 1965 that teenage girls bought 20 percent of all apparel and 23 percent of all cosmetics sold in the United States, but represented only 11 percent of the population (Schnurnberger, 1991).

After World War II, fashionable dress could be compared to a tree trunk that continually divided into more and more branches, each branch representing a different segment of the buying public. Until the 1960s it was still possible to identify one predominant fashion silhouette or shape that influenced most categories of women's clothing. For example, in the 1950s, a natural shoulderline, a fitted bodice or blouse, a narrow waistline, and a full skirt could be seen in daytime dresses, evening gowns, casual sportswear, outdoor clothing, and even underwear. In the 1960s the predominant shaping was loose and unfitted, and hemlines were short, with the shortest skirts called *miniskirts*. Around 1970 the fashion press, led by the influential trade publication *Women's Wear*

Daily, insisted that the **midi skirt** was destined to replace the miniskirt. The midi skirt, also called the **longuette**, was a midcalf-length skirt. Refusal to accept the proposed new styles now spread to mainstream fashion consumers. Many women rejected the style. Groups such as GAMS (Girls Against Midi Skirts) held anti–midi-skirt parades. Consequently, retailers were able to sell only a small part of the large stocks of midi skirts that had been ordered. The fashion press spoke of a period when "anything goes" and declared fashion dead (Figure 18.15).

FIGURE 18.15 Sketch from *Women's Wear Daily*, September 1971, showing hemline lengths that range from mini (far left) to midi (center) to maxi (far right). (Courtesy of Fairchild Publications, Inc.)

Attempts to Curb Fashion Changes

Violation of established norms in dress can cause individuals or groups to feel threatened, especially if the radical new styles are adopted by groups that question existing social values or seek to challenge the status quo. Many of the changes in fashion that began in the United States in the 1960s did just that. Authority was being challenged by "kids" in long hair, African Americans in dashikis and afros, women in pantsuits, and girls in short, short skirts.

Individuals who wore styles outside of the mainstream experienced discrimination. Many office managers forbade women to wear pants to work. Women wearing pantsuits were not admitted to fashionable restaurants. Contemporary Comments 18.1 chronicles the attempts in 1966 of a *Women's Wear Daily* reporter wearing a pantsuit to be admitted to chic Manhattan restaurants. Boys with long hair and girls wearing miniskirts or pants were expelled from school. African-American women who adopted afro styles were subjected to taunts and humiliation about the afro resembling a porcupine. Some employers insisted that women with afro haircuts wear wigs to work (Giddings, 1990). One junior high school student, who wore a long maxi skirt to commencement instead of one of the miniskirts her classmates had selected, was denied participation in commencement (Klemesrud, 1970). Legal challenges overturned most such restrictions, and by the early 1970s the "radical" new styles had become mainstream fashion.

Changes in Fashion Design

In the 1960s, a group of young designers who had trained under men such as Dior and Balenciaga left these established couture houses and opened their own establishments. The most successful of these young men were Yves Saint Laurent, Pierre Cardin, André Courrèges, and Emanuel Ungaro. In the mid-1960s, after becoming established in the haute couture, most of these designers expanded in the direction of ready-to-wear (or as the French call it, **prêt-à-porter**). Both Courrèges and Saint Laurent designed lines of ready-to-wear in the mid-1960s. Cardin had opened a menswear boutique in 1957 and turned his design expertise to a variety of other products as well. In the years since this radical alteration was made in the operation of some of the couture houses, the Paris prêt-à-porter group has become so important that the fashion press goes to Paris not only for the regular shows of the haute couture but also for the opening of the prêt-à-porter collections. The successful ready-to-wear industry in the United States had provided a model for a new business venture for the French couture designers. In turn, the prêt-à-porter provided a new source of fashion ideas for the American fashion industry.

By the late 1960s, franchised boutiques, a new aspect of merchandising the ready-to-wear designs by couturiers, had emerged. These retail boutiques were owned and operated either by the couture house or by independent merchandisers who purchased a franchise and the right to sell the designer's products in a store that carried the designer's name or trade name. For example, Saint Laurent opened the first ready-to-wear boutique in Paris in 1964 under the trade name Rive Gauche.

Ready-to-wear design had a long history in the United States, but except for some individual designers—such as Hattie Carnegie, Claire McCardell, Norman Norell, or Pauline Trigère who gained a loyal following in the 1940s, 1950s, and 1960s—most American fashion designers had been anonymous, working for manufacturers whose trademarks were known to the public. By the 1970s, this had changed. Not only were designer labels a major factor in selling products, but designer-owned firms also became more common. Customers came to know and look for the clothing produced by individual designers whose styles they preferred.

In Italy after World War II, Rome, Florence, and Milan had organized couture houses that showed collections semiannually. In the mid-1970s, the Italian ready-to-wear industry started to hold showings in Milan.

Except for some of the startling designs derived from punk styles by Zandra Rhodes around 1977, the

Contemporary Comments 18.1

FASHIONABLE RESTAURANTS REJECT PANTSUITS

In "Pants and Prejudice," published in Women's Wear Daily, *October 17, 1966, Toni Kosover recounts the difficulties of finding a fashionable New York City restaurant that would allow her admission in her new pantsuit.*

Women can wear the pants but they can't go very far. What's left when you can't eat at the Colony . . . can't dance at El Morocco, and you can't even get through the door at "21."

We tried and even though it hurts us to admit it, we failed. Even in a simple elegant black crepe pantsuit by Victor Joris of Cuddlecoat, we failed. Can you imagine nothing but rejection almost all night long. And just on the basis of appearance.

How sad.

How unsophisticated.

How downright prejudiced.

It starts the other night with our dinner reservation at the Colony. Gene Cavallero just takes one swift glance at the pantsuit.

"I'm sorry but we can't serve you."

"But we have a reservation."

"I am sorry but we can't serve any woman in pants."

"Not even if we sit at a table in the back?"

"No, I'm sorry, if we make an exception this time, we will have to do it all the time." . . .

Who would take us in? Offer us a bit of French cuisine? Perhaps La Cote Basque understands the Modern Woman. . . .

Raymond said, "no," so nicely.

"We don't want any part of it. No one ever tries to come in here in pants. It's not that we are worried about beatniks. To tell you the truth, I prefer women without pants."

And we move back into the night.

At this point we were willing to settle for a drink. Maybe the St. Regis would accept us. It looks hopeful. They watch us skeptically as we glide across the almost empty room. No problems. They serve our drinks. Only it's quiet here and we are still hungry. . . . we drive up to La Caravelle . . . They are looking us over.

A man at one table smiles. "Oh! Look . . . she's wearing slacks."

And then the maitre d,' "The kitchen is closed, now."

Is it really closed, or was it the pantsuit? "It is a little too late for service, and it is not the policy of the house to serve women in pants," says the man. . . .

Before going to El Morocco we stop at "21," where we can barely get in the door before Gary stands before us with his arms crossed and says, "No." . . .

El Morocco is really no better. Angelo has to confer with a couple of others. Finally we tell them we are doing a story . . . and they give us a table which just misses the door by an inch. "If we make an exception for you, we will have all sorts in pants. The drinks are on the house but, please, . . . no dancing and no pictures." . . .

Later on we all go to Yellowfingers, which welcomes us—pantsuit and all. . . .

Which only goes to prove the pantsuit does stand a chance if individuality and fun ever replace status symbols and staring.

1970s had been a relatively quiet period for English design, with a return to classic tailoring and promotion of high-quality cotton products from firms such as Liberty of London and Laura Ashley (Table 18.2).

Labeling and Licensing

In the late 1970s, so-called **designer jeans** were produced by well-known designers. Almost twice as expensive as regular jeans, designer jeans prominently

TABLE 18.2 Influential Designers in Paris and Other Fashion Centers: 1960–1980

DESIGNER	AFFILIATED FIRM	NOTABLE CHARACTERISTICS
FRANCE		
André Courrèges (1923–)	Courrèges, 1961; retired 1995; the firm continues.	Associated with "space age" influences. Ideas included low-heeled white boots, industrial zippers, hard-line minidresses in the 1960s, more feminine styles in the 1970s.
Jules-François Crahay (1917–1988)	Chief designer for Nina Ricci, 1954–1964; head designer at Lanvin, 1964–1984, when he retired and started a ready-to-wear firm.	"Young, uninhibited, civilized clothes"; made glamorous evening pants, jeweled gaucho pants, lavish evening gowns.
Emmanuelle Khanh (1938–)	Especially known for inexpensive ready-to-wear in the 1960s. In 2002, the firm was bought by France Luxury Group.	Very influential in late 1960s among the young, continued to work in 1970s and 1980s in highly individual styles.
Guy Laroche (1923–1990)	Laroche, 1957	Most notice in the couture came in the early 1960s; "back cowl drapes, short puffed hems for evening"
Paco Rabanne (1934–)	Rabanne, 1966. Relinquished creative control of his firm in 2000.	Known for garments made from geometric plastic shapes held together with metal rings. In the 1970s combined other unusual materials.
Yves Saint Laurent (1936–2008)	Chief designer for Dior, 1957–1958; opened own house, Yves Saint Laurent, 1962. Limited himself to couture after sale of the fashion house in 1993; retired in 2002.	Originated many innovative styles; trademark looks included the fisherman's shirt, 1962; trapeze, 1965; see-through blouse, 1968; longuette, 1970; tuxedo dress, 1978; and others. Sometimes called "The King of Fashion" for his preeminent place in the couture.
Emanuel Ungaro (1933–)	Ungaro, first couture collection, 1965; later entered ready-to-wear market as well. After 2001 he did only couture. He retired in 2004. The firm continued under other designers.	Known for geometric, straight, and A-line shapes in the 1960s; 1970s and 1980s styles softer and "more body conscious."
Valentino (c. 1932–)	Valentino, first success, 1962; showed ready-to-wear in Paris from 1975 couture in Rome. Retired in 2008. The firm continued under other designers.	"Noted for refined simplicity, elegantly tailored coats and suits." Also designs menswear.
ITALY		
Princess Irene Galitzine (1916–2006)	First show, 1959; continued to 1968, then sporadically for several years in the early 1970s.	Introduced palazzo pajamas, 1960. Other noted designs include: "at-home togas, evening suits, open-sided evening gowns."
Ottavio Tai Missoni (1921–) and Rosita Missoni (1931–)	Missoni, c. 1953. Children continue to operate the business.	Especially known for timeless knits with distinctive colors and patterns.
Emilio Pucci (1914–1992)	Couture house, Emilio, 1950. Firm bought and reopened in 2002.	Noted for distinctive, colorful prints. Interest in the prints revived in 1990s.
Mila Schoen (1916–2008)	Mila Schoen, 1959 in Milan and Rome. Showed couture collection in Paris in 1991. Remained active after selling business in 1994.	Known for high-quality design and workmanship in women's clothing, menswear, and swimsuits. Active in 1960s, 1970s, 1980s, 1990s.
GREAT BRITIAN		
Jean Muir (1933–1995)	Worked for Liberty, Jaeger; under her own label Jane and Jane, 1962; Jean Muir Inc., 1967.	"Characteristics: soft, classic, tailored shapes in leathers or soft fabrics."
Zandra Rhodes (1942–)	Ready-to wear, began making own designs 1969.	Known for innovative designs, incorporated punk in mid-1970s
Mary Quant (1934–)	Opened boutique and began designing in late 1950s. Still active in 2003.	Influential designs in the mod styles of the 1960s, the miniskirts of the later 1960s. A major factor in making London a fashion center in the 1960s.
Vivienne Westwood (1941–)	Opened boutique with partner Malcolm McLaren in 1974.	Often working with street style and clothes such as punk, new romantic, fetish styles.

TABLE 18.2 Influential Designers in Paris and Other Fashion Centers: 1960–1980 (continued)

DESIGNER	AFFILIATED FIRM	NOTABLE CHARACTERISTICS
UNITED STATES		
Adolfo (1933–)	Opened his own millinery firm, 1962; added then switched to apparel. Apparel design business now closed, but licensing continues.	Known for Chanel-inspired knits; also did menswear.
Geoffrey Beene (1927–2004)	Samuel Winston and Harmay, 1949–1957; Teal Traina, where his name was put on the label, 1958–1962. Opened own business in 1962. Closed wholesale business in 2001, continued to sell to private clients.	"Simplicity, emphasis on cut and line, dressmaking details, and unusual fabrics." Expanded into accessories, menswear, and licensing.
Bill Blass (1922–2002)	After WWII, became head designer for Maurice Rentner Ltd.; eventually became owner and changed the name to Bill Blass, Ltd. Firm continues under other designers.	"Noted for women's classic sportswear in menswear fabrics, elegant mixtures" of patterns and fabrics, and very feminine, glamorous evening wear that contrasts with more mannish daywear. Has design interests in a wide variety of products carrying his name.
Stephen Burrows (1943–)	In 1969 became in house designer at Henri Bendel, showed collection at Versailles in 1973.	Relied on jersey knits and nontraditional closures often in a kind of abstract patchwork.
Bonnie Cashin (1915–2000)	Worked as freelance designer since 1953; started The Knittery for hand knits, 1967.	Specialized in functional clothing, innovative designs especially in outerwear, used knits, tweeds, canvas, and leather.
Oscar de la Renta (1932–)	After working in Paris and New York, opened own business after 1965. Designed for House of Balmain from 1992 to 2002, when he retired but continues to design a New York collection.	Created luxury ready-to-wear; known for "opulent fabrics" for evening wear and "sophisticated and feminine day wear." A variety of other products also carry his name.
Rudi Gernreich (1922–1985)	Worked in California.	Particularly known for sport clothes and for radical styling including a topless swimsuit, and see-through blouses, No-Bra bras in the 1960s.
Roy Halston Frowick (1932–1990)	Designed under name Halston. Opened own business 1968 for private clients, ready-to-wear in 1972. The firm name was revived in 1997.	"His formula of casual throwaway chic, using superior fabrics for extremely simple classics made him most talked about designer in early 1970s."
Charles Kleibacker (1921–)	Started own company, 1963.	Maintained a small business where he could keep control of the making of the bias-cut styles for which he was especially known.
Anne Klein (1923–1974)	Formed Junior Sophisticates, (1951–1964); Anne Klein & Co., 1968. After her death other designers worked under her label.	Noted in the 1960s for "classic blazers, shirtdresses, long midis, leather gaucho pants . . . and slinky hooded jersey dresses for evening."
Calvin Klein (1942–)	Calvin Klein Ltd., 1968. His "designer" blue jeans important in the 1970s. Markets a wide variety of products under Calvin Klein label. Company sold in 2002.	"Considered the foremost exponent of spare, intrinsically American style . . . refined sportswear-based shapes in luxurious natural fabrics such as cashmere, linen, and silk . . . color preferences are earth tones and neutrals."
Ralph Lauren (1939–)	Polo line of menswear, 1967; for women, 1971; and other spin-off firms later. The Polo and Ralph Lauren names are licensed to a number of products.	Came to prominence with wide neckties, known for work with natural fabrics, Western influences, outdoor wear. "classic silhouette, superb fabrics, and fine workmanship . . . attitude is well-bred and confident."
Giorgio Sant'Angelo (1936–1989)	Sant'Angelo Ready-to-Wear, 1966; di Sant'Angelo Inc., 1968. Licensing continued after his death.	"Noted for ethnic themes" and designs "a bit out of the ordinary."
Arnold Scaasi (1931–)	Did ready-to-wear in New York, 1960; switched to couture, 1963; returned to ready-to-wear, 1983, and closed it in 1994, concentrating on made-to-order designs.	"Known for spectacular evening wear in luxurious fabrics."
Diane von Furstenberg (1947–)	Diane von Furstenberg label.	Made major impact in 1970s with jersey knitted wraparound dress with surplice closing. Left the field from 1977 to 1985, then reentered, designing dresses and eveningwear. Moved into telemarketing, and again into design in 1997.

Information about designers already listed in Tables 17.1 and 17.2 (see pages 516 and 517) who continued to be active for all or part of this period are not included in this table.

All quotes comes from Calasibetta, C. M. (1988). *The Fairchild dictionary of fashion* (2nd ed.). New York, NY: Fairchild; and Stegemeyer, A. (1996). *Who's who in fashion* (3rd ed.). New York, NY: Fairchild.

displayed the name of the designer on the posterior of the wearer. With the popularity of designer blue jeans and other logos such as the Lacoste alligator, labels or logos placed on the exterior of garments became a major selling point. The status element in designer labels led to counterfeit designer-labeled products.

As labels became more important in promoting products, the practice of **licensing** a designer's name for use on a wide variety of products also expanded. Licensing has been part of American business since the early 20th century, when the comic-strip character Buster Brown and his dog Tige became enormously popular and closely associated with the Brown Shoe Company. With the advent of television, opportunities for licensing increased. Beginning in the 1950s and continuing into the new millennium, licensing has been especially prevalent in—though certainly not

limited to—children's clothing. Cartoon characters and sports figures, team names, and other logos appeared on all kinds of garments.

Designers of Men's Clothing

Until the 1960s, internationally known fashion designers created women's clothing, whereas well-to-do men patronized custom tailors. Certain brand-name items and particular retailers were known for the quality of their merchandise and classic styling. This was changing. Pierre Cardin had begun to design for men in 1957, and designer John Weitz opened a boutique for men in 1965. Soon others joined them. From this point onward designer styles for men became increasingly important. Throughout the 1970s the practice that had begun in the 1960s for well-known designers to produce a line of men's clothing accelerated, and designer clothes for men became a permanent part of men's fashion.

COSTUME: 1960–1980

Costume Components for Women: 1960–1974

For the first years of the decade of the 1960s, styles showed some uncertainty. Skirts shortened gradually, a trend that had begun in the late 1950s. The earliest examples of new styles were either straight and unfitted or princess style with a slight A-line in which the waist was loosely defined. The **skimmer**, a sleeveless, princess-line style was a popular example of the latter form. The Empire waistline experienced a brief revival around 1960.

By 1964 the transition from New Look–influenced styles to an easy, unfitted line was well established. Gradually shortening skirts had climbed to as much as 2 inches above the knee in the United States in 1966. The term **miniskirt** was coined to describe these skirts, and the term **micro-mini** was applied to the shortest of the short skirts (Figure 18.16).

FIGURE 18.16 Miniskirts are short skirts. Micro-miniskirts are very short skirts worn for both daytime and evening. (David McCabe © 1966 Condé Nast Publications)

All kinds of clothes for women and girls—from dresses to evening dresses and outdoor clothing—had unfitted, short silhouettes. By the end of the 1960s, the fashion industry introduced the **maxi**, a full-length style, and the midi, a skirt that ended about midcalf. However, these styles were not widely worn, and the transition to a new length and silhouette was still several years away in the mid-1970s (see Figure 18.15).

Contemporary Comments 18.2 (page 565) reprints excerpts from *Women's Wear Daily* and the *Wall Street Journal* that follow the progress of the midi from 1969 to 1973.

It was during this period that pants gained acceptability not only as appropriate garments for leisure, but also for all occasions. Blue jeans, first worn by hippies, then picked up by the young, were adopted by mainstream fashion and by 1970 were being worn by men and women of all ages. Pantsuits were worn for work and leisure, and soon after the fashion industry produced other types of pants: knickers, gaucho pants, and **hot pants** (very short pants).

Garments

Brassieres, underpants, slips, and girdles continued to be the most common items of women's underwear. They were made in solid colors and restrained prints in the first part of the decade.

A new garment was introduced, part hosiery, part underwear. Sheer, nylon **pantyhose** were first marketed about 1960 as an alternative to nylon stockings held up with a garter belt or girdle. (The Sears, Roebuck mail-order catalogue carried them in 1961.) Structured in the same way as the opaque, knitted tights worn by dancers, these garments joined underpants and stocking into one garment and became a virtual necessity as skirts became shorter. See Illustrated Table 18.1 for examples of undergarments from the period between 1960 and 1980.

With the advent of short skirts after styles changed in the 1960s, underwear took on a new importance. Wide-legged panties were sometimes worn instead of a slip. Underclothing was manufactured in vivid and striking colors and prints.

The distinction between underwear, footwear, and outerwear became less clear as new garments appeared that combined outerwear and underwear and, sometimes, extended from neck to toe, eliminating the need for stockings. These garments included

- **body stockings**, which were body-length, knitted stretch underwear; and
- **body suits**, similar garments that usually ended at the top of the leg. Some extended from shoulder to toe. Often body suits were designed to be worn with the upper section visible as, or instead of, a blouse. Said one fashion writer, the body suit "takes the place of bra, panties, panty girdle, pantyhose, and a blouse or sweater" ("Fashions of the Times," 1971; see Illustrated Table 18.1).

The ancestor of many of these garments was the **leotard**, a two-piece, knitted, body-hugging garment worn by French acrobat Jules Leotard in the 19th century. Dancers and acrobats adopted this costume, but until a brief introduction of the garment by Claire McCardell in 1943 (which did not catch on), it had never been part of fashionable dress.

Hippies and some radical feminists rejected bras. Some women stopped wearing bras; others bought the No-Bra bra, a design originated by Rudi Gernreich in 1964, which was the underwear manufacturers' answer to the desire of many women for a bra that didn't appear to be there (see Illustrated Table 18.1). The use of girdles diminished.

Acceptance of a new line in suit styles had come earlier than for dresses. By the late 1950s, these were generally made with loosely fitted jackets. One of the more important suits of the 1960s was Chanel's braid-trimmed, collarless, cardigan-style jacket with three-quarter–length sleeves; an A-line skirt; and (often) a blouse with a bow tie at the neck and sleeves extending a little beyond the jacket sleeves (Figure 18.17).

When the first chemises of the late 1950s were introduced, dresses had a rather soft, draped appearance (see Figure 17.18, page 530). By the mid-1960s, many dresses tended to have a harder line (Figure 18.18). Dresses with bodices joined to skirts

FIGURE 18.17 Chanel's cardigan-style suit, made of bouclé fabric and worn with gold jewelry, became a classic style of the 1960s and has appeared in somewhat modified versions ever since. (© Bettmann/CORBIS)

FIGURE 18.18 Styles of the mid-1960s featured lengths well above the knee often characterized by hard, tailored lines. (Bert Stern © 1968 Condé Nast Publications)

were uncommon. Some notable silhouettes for dress styles included

- Empire waistlines (around 1960),
- A-line shapes with dresses flaring slightly from neck to hem,
- dresses cut straight and loose from shoulder to hem,
- dresses falling straight from a yoke at the shoulder, and

- dresses unfitted through the torso and with a flounce joined to the hem of the dress at the knee.

The most fashionable length for skirted garments was above the knee, although more conservative women rarely wore knee-baring styles. Most garments were loosely fitted, without waistline definition. In the early 1970s, bright printed fabrics made from manufactured knitted fabrics were quite popular.

Contemporary Comments 18.2

REPORTS CHRONICLE THE PROMOTION
OF AND RESISTANCE TO THE MIDI SKIRT

Reports from Women's Wear Daily *and the* Wall Street Journal *chronicle the promotion and resistance to the midi skirt.*

Women's Wear Daily, July 7, 1969:
Here's the Lowdown . . . On the Low-down.

The Lowdown Length is the big news for fall.

Paris says so . . . Rome says so . . . London says so.

So does New York.

Designers have been experimenting with lowered hemlines—from below-the-knee to ankle length—for the past five years. The Midi and the Maxi made it . . . mostly in coats worn over pants or short skirts.

The daytime Lowdown has had limited acceptance in New York fall collections. London says the Midi is old news to them . . . the Maxi is where it's happening there now.

Practically everyone agrees it's time for new lengths. It's an addition . . . another choice . . . another facet to the way fashion is moving today.

While the time is right for a new lowdown, it still needs that final stamp of approval from a designer like St. Laurent to make it happen.

And that's just what Yves will do on Monday when he shows his couture collection. St. Laurent has already down the Lowdown in his Rive Gauche fall collection. Now he strengthens his point by doing it for the couture.

Women's Wear Daily, January 14, 1970:
New York. It's just 10 days before the Paris couture collections open.

And the big question on everybody's mind is—what length?

But there's no question about what the news is. It's the Midi. It's the time for it. It's in today's newest mood.

Women's Wear Daily, February 2, 1970:
New York—Hemline War is Escalating

The battle of the hemline rages on.

There are some who see it clearly. Skirts are on the way down.

There are those who are hemming the issue.

Some designers showed short for summer . . . and some buyers bought short.

Some of both are adding inches to the short skirts. And they're missing the point of the Longuette.

You can't add a few inches to a skirt that was designed short and expect to get a new look. The news is lengths are not around the knee. Some women never wavered from that length even at the height of the mini's popularity.

What is news is the skirt that drops a few inches below the knee—or longer still to Midi.

Women's Wear Daily, February 5, 1970:
Longuette Placing SA in a Quandary
By Tom McDermott
New York—The Longuette look has raised more questions than it has answered, according to many SA [Seventh Avenue] dress manufacturers.

It has caused such confusion and doubt among store executives and resident office buyers, they maintained, that retailers are becoming stingy in placing early summer business and holding back on spring orders.

Everyone, it seems, is looking for direction—especially the direction that lengths will take for late spring and summer. The lowdown look has both retailers and producers in a quandary.

Wall Street Journal, October 2, 1970:
Moribund Midi
Woeful Retailers Say the Lower the Hem, the Lower the Sales
Women Call It Sleazy, Dowdy, Depressing; but Designers Say It Will Catch On Yet
Laughed Out of the Office

A *Wall Street Journal* News Roundup
Silence on the Set, please.

We've had months of buildup and lots of heated controversy, but now it's opening night. The notorious midi skirt, much-scorned but also much-promoted, is finally making its debut in thousands of boutiques and department stores across the country. Places everyone. Curtain . . . up!

Ker-plunk.

That's right, fashion fans, that's the sound of the star herself, entering the market place, tripping on her own hemline and falling flat on her face.

That, according to despairing retailers interviewed by *Wall Street Journal* reporters across the country is exactly how it's happening. With crisp weather bearing down and the traditional fall buying season already a couple of weeks old, women from coast to coast are trooping into the nation's retail clothing stores—and trooping right back out, sans midis.

Illustrated Table 18.1

Selected Undergarments for Women and Men: 1960–1980

Designer Rudi Gernreich's "No-Bra" bra in nude tricot for Exquisite Form manufacturer, 1969[1]

Bikini pants and bra, 1969[2]

Bodysuits served as both underwear (1969) and outerwear (1973)[3]

Slip, underpants, and girdle, 1969[4]

Patterned pantyhose, 1967[5]

Left to right: men in jockey shorts and T-shirt, boxer shorts and athletic shirt, long thermal underwear[6]

---

[1] *Women's Wear Daily*, December 10, 1969. Fairchild Publications.
[2] *Women's Wear Daily*, March 6, 1969. Fairchild Publications.
[3] Fairchild Publications.

[4] *Women's Wear Daily*, July 31, 1969. Fairchild Publications.
[5] *Women's Wear Daily*, December 14, 1967. Fairchild Publications.
[6] *Men's Wear*, January 9, 1968. Fairchild Publications.

Long daytime dresses, known as **granny dresses**, were popular among the young in the early 1970s. They apparently derived from mod and hippie styles. Some had design elements that harked back to earlier historical periods; others were cut simply, with elasticized necks, waists, and sleeves (see Illustrated Table 18.5, page 585).

A fashion for sheer, see-through blouses and for dresses worn without underclothing was reported in the press. This had a limited following and did not spread beyond urban, cosmopolitan areas.

A brief flurry of interest in **paper dresses** emerged in 1966 (see Figure 18.11). Scott Paper Company produced some paper dresses as part of a promotion of its products. The manufacturer had no interest in manufacturing paper dresses, but the positive consumer response to the promotion was surprising, and other manufacturers quickly picked up on the idea. The uncomplicated, A-line, unfitted style lines and the vivid, colorful prints popular at this time made the production of acceptable paper styles possible. Interest was brief, however, and the demand for paper dresses declined quickly after 1968, particularly because of the waste these produced.

Matching pants and jackets were introduced just after the mid-1960s for daytime, business, and evening wear. Double-knit polyester fabrics were often used for inexpensive pantsuits; wool double knits, for more expensive versions (see Figure 18.21a). By the late 1960s, pantsuits had surpassed skirted suits in popularity. At a time when controversy over skirt lengths was raging, wearing pants solved the problem of what length to wear very effectively.

Evening dresses were made in both long and short lengths, but short lengths were preferred. As the fitted styles lost their popularity, elaborately beaded bodices or overblouses were worn with long skirts (see Figure 18.8). Trends included straight, short dresses, some in vivid prints (Figure 18.19) and others made of metallic fabrics, or trimmed with sequins, paillettes of plastic, or beads.

In the late 1960s, long evening dresses began to supplant shorter ones. Pantsuits of decorative fabrics

FIGURE 18.19 The vivid colors characteristic of the mid-1960s are seen in this short 1965 cocktail dress. (The Goldstein Museum of Design, University of Minnesota)

with full-legged trousers were also worn for evening, as were wide-legged pants in soft fabrics, and given the fashion name **palazzo pajamas**. They vied with hostess gowns as appropriate to wear for entertaining at home, as well as for formal occasions (Figure 18.20).

Sportswear

A gradual shift in skirt silhouettes occurred. Most tended to be A-line. Many had no waistband but were finished with a facing instead. By the early 1970s, most skirts tended to be mini in length, in spite of heavy fashion promotion of the midcalf-length midi. A few midis were worn, and full-length maxis appeared occasionally for daytime wear, more often in the evening than for daytime.

FIGURE 18.20 Palazzo pajamas in a distinctive print of the type originated by Italian designer Emilio Pucci. (Henry Clarke © 1968 Condé Nast Publications)

In the early 1960s, knitted stretch pants with narrow legs were worn with straight or blouson tops, or knitted tops. Separate skirts and blouses were less important than in earlier decades, having been replaced to a large extent by pants and knit tops.

Pants of all kinds, especially blue jeans were popular (Figure 18.21). The predominant style, called **hip huggers**, had wide, flaring or bell-bottom legs, fitted smoothly across the hip, and was often made with a facing rather than a waistband at the top. These pants were set lower on the hip than the anatomical waistline. The flared bottoms of bell-bottom pants derived from the shape of the pant legs of sailors'

uniforms. These wide-legged trousers were originally designed to make it easier for men to remove their clothing to swim, to pull off the trousers without catching them on their shoes. Hot pants were a feature of the early 1970s.

Tight, figure-hugging, fitted blouses gave way to looser styles, many with straight lines. Turtlenecks were among the most popular separate tops. Their use corresponded with a general interest in knitted fabrics for easy-fitting tops worn over skirts and pants. Young women often wore turtlenecks with jumpers and tights that matched the jumper.

Popular sweater styles included **poorboy sweaters** or tightly fitted, rib-knit styles that looked as if they had shrunk. Matching cardigan and pullover sweater sets and mohair (the wool of the Angora goat) sweaters were fashionable.

Outdoor Garments

Coats tended to be straight and loose, with an easy fit through the shoulders and a rounded shoulderline. Some coats narrowed slightly toward the bottom or, alternately, had a slight A-shape. Up until the end of the decade, coats were short (Figure 18.22). Around 1970 midi, mini, and maxi lengths were all available. Long greatcoats in single- or double-breasted styles with belted and flared skirts in maxi lengths were inspired by the film *Doctor Zhivago* and its early–20th-century Russian styles. Coats in longer lengths were more successful than dresses or skirts. Some manufacturers made coats with horizontal zippers that allowed the wearer to take off sections at each of the mini, midi, or maxi lengths.

Often coat sleeves had a slightly dropped shoulder or were cut in one with the body of the coat. Most were wrist length or shorter.

Capes and ponchos, in short lengths, were popular in the late 1960s as were vinyl-coated fabrics for rainwear (see Modern Influences).

Emphasis on preservation of endangered animals caused some women and men to wear manufactured pile-fabric imitations of fur. Such fabrics were called *fake fur*. Synthetic fibers were used in pile linings

a	b	c	d

FIGURE 18.21 (a) Pantsuit by Gunter (left) and John Anthony (right). (b) "Midipants" that top at midcalf (left) and knickers in suede with matching suede jacket (right). (c) Gaucho pants. (d) Various types of hot pants. (Courtesy of Fairchild Publications, Inc.)

to add warmth. Zip-in linings remained popular, especially for rainwear.

Clothing for Active Sports

Women adopted leotards (long used by dancers for exercising) for aerobic exercises. The company Danskin had sold these garments for years at department-store hosiery counters. Now sporting goods stores were carrying them in a variety of styles and colors, and they were also being worn as tops with skirts. Terminology was not clear cut, and in the March 1979 issue of *Vogue* the editor noted that the terms *body suit*, *maillot* (a one-piece, knitted bathing suit), and *leotard* were used interchangeably.

Leg warmers, loose-fitting footless stockings used by dancers, were worn for exercise sessions and also on the street, a sort of fad among young women.

FIGURE 18.22 The full-length maxi coat of the 1970s co-existed for several years with the miniskirt that fashionable women were reluctant to abandon. Knee-length boots were often worn with miniskirts. (© Bettmann/CORBIS)

For most of the 20th century, clothing had been manufactured that took into account the distinct requirements of certain sports, such as swimming, tennis, golf, and skiing. Considerable variety was evident in bathing suit styles. These ranged from two-piece bathing suits of relatively conservative cut to more scanty bikinis, which gradually became acceptable in the United States. Rudi Gernreich introduced a topless bathing suit in 1964 that he called a monokini (Figure 18.23). Some one-piece bathing suits made in blouson, loosely fitted styles echoed the unfitted lines of dresses.

More people took up downhill skiing. In the mid-1960s skiwear was made in bright colors and prints. By the late 1960s skiers were wearing warm-up pants and overalls with parkas. Synthetic and down fillings were quilted into ski jackets and other sportswear for warmth. Styles worn at the Olympic Games influenced skiwear, and as Olympians looked for styles that enhanced speed, they adopted streamlined stretch-knit ski pants. In 1968 Olympic skier Susie

FIGURE 18.23 Topless wool swimsuit called the *monokini*, designed for Harmon Knitwear in 1964 by Rudi Gernreich, whose designs were often startling. (*Women's Wear Daily*, December 10, 1969. Courtesy of Fairchild Publications)

Chaffee wore a sleek, silver jumpsuit and began the trend toward one-piece **unitard** ski suits.

Knickers and knee-length socks, worn with sweaters and lightweight windbreakers, were appropriate for cross-country skiing, which was becoming popular.

On July 5, 1972, at the tennis matches at Wimbledon, Rosie Casals broke with the tradition of wearing white on the courts: She appeared in a tennis dress decorated with purple scrolls (Figure 18.24). This marked the end of an era, and color entered professional tennis. From this point on, the white tennis outfits required by tennis clubs were replaced with color-trimmed or colored garments. Tennis became an enormously popular sport, and in affluent suburban areas it was common to see women wearing tennis outfits for supermarket shopping.

By the late 1970s the quest for good health through fitness had led many men and women to jog, run, and work out. Manufacturers responded with new lines of warm-up suits, running and jogging clothing, and shoes, especially sneakers. The popularity of professional sports led clothing manufacturers to feature famous athletes in endorsements, advertisements, and TV commercials for clothes and shoe styles based on sports uniforms.

Sleepwear

The variety of sleepwear styles had increased in the late 1950s and 1960s. Short-legged pajamas, short nightshirts, and a wide range of colors and fabrics were added to more traditional styles. The varieties of sleepwear included colorful nylon nightgowns ranging in length from the floor to hip length, "shortie" gowns worn with matching panties, pajamas. Warm robes were made of synthetic-pile fabrics and quilted nylon or polyester fabrics.

Hair and Headdress

See Illustrated Table 18.2 for some examples of hairstyles and hats for the period from 1960 to 1980.

Bouffant hairstyles became stylish in the early 1960s; the fullness was achieved by a technique of massing the hair, called *backcombing*, or adding

FIGURE 18.24 In the 1970s touches of color and some ornamentation appeared at professional tennis matches, and styles for amateurs also became more decorative. (George Freston/Fox Photos/Getty Images)

artificial hairpieces (or both). By the mid-1960s, girls and young women were allowing their hair to grow straight and long. Girls whose hair was not naturally straight pressed the curl out of their hair with clothes irons. The vogue for long, straight hair continued into the early 1970s.

French fashion designers Courrèges and Cardin and English designer Mary Quant had the hair of their models cut in almost geometric styles for their mid-decade collections. English hair stylist Vidal Sassoon also helped make the **geometric cut** a popular alternative to long hair.

More and more women elected to go hatless as a result of lifestyle changes. Bouffant hairstyles also discouraged the wearing of hats. Those hats that were worn included many with large crowns and small or no brims. For the 1961 presidential inauguration Jackie Kennedy wore a pillbox hat designed by Halston, a style subsequently adopted by many women. However, hats never recovered the popularity they had before 1960 and, in general, were more used as practical head coverings for cold weather than as a fashionable accessory.

Footwear

See Illustrated Table 18.3 for some examples of footwear worn in the period from 1960 to 1980.

When advances in technology could produce nylon stockings that fit the leg smoothly and without wrinkles or seams, seamless stockings became popular. Pantyhose gained wide acceptance. Colored and textured stockings, pantyhose, or tights were worn with short skirts. Knee-length, colored socks were paired with miniskirts.

Heels lowered as skirts shortened. By the mid-1970s, toes were more rounded and less pointed. In the early 1970s, platform soles, ranging from small platforms to enormously high ones, were added to all kinds of shoes and boots. Clogs, with wooden soles, were especially popular when platform soles were in vogue.

After the 1920s, boots were worn for functionality in bad weather. During the 1960s women went back to wearing boots as a fashionable part of daytime dress, as they had in the early 20th and 19th centuries. Shown first in the early 1960s, boots were quickly adopted for wearing in the colder months. They ranged from ankle-length, short boots worn with stretch pants to calf-high boots. Boots remained a basic item of footwear, showing annual variations, throughout the period.

Accessories

Notable among widely varying types and shapes were small tailored bags, very large bags with round handles or shoulder straps, and shoulder bags.

Illustrated Table 18.2

Typical Hats and Hairstyles for Women: 1960–1980

Pillbox, 1960

High-crowned,
hunter's cap, 1965[1]

A

B

Hats that revive earlier styles
(a) "Carole Lombard" head cap from the 1930s
(b) 1930s fedora style, 1969[2]

Brimmed velour hat that ties under the
chin, 1970, worn over long, straight hair[3]

Knit ski cap, 1973[4]

Beret 1973[4]

Bouffant hairstyle, 1963[5]

Second half of the 1960s

Corn-row braids, early 1960s

Soft, "natural" hairstyle, 1975–1980

Frizzy curls, late 1970s

Wedge, c. 1976

---

[1] *Women's Wear Daily*, November 16, 1965. Fairchild Publications.

[2] *Women's Wear Daily*, January 1, 1968. Fairchild Publications.

[3] *Women's Wear Daily*, June 19, 1970. Fairchild Publications.

[4] *Women's Wear Daily*, May 5, 1973. Fairchild Publications.

[5] *Vogue*, July 1963, drawing by Henry Koehler. Courtesy, *Vogue*.
Copyright 1963 by Condé Nast Publications

Illustrated Table 18.3

Selected Examples of Popular Footwear for Women and Men: 1960–1980

Women's Shoes

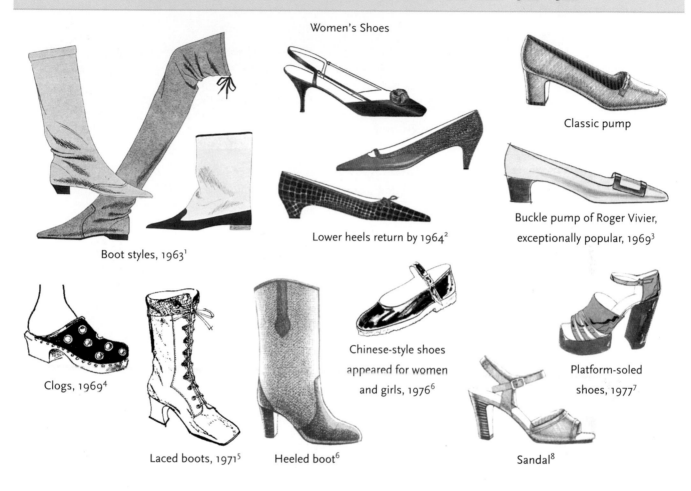

Boot styles, 1963[1]

Lower heels return by 1964[2]

Classic pump

Buckle pump of Roger Vivier, exceptionally popular, 1969[3]

Clogs, 1969[4]

Laced boots, 1971[5]

Heeled boot[6]

Chinese-style shoes appeared for women and girls, 1976[6]

Platform-soled shoes, 1977[7]

Sandal[8]

Men's Shoes

Black patent leather evening shoes, 1965[9]

Sandals with peace symbol[10]

Leather boots, 1969[11]

Platform-soled shoes, 1971[12]

[1] *Women's Wear Daily,* August 25, 1963.
[2] *Harper's Bazaar* and Delman shoes at Bergdorf Goodman, September, 1964.
[3] *Footwear News,* December 16, 1965. Fairchild Publications.
[4] *Footwear News,* July 24, 1969. Fairchild Publications.
[5] *Footwear News,* March 11, 1971. Fairchild Publications.
[6] *Footwear News,* Spring 1976. Fairchild Publications.
[7] *Footwear News,* August 3, 1972. Fairchild Publications.
[8] *Footwear News,* July 20, 1978. Fairchild Publications.
[9] *Footwear News,* December 23, 1965. Fairchild Publications.
[10] *Footwear News,* September 18, 1969. Fairchild Publications.
[11] *Footwear News,* April 3, 1969. Fairchild Publications.
[12] *Footwear News,* September 5, 1971. Fairchild Publications.

Materials included leather and plastic imitations of leather, fabric, and straw (see Illustrated Table 18.4 for examples of popular accessories in the period from 1960 to 1980.)

Jewelry

Popular jewelry items included long strings of pearls or other beads similar to those worn in the 1920s, necklaces of brightly colored stones, small or long hanging earrings, and and an enormous variety of costume jewelry at a variety of prices.

Since the late 1950s, increasing numbers of women pierced their ears. This trend, led by adolescents, accelerated in the late 1960s and the early 1970s. The Montgomery Ward Christmas catalogue of 1974 featured a do-it-yourself ear-piercing device.

Colorful plastic jewelry in geometric shapes complemented the somewhat geometric forms evident in women's clothing. In the latter part of the 1960s large decorative wristwatches appeared, and gold-colored jewelry, especially multiple gold chains, overshadowed colored beads.

Cosmetics

For those who used cosmetics, bright red lipstick was replaced after 1966 by a variety of lighter, paler colors. Mascara, eyeliner, and eye shadow were available in colors ranging from mauve to lavender, blue, green, and even yellow. False eyelashes were commonly used. For the first part of the 1970s makeup, though much used, was supposed to create an "unmade-up" or natural look. Lip gloss was first introduced in 1971.

Changes in Costume for Women: 1974–1980

The unfitted, straight, and short silhouette of the last years of the 1960s continued on into the early 1970s. But by August 1971 the *New York Times* declared that women had the right to wear any length they chose. The longuette, coming to midcalf, was a sharp change from the mini and micro-minis worn at the time, but by mid-decade the very short miniskirt was no longer fashionable (see Figure 18.15). The *New York Times*

noted that "length was not much of an issue" and that designers stressed "what looks best" (Morris, 1978, D9). Long pants were worn as part of pantsuits, worn for casual wear, and worn for formal evening dress. Knickers were popular, as were gaucho pants. Some young women wore very short shorts, called *hot pants* by *Women's Wear Daily* (see Figure 18.21d).

The prevalent silhouette of the mid-1970s and later has been described by fashion writers as "fluid" and "an easier and more casual fit." At the same time the use of softer fabrics molded the body and displayed body curves. An emphasis on fitness made the long, lean, trim, and toned body the ideal of feminine beauty.

Garments

Some women had abandoned bras; most did not. Bras were molded from synthetic fabrics to eliminate unsightly seamlines, which provided a natural appearance under the clinging fabrics so much used during the latter part of the 1970s. Pantyhose with control tops took the place of girdles. See Illustrated Table 18.1 (page 566) for some examples of undergarments from the period between 1960 and 1980.

In 1973 fashion writers spoke of a classic revival. Most dresses were belted or had clearly defined waistlines. Lines were soft, with shaping that followed and revealed body contours (Figure 18.25). By mid-decade skirts had lengthened, and often flared gradually from waist to hem.

Natural fibers in beige and neutral colors replaced the brightly colored manufactured fibers so often seen in the 1960s. Fabrics were soft and drapable; many were knitted. Some examples of popular dress styles included

- dresses that were pulled over the head, had elastic or drawstring waistlines, and slightly bloused bodices; and
- cotton-knit wrap-dresses, a style originated by designer Diane von Furstenberg, that tied shut with an attached belt.

Illustrated Table 18.4

Accessories: 1960–1980

a
b

Accessories adopted by hippies

(a) Headband (b) Hippie or love beads

Man's jewelry:
chain and Maltese cross

Woman's necklace, 1972,
showing Egyptian influences
from museum exhibit
about King Tut

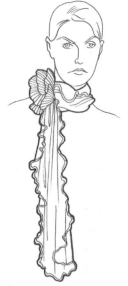

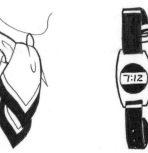

Men's neckties and ascot

(a) Neckties grow wider in the 1970s

(b) Men also wore ascots

Digital wristwatch, c. 1976

Long neckscarf with
lettuce edging, 1977

a

b

a
b
c

Handbags

(a) Women's Chanel bag (b) Woman's handbag in linen and leather (c) Man's handbag, c. 1974

FIGURE 18.25 Diane von Furstenberg's dresses made of printed jersey knits were a popular style of the late 1970s. (Image copyright © The Metropolitan Museum of Art. Image source: Art Resource, NY)

Pantsuits had become a staple in the wardrobes of all but the most conservative women. Sold at widely varying prices and made in fabrics such as knitted or textured polyester and wool gabardine, pantsuits were worn for work and during leisure time as sportswear and for formal evening occasions.

Women in managerial positions in the corporate world were advised in John Molloy's 1977 book *Dress for Success* to avoid pantsuits and to wear a feminine version of the male business suit: a tailored jacket and skirt in a dark color with a blouse similar to a man's shirt. A small bow at the neck was permissible, but a mannish-looking necktie was not advised (Figure 18.26).

As discos replaced elaborate formal dances and parties, evening clothing was not as important as in previous periods. In fact, clothing for discos was decidedly less formal: Some women wore jeans. When skirts or dresses were worn, they tended to be floor length, having replaced the miniskirted evening wear of the 1960s. As with daytime garments, fabrics were soft, clinging, and often knitted (Figure 18.27).

Sportswear

Pants were an alternative to skirts in almost all situations. By 1976 they had moved away from the bell-bottom shape and were narrower in the leg. By 1978, most were pleated or gathered into a waistband, tapering toward the ankle, and cuffed or rolled to ankle length.

FIGURE 18.26
Conservative tailored suits often worn with blouses with a soft tie at the neck were recommended for businesswomen who wanted to succeed in the corporate world. (Courtesy of Fairchild Publications, Inc.)

FIGURE 18.27 Full-length evening dresses were once again popular by the late 1970s, and Halston was one of the most influential designers of these body-hugging gowns often made of silk or synthetic knit fabrics. (Helmut Newton © 1972 Condé Nast Publications)

Jeans were a virtual uniform for casual wear, and designer jeans were very popular among all age groups. Some girls and women, conforming to the body-conscious look of the period, wore exceptionally tight jeans. Young women had to lie on the floor at times in order to zip them up.

By the mid-1970s and later, skirts had more fullness, tended to flare out, and covered the knee by at least several inches. Skirts that wrapped around the body and tied into place and the **swirl skirt**, made from bias-cut strips of multicolored fabrics that were often from India, were part of the ethnic styles that appeared periodically.

For most of the 1970s, blouses were of soft fabrics, often knit. Shoulderlines followed the natural curve

of the shoulder. Many knit tops fell somewhere between a blouse and a sweater. Short- or long-sleeved, made of narrow ribbed knits, these tops fit the body closely and ended a short distance below the waistline. Man-tailored shirts and other blouses that buttoned up the front were worn open at the neck by some women to show that they were braless. The wrap-style closing was popular in blouses as well as dresses. Toward the end of the 1970s and on into the early 1980s, large, loose shirts were worn over pants or skirts. The 1978 film *Annie Hall* had a strong impact on current fashion. It helped popularize not only the combination of layers of separates, including the aforementioned large shirts worn with men's vests, but also pantsuits and men's hats for women.

In 1975 *Vogue* proclaimed the sweater the basis for building a wardrobe. Sweaters with round necks were often worn over tailored blouses, the collar of the blouse visible at the neck of the sweater. The preppy look focused on Shetland wool sweaters. Hand-knitted sweaters were popular.

Long, thigh-length cardigan sweaters usually had a matching tie belt and were worn over trousers or skirts. Another popular sweater style was the sweater twin set, with matching cardigan and belted pullover made from natural fibers (Figure 18.28). Sweaters grew larger and looser in fit. In 1977 Japanese designer Issey Miyake combined oversized sweater tops with narrow leggings.

Among the most popular tops were T-shirts, especially those with written messages. As the focus on fitness grew, sweatshirts in various colors were much worn. Leotards were worn not only for exercising, but also as tops with jeans or wrapped skirts.

As part of the emphasis on preppy-style clothing, single-breasted, tailored wool blazers were combined with pants or skirts and tailored blouses.

Outdoor Garments

Coats, like dresses, followed body lines, flaring out gently below the waist. When sweaters and pantsuit styles featured tie belts of the same fabric, tie-belted

FIGURE 18.28 Among the popular sweater styles of the late 1970s was the twin set, a closely fitted pullover sweater and matching cardigan. This one from Anne Klein (1973) has a low neckline. (Bob Stone © 1973 Condé Nast Publications)

coats, including trench-coat raincoats, became popular. Most coats ended below the knee.

Down or fiber-filled coats, which may have been inspired by either Chinese padded coats or down-filled ski jackets, gained great popularity for winter wear in the late 1970s. Restaurants reported problems in accommodating these large coats in their coatrooms.

Clothing for Active Sports

Tennis clothing was made in a wide array of colors. Bathing suits came in styles ranging from the tiny string bikini, a short-term fad in 1974, to Empire-style, skirted swimming dresses of the same year. In 1975 Rudi Gernreich designed the **thong**, variously described as a "virtually bottomless bathing suit" or

a "glorified jockstrap," cut to reveal as much of the buttocks as possible while covering the crotch. One-piece maillot suits were particularly popular around 1976 and after.

By 1976 the sleek, fitted jumpsuit was popular on the slopes. In 1977 a suit that had the appearance of a one-piece suit but that could come apart with a zipper at the waistline, had been developed. Stretch pants with stirrups worn with puffy parkas were fashionable in 1979. Top fashion designers began to design skiwear in the late 1970s. Downhill outfits grew increasingly colorful and subject to seasonal style changes. Styles in cross-country skiwear did not change markedly.

Sleepwear

Although both nightgowns and pajamas were available, short and long nightgowns predominated. In the winters of the later 1970s, when thermostats were lowered to save energy, warmer fabrics such as cotton flannels, brushed tricot, and all-in-one sleepers like those worn by children gained popularity.

Robes often tied with a sash; they were cut in kimono style or with notched or shawl collars.

Hair and Headdress

See Illustrated Table 18.2 (page 572) for some examples of hair styles and hats for the period from 1960 to 1980. By mid-decade hair was becoming shorter, and for the rest of the decade a soft, natural style was preferred. Media and sports stars helped some fashions in hair. Among the trends were the following:

- Toward the end of the 1970s, some women were wearing their hair in tight, frizzy curls, a style seen on movie star Barbra Streisand in the 1977 film *A Star Is Born*.
- A short haircut called the **wedge** became popular in 1976 after Olympic medal-winner Dorothy Hamill wore the style at the games.
- In the TV program *Charlie's Angels*, Farrah Fawcett-Majors had a full, streaked, blonde mane, a style popular after 1977.

Although hats were not an important fashion item, berets and knit caps were used in colder regions in winter. Head scarves were featured in the fashion press in the mid-1970s.

Footwear

See Illustrated Table 18.3 (page 573) for some examples of footwear for the period from 1960 to 1980. Pantyhose and tights had supplanted stockings for most women and were available in colors and in a wide variety of textures and designs.

By the second half of the decade slender, more graceful shoes with comfortable heels had replaced the clunky platform soles. Boots remained an important item.

Accessories

Wide varieties of accessories of all kinds were available each season. Among those noted in the fashion press were handbags: narrow rectangles, fashionable around 1973; large tote bags after 1976; and large, soft satchels with interesting textures, around 1979. Throughout the period women carried small, square, quilted handbags with chain shoulder straps originally designed by Chanel. Dressed for success women carried briefcases rather than handbags. The emphasis on natural materials led to a strong interest in real leather accessories (see Illustrated Table 18.4, page 575).

Jewelry

Along with natural materials for garments came an interest in real gold and gemstones, in particular gold chains, gold-wire hoop earrings, and **diamonds by the yard**, designer Elsa Peretti's strings of gold chain interspersed with diamonds. In 1973 snakeskin-covered bangle bracelets were something of a fad. Digital watches were introduced in 1976.

Cosmetics and Grooming

In the mid-1970s women worked hard, ironically, at using makeup to create a natural look. Major cosmetic companies developed and marketed complete lines of skin care products. As hairstyles grew in volume, more hair care products were required to hold the styles in place. By the end of the 1970s lipstick shades grew brighter and eye makeup became more obvious.

COSTUME COMPONENTS FOR MEN

Garments

Men's undergarments continued to include boxer shorts, knitted briefs, athletic shirts, and T-shirts. Some changes were evident. In the late 1960s boxer shorts, already available in colors and small printed fabrics, were made in bright prints. The manufacturers of Jockey briefs produced these garments in cotton mesh in 1970 and continued to make the bikini-cut shorts in bright colors. See Illustrated Table 18.1 (page 566) for examples of undergarments from the period between 1960 and 1980.

By the mid-1960s, continental suits were being supplanted by mod clothes: English styles with jackets padded slightly at the shoulders, wider lapels, moderate flare to the skirt, and pronounced side or center-back vents. Jacket fronts had a moderately cutaway shape. Suits with body shaping remained fashionable for the rest of the period (Figure 18.29).

In the early 1970s, lapels were fairly wide, and suits were fitted through the body. Double-knit fabrics in both manufactured and wool fibers were widely used, and trousers tended to flare at the bottom. Suits were both single and double breasted, although single-breasted styles predominated.

In the latter part of the 1970s three-piece suits with vests, in decline since the 1930s, returned. Lapels narrowed and grew longer. The cut was looser. Men's suits were conservatively tailored, usually double breasted, made in dark-color, smooth-textured fabrics.

An upsurge of interest in fashion for men was accompanied by heavy press promotion, and publicists began to speak of a revolution in menswear. *Esquire* in its *Encyclopedia of 20th Century Men's Fashion* declared the stepping out of a peacock from its gray flannel cocoon (Schoeffler, 1974) (Figure 18.30). A spurt in retail sales of men's clothing induced some famous

FIGURE 18.29 Mod styles for men were more colorful and less conservative than styles of earlier periods. Characteristic styles included jackets displaying similarities to those of the Edwardian period, softly tailored shirts, longer hair, and shoes with pointed toes. British band members of "The Who": Bass player John Entwistle, guitarist Pete Townshend, singer Roger Daltrey, and drummer Keith Moon. (Tony Frank/Sygma/ Corbis)

designers of women's clothing to enter the menswear market as well. Pierre Cardin was one of the first.

Suits with **Nehru jackets** appeared on the scene. Based on a traditional Indian jacket that buttoned all the way to the neck with a small, stand-up collar, this garment was named after the Prime Minister of India, Jawaharlal Nehru, who wore the traditional jacket (Figure 18.31). The style lasted about 2 years. The Nehru style had gained notice when, in 1966 after returning from a trip to India, Cardin began to wear gray flannel suits made with Indian-style jackets. After Lord Snowdon (then the husband of Princess Margaret, sister of Queen Elizabeth II of England) wore a formal evening Nehru suit with a white turtleneck, other men combined Nehru jackets with turtlenecks. Turtleneck shirts remained a fashionable item of menswear even after the Nehru suit disappeared.

Sweaters in the 1970s fit fairly close to the body, ending just below the waistline. In the late 1970s sweaters became larger and looser. From the early 1960s on, turtlenecks were accepted as an alternative to the collared shirt. They were available in a wide variety of styles and colors. However, many men still donned collared shirts, especially since some

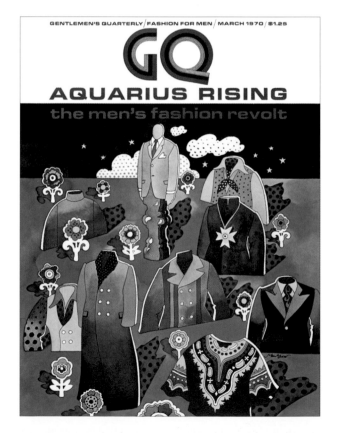

FIGURE 18.30 By the 1970s the "Peacock Revolution" provided men with many colorful alternatives for casual, leisure, and more formal occasions. (John Alcorn © 1970 Condé Nast Publications)

FIGURE **18.31** The Nehru suit, also called the *tunic*, was often worn with a chain, pendant, or other necklace. State Assemblyman Willie Brown of the Haight-Ashbury District of San Francisco appeared at the state legislature wearing love beads and a Nehru jacket over a turtleneck shirt. He reported taking a lot of kidding from his fellow legislators about his attire. (© Bettmann/CORBIS)

FIGURE **18.32** Figured or striped shirts were worn with the very wide neckties that were popular in the early 1970s. David Bowie in landscape print shirt. (© Steve Schapiro/Corbis)

restaurants refused admission to men without neckties (Figure 18.32).

Shirts that were cut and seamed so as to follow body lines, called **body shirts**, were popular in the 1960s. In the early 1970s, many synthetic knit fabrics were used. Collar sizes varied so that shirts would be in proportion to the lapel width of suit collars. Striped and printed shirts were popular.

An alternative to business suits developed for casual wear. Tops and pants were usually made from the same fabrics. The unstructured tops had shirtlike collars or were collarless. Fashionable throughout the 1970s, **leisure suits** were out of style by the end of the decade (Figure 18.33).

The Peacock Revolution had a major impact on tuxedos, which were cut with more body shaping and manufactured in a wide range of colors. Burgundy, green, and brown were especially popular. With these suits men wore shirts with ruffled fronts (Figure 18.34).

Evening jackets and trousers did not always match in the 1970s.

Outdoor Garments

As women's skirts grew shorter, so did men's outerwear. Fur and leather coats and fur-collared coats appeared in the latter part of the 1960s. By the early 1970s coats were made in a variety of lengths, paralleling the mini, midi, and maxi lengths in women's styles.

Casual outdoor garments included western-dress influences during the presidency of Texan Lyndon Johnson, campus or stadium coats that ended below the hip, shorter jackets for bicycling or motorcycling, and quilted jackets filled with down or synthetic fibers.

Sportswear

In the mid-1960s tapered slacks were replaced by those with trouser bottoms that grew wider and included some flared pant legs and wide, bell-bottoms. They

FIGURE 18.33 Leisure suits, often made from polyester knits but also from woven fabrics, became a relatively short-term fashion for men in the mid-1970s. (left: AP Images; right: Courtesy of Fairchild Publications, Inc.)

fit close to the torso without pleats. Blue jeans moved from being work clothes to being fashionable dress by the late 1960s.

Sport jackets generally followed the lines of suit jackets. Styles that were widely used included polyester knits in the 1960s and early 1970s and **safari jackets** and Norfolk-style jackets in the late 1960s and 1970s.

Available in diverse styles, types of sport shirts varied with the seasons: for warm weather, men wore T-shirts and polo shirts; for cooler weather, turtlenecks, velour pullovers and shirts, jacquard-patterned knitted sweaters, and sweatshirts were popular.

Clothing for Active Sports

In the 1960s, the minuscule European knit bikini for men (or, as the Europeans called it, the *slip*) was

FIGURE 18.34 Tuxedos from the 1970s, such as the example here on French singer Claude Francois, showed mod influences in their cut and ruffled shirts. They often had velvet collars and were available in various colors. (© Leonard de Raemy/Sygma/Corbis)

appearing on American beaches. Synthetic knits were used for bathing suits because they dried quickly and were wrinkle-free. In the 1970s suits were made of stretch nylon or cotton in longer lengths called *swim jams*. The Olympics seemed to influence styles in bathing suits, and in 1972 the suit worn by Mark Spitz, American Olympic gold-medal winner, was an important fashion. Throughout the period, men could choose among bikinis and trunks, with race-inspired bathing suits setting the styles.

Until the early 1970s, white predominated for tennis. After this, men as well as women were more likely to wear colored tennis clothes.

Styles for ski clothes changed yearly, moving gradually toward tighter fitting fabrics designed to offer as little wind resistance as possible. For cross-country skiing, men, as well as women, wore knickers with knee-length stockings.

Sleepwear

Pajamas continued to be the major form of sleepwear; they were made with either short or long pants and in vivid solid or printed colors. In the late 1970s when velour fabrics were fashionable, men wore velour robes.

Hair and Headdress

Radical changes in hair length came in the 1960s, beginning as a protest by the young against middle-class values. Hair past the shoulders was chiefly limited to high-school boys and college-age youth or older men wishing to dramatize a personal protest against some aspect of contemporary society. Moderately long hair, beards, mustaches, and sideburns had become accepted styles for all segments of society by the close of the 1960s. The longer hairstyles are often said to have been inspired by the Beatles. Fashion-conscious men began to patronize "hair stylists" rather than "barbers." Longer hairstyles persisted until the late 1970s, when shorter styles returned.

John F. Kennedy did not wear a hat to his inauguration in 1961. Subsequently, hat sales dropped, and hats became a much less important part of men's wardrobes. When hairstyles grew longer, hats became even less important.

Footwear

See Illustrated Table 18.3 (page 573) for some examples of footwear from the period 1960 to 1980. In the 1960s classic styles were supplemented by high shoes and boots, seen for the first time since the 1930s for street wear. By the end of the decade most shoes had somewhat squared toes. As platform soles were added to women's shoes, they were also seen on some, especially younger men's, shoes. After hippie men donned sandals, these entered mainstream men's fashion.

Accessories

Ralph Lauren made 3-inch–wide ties popular in 1967, and ties remained wide until the late 1970s (see Figure 18.32), when they became narrow again. Ralph Lauren came to prominence in 1967 as a designer of men's neckties. He then moved into menswear design, he transitioned into ready-to-wear for women in 1971, and eventually he even entered the home-products market. Lauren provides an illustration of the increasing tendency of successful designers to move easily from one market into another, although more designers have moved from women's design into men's design than vice versa.

Jewelry

Men began wearing necklaces with turtleneck sweaters and shirts. Bracelets and earrings were also seen. The trend seems to have begun with the hippies who wore beads and other decorative jewelry (see Illustrated Table 18.4, page 575).

Cosmetics

With longer hair, products for hair care for men expanded.

COSTUME COMPONENTS FOR CHILDREN

Infants and Toddlers

Clothing for children in this age group tends to change less than for older children. Many of the basic styles of infants' dresses might be called classic, with styles that continue for many decades. This is particularly true of styles produced for the so-called "grandmother" market (older women purchasing for grandchildren), consisting of embroidered or smocked dresses, or suits in cotton or cotton blended with manufactured fibers in pastel colors. Around 1960 basic garments for infants were introduced—stretch, all-in-one, footed terrycloth outfits—and these became a staple in infants' wear. Disposable diapers were introduced in 1960.

As child development experts increasingly stressed the importance of allowing children freedom from physical restraint in clothing, garments for toddlers took into account factors of comfort and safety. Most dresses tended to be loosely fitted, hanging from the shoulders. One-piece or two-piece tops and pants that fastened together at the waist were made for boys. Children at the crawling stage wore corduroy overall-type pants with reinforced knees.

Preschool and School-Age Children

Throughout the decade children's clothing inevitably displayed the same style trends seen for adults. Current events were reflected in children's clothing. As the American involvement in Vietnam grew, the *New York Times* children's fashion supplement of August 14, 1966, featured clothes with military influences. Mod- and hippie-derived styles appeared in the latter part of the 1960s. Fabrics that were washable and required little ironing were preferred, leading to the widespread use of nylon, polyester, acrylics, and blends of synthetics with cotton.

Garan, Inc., developed a new marketing technique for mid-priced children's clothing in 1976. They produced clothing for children 2 years old or older that had animal labels, called *garanimals*. Children could select coordinated outfits by matching, for example, blouses with monkeys on the label with pants with monkeys on the label, or lions with lions, and so forth. This promotion was successful until well into the early 1980s. See Illustrated Table 18.5 for some examples of children's styles for the period from 1960 to 1980.

Costume Components for Girls

Garments

When the full-skirted New Look styles for women began to be replaced by loosely fitted lines in the early 1960s, girls' dresses also gradually took on a looser fit. Slightly A-line, princess-cut "skimmers" were popular as dresses in summer and jumpers in winter. Skirts shortened, ending well above the knee. With the short skirts in cool weather, girls wore long tights in matching or contrasting colors and in a variety of textures. For the duration of the unfitted line, most girls' dresses were either straight, unfitted, sometimes with a wide ruffle around the hem, or gradually and slightly flared from shoulder to hem. When maxi-skirt lengths were introduced for adult women, versions for girls were seen as well, especially for party clothes. In the late 1970s hems lengthened, the silhouette became more fitted, and more belts were used.

Various pants styles were popular. In the 1960s young girls wore stretch nylon pants with narrow legs. At the beginning of the 1970s, pants were more often seen than dresses. Comfort in clothing for girls had clearly become important, as blue jeans and overalls were worn for school and for play. Girls also wore pantsuits. The fashion of pants for girls is another instance of the parallels between adult and children's styles. Whereas in earlier periods pants had been worn for play by girls, they were not generally worn for school until the late 1960s or early 1970s, the period during which adult women began to wear pants to work.

In the early 1960s, a fad developed for adolescent girls to wear **go-go boots**, which were calf length and white.

Hair

Hairstyles for girls were like those for adult women, including long straight hair and, for African-American girls, afros.

Illustrated Table 18.5

Children's Clothing Styles: 1960–1980

Boy's clothing for fall, 1961[1]

Back-to-school advertisement
of clothing for small girls, 1961[1]

Children's outerwear, c. 1966;
on the left, a modacrylic
parka and knit tights, on the
right a melton toggle coat
and blue jeans

Long "granny" dress, a
style that appeared for
girls in the early 1970s[2]

A-line styles, the
predominant line for
girls' dresses and tunics[3]

Dresses from McCall's Pattern Catalog, April 1977

Poncho styles,
popular in the
late 1960s[4]

Leisure suit with bell-
bottom pants for boys[5]

[1] Yelena Safronova.
[2] *Women's Wear Daily*, January 1, 1972. Fairchild Publications.
[3] McCall's® Image Courtesy of the McCall Pattern Company copyright © 2014.
[4] *Women's Wear Daily*, December 1, 1969. Fairchild Publications.
[5] *Women's Wear Daily*, March 15, 1971. Fairchild Publications.

Costume Components for Boys

Garments

Suits for boys were miniature versions of suits for men and included Nehru-style suits and mod-influenced suits. They were often made of polyester. In the 1970s some boys wore three-piece suits, some of which had an Edwardian cut. Sports jackets—often collarless blazers—were worn with short pants by younger boys and with long pants by older boys.

Knitted T-shirts and polo shirts, sometimes with white collars and often in bright horizontal stripes (rugby shirts), were the preferred garment for play. Shirts worn with jackets and suits were like those for adult men.

Hair

The change to longer hair for males was much influenced by the Beatles. Adolescent boys quickly adopted similar styles; some school authorities suspended boys with long hair. As longer hair became the predominant style in the latter part of the 1960s, boys of all ages, like men, wore their hair in a wide variety of lengths.

Costume Components for Boys and Girls

Probably the most important fashion item for both boys and girls was jeans. Jeans and other pants were made with bell-bottom legs from the late 1960s through the mid-1970s. Message T-shirts and clothing bearing licensed logos or other art began to gain importance in the 1970s, and their use accelerated throughout the decade.

Outdoor Wear

Among the more distinctive items of outdoor garments were those made from manufactured fiber-pile fabrics, some of which simulated fur. Boys and girls wore quilted and down-filled jackets, hooded sweatshirts, and vinyl slicker raincoats.

Summary

Themes

Almost all of the themes that were identified in Chapter 1 are found in the 1960s. But those that predominate strongly relate to POLITICS, POLITICAL CONFLICT, and SOCIAL CHANGES. Politics, for example, influenced fashions when the young and popular Kennedy family entered the White House. The 1960s was a period of upheaval in the United States. The civil rights movement, student unrest, women's liberation, and growing dissent over the escalation of the American military commitment in Vietnam were accompanied by changes in fashion that contrasted markedly with the styles of the 1950s. Skirts for women became shorter than in any previous period in the history of western dress. Trousers for women were accepted for daytime and evening wear in place of skirts. Some young men adopted shoulder-length hair for the first time in almost 200 years. Men began wearing more colorful and varied clothing for business and leisure than had been seen since before the 19th century.

Those who study clothing as it relates to social change have pointed out that marked changes in dress often accompany social unrest. The decade from 1965 to 1975 was a period of social upheaval, especially in the United States. It also appears to have been the catalyst for radical changes in attitudes toward fashion that affected not only subsequent styles but also, in the decades to come, would cause profound changes in the organization of systems for originating, producing, and merchandising fashionable clothing.

LEGACIES OF STYLES OF 1960–1980

The miniskirt, first seen in the early 1960s and characteristic of most of the rest of this period, was revived again in the mid-1980s. It had become one

Visual Summary Table

1960–1980

Man: 1960–1970
Greater variety in color and pattern, more decorative mod-influenced styles appear. Turtleneck shirts worn with suits and Nehru suits provide alternatives.

Man: 1970s
Color and pattern continue to be one option for men, along with more traditional business suits. Leisure suits are worn as casual dress in the 1970s.

Women: 1960–1970
By mid-1960s dresses are very short and unfitted. The Chanel suit becomes an important style. Street styles are incorporated into current fashion.

Woman: 1970–1980
Mid-calf-length skirts introduced c. 1970 are unsuccessful. Women retain short skirts, and adopt pantsuits as part of daytime wear.

Woman: 1970s
By mid-1970s, skirts lengthen, and a softer, fitted line replaces the straight, short styles. Punk and African-inspired styles appear.

of the many skirt alternatives from which designers could choose.

In the 1990s fashion designers were also reaching into this decade to borrow ideas from mod styles, op art, and the sleeveless A-line shift. Bell-bottoms, known as flared-leg pants, returned after the millennium. Ideas first seen in the hippie styles, such as recycling and making old clothes new and borrowing from folk and ethnic motifs, styles, and fabrics, have become new again (see Modern Influences).

Blue jeans, not a new style in the 1960s but one that was ubiquitous in this period, never left their prominent position in fashion. They became a fashion staple. With a trend in the 1990s toward casual wear in the white-collar workplace, jeans took on even greater importance. Pantsuits of the 1970s were revived in the 1990s and in the new millennium as a staple in working women's wardrobes.

REFERENCES

Age of Aquarius: Woodstock Music and Art Fair. (1969, August 25). *Newsweek*, 88.

Anawalt, P. F. (2010). Regional dress of Latin America in a European context. In *Berg encyclopedia of world dress and fashion*. http://www.bergfashionlibrary.com/page/encyclopedia/-berg-encyclopedia-of-world-dress-and-fashion.

Bivins, J. & R. K. Adams (Eds.). (2013). *Inspiring beauty*. Chicago, IL: Chicago History Museum.

Burns, R. D. & Siracusa, J. M. (2007). *The A to Z of the Kennedy-Johnson era*. Lanham, MD: Scarecrow Press.

Carter, J. (1977, April 18). Proposed Energy Policy. Retrieved from http://www.pbs.org/wgbh/americanexperience/features/primary-resources/carter-energy/.

Corcuera, R. (2005). Ponchos of the River Plate: Nostalgia for Eden. In R. Root (ed.), *The Latin American fashion reader* (pp. 163–175). Oxford, UK: Berg.

Fashions of the Times. (1971, August 29.) *New York Times*, 1.

Giddings, V. L. (1990). Campus dress in the 1960's. In B. Starke et al. (Eds.), *African American dress and adornment* (pp. 152–156). Dubuque, IA: Kendall Hunt.

MODERN INFLUENCES

Ponchos are square or rectangular garments with center openings that allow the wearer to pull them over the head with the garment resting on the shoulders (Corcuera, 2005). The poncho is an indigenous Andean garment (Anawalt, 2010). Although poncholike garments were worn before the Spanish conquest, most males wore tunics sewn up the sides. The first reference to the open-sided poncho by that name came from a 1629 description of people living in what is now Peru (Meisch, 2005). Ponchos have continued in use throughout Latin America and have come in and out of global fashion throughout the 20th and 21st centuries. This poncholike garment was designed by The Row, the fashion house of Mary Kate and Ashley Olsen. (Giannoni/WWD/Condé Nast)

Kawamura, Y. (2004). *The Japanese revolution in Paris fashion*. New York, NY: Berg.

King, M. L. (1963, August 28). I have a dream . . . Retrieved from http://www.archives.gov/press/exhibits/dream -speech.pdf.

Klemesrud, J. (1970, September 4). They like the way they looked—Others didn't. *New York Times*, 22.

Livingstone, M. (2009). Pop art. Grove Art Online. http://www.oxfordartonline.com/subscriber/article/grove/art/T068691?q=pop+art&search=quick&pos=1&_start=1#firsthit

Martin, R., & Koda, H. (1989). *Jocks and nerds: Men's style in the twentieth century*. New York, NY: Rizzoli.

McCloskey, J. (1970). The men's fashion report: Aquarius rising. *Gentlemen's Quarterly*, 4(2), 109.

Meisch, Lynn. (2005). America, south: History of dress. In V. Steele (Ed.), *Encyclopedia of clothing and fashion* (pp. 45–49). Detroit, MI: Scribner's.

Molloy, J. (1977). *Dress for success*. New York, NY: Wyden.

Morris, B. (1978, July 17). Designers talk about the shade of things to come. *New York Times*, D9.

Plumer, C. (1971). *African textiles: An outline of handcrafted Sub-Saharan fabrics*. East Lansing, MI: Michigan State University.

Polhemus, T. (1994). *Street Style*. New York, NY: Thames and Hudson.

Ross, D. H. (1998). *Wrapped in pride: Ghanaian Kente and African American identity*. Los Angeles, CA: UCLA Fowler Museum of Cultural History.

Schoeffler, O. E. (1974). *Esquire's encyclopedia of 20th-century men's fashions*. New York, NY: McGraw-Hill.

Schnurnberger, L. (1991). *Let there be clothes*. New York, NY: Workman.

Spiegel, I. (1965, June 26). Jewish officials vexed by youths. *New York Times*, 17.

	1980	1981	1983	1985	1987	1988	1989
FASHION AND TEXTILES		Elements of Lady Diana Spencer's wedding dress are extensively copied	Japanese designers show their work at the Paris prêt-à-porter shows		Christian Lacroix opens new couture house		
POLITICS AND CONFLICTS	Ronald Reagan elected U.S. president					George H. W. Bush elected U.S. president	
DECORATIVE AND FINE ARTS	Graffiti gains respect as an art form in the 1980s				The NAMES Project AIDS Memorial Quilt		Development of Adobe's Photoshop program allows manipulation of images
ECONOMICS AND TRADE		Japanese designers Rei Kawakubo and Yohji Yamamoto launch first collections in Paris		Soviet Premier Mikhail Gorbachev proposes plan of openness and economic reform			
TECHNOLOGY AND IDEAS							
RELIGION AND SOCIETY	Increased immigration influences society and fashion designers						

CHAPTER
NINETEEN

The Eighties and the Nineties:
Fragmentation of Fashion

1980–1999

1990	1991	1992	1993	1994	1995	1996

Houses of Dior and Givenchy choose British designers

Germans tear down Berlin Wall celebrating Cold War's end

U.S. war with Iraq in the Middle East

Bill Clinton elected U.S. president

Terrorist attack on World Trade Center

Federal building in Oklahoma City bombed

North American Free Trade Agreement (NAFTA) becomes law

Home shopping allows consumers to shop via television

First custom-fit clothing produced through computer imaging sold at retail by Levi Strauss

No longer was a single style followed universally. Style tribes multiplied, and fashion became more segmented. Often the clothes that originated with style tribes made their way into mainstream fashion. Other influences came from current events, political conflicts, celebrities, motion pictures, television, environmental concerns, demographic changes, and from the past in "retro" or vintage styles. Labels could be a status symbol. Designing, showing, and manufacturing fashionable dress spread around the world. The development of the Internet and personal computer use provided new ways to follow fashion, to acquire dress, and to manage manufacturing in far-flung locations. Advances in sophisticated technological textiles were beginning to blend electronics and dress.

HISTORICAL BACKGROUND

During the 1980s and 1990s, fashion choices were plentiful as a spirit of "anything goes" prevailed. Technology allowed the world to become increasingly connected.

The Cold War Ends

By the 1980s, the strain of the Cold War began to undermine the Soviet system. Mikhail Gorbachev, Soviet premier in 1985, proposed a policy of glasnost (*openness*) and perestroika (*economic reform*) in the hope of saving the communist system. The idea of glasnost spread to the unhappy satellite states in eastern Europe. Moscow could no longer keep them in line without war, a course Gorbachev rejected. Consequently, in 1989 the Soviet control of eastern Europe collapsed and noncommunist governments seized control. The Berlin Wall fell in 1989, and East and West Germany were reunited in 1990 (Figure 19.1).

After hard-line communists attempted a coup in 1991, the Soviet government collapsed. The Soviet Union ceased to exist when Gorbachev ceded power to President Boris Yeltsin; the country joined with other republics to form Commonwealth of Independent States. The Cold War was over.

The Russian republic passed through a crisis as it stumbled from communism toward a capitalistic democracy. A faltering economy, inadequate services, and strikes made the situation worse. Law enforcement suffered because of low pay and inadequate staffing.

One bright spot in Russian political life was that Boris Yeltsin, who had in effect been handed the presidency in 1991, was reelected in 1996 in the first democratic election. Yeltsin pushed through needed economic reforms but could not halt corruption and a fall in living standards. A civil war broke out in the republic of Chechnya in southwest Russia where the Chechens, who were Sunni Muslims, declared their independence. In 1994 Russian forces launched a full-scale invasion only to suffer a humiliating defeat by 1996.

In August 1999, Yeltsin appointed Vladimir Putin prime minister. When Yeltsin resigned as president, Putin, a former KGB colonel, succeeded him. Putin cracked down on the independent press and curtailed the freedom of television and radio. He also took aim

FIGURE 19.1 Built in 1961, the Berlin Wall both physically and symbolically embodied the tensions of the Cold War. Likewise, tearing down the wall both physically and symbolically demonstrated the unification of Germany. (© image BROKER/ Alamy)

at the oligarchs, wealthy Russian business tycoons, whenever they displayed any signs of interest in politics. Putin ordered a resumption of the Chechen war in 1999.

European Union

The European Economic Community (EEC) continued to develop and expand its functions. Steps were taken to encourage trade and investment among EEC members. Barriers to the movement of capital and curbs on financial services were reduced. European passports were issued.

Austria, Finland, and Sweden joined the European Union (EU) in 1995, bringing the total membership up to 15 nations. On March 26, 1995, all border controls were removed between Portugal, Spain, France, Belgium, Luxembourg, Germany, and the Netherlands. Citizens of these countries could cross borders without passport checks. The Maastricht Treaty, effective November 1, 1993, set tough economic standards that each member of the EU had to meet in order to join the European Monetary Union, which established one currency, the euro.

The Middle East

War came again in the Middle East in 1990 when Iraqi armies invaded and conquered Kuwait, a neighbor of Saudi Arabia and a major source of oil for the United States. After Iraq ignored a United Nations resolution demanding that it withdraw its forces, war was legally authorized. Coalition forces, headed by the United States, retook Kuwait and entered Iraqi territory. The Persian Gulf War, code-named Operation Desert Storm, ended after 100 hours of fighting. Unlike previous conflicts that had nightly news coverage, CNN provided nearly 24-hour live broadcasts from the front lines.

After a positive start towards peace between the Israelis and Palestinians in 1993, the peace process once again ran into roadblocks. On November 4, 1995, a religious right-wing Israeli assassinated Prime Minister Yitzhak Rabin as he left a peace rally in Tel Aviv. From this point on, the peace process continued with alternating periods of agreement and disagreement.

Japanese Economic Influences

Not until the 1980s did Americans became fully aware of the growing power of the Japanese economy. By the 1990s, Japanese competition in automobiles and electronic products forced American producers to renovate their plants, cut their payrolls, and introduce new technologies, including robotics. Some American plants producing these goods were moved outside the country in search of cheaper labor. Many companies moved their garment manufacturing operations to areas such as the Pacific Rim.

Japanese fashion designers opened couture houses in Paris and ready-to-wear houses in Paris, New York, and other major cities throughout the world. Hanae Mori was the first to bring her couture collection to Paris in 1977. Rei Kawakubo and Yohji Yamamoto followed with their launch in Paris in 1981 (Figure 19.2). Japan emerged as a world economic power and the major competitor to the United States in world markets.

In the 1990s, the once formidable Japanese economy suffered a severe deflation. Retail and

FIGURE 19.2 Rei Kawakubo at the opening of her Comme des Garçons shop in Henri Bendel in 1983. Kawakubo originally designed almost exclusively in tones of gray and black; she has since inserted touches of color into her work. (Iannaccone/WWD/© Conde Nast)

wholesale prices dropped drastically, real estate prices collapsed, retailers had to compete with cheap imports, and stocks dropped drastically in value. Consumer prices dropped but so did wages. There were some benefits to Japan's deflation. Housing became cheaper. Tariffs dropped and consequently imported food became cheaper. Discounting became more prevalent and discount stores multiplied. Deflation was the force in transforming Japan's economy.

Japanese fashion designers continued to be leaders both in luxury fashion and in ready to wear. Often their designs were described as cutting edge. Adolescent Japanese avidly followed the latest trends in Japanese street clothing. *Manga*, Japanese cartoons, and *anime*, Japanese animation (often of manga cartoons), led young Japanese to engage in *cosplay*, a combination of the words *costume* and *play*, which is dressing up as characters from manga and anime (Figure 19.3). Individuals in other countries became interested, and the practice of cosplay spread beyond Japan. In time, the word *cosplay* came to mean dressing as a character or wearing a costume. Elaborate costumes were created for attending cosplay conventions.

U.S. Political and Economic Developments

Ronald Reagan, former actor and governor of California who was elected president in 1980, endorsed the supply-side, or "trickle down," economic theory, which holds that cutting taxes for corporations and wealthy individuals benefits those lower down on the economic scale and revives the economy. Reagan advocated reduced government spending, an increase in the military budget, and lower tax rates. These lower tax rates did not produce enough revenue, however, resulting in unbalanced budgets and an enormous increase in the national debt. Reagan also instituted policies of deregulation, notably in the airlines and telephone companies, and relaxation of antitrust policies. Reagan's wife Nancy was much admired for her style yet criticized for her lavish spending habits and acceptance of a designer-donated wardrobe from the likes of Galanos, Adolfo, Bill Blass, and other American design heavyweights (Figure 19.4).

FIGURE 19.3 The practice of cosplay, which started in Japan, has spread around the world. Here a youth dressed in cosplay poses in Tokyo. (Kurita Kaku/Gamma-Rapho/Getty Images)

President George H. W. Bush, elected in 1988, was handicapped in fighting a recession, because of the Reagan administration's borrowing. Notable foreign policy events were an invasion of Panama and the Persian Gulf War, following the invasion of Kuwait by Iraq. Rising unemployment and economic recession helped Arkansas governor Bill Clinton defeat Bush in 1992.

Passage of the North American Free Trade Act (NAFTA), which reduced tariffs between the United States, Canada, and Mexico, was an early legislative victory. This agreement established the world's largest free-trade zone.

The Republicans swept to victory in the congressional election of 1994, capturing both houses of

FIGURE 19.4 Nancy Reagan, in her signature color red, and Princess Diana were closely watched for their wardrobe choices in the 1980s and 1990s. (Anwar Hussein/Getty Images)

on April 19, 1995, a bomb set off by Timothy McVeigh wrecked a federal building in Oklahoma City, killing 168, many of whom were children (Figure 19.5).

Energy and Environmental Issues

In 1990, Congress passed the Clean Air Act. Dangers to the environment continued to grow. Depletion of the ozone layer over the Antarctic and a small ozone hole over the Arctic were observed. Many scientists believe that global warming is increasing and caused by human activity. The need to decrease carbon dioxide emissions has been recognized internationally.

The environmental movement was probably responsible, at least in part, for a preference for natural fibers. On March 25, 1990, The *New York Times* published a front-page story with the headline, "The Green Movement in the Fashion World," which described how manufacturers and designers publicize their efforts on behalf of the environment.

FIGURE 19.5 President Bill Clinton and his wife Hillary Rodham Clinton plant a dogwood tree in front of White House in honor of victims of the Oklahoma City federal building terrorist bombing. (Dirck Halstead/The LIFE Images Collection/Getty Images)

Congress for the first time in 40 years. For the first time in 60 years, the welfare system was overhauled, and Congress curtailed unconditional federal cash assistance for the poor. Arguments between President Clinton and the Republicans over the budget, however, led to the federal government being shut down twice, which influenced national elections in 1996.

Helped by a booming stock market, low unemployment, and low interest rates, Bill Clinton won a second term. The Clinton presidency, however, was plagued by scandals about his personal life, which resulted in his impeachment. The Senate voted to acquit Clinton, and he remained in office.

The first terrorist attack within the borders of the United States came on February 25, 1993, when a bomb under the World Trade Center in New York City killed five people and injured more than a thousand. Then

FIGURE 19.6 Knitted cotton dresses, 1996, made from FoxFibre naturally colored cotton. These are two of the colors in which this fiber grows. (Courtesy of Ruth Huffman Designs, Dallas, TX)

Consumer support for environmentally sound products led to the cultivation and sale of naturally colored cottons that did not require dyeing, to the use of organic cotton grown without the use of pesticides, and to fabrics dyed with natural dyes obtained from plants, insects, and minerals (Figure 19.6). Polyester fibers made from recycled soda bottles began to appear in such varied products as T-shirts, baseball caps, and fleece fabrics for active wear and for cold-weather sports.

Animal rights activists began to campaign against wearing fur in the 1980s. The aggressive tactics of the antifur protesters, such as spraying women wearing fur coats with paint, spurred interest in synthetic pile fiber fabrics that simulated furs.

Disposable diapers came under environmental scrutiny. With the introduction of Pampers in 1961, increased numbers of parents used disposable diapers. Debate raged over the impact of massive numbers of disposable diapers in landfills, and some environmentally conscious parents switched to cloth diapers.

Disposal of used clothing in landfills, especially those from synthetic fabrics that are not biodegradable, was another issue that caused some environmentalists to stress recycling used clothing. Some consumers shopped at second-hand clothing stores, but this was often because of fashion interest in antique clothing or a desire to save money, rather than out of concern for the environment.

Business experts expressed the belief that the system of preparing clothing for different seasons had broken down because climate change was reducing the marked temperature differences between seasons. This, in turn, led consumers to stop buying clothing specific to particular seasons. Some major retailers hired climatologists to help them plan their collections and set the time for sales of previous-season merchandise.

The Changing American Family

The peak childbearing years for the baby boom generation came in the 1980s. As a result, children's clothing sales increased. The economic good times of the early 1980s were reflected in the willingness of affluent parents to spend lavishly for what *Newsweek* magazine called **kiddie couture**, and some designers of adult clothing started producing lines for children (Figure 19.7). Increasing numbers of manufacturers of adult clothing entered the children's clothing market through the 1990s.

Changes in the Roles of Women

The 1980s and 1990s saw increased participation and growth in higher paying occupations for women. In

FIGURE 19.7 High-priced, high-fashion clothes for children often were made with style elements similar to those of adults. (© Trinity Mirror/Mirrorpix/Alamy)

departments for clothing, although most manufacturers distinguished men's and women's sizes even in items that were visually identical. Along with major changes for women in career and lifestyle options came a more diffuse view of the social roles of men and women. As such, the taboo against wearing clothing styles traditionally assigned to the opposite sex broke down, and the social norms that required clear differences in men's and women's clothing eroded.

The Computer Revolution

Since World War II nothing has so affected life in the United States as the computer revolution. The uses of computers range from helping engineers design automobiles, buildings, airplanes, and textiles to enabling astronomers to develop theories about galaxies. Extensive computer applications in fashion design and manufacturing aid designers and make

the 1980s the fashion press noted a dichotomy in women's clothing, with conservative, tailored clothing for working hours and glamorous, feminine, and sexy clothing for leisure time. Men's and women's garments for business, called *dressing for success*, were also called **power suits** (Figure 19.8).

Clothing for men and women that was interchangeable in appearance—blue jeans, tailored shirts, T-shirts, sweatshirts, sweaters, blazers, running suits, and sneakers—was attributed by many to changing gender roles. The fashion press called such items **unisex clothing**. Some women shopped in menswear

FIGURE 19.8 Author John T. Molloy was one of the best-known promoters of "dress for success" looks in the 1980s. His suggestions of suit in matching dark fabric, a high-necked blouse, plain pumps, and an attaché case were popular. As the 1990s progressed, greater dressing options for business success were proposed. (Chinsee/WWD/© Conde Nast)

it possible for manufacturers to respond to or create changes in styles almost instantaneously.

With computers, retailers can work more efficiently with manufacturers through **quick response**, the name given to computer-based systems that permit rapid ordering, manufacture, and delivery of goods. Quick response relies on Universal Product Codes. These bar codes facilitate better communication between the producers and sellers of merchandise, ultimately allowing for quicker turnover of merchandise.

Computers also provide retailers with innovative sales techniques through computer imaging. Using this technique, consumers can see themselves in different fashions or hairstyles. The first **mass customization**, custom-fitted clothing produced through computer scanning, was sold in November 1994 by Levi Strauss. Computer software transmitted customers' body measurements to a factory where patterns were cut by robots to the individual's exact measurements and the garments were assembled. Orders were filled in about 3 weeks (Rifkin, 1994).

In the 1990s the potential of the computer increased when Americans discovered the Internet, formerly an obscure communications system or network of computers used chiefly by academics and military researchers. An important communications tool, the Internet serves as a source of information about fashion and provides opportunities to purchase apparel. Lands' End was one of the first apparel firms to enter "e-tailing" in the mid-1990s. The computer revolution and the Internet radically altered how businesses, governments, and industries function.

New Immigrants

A 1965 change in the immigration law had eliminated racially based barriers to immigration. There followed a surge of immigrants from Latin America and Asia, especially from Korea and the Philippines. The end of the Vietnam conflict brought immigrants from Laos, Cambodia, and Vietnam. After the Cold War, immigrants came from eastern Europe and the former Soviet Union. The 2000 census showed that the Hispanic population of the United States had grown to 35.5 million. As a result, many retailers tried to increase their appeal to Hispanic consumers. Between 1980 and 1999 ethnic influences appeared sporadically as fashion designers incorporated design elements from various cultures in their collections (Figure 19.9).

AIDS

Medical researchers of the 1980s grappled with what soon amounted to an epidemic: AIDS—acquired immune deficiency syndrome—a deficiency of the

FIGURE 19.9 Traditional clothing and textiles from various ethnic groups inspired designers. Yves Saint Laurent in his fall/winter collection of 1980–1981 chose to use a Peruvian-derived pattern in this evening dress. (Giannoni/WWD/© Conde Nast)

immune system resulting from infection with the human immunodeficiency virus, (HIV), which French and American researchers had identified by 1984 (Figure 19.10).

It is now believed that AIDS originated about 1959 in what was then the Belgian Congo in central Africa and that the virus, HIV, evolved from a disease found in chimpanzees. Somehow the virus crossed the barrier between species.

The disease is transmitted through sexual contact, blood transfusions, needles shared by drug addicts, accidental needle injuries, and from mother to unborn child. The spread of AIDS to epidemic proportions was the result of dramatic changes in sexual mores, increase in drug use, and increase in international travel.

In the 1980s AIDS became the leading cause of death in New York City among men ages 25 to 44. By 1996, tests of a new combination of drugs were

proving successful in forcing the AIDS virus into remission and giving patients a rebound in health. In tests using these drugs, some patients appeared to be entirely free of the virus after almost a year. The expensive new multidrug treatment is not yet proven to be a cure for AIDS.

The AIDS epidemic has had a devastating impact on the fashion industry. By 1996 a number of top designers (Halston, Angel Estrada, Perry Ellis, Willi Smith), as well as colleagues who were unknown to the public but worked in supporting roles in the fashion industry, were known to have died of AIDS, and there were rumors about the cause of death for still others.

The AIDS epidemic also resulted in economic problems for the industry. Investors were reluctant to provide backing for firms they saw as vulnerable to disruption from the loss of key personnel. This led the financial community to look more favorably on some of the firms headed by women designers, viewed as less likely to succumb to AIDS.

The fashion industry had at first been reluctant to speak out about AIDS because of the effect on business, but this changed. The Design Industries Foundation Fighting AIDS sponsors preventive education programs for those at high risk for the disease, assists with treatment and care services for people with HIV/AIDS, and works to advance public policy initiatives that add resources to private-sector efforts.

CHANGES IN THE FASHION INDUSTRY

The idea that that the fashion industry could no longer dictate styles to its customers had been growing for some time. Developments in the fashion industry between 1980 and 1999 ratified this proposition. Before the

FIGURE 19.10 The NAMES Project AIDS Memorial Quilt was conceived in honor of those lost to the disease and to promote AIDS awareness and HIV-prevention education. The quilt contains 48,000 panels with entries from every state and nearly 30 countries around the world. (© Richard Ellis/Alamy)

1970s, scholars who wrote about fashion generally agreed that fashion trends tended to begin with adoption of styles by the upper class elite, after which the styles trickled down to the less affluent. Often the affluent individuals who began fashions were themselves patrons of the haute couture designers. By the 1960s, when mainstream fashion began co-opting the styles of hippies and young protesters, the notion was taking hold that some fashion influences came from the bottom up.

Initially the number of influential street styles and the young style tribes who originated them (see Chapter 18, pages 548–550) were relatively few. But over the next decades, style tribes proliferated. Analysis of these groups for an exhibit of street style fashion at the Victoria and Albert Museum in 1996 showed that almost half of the groups came together as a result of an interest in some kind of music. The second most important interest bringing groups together was sports. Race, ethnicity, social class, political affiliation, ecological interests, sexual orientation, and drug habits united other groups. As their numbers increased, members easily recognized each other by the clothing they wore. Over time, some new style tribes grew out of other groups in a complex interconnected evolution (Crane, 2000). See Table 19.1, which describes some of the better known style tribes and Figure 19.11 for depictions of the dress of some style tribes.

By 1999, the variety of acceptable options in dress available to consumers was enormous. Clothes could be bought from sources ranging from the haute couture to thrift shops. Style tribes described by Polhemus (1994) and others were mostly adolescents and young adults. Steele (2000) pointed out that affluent adult followers of certain fashion designers (often called **fashionistas**) could also be seen as members of style tribes. This concept could be extended towards many other segments of the consuming public, for example, devoted catalogue customers for merchants such as L.L. Bean and Lands' End, or those who confined their shopping to particular TV networks such as QVC and the Home Shopping Network, or Internet sites (Figure 19.12).

FIGURE 19.11 Dress adopted by some of the more widely known style tribes. (a) Hippies, 1960s and after. (b) Punk, 1970s and after. (c) Goth, 1980s and after. (d) Hip-hop later 1980s and after. (Courtesy of Fairchild Publications, Inc.)

TABLE 19.1 Style Tribes and Their Impact on Mainstream Fashion

STYLE TRIBE	DATES ACTIVE	GENERAL DRESS CHARACTERISTICS	IMPACT ON MASS FASHION
Zooties	Late 1930s into early 1940s	Long jackets, high-cut baggy trousers, bow ties. Mostly adopted by young African Americans.	Disappeared as a result of WWII clothing restrictions. Revived in the early 1980s by some musical groups.
Beatniks	1950s	Originated with poet Jack Kerouac and friends, who wore casual clothes: workshirts, sweatshirts, jeans. Later, Americans followed French existentialists' preference for black. Women wore black tights under black skirts with ballet slippers, black knit blouses or striped knit shirts. Men wore black turtlenecks; grew small beards. Berets a preferred head covering.	Saint Laurent incorporated beatnik-style ideas in 1963, and Ralph Lauren used them as a basis for some designs in 1993.
Teddy Boys	1950s	Elements cut in style somewhat like men's suits of the Edwardian period (1900–1910).	Later, mods adopted similar types of styles for men.
Mods	1960s to early 1970s	Also known as neo-Edwardians.	In 1990s influenced Tom Ford for Gucci (1995–1996), Marc Jacobs, Anna Sui, Helmut Lang, Gianni Versace, Ralph Lauren, and Calvin Klein.
Hippies	1960s	Also incorporated psychedelics and body painting.	1993 Dolce & Gabbana collections included hippie-style beads, patchwork, fringes, and shawls. Kenzo and Saint Laurent also revived.
Skinheads	1970s	In Britain, started as fans of Jamaican music. Shaved heads, heavy boots, clothes associated with manual labor. In United States, skinheads were associated in the public mind with racism, conflict, and aggression. Evening clothes were influenced by mod styles.	Revival of interest in 1976. Dress clothes of skinhead women revived by "purist group of skinheads" in the early 1990s.
Rasta	1970s	Jamaican believers in Rastafarian religion wore large knitted tams; red, gold, and green shirts in the colors of the Ethiopian flag; dreadlocks. Reggae musicians helped spread the styles. As adopted, the styles often included bright-colored, tight clothing, worn with flashy accessories and gold jewelry.	Dreadlocks adopted by many African Americans and some white men and women as hairstyle in the 1990s and after. Designer Rifat Ozbek used Rastafarian dress as basis for clothes in 1991.
Glam	1970s	David Bowie and other musicians adopted androgynous costumes with ornate decorations and fabrics, accessories such as feather boas and platform shoes, dramatic makeup.	Fans of Glam rock stars copied their dress when attending concerts. Glam eventually branched into New Romantics and Goths.
Punks	Mid- to late-1970s and after	Originated with fans of punk rock music. Early punk followers dressed in original ways. Media stereotype developed of their dress as black leather and metal, ripped, safety pins as jewelry, brightly colored hair.	Designer Vivienne Westwood originated designs for early punk musicians and their followers. Has retained its popularity among a segment of young people. Punk revival evident in 1993. Designers Helmut Lang, Thierry Mugler, John Galliano, Jean Paul Gaultier, and Alaia all showed punk influenced styles in mid-1990s.
New Romantics	Late 1970s and early 1980s	Styles often derived from idealized and elegant view of earlier historic period styles in luxurious fabrics.	An offshoot of Glam styles. Certain elements of the more decorative aspects for men's Glam clothing were somewhat similar to typical New Romantic styles. Vivienne Westwood's Pirates Collection in 1981 drew on New Romantics style.

TABLE 19.1 Style Tribes and Their Impact on Mainstream Fashion (continued)

STYLE TRIBE	DATES ACTIVE	GENERAL DRESS CHARACTERISTICS	IMPACT ON MASS FASHION
Goths	1980s and after	Dress derived from literary and art versions of characters in Gothic novels and stories, in which vampires dress in black gowns and accessories. Charles Addams and the TV show *The Addams Family* were especially influential. In the 21st century Cybergoth is an offshoot of Goth.	An offshoot of Glam and New Romantics. John Galliano showed Goth-inspired clothes in his 1992 collection. Influenced Gaultier and Gucci styles. Cybergoth styles are based on futuristic and science fiction and incorporate PVC materials and fetish-style clothing.
Preppies	1979 to early 1980s and after	Based on styles worn at well-known preparatory schools: chinos, Lacoste polo shirts, blazers, D-ring belts, deck shoes.	As a conservative style, it caught on and became popular with both the young and young adults. African American model Tyson Beckford became the face of Ralph Lauren's Polo brand in 1994, influencing urban adoption of the preppy look.
Fashion fetish or pervs	1980s and early 1990s	Stereotypical ideas of dress worn by those involved in sadomasochistic sex led to introduction of leather, rubber, and vinyl clothes; tightly laced corsets; and stiletto heels.	Previously an underground group, some of these styles were incorporated into punk styles and later into Goth styles. Couture designers such as Gaultier, Versace, Mugler, Alaia, Westwood used as inspiration for collections.
Grunge	Late 1980s; early 1990s	Originated as clothes worn by laborers in Seattle (plaid shirts, T-shirts, blue jeans—casual and unkempt); picked up by musicians, surfers. This look of "put-on poverty" was adopted by grunge fans, who liked shapeless print dresses, torn jeans, faded denim vests, and plain shirts.	Designers Jacobs for Perry Ellis, Anna Sui, and others picked up styles c. 1993.
Hip-hop	Late 1980s and after	Origin in the South Bronx with an athletic, street, solo dance style known as break dancing. Boys were called B-boys (break boys) and girls, fly girls. Associated with rap music. Men wore baggy pants and football or baseball shirts, baseball caps turned backward, and high running shoes with untied shoe laces. Clothes were oversized, pants worn low on the waist. Jeweled clips ("grills") were worn on the teeth.	Hip-hop–inspired styles especially popular among the young. Most of the young wore baseball caps backward or do-rags. Designers such as Tommy Hilfiger did well with these design ideas. A number of popular hip-hop musicians branched out into designing and merchandising their own lines of clothing.
Ravers	Late 1980s and 1990s	Huge dance parties, called raves, held outdoors or indoors in large spaces. The drug Ecstasy became associated with raves. Dancers wore T-shirts with smiley faces, or tie-dyed, psychedelic prints, hippielike elements or functional clothes: T-shirts, shorts, sneakers, baseball caps.	Rave influences show up in designs of late 1990s by German designer Walter Van Beirendonck.
Cyberpunks	1990s	Clothing used leather, rubber, PVC, and incorporated technical hardware devices, cables, circuit boards, etc.	Gaultier, 1992–1993, incorporated Cyberpunk ideas in collection.
Emo	1980s and after	Came to wide notice in early 2000s. Adherents described as deeply emotional. Associated with drainpipe jeans for boys and girls, tight T-shirts, makeup.	Sometimes considered to be more fad than fashion.

Sources: De la Haye, A. and C. Dingwall, 1996, *Surfers, soulies, skinheads, & skaters*, Woodstock, NY: The Overlook Press; Polhemus, T., 1994, *Street style*, New York, NY: Thames and Hudson; Takamura Z., 1997, *Roots of street style*, Tokyo: Graphic-Sha.

Postmodernism

Some scholars believe that the movement away from a single predominant fashion ideal toward a variety of fashion segments can be explained by postmodernism, the name given to the culture of the present period by some artists, philosophers, and social scientists. Morgado (1996) explained that postmodernism has been applied to theories about the nature of present-day society, a style of expression in the arts, and certain cultural values and sensibilities. The following

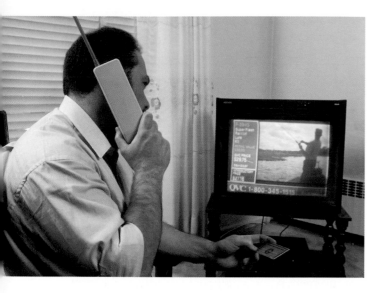

FIGURE 19.12 A man places an order with QVC, the television and online retailer, July 1, 1993, in New York City. The personal computer became essential in businesses, schools, and homes. (Yvonne Hemsey/Getty Images)

examples show how contemporary fashions can illustrate some of the elements of postmodern culture.

- *Rejection of authority.* The rise of street fashion as an influence on mainstream fashion, the absence of a single dominant fashion silhouette, and wearing casual dress in almost any situation are all said to illustrate the rejection of the authority of both social mores and the fashion establishment.
- *Cultural or ethnic groups with irreconcilable differences.* Styles based on ethnic and subcultural dress in both mainstream fashion and within subcultures play an increasingly important role in fashion.
- *The appropriation or juxtaposition of elements from different styles.* The tendency to combine items such as hiking boots with sheer dresses or turning functional objects such as safety pins into ornaments are some examples.
- *The use of symbols without reference to their traditional meanings.* Couturiers have designed high-fashion clothes based on the traditional dress of nuns, monks, and orthodox Jewish groups.

Elements of the Fashion System

Crane (2000) described how the systems of design, production, and distribution of fashions have changed

from 1980 to 1999. She stated that haute couture as a source of fashion inspiration has been replaced by three major categories of styles: luxury fashion design, industrial fashion, and street styles.

Luxury fashion, in this categorization, includes firms that are part of the haute couture and some of the more innovative and expensive ready-to-wear designers. Luxury fashion is not limited to Paris but can also be found in fashion centers such as New York, Milan, London, Tokyo, and other cities. American luxury fashion is rarely made to measure, but it is often sold, Crane said, via designer trunk shows. Trunk shows are held in various cities, attended by wealthy clients who see and try on the clothes. They are hosted by the designer, who can use these opportunities to develop a sense of the needs and wants of this market. Before his retirement, Bill Blass was famous for his use of trunk shows. Other designers have continued the practice.

Crane defined *industrial fashion* as fashion "created by manufacturers, which sell similar products to similar social groups in many different countries, as well as by smaller companies that confine themselves to a particular country or continent" (135). Firms such as Ralph Lauren, Liz Claiborne, and Tommy Hilfiger fall into this category.

Street styles are those originated by urban subcultures or style tribes. Media attention helps spread styles that seem to arise spontaneously or that are adopted by a small group. For example, urban youth in places such as the South Bronx used to wear certain kinds of clothes for street performances of break dancing and rapping. These styles were copied by teens in other places, especially after hip-hop music became popular. In the 1990s Tokyo became known for constant innovation in street styles. Young Japanese avidly participated in fashion that appeared on the street, and items were quickly manufactured and sold by small producers. Japanese newsstands sold weekly newspapers that reported "as seen on the street" fashions, and western fashion entrepreneurs visited Tokyo to observe the fashion scene.

The interconnections between luxury fashion, industrial fashion, and street styles cannot be ignored.

For example, ideas originating in Tokyo street fashion may show up on the runways of Paris haute couture shows or in clothes produced by industrial fashion firms.

The Role of the Haute Couture

Until the 1960s, the Paris haute couture was the undisputed pinnacle of made-to-measure clothing. Its designs set the style trends. (See Chapter 17, pages 513–514, for a description of the structure and functions of haute couture.) This position was challenged during the social revolution of the 1960s when prêt-à-porter (ready-to-wear) designs became more influential. Fashion pundits proclaimed the death of the couture. Morris (1982) summarized this viewpoint, saying, "During the era of miniskirts, T-shirts, and blue jeans, a couture designer seemed as obsolete as a blacksmith" (174).

The couture did not disappear, although its influence waned in the 1970s. By the early 1980s, the couture had made something of a comeback. Wealthy women from oil-producing countries provided a new clientele able to afford couture clothing. Due to Muslim dress restrictions, however, many women from Arab states wore these couture creations only in the privacy of their homes.

FIGURE 19.13 Elements of popular styles can be seen in the 1998 Oscar de la Renta collection, such as tighter fitting silhouettes, an emphasis on the shoulders, sheer fabrics, and sequins. (Chinsee/WWD/© Conde Nast)

The good economic times of the Reagan years (1980–1988) made affluence socially acceptable, and lavish clothing, especially for evening wear, was prominently featured in the fashion press. Designer Christian Lacroix opened a new couture house in 1987, and Oscar de la Renta proposed luxurious fabrics for evening wear (Figure 19.13). Even though the affluent were patronizing the couture, the emphasis of couture designers shifted. In their shows couturiers did not try to compete with prêt-à-porter, but rather focused on more elaborate wear.

Although fashion no longer proposed only one way of dressing, the reaction of fashion designers to this change differed enormously. It was almost as though two divergent schools of thought developed regarding design. Some designers came to be considered classicists. Others saw fashion as a plaything, available for people to use (Figure 19.14). Most couturiers participated in both the couture and ready-to-wear. As Spindler (1996) commented, "The client list [of couture houses] has dwindled drastically, and most see high fashion only as an engine to drive the other businesses at couture houses: ready-to-wear apparel, perfumes, and makeup licenses" (D2).

Changes in the business organization of luxury fashion design also affected fashion. The two most important transformations were the acquisition of couture and ready-to-wear houses by large businesses (conglomerates) and global marketing. In the new world of fashion, it is often most important for a design firm to gain media attention that will help promote not the designs shown on runways but a wide variety of auxiliary products sold worldwide. The more extreme designs seen on the runway often serve as the basis for more realistic garments (Figure 19.15).

Ready-to-Wear

Many of the changes in fashion between 1980 and 1999 came from the ready-to-wear segment of the fashion industry.

The United States

Americans had, by the 1980s, become accustomed to buying ready-to-wear clothes designed by famous

a   b

FIGURE 19.14 The contrast in designer attitudes toward fashion is evident in the difference in these two designs for men's suits. On the left (a), the classic style favored by Armani (*Daily News Record*, September 1, 1996, courtesy of Fairchild Publications, Inc.); on the right (b), a theatrical, three-piece striped suit by Gaultier (*Daily News Record*, September 15, 1994, courtesy of Fairchild Publications, Inc.)

American as well as foreign designers, many of whom had their own businesses. Department stores organized sales floors according to designers or manufacturers so that customers could easily find the clothes from their favorite fashion houses. Specialty chains such as Gap, the Limited, and Talbots also thrived. In the 1990s, department stores increased the design and production of private-label merchandise. Table 19.2 lists some of the major American designers active from the 1980s to 1999.

France

The prêt-à-porter firms established in the 1960s flourished. Many were connected with established couture houses and the couturiers designed the lines. Franchised boutiques sold these ready-to-wear products in cities around the world. Manufacturers purchased licenses to use the couture name on diverse items such as handbags, jewelry, and household linens.

Other designers and firms emerged who created only prêt-à-porter lines. Many of these firms were not French but participated in the French shows because of the attention paid to the two showings each year in Paris. French firms also took part in trade shows in other countries.

Italy

Italians continued to be a strong presence in ready-to-wear and in the couture. Firms such as Biagiotti, Gianfranco Ferre, Versace, Krizia, Missoni, Dolce & Gabbana, Prada, and Soprani in women's wear; Giorgio Armani in menswear and women's wear; Fendi in furs; and Ferragamo and Gucci in leather products developed international reputations for fine design, quality, and workmanship.

FIGURE 19.15 Many runway styles were not likely to appear on the street as shown, such as this dress from the 1997 Givenchy haute couture line. (© Condé Nast Archive/Corbis)

London

In the 1980s British fashion diversified. Unconventional and innovative styles, many derived from street fashions, once again appeared along with the classics. Princess Diana, wife of the heir to the British throne, and Sarah Ferguson, the Duchess of York, helped draw attention to British fashion designers through their patronage. British design got attention in 1996 when British designers were selected as head couturiers at Dior and Givenchy.

Japan

In the 1980s Japan emerged as a major fashion center. A number of Japanese designers, some already internationally known, others relatively unknown outside of Japan, showed their lines at the 1983 Paris prêt-à-porter show. Many of the Japanese designs were radically different from other contemporary fashions and immediately stimulated interest and wide press coverage. *Gentlemen's Quarterly* noted in May 1984 that "Japanese fashion is different. These are clothes that conform to no fashion standards. They seek to abolish form. They hang loosely on the body in oversized, unusual silhouettes. The colors are almost always monochromatic or black" ("Inside Fashion," 1984).

The best-known designers were Issey Miyake, Yohji Yamamoto, Mitsuhiro Matsuda, and Rei Kawakubo. Kawakubo called her firm *Comme des Garçons* (French for "like the boys") and reactions to her designs and those of other innovators ranged from enthusiastic endorsements of the "new wave" to derisive labeling of the loose, dark, unfitted clothes as "bag lady styles."

Throughout the 1980s and the 1990s the Japanese continued to garner attention for both menswear and women's wear. After initially showing extreme styles, many firms became more conservative and more commercial, with the *Daily News Record* reporting in 1989 that many Japanese designers had moved away from idiosyncratic looks in favor of a more wearable approach to design (Godfrey, 1989). At the same time, designers such as Miyake and Kawakubo continued to innovate truly individual styles (Figure 19.16). Table 19.3 lists some major foreign ready-to-wear and couture designers active in the period from 1980 to 1999.

Manufacturing

Many American manufacturers responded to the increasing globalization of the industry by having their merchandise assembled in developing countries.

TABLE 19.2 Prominent European and Asian Designers

DESIGNER	WORKING IN	NOTABLE CHARACTERISTICS OF DESIGNS OR CAREER
ITALIAN DESIGNERS		
Giorgio Armani (1934–)	Ready-to-wear: Showed own menswear collection: 1974; women's wear in 1975.	Known for fine tailoring, easy, comfortable designs. A retrospective exhibit of his work was shown at the Guggenheim Art Museum in New York in 2000.
Gianfranco Ferré (1945–2007)	Ready-to-wear: Established own firm: 1974. Couture: served as designer for Dior from 1989 to 1996.	Brought background in architecture to his designs; high standard of tailoring. His firm continues to produce ready-to-wear in Italy.
Domenico Dolce (1958–) and Stefano Gabbana (1962–)	Ready-to-wear: Focused on womenswear starting in 1985, added knitwear in 1987, beachwear in 1989, menswear in 1990, and a lower priced collection called D&G in 1994.	Described as combining modern styles with romantic and historic references.
Miuccia Prada (1950–)	Ready-to-wear: First showed in 1989. Less expensive collection called Miu-Miu, and men's clothes and accessories.	Clothes said to be "supremely comfortable," and "coming to life on the body."
Gianni Versace (1946–1997) and Donatella Versace (1956–)	Ready-to-wear: First menswear collection: 1979; women's wear later. Since his death in 1997, Gianni's sister Donatella has successfully served as style and image director of the firm.	Known for innovative designs in leather and other fabrics. Donatella works "in the Versace mode of bold prints and forthright sexiness."
FRENCH DESIGNERS		
Azzedine Alaïa (1935–)	Ready-to-wear: Shows only sporadically.	Known for clinging, sexy styles. Helped initiate this trend in early 1980s. Is considered a highly innovative designer.
Jean-Paul Gaultier (1952–)	Ready-to-wear, couture. Creative designer of Hermès from 2003–2010.	Shows nonconformist, exaggerated designs. In 2013–2014, the Montreal Museum of Art organized the exhibit "The Fashion World of Jean-Paul Gaultier: From the Sidewalk to the Catwalk."
Nicolas Ghesquière (1972–)	Couture: Head designer at Balenciaga from 1997 to 2012; from 2013 creative director of the House of Louis Vuitton	Considered to be a young designer to be watched, a "leader of the avant-garde."
Christian Lacroix (1951–)	Couture: Designer for Patou 1981–1987; operated own house 1987–2009; showed 18 couture pieces inspired by Schiaparelli in 2013. Also does ready-to-wear and was creative director for Pucci 2002–2005.	Introduced wide-skirted short gowns in mid-1980s, known for theatrical styles.
Karl Lagerfeld (1939–)	Couture and ready-to-wear: Designs for Chanel (from 1982) and also under his own name.	Tremendously versatile designer. Also designs furs of Italian firm, Fendi.
Thierry Mugler (1946–)	Ready-to-wear: Designed under own label after 1973. Firm closed in 2002. Perfume creator. Designed costumes for Beyoncé's "I Am. . . . Sasha Fierce" world tour.	First known for designs with very broad shoulders, narrow waists. His fashion shows often were considered outrageous.
Sonia Rykiel (1930–)	Ready-to-wear: Opened own boutique, 1968. Introduced shoes and accessories in 1992; Sonia Rykiel Maison debuts 2003.	Especially well known for sweaterlike designs. Later added menswear and children's wear.
ENGLISH DESIGNERS		
Hussein Chalayan (1970–)	Ready-to-wear. Winning awards from early in his career, he added a menswear line in 2002. Has designed or served as artistic director for a number of companies.	His shows are noted for being based on concepts and themes that reflect the designer's thinking about complex ideas.
John Galliano (1960–)	Ready-to-wear: London in the 1980s. Couture: chief designer at Givenchy for couture and ready-to-wear 1995; moved to Dior in 1996. Dismissed from Dior in 2011 due to anti-Semitic and racist remarks.	Initially known for uninhibited, avant-garde styles; evolved to more sophisticated clothing made with great skill.

TABLE 19.2 Prominent European and Asian Designers (continued)

DESIGNER	WORKING IN	NOTABLE CHARACTERISTICS OF DESIGNS OR CAREER
ENGLISH DESIGNERS (CONTINUED)		
Katherine Hamnett (1947–)	Ready-to-wear, founded 1979.	After opening her own business she joined Chloe and later went to Gucci where the line carried her name. She also designs a line of sports clothes for Adidas. Her designs have been described as "figure loving."
Stephen Jones (1957–)	Milliner, founded 1980.	Known for provocative shows and linear tailoring.
Stella McCartney (1971–)	Ready-to-wear designer. McCartney graduated from the design school Central Saint Martins. Named creative director of Chloe 1997. Designed own line 2001; Collection for H&M in 2005; Stella McCartney for GapKids and babyGap debuted in 2009.	Known for original and sometimes eccentric designs. Incorporated punk designs in mid-1970s.
Alexander McQueen (1970–2010)	Ready-to-wear: London. Couture: Named to succeed Galliano at Givenchy in 1996. By 2001, he had left Givenchy and was showing under his own name.	Often working with street style and clothes such as punk, new romantic, fetish styles.
BELGIAN AND GERMAN DESIGNERS		
Martin Margiela (1957–)	Ready-to-wear: Beginning in the 1980s. Head designer at Hermès from 1997 to 2003. Collaboration with H&M in 2012.	Belgian "fashion iconoclast" who makes unconventional clothes. Known for superb tailoring skills; "deconstructionist" styles with seams on outside, etc.
Jil Sander (1943–)	Ready-to-wear; first collection under own label in 1973. Firm bought by Prada in 1999. She left firm a year later and returned in 2003–2004, and then 2012–2012. In 2009 she began a fashion consultancy.	German "minimalist" with emphasis on "design without decoration," "lines and cuts out of the ordinary," and high quality.
Dries Van Noten (1958–)	Initial showing was of menswear. Has since added women's and children's. In 1991 he presented his first runway show of men's ready-to-wear in Paris, his women's wear line a year later. Now has many retail outlets in major cities worldwide.	His designs are described as "simple and sophisticated at the same time."
JAPANESE DESIGNERS		
Rei Kawakubo (1942–)	Ready-to-wear: Showed in Tokyo, 1975; Paris, 1981. Firm is named Comme des Garçons.	One of Japanese designers to make major impact in Paris in early 1980s. Designs are often asymmetrical in shape.
Kenzo (1945–)	Ready-to-wear: Notable in Paris from early 1970s. He retired in 1999 and his firm continues with new designers.	"Designs based on traditional Japanese clothing and made in spirited combinations of textures and patterns."
Issey Miyake (1938–)	Ready-to-wear: Opened own firm in Tokyo, 1970 after studying in Paris; first showing in Paris, 1973. Retired in 1997, but firm continues under other design leadership.	"Combines Japanese attitudes of fashion with exotic fabrics of his own designs."
Hanae Mori (1925–)	Couture and ready-to-wear: well-established in Japan before showing couture collection in Paris in 1977. The firm suffered from the economic downturn in Japan and filed for bankruptcy in 2001.	Notable aspects of her designs are "unusual and beautiful" fabrics with "Japanese feminine motifs . . . evening and at home wear."
Yohji Yamamoto (1943–)	Ready-to-wear: First collection shown in Tokyo in 1976 and in Paris in 1981.	One of Japanese designers to make major impact in Paris in early 80's. Designs with "Japanese sensibility and tradition."

Information about designers already listed in Table 18.2 (see pages 560–561) who continued to be active for all or part of this period is not included in this table.

All quotes from Calasibetta, C. M. (1988). *The Fairchild dictionary of fashion* (2nd ed.). New York, NY: Fairchild Publications; Tortora, P. G., & Keiser, S. J. (2013) *The Fairchild dictionary of fashion* (4th ed.). New York, NY: Fairchild Publications; Stegemeyer, A. (1996). *Who's who in fashion* (3rd ed.). New York, NY: Fairchild Publications; and Stegemeyer, A. (2004). *Who's who in fashion* (4th ed.). New York, NY: Fairchild Publications.

FIGURE 19.16 By 1994 Japanese designers had left the dark designs with which they first came on the fashion scene. Issey Miyake created the "Flying Saucer Dress" in colorful, pleated, polyester. When not in use, the dress could be stored collapsed in accordion-pleated form. (Pierre Verdy/AFP/Getty Images)

Manufacturers moved production off-shore where wages remained lower than U.S. levels. Initially launched in 1983, and expanded in 2000, the Caribbean Basin Initiative allowed duty-free merchandise from Central America and in the Caribbean to enter the United States.

Off-shore production changed apparel manufacturing. In the past, companies manufactured only those styles that were ordered by retail store buyers. Under the foreign production system, orders must be placed before manufacturers know which styles will be most popular, so it becomes especially important for the company to research its customers' preferences carefully. A representative of Liz Claiborne (Daria, 1990, 139) explained,

If we have a sweater on the line and we own ten thousand units of that sweater, and people want to buy fifty thousand units, we can't supply it. We're stuck. On the other hand, if everyone hates it, we're in big trouble.

The Crafted with Pride in USA Council was formed in 1984 to promote domestically manufactured textiles and apparel; however, free-trade agreements continued to stimulate non-U.S. production.

Changes that had been made in 1994 in the General Agreement on Tariffs and Trade (GATT) treaty that regulated imports had mandated a gradual termination of all quotas for imports. At that time predictions were being made that domestic apparel production would be dramatically affected. American apparel manufacturers also expected to see Mexico increase its share of ready-to-wear clothing manufacturing at the expense of domestic production as a result of NAFTA. However, China took much of the business that had been expected to go to Mexico.

Merchandising

Merchandising practices had become as diverse as apparel styles. Beginning in the 1960s and early 1970s small boutiques popped up selling craft and creative fashions. Other boutiques with specialized style orientations appeared in towns and cities across the country. This led many department stores to organize sales floors into small boutiques that featured the clothing of one designer or firm, such as Ralph Lauren or Liz Claiborne. American consumers also purchased clothing from "off-price" retailers (fashion apparel discounters), factory outlets or outlet malls for particular manufacturers, and an ever-increasing number of mail-order outlets. **Bridge lines**, lines at the upper end of the apparel price range and made with fewer details and less expensive fabrics than designer clothing (such as DKNY) appealed particularly to executive women.

Vintage Clothing Used clothing stores had been patronized first by hippies in the 1960s and later by other shoppers who sought "vintage" clothing. Sometimes fashion trends started when shoppers

TABLE 19.3 Prominent American Designers

DESIGNER	AFFILIATED FIRM	NOTABLE CHARACTERISTICS
Liz Claiborne (1929–2007)	Established Liz Claiborne Inc. in 1976. Retired from the company, which continues, in 1989.	Orginally focused on sportswear; expanded to dresses and children's wear. "Philosophy: Simple and uncomplicated designs of mix-and-match separates" in moderate price range.
Sean Combs (1979–)	Created Sean John label in 1998.	Sean Combs, a musician and music entrepreneur, entered design with clothes geared to teens and young adults. Between then and 2003, he earned a number of fashion awards and has become very successful.
Perry Ellis (1940–1986)	Perry Ellis Sportswear established in 1978; Perry Ellis menswear in 1980. Name continues to be licensed in United States and abroad.	Designs described as "young, adventurous, spirited; use of natural fabrics." Designed wide variety of apparel and household textiles.
Eileen Fisher (1950–)	Eileen Fisher, 1984	"Comfortable, loose-fitting separates in natural fabrics with a focus on texture rather than pattern. Committed to fair trade and sustainability issues."
Tom Ford (1962–)	After working at Perry Ellis and other firms, joined Gucci in 1990 and brought clothing design to this firm, which had been mostly leather goods. In 1999 added the post of design director at Yves Saint Laurent. Ford left these positions in 2003 and 2004. Launched Tom Ford Brand in 2005, which distributes menswear, eyewear, and beauty products.	In positions at Gucci and Saint Laurent, Ford was responsible for overseeing design, product development, choosing designers, and the advertising campaigns. Seen as having revitalized the Gucci brand.
Carolina Herrera (1939–)	Established firm in 1981; did her first fur collection for Revillon in 1984, did lower priced ready-to-wear called CH in 1996.	Makes clothes to order for some private clients. Known for elegant clothes. Designed Caroline Kennedy's wedding dress.
Tommy Hilfiger (1952–)	Entered fashion design from retailing, began to design in 1979 and showed under own label in 1984.	Began with styles for men; gained a loyal following among rap and hip-hop musicians and their fans. He expanded into clothing for women, children, and plus sizes.
Marc Jacobs (1964–)	Managed own firm 1986–1988; joined Perry Ellis 1986–1983; showed under his own name after 1994. Artistic director at Louis Vuitton 1997–2013.	Considered a "design prodigy" who was immediately successful in building a reputation as a highly original young designer.
Betsey Johnson (1942–)	Designed for various firms; opened boutique with friends, Betsey, Bunky & Nini (1969); Betsey Johnson Inc. 1978.	Unique and original styles, in particular known for "Basic Betsey," described as "a limp, clinging T-shirt dress in mini, midi, and maxi lengths."
Norma Kamali (1945–)	Established boutique and company called OMO (On My Own) in 1978.	Produces innovative designs for wide variety of prices and markets. Especially known for bathing suit designs and garments made of sweatshirt-type fabric.
Donna Karan (1948–)	After designing for Anne Klein, established own firm and showed first independent collection in 1985. Designs own accessories. Expanded to less expensive line, DKNY, in 1988.	Influential designer in the 1980s and after. Made particular impact with clothes for successful professional women.
Michael Kors (1959–)	Began designing for well-known New York boutique. Opened own ready-to-wear label and in 1997 began designing for Parisian fashion house Celine. He left to focus on his own brand in 2003.	Winner of a number of design awards. Especially known for what has been called "casual chic" styles.
Nanette Lepore (1958–)	Nanette Lepore, 1992	Colorfully patterned clothes described as "free-spirited."

TABLE 19.3 Prominent American Designers (continued)

DESIGNER	AFFILIATED FIRM	NOTABLE CHARACTERISTICS
Mary McFadden (1936–)	Formed Mary McFadden, Inc., in 1976.	Known for designs that utilize unusual fabrics, fine pleating reminiscent of Fortuny, quilting.
Isaac Mizrahi (1961–)	Worked at Perry Ellis, Jeffrey Banks, and Calvin Klein before forming own business in 1985. Closed his business in 1998, worked in television and theater, and reentered fashion design in 2003 doing a lower priced line for Target.	Specialized in luxury sportswear for women and beginning in 1990 for men also. Designs were considered inventive, using unexpected colors and fabrics, while also being comfortable. The 1995 movie *Unzipped* documented his creative process.
Zac Posen (1980–)	Started by making custom designs for private customers, Posen's work was enthusiastically received with his first ready-to-wear show in New York in 2002. Has created a line for Target.	Posen designed youthful clothes with sophistication.
Ralph Rucci (1957–)	Opened Chado Ralph Rucci in 1994.	Invited in 2002 to show in Paris by the Chambre Syndicale, the first American honored this way in 60 years.
Willi Smith (1948–1987)	WilliWear Men, 1978.	Quoted as saying, "People want real clothes. I don't think people want to walk around looking like statements with their shoulders out to there." Introduced graffiti-inspired designs.
Anna Sui (1955–)	Stylist and designer in 1970s, own line marketed in 1980. First runway show in 1991.	Clothes described as a "mixture of hip and haute, romance, and raunch." Clothes priced moderately so that young customers can afford them.
Vivienne Tam (1957–)	Launched first collection in 1982; Vivienne Tam, 1993.	1995 collection of Chairman Mao Tse-tung printed garments caused controversy; asked by computer giant Hewlett Packard to design the first-ever "virtual digital clutch" in 2008.

Information about designers already listed in Table 18.2 (see pages 560–561) who continued to be active for all or part of this period is not included in this table.

All quotes and material from Calasibetta, C. M. (1988). *The Fairchild dictionary of fashion* (2nd ed.). New York, NY: Fairchild Publications; Calasibetta, C. M., & Tortora, P. (2003). *The Fairchild dictionary of fashion* (3rd ed.). New York, NY: Fairchild Publications; Stegemeyer, A. (1996). *Who's who in fashion* (3rd ed.). New York, NY: Fairchild Publications; and Stegemeyer, A. (2004). *Who's who in fashion* (4th ed.). New York, NY: Fairchild Publications.

found designer styles in resale clothing stores that were, in turn, manufactured in new, contemporary versions. Some customers who valued quality and excellent workmanship shopped for vintage designer clothes, often paying more than $1,000 for garments in good condition. Stores that sold used clothing ranged from expensive boutiques to low-cost thrift shops.

An active overseas market for used blue jeans developed. An August 1994 *New York Times* article described the trade in Levi's **501 jeans**. (The number 501 was the lot number given to jeans in 1890 by the manufacturer.) Depending on quality and type, used 501s cost as much as $2,000 in Japan for a pair of "hidden rivets" in good condition (Hofmeister, 1994).

Hidden rivet jeans, made between 1937 and about 1960, have rivets hidden inside the pockets.

New Methods of Selling By the 1990s competition from off-price, discount, and factory-outlet stores, together with ill-advised financing and management decisions, led to the disappearance of many old and well-established department store chains. Catalogues proliferated. TV shopping channels and the Internet were other sources of apparel.

The Growing Teen Market The baby boom generation continued to shape society, but generation X, individuals born from the mid-1960s to 1980, exercised tremendous power in the marketplace. This market, which included teenagers in the 1980s and 1990s as well as a new segment of the children's market called tweens (approximately ages 7 to 14), played an increasingly important role in retailing. Trying to capture this market was not easy, however. Teens tended to be fickle and capricious in their tastes. They got their fashion information from celebrities such as rappers and athletes, magazines, television—most notably MTV—music, and peers. Their loyalty to brands fluctuated, although labels associated with pop music stars did well (see Contemporary Comments 19.1).

The Prominence of Labels

Designer labels for men's clothes had become a selling point by the 1980s. Italian styles, especially those by Giorgio Armani, were widely copied. Japanese designers created men's as well as women's fashions in the early 1980s. By the 1990s, lines of clothing for men carrying designer labels were available in everything from suits and coats to active sportswear and accessories.

Whole stores were devoted to licensed goods from individual companies, such as Disney. Licensing and logos were so important in children's clothing that trade magazines devoted monthly sections to news about licensed goods (see Illustrated Table 19.4, pages 644–645).

In spite of the fragmentation of the fashion market, a number of very successful designers and manufacturers who emerged in the affluent 1980s were in serious financial difficulty by the late 1990s. In her book, *Wall Street Journal* reporter Teri Agins (1999) chronicled the difficulties experienced by many leading fashion industry firms. She identified four trends contributing to the changes in the fashion industry: the movement of women away from fashionable dress and toward practical clothes for their work and lifestyles; the trend toward more casual dress; the devaluation of designer labels; and the success of some designers and manufacturers in focusing on clothes that customers were willing to buy.

FASHION INFLUENCES

Fashion influences of the period derived from historical looks, social groups, and street styles. **Retro**, short for retrospective, styles took their inspiration from the past. Many designers of the 1980s and 1990s looked back, not ahead. Milbank (1989) catalogued revivals in the decade of the 1980s of bustles and crinolines (see Figure 19.15); turn-of-the-century camisoles and petticoats; long hobble skirts; Jazz Age drop-waist chemises; Depression-era looks; World War II large shoulders; 1950s bustiers, toreador pants, and off-the-shoulder stoles; and sheath dresses and minis in Day-Glo colors from the 1960s. In 1995 mod styles returned; designers of 1996 created flapper dresses and Empire waistlines.

Social Groups

Both trickle-down and bottom-up origins for fashion could be seen in the 1980s and 1990s.

The Affluent

Political and Social Elites   For centuries, royal families had influenced fashions, and these individuals continued to capture the imagination of the public, especially when romance was involved. The engagement and 1981 wedding of Prince Charles of England to Lady Diana Spencer thrust "Princess Di" into the fashion spotlight (Figure 19.17). Not only did imitations of her wedding dress become instant best sellers in bridal wear, but the press also kept a running commentary on her wardrobe throughout the 1980s. When Prince Andrew married Sarah Ferguson in 1986, the bride wore a dress with back fullness, a feature that then became fashionable.

After Ronald Reagan's election as president of the United States in 1980, social activities at the White House provided a stage for the display of lavish fashions. Like Jackie Kennedy before her, Nancy Reagan was celebrated for her sophisticated fashion choices but also much criticized for the amount of money she spent on clothing. Neither Barbara Bush, Hillary Clinton, nor Laura Bush caught the

Contemporary Comments 19.1

TWEEN SHOPPING

The importance of the tween and younger market is explained in this New York Times *article written by Ruth La Ferla.*

Chantal William, the owner of the G. C. William boutique on Madison Avenue near 85th Street, looked on in amusement the other day as Romy Schreiber breezed in, her fashion antennae twitching. As Ms. Williams recalled, no sooner had her client crossed the threshold than she made a beeline for a rack of little black dresses, pleading to try on a sleeveless model sparkling with bead. "I picked it out myself, it was my style," Ms. Schreiber said later.

Pressed to define that style, she fumbled for the right word, setting on "cool," an adjective she applied to other items on her most-wanted list, which ran from twin sets and pendant chokers to long skinny skirts, and bell-bottoms and tiny kilts like one she had just acquired by Burberry. Ms. Schreiber also obligingly listed her favorite makes and models—Calvin Klein, DKNY, Kate Moss, and Cindy Crawford—chanting their names in the sing-song rhythm of a small girl skipping rope.

Ms. Schreiber is 9. At an age when many of her contemporaries are decked out in overalls and box-pleated skirts, her own hyper-hip fashion choices conjure up an image that's two parts Posh Spice, one part Diana, the Princess of Wales.

She would recognize a kindred spirit in Kristina Obermeier, 10, who was spied perusing the racks in Saks Fifth Avenue's girls' department. With her blonde hair pulled back in a chignon like her idol, the Olympic figure skater Tara Lipinski, Kristina streaked toward the DKNY rack, leaving her mother in the dust. She gazed Frisbee-eyed at a calf-length column-shaped jumper that could easily pass muster at her parochial school but flirted with fashion just the same. "It's black and I love to wear black," she said, with the authority of a budding style maven. "It goes with everything."

Both girls cultivate a look poised at fashion's cutting edge. Only a few years ago, it would have marked them as members of a hip elite, their tastes outside the mainstream. But to hear the experts tell it, youngest fashion consumers, age 10 and under, represent a huge market, whose profile is rapidly shifting, said Traci Mitchell, the executive editor of *Children's Business*, a fashion trade monthly.

"The majority of little girls want to look grown up and fashion conscious—it's a big trend," Ms. Mitchell said, adding that although parents hold the purse strings, their style-savvy offspring are increasingly making the buying decisions.

Copyright © "Ex/Chic Little Numbers: The Hipless Elite." 1998 by the New York Times Co. Reprinted with permission.

imagination of the fashion press. Hillary Clinton presented conservative fashion choices, while Laura Bush's preferences might be characterized as simple and understated.

Yuppies and Preppies The booming economy of the early 1980s made the acquisition of high socioeconomic status both desirable and possible for many young people. Until the stock market crash had attended before college. The preppy look stressed classic tweed blazers, conservatively cut skirts or trousers, tailored blouses or shirts, and high-quality leather loafers, oxfords, or pumps (Figure 19.18).

Street Styles

African-American Style For a time, the African-inspired fashions that had made headlines in the 1960s were out of the news. In the late 1980s African-influenced styles were back, with much of the impetus for these fashions coming from African-American, inner-city youth and from the rap musicians seen on MTV. They began the practice of wearing Adidas sneakers or high tops with the laces untied, oversized T-shirts, huge gold earrings, and gold chains. They originated the fade, a hairstyle in which the hair was cut very short on the sides, and long on top, and they began to have names, words, or designs shaved on the scalp. When the rock group Public Enemy introduced the song *Black Is Back*, there was a return to black consciousness, and young African Americans began wearing African-inspired, round, flat-

FIGURE 19.17 Prince Charles and Princess Diana on their wedding day, July 29, 1981. (© Trinity Mirror/Mirrorpix/Alamy)

of 1987, yuppies (the nickname applied to *y*oung, *u*pwardly mobile *p*rofessionals who worked in fields such as law and business) strove to acquire high-status possessions. Male yuppies wore Italian double-breasted power suits to work, and female yuppies donned similarly cut women's versions.

Affluent students in Ivy League colleges, who would become yuppies after graduation, and their imitators wore **preppy** styles, a name derived from the private preparatory schools many of these students

FIGURE 19.18 American designers such as Ralph Lauren, Perry Ellis, and Calvin Klein were known for their separates in natural fibers and mixtures of textures. (Chinsee/WWD/© Conde Nast)

topped crown hats and leather medallions with maps of Africa in the colors of African or West Indian countries that were layered four or five at a time over T-shirts (Figure 19.19).

Kente cloth, a traditional, woven fabric that could also be printed, was used in items ranging from dresses to umbrellas. By the 1990s, hip-hop music fans, both white and African American, were carrying leather knapsacks and wearing oversized, baggy pants, matching football or baseball shirts, baseball caps facing backward, and unlaced running shoes. **Dreadlocks**, long hair arranged in many long, hanging twists, were worn by Rastafarian (a religious sect) reggae musicians from Jamaica; some young African-American and white men and women adopted these styles.

Body Piercing and Tattooing Some style tribes incorporated body piercing and tattooing as elements of their dress. Other individuals called themselves *modern primitives* and chose to adopt these forms of ornamentation as a kind of tribute to "traditional peoples" (see Global Connections). By the 1990s and after, body piercing and tattooing were fashionable for both women and men. The scale of tattoos ranged from small decorations not visible to the public to tattoos covering almost all of the body. For those who wanted to participate in the style temporarily, removable imitation tattoos were available.

In the 1990s, many young people were wearing multiple earrings in several piercings in the same ear. For some, adding jewelry to other parts of the body (tongue, nose, lips, navel, nipples, and private areas) was appealing. Jewelry worn in these areas is known as **body jewelry** (Figure 19.20).

FIGURE 19.19 Through the medium of MTV, musical groups such as Salt-N-Pepa broadcast trends of urban America to more rural areas. (Janette Beckman/Getty Images)

FIGURE 19.20 What began with wearing pierced earrings by women and men eventually became a fashion for wearing a wide variety of body jewelry. (Mark Stewart/Camera Press/Redux)

Global Connections

This 19th-century Burmese earplug made of green jasper would have been worn in the pierced ear of a Karan person. Men in Myanmar today typically wear plugs with silver covers, whereas women leave the plugs open. Today piercing is practiced worldwide. The rise of body art modifications in the 1980s and 1990s was inspired by individuals who appropriated practices from the "global supermarket" to show solidarity with other cultures or to set themselves apart. (V&A Images, London/ Art Resource, NY)

Blue Jeans and Denim

Jeans continued to be a staple in people's wardrobes. Even haute couture designers used denim fabrics. Denim was used for jackets, for skirts, and for entire suits. For those who preferred jeans that looked used, textile manufacturers developed techniques for dyeing and finishing that produced a faded or streaked look and a soft texture. Called *pre-washed*, *stone-washed*, or *acid-washed*, these and other jeans were produced in a wide variety of colors (see Figure 19.21).

Old jeans were cut off at the knee and worn as shorts. Manufacturers picked up on this development and sold them as **cut-offs**. By the late 1980s young people were purchasing jeans that had large horizontal tears on the legs. The style had became a Paris street fashion in 1985 and, aided by a 1987 revival of interest in 1960s protest clothing in the United States, was brought to a wider audience in a 1988 music video by

FIGURE 19.21 Actors from soap opera *Days of Our Lives* in 1991 wearing light- and dark-colored denim. Note the higher volume of hair on both the man and woman. (NBC/NBCU Photo Bank via Getty Images)

British rocker George Michael. Taking note of young people in jeans that they had slashed themselves, manufacturers began to make and sell torn jeans.

This phenomenon might be seen as an illustration of a type of status symbol described by Quentin Bell (1973). Social scientists had accepted that conspicuous consumption and conspicuous leisure were symbols of wealth. Bell suggested that a third type of status, which he called **conspicuous outrage**, be added. He argued that economic status could be demonstrated by purchases so outrageous that they showed the buyer had money to invest in something nonfunctional or, as in the case of torn jeans, something contrary to expectations for new and high-priced garments.

The Media

Motion pictures and television continued to influence fashion. Sometimes films or TV shows or personalities inspired a general look or made a particular garment popular. Films with period settings helped to contribute to the focus on retro fashion. Table 19.4 provides some specific examples of influences on fashions from various media in the period from 1980 to 1999.

Music Groups

From the 1970s to the 1990s, rock bands and stars such as Michael Jackson, Madonna, Grace Jones, Annie Lennox, and others had followers who copied their style of dressing. Some music groups have their own designers, while others hire stylists who shop for the clothing they wear during performances. Still other performers change designers often so their look does not become predictable. Designers who work for performers also design for the retail market or operate their own boutiques. In discussing the influences of music on fashion, Conlin (1989, 51) observed, "Teen fashion trends owe much to the music world. Kids pick up styles from concerts and videos and quickly take them to the street." Styles from the street may circulate among the young fans or penetrate the mainstream. The enormous diversity of these styles contributes to the many fashion trends that coexist.

With the growth in the Internet, even those fans living in rural areas were able to easily get information about where to buy clothing like that worn by their favorite musicians and other fans. Some musicians branched out into fashion design. Russell Simmons with Phat Farm, Jay Z and Rocawear, Jennifer Lopez with a line called J. Lo, and Sean Combs, whose Sean John label won a number of menswear fashion design awards, were among the earliest and best-known musicians to enter the design business. After his successes in menswear, Combs moved into designs for women. Since the late 1990s, once a musician has developed a substantial fan base, he or she has often also tried to enter the fashion world. Musicians have an added advantage: They can promote their designs through their performances.

Overweight women and boomers moving toward middle age have felt that they have little in common with the hyper-thin fashion models in fashion magazines. During the mid-1990s fashion models appearing on runways and in magazines looked almost anorexic, and many women wrote to magazines to protest illustrations they felt might be setting a dangerous precedent for impressionable adolescents who admired these "supermodels" (see Contemporary Comments 19.2).

The widespread use of models in advertising and fashion magazines that appeared emaciated, pale, with unkempt hair and large circles under the eyes was inspired by the work of influential fashion photographers. This 1990s trend coincided with an increase in use of hard drugs by celebrities, which the media started to call *heroin chic* in 1995. Eventually the name was applied to this style of fashion photography, and concerns were raised that the elevation of **heroin chic** models to high-fashion status would encourage the use of drugs among young people (Figure 19.22).

Fine Arts

Following her role as editor-in-chief of American *Vogue* from 1963 to 1971, Diana Vreeland became involved with the Costume Institute at the Metropolitan Museum of Art. Vreeland acted as creative director

TABLE 19.4 Media Influences on Fashion: 1980–1999

MEDIA	DATES	STYLE INFLUENCES
Motion pictures	1981	*Raiders of the Lost Ark* gives men's Stetson-type hats brief popularity.
	1983	*Flashdance* makes gray sweatshirt fabric and loose tops over legwarmers a popular fashion.
	1984	*Desperately Seeking Susan* stars Madonna, adding to her fame and fashion influence through use of lace, head ties.
	1985	*Top Gun*, with Tom Cruise, starts a fashion for cropped hair and a military look.
	1986	*Sid and Nancy*, a film about punk rock stars helps maintain interest in punk styles.
	1990s	Disney film productions such as *Pocahontas* and rereleases of earlier Disney animated films result in growth of cartoon characters on children's clothes.
	1994	*Pulp Fiction* actress Uma Thurman begins style for blunt cut, black hairstyle.
	1996	Three films made from Jane Austen novels contribute to a revival in Empire styles.
	1999	Coats worn in *The Matrix* help make trench coats popular in subsequent couture collections.
Television	1978–1991	*Dallas* creates interest in Stetson hats and western attire. Designer Nolan Miller promotes broad and padded shoulders.
	1981	MTV channel broadcasts music videos, cementing the relationship between image and musician. First video shown was "Video Killed the Radio Star."
	1984–1989	*Miami Vice* star Don Johnson sports unshaven look, no socks, and soft pastel shades in unstructured jackets. *Dynasty* spins off a line of clothing bearing its name.
	1990s	*Barney*, the dinosaur on this children's program, becomes popular on children's clothing.
	1994–2004	*Friends* revolves around six main characters living together and working. Rachel, played by Jennifer Aniston, creates eponymously named hairstyle trends.
	1998 to 2004	Series *Sex and the City* attracts women viewers who tune in to see the most current styles worn by the leading characters.
Music and music videos	1980s	Michael Jackson wears one sequined glove on right hand; imitated by teens. Madonna wears sexy outfits, including off-the-shoulder bra straps, torn fishnet stockings, leather, and chains; and imitates Marilyn Monroe's look from the 1950s. With the song "Black is Back" *Public Enemy* helps the revival of African-influenced styles.
	Late 1990s	Spice Girls wear skimpy bustiers and bare-midriff halter tops; copied by fans. Britney Spears becomes major fashion influence for preteens.
	1990s onward	Followers of popular musical styles (examples: hip-hop, grunge, reggae, emo, or other music groups) adopt the styles worn by these musicians.
	Late 1990s onward	Many successful musicians (Sean Combs, Jennifer Lopez, Beyoncé, Justin Timberlake) start their own clothing lines.

Contemporary Comments 19.2

READERS OBJECT TO EXTREMELY THIN MODELS

Some fashion magazine readers took exception to the exclusive use of fashion models who were extremely thin. The following are excerpts from letters to the editor of W, a monthly fashion magazine published by Fairchild Publications, Inc.

February 1996

"I am absolutely appalled by the pictures in the [latest] edition . . . . All the models appear to be anorexic at best and like refugees from concentration camps at worst. With cases of anorexia in adolescents and young women increasing dramatically, I find it almost criminal for this magazine to glamorize girls and women who look like this."

April 1996

"Varied theories and opinions have been offered by celebrated designers regarding the 'depressed' state of fashion today. I would like to offer another.

Much designer fashion does not target a major market: 'plus size' or 'full figure.' . . .

Affluent large-size women attend fashion shows. They shop. They are eager to see how a fashion ensemble could be interpreted for them. As fashion consumers, they are involved in a never-ending quest to find quality, stylish clothes . . .

. . . In our country, more women wear dress sized 12–16 than 0–8."

May 1996

"And if the models in those spreads were animals, you can bet the Humane Society would fine you for starving them and depriving them of exercise."

for 12 exhibits from 1972 through 1985. The extremely popular exhibits included "Balenciaga," "Romantic and Glamorous Hollywood Design," and "The Glory of Russian Costume." Vreeland was able to apply her unique style of fashion marketing to the museum gallery, but she was more interested in sensory impact than historical accuracy (Finamore, 2010).

Retro fashion revived not only styles from previous fashion eras but also drew inspiration for garments and textiles from the work of such artists of the past as Picasso, Velasquez, and Klimt and from such art movements as surrealism of the 1930s and op art of the 1960s. At the same time, contemporary art had an impact when Willi Smith utilized graffiti art, spray-painted on New York subways, in his designs in 1984. Artists working in the medium of fiber and apparel continued to produce striking wearable art designs (see Figure 18.14).

Demographics

White (1996) pointed out that demographic changes appear to have affected the fortunes of the fashion

FIGURE 19.22 Model Kate Moss exemplified the pale skin, dark circles, and angular bone structure popularized in the "heroin-chic" look of the mid-1990s. (Rose Hartman/The LIFE Images Collection/Getty Images)

industry negatively. Apparel spending peaked in 1978 when the baby boomers, some 75 million individuals born between the end of World War II and 1964, were between 15 and 32 years old. Since 1978 spending on apparel has declined and spending on services has increased. Furthermore, as women age, their bodies change. The trend toward increased use of casual clothing may also be related to demographics. Baby boomers grew up wearing jeans and casual clothes. It is probably not surprising that they also welcomed the opportunity to wear those casual clothes to work.

The number of obese adults has increased from 1976 (Ogden, Carroll, Kit, and Flegal, 2014) and continued to grow throughout the 1990s, with similar increases

in obesity among children and teenagers. Plus-sized apparel was available for adults and children.

Casual Lifestyles

The movement of population to the suburbs after World War II and the concurrent growth of casual sportswear contributed to an increase in informality in daily life and dress in the United States. Young people of the 1960s, with their antiestablishment protests, had adopted jeans and other casual clothing as dress for school and for play. Adults followed their example, and sportswear became the major style worn during leisure time. Formal occasions requiring people to dress up became fewer. Cementing the dressing down of America, Oscar nominee Sharon Stone paired a Gap T-shirt with an Armani coat and Valentino skirt at the 1996 Academy Awards. Corporate and conservative businesses, such as banks, continued to require a certain standard of sartorial decorum in the office.

By the 1990s, a number of businesses had instituted policies whereby employees could dress down on **casual Fridays**. In 1996, 90 percent of all companies had at least one casual dress day each week. Spokespersons for the apparel industry felt that the casual dress trend posed a threat to the nylon hosiery industry ("Sara Lee," 1996), to necktie companies, and to suit manufacturers (Adler, 1995). At the same time, sales of men's casual wear increased. From 1990 to 1996, sales of men's shirts, sweaters, and knit tops increased by 31 percent, while khakis, casual dress slacks, jeans, and golf pants were up 36 percent (Steinhauer, 1997; Figure 19.23). As the economy weakened in the new millennium, casual dress for business seemed to be declining somewhat.

High-Tech Fabrics

In the 1980s and 1990s new, so-called **high-tech fabrics** made possible the design of clothing for active sports that took advantage of the unique properties of these fabrics. Waterproof but breathable fabrics were used for running, biking, backpacking, camping, and hiking. Ultrafine **microfibers** made of nylon and polyester were used to make high-performance, water-

FIGURE 19.23 The practice of dressing less formally in the office on "casual Friday" was followed by both men and women. (Photographs courtesy Levi Strauss & Co.)

resistant, soft fabrics for skiwear and other active, outdoor sports. Fabrics made from blends of natural or manufactured fibers and spandex, a high-stretch synthetic fiber, appeared in bathing suits, aerobic leotards and tights, bicycling pants, and skiwear (Figure 19.24). Manufacturers developed special fabrics for competitive swimming that, when warmed by body heat, clung closely to the body, minimizing drag. A silicone finish that repels water helped move the swimmer ahead in the water. Polypropylene, a manufactured fiber that dries quickly and wicks perspiration away from the body, was made into socks and thermal underwear for winter sports.

Although these materials were designed for active sports, designers of high fashion and sportswear

FIGURE 19.24 Activewear outfits, for active sports and working out, use stretch and microfibers and are often made in vivid colors. (R.M. Lewis/NBC/NBC NewsWire)

soon utilized some of these fibers and concepts. Stretch fabrics became a major factor in fashion. Body-hugging, knitted leggings, leotards, and body stockings were included in many couture and ready-to-wear collections beginning in the late 1980s. Eventually fabrics for classic garments such as tailored blouses and shirts, blazers, fitted skirts, and pants incorporated stretch yarns to assure a better fit.

New advances in textile technology had an impact on fashion. Teflon-coated fabrics that resisted staining were marketed, performance of fabrics that do not require ironing improved, and washable leathers were obtainable. **Lyocell,** a new form of rayon, was developed that is more environmentally friendly. In the 1990s, garments made from Tencel and other trademarked lyocell fibers were available. T-shirts with temperature sensitive pigments were marketed as Hypercolor and were immensely popular in the early 1990s. One Japanese firm showed a prototype of a jacket with a computer screen in the sleeve. This paved the way for 21st-century wearable technologies. See Contemporary Comment 19.3 for a discussion of solar-powered clothing.

Fashionable Fabrics

Fabrics fueled other fashion trends: voided velvet, a fabric in which sheer background alternates with designs in raised velvet pile; op art prints; and animal prints, especially leopard, wild cat, tiger, cow, and zebra designs. Stretch knit and woven fabrics made with elastomeric yarns of spandex were used in many kinds of garments.

The Fitness Craze

Interest in fitness continued to stimulate the growth of clothing for running, jogging, and exercising. The distinctions between clothing for active sports and sportswear for nonsports activities blurred (Figure 19.25).

In the past, one pair of athletic shoes or sneakers had been sufficient for almost any kind of sport activity and for casual wear. It is almost impossible to overestimate the importance of sneakers in the 1980s, 1990s, and after. In 1980 when New York City experienced a transit strike, women walking to work wore sneakers and carried their more dressy work shoes, changing once they got into the office. When the strike ended, the practice continued, and many women wore sneakers as they traveled to work.

Expensive sneakers became a status symbol among inner-city youth; incidents were reported in which sneakers and other high-status garments were stolen, and young men killed to obtain the prized items (Berkow, 1990). By 1995 retro fashion had taken hold even in sneaker styles with revivals of 1950s and 1960s sneaker styles. In addition to a huge variety of sneakers, there were also tennis shoes, running shoes, jogging shoes, walking shoes, and hiking boots. Recognition of the important place of active sportswear in the fashion industry came in the mid-1990s as well-known designers began designing lines of active sportswear. Rarely did people use sportswear exclusively for athletic activities. An example of this was the jogging suit. Usually made of knitted fabric as pants with an elasticized waistband and a matching top that either closed with a zipper or pulled over the head, this easy-to-wear, comfortable garment was adopted for casual and leisure wear not only by athletes but also by older Americans and others whose participation in active sports was often quite limited (Figure 19.26).

FIGURE 19.25 This 1993 acrylic microfiber shirt and pants ensemble was typical of the use of manufactured fiber microfibers in sportswear. (Courtesy of Jack Mulqueen, manufacturer)

Contemporary Comments 19.3

NEW SOLAR-POWERED JACKET CHARGES YOUR DEVICES WHILE OUTSIDE BY ZEGNA

This article by Stefan Anitei discusses solar-powered products that charge technological devices when exposed to the sun's rays.

You just love drinking your coffee outside on some bar's sunny terrace. But what do you do if your iPod's or your mobile phone's battery is low? Well, now technosexuals (or "technological geeks," if you like) that love to spend time in open air will see their dream come true. This is better than the solar-powered backpacks and solar-paneled LCD mobile phones from Motorola.

The Italian fashion house Ermenegildo Zegna Holditalia S.p.A. (Zegna) will release the Solar-Powered Jacket, the most practical and best-looking method to charge your mobile gadgets. The Italian firm presented the model in September 2007 in Florence, Italy, taking fashion to a whole new level.

The jacket can charge every small gadget you might own, from cell phone and iPod to even tiny vacuum cleaners for keyboard ($12) or eight-inch (16 cm)-tall minirefrigerator ($30) (that can chill one can of soda). Yes, sun heat to cool down your drinks . . . what can be better than this?

The silvery-gray bomber jacket is made of a breathable fabric named Microtene. Two-inch-by-three-inch (5 cm x 7.5 cm) silicon-based polycrystalline solar panels are embedded in the jacket's removable Nehru-style collar, being capable of converting 1 watt of sunlight. And there are no bulky wires in your pockets, as all power is sent through conductive textiles that flex, following your body's movements.

The energy can be used to directly charge your device or through wires sent to a battery in the breast pocket having the size of a card deck (70 x 60 x 13 mm, 100 g), to store power for later use. A 5-volt USB connection charges your iPod and a 6-volt connection charges your mobile for about four hours, but the battery is completely loaded in eight hours of sun exposure. "The Solar JKT is based around Interactive Wear AG's iSolarX technology, and sports a number of solar modules around the neoprene collar that can pass energy through conducting textile leads for storage in a buffer battery or to charge a connected device directly" reported *Engadget*. Some are worried about the price of the jacket. Well, you know how Italian designers' products always have high prices . . .

In the end, that's exactly what we needed after smart fabrics, like that one developed by New Zealand firm Zephyr and offering data on our heart beat, skin temperature, posture, activity and breathing rate. The smart fabric allows athletes to determine their performance by measuring in an extremely simple way their physiological reactions.

Anitei, S. (2007). New solar-powered jacket charges your devices while outside. Retrieved from www.softpedia.com

COSTUME: THE EIGHTIES AND THE NINETIES

Several schools of design emerged in the 1980s and 1990s. Although these designs may not have fully appealed to the average consumer, they did have an impact on other designers.

Costume Components for Women

Japanese influences, for example, were evident in the popularity of blacks and grays, and the innovative cuts typical of the Japanese were reflected in the work of other designers. Inspired by Japanese fashion designers, Martin Margiela, a Belgian designer, became one of the best-known **deconstructionists,**

FIGURE 19.26 Jogging suits, originally designed for athletes, were widely adopted as comfortable leisure wear by men and women of all ages and sizes. (Gary Null/NBC/NBCU Photo Bank via Getty Images)

designers who made clothes with seams located on the outside, linings that were part of the exterior, or fabric edges left unhemmed and raw. As with the Japanese, these edgy designs had an impact on mainstream design in subtle ways (Figure 19.27).

By the latter years of the 1990s, influential designers who were called **minimalists** made styles in neutral or darker tones that had little ornamentation and good lines (Figure 19.28).

A few trends were identifiable within the many varying fashion segments. The 1980s had begun with an indication of change. Shoulders and sleeves were larger, with shoulder pads added to everything from daytime dresses to sweaters for casual wear and evening dresses (Figure 19.29). The fashion for large shoulders continued into the early 1990s, after which shoulder lines became smaller and more natural.

The 1980s ushered in a period of greater interest in the body that continued into the 1990s. Skirt lengths gradually decreased. Tightly fitted dresses were made from spandex stretch fiber blends (Figure 19.30). Not only were many items made with cutouts or bare midriffs, but throughout the 1990s lace and sheer fabrics were fashionable (Figure 19.31). Designers showed these garments with little or nothing underneath; however, most women wore transparent dresses as an outer layer over a more opaque garment and stores ordered such items with linings.

FIGURE 19.27 Belgian designers Martin Margiela and Ann Demeulemeester, whose fashion design shop is shown here, are known for creating clothing in the deconstructionist style, in which parts of the garment are left unfinished or appear to be coming apart rather than being assembled. (Maurice Rougemont/Gamma-Rapho via Getty Images)

FIGURE 19.28 Minimalist garments such as Jil Sander's 1993 jacket with pants are simple, unadorned, and well-cut designs. (Streiber/WWD/© Conde Nast)

FIGURE 19.29 In the early 1980s, designers such as Thierry Mugler shortened women's dresses and added broad, exaggerated shoulder pads. (Courtesy of Fairchild Publications, Inc.)

Short skirts and miniskirts reappeared in the 1980s. Throughout the 1990s these were seen side by side with skirts of many different lengths. The most common choices were between very short skirts and those that reached to below the calf. Long, straight skirts had long slits. Many dresses, skirts, and pants were fitted and tight until the early 1990s. By the mid-1990s pant legs had become wider, and short, full skirts appeared.

During the late 1990s, it had become more and more difficult to identify any one look, or predominant silhouette. Individuals were likely to dress in styles acceptable to their peers. If the peer group was attuned to current fashion trends for that group (as adolescents, media stars, or avid followers of high fashion were likely to be), fashionable styles came and went quickly. For other women, the same basic, classic styles might be worn year after year, with more current fashions showing up in clothing for special occasions or in hems moving slightly up and down from one year to another.

Underwear

While the same general repertoire of undergarments continued in use, frilly, feminine underwear made a comeback. Victoria's Secret, a national chain, was quite successful, selling colorful lace- and ribbon-trimmed undergarments and sleepwear.

When clothing became more form fitting in the 1990s, undergarments provided more support and shaping, with modern versions of corsets and even bustles. The latter were padded panties with trademarks

FIGURE 19.30 In the mid-1980s and later, short, tight dresses made of fabrics that blended stretch fiber spandex with other fibers were one of the available style options. (© Pierre Vauthey/Sygma/Corbis)

FIGURE 19.31 Sheer styles of the 1990s were shown by designers with little or no underwear beneath. Some sheer dresses, like the one on the left, created a layered look. (© Pierre Vauthey/Sygma/Corbis)

such as Rear Riser or Butt Booster. (See Illustrated Table 19.1 for some examples of undergarments from the period between 1980 and 1999.) When bodice styles were cut low and intended to show cleavage, special bras were designed to provide the needed uplift. Some undergarment styles, such as the bustier worn as a strapless blouse, continued to be popular, and camisoles were worn as blouses, or peeked out through sheer fabrics, or were visible at the edges of garments.

Garments

Although no one silhouette or skirt length predominated and the range of fabrics used was very wide, a few trends in fabric use were evident. Rayon fabrics,

out of fashion since the end of World War II, returned to popularity in the 1980s and 1990s. Floral-patterned rayons, many reminiscent of fabrics of the 1930s, were popular. Printed rayon dresses often had Empire waists and buttoned down the front. Although natural fibers were preferred over synthetics by many people, Lycra spandex was used extensively in blends with other fibers for stretch fabrics. Very fine polyester microfibers were made to look and feel like silk.

Diverse dress styles from which women could choose included classic shirtwaist dresses or long dresses unfitted through the bodice and joined to gathered skirts at a dropped waistline (a 1920s revival). Sweater dresses; T-shirt dresses; sweatshirt dresses; and short, tight dresses made with spandex stretch fibers could be found, as could chemise or shift

Illustrated Table 19.1

Selected Undergarments for Women and Men: 1980–1999

Sports bra, 1979[1]

Popular uplift
Wonderbra, 1994[2]

Nylon lace-string
bikini and bra, 1990[3]

Thong underpants, 1987[4]

"Bottom-enhancing"
underpants, 1996[5]

Men's striped
bikini, 1987[7]

Men's patterned boxer
shorts, 1987[6]

Men's Jockey® shorts and athletic shirt, 1987[7]

---

[1] *Women's Wear Daily*, August 30, 1979. Fairchild Publications.

[2] *Women's Wear Daily*, May 5, 1994. Fairchild Publications.

[3] *Women's Wear Daily*, May 10, 1990. Fairchild Publications.

[4] *Women's Wear Daily*, November 11, 1987. Fairchild Publications.

[5] *Women's Wear Daily*, April 8, 1996. Fairchild Publications.

[6] *Daily News Record*, January 6, 1987. Fairchild Publications.

[7] *Daily News Record*, January 7, 1987. Fairchild Publications.

FIGURE 19.32 The shorts suit, shown here in a version by Giorgio Armani, was an alternative to the skirted suit in the latter part of the 1980s. (*Women's Wear Daily*, October 16, 1990. Courtesy of Fairchild Publications, Inc.)

to shorten, some women switched to pantsuits, which made a comeback in the 1990s.

After 1987, when the style was introduced by Giorgio Armani, a suit consisting of shorts and a matching tailored jacket called the **shorts suit** was worn as an alternative to the skirted suit (Figure 19.32). In the mid-1980s, the traditional Chanel suit was revived by designer Karl Lagerfeld, who became designer for the Chanel firm after 1982. Lagerfeld took the basic Chanel formula and updated it imaginatively with vivid colors and his own individual touches. Some versions were made more for the fashion show runway than for the street. By 1990 jackets were long. With them women wore short, slim skirts or pants. In previous decades, maternity wear had been loosely fitted, but by the late 1990s, maternity clothes followed the body curves of pregnant women.

Evening Wear

Dresses for evening were among the most interesting designs produced in the 1980s by a revived French couture. These designs influenced ready-to-wear formal clothing as well. The glamour of evening clothing contrasted with the conservative clothing recommended for daytime wear for career women. Evening dresses had a great deal of glittering embroidery, sequins, and beading. Colors were bright and fabrics were ornamented with vivid woven or printed designs.

Around 1985 Christian Lacroix, designing for Patou, produced a design nicknamed **le pouf** (Figure 19.33a). It had a wide, puffy skirt with a light airy appearance. Shown in both short and longer styles by Lacroix, it was copied widely, especially in shorter lengths. Other wide-skirted, short styles were known as **mini-crinolines**. By the late 1980s the wide-skirted evening dresses were superseded by tightly fitted, short evening dresses that were either strapless or had tiny shoulder straps and made from stretch fibers. Simple slip dresses of soft crepe fabrics were often worn in the 1990s and maintained their popularity after the millennium (Figure 19.33b).

By the mid-1990s the full-skirted, short, strapless evening dress was back. Lace or elaborately decorated

dresses, usually sleeveless, and ranging from fitted to full tentlike styles. Young women wore delicate, sheer dresses over other garments and combined them incongruously with hiking boots or sturdy sandals. Coordinated ensembles of dresses worn with short to almost full-length jackets or coats were also seen.

Tailored suits worn with a tailored blouse were considered appropriate wear for business women, although by the latter part of the 1980s these suits were somewhat less uniformlike and more diverse. Some were collarless, cardigan style. Skirts grew shorter, but working women were cautioned against wearing their skirts too short. Around 1987 when skirts were growing very short, the length recommended for the office was "just above the knee." When skirts continued

FIGURE 19.33 Between 1985 and 1996, evening dresses included a wide range of styles. (a) Short, wide-skirted mini-crinoline dresses from Jean Patou's autumn/winter 1986–1987 fashion show in Paris (© Pierre Vauthey/ Corbis/Sygma); (b) Short, bare evening dress from John Galliano's 1991 spring/summer ready-to-wear collection (© John Van Hasselt/Sygma/Corbis); (c) Long gowns with cutouts or bare shoulders from Valentino's winter 1993 haute couture collection (© Pierre Vauthey/Corbis/Sygma); (d) Retro fashions based on beaded dress styles of the 1920s from Givenchy's couture spring/summer 1998 collection. (© Condé Nast Archive/Corbis)

bustiers were worn for evening in the 1990s. So, too, were long, fitted evening dresses. Black was a popular color. These long gowns might be strapless, sleeveless, with one covered shoulder, or with peekaboo cutouts (Figure 19.33c). Some dresses of the mid-1990s had interesting details that were visible at the back. In the late 1990s Givenchy showed flapper-style beaded evening dresses (Figure 19.33d).

Outdoor Garments

By the end of the 1980s, longer down coats were replaced by short, casual down jackets. Both real and imitation fur coats were worn throughout the period. In the 1990s furs became less bulky, and some were brightly colored. Large, oversized coats, perhaps inspired by Japanese design, were worn over narrow dresses and suits in the early 1980s, but by the mid-decade many coats were neat and not overly wide. Lengths varied. Some were quite long, and shorter lengths were also available. By the late 1980s shorter coats were being worn, especially with pants.

Throughout the 1990s, wrap coats and trench coats were popular (Figure 19.34). In 1996, the idea of "between season" coats was revived, and a design originated by Chanel in the 1960s was widely copied.

Sportswear

Pants and Skirts Culottes, or divided skirts, were worn on and off throughout the 1980s. Toward the end of the 1980s, spandex was used to make tight-fitting stretch tights or leggings. Some of these covered the entire leg including the foot, others extended to the ankle, and still others ended at mid-calf or around the knee. Some were made in bright prints such as those designed by Emilio Pucci. These were worn with large, loose T-shirts, with sweaters, or under miniskirts.

Pants were slender at the beginning of the 1990s, then started to widen. By 1994 some pants had grown quite wide and had large cuffs. Towards the end of the decade, narrow pants with a flat front were popular (see Figure 19.34); however, pleated full pants were still available.

FIGURE 19.34 Austrian-born American designer Helmut Lang's 1997 collection featured a trench coat with mix-and-match separates. (© Condé Nast Archive/Corbis)

Blouses, Sweaters, and Other Tops Early in the 1980s sweatshirts became a big fashion item. American designer Norma Kamali originated a line of clothes inspired by the knitted fabric used in sweatshirts. The styles not only included traditional sweatshirt design features but extended to skirts, dresses, and even evening wear (Figure 19.35).

Blouse styles of the mid-1980s ranged from tailored designs used with business suits to blouses and sweaters with standing collars finished with a ruffle at the top and sleeves gathered into the armscye and with puffed sleeve caps that looked as if they owed their inspiration to the Gibson Girls. Other notable styles of the 1980s and early 1990s included shirts cut large though the shoulders and full through the body, which were often worn as over blouses with pants or skirts.

FIGURE 19.35 Norma Kamali's sweatshirt fabric designs were exceptionally popular. Here an oversized turtleneck (1981) is worn as a dress. (Paul Arnato © 1981 Condé Nast Publications)

1950s: a pullover and matching cardigan. More expensive versions were made from cashmere. Some T-shirts and knit tops were made to fit tightly. Turtlenecks, never altogether abandoned, became more important again (see Figure 19.34).

Clothing for Active Sports

As a result of the promotion of fitness, running suits, warm-up suits, and jogging and exercises suits proliferated and were worn as casual streetwear as well as for exercising. In the early 1980s sweat shorts were worn over sweatpants or tights. Spandex-blended stretch fabrics were used for everything from brightly colored leotards to bathing suits and ski suits. Synthetic fleece fabrics provided good insulation in cold weather for outdoor activities. Making polyester fleece from recycled soda bottles was seen as an ecological advantage.

Swimming   A new bathing suit style appeared, cut with a high, inverted V at the sides over the hip, the cut reaching almost to the waistline (Figure 19.36). This high side was often combined with a deep V in

T-shirts ranged from basic cotton tees to those made in handsome fabrics and with embroidered, sequined, and beaded decorations. Fine-gauge cotton or silk knit T-shirts were being worn with suits as distinctions between work and play clothes broke down.

Fair Isle patterns and knitted pictures appeared on sweaters in early and mid-1980s, but after this, sweaters were more likely to be plain or have overall patterns.

One of the most popular blouse styles of the early 1990s was a frilly, white blouse with large sleeves. Sometimes it was worn with slim, black pants for evening. Sweater sets were similar to those of the

FIGURE 19.36 A new, high-thigh cut for bathing suits, originated by Norma Kamali, influenced bathing suit styles of the 1980s. (*Women's Wear Daily*, February 27, 1985. Courtesy of Fairchild Publications, Inc.)

the front or back of the suit. Bikinis, including those with thong bottoms, continued to be an option, as did more conventional one-piece suits. In the late 1990s, the tankini, a two-piece suite with tank top and separate bottom, was introduced. Holly Brubach, writing in *The New Yorker* (1991, 72), noted, "Those days of consensus, in swimsuits as in fashion, are gone. Today all the options exist simultaneously."

Skiing   Olympic skiers used skin-tight, hooded ski suits in vividly colored fabrics made from high-tech fibers that minimized wind resistance. Styles for recreational skiers utilized some of these ideas but were more fashion oriented with bright Day-Glo colors dominating until the late 1980s when softer, more pastel colors were preferred.

In the 1990s ski clothing styles also reflected the trend to retro fashion. Ski styles of the 1960s and 1970s were revived, which included tight, knit sweaters with racer stripes, quilted down parkas, flared stretch pants, and short, snug jackets. At the same time there was a fad for wearing ski goggles pushed up on the head.

Tennis   Women wore knitted tops (often white) with either skirts or shorts in white or colors. In 1985 Anne White wore a skin-tight, white jumpsuit to play her first match at the Wimbledon tennis tournament and was banned from wearing the garment for subsequent matches. The authorities said the garment was "not traditional tennis attire."

Sleepwear

Choices for sleepwear ranged from footed all-in-one sleepers to frilly, feminine nightgowns in fabrics ranging from silk to brushed nylon tricot. In the mid-1980s and 1990s both short and long T-shirts were worn as nightshirts.

Robes included long or short fleece styles made from colorful, high pile or velour knits made from manufactured fibers and long and short quilted robes.

Hair and Headdress

In the 1980s and 1990s, hairstyles reflected the diversity of the current fashion. Very full, curly, and frizzy hair in both longer and shorter lengths continued. In the mid-1980s, those who wanted to expcriment with punk styles could use washable sprays to color their hair. By the end of the 1980s some women were wearing their hair very short, and in some cases men and women wore the same haircut. The 1990s saw a return to popularity of long, straight hair, another 1960s revival.

In the late 1990s hair was sometimes curled and full in order to make the head appear bigger. Tousled hair was called **bed hair**. Young girls tied their hair into ponytails at the back of the head, purposely allowing wisps and strands of hair to escape. When popular celebrities cut their hair short, some women followed.

Beginning in the mid-1980s, hat sales rose as much as 15 percent each year. Young people were more likely to wear hats than were older persons. Hats were still used more to keep the head warm than as a fashion statement. With publicity about the need to protect the skin from ultraviolet light, hats were also worn as protection against the sun. Nevertheless, a variety of ways of decorating the hair could be observed. In 1985, headbands appeared in summer; in the late 1980s, hair bows appeared. In 1988, scarves or small elastic bands with ribbon or fabric decorations attached were tied around the hair. After Bill Clinton's election in 1992, some women wore headbands similar to those worn by Hillary Clinton. Elastic bands covered with fabric (for confining ponytails) were called **scrunchies** (Figure 19.37).

Footwear

As skirts grew shorter toward the end of the 1980s, lower heeled shoes were worn. Throughout the 1980s and 1990s sneakers of all kinds were worn for sports and leisure.

The 1990s provided considerable variety in footwear. Many of the styles were revivals of earlier styles. They included platform-soled shoes revived in 1992 that had wedge or large, square heels; stiletto heels; and two-tone, spectator-style shoes that were often black and white. In the 1990s, boots made a major return. Important styles ranged from thigh-high boots to hiking boots.

FIGURE 19.37 Actresses from the TV show *Full House* wear their hair straight, the youngest girl in a scrunchie. They demonstrate the diversity of children's wear styles for girls—from knit sweaters to floral prints. (ABC Photo Archives/ABC via Getty Images)

Many young people wore Doc Martens laceup boots, which had first been made in 1946 for physician Klaus Maertens. After hurting his foot skiing, Maertens had the shoes made with air pockets in the soles to ease pressure on his feet. The style, licensed to R. Griggs & Co. in 1959, first came to the attention of the fashion world when it was adopted by skinheads and punks in the 1960s and 1970s.

Pantyhose were either opaque or sheer. Some were patterned and others had beaded, sequined, or other decorations applied. By the mid-1990s opaque stockings without texture or pattern were more fashionable. See Illustrated Table 19.2, page 634, for some examples of footwear for the period from 1980 to 2008.

Jewelry

Small, diamond solitaire ear studs were very popular in the 1990s. By the late 1990s, costume jewelry made in bright colors became fashionable. Large, dangling earrings, called *chandelier earrings*, were especially popular. Necklaces made from cultured pearls strung on a transparent cord made it appear that the pearls were lying on the wearer's neck without any support. Chokers were also popular.

Accessories

Among the most notable of the many fashionable accessories of the 1980s were shawls and large scarves, often worn over coats. In 1983 Swatch watches became a fad and maintained their popularity in the ensuing years. Quilted leather handbags remained popular in the 1990s and after. Small duffelbaglike backpacks replaced handbags for some women. As cell phones became more popular, handbags and business cases started to come with special compartments for them. See Illustrated Table 19.3 for examples of popular accessories from 1980 to 1999.

Cosmetics and Grooming

The natural look of the 1970s was replaced in the 1980s by more obvious makeup. Lipstick was darker, often with a still darker outline at the edges of the lips. In order to have the full, pouty lips popular in the 1980s, models and other women had silicone injections. Pale, powdered skin was preferred to a tanned look. The connection between sun exposure and skin cancer was probably responsible for making suntans unfashionable.

A variety of hair care products was needed to maintain the fashionably tousled hairstyles, and as a result hairstyling mousses, gels, and sprays proliferated.

Street fashion focused interest on tattooing and body piercing for the attachment of ornaments. To participate in these fashions without making permanent changes in their bodies, individuals could buy clip-on rings for navel and nose and decal tattoos that washed off.

Costume Components for Men

The so-called Peacock Revolution of the 1960s had focused attention on men's clothing and the menswear industry. From that time on men, like women, had

Illustrated Table 19.2

Selected Examples of Popular Footwear for Women, Men, and Children: 1980–1999

Many women's shoes for 1989 were cut high across the instep[1]

Suede moccasins with low backs
came in many colors[3]

Athletic shoe styles for men, women, and children
proliferated as "fitness" became more important[2]

Boot styles[5]

a   b

Two examples of classic men's loafers,
often associated with "preppy" styles[6]

Retro fashion extended to shoes in the 1990s
with the revivals of interest in (a) Black-and-white
"spectator shoes" and (b) Platform soles[4]

---

[1] *FNM Viewpoints*, January 1989.

[2] Buyer's Guide, *Footwear News*, September 22, 1975. Fairchild
Publications.

[3] *Footwear News*, July 31, 1995. Fairchild Publications.

[4] *Footwear News*, August 10, 1992. Fairchild Publications.

[5] *Footwear News*, January 23, 1994. Fairchild Publications.

[6] *FNM Viewpoints*, February 1987.

---

more choices among clothing options, and fashion segmentation increased. Although the corporate world still required traditional business attire in the 1970s and 1980s, there was wide latitude in acceptable dress for social occasions and leisure activities. Then in the 1990s, changes in dress policies made casual dress acceptable in many business settings as well.

Separates became more important. Since World War II, the differences between clothing for active sports and sportswear were lessening. Even dress clothing had become sportier.

Boutiques sold designer clothing for men, and more designers of women's clothing began to design lines for men. Men's styles also provided inspiration

Illustrated Table 19.3

Accessories: 1980–1999

Mufflers

Large shawl-type scarf

Neck scarf

Boa, made from
yarn hoops, c. 1999

Silk head scarf

Women's jewelry, 1996–1999
(a) Chandelier earrings, (b) Bib necklace (c) Cuff bracelet

Women's handbags
(a) Gym bag, (b) Backpack, (c) Duffle bag, (d) Tote bag, (e) Pouch handbag, (f) Handbag, and (g) Multimedia bag

for women's clothing for work and for play in the 1980s and after.

Garments

The same basic items of boxer shorts, briefs, and undershirts continued to be worn, with innovations in color and cut. In 1984 the classic brief was first made in colors. Interest in hiking and camping increased in the 1980s, and soon thermal underwear for cold weather was produced in cotton, wool, silk, and polypropylene. These products were manufactured for both men and women. See Illustrated Table 19.1 for examples of undergarments from the period between 1980 and 1999.

A change in silhouette for men's suits came about with an emphasis on Italian styling, especially fashionable in the 1980s. These suits had wide shoulder lines; the fit remained easy.

In the 1990 *Time* magazine article "The Bonfire of the Business Suit" it was reported that the loose-fitting sack suit, the staple of men's business suits in the medium price range for conservative American men for many years, was "fading fast" (Cocks and Fallon, 1990, 83). Citing large financial losses by American ready-to-wear men's suit manufacturers, interest in English styling that was narrower at the waist, wide at the shoulders, and had side vents rose. Suspenders were used to hold up trousers. French and Italian suits, with slightly softer tailoring, were also noted as fashionable (Figure 19.38a). Color ranges were broadening, too. By 1996, a more structured line in suits was apparent. Some Italian suits even had stretch fibers incorporated to maintain a line that was closer to the body (Figure 19.38b).

Men could buy dress shirts in a wide variety of colors and patterns. In the early 1980s colored or printed shirts with white collars were especially popular. Collar sizes varied, their proportions suited to the proportion of jacket lapel widths. Striped shirts were being worn with patterned neckties in the 1990s. Italian designer

FIGURE 19.38 The softer styles of the (a) Armani jacket of 1996–1997 (Luca Bruno/AP Images) are in contrast to the slimmer silhouettes of (b) the 1998/99 collection by Miuccia Prada (Antonio Calanni/AP Images).

Giorgio Armani showed some of his suits of the 1980s worn with T-shirts. By the 1990s men working in informal settings or for leisure were wearing a variety of informal shirts with business suits. The trend toward increasingly casual clothing was evident in suits, composed of matching denim or cotton pants and jackets fashionable in the period (Figure 19.39).

Sportswear

Sports jackets generally followed lines of suit jackets, easy in the 1980s, then more fitted again in the 1990s and gradually looser again. Some of the more popular styles included double-breasted blazers and wool tweeds, especially in the early 1980s when natural fibers were popular. These were often worn over a sweater or a fabric vest. Linen jackets were made in light or bright colors for summer in the 1980s, and tweed, checks, and plaids were popular in the 1990s.

Pants styles for casual wear ranged from blue jeans to tailored slacks. Along with traditional, conservative styles, some innovations can be identified. In the early 1980s some pants tapered to the bottom and closed with Velcro fasteners at the ankle (Figure 19.40a). By the latter 1980s trouser fronts had pleated fullness and a loose, easy fit. *Gentlemen's Quarterly* in the 1990s regularly showed cross sections of pants styles. All of these pants had pleats, although the style of the pleats was not the same for all trousers. Most had cuffs. The styles included the following:

- slim, narrow at ankle;
- wide all the way to the hem;
- cargo style, with large patch pockets on the side;
- high waisted and tapered to the ankle; and
- casual with suspender buttons and no cuffs.

By 1996, pleats were disappearing, and dress trousers were tighter. Casual pants alternatives, however, picked up some style features from hip-hop style and were fuller, baggier, and lower on the hip (Figure 19.40b). Cargo pants maintained their popularity.

The basic sport shirt styles continued to be T-shirts; woven, short-sleeved styles; and polo knit shirts. Summer wear included tank tops. For cooler weather,

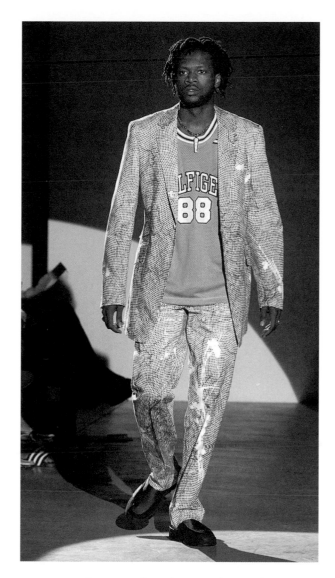

FIGURE 19.39 Entertainer from the musical group the Fugees wears an indigo and white stretch cotton suit over a mesh basketball jersey in the spring 1999 collection of designer Tommy Hilfiger. (Richard Drew/AP Images)

men wore turtlenecks, velour pullovers and shirts, jacquard-patterned knitted sweaters, and sweatshirts. Sweaters of the 1980s were loosely fitted and made in a wide variety of knits made from natural fibers in earth tones and brighter colors (Figure 19.41). In the 1980s, mesh shirts worn by football players were added to casual sportswear.

Evening Dress

Tailcoats were worn by musicians and other stage performers and occasionally for weddings. Almost all

FIGURE 19.40 (a) Men's sportswear styles of the early 1980s were broad shouldered, pants often tapered to the ankles to close with Velcro, zippers, or tabs (*Daily News Record*, June 22, 1981, courtesy of Fairchild Publications, Inc.); (b) By the 1990s, as seen in the styles designed by Tommy Hilfiger, a more casual combination of madras shorts or short trousers and sports jackets worn with loosely fitting white or madras shirts were popular. (Chip East/Reuters/Corbis)

other formal evening dress, men wore tuxedos. Their fit varied in much same way as that of daytime suits (Figure 19.42). Evening dress colors were diverse. By the mid-1990s, white dinner jackets were featured in men's fashion magazines.

Outdoor Garments

Hemline lengths of coats for business and dress were similar to those of women. The fit of overcoats followed the fit of suit jackets.

Some of the more popular casual outdoor wear included leather motorcycle jackets, western-style split cowhide with pile-lined jackets (or simulated synthetic pile versions), and down-filled vests and jackets. Parkas were also worn.

FIGURE 19.41 Sweaters such as the ones designed by Koos Van Den Akker of the label KOOS were popularized by Bill Cosby on the *Cosby Show*. (Ron Galella/WireImage)

FIGURE 19.42 Evening wear of the late 1980s shows the large-shouldered looser fit, characteristic of much of men's clothing from this period. (*Daily News Record*, February 6, 1989, Courtesy of Fairchild Publications, Inc.)

Polhemus (1994) cited black leather **Perfecto motorcycle jackets**, made by the Schott Bros company, as examples of street fashions that bubble up into mainstream fashion. Such jackets had been symbols of rebellious youth ever since Marlon Brando wore one in the 1953 film *The Wild One*. Gradually, through the 1970s and 1980s, these jackets became normal apparel, helped along by their adoption by rock musicians. By the 1980s and 1990s this jacket, and leather vest, was appearing in shows by the haute couture, and its transformation into mainstream fashion was complete.

Clothing for Active Sports

For swimming, men could choose from a wide range of styles that included the extreme thong, bikinis, briefs, and boxer trunks. After the end of the 1980s stretch fabrics were used. As surfing got more attention, so did loose and long surfer shorts. In 1990, Jockey introduced a string bikini for men.

Warm-up suits, popular as a result of jogging and running fads, were important garments from the early 1980s forward. Gym shorts and sweatpants were worn for athletics and as casual sportswear in the 1980s and 1990s. From the mid-1980s and after, spandex bicycling shorts were worn. The knee-length styles worn by Tour de France competitors set the styles.

By the 1980s colors were much in evidence in tennis clothing. Skiing styles changed yearly, with gradually tighter fit and fabrics designed to offer as little wind resistance as possible. Bob Ottum, writing in the February 27, 1984, issue of *Sports Illustrated*, observed that the Olympic ski uniforms of that year were so tight that "the next step can only be to line up the racers naked at the starting gate and spray paint them" (23). Cross-country skiing continued to be popular. Knickers or tightly fitted pants made of high-tech synthetic fibers were worn for competitions, while amateurs wore wool or corduroy knickers with knee-length stockings. By the 1990s and after knickers had largely been replaced by manufactured fiber stretch pants.

Interest in snowboarding grew rapidly after 1990. Unlike skiers, snowboarders wore loosely fitted, well-insulated clothing. Most often it was two pieces, and top and bottom were different in color. Popular colors varied from season to season (Figure 19.43).

Sleepwear

The most widely used pajama styles tended to be high-necked pullovers, V-neck pullovers, or shirt-collar tops with pants. Some robes were made in collarless kimono styles; other had shawl collars. In the 1980s, there were matching terry robes and shorts.

Hair and Headdress

Shorter hair predominated throughout the 1980s, although hair of all lengths was still seen. Men's hair stylists in the late 1990s used hair care products to make men's hair stand up into a tousled effect.

Hats were not worn a great deal except in cold weather. For sports, men wore caps. In the 1990s

FIGURE 19.43 Snowboarders prefer looser fitted and more casual clothing than downhill skiers. (Nathan Billow/Allsport)

baseball caps, worn backward by younger men, became exceptionally popular. Perhaps as male baby boomers were aging, baseball caps were useful to hide receding hairlines. Traditional hat styles were not something they were comfortable with; baseball caps could be related to their nostalgia for the past.

Stetson-style hats experienced a brief revival during the popularity of the TV program *Dallas*, set in Texas, and snap-brim felt hats, in the early 1980s after the release of the film *Indiana Jones and the Raiders of the Lost Ark*.

Footwear

See Illustrated Table 19.2 for some examples of footwear for the period from 1980 to 1999. Stockings were available in wide variety of knit fabrics, colors, and patterns. When the lead actor, Don Johnson, wore shoes without socks on the 1980s TV series *Miami Vice*, some men imitated him.

Boots remained fashionable throughout the 1970s. In the 1980s various types of sneakers, both high and low, were important, as were western boots and hiking and walking shoes. The wide variety of shoes in the 1990s ranged from wing-tipped styles and two-tone shoes to sturdy hiking boots and included a vast array of sneakers. The casual focus was evident in shoes in 1994. One shoe company introduced a line for casual Fridays, and sales of loafers and sporty oxfords increased. Rock stars were responsible for the popularity of some casual shoe styles, such as driving shoes and foam-soled, suede-laced oxfords.

Accessories

In the late 1980s floral ties gained popularity, and ties grew wider again, remaining wide into the 1990s.

Jewelry

Although more men were wearing jewelry, including gold chains and earrings, advice manuals about appropriate attire for business generally counseled men to wear only wedding or signet rings, conservative watches with leather bands, tie clips or stickpins, and cuff links.

Cosmetics and Grooming

In 1987, $1 billion was spent on men's toiletries, $560 million of which was for fragrances and aftershave lotions, double that of ten years before (Lord, 1987). More skin-care products were also available. Many men had their hair "styled" at unisex beauty parlors rather than "cut" at barber shops.

Actor Don Johnson generally appeared on *Miami Vice* with several days' growth of beard. Soon fashion models, popular musicians, some fashion-conscious students, and men whose jobs permitted it were cultivating an unshaven look—a style that persisted off and on throughout the 1990s. Special razors could be used to maintain the stubble from several days' growth of beard (Figure 19.44).

COSTUME COMPONENTS FOR CHILDREN

Throughout the period children's clothing, even for tots as young as 1 to 3 years, displayed clear reflections of adult styles in silhouette, hemline length, and preferred fabrics. As soon as a new style was introduced for adults, it was likely to be made in child-sized versions. High-priced, high-fashion lines of clothing for children of all ages were being made by many more firms as children dressed like small adults (see Contemporary Comments 19.1, page 613). Retro fashions were

FIGURE 19.44
This 1990s advertisement exemplifies the "no ties" casualness of the 1990s. (Courtesy of Advertising Archives)

Costume Components for Infants and Preschool-Age Children

For many decades it had been customary to dress very young children in soft pastel or light colors. Patterned fabrics were made in small scale. The conventional wisdom had been that these colors best suited the delicate complexions of small children and that small-scale patterns were better on small people. Children were rarely dressed in black. A major shift occurred in the 1980s when vivid, multicolored clothing styles were introduced for even the youngest children (Figure 19.45). From this point consumers could find both bright colors and pastels for children.

Among the more popular items for infants cited by retailers in the 1990s were rompers for warm weather and one-piece outfits and coveralls for colder weather. Bubbles, one-piece outfits with extra width in the shaping that gave them a rounded effect, were popular for infants and toddlers. When an early 1990s public TV show for preschool children featured a

designed for children as well as adults. In 1990 the *New York Times* noted a tendency for baby-boomer parents to dress their children in styles reminiscent of the 1960s, styles also promoted for adults (Leinbach, 1990). Trade magazines for the children's wear industry cited street fashion styles and retro styles, especially mod, as important influences in 1996.

TV channels, such as MTV, and TV shows such as *Sesame Street* also influenced children's clothing (Leinbach, 1990). Cartoon and comic-strip characters were extensively licensed to children's clothing manufacturers and appeared on garments ranging from sweatshirts to sneakers. This trend accelerated during the 1990s.

FIGURE 19.45 By the 1980s, traditional pastel colors for the very young had been augmented by vivid, multicolor designs. (Oberto Gili/© 1989 Condé Nast Publications)

purple dinosaur named Barney, the dinosaur logo appeared on preschoolers' clothing. By 1996 animal and vegetable prints were popular.

Toddler-sized versions of hiking boots appeared in the 1990s, along with small-scale versions of popular sneakers.

The 1953 Flammable Fabrics Act and subsequent amendments have required that children's sleepwear sizes 0–14 meet certain flammability standards. In order to achieve a nonflammable fabric, manufacturers have had to either use certain manufactured fibers that are not inherently flammable or apply special finishes to cotton and cotton blends. When one of the chemical finishes, TRIS, was found to possibly be mutagenic, the public became suspicious of flame-retardant finishes. As a result, some parents bought loose cotton T-shirts or other undergarments for children to use as sleepwear. However, loose-fitting garments are more likely to catch fire than tight-fitting sleepwear. Therefore, in 1996 changes were made in this legislation to exempt tight-fitting sleepwear for children from regulation to encourage parents to purchase safer, fitted sleepwear. Sleepwear for children under 6 months was also excluded from the standard, based on the rationale that children so young are not mobile enough to come close to sources of ignition.

School-Age Children: Trends Affecting Boys and Girls

In the 1990s many U.S. schools reacted to conflicts arising from gang-color–related outfits by requiring students to follow a dress code. As more adult clothing became unisex in nature, so did clothes for children. Knitted fabrics were extensively used in clothing throughout the period, especially those made from manufactured fibers or blends that were easy to launder. Vividly colored fabrics with large-scale prints, stripes, and checks were used, especially during the late 1980s and the 1990s (see Figure 19.37).

Garments

T-shirts remained a major clothing item for boys and girls. Interest in licensing and logos grew year by year, and from after the late 1990s, sports and entertainment logos were everywhere. T-shirt messages reflected current issues such as global warming and ecology.

Both boys and girls wore pants for almost all occasions, and blue jeans continued to be enormously popular. Bell-bottom pants from the 1960s were revived in the early 1990s and continued to be important as the fashion for bare midriffs spread to younger children. Spandex was used to make tight-fitting pants for girls. Boys adopted loose-fitting, large hip-hop styles.

As warm-up suits became popular for adult wear, they also penetrated the children's market. Active sports clothing with spandex for stretch, such as bicycling pants, were popular as were manufactured fiber fleece fabrics for outdoor wear. Sometimes these fabrics were used as linings for warmth or as the outer layer.

Bathing suits were like those of adults. When the high-cut bathing suits for women were introduced in the 1980s, suits for little girls also incorporated these lines. In the 1990s rumba suits, bathing suit styles from the 1950s with ruffles across the backside, were revived.

Footwear

In the 1990s the most important types of footwear were boots and sneakers. Rain boots were available in bright colors.

Accessories

By the 1990s both boys and girls carried books to school in backpacks. Many backpacks had logos, and local fashions played a role in what type of backpack was most desirable. When violent incidents began to occur in some schools, pressure mounted to require students to bring clear plastic backpacks so that it would be evident if the bag contained any weapon.

Costume Components for Girls

In the 1980s hem lengths were variable and included lengths from several inches above the knee to knee length. By the late 1980s and 1990s some dresses ended several inches below the knee, others were short.

In the 1990s, preteen girls wore layers. Blouses hung out over skirts or pants, and vests over the blouses. Specific styles that appeared frequently included sweatshirt dresses, jumpers, and dresses with dropped waistlines. Many dresses for more formal occasions had lace or other decorative collars and trimmings. Prints were popular for summer; velveteen, for winter.

Other popular items included a wide variety of shorts and longer pants, knee-length or longer tights worn with large T-shirts, jump suits, and jogging suits.

Costume Components for Boys

Influences from sports were strong in boys' clothing. Among the more important styles were baseball players' jackets and caps, rugby shirts, and fashions endorsed by sports figures. Sports logos appeared on clothing ranging from caps to jackets.

Among the adult men's styles that had a strong influence on boy's clothing in the 1980s were safari and western styles, men's leisure suits, and natural-look fabrics. As menswear became more casual in the 1990s, boys' dress clothing reflected this trend and focused on blazers and jeans or chinos. See Illustrated Table 19.4 for some examples of styles for children in the period from 1980 to 1999.

Summary

Themes

In looking at the themes identified in Chapter 1, examples of many themes are found in the styles of 1980 to 1999: the impact of POLITICS through the influences on style of POLITICAL LEADERS and their families such as Nancy Reagan and Princess Diana; the introduction of styles with military influences when POLITICAL CONFLICTS took place, such as the first Persian Gulf War and strife in Somalia, Bosnia, Afghanistan, and Iraq; and ECONOMIC EVENTS such as the GATT and NAFTA treaties and their impact on the American apparel industry. One theme that needs more detailed examination in this period is FASHION itself.

Fashion, broadly defined as a taste shared by many for a short period of time, first appeared in the Middle Ages when social and economic conditions in western Europe provided fertile ground for its growth and development. With succeeding centuries, fashion change accelerated. By the 19th century, major fashion changes were coming about every 20 years. The development in the 20th century of a complex industry that to some extent manipulated the social phenomenon of fashion and a population that was economically well off enough to follow the latest styles resulted in still shorter fashion periods, lasting 10 years or less.

Illustrated Table 19.4

Children's Clothing Styles: 1980–1999

Many items of children's clothing reflected adult styles, 1985

Dresses from
Simplicity pattern
catalog, March 1989[1]

Licensed cartoon characters were an important part of children's
clothing. T-shirts and sweatshirts, often oversized and worn over
narrow tights, were popular for adults and children, 1985[1]

Through licensing agreements between Sears, Roebuck and Co.
and the fast food chain McDonald's in 1987, a line of casual
sportswear for children called McKids was produced[1]

---

[1] *Children's Business,* October 1985. Fairchild Publications.

Illustrated Table 19.4

Children's Clothing Styles: 1980–1999

Children's styles of the 1990s and 2000s
echoed adult styles

Throughout the 1970s and
1980s jeans and other clothes
made of denim, including
stone-washed denim, were
especially popular with
adolescents[2]

Retro styles for adolescents
included poodle-skirt revivals
of the 1950s[3]

Short and long garments, called "bubbles," with
gathered pants were among the best-selling
items for very young children in the 1990s

Plus sizes for overweight
children became available

[2] *Women's Wear Daily,* September 3, 1985. Fairchild Publications
[3] *Women's Wear Daily, Youth,* July 27, 1987. Fairchild Publications

From post–World War II until the 1960s, consumers who wanted to purchase clothing that did not conform to mainstream fashion trends had few choices. With the 1960s, that began to change.

It is not that fashion change disappeared. As in earlier periods, in the decades since 1960 some generalizations can be made about similarities of clothing styles for women, men, and children. One generalization is that when a trend clearly predominated, it may be seen in clothing for women, men, and children. For example, when an unfitted silhouette without a defined waistline was popular for women in the latter part of the 1960s, the same silhouette appeared in girls' clothing. Both men's and women's garments grew wide at the shoulders in the early 1980s. Hemline location is another general trend that has often been evident in clothing for both sexes and all ages. When women's and girls' hems were long in the 1940s, men's overcoats tended to be long, but as women's and girls' hemlines grew short in the 1960s and early 1970s, men's overcoats also shortened, as did boys.' When almost any length of skirt was acceptable in the 1990s for women, hemlines in men's overcoats and girls' dresses also became variable.

Popular fabrics are generally popular across age and gender lines. The polyester knitted fabrics of the 1960s showed up not only in women's and girls' dresses, pants, and sportswear but also in men's and boys' suits, sports jackets, and trousers. Denim as a fabric and blue jeans as a garment were used by everyone throughout the period, and when natural fibers returned to popularity in the 1980s and 1990s, it was for all consumers. Hairstyles for adult women and for young girls tended to be similar, as did hairstyles for adult men and boys.

Influences from current events, the media, and new fashion designers usually appeared widely. Some examples include the western styles of the 1970s, designs inspired by the film *The Great Gatsby* in 1974, Japanese designer ideas from around 1980, and retro fashions seen from the 1980s and 1990s. Many American and foreign designers produced both men's and women's lines.

Although these common threads that tie together clothing for all ages and both sexes continue to be evident, something happened to fashion in the late 1960s. American society was questioning many of its assumptions about issues as diverse as politics and government, race and ethnicity, the arts, and morality; the old rules about fashion were also being questioned.

The previous world of fashion, in which conformity to the predominant silhouette and skirt length was a mark of sophistication, disappeared. Fashion had never been totally predictable, but the industry had developed a structure and a means of production and distribution that relied on customers who would, at least, follow the latest major trends from the international style centers. A more diverse, more segmented marketplace replaced the fashion industry that once spoke with a single voice.

The fashion industry was far from dead; instead, it was transformed. Entrepreneurs in the fashion industry are well aware that they must satisfy their customers' preferences if they wish to survive. Consumers have gotten used to having a wide variety of fashion goods from which to choose. This expectation—together with the development of new computer-based technologies that enable manufacturers to adapt more rapidly to style changes and the proliferation of specialized retail outlets—is likely to sustain the desire for and the availability of a wide variety of diverse styles from which to choose.

NEW VIEWS OF FASHION

Many analyses of fashion in this period focus on the extreme nature of the designs that came from the best-known designers in Paris and other fashion centers. Some of the more bizarre styles are said to reflect the anxieties of contemporary society. Examples include designs by Belgian Martin Margiela who showed garments with mold and bacteria growing on fabrics and the controversial collection by John Galliano for Dior called *The Tramps*. Inspired by the homeless people of Paris, it featured tattered gowns. Such designers are viewed by some scholars as avant-garde

Visual Summary Table

Major Styles c. 1980–1999

Women: 1980–1995
Trends that influenced mainstream fashion included wide, padded shoulders and shorter skirts.

Women: 1990s and after
Spandex added to many fabrics provided a tight, close fit. Shoulders narrowed somewhat.

Women: 1995–1999
Skirts of many lengths could be found. Often hemlines were uneven. A layered look was also fashionable.

Men: 1980–1999
Business suits had wide shoulders and an easy fit until the latter half of the 1990s when the incorporation of stretch fibers made for more fitted garments.

Men: 1990s and after
Casual dress for business became more widely accepted.

Men: 1980–1999
Emphasis on fitness made activewear an important part of men's wardrobes.

Men: 1980–1999
More colorful and decorative clothing continued to be an option for men.

artists whose medium of expression is dress. Just as the creators of avant-garde art, music, sculpture, and architecture may be seen by the general public as outlandish and incomprehensible, so too the designs in fashion shows may seem unconnected to the lives of most consumers.

Caroline Evans in *Fashion at the Edge* (2003) argued that extreme fashion expresses anxieties, alienation, and loss in a time of rapid social, economic, and technological change. Evans noted that it is a new development to have fashion "speculate about identity and community in a changing world" (5).

But the fashion industry has become a global enterprise, and those who design at the highest level, though often the most visible, are just one part of this enterprise. Street styles that originate outside the organized fashion system as well as high fashion are among the sources of design ideas. Fashion, with its dual elements of public acceptance and change, has long provided individuals with the opportunity to conform and express individuality at the same time (see Modern Influences). Fashion continues to fuel changes in dress in the western world.

REFERENCES

Adler, J. (1995, February 20). Have we become a nation of slobs? *Newsweek*, 56.

Agins, T. (1999). *The end of fashion*. New York, NY: William Morrow.

Bell, Q. (1973). *On human finery*. Philadelphia, PA: West.

Berkow, I. (1990, May 14). The murders over the sneakers. *New York Times*, C6.

Brubach, H. (1991, September 2). In fashion. *The New Yorker*, 72.

Cocks, J., & Fallon, K. J. (1990, November). The bonfire of the business suit. *Time*, *136*(22), 83.

Conlin, J. (1989, April 20). Gonna dress you up. *Rolling Stone*, 51.

Crane, D. (2000). *Fashion and its social agendas*. Chicago, IL: University of Chicago Press.

Daria, I. (1990). *The fashion cycle*. New York, NY: Simon & Schuster.

Evans, C. (2003). *Fashion at the edge: Spectacle, modernity, and deathliness*. New Haven, CT: Yale University Press.

Finamore, M. T. (2010). Vreeland, Diana. In V. Steele (Ed.), *The Berg companion to fashion* (pp. 715–716). Oxford, UK: Berg.

Godfrey, D. (1989, September 6). U.S. buyers find mixed messages in Paris. *Daily News Record*, *176*(19).

Hofmeister, S. (1994, August 22). Used American jeans power a thriving industry abroad. *New York Times*, 21.

Inside fashion. (1984, May). *Gentlemen's Quarterly*, 39.

Leinbach, D. (1990, March 4). Trends in children's fashions (Part VI). *New York Times*, 52.

Lord, S. (1987, June). The masculine presence. *Vogue*, 187.

Milbank, C. (1989). *New York fashion: The evolution of American style*. New York, NY: Abrams.

Morgado, M. A. (1996). Coming to terms with postmodern: Theories and concepts of contemporary culture and their

MODERN INFLUENCES

Japanese designer Nozomi Ishiguri founded his atelier in 1998 and worked for Comme des Garçons. His 2014 ready-to-wear collection mixing textures and patterns is reminiscent of the 1990s as is the pairing of turtleneck under a jacket and short-suit outfit. Ishiguri designs unisex clothing, another element borrowed from the 1990s.

(Giannoni/WWD/Condé Nast)

implications for apparel scholars. *Clothing and Textiles Research Journal, 14*(1), 41.

Morris, B. (1982, March 7). The case for couture. *The New York Times Magazine,* 174.

Ogden, C. L., Carroll, M. D., Kit, B. K., & Flegal, K. M. (2014). Prevalence of childhood and adult obesity in the United States, 2011–2012. JAMA, *311*(8): 806–814.

Ottum, B. (1984, February 27). Notable triumphs, wrong notes. *Sports Illustrated,* 23.

Polhemus, T. (1994). *Street style.* New York, NY: Thames and Hudson.

Rifkin, G. (1994, November 8). Digital blue jeans pour data and legs into customized fit. *New York Times,* A1.

Sara Lee hosiery executive tells symposium attendees 'casual dress trend poses threat to hosiery industry.' (1996, October 21). *Southern Textile News,* 7.

Spindler, A. M. (1996, January 22). Investing in haute couture's lower-brow future. *New York Times,* D2.

Steele, V. (2000). Fashion: Yesterday, today, and tomorrow. In N. White & I. Griffiths (Eds.), *The fashion business* (pp. 7–20). New York, NY: Berg.

Steinhauer, J. (1997, April 9). What vanity and casual Fridays wrought. *New York Times,* A1.

White, C. R. (1996, October 6). As the way of all flesh goes south. *New York Times,* Section 4, 16.

	2000	2001	2002	2004	2006	2007
FASHION AND TEXTILES	U.S. retailers acknowledge and respond to changing demographics					
POLITICS AND CONFLICTS	By Supreme Court decision, George W. Bush becomes president	Terrorists attack the United States on September 11				
DECORATIVE AND FINE ARTS		Movies such as *Lord of the Rings* and *Harry Potter* rely on special computer effects		Google announces plans to convert 15 million books into searchable, digital format	*An Inconvenient Truth*, a movie about climate change, becomes international hit	
ECONOMICS AND TRADE			Euro coins and banknotes become currency for EU			The Great Recession impacts U.S. and world markets
TECHNOLOGY AND IDEAS	AT&T introduces text messaging via mobile phone				*Time* names "You" its Person of the Year, because of the prevalence of user-generated online content	iPhone launched
RELIGION AND SOCIETY				Same-sex marriage legalized in Massachusetts		

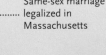

CHAPTER TWENTY

The New Millennium

2000–2014

2008	2009	2010	2011	2013

Fashion blogs become mainstream component of the fashion press

China hosts Olympic Games

Barack Obama elected 44th U.S. president

A revolutionary wave of protests, part of Arab Spring, sweeps the Middle East

The Metropolitan Museum of Art's Costume Institute celebrates designer Alexander McQueen

Occupy Wall Street protest movement begins in New York's financial district

Bangladesh tragedy brings attention to unsafe garment factory working conditions

First Lady Michelle Obama and the Duchess of Cambridge have become style icons

The September 11, 2001, attacks on the United States had a far-reaching impact. The ensuing conflicts in the Middle East influenced both domestic and international politics. In fashion, the variety of styles available for women, men, and children flourished with a multitude of sources including designers, celebrities, and Internet blogs and videos. Although apparel conglomerations and mergers increased, niche producers also succeeded, particularly in ethnic and plus-size markets. Technological innovations moved fiber and fabric performance forward, while designers found inspiration for silhouettes in the previous century.

HISTORICAL BACKGROUND

The European Economic Community developed and expanded its functions as trade and investment among members increased. Barriers to moving capital and curbs on financial services were reduced, and citizens of participating countries began using European passports. Beginning in 2002, euro notes and coins were issued. By 2013 membership expanded to include 28 countries, with 18 of the member states using the shared monetary system. But beginning in 2009, countries in the euro zone's underperforming economies, including Portugal, Spain, Italy, and Greece, threatened one of the fundamental aims of the currency union: to create a single market with an integrated economy.

Russia

Elected president of Russia, Vladimir Putin served from 2000 to 2008. He then served as prime minister from 2008 to 2012. Following a change in the law, Putin began an unprecedented third term as president in 2012. The forceful 2014 annexation of Crimea, a peninsula south of Ukraine, provoked the greatest tensions between Russia and the west since the height of the Cold War.

The Middle East

After the terrorist attack on the World Trade Center on September 11, 2001, the United States together with the United Kingdom attacked Afghanistan in October 2001 with the purpose of finding and eliminating the terrorist group al-Qaeda, which was responsible for the attack.

U.S. forces, with the support of British troops, invaded Iraq on March 20, 2003. The announced aim of the invasion was to disarm Iraq, because it was believed that Iraqi leader Saddam Hussein held massive supplies of chemical and biological weapons and other weapons of mass destruction. In addition, the allies sought to overthrow Hussein's government and free the Iraqi people.

On May 1, 2003, from the deck of the USS *Abraham Lincoln*, President George W. Bush announced the end of the campaign and the defeat of the Iraqi forces. Allied forces had been unable to locate any weapons of mass destruction. In the days following Bush's announcement of the end of the war, American and coalition troops suffered almost daily attacks resulting in more casualties than were suffered before May 1. Hussein was captured in December 2003. He was tried and found guilty of crimes against humanity and was hanged on December 30, 2006. The withdrawal of American military forces from Iraq began in June 2009 and was completed under the orders of President Barack Obama in December 2011.

Throughout the Middle East, a revolutionary wave of demonstrations and protests, dubbed the Arab Spring, began in December 2010 (Figure 20.1). By 2013, leaders were forced from power in Tunisia, Egypt, Libya, and Yemen, with civil uprisings in Bahrain and Syria, and protests in Algeria, Iraq, Jordan, Kuwait, Morocco, and Sudan (Hubbard and Gladstone, 2013).

The United States

The 2000 presidential campaign ended with Vice President Al Gore ahead in the popular vote and Governor George W. Bush of Texas holding a slim lead in the electoral vote. The outcome of the national election hinged on the final vote in Florida. Because of the closeness of the vote, Florida law required a recount of the ballots. Problems in counties that used punch cards resulted in questions about the accuracy

FIGURE 20.1 Women of all ages, classes, and religions participated in the Arab Spring protests. (Khalil Mazraawi/AFP/ Getty Images)

of the counts. The Bush campaign appealed the case to the U.S. Supreme Court. The court, by a five-to-four majority, ruled in favor of Bush, who then became president of the United States. George W. Bush was reelected on November 3, 2004.

On August 29, 2005, Hurricane Katrina, described as the most severe natural disaster in United States history, struck the Gulf Coast states of Louisiana, Mississippi, and Alabama. The destruction was widespread, with 50 percent of the city of New Orleans submerged after the levees holding back the gulf waters failed. There was widespread criticism of the slow reaction of the federal government to this disaster.

Democrats gained control of both houses of Congress in the midterm elections of 2006, ending

almost ten years of continuous Republican control. A substantial number of voters were worried about the continuing war in Iraq. With Democrats in control of the House of Representatives, Nancy Pelosi became the first woman elected speaker on November 16, 2006.

Triggered by the collapse of a credit bubble in which institutions lowered their standards to qualify more home borrowers for sub-prime loans, the United States experienced the 18-month Great Recession from December 2007 through June 2009 (U.S. Bureau of Labor Statistics, 2012b). During this time, private consumption declined for the first time in nearly two decades and unemployment reached 9.5 percent. Despite these economic hardships, the mention of retail therapy or purchasing items to improve mood increased in advertisements and editorials across the nation.

In 2008, the United States elected Barack Obama as the 44th president, the first of his two terms in office. The first African American elected to this position, President Obama also made history with passage of the Affordable Care Act, a health care reform bitterly contested yet ruled constitutional by the U.S. Supreme Court. Often compared to First Lady Jacqueline Kennedy, President Obama's wife Michelle endorsed up-and-coming American designers and paired classic yet updated styles such as triple-strand pearl necklaces with sleeveless shifts (see Figure 20.13). For a list of prominent designers of the period, see Table 20.1.

During the 2009 inauguration Michelle Obama wore a coat and dress designed by Cuban-American designer Isabel Toledo with gloves from retailer J. Crew. This pairing of high and low fashion led to much emulation and earned Obama the moniker "everyday style icon" (Betts, 2011).

Energy and Environmental Issues

In the 21st century, as concerns about climate change increased, manufacturers advertised products made from environmentally friendly fibers. Some, such as hemp, were promoted for requiring fewer pesticides in their cultivation and being biodegradable. Others, such as soy silk, corn fiber, and milk fiber,

TABLE 20.1 Some Prominent Designers: 2000–2014

DESIGNER	WORKING IN	NOTABLE CHARACTERISTICS
Altuzzara (1983–)	Women's ready-to-wear; launched line in 2008; announced Target collection in 2014.	Sophisticated and easy to wear.
B. Michael (1957–)	Menswear and women's wear; launched millinery in 1989; couture in 1999.	Focuses on the quality of the garment's cut, fit, and silhouette.
Manolo Blahnik (1942–)	Shoe designer, products sold in specialty stores and Blahnik boutiques.	A prodigious designer; most popularly known for footwear for 2006 film *Marie Antoinette* and shoes worn in the *Sex and the City* TV show and 2008 film.
Thom Browne (1965–)	Thom Browne label launched in 2001, contracted with Brooks Brothers to design high-end unisex collection for Black Fleece in 2007, launched eyewear in 2011.	Narrow-cut suits, sometimes in plaid paired, with high-water pants or shorts.
Tory Burch (1966–)	Ready-to-wear women's clothing, handbags, shoes, jewelry. Tory Burch, 2004.	In the tradition of Ralph Lauren, Burch is "one of the most successful examples of marketing a stylized version of oneself as a ready-to-wear lifestyle."
Sarah Burton (1974–)	English fashion designer, currently creative director of fashion brand Alexander McQueen.	Winner of Designer of the Year Award at the 2011 Vogue British Fashion Design Awards and wedding dress designer of Kate Middleton, Duchess of Cambridge.
Doo-Ri Chung (1973–)	Ready-to-wear: Doo.Ri , 2001, left label in 2012. Created capsule collections for J. Crew and Gap; sells her line to exclusive stores such as Barney's New York. Launched lower price line Under.Linge in 2009.	Jersey, shocks of color in subdued palette.
Alber Elbaz (1961–)	Design assistant for Geoffrey Beene, designer for Guy Laroche, Head women's wear designer at Yves Saint Laurent Rive Gauche, Creative Director for Lanvin, 2001.	Classic shapes, in flattering colors and the use of deconstructed details.
Patricia Field (1942–)	Costume designer, stylist, fashion designer.	Costume designer for *Sex and the City*, *The Devil Wears Prada*, and *Ugly Betty*.
Prabal Gurung (active 2003–)	Launched own label in 2009, partnered with Target for capsule collection in 2013.	His goal is to create "clothes that make women look beautiful rather than following the latest trend."
Christopher Kane (1982–)	Launched own label in 2006; expanded into menswear in 2010; designed three capsule collections for Topshop and one for Versus.	Known for inventive and imaginative designs.
Naeem Khan (1958–)	Apprenticed for Halston; Launched own line in 2003.	"Designs dresses, gowns, and chic separates that often feature hand-embroidery that reflects his [Indian] heritage."
Reed Krakoff (active 1996–)	Joined Coach in 1996; Created own line of ready-to-wear, handbags, and shoes in 2013.	"Focus on sportswear that juxtaposes utility and femininity."
Monique Lhuillier (1971–)	Upscale, bridal company: Lhuillier, 1996; expanded into evening wear in 2001 and ready-to-wear in 2003.	"Her silhouettes are dramatic but soft, often with a juxtaposition of fabric textures."
Phillip Lim (1973–)	Ready-to-wear: Launched 3.1 phillip lim, 2005 with business partner Wen Zhou.	Designs "real clothes that people wear—pretty, but cool and chic without the high price of designer brands."
Christian Louboutin (1964–)	Shoe designer, first opened shop in Paris in 1992.	Known for slim and pointy-toed silhouette and signature red soles.
Marchesa (Designers Georgina Chapman, 1976– , and Keren Craig, 1976–)	Launched by two British designers in 2004.	"The label specializes in high fashion evening wear with an eclectic aesthetic."

TABLE 20.1 Some Prominent Designers: 2000–2014 (continued)

DESIGNER	WORKING IN	NOTABLE CHARACTERISTICS
Thakoon Panichgul (1974–)	Ready-to-wear: Thakoon, 2004	Etheral and urban styles influenced by eastern heritage.
Preen (Designers Justin Thornton and Thea Bregazzi)	Launched in 1996	Known for clean, fluid lines and futuristic elegance.
Proenza Schouler (Lazaro Hernandez, 1979– ; Jack McCollough, 1979–)	Proenza Schouler, 2002	"Classic silhouettes with a twist for grown-up women;" emphasis on spare silhouettes in subdued colors.
Gareth Pugh (1981–)	Couture, 2005	Fashion as performance art; "cast as enfant terrible of the British fashion industry."
Tracy Reese (1964–)	Sportswear; 1987 launched own company, then design director at Magaschoni; relaunched own company Tracy Reese Meridian.	Ultrafeminine Tracy Reese and more moderately priced Plenty. Her specialty is dresses, but she has expanded into cosmetics, shoes, handbags, and home furnishings.
Narciso Rodriguez (1961–)	Ready-to-wear launched in 2003 with business partner Nicola Guarno; designer of diffusion line Robbi & Nikki.	Known for excellent tailoring and feminine, wearable designs.
The Row (Ashley and Mary Kate Olsen, 1986–)	Established in 2006 and has expanded to include eyewear and handbags.	Focus on fine fabrics and fit, in 2012, the Council of Fashion Designers of America named the designers the Womenswear Designers of the Year.
Jonathon Saunders (1977–)	Debuted in 2003.	Known for his work with prints and use of traditional silk screening techniques. Received the Scottish Fashion Designer of the Year in 2005.
Raf Simons (1968–)	Belgiun furniture designer; launched menswear line in 1995, creative director at Jil Sander 2005–2012, artistic director of haute couture, ready-to-wear, and accessories at Christian Dior 2012.	Emphasis on modern proportions, and new fabrics and techniques.
Riccardo Tisci (1974–)	Named Creative Director for Givenchy women's wear and haute couture 2005; named menswear and accessories designer of the Givenchy men's division 2008.	Known for Gothic leanings and minimalism.
Philip Treacy (1967–)	Milliner of couture and ready-to-wear hats.	Fascinated by surrealist themes, in 2005 created hats for the wedding of Prince of Wales and Camila Parker Bowles.
Isabel Toledo (1961–)	Showed first designs in 1985.	"Considered a 'hands-on' designer whose clothes have avant-garde appeal."
Iris van Herpen (1984–)	Haute couture label 2007, ready-to-wear 2014.	Time chose a van Herpen 3-D printed dress as one of the 50 top inventions of 2011.
Alexander Wang (1984–)	Ready-to-wear: Alexander Wang, 2007	Known for "model off duty look": comfortable outfits that appear classic and chic and thrown together.

Information about designers already listed in Tables 19.2 and 19.3 (see pages 607–608 and 610–611) who continued to be active for all or part of this period are not included in this table.

Sources: Alford, H. P., & Stegemeyer, A. (2010). *Who's who in fashion* (5th ed.). New York, NY: Fairchild Publications; Tortora, P. G., & Keiser, S. J. (2014). *Who's who in fashion* (4th ed.). New York, NY: Fairchild Publications.

were regenerated from natural materials. **Tencel**, regenerated from wood chips, was made by a process that polluted than its closest fiber relative, rayon. Manufacturers and retailers often touted bamboo as a "green" fiber. However, in 2013 several retailers, including Amazon, Macy's, and Sear's paid monetary penalties to the Federal Trade Commission (FTC). The FTC charged these retailers with violating the Textile Products Identification Act and the FTC's textile rules by labeling rayon products *bamboo* to appeal to environmentally conscious consumers.

In 2003, animal rights activists presented a fashion show of synthetic fur fashions in the hopes of encouraging women to wear imitation rather than real fur. Although these activities did not totally eliminate fashion interest in fur, fashion designers increasingly turned to faux fur and leather (Figure 20.2). Technological advances improved the look and feel of imitation goods, with significantly lower price tags than the animal products. The importation of products such as tortoise shell, ivory, crocodile skin, and other products on the endangered species list was banned, with limitations placed on the sale and export of live coral.

The Changing American Family

By 2011, 58 percent of women were in the labor force. The share of working mothers accounted for nearly three quarters of women with children at home. The number of women who were their families' sole or primary breadwinner also soared, to 40 percent in 2013 from 11 percent in 1960. Despite these gains, the Bureau of Labor Statistics (2012b) reported that wage disparity continued, with working women earning just 82 percent of men's salaries. Perhaps because of women's labor engagement and higher levels of education, the birthrate hit its lowest point in 2012.

Monumental changes came to the look of the traditional family when Massachusetts became the first state to legalize same-sex marriage in 2004 (Figure 20.3). By 2013, the U.S. Supreme Court ruled that a 1996 law, the Defense of Marriage Act, forbidding the federal government from recognizing

FIGURE 20.2 Furs took on new colors and textures especially in the years after 2000, as new techniques for handling fur developed. (Miranda/WWD/© Conde Nast)

same-sex marriages, was unconstitutional. By 2014, 26 states, plus the District of Columbia, allowed same-sex marriage, causing a boon to wedding and related industries in these states. Public support grew considerably, exemplified by President Obama's declaration, the first for a sitting president, for support of legalizing same-sex marriage.

Changing U.S. Demographics

In 1960, the U.S population was 85 percent Caucasian. The Pew Research Center statistics estimated that by 2060 it will be only 43 percent white. This cultural shift is reflected in the 2013 Super Bowl ads of three global brands: Coke, Chevrolet, and Cheerios incorporated their appeal to these consumers. In markets with large Latino populations, some major retailers such as Target and Walmart used bilingual signs and product mix more attuned to the preferences of Mexican, Cuban, Puerto Rican, and other Hispanic consumers. Retailers also partnered with Hispanic celebrities to increase this market base (Figure 20.4). In 2003, Kmart introduced a new line of fashions named for Thalia, a popular Mexican singer, and in 2011 the retailer partnered with Sofia Vergara, the Columbian-born actress of TV show *Modern Family*. Kohl's offered two apparel collections featuring Jennifer

FIGURE 20.3 Throughout the 2000s, state governments extended marriage rights to same-sex couples. In 2011, the ban on gays serving in the U.S. military was lifted with the repeal of the 1993 "don't ask, don't tell" policy. Some wedding-related businesses benefit commercially from same-sex marriages. (Nigel Roddis/Getty Images)

FIGURE 20.4 American retailers in the 21st century pay particular attention to the growing Hispanic population. Entertainer Jennifer Lopez maintains clothing lines and perfume sold in major department stores such as Kohl's and Macy's. (© Everett Collection Inc./Alamy)

interracial and same-sex families in portrayals of what one voice-over declared as "the new us."

After four decades of rapid growth (Brown, 2014), the number of Latino immigrants in the United States reached a record 18.8 million in 2010. As of 2012, the U.S.-born Latino population numbered 53 million individuals and continued to grow at a faster rate than the immigrant population.

The spending power of the Hispanic population, $1.2 trillion in 2012, was larger than the economies of all but 13 countries in the world (Humphreys, 2013). Retailers from apparel to food service tried to increase

Lopez and Marc Anthony. Other retailers, including Macy's, marketed to Latinos via *People en Español* and by running TV ads on the Univision and Telemundo networks.

In 2006, 24 million baby boomers were older than 50, and 27.5 percent of the population consisted of baby boomers. Since 1978 spending on apparel declined and spending on services increased. Furthermore, as women age, their bodies change. The trend toward increased use of casual clothing may also be related to demographics. The baby boomers grew up wearing jeans and casual clothes. It is probably not surprising that they welcomed the opportunity to wear these casual clothes to work.

According to *Women's Wear Daily*, since 2005, the average dress size in America has grown from a size 12 to 14. Though select stores such as Forever 21, H&M, and Ann Taylor have released plus-size clothing, the plus-size market represents just 18 percent of total revenue in the women's clothing industry. Efforts to promote plus-size retailers include New York's Full Figured Fashion Week, which spans 6 days and features fashion shows and shopping events, and London's Plus Size Fashion Weekend (Figure 20.5). In 2014, Isabel Toledo presented a collection for plus-size retailer Lane Bryant. For her first time designing for this market, Toledo commented: "Maybe this category has not been addressed as much, but that's changing.

Women of all types are great customers if they love fashion" (Shapiro, 2014, E6).

The backlash against hyper-thin models developed after the 2006 deaths of several young anorexic Brazilian fashion models. Models considered excessively thin were banned from Spain's most influential fashion show. Although other voices were raised in support of Spain's action, such direct action was limited, and very thin fashion models continued to be the norm.

The Digital Revolution

The computer revolution and the Internet are profoundly changing the way business, government, and industry function.

Virtual Internet sites provide a venue for the pursuit of fashion. These sites consist of imaginary environments that participants can develop and where they can create individual characters called **avatars**. Similar in many respects to computer games, these virtual environments, which have proliferated in the 21st century, provide opportunities for engaging with fashion by selecting or designing clothes for avatars. The real-world fashion industry soon recognized virtual worlds and their potential as sites for advertising, information, and building a potential clientele. Designers such as Donna Karan and Vivienne Tam, as well as retailers, opened "stores" where customers

FIGURE 20.5 Models in a mix of product categories from sports to evening wear wait backstage at London's 2014 Plus-Size Fashion Weekend. (Andrew Cowie/AFP/Getty Images)

use virtual money to purchase fashions in which to clothe avatars. There have also been competitions for fashion design in which the winning designs have been manufactured and available for purchase in real-world stores.

Fashion **blogs**, personal website pages devoted to opinions, ideas, photographs, and links to other websites, are an increasingly important means of fashion information. In describing a 13-year old blogger being seated in the front row at a 2009 Marc Jacobs show, *New York Times* style-section writer Eric Wilson (2009) wrote: "Fashion bloggers have ascended from the nosebleed seats to the front row with such alacrity that a long-held social code among editors, one that prizes position and experience above outward displays of ambition or enjoyment, has practically been obliterated" (ST1). Creators, promoters, and sellers of fashion regularly post blogs, and the medium has become a mainstream component of the fashion press (Figure 20.6).

Social networking sites, also referred to as **social media**, provide users their own unique "space" in which they can connect with others. These sites include ones that are business related (e.g., LinkedIn), social related (e.g., Twitter and Facebook), provide location-based services (e.g., Foursquare), and provide visual communication (e.g., Instagram, Pinterest, and Flickr). YouTube has also provided a means for shoppers to share their "hauls," or beauty and fashion purchases, some of whom receive sponsorship from designers and brands.

Large and small brands, as well as entrepreneurs, fashion bloggers, and everyday consumers, use social media (Figure 20.7), changing how fashion is designed, consumed and reported. Some designers create for the two-dimensional image that shoppers consume without considering the tactile or even matters of quality construction. Designer Alexander

FIGURE 20.6 Fashion blogs have become a mainstream component of the fashion press such that *Lucky* magazine hosts a multi-day fashion and beauty blog conference. (Bryan Bedder/Getty Images for Lucky Magazine)

FIGURE 20.7 Chanel posted an invitation to the Chanel Shopping Center on Facebook and Twitter prior to its 2014 runway show at a staged supermarket. (Giannoni/WWD/Condé Nast)

Wang commented that in designing a collection "We try to think of the pictures that are going to come out online" (Schneier, 2014). With the speed and ubiquity of social media, copies or knock-offs appear nearly simultaneously to the runway or award show premieres of the designs.

Elements of the Fashion System

The global fashion industry includes collaborations from designers, manufacturers, merchandisers, and retailers from all over the world. In the 21st century, the industry is characterized by short product-life cycles, erratic consumer demand, an abundance of product variety, and complex supply chains (U.S. Bureau of Labor Statistics, 2012a).

Design

In the 21st century, the design process is influenced by the work presented in collections in cities such as Paris, Milan, and New York, as well as trade shows. Some designers use fashion consulting services to analyze and predict the popularity of street trends. Perhaps most important to large retailers, technologies such as computer-aided design (CAD) systems help reduce the time for making patterns and enable electronic storage of the design for later modifications. Software such as Product Lifecycle Management improves communications throughout the supply chain, ultimately reducing production cycle time.

Production

By 2008 it was evident that both the apparel and the textile industries in the United States had suffered severe economic losses. Many apparel producers choose lower cost, off-shore production in Asia and Latin America. In order to meet foreign competition some American manufacturers exploited workers, often immigrants, who worked in sweatshops in metropolitan areas of the United States. Protesters have made the abusive working conditions and low pay of some foreign workers an issue, especially targeting those firms selling high-priced merchandise. Anger and outrage accompanied the 2013 collapse of a

Bangladesh building that killed 1,127 garment factory workers (Figure 20.8).

Apparel production in the 21st century has sped dramatically. Fast fashion retailers Zara and H&M turn over the items in their store in as few as 14 days as compared to the 90-day cycle of competitors. These stores have seen increased sales as they appeal to Internet-savvy consumers aware of the latest trends but unwilling to spend large amounts of money on the newest fashions (Pasquarelli, 2012). Retailers such as Target have imitated the "shop within a shop" strategy

FIGURE 20.8 A woman holds up a portrait of her loved ones at the site of the garment factory building that collapsed in Bangladesh. Bangladesh's garment industry is the mainstay of the economy and worth upwards of $20 billion annually. (Wong May-E/AP Images)

of H&M which tests the market by presenting trend-sensitive styles in limited quantities.

Retailing

In the 21st century, retail consolidation has shifted the industry power from apparel manufacturers to larger and more powerful retailers. Deals such as The Gap Store Inc.'s $130 million purchase of luxury boutique chain Intermix Holdco, Inc., enabled these brands to break into new segments of the industry with less risk. Fewer and stronger retail firms are able to negotiate more favorable terms with manufacturers involving price, service, and product.

CHANGES IN THE FASHION INDUSTRY

By 2000, consumers enjoyed an enormous variety of options in dress. Clothes could be bought from sources ranging from Internet retailers to haute couture to thrift shops. The fashion industry, which has always been a perilous business because of the unpredictability of fashion changes, found it was no longer possible to simply copy new trends originating with the top designers. Instead, manufacturers tended to focus on niche or specialized markets aimed toward people from particular geographic areas, ages, social classes, ethnicities, or lifestyles.

The Internet and Multichannel Retailing

According to the U.S. Census Bureau, nearly 75 percent of U.S. households have Internet access. E-commerce transactions grow each year, with clothing and clothing accessories the leading category of items purchased online. Liberal return policies, free or low-cost shipping, and navigation tools such as zooming have lowered consumer risk in making purchases based on sight rather than tactile feel. The Internet has shaped and accelerated fashion cycles. Perhaps because of the dominance of established brick-and-mortar companies, such as Lands' End, in online apparel sales, **multichannel retailing** or the integration of physical stores, websites, and catalogues have become increasingly important to retailing establishments.

Vintage Clothing

By 2002, specialty manufacturers were making replicas of well-worn jeans. All of the worn spots, tears, repairs, and stains on an authentic pair of used jeans were reproduced on a new pair and sold from $150 to $200. These sales of "new vintage jeans" represented about 3 percent of the jeans market, but mass-market retailers such as Gap soon started selling distressed jeans for less than $50 (Bunn, 2002). In 2013, the duo Macklemore and Ryan Lewis skyrocketed to the top of the Billboard charts with their ode to the thrift shop, which celebrated the joys of the bargain bin. Distressed denim looks continue for menswear and women's wear (Figure 20.9).

The Changing Teen Market

By 2000 it was evident that the teen market and a new segment of the children's market called **tweens** (approximately ages 7 to 14) played an increasingly important role in retailing. In 1995 there were 4,000 stores aimed exclusively at teens. By 2003, this number increased to about 10,000 (Rozhon, 2003). Michael Wood, vice president of Teenage Research Unlimited, was quoted in a *New York Times* article saying, "The teen market has exploded in terms of size and direct spending power" (Seymour, 2007, NJ8). Trying to capture this market was not easy, however. Teens tended to be fickle and capricious in their tastes. They got their fashion information from celebrities (such as rappers and athletes), magazines, television, music, and peers. Their loyalty to brands fluctuated, although labels associated with pop music stars did well. Price was important.

By 2014, news reports wondered "Where did the teenage market go?" Mainstays in the industry Abercrombie & Fitch, American Eagle Outfitters and Aéropostale, which dominated teenage closets for years, have fared worse than others in the retail industry. Increased competition from retailers TJ Maxx and Forever 21 has had a negative impact on discretionary spending on clothing at a time of high unemployment within the age group.

FIGURE 20.9 Twin brothers Dean and Dan Caten of Dsquared2 present denim distressed looks for men and women. They mix textures and layer a button-down shirt, colorful sweater, and woolen safari jacket. (Giannoni/WWD/© Condé Nast)

Distribution of Fashion Information

With the rapidity of communication in the 21st century, ideas move easily from one area to another. For example, ideas originating in Tokyo street fashion may show up on the runways of Paris haute couture shows or in clothes produced by industrial fashion firms. In describing the importance of the Internet to consumer spending habits, analyst Matthew McClintock stated:

> Ten years ago, [consumers were] buying from the select items that the C.E.O. [of companies] thought would be

popular nine months ago. Today . . . you can go online and find cool [clothes] and have [them] delivered to you in two days." *(Harris, 2014, B1)*

THE ORIGINS OF MAJOR FASHION TRENDS OF 2000–2014

Crane (2000) effectively summarized how and why fashion in the new millennium had become so diverse: "Different styles have different publics; there are no precise rules about what is to be worn and no agreement about a fashion ideal that represents contemporary culture" (135). Some 2000s styles were based on mod, punk, miniskirts, and op art prints as well as on 1950s, 1970s, 1980s, and 1990s styles. In a *New York Times* article from 2013, Lauren Sherman, executive digital editor of *Lucky* magazine, thinks that the democratization of fashion has diffused identifiable trends. "It's more about having a personal style now, with the advent of 'Project Runway,' 'America's Next Top Model' and personal style blogs everyone feels like they can judge what's happening . . . Clothes are like ingredients" to mix and match (Wayne, 2013, ST1). Nonetheless, politics, the arts, and technological advances continued to contribute to and be influenced by fashion.

Current Events

Current events often inspire particular fashions or clothing practices. The impact of the tragic events of September 11, 2001, on fashion was largely economic. Demand for clothing dropped sharply and many manufacturers had to lay off significant numbers of workers. To stimulate the industry, the Council of Fashion Designers of America and *Vogue* launched "Fashion for America: Shop to Show your Support" (Ribitzky, 2001). These efforts aided, in part, the short-term economic recovery of the United States (Pham, 2011).

The tragedy also inspired specific styles. Clothing ornamented with American flags appeared everywhere, providing a means of making a patriotic statement. As the United States entered war in the Middle East, military influences appeared in civilian dress. Cargo pants were fashionable, especially among the young. Trench coats and battle jackets appeared on Paris runways. Styles ranging from cargo pants to women's sheer blouses were made from fabrics decorated with camouflage prints. At first these prints were made in the traditional camouflage mixes of tans, browns, greens, and grays, but by 2003 and after, they also appeared in mixes of vivid colors, even for children, with no pretense that these patterns would blend into any natural background (Figure 20.10).

As a result of the conflicts growing out of the attack on the World Trade Center on September 11 and the role of radical Islamic terrorists in those attacks, some Americans eyed individuals in traditional Islamic suspiciously. Muslim women who wanted to wear fashionable dress and also follow the teachings of their religion worked creatively to wear current styles in combination with dress in line with their religious beliefs. A headscarf, called **hijab**, was one of the garments that devout women wore in combination with acceptably modest contemporary styles (Figure 20.11).

The black and white headscarf called a **kaffiyeh** has been associated with the late Yassir Arafat and his Palestinian countrymen. During many years and from time to time some Americans have adopted this item of dress, and it is often seen as a symbol of solidarity with the Palestinians. In 2007 some young women in urban areas started wearing the scarf around their

FIGURE 20.10 Utilitarian when used on vests, parkas, and pants, camouflage is high fashion when designed with bright colors and interesting details as used in 2012 by Giambattista Valli. (Giannoni/WWD/© Condé Nast)

FIGURE 20.11 A model wears a hijab with designs by Hannie Hananto during Jakarta Fashion Week 2014. Indonesia is the largest Muslim country in the world. (Robertus Pudyanto/Getty Images)

necks, and political controversy ensued. Many of the young women interviewed were unaware of its political implications. One, quoted in the *New York Times*, said, "I'm not too up to speed in what's going on in the Middle East. It's [the headscarf] an aesthetic thing" (Kim, 2007). As a result of the controversy over the scarf, many of those who wore it only as a new fashion gave it up.

Clothing has been worn in protest against politics and the social milieu in many historic periods. But by the 2000s, it was difficult to engage in clothing-based protest against the current establishment. The disappearance of widely accepted norms of dress had robbed protest clothing of its ability to shock or startle. Almost the only way to really get a message across was to wear a T-shirt with a clearly printed word or phrase (Givlin, 2002) (Figure 20.12). Such was the case in the Occupy Wall Street protests that began in New York City, September 2011 and spread to other cities and some countries around the world to rally against the social and economic income inequality between the wealthiest and the 99 percent of the rest of the population.

Political Leaders and Celebrities

Continuing the trend that started in the early 20th century, celebrities and political leaders were much admired and followed for their fashion choices in the 21st century. The fashion statements made often had an impact on the fashion industry. For example, when First Lady Michelle Obama appeared on the *Tonight Show* wearing a J. Crew ensemble, traffic on the retailer's website increased significantly, and the outfit sold out immediately. Macy's fashion director Nicole Fischelis commented that the bright-colored cardigans, sleeveless sheath dresses, and the pencil skirts Obama favored were among the best-selling items in the store. According to Bloomingdale's fashion director Stephanie Solomon, the First Lady's choice in clothing "influences the decisions of every single buyer that goes into a showroom" (Gregory, 2009).

Similarly, the Duchess of Cambridge positively influenced fashion, resulting in British fashion

FIGURE 20.12 Message T-shirts can relay important (and not so important) information with humor. (John Parra/Getty Images for petiteParade)

designers making inroads into the United States. In her 2011 wedding to Prince William, Kate Middleton wore a dress designed by Alexander McQueen's creative director Sarah Burton. Much copied, this and other fashion choices from British designers Jenny Packham and Roland Mouret have proved the "Kate effect" on fashion sales (Figure 20.13).

Although celebrities often make more daring fashion choices than politicians, they also sway fashion, particularly the choices of young people. Musical entertainers, film and television stars, and professional athletes are closely followed for their personal and professional style choices. Some, such as actress Chloe Sevigny and musician Lady Gaga, become muses to fashion houses. Others become

FIGURE 20.13 In her first official engagement as Duchess of Cambridge, Kate Middleton wears a tan sheath dress when meeting First Lady Michelle Obama. The brand Reiss reported its website crashed, and when it reopened, the particular dress style sold out immediately. Michelle Obama became an equally powerful influence on 21st-century fashion. (Toby Melville—WPA Pool/Getty Images)

the paid "face" or spokesperson of a brand, such as Sarah Jessica Parker for Garnier and Gap. Others still, including former child TV stars Ashley and Mary Kate Olsen and Victoria Beckham, formerly of the Spice Girls, successfully parlay their fame into

fashion brands (Gibson, 2012; Figure 20.14). The shift from using models to using celebrities in fashion magazines, a decision attributed to *Vogue*'s editor Anna Wintour, demonstrates the importance of celebrity on fashion. Table 20.2 provides some specific examples of influences on fashions from various media during the new millennium.

The Arts

Until recently, the integration of tattoos into the art world was mostly confined to performance art. But today, tattooing, much like graffiti, has been increasingly embraced, particularly in areas where art meets fashion (Randall, 2013). The Musée du Quai Branly in Paris, a prestigious art institution, exhibited "Tatoueurs, Tatoués" (*Tattooists, Tattooed*) in 2014.

FIGURE 20.14 Madonna launched her Material Girl collection with daughter Lourdes. Celebrities often use themselves to market their goods. (© Everett Collection Inc./Alamy)

TABLE 20.2 Media Influences on Fashion: 2000–2014

MEDIA	DATES	STYLE INFLUENCES
Television	2003–2007	*Queer Eye for the Straight Guy* featured "make-betters" of men's fashions, home decor, grooming, and culture.
	2003–2013	*What Not to Wear* presented makeovers, may have inspired interest in career of styling.
	2004–2013	Fashion designing reality show *Project Runway* introduces many Americans to the fashion design process.
	2007–	*Mad Men*, set in an advertising agency in the 1960s, influences retro fashions such as floral dresses and trim suits. *Mad Men* capsule collections introduced in Banana Republic.
	2007–	Reality television shows such as *Keeping Up with the Kardashians* and *Jersey Shore* impact hairstyles and revealing clothing choices.
	2007–2012	*Gossip Girl* influences a resurgence of preppy and collegiate looks such as blazers, polo shirts, argyle, for the youth market.
	2010–	*Pretty Little Liars* characters popularize stripes, leather jackets, trench coats, and feather earrings.
	2012–	The main character of *Scandal*, Olivia Pope, played by Kerry Washington, wears tailored separates in pastel colors, with dainty jewelry.
Internet	2002 and on	The Internet, including e-commerce, fashion blogs, social media, and YouTube postings, influences the design, marketing, and promotion of fashion.
Motion pictures	2000	In *Erin Brockovich*, actress Julia Roberts wears special bra that gives a natural look and cleavage to flat-chested women.
	2001	*Moulin Rouge* contributes to a fashion for lace, Edwardian clothing, and bustiers.
	2001–2011	The *Harry Potter* books and later the eight films based on the books lead to increased sales of spectacles to teens.
	2006	Film version of *Lord of the Rings* contributes to some fans' adoption of hairstyles similar to those in the film and medieval-inspired fashions and jewelry.
	2006	*The Devil Wears Prada* is based on a 2003 novel of the same name, written by former assistant to *Vogue's* editor-in-chief Anna Wintour.
	2008 and 2010	Fashions in the filmed version of *Sex and the City* and *Sex in the City* 2 are eagerly viewed by fans of the television series.
	2009	Documentary feature film *The September Issue* gives a behind-the-scenes look at making of *Vogue*.
	2012, 2013	The *Hunger Games* films series based on the trilogy of books of the same name features leather detailing, mesh, and boots.
	2013	*The Great Gatsby* inspires 1920s looks.
Popular music and popular music videos	2000s	More musicians and popular singers entered the fashion business, including Gwen Stefani's L.A.M.B. line (launched in 2003), Jessica Simpson (2006), Beyoncé (2006), Victoria Beckham (2008), Madonna (2010), Kanye West (2012), Adam Levine for Kmart (2014).
	2000s	Followers of popular musical style (examples: hip-hop, country, reggae, indie-pop) adopt the styles worn by these musicians.
	2000s	Individual musical entertainers such as Beyoncé, Eminem, Rhianna, and Miley Cyrus are closely followed for their fashion choices.
	2000s	Clothing companies design garments, ranging from outerwear to sportswear, with MP3 pockets and holes for headphone cords to pass through.

Once a rarity, exhibitions of fashion in fine art museums are now commonplace. Following his death in 2010, the Metropolitan Museum of Art's Costume Institute celebrated the late Alexander McQueen's extraordinary contributions to fashion (Figure 20.15). Other designer retrospectives included the Brooklyn Museum's *The Fashion World of Jean Paul Gaultier: From the Sidewalk to the Catwalk* and the Philadelphia Museum of Art's *Patrick Kelley: Runway of Love*. Some museums focus on a theme, geographic location, or particular style, such as Victoria and Albert's *The Glamour of Italian Fashion, 1945–2014* or the Kyoto Museum's *Future Beauty: The Tradition of Reinvention in Japanese Fashion.*

Technological Advancements

As the new millennium advanced, the variety of technologically enhanced fabrics and garments increased. In *Fashionable Technology*, Seymour (2009) assigned items of dress that incorporate technology a place on a range extending from expressiveness at one end to functionality at the other. For example, high-fashion items may be placed at the expressive end of the range, whereas dress for specific types of work in fields such as medicine may rest at the functionality end of the scale (Tortora, 2015).

Developments in a wide range of technical fields stimulated new styles. Well-known fashion designers such as Armani, Prada, Cavalli, and Dolce & Gabbana included a mobile phone as part of their fashion collections (Fortunati, 2010). Technological advances include three-dimension printing and laser cutting (Figure 20.16). With advancements in sewable electronics, textile engineers can incorporate solar panels mounted on outerwear that can store energy to recharge a mobile phone and T-shirts that monitor vital signals such as heartbeats. (See Contemporary Comments 20.1 for a discussion of this technology as applied to accessories.) As textile technology advances, new products will continue to combine electronic gear and fashionable and functional dress. Forward-thinking designer Hussein Chalayan (as cited in Quinn, 2002, 32) anticipated this phenomenon: "The fashion audience doesn't really know about technology. . . . but they soon will."

Sports and Activewear

Rarely did people use sportswear exclusively for athletic activities. In 2008 high-end manufacturers of clothing for active sports such as Adidas and Puma were promoting a full range of clothing from accessories to footwear designed by such well-known designers as Stella McCartney, Yohji Yamamoto, and Alexander McQueen. Trade newspapers such as the *Daily News Report* noted that design for the sportswear

FIGURE 20.15 British designer Alexander McQueen often used traditional techniques of embroidery, lace making, and metal working to create radically modern designs. (Image copyright © The Metropolitan Museum of Art. Image source: Art Resource, NY)

FIGURE 20.16 Iris Van Herpen creates dresses using three-dimensional printing technology. Her partnership with United Nude's Rem D. Koolhaas and Stratasys led to shoes in her Wilderness Embodied 2013 show that resembled tangled tree-root webs. Iris van Herpen uses techniques she calls "the artisanal and the technical." (Giannoni/WWD/Condé Nast)

market was influencing the active sportswear market and that consumers desired garments that would take them from the gym to the hiking trail to casual social events. Even for professions and occasions that require

FIGURE 20.17 Street wear and sportswear collide in the spring 2014 DKNY pairing of a blazer, patterned sweater, lounge pants, and baseball cap. (Iannocone/WWD/Condé Nast)

more formal attire, it has become commonplace to see sportswear-inspired fabrics and styles (Figure 20.17).

COSTUME COMPONENTS: 2000–2014

Costume Components for Women

Many of the trends of the early 1990s continued into the last half of the decade and on into the early 2000s. During the 1990s, it had become more and more difficult to identify any one "look" or predominant silhouette. Individuals were likely to dress in styles acceptable to their peers. If the peer group was attuned to current fashion trends for that group (as adolescents, media stars, or avid followers of high fashion were likely to be), fashionable styles came and went quickly. For other women, the same basic, classic styles might be worn year after year, with more current

Contemporary Comments 20.1

START-UP DISGUISES WEARABLE TECH AS JEWELRY

In a New York Times *blog from 2014, writer Nick Wingfield introduces the reader to a start-up company that creates wearable technology disguised as jewelry.*

There are two broad strains of wearable technology emerging: the doo-dads that proclaim their techiness from the wrists, faces and other body parts that they are fastened to, and those that try to conceal that quality.

Cuff, a new wearable start-up in the San Francisco Bay Area, is making products firmly in the latter category. Earlier this week, the company unveiled a line of accessories that look more like the jewelry featured in an issue of Vogue, than hardware from the pages of Wired. There are bracelets made of leather and metal with names like The Lena, The Carin and The Mia, necklaces (The Lisa, The Soleil) and keychains (The J and The G).

These are not, in short, Google Glass or Samsung's Galaxy Gear, the high-tech eyewear and smart wristwatch that telegraph their nerd cachet as if they were screaming it through a megaphone.

Cuff's line of accessories, which range from $50 to $150, don't try to do as much, technology wise, as those other wearables do. They act a bit like remote controls for the smartphones that they connect wirelessly to and on which they depend for access to the Internet. Initially the company is emphasizing personal security as one of the main uses of the devices, Cuff's founder, Deepa Sood, said in an interview.

A woman who encounters a threatening situation on the street or elsewhere can press her finger to a Cuff bracelet on her wrist, which will then send an electronic distress signal to one or more people she has authorized through the Cuff app to receive those messages. The signal will reveal her physical location.

A senior citizen can do the same if they've fallen and can't get up. A wearer of a Cuff accessory can program any number of other actions to occur on their smartphones—for instance, a tap of the wrist can send an automated message alerting family that the wearer is driving home. A text message or email from a spouse or parent can vibrate the accessory.

The technology inside the accessories includes a battery that lasts a year so people don't have to recharge them constantly. There's an accelerometer chip inside them which will allow Cuff to later turn on walking- and sleep-monitoring functions like those in the Jawbone Up, a bracelet that people use to keep track of their daily activity levels.

Underlying all of the Cuff accessories is a belief that there needs to be a higher fashion quotient to wearable technology if people, especially women, are to wear them, said Ms. Sood, who was previously the vice president of product development at Restoration Hardware, the furniture retailer.

"There's this aesthetic vision that technology doesn't have to scream technology," said Ms. Sood, who has long made jewelry on her own. "That was super appealing to me."

Wingfield, N. (2014, February 21). Start-up disguises wearable tech as jewelry. *New York Times*. Retrieved from http://bits.blogs.nytimes .com/2014/02/21/start-up-disguises-wearable-tech-as-jewelry/

fashions showing up in clothing for special occasions or in hems moving slightly up and down from one year to another. From the turn of the millennium, the variety of fashions increased, and customers could find almost any variation they wanted in these garments. If one skirt length was not to their taste, shoppers could find another or alter their garments to achieve the look they desired.

Garments

Mirroring the fragmentation of the industry, women's wear continued to offer numerous looks at once. General trends continued mixing levels of formality, achieved by pairing garments such as leggings with blazers and using different colors, textures, and patterns. Certain printed designs continued to be fashionable throughout the period. Examples include camouflage, prints that simulate animal fur, and brightly colored stripes. Leather and leather detailing was much in use for garments ranging from skirts to coats. Asian influences appeared, showing up in banded collars, dresses and jackets cut like the Chinese cheongsam dress, and beautifully embroidered silk kimonos (Figure 20.18).

Retro styles continued to emerge. In 2007 fashion writers spoke of the strong showing of 1950s influences in "ladylike" dresses. Baby-doll and trapeze-style dresses appeared, and in 2008 so did revivals of styles reminiscent of those worn by Jacqueline Kennedy as first lady in the 1960s. In 2012, retailers provided offerings culled from multiple decades simultaneously. Pencil skirts with cardigan sweaters reminiscent of the 1930s, ankle-length slim pants evocative of the 1960s, neon colors suggestive of the 1980s, and sleek pant suits from the 1990s coexisted (Figure 20.19). The styles were not exact copies of the past but were refreshed with new fabric treatments and modifications in cut. High-fashion designers also

FIGURE 20.18 Interest in east Asia is evident in garments such as this kimono designed by Valentino. (Giannoni/WWD/© Condé Nast)

FIGURE 20.19 Pant suits, introduced in the second half of the 1960s, have become a staple in many a woman's wardrobe. Armani has become known for the soft jackets and comfortable pants he has designed since the 1970s. Armani 2014 RTW fall collection. (Elgort/WWD/© Condé Nast)

looked to the past for inspiration and turned to art by painters such as Botticelli to classic designers such as Balenciaga and to historic periods such as the First French Empire.

Daytime Garments

By 2005 a style trend nicknamed **boho** had taken hold and persisted for several years. The term, derived from the word *bohemian*, was in a sense a revival of the ideas that were part of upscale, hippie-influenced clothes of the 1960s. Vibrant colors, softly flowing fabrics, and combinations of variously patterned fabrics were all part of this style (Figure 20.20).

In addition to button-down blouses and knit tops, there were ultrafeminine blouses in peasant style, some of which were ornamented with ruffles and frills. A popular neckline style was the funnel neck, similar in appearance to a turtleneck, but wider. Tops were cut like the men's athletic shirts nicknamed **wifebeaters**, a term that came from the style of undershirt worn by Marlon Brando when he played a violent working-class husband in the play and film *A Streetcar Named Desire*.

Skirts could be found in almost any length. Some were A-line; some were short, tight miniskirts; others were long, slender skirts, called pencil skirts. Latin-inspired ruffled skirts were also evident.

Like skirts, pants showed considerable variability. Bell-bottoms revived from the 1960s were often made with a dropped waist. Other styles included tight-fitting pants with spandex, tailored pants with legs of moderate width, and, in 2003, a style of pants made with ties or a belt at the bottom hem. **Capri** pants (Figure 20.21a) became a wardrobe essential. Throughout the period, but especially after the invasion of Iraq, **cargo pants** and **combat shorts** were often made in camouflage prints or solid-colored fabrics (Figure 20.21b). The large cargo pockets on these pants and shorts were popular, in part because they made a convenient storage place for cell phones, which had become ubiquitous (Figure 20.22). Solid-colored trousers in bright colors and patterned pants were popular from 2012 onward. Denim jeans continued in popularity, worn for both casual wear and for some even appropriate for business attire (Global Connections).

As the decade progressed, short dresses, skirts, or hip-length tops were often worn over blue jeans, with knitted spandex leggings, or with lighter weight footless tights or pantyhose. Even maternity wear favored close-fitting styles, some with Empire styling to highlight the growing "bump" (Figure 20.23).

FIGURE 20.20 Upscale hippie styles of the 1960s probably inspired these softly flowing fabrics in vibrant colors. (Centano/WWD/© Condé Nast)

FIGURE 20.21 High-fashion designers did not limit themselves to lavish gowns but also designed sportswear and leisure wear styles. These included (a) capri pants by Dior for spring 2008 resort (Aquino/WWD/Condé Nast) and (b) cargo pants by Wunderkind in spring 2009 (Giannoni/WWD/© Condé Nast).

FIGURE 20.22 The pockets of cargo pants are helpful in carrying 21st-century mobile technology. Apple described the iPhone as three products in one handheld device: a mobile phone, an iPod, and a wireless communication device. The devices for making phone calls, sending text messages, taking photographs, and searching the Internet are ubiquitous. (Stesh/Shutterstock)

workforce, they also procured their own jewelry as both accessories and investment pieces (Beckett, 2014). In part because of concerns that newer diamonds, so-called *conflict* or *blood diamonds*, might have been used to help finance civil wars in Africa, heirloom engagement rings were increasingly an option for couples.

Hair and Headdress

Both wavy and straight looks were popular. For length enhancement, extensions were sold in beauty parlors, online, and in mall kiosks. Around 2008, celebrities Victoria Beckham and Katie Holmes sported graduated bobs with ensuing popularity for the style through 2014. Singer Rihanna was followed for her constantly changing hairstyles, from pixie cut to fishtail braids to asymmetrical haircuts. Professional and working women preferred natural or at least natural-looking shades with multidimensional high- and lowlights. Celebrities such as Kelly Osbourne, daughter of rocker Ozzy and a co-host of TV series *Fashion Police*, popularized pastel colors in purple shades and grays even on younger women. Ombré styles, popular in denim in the 1990s, resurged in women's hair (Figure 20.29).

Headwear included baseball caps for younger women and knit, fleece, and soft-crowned caps for colder weather. Headbands became popular again in the 2000s popularized by a character on the TV show *Gossip Girl*. Even donned by former First Lady and Secretary of State Hillary Clinton, the accessories could be knit or bejeweled and worn across the forehead, on the head, or more like a turban.

Cosmetics

Women continued to enhance their looks with makeup products. Over the counter creams as well as dermatological treatments, ranging from microdermabrasion to injections of the toxin Botox, promised to erase wrinkles for more youthful appearances. With knowledge of the harmful effects of the sun and improved formulations, more women achieved a tanned complexion with self-tanning lotions.

FIGURE 20.29 Ombré, long, wavy hair and more natural makeup on the left are contrasted with purple, short shaved hair and brighter makeup on the right. (Stephen Lovekin/E! Entertainment/NBCU Photo Bank via Getty Images)

Costume Components for Men

Specific menswear garments continued from the late 1990s, but enhanced attention was paid to the fit of the garment, favoring slimmer silhouettes. At least according to media reports, men paid increasing attention to grooming and purchasing their own clothes in the 2000s. Though some men have always cared about their appearance, in the new millennium the numbers of products and advertisements targeted to male consumers increased.

Garments

The same basic items of boxer shorts or briefs and undershirts continued to be worn. Burberry plaids were so popular in the 2000s that they were even used for the waistband on some men's boxer briefs.

Around 2000 shirts in darker shades of colors were worn with neckties in lighter shades and patterns of the same color. Asian influences showed up in men's shirts made with band collars. Striped and patterned shirts, including Hawaiian prints, were featured. Pinstripes were again popular in 2007 through 2008.

By 2000 suits tended to be dark, slim in cut, and had either three or two buttons (Figure 20.30). In summer men could wear unpressed linen suits, with a somewhat rumpled look. Preppy styles were revived in 2007. Closer to 2008, suits had a less tailored, more casual look. By 2010, there were reports that although the casual dress look may have remained the preferred style for men, fashion trends dictated a return to the "dressed up man" signifying success. Men were interested in apparel specifically designed to hold electronic gear such as iPods, BlackBerries, and digital cameras.

Denim jeans, though commonplace for casual wear, were increasingly worn for dressy events, particularly when worn with blazers and button down shirts (see Figure 20.9). Jeans in dark washes, with distressed and embellished looks, were particularly popular for the fashionable set. With extra washes and trims also came high prices.

FIGURE 20.30 Closer fitting three-piece styles were popular in 2009 and resurged in 2014. (Aquino/WWD/Condé Nast)

Sportswear

A sportswear look also donned by women and children, the **hoodie** was popular and often included sports or brand logos (Figure 20.31). Hoodies were manufactured in a wide variety of weights and styles from lightweight jersey to vests to fleece lined jackets.

The basic sport shirt styles continued to be T-shirts, polo shirts, and woven short-sleeved styles. Many T-shirts and sweatshirts were decorated with words or phrases or sports logos.

For activewear, nylon track jackets, pants, and shorts were popular. For more serious athletes, fabrics that promoted advanced wicking of sweat and compression support prevailed.

Evening Dress

Formal wear included the traditional black tuxedo (see Figure 20.25). Fit was key to achieving a modern look. For less formal outings, blazers and sports suits in tweed and herringbone patterns were popular.

Hair and Headdress

A wide variety of hairstyles could be seen on male fashion models. Very short hair and even shaved heads were seen often in the 2000s, possibly a military influence. Baseball caps were popular. A variation, called a **trucker's cap**, that had a foam section at the

FIGURE 20.31 Mark McNairy's 2014 collection included hoodies, plaid jackets, and cargo camaflouge pants. Tattoos peek out underneath the garments. (Chinsee/WWD/Condé Nast)

FIGURE 20.32 The trucker cap is complemented by a track jacket; slim, low-fitting pants; brightly colored sneakers; and a neat, but "unshaven," beard. (GONZALO/Bauer-Griffin/GC Images)

front of the crown and mesh around the rest, was being worn by the middle of the first decade after 2000 (Figure 20.32).

Younger men and boys copied other hairstyles, such as the shag, the longer side-swept hair inspired by Justin Bieber, or the faux hawk sported by soccer star David Beckham.

Footwear

Athletic footwear continued and diversified to include bright and neon colors. For professional wear, men could choose classic leather oxfords, suede half boots, and loafers. For casual wear, flip-flops, slides, and boat shoes were available in leather, cloth, and synthetic materials.

Accessories

Articles about men's fashion in 2007 proclaimed the return to popularity of neckties, after a period when they were less important. They were described as low-key and narrow.

Tattoos became more commonplace, often peeking from behind shirt collars or under sleeves (see Figure 20.31).

Jewelry

Commonly worn jewelry included rings and watches. For business wear, lapel pins and tie clips were common. Bracelets, necklaces, and earrings were enjoyed by some. However, style columnists suggested as a general rule to err on the side of understatement. In the late 1990s and early 2000s, rubber wristbands first popularized by Lance Armstrong's LiveStrong Cancer Foundation were nearly ubiquitous. Available from the 1980s, more rap stars donned full-mouth metal "grills," or jewelry worn over the teeth in the mid-2000s. They are far from commonplace outside of major cities and celebrity culture.

Cosmetics and Grooming

Some men and boys imitated professional athletes who shaved their heads and wore goatees. After 2000 facial hair was still much in evidence. Some men grew moustaches, sometimes with goatees and a **soul patch**, a small patch of hair centered beneath the lip, or **circle beards**, moustaches combined with rounded goatees. Grooming aids including hair styling creams and skin care products proliferated in the 2000s.

COSTUME COMPONENTS FOR CHILDREN

In November 2003, trade magazines emphasized authentic urban looks (i.e., cargo-pocket styles, T-shirts, large and loose dress shirts, and jackets) for children like those produced for adults. Children's clothing mimicked in many ways the casual styles of adults with jeans, shorts, T-shirts, and baseball caps (Figure 20.33).

Infants and Preschool-Age Children

By the millennium the technology for making fire-retardant fabrics had improved, and as a result manufacturers were producing more fashionable sleepwear styles that complied with the U.S. Consumer Product Safety Commission's regulations. Underwear and T-shirts, particularly for boys, featured Spiderman, Batman, and other cartoon characters.

School-Age Children: Trends Affecting Boys and Girls

When preteen and adolescent girl fans of singer Britney Spears began wearing sexy and skimpy clothing in 2003, some schools imposed dress codes requiring that skirts be no shorter than a specified length (e.g., 4 inches above the knee) or banned tube tops or tops with spaghetti straps. Some schools experienced resistance to dress codes and uniforms, however, from parents as well as students.

Dolls based on characters in the *American Girl* book series became very popular, and by 2003 it was possible for girls to dress like their dolls, because look-alike clothing was marketed by the company. In 2008, retailer Target carried clothing based on that of another popular series, *Fancy Nancy*.

Swimwear for girls ranged from bikinis to tank suits and even suits with built-in flotation devices. Boys tended to wear trunks, often in bright colors or prints. As concerns mounted about risks to health from

FIGURE 20.33 Children's wear included many of the styles seen in casual adult wear. Bright colors for both boys and girls were commonplace. (Courtesy of Ian Lin)

overexposure to sun, manufacturers promoted swim shirts (Figure 20.34).

Trends for teenagers and college-age youth included low-rise jeans, miniskirts worn with leggings, matching velour zip-up sweatshirts and pants, and oversized glasses.

Footwear

By 2000 there were shoes with wheels inset into the soles called **wheelys**. The removable wheels allowed children to glide down the street as if on roller skates. Some schools found them disruptive and banned them during school hours. Other footwear included sneakers, flip-flops, ankle boots, and oxfords. Stride-Rite, Keds, Weebok (owned by Reebok), and Toddler University were major brands in children's footwear.

FIGURE 20.34 Children in 2011 wearing a range of swimwear, from bikini style to board shorts with rash guard shirts. (Author's collection)

Summary

Influences from current events, the media, and new fashion designers appeared widely. Some examples of POLITICS AND CONFLICT include the use of American flags on clothing following the September 11, 2001, tragedy and the stylistic influences of First Lady Michelle Obama and the Duchess of Cambridge. ECONOMIC EVENTS of the Great Recession influenced personal spending on clothing, but also, perhaps, invigorated interest in second-hand clothing, mixing and matching styles, and the notion of shopping trends that fit within an existing wardrobe. The theme of TECHNOLOGY is quite evident in the 2000–2014 period with innovations in the functionality of clothing, valued as much for the tasks they perform as their mere aesthetics. The role of the Internet in acquisition and promotion of clothing has never been stronger, with no end in sight.

NEW VIEWS OF FASHION

As the millennium marches on, philosophers, sociologists, economists, art historians, historians, and others from fields related to design, apparel, and textiles have flooded the market with books and coverage about fashion. The field has never been more ripe for study and participation than today.

Dress in the 21st century is increasingly segmented according to age, social or economic class, ethnicity, occupation, recreational preferences, and musical tastes. To complicate the picture, specific fashions may move from one segment to another, movements facilitated by the fashion press and other media, such as personal blogs.

Fashionable dress in the first decade of the 21st century might be compared to a river constantly moving onward, a river that divides into many narrower channels. These streams separate, cross, come together, and separate again, and yet that larger river made up of these different parts continually moves on (see Modern Influences).

Visual Summary Table

Some Major Styles c. 2000–2014

Slim ankle pants and leggings are worn with layered tops and jackets.[1]

Pant suits, first introduced in the second half of the 1960s, remain a staple in many women's wardrobes.[1]

Cardigans worn with sheath dresses or pencil skirts were revived from the 1960s[1]

Short dresses worn over blue jeans, c. 2007

Underwear styles worn as outer garments, c. 2000–2008

Casual men's styles included cargo pants and hoodies.[1]

More formal styles for men included three- and two-piece suits as well as tuxedos.[1]

[1] Yelena Safronnova

MODERN INFLUENCES

"The past is prologue." "There is nothing new under the sun." Like the consumer, fashion is never immune to what has gone before, and the past exercises a strong pull on the imaginations of the fashion designers of the 21st century. Pictured here in summary are Modern Influences drawing on each of the six parts of this book.

Part One: The ancient world is represented by the one-shouldered, toga-inspired dress designed by Elie Saab. (Giannoni/WWD/© Condé Nast)

Part Two: The Middle Ages is recalled by a shift designed by Abaete that appears to be made of something like chain-mail worn with a hood that might have been familiar to a crusader or monk. (Iannaccone/WWD/© Condé Nast)

Part Three: The Renaissance lady of Italy would have been perfectly at home in this flowing gown of satin with its jeweled ornamentation by Karl Lagerfeld. (Giannoni/WWD/© Condé Nast)

Part Four: Ruffs framed the faces of both women and men at the beginning of the 17th century and have been revived in women's fashions by designers ever since, including this one from the collection of Gareth Pugh. (Giannoni/WWD/© Condé Nast)

Part Five: Gentlemen of early to mid-19th century would have recognized the tailcoat of this orange and white jacket. They would also have been familiar with the trousers—a new development for men who abandoned the knee breeches of the previous century in the early 1800s. Designed by Jean Paul Gaultier. (Giannoni/WWD/© Condé Nast)

Part Six: The influence of Coco Chanel lives on in structured suits designed by Karl Lagerfeld for the House of Chanel. (Giannoni/WWD/© Condé Nast)

REFERENCES

Akou, H. M. (2013). A brief history of the burqini: Confessions and controversies. *Dress, 39*(1), 25–35.

Beckett, K. (2014, May 15). What women buy when they treat themselves. *New York Times.*

Betts, K. (2011). *Everyday icon: Michelle Obama and the power of style.* New York, NY: Potter Style.

Brown, A. (2014). The U.S. Hispanic population has increased sixfold since 1970. Retrieved from Pew Research Center at http://www.pewresearch.org/fact-tank/2014/02/26/the-u-s-hispanic-population-has-increased-sixfold-since-1970/.

Bunn, A. (2002, December 1). Not fade away. *New York Times Magazine*, 60.

Crane, D. (2000). *Fashion and its social agendas.* Chicago, IL: University of Chicago Press.

Eicher, J. B., Evenson, S. L., & Lutz, H. A. (2000). *The visible self: Global perspectives on dress, culture and society* (2nd Ed.). New York, NY: Fairchild Publications.

Fortunati, L. (2010). Wearing technology. In J. Eicher (Ed.), *Encyclopedia of World Dress and Fashion*, http://www.bergfashionlibrary.com/page/encyclopedia/-berg-encyclopedia-of-world-dress-and-fashion.

Gibson, P. C. (2012). *Fashion and celebrity culture.* New York, NY: Bloomsbury Academic.

Givlin, R. (2002, April 19). From bellbottoms and beads to casual Friday protest apparel. *Washington Post*, p. C01.

Gregory, S. (2009, May 6). Can Michelle Obama save fashion retailing? *Time.* Retrieved from http://content.time.com/time/business/article/0,8599,1895631,00.html.

Harris, E. A. (2014, February 1). Retailers ask: Where did teenagers go? *New York Times*, B1.

Hubbard, B., & Gladstone, R. (2013, August 15). Arab Spring countries find peace is harder than revolution. *New York Times*, A11.

Humphreys, J. M. (2013). *Multicultural economy.* Athens, GA: Selig Center for Economic Growth, University of Georgia.

Kim, K. (2007, February 11). where some see fashion, others see politics. *New York Times.*

Maynard, M. (2010). Globalization and dress. In J. Eicher (Ed.), *Berg encyclopedia of world dress and fashion.* Oxford, UK: Berg.

Pasquarelli, A. (2012, May 14). Fashion gets fast. *Crain's.*

Pham, M-H. T. (2011). The right to fashion in the age of terrorism. *Signs, 36*(2), 385–410.

Quinn, B. (2002). *Techno fashion.* New York, NY: Berg.

Randall, E. (2013, May 8). Tattooing makes transition from cult to fine art. *New York Times.*

Ribitzky, R. (2001, October 23). Fashion designers try to draw shoppers. *ABC News.*

Rozhon, T. (2003, February 9). The race to think like a teenager. *New York Times*, Section 3, 1.

Schneier, M. (2014, April 10). Fashion in the age of instagram. *New York Times*, E4.

Seymour, L. (2007, April 22). Tweens "r" shoppers. *New York Times*, NJ8.

Seymour, S. (2009). *Fashionable technology.* Vienna: Springer Vienna Architecture.

Shapiro, B. (2014, March 27). Isabel Toledo and Lane Bryant see a plus in collaboration. *New York Times*, E6.

Sherman, L. (2014). For the activewear market: There's no way but up. *The Business of Fashion.* Retrieved from http://www.businessoffashion.com/2014/01/activewear-lululemon-nike-hm-sweaty-betty.html.

Tortora, P. G. (2015). *Dress, fashion and technology: From prehistory to present.* New York, NY: Bloomsbury.

U.S. Bureau of Labor Statistics. (2012a). Fashion. Retrieved from http://www.bls.gov/spotlight/2012/fashion/#.

U.S. Bureau of Labor Statistics. (2012b). The recession of 2007–2009. Retrieved from http://www.bls.gov/spotlight/2012/recession/pdf/recession_bls_spotlight.pdf.

Wayne, T. (2013, January 6). What will induce nostalgia in 2033? *New York Times*, ST1.

Wilson, E. (2009, December 27). Bloggers crashed fashion's front row. *New York Times*, ST1.

BIBLIOGRAPHY

See *Survey of Historic Costume Student Study Guide* for books related to specific periods.

DICTIONARIES AND ENCYCLOPEDIAS, GENERAL REFERENCES, AND SURVEYS

Anawalt, P. R. (2007). *The worldwide history of dress*. New York, NY: Thames and Hudson.

Arnold, J. (1977). *Patterns of fashion* (Vol. 1: 1660–1860, Vol. 2: 1860–1940). New York, NY: Drama Books.

Ashelford, J. (1996). *The art of dress: Clothes and society, 1500–1914*. New York, NY: Abrams.

Boucher, E. (1987). *20,000 years of fashion*. London, UK: Thames and Hudson.

Bradfield, N. (1997). *Historical costumes of England, 1066–1968*. Quite Specific Media.

Braun, L., & Schneider. (1975). *Historic costume in pictures*. Mineola, NY: Dover.

Braun, L., et al. (1982). *Costume through the ages*. New York, NY: Rizzoli.

Breward, C. (1995). *The culture of fashion: A new history of fashionable dress*. New York, NY: St. Martin's Press.

Brooke, I. (1973). *A history of English costume*. New York, NY: Theatre Arts Books.

Cassin-Scott, J. (1994). *The illustrated encyclopedia of costume and fashion: From 1066 to the present*. UK: Studio Vista Books.

Cunnington, C. W., Cunnington, P., & Beard, C. (1960). *A dictionary of English costume, 900–1900*. London, UK: A. & C. Black.

Davenport, M. (1948). *The book of costume* (Vols. 1–2). New York, NY: Crown.

Davies, S. (1995). *Costume language: A dictionary of dress terms*. New York, NY: Drama Books.

Eicher, J. (Ed.). (2010). *Berg encyclopedia of world dress and fashion* (Vols. 1–10). Oxford, UK: Berg Publishers.

Gavenas, M. L. (2008). *The Fairchild encyclopedia of menswear*. New York, NY: Fairchild Publications, Inc.

Gleba, M., & Nosch, M. (2007). *Dressing the past*. New York, NY: Oxford University Press.

Laver, J. (1985). *Costume and fashion: A concise history*. New York, NY: Thames and Hudson.

Newman, H. (1981). *An illustrated dictionary of jewelry*. London, UK: Thames and Hudson.

O'Hara-Callan, G. (1998). *The Thames and Hudson dictionary of fashion and fashion designers*. London, UK: Thames and Hudson.

Payne, B., Winakor, G., & Farrell-Beck, J. (1992). *History of costume*. New York, NY: Addison-Wesley.

Ribeiro, A. (1986). *Dress and morality*. New York, NY: Holmes & Meier.

Ribeiro, A., & Cumming, V. (1990). *The visual history of costume*. New York, NY: Drama Books.

Schoeffler, O. E. (Ed.). (1973). *Esquire's encyclopedia of 20th century men's fashion*. New York, NY: McGraw-Hill.

Steele, V. (Ed.). (2005). *Encyclopedia of clothing and fashion* (Vols. 1–3). New York, NY: Thomson Gale.

Steele, V. (Ed.). (2010). *The Berg companion to fashion*. New York, NY: Berg.

Stibbert, F. (1968). *Civil and military clothing in Europe*. New York, NY: B. Blom.

Tortora, P., & Kaiser, S. (2014). *Fairchild's dictionary of fashion* (4th ed.). New York, NY: Fairchild.

Waugh, N. (1968). *The cut of women's clothes, 1600–1930*. New York, NY: Theatre Arts Books.

Yarwood, D. (1975). *European costume: 4000 years of fashion*. New York, NY: Larousse.

Yarwood, D. (1978). *The encyclopedia of world costume*. New York, NY: Scribners.

American and Canadian Costume

De Marly, D. (1990). *Dress in North America*. New York, NY: Holmes & Meier.

Earle, A. M. (1970). *Two centuries of costume in America* (Vols. 1–2). Mineola, NY: Dover.

Earle, A. M. (1974). *Costume of colonial times*. Detroit, MI: Gale Research Company.

Farrell-Beck, J., & Parsons, J. (2007). *20th century dress in the United States*. New York, NY: Fairchild Books.

Gummere, A. M. (1968). *Quaker: A study in costume*. New York, NY: B. Blom. (Reprint of 1901 edition)

Hall, L. (1992). *Common threads: A parade of American clothing*. Boston, MA: Bulfinch Press.

Milbank, C. R. (1989). *New York fashion: The evolution of American style*. New York, NY: Harry N. Abrams.

Modesty to mod: Dress and undress in Canada, 1780–1967. (1967). Toronto, Canada: Royal Ontario Museum.

Routh, C. (1993). *In style: 100 years of Canadian women's fashion*. Toronto, Canada: Stoddart.

Warwick, E., Pitz, H., & Wykoff, A. (1965). *Early American dress*. New York, NY: Bonanza Books.

Worrell, E. A. (1975). *Early American costume*. Harrisburg, PA: Stackpole Books.

Wright, M. (1990). *Put on thy beautiful garments: Rural New England clothing, 1883–1900*. Montpelier, VT: Clothes Press.

Children's Costume

Brooke, I. (2003). *English children's costume: 1775–1920*. Mineola, NY: Dover.

Ewing, E. (1977). *History of children's costume*. London, UK: B. T. Batsford.

Moore, D. L. (1953). *The child in fashion*. London, UK: B. T. Batsford.

Paoletti, J. G. (2012). *Pink and blue*. Bloomington, IN: Indiana University Press.

Rose, C. (1989). *Children's clothes*. New York, NY: Drama Books.

Sichel, M. (1990). *History of children's costumes*. Oxford, UK: Chelsea House.

Worrell, E. A. (1981). *Children's costume in America, 1607–1910*. New York, NY: Scribners.

Men's Costume

Chenoune, F. (1993). *A history of men's fashion*. Paris, France: Flammarion.

DeMarly, D. (1985). *Fashion for men: An illustrated history*. New York, NY: Holmes & Meier.

Harvey, J. (1996). *Men in black*. Chicago, IL: University of Chicago Press.

Herald, J. (1997). *Men's fashion in the twentieth century*. London, UK: Chrysalis Books.

Hochswender, W. (1993). *The golden age of style from Esquire*. New York, NY: Rizzoli.

Martin, R., & Koda, H. (1989). *Jocks and nerds: Men's style in the twentieth century*. New York, NY: Rizzoli.

Waugh, N. (1964). *The cut of men's clothes, 1600–1900*. London, UK: Faber and Faber.

Zakim, M. (2003). *Ready-made democracy: History of men's dress in the American republic: 1760–1860*. Chicago, IL: University of Chicago Press.

SPECIAL TYPES OF COSTUME ACCESSORIES

Armstrong, N. J. (1974). *A collector's history of fans*. New York, NY: Crown.

Black, J. A., & Garland, M. (1974). *Jewelry through the ages*. New York, NY: Morrow.

de Castelbajac, K. (1995). *The face of the century: 100 years of makeup and style*. New York, NY: Rizzoli.

Ewing, E. (1982). *Fur in dress*. London, UK: B. T. Batsford.

Flower, M. (1973). *Victorian jewellery*. Cranbury, NJ: S. Barnes.

Foster, V. (1982). *Bags and purses*. London, UK: B. T. Batsford.

Jewelry through 7000 Years. (1976). London, UK: British Museum.

Peiss, K. (1998). *Hope in a jar: The making of America's beauty culture*. New York, NY: Henry Holt, Metropolitan Books.

Pointer, S. (2005). *The artifice of beauty: A history and practical guide to perfume and cosmetics*. Brimscombe Port, Stroud, UK: Sutton Publishing Limited.

Shields, J. (1988). *All that glitters: The glory of costume jewelry*. New York, NY: Rizzoli.

Stera, D. F. (Ed.). (1992). *Jewels of fantasy: Costume jewelry of the 20th century*. New York, NY: Abrams.

Tortora, P. (2003). *The Fairchild encyclopedia of fashion accessories*. New York, NY: Fairchild Publications, Inc.

Footwear

Brooke, I. (1976). *Footwear*. New York, NY: Theatre Arts Books.

Farrell, J. (1992). *Socks and stockings*. New York, NY: Drama Books.

Rexford, N. E. (2000). *Women's shoes in America, 1795–1930*. Kent, OH: Kent State University Press.

Ricci, S., & Maeder, E. (1992). *Salvatore Ferragamo: The art of the shoe, 1896–1960*. New York, NY: Rizzoli.

Riello, G., & McNeil, P. (2006). *Shoes*. Oxford, UK: Berg.

Swann, J. (1982). *Shoes*. London, UK: B. T. Batsford.

Walker, S. A. (1978). *Sneakers*. New York, NY: Workman.

Hats and Headdress

Ginsburg, M. (1990). *The hat*. Hauppauge, NY: Barron's.

Jones, D. (1990). *Haircuts: Fifty years of styles and cuts*. New York, NY: Thames and Hudson.

Severn, B. (1971). *The long and short of it: 5000 years of fun and fury over hair*. New York, NY: D. McKay.

Underwear

Carter, A. (1992). *Underwear: The fashion history*. New York, NY: Drama Books.

Ewing, E. (1990). *Underwear: A history*. New York, NY: Drama Books.

Farrell-Beck, J., & Gau, C. (2002). *Uplift: The bra in America*. Philadelphia, PA: University of Pennsylvania Press.

Martin, R., & Koda, H. (1993). *Infra-apparel*. New York, NY: Abrams.

Steele, V. (2001). *The corset: A cultural history*. New Haven, CT: Yale University Press.

Waugh, N. (1954). *Corsets and crinolines*. New York, NY: Theatre Arts Books.

Armor

Blair, C. (1958). *European armour*. London, UK: B. T. Batsford.

Blair, C. (1962). *European and American arms, 1100–1850*. London, UK: B. T. Batsford.

Wilkinson, F. (1973). *Arms and armour*. New York, NY: Bantam Books.

Clothing for Special Occasions

Cunnington, P., & Lucas, C. (1972). *Costume for births, marriages, and deaths*. New York, NY: Barnes and Noble.

Cunnington, P., & Mansfield, A. (1969). *English costume for sports and outdoor recreation*. New York, NY: Barnes and Noble.

Kidwell, C. (1968). *Women's bathing and swimming costume in the United States*. Washington, DC: The Smithsonian Institution Press.

Mackay-Smith, A., Druesdow, J. R., & Ryder, T. (1984). *Man and the horse: An illustration of equestrian apparel*. New York, NY: Metropolitan Museum of Art.

Poli, D. D. (1997a). *Beachwear and bathing costume*. New York, NY: Drama Publishers.

Poli, D. D. (1997b). *Maternity fashion*. New York, NY: Drama Publishers.

Probert, C., & Lee-Potter, C. (1984). *Fashion in Vogue since 1910: Sportswear*. New York, NY: Abbeville Press.

Taylor, L. (1983). *Mourning dress: A costume and social history*. Boston, MA: Allen and Unwin.

Zimmerman, C. S. (1985). *The bride's book: A pictorial history of American bridal gowns*. New York, NY: Arbor House.

Occupational and Working-Class Dress

Barsis, M. (1973). *The common man through the centuries*. New York, NY: Ungar.

DeMarly, D. (1987). *Working dress*. New York, NY: Holmes & Meier.

Williams-Mitchell, C. (1983). *Dressed for the job: The story of occupational costume*. Poole, Dorset, UK: Blandford Press.

STAGE AND SCREEN COSTUME HISTORY

Bailey, M. J. (1982). *Those glorious, glamour years: The great Hollywood costume designs of the thirties*. Secaucus, NJ: Citadel.

De Marly, D. (1982). *Costume on the stage*. New York, NY: Barnes and Noble.

Landis, D. N. (Ed.). (2013). *Hollywood costume*. New York, NY: Harry Abrams.

La Vine, W. R. (1982). *In a glamorous fashion: The fabulous years of Hollywood costume design*. New York, NY: Scribners.

McConathy, D., with Vreeland, D. (1976). *Hollywood costume*. New York, NY: Abrams.

PERIODICALS REPORTING COSTUME HISTORY AND RESEARCH

Clothing and Textiles Research Journal. Journal of the International Textile and Apparel Association

Costume. Journal of the Costume Society (Britain)

Dress. Journal of the Costume Society of America

Fashion Theory. Journal of Dress, Body, and Culture

Textile History

CIBA Review (no longer published)

Fashion Magazines and Newspapers

Ackermann's Repository of the Arts. London, UK: 1890–1929

Almanach des Modes. Paris, France: 1814–1822

La Belle Assemblée or Bell's Court and Fashionable Magazine. London, UK: 1806–1818

Cabinet des Modes. Paris, France: 1785–1789

Daily News Record. New York, NY: 1892–2008

Delineator. New York, NY: 1873–1937

Demorest's Monthly Magazine. New York, NY: 1865–1899

Ebony. Chicago: 1945 to present

Elle. Paris, France: 1945 to present

Esquire. New York, NY: 1933 to present

Essence. New York, NY: 1970 to present

La Galerie des Modes. Paris, France: 1778–1787

The Gallery of Fashion. London, UK: 1794–1803

Gentleman's Quarterly (GQ). New York, NY: 1957 to present

Glamour. New York, NY: 1939 to present

Godey's Lady's Book. Philadelphia, PA: 1830–1898

Harper's Bazaar. New York, NY: 1867 to present

Journal des Dames et des Modes. Paris, France: 1797–1839

Le Journal des Demoiselles. Paris, France: 1833–1904

L'Officiel de la Couture et de la Mode de Paris. Paris, France: 1921 to present

M. New York, NY: 1983–1992

Mademoiselle. New York, NY: 1935–2001

Menswear. New York, NY: 1890–1983

Mirabella. New York, NY: 1989–2000

Les Modes Parisiennes. Paris, France: 1843–1875

Peterson's Magazine. Philadelphia, PA: 1837–1898

Petit Courrier des Dames. Paris, France: 1822–1865

Sir. Amsterdam, Netherlands: 1936 to present

Vanity Fair. New York, NY: 1913–1936 and 1983 to present

Vogue. New York, NY: 1892 to present

W. New York, NY: 1971 to present

Women's Wear Daily. New York, NY: 1910 to present

INDEX

689

The Modern World